HISTORY OF THE LOW COUNTRIES

History of the Low Countries

edited by
J.C.H. Blom, E. Lamberts

translated by
James C. Kennedy

Berghahn Books
New York • Oxford

First published in 1999 by

Berghahn Books

Library of Congress Cataloging-in-Publication Data
Geschiedenis van de Nederlanden.   English.
    History of the Low Countries / J.C.H. Blom and E. Lamberts, eds.
    translated by James C. Kennedy.
        p.   cm.
    Includes bibliographical references and index.
    ISBN 1-57181-084-6 (hardcover : alk. paper). -- ISBN 1-57181-085-4
    (pbk. : alk. paper)
    1. Netherlands--History.   2. Belgium--History.   I. Blom. J. C. H.,
    1943- .   II. Lamberts, Emiel.
    DH131.G4713   1998
    949.3--dc21   98-22708
                                                                            CIP

British Library Cataloguing in Publication Data
A catalogue record for this book is available from the British Library.

Printed in the United States on acid-free paper.

This publication has been made possible with financial assistance from the
Prins Bernhard Foundation, the Netherlands.

Contents

Translator's Note

This translated text is a slightly amended version of the *Geschiedenis van de Nederlanden*. In some chapters, paragraphs have been redrawn, and, in a few instances, shortened or amplified for clarity. Keeping these minor changes in mind, the reader of the *History of the Low Countries* may have every confidence that the content and style of each author has been preserved.

One note about the spelling of proper nouns: Dutch and Flemish names and places have been kept in the original wherever possible, in line with current sensibilities on this matter. I have, for example, used Nijmegen rather than Nimwegen (traditionally used by German and English speakers). Flemish-speaking towns, once known to Anglophones by their French names, are noted here by their Dutch names (e.g., Kortrijk instead of Courtrai). The same rule applies to the River Maas (not Meuse). Only in the cases of two famous towns (Bruges and Ypres) have I chosen to retain the French variant, since this is how they are best known to Anglophones.

I also have elected to use specific English variants (Brussels and The Hague, for instance) in all cases where these are still commonly in use among English speakers. In those instances where towns were once well-known to Anglophones by their own spelling, but no longer are, I have reverted to present-day spellings (Douai and Tournai, instead of Douay and Tournay). Finally, it is important to note that medieval historians sometimes use geographical terms different from modern historians. For this reason, Friesland replaces Frisia after Chapter 3, just as Gelderland (the province) replaces Guelders (the duchy). Wherever confusion might ensue, I have provided alternate spellings in parentheses where the name is first encountered.

Finally, there is the problem of "the Low Countries." Is the term plural or is it singular? *Nederlanden* is plural in Dutch, and given that the region has often been divided politically and culturally, it seems appropriate that the plural be used in most cases. Still, part of the ambition of this book is to treat the region as a whole, to see unity in diversity, and when the Low Countries is treated by an author as a single entity, I have opted to translate the term in the singular.

James C. Kennedy

Preface

This book sketches the history of Europe's Low Countries, present-day Belgium and the Netherlands. There is more than sufficient reason to put the region's history into a single narrative. It is true that "the Low Countries" possessed clearly delineated boundaries only after 1500, and that they constituted a single political unit for but short periods of time. Still, in many respects they demonstrated common traits and underwent similar developments that differentiated them from surrounding countries. The social and economic similarities evident throughout most of the region stem from the High Middle Ages, when the Scheldt, Maas, and Rhine delta area became an important center of trade. Next to Northern Italy, the Low Countries became the most urbanized and prosperous region in Europe. Its political system exhibited, from relatively early on, a degree of representative government that differed from the more feudal arrangements then existent in much of Europe. Internationally, the region served both as a mediator for and a buffer to the surrounding great powers, France, England, and Germany. The Low Countries also fulfilled a similar role in cultural life. Overwhelmingly bourgeois in character, its culture was characterized by a determination to control nature and a commitment to the visual arts, its most striking artistic legacy. A single language, Dutch, linked people across political boundaries, enhancing cultural points of contact across the region. In recent decades, Belgium and the Netherlands have become increasingly involved in the broader process of European integration, in which they often share the same interest and follow parallel policies. A single history of the Low Countries helps reveal these parallels and similarities, even while retaining an eye for the equally important differences.

An extensive historiography of the Low Countries' common past already exists in Dutch, most impressively, perhaps, in two extensive, multi-volumed histories, entitled the *Algemene Geschiedenis der Nederlanden*. They never found a broad public, however, and, because of the language, they remained closed to most foreigners. This book is designed to correct this inconvenience. The authors, all of them experts in their own fields, have presented the latest historical research in both a comprehensive and abbreviated form, appropriate for university students and a wider, interested, international public.

Each of the book's eight chronologically based chapters, then, has been written by a different author, and the chapters show clear differences in approach, interpretation, and style. Any disadvantage in this approach is outweighed by the advantage of the great expertise each author brings to his subject. Indeed, it made eminent sense to give the authors a high measure of freedom in writing their chapters, so that their expertise could be maximally utilized. At the same time, the editors and the translator have attempted to streamline the book, both in content and style.

Political developments receive the most attention in this survey. In defense of this approach, we cite the great Dutch historian Johan Huizinga, who wrote to the budding historian Jan Romein in 1925: "I often sigh: Doesn't the wider public actually learn the history of civilization best through a well-structured political history?" Economic developments, too, receive much space. The connection between politics and economics leads to an examination of social relations and cultural developments, in which religion almost invariably played a large role.

In all of this, the editors hope that they have succeeded in creating a clear and highly readable survey. An epilogue, dealing with unity and diversity of the Low Countries, has been supplied to provide the reader with a short overview of major historical developments.

Finally, the editors and authors express their thanks to those who aided them in bringing this book to press, as well as to those who, through their comments and other assistance, helped prepare the final text: Ms. M.C. le Bailly, Prof. C. Fasseur, Prof. P.H.D. Leupen, Prof. J. de Maeyer, Prof. L. Noordegraaf, Dr. P. Pasture, Ms. M. Pluymers, Prof. P. de Rooy, and Dr. J. Talsma. Dr. J. Kennedy's services as translator, including his advice on accomondating the text for an international public, were most important. Thanks are due also to the Prins Bernhard Fonds and the Fonds Louis Lamberts Van Assche, which provided financial support for the translation.

J.C.H. Blom and E. Lamberts

The oldest remnants of human habitation in the Low Countries are menhirs, prehistoric monuments from the Neolithic Age. Some of the finest exemplars can be found north of Havelte in Drenthe province, the Netherlands.

1 A Long Beginning

The Low Countries through the Tenth Century

L.J.R. Milis

The first historical records for "the Low Countries" date back to the arrival of the Romans from the south in the first century B.C. With the invasion of the Germanic tribes, the Roman Empire collapsed, and one of these tribes, the Franks, succeeded during the fifth century in establishing a strong kingdom, with Paris as its capital. Under the Merovingian kings, as they were called, Roman and German customs and laws coexisted. After the Merovingians were cast aside in the eighth century by a new dynasty, the Carolingians, royal power shifted from Paris to Aachen. Charlemagne and his son Louis the Pious aimed both at administrative centralization and the Christianization of society. The growth of central authority also cultivated new cultural life among the empire's elites.

The Carolingian Empire, however, soon collapsed under its own weight, from a lack of finances (which led to feudalism) and through the old Germanic custom of dividing royal territory among sons. The border between the two realms that resulted from the division – France and Germany – ran across the territory of what became known as the Low Countries in later centuries.

1. Celts, Romans, and Germans

A Geography of Prehistoric Times

The "Low Countries" did not constitute a coherent whole throughout most of the region's history. Even today, the Low Countries remain politically and culturally fragmented, with their inhabitants speaking Dutch, French, Frisian, and German. It is even more difficult to give the region set parameters in earlier ages, when tribes and kingdoms stretched across expanses not limited to the present states of Belgium, Luxembourg, and the Netherlands. For historical reasons, parts of northern France and western Germany also should also be included in the "Low Countries," but the term must remain both broad and fluid, a convenient label for a region which has seldom, if ever, composed a unified whole.

A brief word should be said first about the Low Countries in prehistoric times. To what degree were they formed by natural factors and by human initiative? Geographically, most of the region is an extension of the plain of the Lower Rhine, itself part of the Northern European Plain. Only the south and southeast consist of hills and low mountains. The Ardennes, linked to the Eiffel, formed a daunting natural barrier, cut only by the Rhine. All great geological changes had occurred by the time of the Quartair, and only the surface remained vulnerable to change, transformed over time by colder periods or ice ages.

Roughly speaking, the Low Countries can be partitioned into three geographical areas: the elevated interior, the coastal zone, and the river region in the middle of the present-day Netherlands. Finer distinctions, however, do greater justice both to geological and historical

Reconstruction of the "temple" in Bargeroosterveld, Bronze Age, ca. 1050 B.C. (Drents Museum, Assen).

differences. Geologists can delineate a series of zones, starting in the southeast and moving northwest. The fertile marl area of southeastern Belgium, bordering on France and Luxembourg, comes first; it has been inhabited since the Stone Age. Adjacent to it lie the heavily forested Ardennes, which, in contrast, barely tolerated human settlement during the colder climactic spells. Then come the limestone formations along the Maas (Meuse) as it flows toward Limburg, whose caves and grottos have offered evidence of continuous settlement since the Stone Age. To the north lies the Leem (Loam) district, stretching from Artois to Limburg, which attracted early settlement through its fertility and the abundance of flint for the making of artifacts. From there a broad belt of sandloam and sand follows, from coastal Flanders through the Campine, north to the Netherlands's river region and up to the Drenthe plateau in the northeastern Netherlands. This type of land promises easy cultivation, but is, in the long run, infertile and barren, and subject to sand-drift. Overgrazing often led to unproductive heathlands replacing its forests. The rest is coastal area, vulnerable to sea erosion. Parts of the coastal region have amassed elevated sand deposits, which have checked the power of the sea. The great estuary formed by the Scheldt, Maas and Rhine (or Helinium as it was called in Roman times) was constantly subject to topographical change and also, from the Middle Ages on, to human influence. Before dredging, draining and dike-building, human life was viable only on elevated ground such as the *terpen* (artificial mounds) which still mark the Frisian landscape.

Roman Rule and Germanic Migration

Written documentation of what we call the Low Countries begins in 57 B.C., when the Roman political and military leader, Julius Caesar invaded Gaul and subjected it. But the watershed between recorded history and prehistory, once uncontested by historians, gradually has become arbitrary. The distinction itself stemmed from a time when archaeology had not yet developed and when historians could not go beyond texts in searching for the past. Such a time, however, is now gone, and the picture that archaeologists have given of the centuries before Caesar's arrival is no poorer than that of the centuries which followed it. We now know that by the seventh century B.C., the so-called Halstatt culture had begun to use iron, and the La Tène culture, which replaced it two centuries later, shows recognizably Celtic forms. Both cultures made their impact on the region, particularly in the south, where there are signs of sizable towns (*oppida*, or fortified settlements like those on the Kemmelberg in West Flanders) and of social stratification (a prosperous ruling class). Already by the second century B.C., Germans had settled throughout the area, the result of westward migration.

In A.D. 47, the Rhine (or more particularly, the Old Rhine) became the border between the Roman imperium and Germania; it separated a centralized, well-organized but ethnically diverse state from a loose conglomeration of tribes with a common language, culture, and religion. Along the Rhine and thus also in the Low Countries, native Celts and Germans came into contact with the heterogeneous soldiers and traders of the Roman Empire.

The Low Countries in the Late Roman Period.

Roman colonization brought new forms of administration to the Low Countries. The area to the west of the Scheldt and upper Maas was part of the province called *Belgica secunda*, for which Rheims served as capital. Boundaries of the subprovincial *civitates* seem to have corresponded at least partly with the pre-Roman territories of various tribes, including, among others, the Nervii, Menapii, and the Tungri. The chief administrative centers, such as Cambrai, Arras, and Tournai, would even survive the collapse of urban life in the early Middle Ages. To the east of *Belgica secunda*, stretching to the middle and lower Rhine, lay the province *Germania secunda*, with its capital at Cologne.

The Franks

German migration, long an important pattern, reached its high point between the third and fifth centuries A.D. Germanic tribes moved into the Roman Empire, established themselves, and disrupted Roman structures and institutions. To stave off this migration, the Romans had long depended on Germanic tribes within the Empire. The most famous were the Batavians, whose name became linked to the national identity of the Netherlands. But it is the role of the Franks which would prove particularly crucial. They would use the region as a funnel to "Gaul," which they would gradually transform into "France." Although considered a tribe, the Franks hardly formed a unified whole. Their name, first used in the middle of the third century, probably refers to a group of smaller tribes centered between the Rhine and Weser Rivers, including the Salians, Chattuari, Bructeri, and Chamavi, names which soon disappeared from history. Little of their culture is known because Roman chroniclers themselves knew so little about them, and the bishop Gregory of Tours, author of the sixth century *History of the Franks*, did not have much to report about them, due to a dearth of written sources, a weak oral tradition, and Gregory's own purpose, which concerned itself only with the ruling dynasty.

Frankish warriors – in the tradition of many Germanic tribes – also chose to join the Roman army. Imperial policy, aimed at checking further Germanic migration, necessarily pitted Germans against Germans as the once-mighty empire devolved into dictatorship, military rivalries, and civil war. The significance of the Franks does not rest, however, on their presence in the army – although some Frankish leaders attained high rank – but in their migration. By the mid-fourth century, Salian Franks were living in the Betuwe, between the Rhine and Waal, and later in Toxandria (the Campine), south of the Maas in Roman territory. Within the empire, they were recognized as *foederati*, federated with Rome, and in this position they absorbed Chamavi and Bructeri into their tribe. Frankish presence near the border, lasting several centuries, may explain their success in integrating so well into the Roman Empire. A certain amount of acculturation must have occurred, all the more after the Franks moved south and made Paris the center of their power.

Saxons and Frisians

Two other Germanic tribes, the Saxons and Frisians, also proved to be important to the history of the Low Countries. Both tribes hailed from northern Germany, and they, too, were sucked westward in the great migration. Much of their historical significance, of course, lies in their maritime role; Saxons and Angles, with Jutes and Frisians in their wake, established themselves in late Roman Britain. But their kinfolk also settled in the Low Countries. Several villages near Boulogne, for instance, with a name ending in *-thun* (enclosure), denote Saxon origins, and when the declining empire built fortifications on both sides of the Channel to keep out the rising number of Germanic invaders, they called the coast *Litus saxonicum*. The Frisians occupied almost all of the region north of the Rhine, and there is much to suggest that by the sixth century, their settlements extended as far south as Antwerp.

Our understanding of the late Roman and early medieval period, however, must unfortunately remain incoherent. Archaeology certainly has supplemented the scant written sources, but it provides an entirely different kind of information, and is often difficult to incorporate into what the written documents say. Excavations unearth clues about every day life and death, whereas the documents report only unusual events to which its authors attached eternal significance.

2. The Merovingian Period

Change and Continuity

In 406, when the Rhine froze, large numbers of Germans moved into Gaul, destroying towns and scattering the native population. Saint Jerome reports that Arras, Boulogne and Tournai were among the places affected. The Roman practice of stemming the German tribes with other Germans had thus failed. The Franks, who had lived relatively quietly in Toxandria, now moved south, upstream along the Scheldt. Under King Chlodio, they seized Tournai and Cambrai around 430, and Arras fell shortly thereafter. Small kingdoms were established, headed by kings who sometimes governed in the name of Rome, sometimes on their own authority.

More important than these military and political movements is the question whether these developments led to different patterns of settlement. At least a portion of the native Gallo-Roman population deserted their settlements. Aerial photography and archaeology have proven that the old rural settlements, the *villae* of the Roman period were abandoned on a large scale; unearthed coin hoards at the *villae* show that refugees had hoped to return to their homes. For decades historians and archaeologists have debated to what extent the Roman patterns of settlement continued. It seems now that most land remained, without much interruption, under cultivation – but along different organizational lines, since the structure of the Germanic settlement, farms and villages diverged considerably from the Roman one. Although Frankish settlement was relatively dense in the southern part of the region (as far south as the Somme), no area became very heavily populated, since even the largest Germanic tribes never exceeded several tens of thousands of people. The names of villages and hamlets, both past and present, give us a good indication of migration patterns. Often, two cultures and two languages, Roman and Germanic, existed side by side. Settlements in the Arras area dating from the fifth and sixth century illustrate this: places ending with *-iacas* and *-iaca*, *-curtis* (now *court*) and *-villa* (now *ville*) suggest the existence of a broad bilingual zone inhabited by Gallo-Roman autochtones and Frankish migrants. Place names ending with *-inga* and *-haim* (now *-gem* or *-hem*) or a combination of both are centered on Boulogne and the Scheldt region, suggesting intensive Frankish and (later) Saxon settlement. For example, the village of Petegem (situated near Oudenaarde) was originally *Patjinga haim*, meaning the "dwelling of the Patjo people." The anthroponymic quality of most toponyms suggests that Frankish villages were organized around a paterfamilias and his small clan of relatives and tenants, seldom more than several dozen people. The survival of Latin and its Romance successors in the south, and the persistence of Roman (and even Celtic) place names prove at least some continuity with older settlements.

This continuity – greater in the south than the north – had a considerable impact. It explains the rise and development of the Franco-Dutch language boundary in the southern part of the region, a phenomenon of fundamental importance to the later history of the Low Countries. At first Germanic migration into Latin territory made the line quite loose and porous, forming no impediment to strong economic, political, and even cultural ties across the boundary. As a result, the Low Countries would be characterized in later centuries by a high level of cohesion, political splintering and cultural diversity notwithstanding. Frankish and Saxon became the dominant languages in the regions where their presence was strong. The language boundary between Romance and Germanic tongues – with the exception of the southwest – remained remarkably stable through the centuries. In the southwest (toward the Canche and the Somme) the Germanic tongue did not survive, despite the rather dense settlement. There, Romance assimilation was greater, so that by no later than the ninth century a clear language border was discernible, a line which moved north in later centuries.

Political continuity was strongest in the south. The Germanic kings gradually established authority in their capitals, cities of the old Roman *civitates*. Clearly, their purpose was to rule – if that is the right word – their kingdoms along the lines of Roman law and administration. A generation later, Chlodowech (483?-511) did the same thing when he captured Paris and ensconced himself in the heart of the old Roman *cité*. Further administrative continuity appears in the appropriation of Roman state property and finances, the *fisci*, by the Frankish kings, and in the minting of their coins (first done at Soissons at the end of the fifth century), imitating Roman example.

The old and the new continued in social relations as well. Two types of nobility were discernible: the Germanic and the Gallo-Roman. In time, they merged, since there were no prohibitions (as with the Visigoths) on intermarriage. In addition, there were freemen and all kinds of villeins. Slavery, too, lived on, through birth or through capture, and slaves were part of the "merchandise" that made Cambrai an important center of long-distance trade. Christianity would eventually all but eradicate slavery, at least for Christians. Whether some medieval forms of tenancy differed much from slavery, however, is questionable.

The spread of Christianity owed much to the organization and communication networks of the Roman Empire, and by the mid-fourth century at least, a bishop, Servatius, had been installed at Tongeren, an important Roman center near the Maas, Rhine and Moselle. Later names of bishops or missionaries are reported at Bavay (likely) and

Tournai (certain). The new faith, introduced under Roman rule, probably did not establish deep roots in these turbulent times, least of all among the Germanic tribes. But it did not entirely disappear during the great migration, either (for example, there is proof of its persistence in Tournai and Maastricht), whereas pagan religions, already an admixture of Celtic, Roman, and Germanic beliefs, now incorporated some Christian elements. But the social impact of Christianity's demanding monotheism was still far off, and systematic attempts at conversion would not occur until the sixth century, after the empire long had disappeared and been replaced by the tribal kingdoms, of which the Frankish was the most important.

Frankish Rule

The formation of the Frankish Kingdom was the work of Chlodowech (Clovis in the old textbooks) of the Merovingian dynasty. He managed to push his territory to the south of Gaul, reaching just shy of the Mediterranean, mostly at the expense of his vanquished enemies like the Gallo-Roman Syagrius, the Burgundians, the Alemans, and the Visigoths. Paris became the Frankish capital, shifting the center of Frankish power to the south. Most Franks, however, settled north in the Low Countries, leading over time to a widening cultural divide with the ruling Frankish families far to the south.

The Frankish Kingdom was an amalgam. The king had to be a powerful leader whose authority rested on his personal successes. Nominally, however, Frankish kings continued to pledge their loyalty to Rome, the capital of a defunct empire. At the same time they were bound by the advice of assemblies of Frankish freemen and by tribal legal traditions. The Germanic tribes followed customary law, delivered orally, which, as the name suggests, determined law according to accepted practice – a stark contrast to the written and codified law of the Romans. In such a fluid situation, Chlodowech's multicultural kingdom relied far more on family ties than on an abstract conception of political identity; not the "territorial" but the "personality principle" was the leading juridical system. Within one and the same kingdom, each tribe practiced its own customary law, the Franks employing, for instance, the *Lex Salica* and *Lex Ripuaria*.

Upon his death, Chlodowech's kingdom was divided by his four sons – a move revealing the lack of statecraft in the whole Frankish period. Royal power was considered an inheritance, to be divided like any other part of an estate. This arrangement would remain a burden on the Frankish kingdom through the ninth century (or sometimes later), for it subjected the size of the kingdom to the number of dynastic heirs in each generation. The Merovingians, however, did continue to expand; Chlodowech's sons reached the Mediterranean, and both Chlotarius (d. 561) and Dagobert I (625-639) temporarily achieved unified control over much of their split kingdoms. Expansion and fragmentation existed side by side; territorial development continued, apparent in the Low Countries by the temporary existence two kingdoms: Neustria, between the Seine and Scheldt, and Austrasia, centered along the Maas and Rhine.

DE NEDERLANDEN ONDER DE MEROVINGEN

Grenzen van
stammengebieden

NOORDZEE

FRIEZEN

SAKSEN

Utrecht

Dorestad

Nijmegen

Brugge

Keulen

Gent

Aken

Kortrijk

Luik

Terwaan

Doornik

FRANKEN

Kamerijk

Trier

Soissons

Reims

Parijs

The Netherlands under the Merovingians.

The Frisians

King Dagobert deserves more attention. Under his rule the Franks attempted – with mixed results – to subdue the Frisians. This policy had several aspects; first, it aimed at political expansion. At a time when land was the chief source of revenue (and power), the motive for this is obvious enough. Moreover, the Frisians exercised control over Dorestad which, situated on the Crooked Rhine, was one of the most famous trade centers of the early Middle Ages. Together with Birka

(Sweden), Haitabu (Schleswig) and Quentowic (on the Canche, in the extreme southwest of the Germanic language area and of what we call the Low Countries), Dorestad generated much of the trade in the North Sea and Baltic. Excavations of its site (near present-day Wijk-bij-Duurstede) give a good idea of its harbor and the settlement of that time. Control of Dorestad and nearby Utrecht would give the Franks a greater share of the maritime trade. Their quest was not an easy one – the region switched hands several times – but by the eighth century the Franks decisively exercised authority over the area. By the next century, however, Vikings periodically destroyed and occupied these commercial centers.

The third reason for Frankish expansion in Frisia stemmed from religious motives. Chlodowech's conversion to Christianity around 500 paved the way for a "second Christianization" of the region. The early church had been largely urban in orientation, but this proved to be inadequate in the predominately agrarian world of the Germanic tribes. Although the bishoprics in the old *civitates* were sometimes left vacant for decades, there are nonetheless signs of a persistent Christendom. Moreover, the new wave of missions were supported by the Merovingian kings, who called upon missionaries from Gaul, Ireland, and England. The missionary Saint Amand was particularly significant for the Scheldt region. Dagobert granted Amand a *fiscus* at Elno (now St. Amand-les-Eaux in northern France), where he founded an abbey before 639. From there his companions moved north, down the Scheldt, to Ghent (where they established the Saint Bavon and Saint Peter abbeys) and Antwerp. Irish and (later) English monks also came to the continent in order to practice their ideal of self-imposed exile. Columbanus is undoubtedly the most high profile of these monks on a European scale, but Willibrord was more important for the Low Countries, becoming the "archbishop of the Frisians" (695-739). His work coincided with the growth of Frankish power in the region, and there can be no doubt about the connection between territorial expansion and missionary activity. In any event, one must not imagine that the missionaries accomplished great spiritual changes; the first phase of conversion consisted purely of the acceptance of Christian ritual. The inner recognition of theological and moral values was a process which took centuries.

The attempt by Merovingian nobility to find legitimacy in Roman antiquity has already been mentioned. When the burial place of Childerik I (d. after 477) was excavated in Tournai during the seventeenth century, Roman symbols of authority were found alongside traditional Germanic weapons. Chlodowech clothed himself in purple – the color of emperors – and received the honorific title of consul from the Byzantine emperor. None of this, however, was more than show, and the idea of a "state" steadily dissipated. Despite royal efforts to collect tolls and taxes, revenues continued to decline and the role of coinage suffered from a lack of bullion and a slowdown in trade. Land, therefore, became the exclusive standard of value, and the measure with which kings rewarded loyalty and services. The old system of exchanging land for political support, practiced by both the Romans

The holy Amand, missionary bishop in the Merovingian period, hands over his testament to St. Baudemundus. Illuminated manuscript from the Vita Sancti Amandi *(twelfth century). (Bibliothèque Municipale, Valenciennes.)*

and Germans, was now further expanded. The feudal system would later develop out of these ties.

Mayors of the Palace

Merovingian kings entrusted their estates to so-called mayors of the palace who began to assert their own power around 700. Thus the rivalry between the Frankish kings was compounded by the rivalry with their mayors. The Austrasian mayors – the Pepinians – would gradually increase their authority at the expense of the mayors of other kingdoms and ultimately to the detriment of the Merovingian kings themselves. The Austrasia-based campaigns against the Frisians offered new opportunities for such mayors as Pepin I, whose estates, a backwater since the days of Chlodowech, now became a center of power. When one of Pepin's descendants, Charles Martel, confined the Muslims to Iberia by defeating them near Poitiers (732), his dynasty's

The grave of the Frankish king Childerik I, St. Brixius Church, Tournai. The horses in the photograph were buried with the king as gifts.

prestige was further enhanced. In the long run, the victory made their seizure of the Frankish throne possible, a feat accomplished by Charles's son Pepin III.

3. The Carolingian Period (Eighth and Ninth Centuries)

Anointed Kings and Crowned Emperors

The triumph of Pepin III led to a new phase in the history of the Frankish realm. In 751, the Lombards, a Germanic tribe in northern Italy, threatened the pope and his *Patrimonium Petri*, the core of what later became the Papal States. Pepin came to the rescue, and the pontiff, in return, anointed him "king of the Franks" (*rex Francorum*) – in effect legitimating Pepin's recent coup against the Merovingian king Childerik III. The anointment, following biblical precedent, symbolized the beginning of a new royal dynasty that would pursue policies of truly European dimensions for almost a century. In the end, though, it would collapse due to a series of weaknesses, some inherent in the character and structure of the Carolingian Empire itself, and some a result of external factors.

The Pepinians had expanded their power in Austrasia by a kind of spoils system, in which administrative and ecclesiastical functions – not to mention land – were parceled out to local nobility in order to gain their sympathy and support. In this way, they provided the incentives to wage a successful war, evident in Pepin III's 734 victory over the Frisians, which led to the first sizable Frankish expansion to the north. Victories over the Lombards and the establishment of a protectorate over Rome provided the Frankish leaders with more new opportunities. Closer to home, Charlemagne, Pepin's son and heir, had engaged the Saxons in a brutal conflict. Under his rule, the Empire of the Carolingians – now named after Charlemagne – stretched from the Pyrenees to the Danube and from Frisia to central Italy. This territorial expansion encouraged both royal ambition and nostalgia for an idealized Roman past, and in 800 the pope crowned Charlemagne "Emperor" (*Imperator*) – to the dismay of Byzantium – the true successor of the old Roman Empire. More than its Merovingian predecessor, the new empire suffered under the ambiguity of being a kingdom structured by Germanic tradition and at the same time possessing aspirations to continue the Roman state. Charlemagne's ambitious Roman – and Christian – ideal was expressed in the edict *Capitulare missorum generale* (802), in which he, as trustee of the Earthly City, was to promote justice and righteousness throughout the whole Empire so that it might resemble the Heavenly City.

Charlemagne's restoration of the old *imperium*, however, was little more than a dream; the Germanic past and its values continued to live on. The tradition of dividing the kingdom after the king's death remained intact, and it was purely coincidental that Louis the Pious was Charlemagne's sole surviving son, thus inheriting the whole empire in 814. Another more structural problem was communications; how could an empire of this size adequately be administered on a road system which dated back to Roman times? Lack of financial sources, too, proved to be a major problem. Weakness in commerce, including a trade deficit with the Byzantine and Islamic worlds, had made precious

Bronze statue of a Carolingian nobleman, possibly Charlemagne, 8th century. (Musée du Louvre, Paris.)

metals scarce. Gold coins disappeared, and the gold and silver wares that the church possessed were not in economic circulation. They only drew the unwelcome attention of the Vikings.

The Beginnings of Feudalism

Effective administration – the aim of Charlemagne and Louis – thus could only be realized by rewarding land and its income to those who performed royal service, an arrangement which soon developed into feudalism. A fief – in Latin a *beneficium* or *feodum*, as it was called from the tenth century onwards – usually consisted of an estate, dispensed by a "lord" (who asked for services) to a *vassus*, or "man" (who would perform those services). The lord continued to own the land, and the vassal enjoyed all its fruits – a contract which ended upon the death of either, or in the case of disloyalty. Indeed, this system of patronage rested on loyalty and is reminiscent of its roots in the old Roman *clientela*. It should be noted that this arrangement remained restricted to the nobility; it had nothing to do with obligations levied on peasants within what is commonly called the manorial system (see below). Feudalism, designed to increase the power of central authority (by fostering administrative and military reliability) eventually had the opposite effect. Under pressure from the vassals, the system became increasingly hereditary, and in 877, it became legalized as such by the "Capitulary of Quierzy" in the western part of the Empire (West Francia). The permanence of fiefs jeopardized the existence of a unified empire and strong government.

The Division of Kingdoms

This impossibility of strong government was already evident in the Treaty of Verdun (843), in which the sons of Louis the Pious (who had died in 840) divided the empire among themselves. Lothar I, the eldest, received the title of emperor, and, in addition to northern Italy, inherited the territory roughly between the Rhine on the east and the Scheldt, Maas, Saône, and Rhône on the west. This was Middle Francia; Charles the Bald received West Francia, and Louis the German, East Francia. This division would prove very important for European history in general – influencing a long-standing rivalry between France and Germany – and for the Low Countries in particular. The middle kingdom of Lothar stretched from central Italy to Frisia, and included not only Rome but the "new Rome" of Aachen (Aix-la-Chapelle), Charlemagne's seat of government. Most of the Low Countries belonged to the central kingdom (only a small portion to the west of the Scheldt belonged to France). It included political and trading centers in the Maas and Rhine area with a strong Roman tradition and vital but elitist culture: Aachen, Liège, Maastricht, and Nijmegen. The kingdom also included huge marshes, like the area west of Utrecht, that would have to be saved from the sea in later centuries.

With Lothar's death in 855, dynastic fortunes took yet another turn: his kingdom was divided among his three sons. His second son and namesake inherited the northern part, situated between Frisia and the Jura, called *Lotharii regnum*, Lotharingia (still surviving in the

Regional boundaries of the Frankish Kingdom.

French as Lorraine). It is not necessary here to enumerate all of the territorial changes, but Lotharingia's eventual annexation by the German king Henry the Fowler in 925 was of lasting importance. With this annexation, the Scheldt became the boundary between France and Germany. The area west of the Scheldt – i.e., Flanders and Artois – was officially (hardly in reality) bound to France until the sixteenth century; some areas to the east continued to belong, at least formally, to the German "Holy Roman" empire as late as the nineteenth century. But this situation did not prevent the Low Countries from developing an economic, cultural, and political life of their own in the late Middle Ages.

Invasion of the Vikings

One more vulnerability of the Carolingian Empire must be mentioned: the invasions of the Vikings, whose seaborne rovings carried them from Canada to Baghdad. The speed of their raids and the slowness of the Carolingian defense system prevented effective checks against them until around 860, some six decades after their first incursions. An assessment of their impact depends upon whether one considers archaeological evidence or the written reports. The former has revealed a dynamic, commercial people with an interest in creature comforts and beauty; the latter stressed their cruelty and ferociousness.

In the course of the ninth century, Vikings (mostly Danes) were able to sail from the Atlantic and North Sea down the Seine and Rhine, and all the rivers in between. Written accounts like the *Annales Regni Francorum* and the *Annales Bertiniani* report many raids against Quentowic, Saint-Omer, and Arras, against Antwerp, Ghent and Tournai, and against Witla (a vanished settlement near Rotterdam), Utrecht, and Dorestad. Frisia was the preferred destination, and in 826 Louis the Pious was compelled to grant the Danish kings Harald and Rorik feudal rights there. A defense against the Danes developed slowly, and the strengthened walls of, for instance, Arras and Saint-Omer reduced the Danes's menace in the 880s. Even more effective were the circular fortifications built along the Flemish and Zeeland coasts, from Bourbourg to Burg-op-Schouwen. When Arnulf of Carinthia defeated the Normans at Leuven (Louvain) in 891, the Viking threat came to an end, at least in the Low Countries. The central authority of the Carolingian kingdoms had proven powerless to stop them. Hence local lords, already profiting from their newly hereditary fiefs, strengthened their position further by serving as protectors against the Vikings. Once administrators in service of the Carolingians, they became independent potentates, some of whose descendants, in the course of decades or centuries, would become dukes and counts ruling sizable principalities.

Ideal and Reality

"Land is power": this adage illustrates that – apart from very limited long-distance trade in slaves, weapons, cloth, and earthenware – the economy remained limited to agriculture. Although the Frisians generated some trade ("Frisian cloth," even when it may have been produced in Flanders, is mentioned in several sources), the economy was overwhelmingly confined to the system of autarky imposed by primitive agriculture and the lack of communications, producing what people consume and vice versa. This led to the manorial system in areas capable of generating both crops and livestock. On a village by village basis, dependent peasants would work on the manor of their lord in exchange for part of what they raised. In this fashion, a balanced system of agricultural exploitation was possible, as evidenced in several royal and ecclesiastical inventories of the period. This static system, however, led to the immobility of the peasants' social and legal status. Whether freemen or serfs, the peasants were bound to the land, and immobility in general was considered a moral good, the result of growing Christian influences.

Attack on a city, possibly by Vikings;
sketch from the "Utrecht Psalter," ca.
800. (Universiteitsbibliotheek, Utrecht.)

Charlemagne and his son Louis the Pious, for instance, had been remarkably influenced by their clerical counselors. The lower classes were far from being thoroughly christianized, and the last mention of pagans in the area dates back to the early eighth century. The church's organization increasingly expanded in the Low Countries. The role of the missionary Boniface was crucial in this respect, despite his difficulties. When he arrived from England in 716, the task of converting the Frisians was just as pressing as it had been under Willibrord a generation earlier. Operating out of Utrecht, Mainz, and the abbey he founded in Fulda, Boniface's extended efforts were slow and ran into resistance; the Frisians murdered him at Dokkum in 754.

Carolingian organization aimed at uniformity, conforming to medieval opinions of an ideal Christian state. This systematization expressed itself in various aspects of society. The Carolingians, for example, actively created legislation (as seen in the *capitularia*) to influence the passive customary law of the Germanic tribes. The *missi dominici*, traveling royal envoys, also exercised control over the local authorities in the *pagi* (or *gouwen*), ruled by counts in the name of the emperor. Actual names like Oostergo and Westergo in Frisia and Hainaut (Henegouwen in Dutch) are reminiscent of this medieval organization.

The ideal of unification was also apparent on the religious level. In the Merovingian period, the quality of monastic life reflected Irish or Anglo-Irish origins, including an interest in missionary activities. From such centers as Torhout (near Bruges), missionaries were sent out to the Frisians and Saxons. The Carolingians, however, insisted that all monks follow the Rule of Saint Benedict – stemming from sixth-century Italy – which led to a Benedictine monopoly in monastic life for many centuries. Clerics living in urban areas were asked to abide by the more

An aerial view of Middelburg reveals the circular fortifications built at the end of the ninth century.

flexible rule established by Saint Augustine around 400. It should not come as a surprise that the emperor or king frequently involved himself in religious matters. Separation of church and state did not exist, and the rulers regarded it as their responsibility to God to promote church life, in the footsteps of the first Christian emperor of Rome, Constantine. But the easy demands placed on the village clergy and the apparent failure of, for instance, planned but apparently not implemented general primary education, show the deep chasm between ambitious policy and reality.

Because of the Austrasian origins of the dynasty, the region between the Maas and Rhine played a central role (see above) in the formation of elite Carolingian culture. The still-impressive palace chapel in Aachen was the most beautiful and prestigious construction that the Carolingians were able to build, although both its conception and materials were borrowed from the Roman past. Moreover, the court, nobility, rich abbeys, and churches patronized the creation of brilliantly decorated manuscripts, some of them following the Byzantine model of golden letters on purple parchment and bound with precious stones and gold. Given the Carolingian vision for unity, it is not surprising that they devoted much attention to the quality of content: the Bible was submitted to textual criticism to make it error-free, and the "Carolingian minuscule," a uniform and simple script, developed. These measures intended to make the transmission of knowledge, specifically that of the Bible, more accurate and more quickly disseminated.

And yet this period should be characterized as "the disillusioned hope of the Carolingians": their efforts were great, but their means were modest, and the time span to achieve it far too short.

4. The "Iron" Tenth Century

Even if the Low Countries were central to the Carolingians because of Aachen and several other cities, it is still impossible to attribute a coherent character to them during that time. And even if such a character existed, the meager sources give no evidence of it. More information on the tenth century is available, although this should not be exaggerated. For example, the yearly average of preserved charters originating in present-day Belgium is 6.7 for the tenth century, compared to 1.2 in the seventh, 3.0 for the eighth and 3.7 for the ninth. But averages for later centuries are strikingly higher: 17.7 for the eleventh century and 110.7 for the twelfth! Even though charters are not the only written sources – there are also annals and chronicles – these statistics give a good idea of the limitations of the information, in number, in type, and in scope. Whole swaths of early medieval society remain beyond the reach of historians, and these figures clearly demonstrate why a wider view is only feasible from the twelfth century onwards.

The implosion of the Carolingian Empire had all sorts of consequences. Old regions regained their former names and cultural identity, such as Aquitaine and Burgundy. For the Low Countries, however, Merovingian names like Neustria and Austrasia had fallen into disuse and new names had not yet achieved geographical coherence, if they existed at all. The *pagus Flandrensis* (Flanders district), for example, only indicated the area around Bruges, rather than the much larger political unit that would later bear its name. Lotharingia owed its name to its ruler, Lothar II, and any connection with passed-on tradition was wholly absent. In any event, boundaries in the Low Countries were not imposed by economic conditions, political traditions or cultural identity. The Scheldt boundary between East and West Francia, however, even when drawn in 925, was not new, in the sense that it had long divided Roman *civitates* and Celtic tribes, and continued to divide bishoprics. In general, rivers, particularly in a time of tenuous communication, were crucial to establishing what unity there was. Without any precedent in history, the people of the Low Countries would gradually, imperceptibly, integrate as a result of these rivers. From the rich grain fields of Artois and the hills of southern Flanders, across the bogs of Holland and Utrecht, to the saltings and meadows of Frisia, rivers brought trade, trade which would increase in volume over the years.

These new developments, begun in the tenth century, took place during a new political marginalization of the Low Countries. The Carolingian axis Aachen-Rome declined in importance, as first Orléans and then Paris became centers for France, and as German kings established their own changing political centers. Neither the weakened central authority in East or in West Francia had vital interests in the Low Countries; this explains why powerful nobles were able to expand their own regional power. Economic dynamics, stimulated by the rivers, the sea, and – in the south – by the old road system, strengthened this tendency.

Still, we must refrain from determinism. The sometimes dry story of how the different counties and duchies developed, slowly but steadily, should tell us that political developments could have gone in a myriad of directions. For example, the history of Flanders, even as late as the twelfth century, gives no indication that it would ever form a political federation with the principality of Guelders, and the reverse is equally true.

Example of the medieval art of illuminated manuscripts: the evangeliary of Hugo d'Oignies, 1228-1230.

The reference to Flanders is not arbitrarily chosen in this section on the "Iron Century." The first and important reason for choosing it is that West Francia – earlier than East Francia – experienced the decentralizing effects of feudalism. After the late ninth century, it was no longer customary to find kings from the traditional Carolingian dynasty but to find them from the dukes of Francia (Ile-de-France). This indicates that the nobility, hitherto having served the emperor or king, gradually changed their offices to suit their own interests, and in so doing changed kingship into a local affair. The growing power of the counts of Flanders also fits into these developments, which included efforts at self-legitimation, even through the invention of legendary ancestors. The first count, Iron Baldwin (863/4-879) laid the basis for his power by eloping with the daughter of Emperor Charles the Bald, a proven method for social climbing. His domain included not only Bruges but the area around Ghent. An increasingly successful leader against the Vikings and the tutor of the Carolingian heir Louis the Stammerer, Baldwin was clearly a rising star in the political firmament, a situation he used to further undermine central authority and dispense with ambitious rivals. His son Baldwin II (879-918) completed the transformation of the count of Flanders's status from that of a royal administrator to that of a territorial prince, just as other regional potentates in other parts of France did. For more than a century, the Flemish counts won territory to the south, taking old towns (Arras), prosperous abbeys (Saint Bertin's), and rich granaries. Under Arnulf (918-965), they reached the limits of southern expansion when they took Amiens on the Somme. There Arnulf's move southward was checked by Normandy, a duchy established by the Viking leader Rolo in 911.

Further expansion, therefore, implied shifting forces to the east. But the territory of East Francia directly east of the Scheldt had undergone its own changes. There the Carolingians had died out in 911, and the great nobility offered the crown to the duke of Frankenland, who, with the dukes of Bavaria, Saxony, and Swabia, each presided over parts of Germany named after the great tribes. When Henry the Fowler was elected king in 919, the basis was set for German expansion. His descendants, Otto I, II, and III (936-1002) renewed the vision for a *Renovatio Imperii* in which the Roman Empire was to be restored. To further this end, they developed the "Imperial Church," in which bishops were entrusted with ruling principalities. By appointing them, the Ottonians hoped to overcome the effects of hereditary feudalism which had so jeopardized central authority. But the Ottonians – as *Roman* Emperors – devoted a great deal of interest and resources to their position in Italy; accordingly, they squandered the opportunity to strengthen their power north of the Alps, where the process of fragmentation continued. Whereas French royal power began growing steadily in the later Middle Ages, creating a strongly unified state, the unification of Germany did not occur until the nineteenth century.

Lotharingia did not have the cohesive ethnic identity found in the German duchies, and an attempt to create an independent kingdom failed at the end of the ninth century. The Imperial Church, however, did shape its future in the tenth century; Otto I named Bruno, his brother and archbishop of Cologne, duke of Lotharingia (953). After Bruno's death, the duchy was split in two: one part, Upper Lotharingia, eventually became French Lorraine, the other, Lower Lotharingia, corresponds with the greater part of the Low Countries (the areas west of the Scheldt excepted, of course). Lotharingia's lack of increased cohesion deepened as local nobility successfully resisted imperial control. It never was a stable political entity, and in the eleventh century it broke further up into fiefs.

Gravensteen, Ghent. Its appearance today is close to how it looked at the end of the twelfth century. The most imposing of all medieval castles, Gravensteen was inspired by Krac de Chevaliers, the famous crusaders' castle in Syria.

2 Counts, Cities, and Clerics

The Eleventh, Twelfth, and Thirteenth Centuries

L.J.R. Milis

Between the eleventh and thirteenth centuries, the Low Countries underwent a political, economic, demographic, and religious metamorphosis. Despite political fragmentation, a number of feudal lords managed, with the help of cities and at the expense of other nobles, to install a more centralized authority over larger territories.

The development of the cities was stimulated by more intense trade and by population growth. Increases in population led to the reclamation and drainage of once nonarable land. Over a century, these developments spread from the southwest northwards, via Flanders, Hainaut and Brabant, to Holland and further east.

The church reformed itself at the instigation of Gregory VII, becoming a more effective institution; Christian belief itself became more internalized. Culturally, the monopoly of the church was eventually broken by the rise of the merchant class in the cities.

1. Political Fragmentation

Writing a political history of the Low Countries from 1000 to 1300 is a most daunting task: it is almost impossible to give an overview. There are no "Low Countries" to speak of, only a patchwork of domains, some larger, some smaller. They came and went, not so much because of socioeconomic factors, but by the vicissitudes of dynastic politics practiced by local lords. Eventually, a number of these smaller domains grew into larger principalities. The power of the greater nobles (such as counts and dukes) who controlled them depended on several factors: the limited extent of central authority that remained from the Carolingian period, their relations with the lesser nobility under them and with the new urban elite, and finally the level of cooperation or rivalry among themselves. The strongest among them would exploit their strength; the weakest could only hope to thwart the strong.

Economically, the period began auspiciously; between 1050 and 1250, the regional economy expanded considerably, but declined thereafter. Political developments, too, became increasingly influenced by socioeconomic trends, which included the increasing importance of trade, the rise of guilds, the cities, coinage, and greater social mobility. Three participants – the greater nobility, the lesser nobility, and the urban elites – played a power game of musical chairs, which the lesser nobility would lose, paving the way for the centralization and larger economies of scale strongly evident in the thirteenth century. Still, the influence of the lesser nobility persisted for centuries, demonstrating that their traditions and established prerogatives continued to function as effective brakes on far-reaching centralization.

Flanders's Lead

Flanders's beginnings have already been described: a district on the northern edge of France, its counts were able to build an independent power base and expand their territory at the expense of its neighbors. When expansion was blocked to the south, the counts of Flanders saw new opportunities in the Holy Roman Empire lying to the east of the Scheldt, in Lotharingia. Baldwin IV and V (988-1067) managed to seize the Land of Aalst and the islands of Zeeland in the Scheldt estuary. Why mention these relatively small gains? In the first place, it illustrates an important ambiguity: a vassal (the Flemish count) now formally recognized two lords (the French and the German king), showing that the basis of feudalism, loyalty to the lord, one lord, was actually subordinate to the self-interest of the vassals. In the second place, Flanders would now increasingly participate in Lotharingian power struggles and the formation of new principalities. This would ultimately produce the unity-in-diversity characteristic of the political landscape of the Low Countries.

In the eleventh century, Flanders was the only fully developed political unit in the region. Baldwin V further strengthened his own control by building fortresses commanded by castellans, who represented the count locally. In contrast, castellans were introduced in Holland only a century later. They too, however, were feudal vassals with hereditary claims, meaning that they were often untrustworthy. But no other system was yet possible; no lord possessed enough money to pay a loyal corps of administrators, nor was there as yet a mentality to make such reforms.

By the eleventh century, the counts of Flanders also took measures to develop the barren interior that was later called, in half-legendary terms, "the Merciless Forest." They founded or stimulated the growth of cities like Ypres and Lille, and built at least some roads and canals for the first time since the collapse of the Roman Empire. The count granted the first city charters and privileges (to Gerardsbergen and Aire) about the same time that the bishop of Liège first granted a charter to the city of Huy (1066). This meant that cities became exempted from the power of the local nobility and that their citizens received special privileges guaranteed by statute. The dominance of Flanders was also evident elsewhere – institutionally, economically, culturally – and its lead established a pattern: for centuries, almost all social and political developments in the Low Countries moved from the southwest (Flanders) to the northeast.

Political Life in Lotharingia

Most of the principalities which later constituted the Seventeen Provinces of the Netherlands were part of politically inchoate Lower Lotharingia, where political organization remained weak. Only in the south, in Hainaut, which bordered Flanders, was there a relatively high level of political cohesion. Looking at a map of the eleventh century Low Countries, one would be able to spot Flanders and Hainaut quite easily, but a lot of imagination would be required to distinguish the other regions. Already in the beginning of the twelfth century, a poet in Saint-Omer could write a poem hailing "his" Flanders (*De laude Flandriae*), while many regions in Lotharingia scarcely possessed a proper name.

Elsewhere, this political backwardness elsewhere was due to the Ottonian system practiced by the Holy Roman Emperors, who continued to exercise real power in the region by appointing loyal bishop-princes in Liège, Utrecht, and Cambrai. These bishops, who together had ecclesiastical authority over the region, maintained central authority for the Ottonians. The bishop of Liège ruled a territory along the Middle Maas, between Huy and Maastricht, which only partially corresponded with his bishopric. It would remain badly splintered and would never become part of the Seventeen Provinces. It was not until 1794 that invading French armies put an end to the bishop's temporal power.

The bishop of Utrecht, whose diocese roughly corresponded to the Netherlands of today, presided over a territory called the Sticht: the Lower Sticht, approximately the same as the present province of Utrecht; and the Upper Sticht, including Drenthe, Overijssel and the city of Groningen. Cambrai, although in German territory, lay in the ecclesiastical province of Rheims, in France. Here, too, the bishop received a temporal mandate over lands called *le Cambrésis*, but these lay within the sphere of influence of the counts of Flanders, not the Holy Roman Emperor.

DE ZUIDELIJKE NEDERLANDEN OMSTREEKS 1100

The Southern Netherlands around 1100.

In any event, German imperial control over the sees declined with the Concordat of Worms (1122), which ended the Investiture Controversy between the emperor and the pope by taking away the emperor's prerogative to appoint bishops. In fact, it signalled the end of most imperial interventions in the Low Countries. The emperors of the Holy Roman Empire still considered it an important symbolic privilege to appoint the duke of Lower Lotharingia, but in reality it was an honorific title with no fixed content or authority. In the eleventh century, these dukes belonged to the noble family of Ardennes, whose power was centered in Verdun. Their most famous representative was Geoffrey of Bouillon, who was known as the "Guardian of the Holy Sepulchre" after the Crusaders' seizure of Jerusalem in 1099. In 1101, this ducal title was transferred to the counts of Limburg (centered east of Liège) and in 1106 to the count of Leuven (Louvain). They would later become the dukes of Brabant.

If occasionally emperors did decide to intervene in the Low Countries, hereafter, it was because they intended to enforce their titular control over the region. Frederick I Barbarossa (1152-1190) boldly imposed his own candidate, Raoul von Zähringen, for bishop of Liège in 1167. But the emperors were usually too preoccupied with Italy – where their claim to be Roman emperors ran afoul of the wealthy Italian city-states and an increasingly powerful papacy – to spend much energy in the north. After 1198, all German influence in the Low Countries ended when two families, the Hohenstaufen and the Welfs, battled over the imperial throne, throwing the German lands into chaos and division.

1237 Dutch translation of the charter, granted in 1165 and lasting until 1177, by Philip of Alsace to the city of Ghent. (Rijksarchief Gent.)

When a count of Holland, William II, was elected emperor in 1247, it was because of his weakness, not his strength; his political interests remained wedded to Holland, and he died in an expedition against the Frisians.

As in Flanders, regions in Lotharingia coalesced around important political and economic centers: in Hainaut, it was the city of Mons; in Brabant, Leuven. Not surprisingly, expansion often led to military conflict, based on legitimate and invented claims to territory by the respective nobility. Dynastic considerations were paramount well into the thirteenth century, as evidenced by the importance of political marriages, which were supposed to secure the future of each dynasty. Church prohibitions against incest (used in a broader sense than nowadays) were therefore often evaded by nobility who were anxious to solidify and expand their position.

Gradual Consolidation

The consolidation of territory in the late Middle Ages in fact suggests that marriage, rather than war, was the more effective way for counts and dukes to expand their power. The temporary union of Flanders and Hainaut under Baldwin VI (1067-1070), and under Baldwin VIII and his descendants (1191-1280) are examples of this, just as the "personal union" of the Avesnes dynasty, which would unite the fortunes of Hainaut and Holland in a later period. Of all the high nobility of the Low Countries, it was the Flemish counts of the House of Alsace, Thierry (1128-1168) and Philip (1168-1191), who were the most active and successful in international politics. Both were involved in the Crusades. Moreover, Philip wielded power as the tutor of the crown prince of France, Philip II Augustus, and by ruling (through his wife) the county of Vermandois, which bordered on the lands of the French crown. Later, he married a Portuguese princess who called herself "Queen" Mathilda, another sign of Philip's power and international ambition.

Count Diederik of Alsace and his consort Sybille of Anjou; sketches by Anton de Succa from 1602. (Koninklijke Bibliotheek, Brussels.)

All of this also demonstrates the continuation of feudal interests, but in the long run the counts of Flanders were not blind to new – and opposite – developments. In a time of great economic expansion, they founded cities and granted them rights at the expense of local nobles. With their new wealth which resulted from increased income, they were able to hire (and fire) a new type of administrator, the bailiffs, who carried out their instructions and implemented justice. Rendering verdicts remained in the hands of aldermen, town inhabitants who were appointed by the counts. These developments turned Flanders from a feudal principality into a kind of mini-state (even though the word "state" is anachronistic and should be used advisedly here). Elsewhere, these changes occurred more sluggishly. Appointed bailiffs did not arrive in Holland until the time of Floris V, an active count who can be compared to Philip of Alsace but who lived a century later (d. 1296). Here, as in Flanders, feudal tradition and economic realities existed together in a precarious balance. When making decisions, Floris was compelled to consider England, whose production and export of wool was becoming indispensable to the economy in the Low Countries.

The counts of Flanders suffered from strained relations with their cities, whose ambitions showed similarities with those of the Northern Italian city-states. In Brabant, relations were more amicable, owing to the relative weakness of the dukes of Brabant and the modest size of the cities, which included Leuven, Brussels, and Antwerp. Moreover, both parties in Brabant stood to gain by controlling the transportation of goods, from Bruges to the Rhineland and points further east. By the late twelfth and thirteenth centuries, this trade was growing sizably in volume, and Brabant sought to control this trade by expanding eastward, challenging the power of Liège and Limburg. In 1204, Brabant received authority to rule over Maastricht (at the expense of the emperor), and won even more territory in the Battle of Woeringen (1288) at the expense of Liège, Guelders and the archbishop of Cologne. After this, Cologne could no longer play a political role in the Low Countries, and with the duchy's annexation of Limburg, Liège became hemmed in by Brabant. As a result, Brabant became the most powerful entity in the Low Countries in the late thirteenth century, as Flanders was bogged down in conflicts with France and faced growing economic problems.

In particular, Brabant was blessed with a quiet northern border which it shared with Holland. (Sometimes conflicts did arise; for instance, they struggled for control of Dordrecht, then the most important city in the north.) Holland, which only developed slowly between the eleventh and thirteenth centuries, followed the pattern established by Flanders and Brabant. It fought a protracted conflict with Flanders over the Zeeland islands at the mouth of the Scheldt until these islands permanently came under Holland's rule in the early fourteenth century. The history of Holland can said to have begun in the early eleventh century, when a local nobleman, Dirk III, defeated a German force at Vlaardingen (near present-day Rotterdam) in 1018. The rising political power of his descendants depended upon the reclamation of Holland's soggy landscape; the barely inhabitable area was turned into arable land, and waterways were developed for easy communication. Controlling the water was essential, and methods to do this were hard to develop. The boundaries of Holland were barely delineated, but they extended roughly from the saltings of what later became South Holland and Zeeland northward, and eastward through the bogs and clay-like lands along the Rhine until they reached lands controlled by the bishop of Utrecht. In the north, the counts of Holland faced the West Frisians, and it was not until the end of the thirteenth century that Count Floris V of Holland decisively defeated them.

One of the more difficult problems in researching the Middle Ages is determining how sensitive its political leaders were to the desires of their subjects. Whatever the case, it is clear that the land reclamation directed by the counts of Holland clearly helped the population. It soon

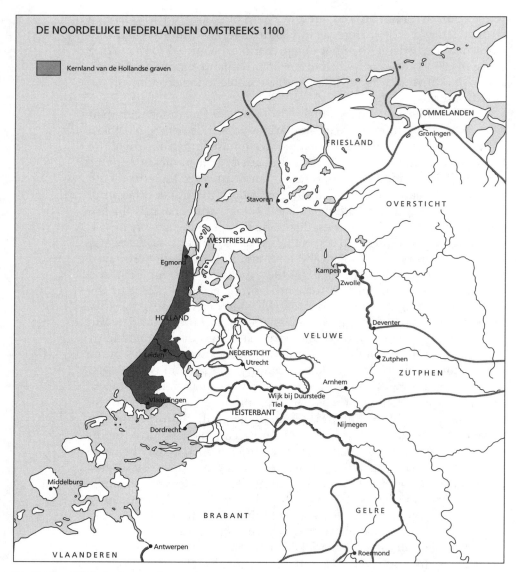

The Northern Netherlands around 1100.

became apparent, however, that this required large scale organization and vast resources. Dike reeves imitated Flemish techniques in the construction and maintenance of dikes, but it was not until the establishment of cities and their wealth— in which Holland's counts followed Brabant's pattern of actively founding cities – that Holland developed into an important regional power.

When the cities did come, wherever they came, the losers were almost invariably the lesser nobility. Only in the more socially static eastern parts of the Low Countries, as in Guelders or Cleves, did the lesser nobility remain important power brokers for awhile longer because of the lack of large, ambitious cities. The decline of the lesser nobility was already apparent in Flanders in 1127, when one such family succeeded in killing count Charles the Good, but paid dearly for doing so rather than reaping the gains they anticipated. In Holland, too, the lesser nobility managed to murder Floris V in 1296, but could not break the power of the counts. In most areas, counts forged powerful coalitions with the cities, whose newfound wealth through trade and the wool processing made them desirable and important allies. The combination of feudal allegiances and urban commerce had a powerful – and complicated – effect on political life, particularly in Flanders, whose nominal feudal fealty to France belied its economic dependence on the English wool supply.

In 1191, when Philip of Alsace died childless, Flanders was a well-administered country, more akin to the well-developed political system in Norman England than to the less efficient kingdom of France. Still, there was a considerable chasm between the interests of the counts and the land as a whole. Philip's successors, who also ruled over Hainaut, used their possessions as springboards for foreign adventure; Baldwin IX even became Latin emperor in Constantinople during the Fourth Crusade. In 1214, however, the French king Philip II Augustus defeated the Flemish count and his allies (the English king, the emperor, the duke of Brabant and the count of Holland) at Bouvines, demonstrating the military primacy of France. The battle signalled the decline of Flanders, and its leading role in economic development was soon eclipsed.

All the major powers of the Low Countries had fought together at Bouvines, but it would be a mistake to interpret this as growing regional unity; each ruler had chosen to fight for his own reasons, and drifted apart after Bouvines. Other trends, however, continued. By the thirteenth century, the merchant class had begun to influence the administration of various local powers. In Flanders, the patricians, the wealthiest burghers of the cities, enjoyed an increasing role in the selection of the magistracy. A centralized council of aldermen (the *scabini Flandriae*) was established, representing the big cities. By the twelfth century, Liège and Utrecht had also developed institutions which guaranteed a voice for the merchant class.

In the long run, only Frisia had escaped both the feudalism and the urbanization which had transformed most of the Low Countries. Its social organization and cultural climate (which we know from the centuries-old Frisian law written down in the thirteenth century) were most similar to Britain and Scandinavia, who were important trading partners with Frisia. Powerful landed nobility scarcely existed, and the counts of Holland found it exceedingly difficult to assert their authority over the Frisians. However, to say that the Frisians were democratic, at least in the modern sense, is fallacious; the large cattle owners and important traders possessed most of the wealth – and accordingly, most of the political power.

This overview is necessarily superficial as it reduces many events down to general trends, and generalities do injustice to complex historical realities. At any moment, developments could have taken an entirely different turn: Flanders, for instance, might have become completely subservient to France; Frisia might have remained part of northern Europe; or Guelders, Cleves, and Luxembourg might have become an integral part of central Europe. Premature deaths and childless marriages often effectively blocked the great nobles' ambitions for larger, centralized authority, and in almost all cases, centralization was not pursued out of any political or social ideal but out of the nobility's concern for their dynasty's future. If any regional unity or cohesiveness existed in the thirteenth-century Low Countries, it was because of a coincidence of divergent interests, riven together by geographical conditions, particularly the tangle of rivers and the proximity of the sea. That many of the regional interactions, including economic contacts, were coupled with violence only proves this point. Sometimes allies and partners, sometimes rivals and enemies, the inhabitants of the Low Countries acted with a strange mix of conflict and cooperation.

2. Economic and Social Relations

The "renaissance of the twelfth century," a phrase coined around 1930, was intended to characterize the cultural and intellectual rebirth of the period. Now it is used to describe a much broader series of developments – including economic, political and religious change – which occurred between 1050 and 1250. Very few periods in the history of Europe and the Low Countries witnessed as much change as these two hundred years, and it is only a slight exaggeration to say that the world of 1250 bore little resemblance to the world of 1050. Economic changes were at the center of this metamorphosis, which consisted largely of changes in farming, and in the increasing importance of trade and commerce. These changes exerted a tremendous impact on the social fabric of the Low Countries.

To what extent was this economic takeoff dependent on earlier factors and developments? A definitive answer is hard to provide, given the lack of evidence and the difficulty of its interpretation. For example, innumerable shards of pottery can be found at any archaeological site – incontestable signs that earthenware was an important part of trade and the material culture of every village. But written evidence about these artifacts is extremely rare, as it is in many instances. Written sources for the twelfth century become more numerous, but historians must avoid thinking when items were reported for the first time they were only then being used for the first time.

Demography, Agriculture, and the New Lands

The Carolingian manorial system assumed a closed universe, with a systematic and strongly hierarchical organization, both socially and legally. It also assumed the presence of large landowners overseeing manors whose contours would remain static. Still, there is evidence that around this time, limited amounts of new land were being developed for agriculture, perhaps a reaction to soil exhaustion or demographic pressure. Certainly soil depletion was a very serious problem at this time, a condition that was worsened by the lack of livestock (except for the meadowlands of Frisia and parts of Holland), whose manure was essential to productive crop-planting. Livestock became more numerous in the eleventh and twelfth centuries, but excavations suggest that beef remained a limited source of nutrition for the common people.

Demographics, too, played an important role in the search for new land. It is estimated that the population of Picardy (in northern France) grew between 0.12 percent and 0.72 percent a year during the twelfth and thirteenth centuries. The growing population could only be fed in two ways – with higher yields or with more land under cultivation. This leads to the chicken-or-the-egg question: did higher yields allow for a population increase, or did the increase in population foster greater inventiveness? No simple answer can suffice, but some historians have pointed out that new agricultural techniques came (or were reported) later than demographic growth, suggesting that the latter is true.

The heavy plow – which replaced the much older "scratch" plow – made the cultivation of wet soil possible, as did the switch from wood to iron implements. The harrow, too, proved an important innovation. Moreover, farmers now used the three-field system (replacing the old two-field system) in which fields were divided into those containing winter crops (wheat and rye), summer crops (barley and oats), and those lying fallow. The following year, the fields were rotated. By cultivating different kinds of crops, this system also provided protection against failed harvests, and brought about a more varied diet, which including more vegetables. The threat of hunger declined and people became more resistant to illness. Horses – once solely associated with knighthood – now became draught animals with the invention of effective halters. Use of oxen declined correspondingly, but disappeared only gradually. Through these changes, the ratio of seed to harvest rose from 1:2.5 in the ninth century (for the imperial lands of Annappes near Lille) to 1:14. More people could be fed, and hunger gradually disappeared from the experiences of twelfth century people. Famine could reappear, however, after prolonged periods of bad weather (as happened in 1124-1126 and 1196-1198), when stored supplies were depleted.

This agricultural transformation started with the massive clearing of new lands and continued from the eleventh century onwards. This process had already modestly begun during the Carolingian period, as lords and peasants deforested their own domains – insofar as the inflexible organization of the manor permitted it. The large-scale cultivation of new lands that took place from the eleventh to thirteenth centuries continues to determine the still-existing patterns of settlement in the Low Countries. Modern urbanization and the reclamation of the Zuyder Zee in the twentieth century, however, have dramatically changed this landscape.

The creation of polders – meadowlands below sea level – was one important form of land reclamation. Profiting from a lowered sea level, coastal inhabitants were able to build a series of dikes, from the River Aa in the south, to East Frisia beyond the Eems. The saltings, first used as temporary sheep pastures, could now be protected by dikes and desalinated, turning them into productive meadows. Wastelands along the coast traditionally belonged to the higher nobility, who had usurped coastal rights from the kings. Worthless land now became potentially valuable, and in the twelfth and especially thirteenth centuries the high nobility granted uncultivated lands, including many near the sea, to abbeys. Dikes were sizable projects and demanded high maintenance, and many parts of Utrecht and Holland – including the low-lying peat bogs exploited for fuel – required sluices and canals to control water levels. Dike reeves were appointed to oversee district water authorities, who tried to keep the system in good order. At least several counts of Holland found these improvements important enough to personally promote them; in 1165, Count Floris III tried to dam the Rhine at Zwammerdam, initiating a conflict with the bishop of Utrecht which required the mediation of the emperor Frederick Barbarossa. By the thirteenth century, there were overarching water authorities responsible for water control throughout a whole region; the Rhineland Council, headquartered in Leiden, is the best known (and still extant) example.

In the interior, inhabitants cleared forests and established new villages, indicated by the suffix -*rode* (in Dutch) and -*sart* (in French) or evident in such suffixes as -*bos(ch)*, -*hout*, and -*woud*, meaning wood. Heaths were also settled, but the new inhabitants seemed to prefer deforestation or poldering where that was possible; these lands were more productive, and some heaths were thus ignored for centuries. This pattern is easily discernible on old (and even new) maps as a series of long but narrow cultivated parcels of land (*Langstreifen* in German) which perpendicularly lay out to new roads. From the thirteenth century on, settlers from Flanders and Holland also migrated to Central and Eastern Europe – primarily to Slavic regions once within the Holy Roman Empire's sphere of influence. In this process of *Ostkolonization*, the settlers took advantage of new farming techniques and benefitted from a privileged social and legal status.

However well a Carolingian manor might have been regimented in theory (most peasants were supposed to be given some thirty-five acres), local conditions must have varied considerably. Only scanty information exists on how or if this system worked in practice, and even less on how manorial inhabitants perceived their lot in life. But we do know that the system was too static to endure for very long, since it offered few opportunities for mobility, social improvement, or differentiation. Moreover, it seems logical that peasants spent more energy on their own acreages than on the land belonging to their lord; and it is quite likely that the low yields of these lands made manors unprofitable. Therefore, by the late Middle Ages the villages' communal lands – which stemmed from the collective exploitation of the manor – were often subdivided into individualized units.

Population pressures alone threatened the stability of the manor, since the land could not be infinitely subdivided among its tenants. Demographics thus put an end to a static agrarian pattern in Europe. Pressures to cultivate new lands brought more mobility, and those who thought they could profit from these new agricultural ventures were obligated to find settlers (often called *hospites*, or guests) to do the work. Most received better terms of tenancy than those to which they had been born. New settlers often paid no rent during the clearing of land, and performed no work obligations on the lord's land, as was usually required on the old manors. The high expectations of the new settlers can be deduced from a name such as "Kockengen" (near Utrecht), which is playfully similar to "Cockaigne," land of plenty. Written contracts enumerating the terms of lease appear at the end of the twelfth century – an illustration of a society that had come to believe in changing socioeconomic relations that could be legally established by contract. In this society, "tradition" and the trustworthiness of the spoken word were no longer completely taken for granted.

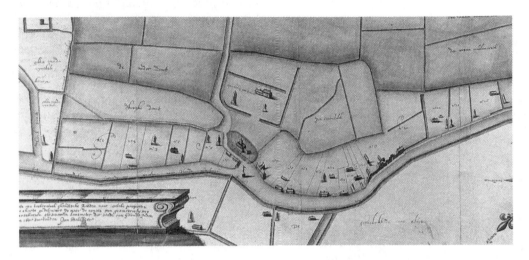

The colonist village of Kluizen, founded in the twelfth century by the Abbey of Ename and the count of Flanders, in a seventeenth-century map. Kluizen is an example of the systematic cultivation of land throughout the 1100s. (Rijksarchief Ronse.)

In the power vacuum that had followed Charlemagne's reign, the manorial *seigneurie* had become not only economically but also socially and legally dominant. However, now these lords were compelled to grant new freedoms to the serfs. Fearing that peasants would leave the manors for attractive new opportunities, great landowners drastically reduced the service obligations of their serfs – in some cases from three days a week to three days a year. Gradually, landowners's other obligations – payments in kind – were replaced by cash payments, made possible by an increasing money supply. This supply and the growth of trade led to inflation which undermined the value of the payments demanded from the peasants that had been established by custom. This in turn led to the economic decline of the manorial lords – the bulk of the lesser nobility – and with it, their political and juridical power. Both the manorial system and the feudal system supported by it declined, although some vestigial components of manorial obligations lasted until the French Revolution.

Bringing new lands under cultivation required some degree of planning. Forests, for example, could not be completely chopped down, since wood was always required for housing and for heating. Communal lands required management and conservation, and in some cases this was left to the tenants themselves, who in the northeast formed district councils to oversee these lands.

By the thirteenth century (if not earlier), tenants increasingly paid rents on the farms instead of payments imposed by custom. In most cases, the owner and tenant would draw up leases which were to last for three years, or some multiple of three years. This reflected the three-field system, in which the ground was to be, after three years, in the same condition as it had been at the beginning of the lease. These agreements – increasingly written leases – also delineated the rights and responsibilities of each party. In some cases, reconsideration of the terms at the end of the contract worked in favor of the owner, as in the case of bad land, in some cases in favor of the tenant, as when labor was scarce.

It may seem that these developments had little to do with the other great phenomenon of the "twelfth-century renaissance": the growth of cities. Nothing is less true. The same conditions necessary for agricultural expansion and social emancipation —demographic and agricultural surplus – created sizable numbers of people who were no longer needed for work in the production of food. Rising agricultural productivity, therefore, did not only provide more food for more people; it allowed a large segment of the population to be engaged in nonagricultural activities. Moreover, the rise of cities – far more pronounced in the Low Countries and northern Italy than anywhere else in Europe – was not only dependent on commerce and trade, but also on the ability of these nascent urban centers to maintain reliable food supplies. Without sufficient food from the nearby hinterlands, or the existence of well-developed trade routes, the growth of cities would have been impossible. The large Flemish cities were heavily dependent on massive imports of grain from nearby Picardy, just as in later centuries the region relied on the granaries along the Baltic (Germany and Poland). The internationalization of agricultural markets was thus essential for the growth of Netherlandic cities, but at the same time it made the region more vulnerable to international developments.

Cities, Trade, and Commerce

In the early Middle Ages, town life had been very limited. Some larger Roman cities had survived the end of the empire, some as the seat of a bishop, but they all suffered from a loss of importance and size. A few "mushroom cities," like Dorestad and Quentowic, had thrived through the North Sea trade during the Frankish period only to disappear in the tenth century, when Viking aggression and changes in the local water-control system seem to have contributed to their demise. Dorestad's role was taken over by the more modest settlements of Tiel, Utrecht, and Deventer, and Quentowic's by Montreuil-sur-Mer.

Historians generally assume that most large medieval cities sprang up as a result of the revitalized trade that began in the eleventh century. This is certainly true of thirteenth-century cities in the north of Brabant and in Holland, which were deliberately established by the dukes and counts for commercial (and fiscal) purposes. In the south, the picture is more complicated; scholars now tend to date the cities of Flanders, Hainaut, Artois, and those on the Middle Maas earlier than they once supposed. Archaeologists have recently concluded through shards, profiles, and coloration that these cities had earlier beginnings than written documents could confirm. As a result, we now know much more about such cities as Ghent, Bruges, Antwerp, Nijmegen (Nimwegen), and Douai. Few general patterns have emerged from the data so

far, but undoubtedly the growth of these communities depended on
their proximity to navigable rivers and roads. Their function as regional
markets best explains their geographical location, or at least their
growth. Various factors determined the rhythm of their expansion: their
wares had to sell – not necessarily an easy requirement in the static agricultural society of the manorial period – and farming had to be productive enough to support nonagricultural workers. It is clear, in fact, that
the cities came into existence only in the areas where agricultural production really had increased, or where imports were easily accessible.
Grain was a vital component of this urban trade, but wine (from Poitou,
the Rhine, and the Moselle), fish, and salt (indispensable for the preservation of food) were equally important. Large consumers often tried to
guarantee their own supply; for instance, churches and abbeys in the
Low Countries would establish their own vineyards in the Rhineland
and, as a consequence, organize their own transportation.

The increase in transportation made levying tolls more lucrative.
Political authorities had long maintained the right to demand tolls, and
in the years of decentralization these rights were usurped by the local
nobility or by ecclesiastical institutions. Now these tolls, first on the
rivers and then on the roads, became an important source of income,
and some lords became dependent on tolls to supplement the agricultural income from their domains. Tolls increased as the profitability of
commerce increased, and tradespeople began resenting these indirect
taxes. This resentment is evident, for instance, in an Antwerp legend
from a later date, in which the hero Brabo cuts off the hand of the giant
Antigoon, who levied tolls on the River Scheldt. But it is also manifest
in real historical events, as when traders in Tiel rebelled against the toll
imposed by Dirk III of Vlaardingen as early as the eleventh century.

In their early stages, these "cities" hardly deserved the name.
Ename (near Oudenaarde) flourished around 1000 as a fortress and
trading center, and one contemporary source called it "the most important strongpoint in the Lotharingian kingdom." Yet archaeologists think
that it could not have held more than several hundred inhabitants. Significant population growth occurred only in the twelfth and thirteenth
centuries, so that by the fourteenth century (when the population was
already in decline) Ghent numbered some sixty thousand people – the
second largest city (after Paris) north of the Alps.

Foodstuffs were not the only units of transaction in these cities.
Increasing demand for iron, as from farmers, required that it be imported
from Germany. Dinant specialized in *dinanderie*, utensils made of copper or brass. The lumber trade was also substantial, and by the early
twelfth century it was conducted on such a large scale that the Flemish
count was compelled to issue restrictions on unreasonable deforestation. Textiles, however, were the most important sector for trading and
commerce. Whether the "Frisian cloth" of Carolingian times really came
from Frisia or was actually produced in Flanders is not important; its
production more or less followed the same pattern: in the quiet season,
sheep were shorn and the wool spun and woven, first for private use
and then for the market. Wool production became increasingly sophis-
ticated, with the use of mills for energy and the specialization of labor

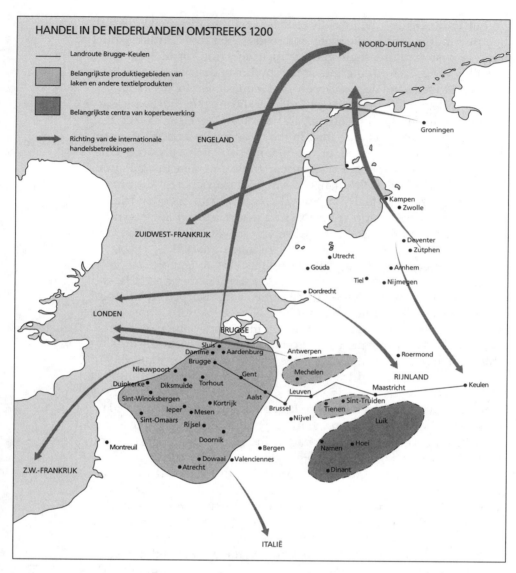

Trade in the Low Countries around 1200.

into washers, shearers, weavers, and fullers. Increasingly, too, this became an urban activity, setting a centuries-long pattern in which large-scale urban production competed with smaller centers in less developed (and less expensive) areas. Both domestic and foreign demand for woollen goods grew, and it eventually outstripped the local supplies of wool. This necessitated the purchase of foreign wool, first from England (the earliest surviving reference dates from 1113) and later from Spain.

As the economy of the Low Countries internationalized, its political structures also changed; international relations, once the preserve of the great nobility as they fought for patrimony, was now increasingly determined by the surging and ebbing profits of merchants. In this way, too, the nobility, the masters of the countryside, were threatened by the

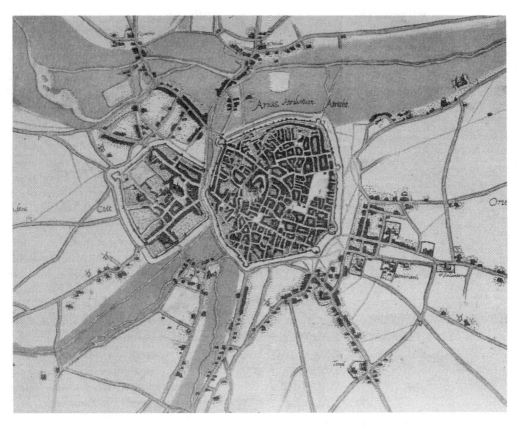

Arras is an example of medieval urban growth. To the left is the old Roman cité, seat of the bishop; to the right the medieval city centered around the Saint Vaast's Abbey. The map was drawn by Jacob van Deventer in the mid-sixteenth century.

burghers, the masters of the cities. But it was only toward the end of the thirteenth century that the great nobility changed their own policies to accommodate the interests of the burghers.

Just as the settlers of the new lands did, city dwellers cherished their new freedom. Freedom at that time meant the rights and privileges which set them apart from inhabitants of the countryside. City dwellers would sometimes christen privileged areas of their community with the name "freedom"; in Hoogstraten, "Freedom" is still the name of the main street. This desire precipitated a whole host of privileges and charters, granted first orally, then in writing, by the great or local nobility.

The quality of these urban charters varied considerably, depending on the varying balance of power between town and nobility. Nonetheless, some general observations can be made on the basis of the hundreds of charters issued between the eleventh and fourteenth centuries. Citizenship and its privileges were restricted to those living within city walls, as a way of controlling immigration to the cities. These burghers (those living in the *burg*) eventually formed the basis for an urban oligarchy, in which the most economically powerful families became the political elite of the city. This process happened in various ways throughout the Netherlands, according or contrary to the will of the great nobility and almost invariably against the wishes of the artisans. The local nobility were usually powerless to stop the rise of this oligarchy; this demonstrated the sharp increase in the power of the new urban elites.

All of the town charters also indicate a growing rationalization of law. Trial by ordeal (obtaining evidence through the use of boiling water or glowing iron) and the oath of innocence were replaced by witnesses and official prosecutors. Civil authority, now held by the dukes, counts, and the municipal magistracy, thus increased these men's grip on power. All had a compelling interest in maintaining peace and reducing violence – especially the organized vendettas among warring clans, who were accustomed to taking justice into their own hands. However, it would be going too far to say that the great urban families now refrained from all vendettas.

As mentioned before, the counts and other high nobility benefitted from the rise of cities as they increased the wealth of their lands. After the first phase of city building, in which merchants and traders established promising intersections of commerce (often under the protection of nearby castles or abbeys), the great nobility began to establish their own cities. In Flanders, Philip of Alsace founded settlements like Gravelines, Nieuwpoort, and Biervliet in the third quarter of the twelfth century. The dukes of Brabant and counts of Holland did the same, only later; in recent years, many Dutch cities have celebrated their seven hundredth anniversaries. Many of the cities in Holland copied the statute of Leuven in Brabant, making them "daughter cities," which were supposed to consult with Leuven when faced with legal problems.

The Hanse System

Many cities were dominated by high-volume foreign traders. These traders were vulnerable to feudal rivalries, economic politics and the particular vicissitudes of their own business. Many of them, therefore, formed trade associations, and their cities also formed hanses. The term "hanse" originally referred to a fee which wholesale traders had to pay before they could sell in a city or region. Originally private associations, they eventually came under the guardianship of the city councils. By the twelfth century, Ghent had a hanse for trade with the Rhineland and Saint-Omer had one for trade with England and France. By the thirteenth century there were large intercity organizations for trade; the Flemish Hanse of London was headed by the city of Bruges and regulated trade with England and Scotland. In the later Middle Ages, the Great Hanse became an all-important organization for trade in the Baltic. Cities in the eastern Netherlands like Kampen, Zwolle, and Zutphen owed their prosperity, if not their existence, to their location on important inland waterways, which facilitated commerce with Hamburg and Lübeck. Many Frisian coins have been found in excavations near the Baltic, suggesting that cities like Stavoren and Groningen were important commercial centers.

The sheer size of the textile trade – the importation of wool, its processing, and its export and sale – led to the rise of so-called trade capitalism. Begun by individual clothiers – Jehan Boinebroke of Douai in the thirteenth century was an example of the richest – this trade capitalism was a fixed system of international contacts among traders, in which the organization of annual fairs was an important component. By the twelfth century, annual fairs were held in Champagne and Flanders (including the cities of Ypres, Lille, Bruges, Mesen, and Torhout) in which traders from throughout northwest Europe and Italy came to buy and sell cloth for spices, alum, and dyes. Guaranteed safety was a prerequisite for these fairs, and "peaces" were declared by the political authorities whenever fairs were held. That such public order was possible is itself indicative of the rising power of the great nobility, as well as the importance of trade as a source of revenue.

Internationalization of the economy demanded a new and better money supply. Until the thirteenth century, only small silver pennies were minted, traditionally worth one loaf of bread. Now there was also the *grote* (the "big"), worth twelve pennies, and better suited to larger transactions. New Venetian and Florentine gold coins also impacted markets in the Low Countries – the name of the present-day Dutch currency, florins or guilders, is a reminder of this. The most important innovation, however, was the introduction from Italy of fair certificates, an early ancestor of paper money.

The transportation of goods improved as demand increased. The movement of wares along rivers and across land to Italy was not especially easy or safe in the thirteenth century, but Mediterranean skippers, equipped with better ships and navigation systems, could now sail around Gibraltar with a high degree of reliability. The port of Bruges became the center of so-called passive trade, in which its merchants could make a handsome living as middlemen, loading and unloading transports en route to other destinations. They no longer needed to do their own trading, but the power and influence of the city, or of Flanders, was in no way undermined by this new, more "passive" role.

Guilds and Trades

Just like traders, artisans, too, found it advantageous to establish their own organizations. Unlike modern unions, they were not organized according to their position in the production process, but according to profession. Masters and apprentices were thus in the same association as long as they were both butchers or fullers. Originally intended as charitable associations designed to help the sick or families of deceased members, these professional associations increasingly aimed at regulating labor and protecting collective interests. They sought to maintain high standards in order to ensure quality products and their own reputations; in the textile sector, for instance, a reputation for high quality was absolutely essential for selling goods in foreign countries. Yet the primary motivation behind these guilds was protectionism – preventing the unregulated entry of new artisans, the introduction of new techniques (such as the spinning wheel) and the competition of new and cheaper rivals in other cities. The guilds' importance in the labor markets – particularly those attached to textiles – increased their political power, and ultimately brought them into conflict with the powerful merchant associations controlled by the city oligarchs. By the late thirteenth century, these social tensions between the artisans and the oligarchs became conspicuous. A number of factors contributed to serious social shifts and economic dislocations, particularly the growing imbalance between supply and demand, aggravated by a sharply rising population. The Kokerulle Revolt in Ypres (1280) and the Moerlemaaie Revolt in Bruges (1281) are the most important indications of urban conflict. However, it was only after the Battle of the Golden Spurs (1302), when a Flemish militia, mostly of urban origin, defeated a French army of knights, that some of the great nobility began to grant greater powers (in some cases, temporarily) to the artisans and the lesser merchants.

3. Religious and Cultural Life

Most historians characterize the church history of the post-Carolingian period (roughly 900-1050) as a time of decline and decay, due to widespread lay interference in church life. This interference cannot be denied, but it should be seen in its context. The separation of church and state – the modern norm which forms the basis for this negative judgment – was never a medieval concept. Rather, it was customary to believe (especially in the Carolingian period) that the prince (ideally the emperor) exercised both temporal and spiritual authority for the benefit of his subjects. Reality was often, if not usually, different, but this belief remained an ideal nonetheless. When the papacy attempted to achieve supremacy over the emperors of the Holy Roman Empire in the last half of the eleventh century, it justified its infiltration of the political sphere along the same lines. Thus the theocratic ideal, first with the emperor, then with the pope, as the supreme authority, continued to command respect.

Priests and the religious orders exercised great influence on conceptions of the cosmos (God, the world, and humanity), and they also tried to translate these into moral prescriptions. Since they held an effective monopoly on writing, we must rely almost exclusively on them, and a distorted picture of the period results. They scarcely wrote about the ordinary laity, and it is therefore risky to make many judgments about the common people's religion and their culture. Only in the twelfth and especially the thirteenth centuries did this clerical monopoly on writing end, giving a more varied and thus more nuanced picture of how society worked. Accordingly, when speaking of church, religion, and culture in this period, we must be cautious.

The Church

As regional nobility assumed the powers once belonging to the Carolingians, they also sought greater control over church life. The oldest abbeys (like Elno, dating from the early seventh century) had been founded by the Merovingian kings or at least with their support, and it was customary for founders to retain a considerable say in the election of abbots and the use of the abbey's resources. The Carolingians did not change this practice; they appointed trusted friends and family as bishops and even appointed laymen as abbots, although this did not necessarily mean that they chose impious or incompetent persons. With the demise of the Carolingians, social and juridical elites assiduously sought to found their own ecclesiastical institutions (prompting German medievalists to speak of a *Eigenkirchenwesen*). In establishing and maintaining the abbey at Egmond, for instance, the counts of Holland (before they gained this title) retained their rights as founders; the abbey was to be used for the material and spiritual benefit of their own dynasty.

The popes in Rome detested what they saw as the usurpation of their prerogatives, and with the election of Gregory VII in 1073, the church struck back. At the center of his "Gregorian" reform was the Investiture Controversy with the emperor, in which the papacy sought both to deepen the spiritual life of the church and to reclaim the political power the emperor possessed in appointing his own bishops (see last section). This polemical embroglio lasted nearly half a century and ended in a compromise outlined by the Concordat of Worms (1122). The emperor renounced his right to invest (appoint) bishops and hence lost an important political power; the ancient practice which dictated that bishops be chosen by the clergy and the people was not reintroduced, either. Rather, the clergy of the cathedrals (the canons) now became the central players in the election of bishops, and most of these higher clergy were scions of prominent noble families. Often a bishop was elected from among their ranks. The election procedure for Utrecht's bishop was more complicated: the clergy of the city's five churches formed an electoral college with the chapter deans of Tiel, Deventer, Oldenzaal and Emmerich. Later, in the thirteenth century, the popes appointed bishops directly. That clerics were now able to appoint other clerics (even the pope was chosen by the college of cardinals from 1059 on) did not, however, mean the end of lay interference in their election. Previously, the owners of a church chose their own clergy; now, the right of patronage emerged as the owners proposed candidates to the bishops, who were expected to formally appoint them. Nor was this practice restricted to important churches; it routinely occurred in most village parishes.

The church's position was also strengthened when it regained possession of tithes, a tax assessed on the harvest and on livestock increases – and paid to the church to support the clergy, help the poor, and for other sundry purposes. Lay owners of churches had long controlled this revenue, on the grounds that the churches belonged to them. But strong pressures on these owners to return the tithe to the church, facilitated by feelings of guilt (made possible by a deeper religious life among the laity) and the landowners' own financial difficulties, resulted in a massive surrender of the tithe to the church from the late eleventh through the twelfth centuries. In the long run, the monasteries gained the most from this shift – they had been most active in this campaign – and not the original possessors of the tithe rights, the parish churches.

The spiritual aspects of the Gregorian reforms (outlined in the section on religion below) were succeeded in the twelfth and thirteenth centuries by a more structured ecclesiastical organization, which stemmed from a new appreciation for legal and rational thought. The role of the secular clergy in society increased significantly, both externally and internally. The appointment of priests and an expanding network of parish churches accommodated the new population and new settlements, solidifying the presence of a functional church organization among the faithful. Church offices were also rationalized: archdeacons, who assisted bishops in canon law and were appointed for life, were increasingly replaced after 1200 by officials who could be dismissed from their offices. This paralleled the same development in secular government, where functionaries like bailiffs could be dismissed. These ecclesiastical clerks, diocesan judges par excellence, were classic examples of the new church bureaucracy. A French and English invention, their appearance in the Low Countries came via Tournai at the beginning of the thirteenth century. Clergy also gathered in synods to discuss the condition of their diocese and moral questions. These synods existed before the thirteenth century, but it seems it was only then that they began to function adequately. Moreover, bishops (or their representatives) visited their parishes in an effort to control the effectiveness of pastoral care. In the large parishes, ecclesiastical courts (the *seends*) punished public offenders, and they proved reliable weapons in religious – and social – control. Finally, it should not be forgotten that many important aspects of law – including the moral norms governing marriage – belonged under the jurisdiction of the church.

Religion

How did these organizational developments within the church square with religious belief? This is an important question for this period. In the early Middle Ages, the region's people had been forcibly converted, and Christian faith was accordingly superficial. This remained the case for some time – there were few other sanctions than force and especially the threats of eternal damnation – but eventually this situation was changed through the emergence of two developments. In the first place, Christianity became a more functional religion as its own theology and morality developed further, and as it absorbed pagan elements which made the faith more accessible to the common people. Pagan practices were either directly assimilated into Christianity or they coexisted as superstitions, particularly those practices designed to stave off sickness or death and those predicting the future. Belief in pagan gods, however, disappeared during this period.

The second remarkable development was the internalization of the Christian faith, which now nestled in the hearts and minds of the common people. The process of internalization was difficult, however, and it partly depended on the quality of the clergy. It was not until the thirteenth century that priests were able to influence the mental and emotional behavior of their parishioners, largely through the introduction of homilies and the enforcement of confession. In these respects, developments in the Low Countries scarcely varied from trends throughout Western Christendom.

This religious internalization would not have been possible without the earlier existence of a religious elite, particularly those in the monastic orders. Since the Carolingians, monasteries were compelled to follow the Rule of Saint Benedict, which stressed order and balance, the obedience of the monks, the pious example of the abbot, and the avoidance of spiritual excesses, such as extreme fasting and isolation. The rule, however, made no arrangements for the creation of orders or of a larger hierarchical structure, and as a result individual monasteries were vulnerable to the material and spiritual forces outside their walls. Some historians have maintained that the post-Carolingian period witnessed a decline in monastic life as a result of lay interference, a condition aggravated by the Vikings, who looted many monasteries and scattered their monks.

Concepts such as "growth" and "decay" are difficult to apply, and they often cultivate cliched pictures of the past. Nonetheless, the monasteries had crumbled under pressures from a number of threats and were clearly in need of reform. Some reforms stemmed from Lotharingia as early as the tenth and eleventh centuries, most notably those initiated by Richard of Saint-Vanne (near Verdun). The religious dynamics in the Low Countries themselves help explain why the monastic reform of Cluny in Burgundy (begun in 910), with its powerful impact throughout much of Western Europe, only made a delayed entry into the Low Countries, at the end of the eleventh century. And even where the Cluniac reform did influence monastic life, as in the abbey of Egmond, its effects were limited; its customs regulating monastic life were accepted, but few heartily endorsed Cluny's strongly centralized organization.

Religious Life

These reforms, primarily concerned with conforming monastic practice to monastic rule, expressed themselves in the ranks of the "black" Benedictines, named so after the color of their habit. The abbeys and their inhabitants remained anchored in the feudal structures of society. The most radical religious figures were the hermits, who, in their search for authentic spiritual experience, preferred living in the wilderness. They were both products of, and opposed to, the socioeconomic and demographic expansion of the eleventh and twelfth centuries.

Some reformers opted for the Rule of Saint Augustine, which was shorter than the Benedictine Rule observed by others. Both rules were remarkably clear and well-formulated, and the reform implied literal interpretation. But to regulate everyday situations monasteries relied upon their own *consuetudines* (written or oral customs) to supplement the Rules. Some of these customs developed emphases that were different from the rules they were supposed to augment. The Cluniac reformers, for instance, stressed manual labor as a way to maintain the Benedictine emphasis on balancing soul and body, but their reforms were undermined by the extensive liturgical practices in the monasteries. The founders of the Burgundian abbey Cîteaux – members of the new Cistercian order – curbed these practices. After 1115 scores of abbeys throughout the West (and in the Palestine of the Crusaders) would be established which insisted on the literal interpretation of their rule. It is striking that the Cistercian order arrived relatively late in the Low Countries; the first was established at Vaucelles (near Cambrai) in 1132, and by 1163, the Cistercians founded Klaarkamp in Frisia.

Cistercians were famous for building dikes and cutting forests. They were not, as is sometimes assumed, the chief impulse behind the cultivation of new land that characterizes this period. The nobility already tried to attract colonists, one of the reasons why the emperor of the Holy Roman Empire crossed swords with Dirk III of Holland in 1018. Cistercians preferred the wilderness for spiritual reasons, and the nobility was generous in granting them wasteland. They were quite successful in converting these grants into arable land; the monks of Ter Duinen and Ter Doest did this along the Flemish coast and Klaarkamp in the north. The monks themselves were socially isolated, since their primary concern was self-sanctification. The heavy work was therefore done by lay brothers or *conversi*, laity regulated by religious statute. They usually stemmed from the lower classes, and lived in separate dwellings, apart from the monks.

Some religious movements began in the Low Countries. The most important was begun by the canon Norbert of Xanten who, after a time as itinerant preacher, established a settlement in the forest at Prémontré (near Rheims). This would become the cènter of the Norbertine or Premonstratensian order. The first monastery founded in the Low Countries was at Floreffe (Hainaut) in 1121, and by 1300 they established another twelve, including some which still exist (such as Tongerlo and Berne). This order spread throughout Europe.

Quite often the line between orthodox and heretical reform movements was vague, and the criteria for being considered heretical varied. The first trace of heresy in the Low Countries occurred at Arras as early as 1025, but the most famous instance concerned Tanchelm, a controversial and bizarre preacher who was active in Zeeland and Antwerp. Whatever one thought or thinks of his deviant religious practices, they certainly demonstrated a critical kind of thinking which was unusual for that age.

The reform movements led to the founding of numerous monasteries, but they provided no answer to the greatest social challenge of the twelfth century: urbanization. On the contrary, the hermits, Cistercians and other movements sought solitude and escape from a world which was changing and which was afraid of change. The foundation of the Crutched Friars at Huy in 1210, who were regular canons, did not change this picture. A twelfth-century innovation was exemplified in the Knights Templar, Knights of Saint John, and Teutonic Knights, which combined religious calling and knighthood in order to fight the "infidel" in Palestine and Slavic Europe. While their military role was important for some time, their religious influence was not. These orders possessed numerous houses in the Low Countries; the Knights Templar were centered in Flanders, oriented as it was toward France, while other orders in the north and east were more oriented toward Germany.

It was the mendicant orders who focused on the cities in the second quarter of the thirteenth century. This was not the original purpose of their vocation, but as they chose to live on alms, they were compelled to live in urban centers. The mendicants (or friars) thus broke with the traditional form of monastic poverty, which rejected private property but not the collective wealth of the monasteries. The friars rejected even this, at least in their first phase of existence. Eventually, however, they were undermined by their own success, as the increasing number of real paupers looking for alms challenged the mendicants' begging practices during the prolonged depression of the late thirteenth century.

The Franciscans and Dominicans were the two most important mendicant orders. The former were named for the charismatic Francis Bernardone of the Umbrian city Assisi, in about 1226. As the son of a wealthy merchant, Bernardone committed himself to a life of poverty, and as disciples multiplied around him, he felt it necessary to write a rule. Within a few years, Franciscans had spread across all of Western Christendom. They first moved into the Low Countries from France via Lens (1219) and from Cologne to Saint Truiden, Tienen, and Diest (1220). It was not until 1242 that they settled in the north, in Utrecht. The Dominicans had a different history, although their success was no less marked. The Spaniard Dominicus de Guzman established an order characterized by learning, and this trait made them particularly adept in combatting heresy, as evidenced in their activities against the Cathari in southern France. The Dominicans' role in the Inquisition also impacted the Low Countries as early as 1236, when they purged the notorious Robert le Bougre. Their pursuit of knowledge and rational faith made them the most important scholars and teachers of the new universities of the thirteenth and fourteenth centuries. Like the Franciscans, the Dominicans moved into the Low Countries from south to north: first Lille (1224), Ghent and Leuven (1228), and then Utrecht (1232). Dominicans were active in the cities, too, since their pastoral concerns could be implemented there. Preaching was a central part of their mission, and for this reason the Dominicans also became known as the preacher's order. The Carmelites, Augustinians and the so-called Magpie friars were other important mendicant orders in the Low Countries.

The Beguines

Women have not yet been mentioned in this constellation of religious orders. Convents existed beginning in the Merovingian period, but they were more elitist and exclusive than the male cloisters. Neither the Carolingians nor even the "twelfth-century renaissance" changed this situation; in practice (if not legally) convent entry was reserved for the nobility. But growing religious internalization also affected women and by the late twelfth century many Cistercian convents were established for women of modest means. Orders like the Daughters of God catered especially to "converted" prostitutes.

After 1200 there are reports of women living together in small, spiritually oriented communities. These devotees developed into beguines during the second quarter of the thirteenth century, becoming the most important expression of women's religiosity in the Low Countries. Unlike nuns, beguines were free to give up their religious state. Historians debate whether the sizable beguine movement was concocted by a male-dominated society as a remedy to a female surplus population, or whether it was motivated by religious calling. In fact, one interpretation does not exclude the other. Beguine communities were undoubtedly more democratic, recruiting women from all walks of life. Most cities, beginning with Liège, Huy, and Nivelles, had at least one beguine court within their walls. The beguine movement is often characterized as particular to the Low Countries, but this is incorrect. Similar pietistic groups appear along the Mediterranean, and in France and Germany. Only in the Low Countries, however, did they survive their abolition which was decreed in the early fourteenth century by the Council of Vienne. The rise of mysticism – either as a mode of women's spirituality or as an important literary genre – would be hard to explain without the beguines. The depth of beguine spirituality differed considerably, however, ranging from the exquisite spirituality expressed by the "first" beguine, Marie d'Oignies (who died in 1213) to the saccharine piety of the later centuries.

Culture

"Culture," of course, has numerous meanings, and one must make use of the word carefully. Here it refers to artistic and intellectual expression. Buildings and objects, in the same way as written documents, inform us chiefly about the higher social strata. They were made of durable materials and were kept because of their value. Moreover, they have in common the fact that they all survived war, fire, and other ravages. For instance, the preservation of churches like Saint Servatius and Our Lady's in Maastricht, or manuscripts like the Utrecht Psalter or the Evangeliary of Averbode, depended on their durability and a continued appreciation for their function and value. Any object not meeting these criteria did not survive. Obviously archaeology gives them supplementary information, but literally in bits and pieces. Thus any discussion about "culture" is largely confined to elite culture.

Language

The same is true for the most fundamental aspect of culture: the language. Almost all of the preserved texts dating before 1200 are in Latin, since the clergy had a monopoly on learning and writing. All documents – theological tracts, historical works, liturgical books, deeds – were written in this language. If the laity required any written deed to demonstrate their rights, the clergy had to draw it up.

Few exceptions to this rule exist, and most of them are literary works. The "Wachtendonck psalms," for instance, stem from the Carolingian period, and the works of several twelfth-century poets have been preserved, including the Dutch-speaking Hendrik van Veldeke. He wrote *The Legend of St. Servatius* (the patron saint of Maastricht) in the 1160s. Walter of Châtillon was active in the Francophone area around Lille. Their texts spoke of knights and saints, and were oriented toward a public with no access to Latin. Knowing Latin was necessary in ecclesiastical matters, administration, and law, since most public and private transactions, even if they occurred in the vernacular, were written down in Latin. Undoubtedly oral literary production in the vernacular was far more widespread than the bits which came to be written down and preserved. Historians know of the existence of a ninth century Frisian poet named Bernlef and of stories ordered written down by Charlemagne, but these stories have not survived.

Hendrik van Veldeke, fourteenth century illumination from the Codex Palatinus Germanicus. *(Universitätsbibliothek, Heidelberg.)*

We have mentioned only in passing that the Low Countries was divided into four language regions: Dutch, French, Frisian, and German. The variations of Dutch spoken in the east, from Maastricht to Cleves and north to Coevorden, hardly differed from the German spoken further to the east. Only much later, with the development of linguistic standards – made possible with the rise of national states – did language boundaries become less fluid. Even in late medieval times, traders from Lübeck or anywhere in northern Germany had few problems understanding their counterparts in Deventer or Bruges. The case was probably similar in the southwest. As long as Calais or Saint-Omer remained Dutch-speaking – which they did until the late Middle Ages – their inhabitants had relatively little difficulty communicating with the English across the Channel. In the southwest, however, Dutch slowly gave way to French, a process evident from the ninth century onward, and later precipitated by powerful French political and cultural influences. Even now, in French Flanders, where some residents still speak a Flemish dialect, this process is still under way. A similar shift took place in the north, although this time in favor of the Dutch and to the detriment of the Frisian language. Frisian had originally been spoken along a lengthy coastal strip, from the Zwin to the Weser, but was eventually reduced to the contemporary province of Friesland. The collision of languages in the Low Countries and the numerous contacts

among their inhabitants led to many derivations which are more noticeable in the region's dialects than in the vernacular standards.

Art

As we have already suggested, the church enjoyed a monopoly on high
culture and durable materials. Almost all of the preserved buildings
dating before 1200 are churches. The church usually had few problems
amassing funds for its buildings, as they were built for the eternal glory
of God and as a dwelling place for his servants.

Architecturally, two areas of the Low Countries figure more
prominently than the others. The river region along the Rhine and Maas
continued (through the thirteenth century) to express the architectural
élan of the Carolingians and the German Ottonians, whose centers of
power lay upstream. The churches of Maastricht, Saint-Barthélemy's in
Liège, and the abbey of Nivelles are stout edifices with a German influence suggestive of the (much bigger) imperial cathedrals in Mainz,
Speyer, or Worms. The other area is the Scheldt Valley in Flanders,
where French influence is obvious. The cathedral of Tournai, with its
majestic towers, is unquestionably the most sublime example of this
style. The presence of suitable stone quarries in both regions promoted
the construction of large buildings.

Church of Our Lady in Maastricht, an
example of Romanesque ecclesiastical
architecture in the Rhine-Maas region.

Builders in areas without these stone deposits – including most of
the low-lying regions from the Flemish coast to Groningen in the north
– were obliged to use wood. These structures had a very poor survival
rate, and even archaeologists have had limited success in discovering
traces of their existence. Where possible, inhabitants used tuff, exemplified by the small church in the Frisian village of Hijum. In the long
run, brick would replace wood – itself in short supply in some areas –
but it was not until the thirteenth and fourteenth centuries that large
brick edifices appeared, as evident in the (excavated) Cistercian abbey
of Ten Duinen near Veurne in western Flanders.

Buildings with less exalted and more profane purposes were less likely to survive over time, and few of them had any aesthetic pretensions. Castles or fortresses were originally made of earthen and wood walls, and later improved by stone, usually at the behest of the great nobility. The count's castle in Ghent is certainly the most imposing example of this genre, enlarged in 1180 by Philip of Alsace, who modeled it after the Crusaders' castles in Palestine. It was supposed to dampen the "pride" of Ghent's burghers, who were notorious and feared for their independence of spirit and financial means.

Sculpture of this period produced few remarkable achievements. Tournai stone provided the material for sculptured baptismal fonts, some of which have survived in England (like the one in Winchester). Tympana and capitals with scenes from the Bible and daily life, the charms of French Romanesque art, are almost entirely absent (the exception being the Porte Mantille in Tournai). The most valuable product is the so-called *Ruprecht's Madonna and Child* in Liège, reflective of the Byzantine style in vogue among the Ottonians. In contrast, gold, silver and brass artwork were of international quality; Reinier of Huy's baptismal font (around 1115) in Liège, and Nicholas of Verdun's reliquaries (early thirteenth century) in Cologne and Tournai are the most significant examples.

Only a very few paintings of the period have been preserved. Some mural paintings have survived, and building restoration leads to the discovery of fragments. This form of art is best preserved in the Scheldt Valley, in cities like Tournai and Ghent (the Abbey of Saint Bavon). Manuscript illumination was a more widely practiced form of art – and more widely preserved; the abbeys and large churches exchanged manuscripts, fostering a level of production which ensured that scores of them, in good condition, now enrich many of the world's libraries and museums.

As in France, Gothic became the style for architecture and sculpture at the end of the twelfth century. Flanders's orientation toward the Ile-de-France, the center of French power, explains why the Gothic architectural forms of Saint-Denis near Paris (built in 1140) were soon emulated in the cathedrals of Arras (1160; destroyed after the French Revolution) and Liège (1185). There were regional flourishes on the style, such as the Scheldt Gothic, centered on Tournai (Our Lady of Pamele in Oudenaarde is a balanced example), and the tall, lace-like Brabantine Gothic, which developed later, in the fourteenth century. Monumental buildings were no longer only churches; the dominant urban classes wanted proper civic buildings: city halls for councillors' meetings, and belfries to function as sentinel posts and as repositories for the city charters. Bruges's bell tower is unquestionably the most impressive of the genre. Some urban centers began to strongly resemble the northern Italian cities.

A Written Culture

After 1200, the cultural monopoly of the church broke up. The nobility's cultural contacts with Islam, the growing pride of the urban patricians, the growing size of government, trade, and a money economy all demanded more durable expressions of culture. The laity increasingly used writing, anticipating the advent of the printing press in the fif-

Reinier of Huy's baptismal font (1107-1118), a highpoint of Romanesque art.

teenth century, which would vastly expand the limited scope of hand-copied texts. An early and important sign of this shift is the growing use of the vernacular in documents. The city charter of Chièvres (Hainaut), dating from 1194 and written in French, is the earliest surviving example of an official document in the vernacular. The oldest Dutch-language documents were written a few decades later, including such ordinances as the Lepers' House in Ghent (1236), or the city charter of Middelburg in Zeeland (1254). This precedent was later followed in areas to the north and east (according to the general pattern of cultural transmission), in Brabant, Utrecht, Loon, and Cleves. In the far north, however, use of the vernacular in documents came earlier, as it did in much of Northern Europe. We know of the Frisian-language "Seventeen Charters" from a thirteenth century manuscript, but the original text was written around 1080, a century before the charter of Chièvres.

The language of the elites was not necessarily that of the common people; Philip of Alsace, a Francophile, appointed the French poet Chrétien de Troyes as his court poet; duke Henry III of Brabant (1248-1261) also wrote French poems – although his son John I (1267-1294) composed in Dutch. Flanders set the literary standard in the thirteenth century for Dutch-language poetry. The most famous poet of the period was Jacob van Maerlant (ca. 1225-after 1291), who produced the hagiographical *Life of Saint Francis*, as well as didactic works (the *Spiegel Historiael*, an adaptation of Vincent of Beauvais's Latin encyclopedia and the *Rhymed*

Bible). The touching miracle play *Beatrijs* (anonymous) and epic stories with feudal motifs (such as *Karel ende Elegast*) also appeared at this time. Some of the stories pointed back to antiquity, such as Maerlant's *The Deeds of Alexander*, others looked over to the Islamic world (*Floris ende Blancefloer*), or back to Arthurian legend. In most cases, these were reworkings of French models. French culture, in fact, exerted considerable influence in Dutch-speaking areas, thanks to the literary center of Arras, which sustained poets like Jean Bodel and Adam de la Halle. Poet societies sprouted up (such as Puy Notre-Dame), and were the origins of more elaborate chambers of rhetoric that would appear later on. The masterpiece of Dutch literature is unquestionably *Van den Vos Reynaerde*, largely exceeding the quality of its French model. A beast-epic, it had been preceded in the eleventh century by a Latin work, *Ysengrimus*.

The nobility used history to legitimate their own dynasties. The oldest Dutch-language example of this is the *Rijmkroniek van Holland*, attributed to Melis Stoke, the oldest part dating from the time of the powerful Floris V (late thirteenth century). The most typical contributions of the Low Countries to European culture, however, were mystical works. Early examples include Rupert of Deutz (died 1129) and William of Saint-Thierry (died 1149), who stressed the consuming love of God and insisted that rational understanding of faith must yield to faith itself. Some women – and this testifies to their increased social and religious presence – wrote down their spiritual experiences. Hadewijch of Brabant, the most important of them, was (not surprisingly) a beguine; her *Visions* ranks among the best of all medieval European literature. Beatrice of Nazareth (died 1268), a Cistercian nun, is worth mentioning for her *Seven Manners of Love*. For her, this love was striving to attain unity with Christ the Bridegroom, who increasingly became the Dying Son for whom the Holy Mother wept. Marguerite Porete, a French-speaking beguine from Valenciennes, was declared a heretic and burned at the stake for writing *Mirror of Simple Souls*. Mystics could not always be relied upon to follow religious orthodoxy.

It is remarkable that the Low Countries were late in developing universities, which did so much to change the intellectual landscape of Europe. Promising cathedral schools of the twelfth century, which were important in the cultural life of the Low Countries, never developed into universities as they did elsewhere. Liège in particular had been intellectually important in the eleventh and early twelfth centuries, and was called "the Athens of the North." But the city's diminishing importance as a center of the imperial church and its inability to adapt to new patterns of thought (like scholasticism) greatly diminished its role. Students from the region preferred the University of Paris, and, when it was established in the fourteenth century, the university in Cologne.

Was the absence of a university caused by the political fragmentation of the Low Countries, and by the region's small size, in comparison to Germany and France? Or was it caused by the dominance of an entrepreneurial spirit, more interested in profit in commerce and craft than in study? Both features were the most striking characteristics of the Low Countries at the close of the thirteenth century.

Massacre of the Innocents in Bethlehem *by Pieter Brueghel. This picture is most often associated with the harsh methods used by Alba's soldiers to repress the revolt in the Low Countries. (Kunsthistorisches Museum, Vienna.)*

3 The Formation of a Political Union, 1300-1600

W.P. Blockmans

During the crisis of the fourteenth century, some of Europe's great powers struggled for control of the Low Countries. Both the Holy Roman Emperors and the French kings, titular lords over the region, collided with each other; and the English, who had important economic interests in the region, also tried to exert influence.

Through its geography and a high level of regional interdependence, the Low Countries became, after Northern Italy, the single most important economic area in Europe, with Flanders as its center. Its economic growth also coincided with the rise of bourgeois culture – an exceedingly important social development in both regional and European history.

Urban and regional conflicts erupted continuously, and guilds attained a high level of influence in the fourteenth century. As most of the Low Countries came in turn under the control of powerful Bavarian, Burgundian, and Habsburg dynasties, the region became subject to greater centralization – and increasingly resistant to it. Under the Habsburgs, these conflicts reached a climax, as the local authorities' fight against centralization ultimately expanded into open revolt. It was a struggle complicated by continuing conflicts between city leaders and the central government – and by the rise of Protestantism. That the Dutch Revolt of the sixteenth century would lead to the division of the Low Countries is something no one could foresee, for it was the urbanized regions of both the north (the present-day Netherlands) and the south (present-day Belgium) that resisted Habsburg Spanish authority most fiercely.

Since the fourteenth century, the Low Countries has continuously played a central role in European history. For the last seven hundred years, one of its regions has usually taken a leading position in the history of the continent. These regional powers *shifted or were displaced over time, but the Low Countries, with its strategic coasts and rivers, never lost its importance. It is striking that while the Low Countries exercised great influence in Europe through its economic and cultural vitality, regional politics and government were largely directed from abroad. The houses of Bavaria, Burgundy and Habsburg, governing from their less economically developed homelands, provided an important political dynamic in the Low Countries. The tension between the process of political unification, imposed from outside by these ruling houses, and the Low Countries' own cultural and economic traditions forms the theme of this chapter.*

1. The Fourteenth Century: The Age of Uncertainties

Introduction

Throughout Europe, the fourteenth century was a time of deep crisis. Population growth, sustained for three centuries, came to a halt as unmistakable signs of overpopulation became manifest: exhaustion of the new agricultural lands, the rising price of grain, and widespread hunger. After 1348, this situation was aggravated by plagues which recurred, on average, every decade. Between 1300 and 1400, the population of Europe declined by at least a third, and in some areas by half. At the same time, the young states of Western Europe, in efforts to solidify and increase their power, engaged in near-perpetual warfare, which not only led to death and pillage but to an exceedingly heavy tax burden on the population, made worse by the devaluation of coinage. Much of the trade that had led to earlier prosperity dried up, precipitating further pauperization of the population and triggering serious revolts, both in the towns and in the countryside. The church leadership, too, proved incapable of offering solace in these confusing times. In 1309, the papacy was obliged to move from Rome to Avignon under the direction of the French king, and its return to Rome in 1378 only fostered rivalries between various popes and antipopes, each declaring to be the one and only true heir of Saint Peter.

These important European developments also reverberated in the Low Countries. At the mouth of great rivers, the Low Countries became the outlet for tensions in the European hinterland. The king of France exercised his authority in Artois and Flanders, while the German emperors, at least in theory, retained similar rights over the rest of the Low Countries. The rivalries between the European monarchs – and in particular between the English and the French kings – soon made its mark on the history of the Low Countries.

Tottering Dynasties

By 1300, many of the Low Countries' ruling dynasties faced new problems stemming from intensified internal and external conflicts. The fighting between the counts of Flanders and Holland over the Zeeland islands, which began in the twelfth century, has been mentioned in the last chapter. Flanders considered possession of the islands imperative, since they lay in the Scheldt delta and hence along Flanders's most important trade route. Nor were the English kings uninterested in securing the estuary for themselves. In 1290, these regional rivalries grew more acute when the Flemish count, Guy of Dampierre, briefly imprisoned count Floris V of Holland in order to compel him to come to amicable terms. Floris had sought to undermine his Flemish rival by securing support from the ruling Avesnes family of Hainaut – archenemies of the Dampierres – and from the king of France, who was eager to exercise real power over his nominal subjects in Flanders.

This precipitated intervention by the English, who were – not for the last time – concerned with the fate of the Low Countries. King Edward I of England, who did not wish to see the Scheldt estuary fall into the clutches of the Avesnes-Holland-France axis, kept the young heir of Holland, John I, at his court and in 1296 commissioned several noblemen with grudges against Floris to take him prisoner. This plot soon led to Floris's murder at Muiderberg, creating a power vacuum in Holland which the English king, the counts of Flanders and Hainaut, and the nobility of Zeeland all tried to turn to their advantage. John of Avesnes, count of Hainaut and a first cousin of Floris, had the strongest claim to act as regent for Floris's son John, and he assumed these powers in 1299. When young John died two weeks later, John of Avesnes became the count of Holland and Zeeland, inaugurating a personal union between Hainaut and Holland-Zeeland which lasted half a century. When the king of the Romans appeared at Nijmegen (Nimwegen) in 1300 to assert his authority over this transfer, the newly installed count John simply chased him away. Such a cavalier dismissal of the king of France would not have been possible in those days.

Flanders

Count Guy of Dampierre could hardly have considered the triumph of the Avesnes, which now threatened him from both the north and the south, as good news. But the Avesnes dynasty was a secondary problem compared to the resurgent power of France under King Philip the Fair. In 1285, Philip acquired the county of Champagne, and in 1294 he launched a war against England over the possession of Gascony, in southwest France. Nor did the French king avert conflict with Pope Boniface VIII, which ended badly for the pontiff. Finally, Philip all too gladly interfered in Flemish affairs as a way to undermine Guy's authority and subject this rich domain to his control. The French monarch held several trumps which helped him to do this. As vassal to the French king, the count of Flanders was technically obliged to lend all aid and service to his suzerain. Moreover, the French crown was the supreme judge over most of Flanders, a judicial authority exercised by the Parlement of Paris, which served as an appellate court for all areas nominally under French suzerainty. In 1294, unhappy burghers of Ghent protested to the Parlement against Guy's having ceded the monopoly of power to the city patricians (its wealthiest merchants). The Parlement ruled in favor of the protesting Ghentenars, nullifying Guy's agreement with the patricians which had given the count an important source of revenue. Moreover, the king called his vassal Guy to Paris and held the count there for months until he renounced his alliance with England. Philip also successfully insisted that Guy end Flemish trade with England, and by 1295, the Flemish textile industry was without wool.

Philip continued to apply pressure; using the complaints of Flemish patricians, Philip's Parlement found Guy guilty of disobeying royal commands in 1296, and divested him of authority over Flanders's five large cities. After so many humiliations, the count was desperate and was forced to find support among the urban artisan guilds – the same people who had opposed him in Ghent two years earlier. Having forged a coalition with the loyal nobility, the artisans and lesser burghers, Guy sealed an alliance with England in January 1297, which included both military assistance and the resumption of trade. Two days later, he sent two abbots to Paris to officially renounce his fealty to the French king.

In June 1297 a French army of knights invaded Flanders, quickly seizing Kortrijk (Courtrai), Lille and Bruges – cities that were surrendered by the pro-French patricians within their walls. The truce of the following October between the king and the count led to the de facto division of Flanders, lasting until January 1300. In the count's territory, new city leaders, supported by the guilds, ended the power of the once all-powerful patricians. Douai and Ypres remained loyal to the count, although they were cut off from the count's center of power in Ghent. A new French offensive, launched in January 1300, succeeded in taking all of the remaining Flemish bulwarks within a few months. The county of Flanders ceased to exist, and the territory was placed under a French governor. For the time being, the House of Dampierre was relegated to ruling over the tiny county of Namur.

The Other Principalities

Political conditions among the various principalities of the Low Countries contrasted sharply with each other. The administrative organization of Flanders was well-developed, and Brabant and Hainaut were not far behind. But the eastern and northern regions were far less politically centralized, and the prerogatives of local authority would remain very strong for centuries. Liège and Utrecht, as bishoprics, were subject to even greater political instability than their secular neighbors. Pope Boniface VIII (1294-1303) was very active in selecting bishops, intentionally circumventing the rights of the cathedral canons to choose their own candidates. At the same time, neighboring nobility also made every effort to elevate one of their own to head these bishoprics. The prince-bishops of Utrecht and Liège thus followed one another in quick succession, behaving in a manner scarcely different from their secular counterparts; in 1301, for instance, bishop William Berthout of Utrecht died in a war against Holland.

North Netherlandic calendar from the fourteenth century. (Koninklijke Bibliotheek, The Hague.)

Many of these conflicts stemmed from the vicissitudes of feudalism. The nobility regarded their lands as family possessions which should be expanded wherever possible, an aspiration which by no means excluded abducting rivals or waging war. They divided territories or unified them by agreement, always to the detriment of weaker rivals, who sometimes saw their lands entirely swallowed up by more powerful entities. In 1288, for example, the duke of Brabant assumed direct control over the small duchy of Limburg, and in 1366 the tiny county of Loon was ingloriously absorbed into the prince-bishopric of Liège. The struggle for power among the nobility had an appreciable impact on society as well, since the nobility's strategies for conquest and their dependence on wartime resources necessarily impacted the population at large – an impact felt all the more in the fractious fourteenth century. The destructive effects of war led burghers to try to limit the power of the nobility, a trend already evident in the eleventh and twelfth centuries (and mentioned in the last chapter). It was only after 1300, however, that a much more sizable political and social movement emerged, largely in Flanders, which would effectively check the power of the greater nobility.

Peasants in the field, as depicted in the early fourteenth century by a Flemish book of hours. (Koninklijke Bibliotheek, The Hague.)

Social Tensions

The great Flemish cities must have reached the apex of their population around 1300, a level of density that they would not achieve again until the eighteenth century. We possess relatively accurate estimates for Ghent and Bruges, but only from the middle of the fourteenth century, when the great famine of 1315 to 1317 and the first of the plagues had already taken their toll. During the extended famine, the authorities in Bruges were obliged to inter two thousand bodies, taken from the streets, at their own expense. In Ypres, the figure was twenty-eight hundred in 1316 – fully a tenth of the city's population. It seems safe to assume that many other bodies were not interred, and were abandoned in their homes by families and friends. In the first half of the fourteenth century, many other Flemings died during military campaigns or emigrated. All of these factors contributed to the substantial depopulation of Flanders between 1300 and 1350.

Social dislocations also stemmed from economic rivalries. Only the northern Italian cities could match the size of Flemish urban centers, which were, by fourteenth century European standards, enormous. In 1300, Ghent contained sixty-four thousand inhabitants, Bruges forty-six thousand, Arras and Lille boasted thirty thousand, and Ypres perhaps twenty-eight thousand (although actual numbers may be about 10 percent greater than these figures). Moreover, by the middle of the four-teenth century, many smaller cities also existed, including Kortrijk, Béthune, and Hesdin, which counted ten thousand residents each. Urbanization went hand in hand with the rise of the textile industry, which employed at least half and as much as two-thirds of the popula-tion in most cities. An advanced level of specialization had made it pos-sible for the industry to sell goods of unrivaled quality and variation, and Flemish cloth was widely known and appreciated from the Baltic to the eastern Mediterranean.

The Flemish textile industry traditionally lay in the hands of the great wholesale merchants who formed the patrician class that con-trolled the Flemish cities. Occasional revolts by lesser merchants and artisans in the late thirteenth century had done little to undermine their monopoly on power, and the patricians refused to give these groups their own independent organizations. Only after 1280 was the count of Flanders able to force city administrations – which were controlled by the patricians – to keep public accounts of their expenditures. The patri-cians' domination of the magistracy, which they openly used for their own ends, also fostered resentment. A 1297 survey of 103 prominent burghers of Ghent reveals the patricians' total grip on the legal system, which gave no assurance of justice to outsiders but treated their own members with great leniency.

The growing political strains between the Flemish count and the French king gave the artisans an opportunity to place their struggle against the patricians in a broader context. While the patricians sought royal help in their struggle against the count, the high nobility and the antipatrician urban reformers formed a broad coalition around the count. The French occupation of 1300 also cultivated a hatred of for-eigners and fomented greater cultural conflict. The urban patricians long had preferred to speak French – which separated them from the Dutch-speaking common people – and the French occupation added a cultural dimension to the political tensions in the cities.

The First Revolution

This explosive situation led to violence when, on 1 April 1302, the mag-istrates of Ghent reintroduced an excise tax which Philip the Fair had abolished upon his triumphant entry into the city two years earlier. Resistance to the tax was punishable by death or banishment. In protest, textile workers went on a massive strike. Patricians countered by send-ing armed parties to working-class districts in order to force them back to work. Leaders of the protest summoned their followers by drums, instructing them to assemble their weapons at home and join under the banners of their respective trades. Artisan militias had existed for some time, organized for occasional service to the count, but mobilizing them without authorization was unlawful. Soon ten thousand textile work-ers, protected with helmets and armored breastplates, marched on the Friday Market, driving several hundred patricians before them. Some drowned with their horses in the River Leie, others managed to escape to the city fortress of Gravensteen. After a bloody siege in which thir-teen were killed and a hundred wounded, the patricians were obliged to surrender and swear loyalty to the common people. The French governor, detecting similar urban unrest in Bruges, realized that his troops could not hold both cities, which together totaled far over one hundred thousand inhabitants. He accordingly gave in to all the demands of the Ghentenars, but assembled his army near Bruges for military action.

In Bruges, a grandson of the now imprisoned count, William of Gulik, proclaimed himself regent in the name of Guy. In doing so, he gave the revolt not only leadership but legitimacy beyond local grievances, leading his forces under banner of the Lion of Flanders. When the French army, with overwhelming force, seized Bruges on 17 May 1302, William's followers regrouped within the city as a clandestine resistance force. The next morning, as the church bells rang for matins, they surprised the enemy and slit the throats of at least 120 Frenchmen, as well as scores of nobility from Hainaut and local patricians. The governor and the French chancellor, with the help of their bodyguards, only just managed to escape with their lives.

The Battle of the Golden Spurs

Political polarization was now total. The French nobility, shocked at this ungentlemanly outrage, prepared to take bloody vengeance by amassing an army for invasion. Count Guy of Namur, son of the deposed count of Flanders, merged his small army of knights with William's army, turning western Flanders into a bulwark of resistance. With the hated patricians gone, the lesser merchants and artisans assumed control of the cities. Only in Ghent did the patricians manage to hold on, as a result of the concessions they had made in April.

The social composition of the rebel army in western Flanders is evident in the kinds of troops they were able to muster near Kortrijk on 11 July 1302. The Flemish had only 400 to 600 knights, most from Namur and Zeeland (the latter under John of Renesse); the rest were 8,000 to 10,000 foot soldiers, mostly from Bruges and the countryside (only a few hundred came from the other cities). The French army counted 2,000 to 2,500 heavily armed knights and an additional 4,000 to 5,000 archers and auxiliary troops. At best, the Flemings had 11,000 troops to stand against a French force of at most 7,500, but mounted knights were considered so superior that one of them was reckoned equal to ten foot soldiers. The soggy terrain near Kortrijk prevented the French knights' horses from galloping, however, and they were unable to jump over the stream that separated the armies. As they sunk in the ooze, many French knights were massacred by Flemish peasants unfamiliar with the time-honored custom of holding knights for ransom.

The defeat of a professional, well-equipped cavalry by a militia of foot soldiers signalled an important turn in military history. Since the collapse of the Roman Empire, horse soldiers had been the dominant weapon in war. Now it seemed that a large army of artisans and peasants were more than a match for mounted knights. Part of their strength lay in a deep commitment to their own cause, their own rights, their own people, while the knights primarily regarded battle as a sporting competition. The difference in the two armies also symbolized the differences between two visions of society.

The Flemish victory at the Battle of the Golden Spurs, named after the booty they amassed after the fighting, meant that Flanders regained its independence after five years of French domination. The significance of this victory for Netherlandic culture is hard to assess, but is not easily overestimated, given the centrality of Flanders in the medieval Low Countries. Flemish now became the county's official language. Moreover, the battle signalled a substantial shift in power away from the old Flemish elites, the feudal lords and city patricians, and toward the lesser merchants and artisans. They restored the Flemish count to his place, but they also wanted him to reward them with new social and political rights. In the glow of victory, Guy of Namur and William of Gulik granted the craft guilds in Bruges rights to their own autonomous associations and a role in the administration of the city. The large merchant guild, which had hitherto regulated the economic life of the city, lost its monopoly. Each guild could now set their own regulations, after consultation with the city administration. Both descendants of count Guy maintained their leadership over the army, which now consisted of strong representation from Ghent and Ypres, and drove the patricians from the French-speaking Flemish cities of Lille and Douai.

The Battle of the Golden Spurs, from an illumination in the Grandes Chroniques de France. (Koninklijke Bibliotheek, Brussels.)

The events in Flanders between 1297 and 1302 marked nothing less than a social and political revolution. The demands of the artisans, supported by dissident burghers and the desperation of the Dampierres, had led to the overthrow of the whole political and economic system in the Flemish cities. The political successes of the Flemish guilds soon spread to other regions. In Liège, Mechelen (Malines), and in the Brabantine cities, the artisans and lesser merchants also revolted, demanding rights to form their own organizations. The same social conditions which made Flanders ripe for change also existed in Liège, where the rivalries among the bishop, the canons and the patricians led to the participation of the artisans in city politics. Guilds had already existed since 1288, but now, in 1303, half of the city administration was reserved for their representatives. In Brabant, however, the patricians – with the help of the duke – managed to roll back the guilds' early gains, so that by 1306 the city administrations were again in the hands of the patricians. This effectively checked the Brabantine guilds' hopes for social and economic emancipation. The reasons for their failure are obvious enough: the duke was more politically secure than the Flemish count, and the Brabantine cities were smaller, lacking the critical mass of workers so crucial to the Flemish outcome. Moreover, the textile industry itself was smaller, more flexible, and less susceptible to the Anglo-French rivalry present in the Flemish conflict. The ambitions of the artisans and lesser merchants were thus stymied in Brabant.

In 1303 and 1304 count Guy of Namur led the Flemish army against his archrivals in the House of Avesnes, which now ruled over Holland-Zeeland and the bishopric of Utrecht. The Scheldt estuary again became a focus of conflict, but Guy proved unable to make much headway in his campaigns. Nonetheless, the war prompted the Dutch Avesnes to grant recognition to the guilds in their most important cities, Dordrecht and Utrecht, and gave them a say in city affairs – an important right they would retain for centuries. But in the other cities of the North, the artisans remained unable to obtain the same rights as their Flemish colleagues.

Political Structures and Culture

The major political changes wrought by the revolution of 1302 did not usher in a new period of peace, however. The old elites, as in all revolutionary situations, tried to regain as much power as circumstances would allow. In Flanders and Liège, where the conflicts were sharpest, the political situation would remain unstable for decades. In each region, however, the patterns were different, determined by different experiences. These differences led to variations both in political institutions and in the quality of public life. Once a pattern of conflict had been established, it tended to repeat itself, even as circumstances changed, and past attainments continued to direct the ambitions of competing constituencies. The independent Flemish city republics of the mid-fourteenth century, for instance, would serve as an inspiring example for the Calvinist Republic of Ghent (1578-1584) and for the resistance against Emperor Joseph II's policy of centralization (1789). The wide divergence of the institutional histories of each region, from north to south, would characterize political life in the Low Countries until the end of the eighteenth century. For that reason, it is important to examine the parameters of political conflict and traditions in each key region.

Constitutional Safeguards

Liège

In three principalities, it became the custom to enshrine the results of civil conflicts in solemn, written documents, which were drawn up to prevent further trouble. In 1253, the prince-bishopric of Liège issued a charter guaranteeing the people's right to select two of their own "masters." Civil strife was always just below the surface in tumultuous Liège, and city leaders were anxious to conclude a new "peace" whenever armed conflict threatened to plunge Liège into open war. The hostile parties invariably included the bishop, the chapter, the patricians, and the guilds; rivalries were often energized by the interventions of papal legates (supporting the bishop) and the regional nobility (opposing the bishop). These conflicts were particularly sharp during the selection of a new bishop. In 1312, two hundred patricians (including ten of the fourteen magistrates) were killed in the church of Saint Martin after they had taken refuge there following an aborted attack on the chapter, which had sided with the guilds. The "peace" that followed put the city administration, at least formally, into the hands of the guilds. Successive bishops attempted to undermine this far-reaching accord, which in turn triggered renewed resistance by the guilds. The Council of the XXII was established to give the whole territory an even-handed administration, but it was frequently rendered powerless by factional intrigue and was often inactive. Class conflict remained the central hallmark of political life in Liège, a situation made worse by the bloody incursions of foreign armies.

Brabant

Brabantine politics, too, were characterized by "constitutional" efforts to maintain social peace, although its political landscape was much less violent. The constellation of power in Brabant differed from Liège. In the thirteenth century, the dukes of Brabant had continued to battle powerful local barons, who controlled large tracts of land and even some cities. The duke was obliged to seek allies among the urban elites, who in turn demanded greater economic and administrative autonomy. The power of the cities increased during the numerous conflicts over ducal succession; between 1248 and 1430, only two of the nine successions to the throne went uncontested. In some cases, there was no clear heir; in others, the successor was a minor or a woman whose foreign husband caused suspicions among Brabantine elites. Taking advantage of these uncertainties, the Brabantine cities formed alliances with each other and became increasingly influential in the administration of the duchy.

When duke John II died in 1312, he left a son too young to rule; this prompted urban elites to create the Council of Kortenberg, in which urban representatives enjoyed a majority over the nobility. The Council oversaw the restoration of the duchy's finances, which had suffered from so severe a debt that Brabantine traders traveling abroad had been arrested. Furthermore, the Council officially proclaimed that the duke's subjects were free to disregard his authority if he should ever transgress a law. Only by righting his wrong could the duke again appeal to the loyalty of his subjects. This arrangement was incorporated into the solemn acts of inauguration known as the *Blijde Inkomst* (or *joyeuse entrée*) in which each new duke drew up an arrangement with his subjects under which he pledged himself to rule. Not all dukes, of course, were equally scrupulous in keeping these "constitutions," nor were their subjects always in a position to defend their rights. Moreover, the Council of Kortenberg, like the XXII in Liège, only functioned when central authority was weakened or challenged, as when the duchy was threatened by a coalition of regional rivals from 1332 to 1334. But the precedent of 1312 was an important development: it established a peaceful mechanism by which, with each inauguration, the rights and obligations of ruler and ruled were clearly delineated. The arrangement would last until 1794.

The Brabantine "constitution" of 1356 became the model for future acts. In 1355, the impending death of duke John III caused urban leaders to seek an alliance with the Brabantine nobility. They feared that Brabant would be divided among John's three daughters and that the husband of the eldest, Wenceslas of Luxembourg, would try to bring Brabant into the orbit of his brother, Emperor Charles IV. Joanna and Wenceslas tried to allay these fears in February 1356 when they promised in their act of *Blijde Inkomst* to respect the indivisibility of Brabant, restrict foreign influences, and maintain the influence of the cities in ducal policy. This did not guarantee peace and tranquility, however; Louis of Male, count of Flanders and married to another of John's daughters, invaded Brabant to secure his portion of the inheritance. The States of Brabant (the representatives of the clergy, the nobility, and the cities) recognized his claims, and ceded Mechelen and Antwerp to him. The States, therefore, had violated the act of *Blijde Inkomst*, which was in turn violated by Joanna and Wenceslas. Broken by both sides and legally dead, the text of the 1356 document – including the indivisibility of Brabant – nonetheless became the basis for all future "constitutions."

Utrecht

The bishopric of Utrecht, known as the Sticht, also developed a tradition of interclass agreements legitimated by ceremonial statute. The power of the bishop declined to such an extent in the first half of the fourteenth century that in 1331 William II of Holland and Ronald II of Guelders resolved to place the Sticht under their own guardianship, each receiving a part to pay off the bishop's debts. As in Brabant, financial debt and foreign intervention proved powerful incentives for the bishop's subjects to become active in the political life of the bishopric. The territorial integrity of the Sticht, and particularly the maintenance of the castles at its borders, so concerned the burghers that the bishop was obliged to grant them new political and military powers in 1363, which were expanded by his successor in 1364. The Land Charter of 1375 was the most extensive version of these privileges, granted by Bishop Arnold during new hostilities with Holland. The burghers were now given a say in declarations of war, and – in a far-reaching article that was unheard of elsewhere – they gained the right to try the bishop's representatives for violating the charter.

But this did not stop the duke of Guelders, William of Gulik, from violating the Charter in 1389 by seizing Salland and Twenthe from the bishop, or from intensely interfering with the installation of Bishop Frederick of Blankenberg (1393-1423). Frederick managed to consolidate Utrecht's power, however, and expanded his sphere of influence to include Groningen, Friesland (Frisia), and Drenthe.

Party Strife

Holland

During the first half of the fourteenth century, the counts of Holland ruled from afar. Count William III of Avesnes (1304-1337) was native to Hainaut, spoke French, and had married into the French royal house of Valois. He was most interested in European power politics, and managed to marry his daughters to King (later Emperor) Louis the Bavarian and King Edward III of England. One of his successors, Wenceslas, married Joanna, heir to Brabant. The Avesnes left the administration of far-flung Holland and Zeeland to the nobility who chiefly ruled according to their own interests. The nobility's ambitions went largely uncontested by the burghers, whose cities were small; and by the clergy, whose power was centered in the bishopric of Utrecht, outside of Holland. The weakness of Holland's cities and the clergy explains why no class conflicts of the magnitude experienced in Liège and Flanders ever shook the county in the fourteenth century. Rivalries among noble families, however, were intense, and led to cycles of vendettas. These rivalries had been partly curbed elsewhere by the church-sponsored "Truces of God," begun in the eleventh century, but the clergy were so weak in Holland that they were powerless to prevent these conflicts.

Count William IV (1337-1345) was the very incarnation of the ideal knight, having joined three crusades against the pagan Borussians and having traveled once to the Holy Land. He died in a campaign against the Frisians, which he had launched to redeem the honor of his ancestor, William II. All these expeditions taxed the resources of the counts, who granted the cities new privileges in exchange for military financing. This gave the counts only short-term benefits as they squandered their own assets and political powers in order to fuel their military campaigns.

The counts' debt-ridden ledgers led to a political crisis after William IV's death in 1345. William III's daughter Margaret, who was married to Louis the Bavarian, pawned Hainaut, Holland, and Zeeland to her husband as a way of raising money. Margaret had already incurred the wrath of some of her subjects, including burghers in the increasingly powerful city of Dordrecht, for the lavish gifts she bestowed on her favorites. But her problems only worsened after she left for Bavaria in the wake of her husband's death and political problems in the Empire, leaving her thirteen-year-old son William behind as "stadholder" (appointed to "hold" the counties in the name of the sovereign). The bishop of Utrecht saw her absence as an opportunity for war against Holland, and this generated further political confusion. When Margaret returned in 1350 to resume direct control over her lands, only some of the nobility were willing to support her; the rest preferred to give their allegiance to her son. In the civil war which ensued, the *Hoeken* (Hooks) favored Margaret's return to power; the *Kabeljauwen* (Cods) the rule of William. By 1351, the son had won the struggle for power, becoming Count William V. He soon angered some of his own followers, however, by repealing the lucrative trading rights he had previously given to cities like Dordrecht.

Both the Hoeken and the Kabeljauwen found their base of support in important noble families, and each had ties in the cities. Because of the close connections between the nobility and the nascent urban elites, the lines of conflict were not defined by class, but by family. Long-standing local rivalries between families became the basis for choosing sides between Margaret and William. Once unleashed – the political crisis of 1350 was more of the catalyst than the cause for the conflict – the enmity between the Hoeken and the Kabeljauwen became the basis for which *all* political squabbles in Holland (and to a lesser extent in Zeeland) were fought. In 1392, a string of vendettas broke out as Count Albrecht and his son struggled for political power, a conflict which was muddied by the ambitions and intrigues of the father and son's own courtiers. Each faction was forced to identify with either the Hoeken or Kabeljauwen, no matter what their real allegiance or aims were. Even with the advent of new social and political rifts in the fifteenth century, these two parties remained reliable fixtures in the contentious political landscape.

Guelders

In the county of Guelders – elevated to the status of duchy after 1339 – conditions were similar to those in Holland: there were contested successions and a social structure in which the nobility continued to play the dominant role. As in Holland, the cities were too small and the clergy too weak to offer an effective counterbalance to the nobility. Only a strong central authority could provide a check on the nobility, but this was long in coming.

In 1343, two underage claimants to the duchy, the brothers Ronald and Edward, precipitated a struggle for control by two warring parties. It was a conflict stimulated by the tensions caused by the Hundred Years' War (between France and England) and (after 1350) by the bitter rivalry between the Van Heekerens and the Van Bronkhorsts, two prominent families in Guelders. One side supported Utrecht in their war against Holland; the other side aligned with Holland. This internecine struggle continued until 1361, when the younger brother Edward was recognized throughout Guelders as the duke and managed to imprison his brother Ronald. This coup only led to a war with Brabant, since Ronald was married to a sister of Joanna (then ruling Brabant). In 1371, Edward was killed at the Battle of Bäsweiler, and his brother survived him only by a few months. The cycle repeated then itself: neither brother had produced an heir, and two of their aunts now claimed the throne of Guelders, leading their respective parties into a new conflict. Emperor Charles IV intervened by proposing his own candidate, William of Gulik, but it was not until 1379 that William was able to impose his authority over the whole duchy. William's rule and that of his successor and brother Ronald IV (1402-1423) consolidated central authority in Guelders – despite interminable border disputes with Brabant, Holland and the Sticht. The union of Gulik and Guelders during their reign also strengthened their grip on both duchies.

The Creation of the Flemish City-States

France did not let the radical turn taken in Flanders after the Battle of the Golden Spurs go unchallenged. The French king launched a new offensive in 1304 which met with considerable military success. In the Treaty of Athis (1305), the count of Flanders – in exchange for French recognition – was obliged to grant amnesty to the pro-French patricians, pay a sizable indemnity, and cede land to France. The French-speaking castelines (châtellenies) in Flanders (Lille, Douai, and Orchies) were surrendered to the French crown in 1312. The patricians attempted to use the treaty to retake their lost privileges and temporarily succeeded; between 1319 and 1337, they largely controlled the cities of Ypres and Ghent.

The newly powerful Flemish artisans, lacking administrative experience, made numerous missteps which undermined their political authority. Moreover, they hardly constituted a monolithic bloc; in Ghent, the two largest guilds – the weavers and the fullers (counting 5,100 and 3,400 members respectively) – alternated between forming coalitions and fighting each other in the streets as political power flowed and ebbed among the various guilds. This volatile situation ended in 1360, when the weavers and their allies were able to exclude the fullers from direct political participation in Ghent. In a three-way pact which lasted until 1540, the wealthy burghers or *poorters* (the patrician remnant), the weavers and smaller guilds in the textile industry, and a coalition of lesser merchants and artisans divided the city administration among themselves. The *poorters* were allocated only six of the twenty-six seats in the magistrate benches, but their representatives exercised influence beyond their numbers.

The other Flemish cities employed less extreme measures to achieve a political equilibrium. In Ypres, the fullers joined with the *poorters*, weavers, and other guilds in a power-sharing agreement. In Bruges, it was much the same, although the textile guilds were weaker and the *poorters* stronger, controlling nine of the twenty-eight magistrates. The city population – in contrast to the tripartite model of Ghent – was divided into nine parts, each consisting of guilds and trades which, in a complicated system, were each allocated a number of magistrates. It is quite remarkable that all of these political systems were largely successful in bringing urban peace to cities which had been racked by bloody conflict for decades. From the 1360s on, the problems confronting the Flemish cities were channeled through these governing organs, which proved quite effective in diffusing numerous crises.

The Flemish Peasants' Revolt

The peasant population, although it supplied most of the manpower for the campaign of 1302, benefitted the least from the new constellation of power in Flanders. Confronted with the large indemnity to France and the return of the arrogant patricians, the peasants of the western Flemish polders rebelled. They were not the poorest segment of the populace, but they refused to surrender the freedoms they believed had been compromised, and unleashed what would become the first of three fourteenth century peasant revolts in Western Europe. From 1323 to

1328, the Flemish peasants established their own government, which was primarily set up to oppose the large ecclesiastical and noble estates. Reprisal followed reprisal as castles were torched and villages plundered, giving the conflict an exceedingly brutal character. The pope's use of the interdict against the rebels only heightened their anticlerical feelings. Under the capable leadership of Klaas Zannekin, the peasants marched on Ypres and drove out the ruling patricians.

The rebellion was able to last for so long because the city of Bruges was also rebelling against the young count of Flanders, Louis of Nevers. The count was in a terrible predicament, but infighting among the Flemish cities – the ruling patricians in Ghent backed the count – gave Louis necessary breathing space, and in 1328 the peasants were crushed by a French army that had come to the count's rescue. Rebel property was systematically confiscated, Bruges was shorn of many of its privileges, and the count's administrators used the peasants' defeat to increase the judicial and financial powers of the central administration.

City-States

The commencement of the Hundred Years' War between England and France in 1337 had immediate consequences for Flanders. The principality traditionally cultivated good relations with England, since it relied on imports of English wool and on exports of finished goods to English markets. It remained, however, a fief of the French king. The pro-French count, Louis of Nevers, soon felt the political fallout of the war and fled the country, dying in the service of the French king at the disastrous Battle of Crécy (1346). Pro-English factions took over; in 1337, Jacob van Artevelde rose as a tribune in Ghent, and in 1340, he publicly hailed the English king Edward III as king of France on the city's Friday Market. In 1339, the count was replaced by a stadholder, the Lombard banker Simon de Mirabello, who had lent Ghent large sums of money.

With the count's departure, the powerful cities of Ghent, Bruges, and Ypres were able to divide Flanders among themselves, each carving a sphere of influence over the countryside and over the smaller cities. The cities' policies amounted to imperialism of the most obvious sort, with each city not hesitating to impose its will in those areas it dominated. Ghent, Bruges, and Ypres each introduced discriminatory legislation designed to protect their own textile industry at the expense of the smaller cities and villages. If their laws were not obeyed, they sent militias to destroy the looms and fuller tubs of their opponents. Burghers from the three cities were given the right to be tried only by their own magistrates, even if it involved a matter in the countryside. These burghers paid no taxes on their possessions in the villages and the countryside, and were exempt from military service. The peasantry was forced to sell a portion of its grain (a third of the crop, in some cases) directly to the "capital" city in order to ensure sufficient supply and a low price for the urban population. In this way, the economic malaise of the big cities, made worse by the Hundred Years' War, was unwillingly shouldered by the hapless smaller cities and villages of Flanders.

The three cities formed a consultation committee, the Three Members of Flanders, which attempted to coordinate a common political course which would subject all of Flanders to their will. Divergent interests, however, soon made it difficult for them to pursue a common cause. The power monopoly of the three cities declined somewhat after 1348, when a new count of Flanders, Louis of Male, was welcomed by the population of Aalst, a city which had suffered greatly under the lordship of Ghent. Louis's tactful diplomacy was instrumental in securing his recognition by the other cities, and he restored a measure of stability and peace to the county.

With his support, the extensive and wealthy rural districts around Bruges, the scene of the peasant revolt in the 1320s, became influential in the administration of Flanders. In granting this region greater representation, the area's large landowners provided a conservative counterbalance to the domination of Ghent, Bruges, and Ypres. The Three Members thus became the Four Members of Flanders, each participating energetically in the new Flemish administration established under count Louis. These four regional powers required no solemn "constitutions" of the kind valued in Liège, Brabant, and Utrecht; everyone knew that Flanders could not be ruled without their cooperation. Together, they paid (at least in theory) more than half the taxes of the whole county; Ghent's budget alone exceeded the count's income. Their influence, however, depended on the degree of unity among themselves, and it was precisely a lack of unity that remained their Achilles' heel.

Economic Reorientation in the Low Countries

In the course of the fourteenth century a significant shift took place in the economic structure of the Low Countries. Given the region's strong commercial ties with the rest of Europe, it is not surprising that the changes occurring elsewhere on the continent also happened in the Low Countries. Of course, we should not overestimate the influence of these economic links; as much as two thirds of the population lived in the countryside, and were less affected by this international trade. In any event, maritime trade remained modest in scope. Nonetheless, the Low Countries was an important region in an international economic system which was interdependent and hence vulnerable to disruption. Decline in one economic sector led to decline in others, with serious effects both for cities and rural villages.

For this reason and others, it would be incorrect to view the cities and the countryside as two distinct worlds. Cities separated were not only dependent on agricultural surplus for their survival; they also helped determine agricultural production. For instance, the presence of nearby cities prompted peasants to plant more and to specialize in order to meet the diverse tastes and needs of the urban market. City merchants also affected rural life by purchasing land and by investing in cattle. These owners often leased their land, and affected production by insisting on more efficient methods and by demanding a direct share of the produce obtained from their lands. This was not restricted to food. Peat, increasingly used as a heating fuel, was harvested on an extensive scale and inexpensively transported to the cities by a network of new canals. Urban demand for peat was so high that agricultural production in parts of Holland, Zeeland, and the Flemish polders declined as landowners literally turned their fields over for peat cutting.

The grain fields of Artois, Hainaut, and Picardy were largely oriented toward the great Flemish cities, which could be easily supplied by sending cargo ships down the navigable rivers. Exceptionally high wheat yields were reached in present-day northern France, where rich loam- and chalk-based soils were expertly strewn with cattle manure. Cattle from the vicinity of Ath, Valenciennes and Mons found a large market in Flemish consumers. In all of these cases, urban demand spurred higher production and greater specialization; at the same time, it must be added that Flemish cities never could have reached their size without the proximity of these rich agricultural hinterlands.

In summary, the cities and the countryside had a symbiotic relationship, in which urban commerce depended on the level of agricultural production; and the countryside changed its production to accommodate the demands of the cities. It is clear, for instance, that the extensive textile industry in Artois, Flanders, Brabant, and Holland (in this chronological order) could only successively develop because they were able to import sufficient wool from rural parts in Artois, England, Scotland, Ireland, and (later) Castile – regions prepared to meet the growing demand for wool. This was no less true in the nonagricultural sector: the large-scale construction of the Flemish and Brabantine cities created work for the quarrymen and woodcutters of Hainaut, Namur, and Luxembourg. Urban demand for lumber also stimulated logging in Scandinavia and along the Baltic coast. Even though international trade was limited in volume, such trade still provided work for anywhere from half to two-thirds of the artisans in the big cities, and these estimates do not include secondary commercial sectors, which were dependent on the employment of the artisans.

In the fourteenth century, the demand for international trade rose so sharply that the old modes of transportation along rivers and roads proved inadequate. Moving goods by sea now proved cheaper and faster. After 1277, galleys from Genoa, Pisa, and Venice routinely sailed to Bruges and Southampton, circumventing the Alps. This led to a decline in the annual fairs in Champagne and Flanders, which had thrived on the inland trade; but it transformed the harbor city of Bruges into the most important economic center of northwestern Europe. Similarly, towns along rivers like the Maas and IJssel lost their commercial advantage to settlements closer to the coast, including Antwerp, Bergen op Zoom, and Amsterdam.

Population, Standard of Living, and Economy

Like elsewhere in Europe, the population of the Low Countries declined considerably over the course of the fourteenth century. It is possible that, despite the high cost of food, the population rose again after the famine of 1315-1317, but the Black Death of the late 1340s plunged Friesland, the IJssel region, Liège, Brabant, Hainaut and Flanders into desolation. In the late fourteenth century, a plague came every ten years, and in some regions (like Holland) these recurring plagues were more deadly than the original. The loss of life could not be restored by the birth rate; in eastern Flanders, the death rate among women was so high between 1350 and 1400 that men outnumbered them by 20 to 30 percent. As a result, women married earlier and the average age for marriage dropped for both sexes: twenty for men, and several years younger for women. With the decline in life expectancy, records suggest that the number of children plummeted by 16.5 percent to 22 percent among the burghers of Oudenaarde, and the decline must have been even greater among poorer segments of the population.

Yet paradoxically trade volume rose during this time when Europe's population was reduced by at least a third. The reason for this is both complex and straightforward: the massive death toll increased the standard of living for the survivors. In general, they had more money and their real wages were higher than those of previous generations. This flush of money – coupled perhaps with the hedonistic abandon which can accompany times of great uncertainty – stimulated demand for luxury goods. It was precisely these goods which tended to be shipped over long distances, since their high price justified the transportation costs. Thus the demand for luxury goods, which often required specialized labor, barely declined. Shipping, however, became more expensive because the scarcity of labor pushed up wages. In order to cut these costs, larger ships were built. Despite the risks of storms, rocks and piracy, high-volume sea-going vessels were more profitable than land transport, which had its own dangers and was far more labor-intensive. Once the new class of ships had established trade routes, skippers further increased their profit by streamlining their operations, making additional stops (at the little-used Iberian harbors, for instance) and filling their vessels with cargoes in both directions. Supply creates demand, and increased shipping capacity provided the basis for further commercial expansion.

Acrobats, table pleasures and games. Flemish illumination from Li ars de l'amour, de vertu et de boneurté, *ca. 1300. (Koninklijke Bibliotheek, Brussels.)*

Commercializing Holland

While the total population declined, there are indications that some cities lost less than the surrounding countryside. It seems likely that urban losses were partly compensated by migration from the country-side, as people benefitted from the higher wages and greater living space that the cities now afforded. This trend was strongest in Holland because of another factor: the decline in arable land. Low-lying fens, which had been drained for centuries, were slowly sinking, requiring more intensive – and costly – drainage techniques. Moreover, in the long run the lands had proven unsuitable for growing heavy grains like wheat and rye. Switching to barley and oats sometimes worked, but usually the only viable option was relegating the land to grazing. Graz-ing required less human labor, which meant that by the late fourteenth century – despite the overall decline in population – the Dutch coun-tryside was relatively overpopulated, with a large segment of the pop-ulation looking for new employment.

Water Control

The extensive use of peat as a fuel created problems for the areas in which it was cut. The ground under the peat was often of mediocre quality, and removing the peat sometimes precipitated flooding. This was particularly a problem in Holland: when people drained the fens, the ground dried and shriveled and sank considerably, sometimes by meters in the space of a few decades. The traditional ways of draining water out of these sinking lands became useless, and the inhabitants were compelled to build new and better dikes; they also developed a system of locks which could be opened at low tide. By the early fif-teenth century, they had created hoisting devices which were driven by windmills.

Much of the land that was made arable by human effort could only continue to be arable with extensive improvements and better organization. Since the thirteenth century, local boards had regulated the water system (see last chapter); these public organs, while nomi-nally under the count, functioned autonomously. The reason for their autonomy was a practical one: local inhabitants who were confronted with local problems, and they had the most experience in solving them. The whole system of dikes, channels, locks, and canals could only be maintained by a tightly run organization which assessed costs and responsibilities proportionately and enforced regulations. Land-owners paid according to the amount of land they had in the pro-tected areas, but were also assured a say in the decisions of the water authorities. In this way, individuals became responsible for a system of collective security. This arrangement cultivated a mentality, devel-oped over centuries, which valued the rational consideration of means and ends, the careful administration of the collective enterprise, and a decision-making process which included all participants. This men-tality became characteristic of many groups in the northern Low Countries, and was also an important precondition for the expansion of Dutch commerce.

Rural Trades and Guilds

A segment of Holland's rural population, facing unemployment, left for the cities in search of work. Others, however, developed new trades and crafts within the rural villages. The most obvious examples of this are cheese making and other forms of dairy production; we know that by 1358 there was already a large surplus of dairy products available for export. By this time, traders from Holland had already secured the right to supply the city of Antwerp with all kinds of dairy products, "fat wares," hides, and specialized agricultural goods like coleseed, mustard seed, turnips, honey, and hemp (ropers were also important artisans in Holland). From toll records and other documents, we know that these traders exercised their rights to the fullest; merchants from Holland very frequently traveled down the Schelct to unload their goods in the Brabantine cities. On the return trip, they would fill their ships with the grain that was scarce in their own land.

Fishing

Other economic sectors in Holland also grew during the general European depression of the late fourteenth century. Traditionally, inhabitants of the coast had used fishing and trading to supplement the meager existence they derived from farming. Now, in a time of agricultural decline, both occupations gradually became more central to the economy of the coast. By 1400, herring had become an important source of income. Hollanders first fished for the herring in the Skagerrat and sold much of their catch at the fairs of Skånor in southern Sweden, where they had gained the right to trade in 1370. By the end of the century, however, German fishermen drove them from the region, and the Hollanders, along with their counterparts from Zeeland and Flanders, found new herring shoals north of Scotland. In their long trips home across the North Sea, the fishermen effectively preserved the herring by cleaning and pickling them. Herring was thus able to become a valued product on the European market, where tastes had become more expensive since mid-century. The toll at Dordrecht recorded that 6.5 million herring were shipped upstream between 1380 and 1384, indicating the vast size of the fishing industry.

Salt

The preparation of both herring and cheese required salt. At first salt had been obtained by burning the salt peat found along the Maas River and the Scheldt Estuary. By 1400, however, the demand for salt had risen so sharply that these sources proved insufficient. Evaporating seawater now became the preferred method of obtaining salt, and the inhabitants of Bourgneuf Bay and La Rochelle in France soon specialized in this production. This salt, however, was too coarse for pickling herring, and entrepreneurs from Holland and Zeeland made a new business of importing French salt in bulk and refining it by boiling it with the peat from their own region. In doing so, they established both a supply and market for refined salt which grew rapidly in the fifteenth and sixteenth centuries.

Overseas Trade

The cities of Holland also developed other export goods, chiefly beer and cloth. Holland had a natural advantage in brewing beer, since the ingredients necessary for its production – barley, oats, water, hops and peat fuel – were available from nearby sources. Dutch brewers simply imitated the process developed in Bremen and Hamburg, and soon Harlem, Gouda, and Delft formed their own export capacity. Their most important market was Flanders, where the impurity of the water had a negative effect on the quality of local beer. Amsterdam and Leiden became key centers for the export of cloth. Although Dutch items differed little from the Flemish and Brabantine products on which they were based, cloth from Holland was cheaper because of lower wages and fewer regulations in the textile industry – a substantial advantage in the cloth trade.

The success of these export enterprises depended both on regional shipbuilding and on a labor pool willing to sail the ships, and Holland supplied both. At the same time, these new exports were also driven by Holland's inability to produce enough grain for its own population. Dutch merchants were compelled to find the grain in far-flung markets: first Antwerp, then Artois and Picardy and finally the granaries along the Baltic. By the late fourteenth century, they made frequent trips to Danzig, Königsberg, and Livonia in order to benefit from the abundant rye harvests in the eastern Baltic. In exchange, they offered their own cloth, herring, and (from the beginning of the fifteenth century) salt. Eventually, however, Hollanders expanded their business by transporting the cargoes of third parties, and in this they proved so successful that they thrived at the expense of the German Hanseatic League, which had hitherto dominated trade in the Baltic. Nor did Hollanders confine their activities to the Baltic; they soon established regular routes to England and along the Atlantic coast. The Hollanders further adapted to this trade by developing larger, faster, and more efficient ships. Through all of this, they managed to turn a serious handicap – a perennial grain shortage – into a vehicle for economic growth, in which they both exported their own goods and offered their shipping services. This economic growth would form the basis for the Dutch Republic's commercial system during the golden age of the seventeenth century.

Regional Complementarity

Holland's rising commercial success cannot be understood apart from its surrounding regions, however. After all, brewing beer and pickling herring were techniques learned from the German Hanseatic cities, and Dutch cloth production was based on methods developed in Flanders and Brabant. Holland was dependent on the southern Low Countries both as a market for its beer and dairy products and as a source for its grain. Thus Holland benefitted from important commercial contacts with the regions which had developed earlier. With the new importance of Holland and Zeeland, however, the cities along the IJssel (in the eastern part of the Netherlands) declined. These cities had been important links between the German cities and the Flemish coast throughout the fourteenth century, but they now stagnated. Shipping shifted from their inland waterways to the sea (now a faster route), and the IJssel cities were also disrupted by unfortunate geographical changes, as when silt ruined the harbor of Kampen. Perhaps most important, the IJssel cities did not have the critical mass of population necessary to generate the kind of import-export economy that had developed in Holland. Nonetheless, Deventer's four annual fairs (first mentioned in 1340) remained economically important through much of the fifteenth century, serving as a commercial nexus between Holland, the Lower Rhine, the Westphalian Hanseatic cities, Flanders and Brabant.

Regional complementarity also played an obvious role in the affairs of Flanders. During disputes, when the Hanseatic League boycotted Flanders, its most privileged trading partner, the count of Holland offered the League new privileges in nearby Dordrecht in 1358, 1363, and 1389 which rivaled those it obtained in the Flemish city of Bruges. Despite these gains, Dordrecht did not supersede Bruges as a trading center. In the first place, Bruges was so well-established as a hub for the Hanseatic League – in the fourteenth century, scores of prominent international traders based their operations there – that the League never seriously thought of abandoning Bruges. For the same reason, efforts by Albrecht of Bavaria, the count of Holland and Zeeland, to attract Italian and Iberian merchants to Dordrecht failed. The commercial potential of Bruges, strong until the end of the fifteenth century, was so much greater than anything Dordrecht could offer that the League only used Dordrecht as leverage in its disputes with Flanders. (It is worth noting that Kampen, a Hanseatic city under the bishop of Utrecht, never took part in the League's blockade of Flanders.) Although the Flemish maintained their economic primacy in northwestern Europe, Hollanders used the years of the boycott (from 1358 to 1360 and from 1388 to 1392) for their own commercial gain.

The regional economic advantage Flanders had enjoyed since the eleventh century continued until the late fifteenth century, but by the thirteenth century Brabant had already become a formidable rival to Flanders in the production of cloth. In the fourteenth century, Brabantine trades and guilds were less protectionistic than their Flemish counterparts, and their wages and prices were lower. Moreover, Brabantine cities strictly monitored the quality of their products in order to prevent imitations by smaller competitors. As a result, cloth produced in Leuven (Louvain), Mechelen, Brussels, and other cities sold well throughout Europe in the fourteenth century, from the Baltic to the Mediterranean. Mechelen reached its highest output in 1333 with 30,000 cloths produced, or 720,000 el (of lengths between seventy and eighty centimeters). In Leuven, the oldest figures date from 1345: 14,000 pieces or 756,000 el (of lengths varying twenty-seven to fifty-four centimeters) were produced that year – but by this time production was already in decline. By 1368, it had declined to 475,000 el and for decades thereafter production remained at the low level of 30,000 el.

These figures illustrate how impressive textile production had been. The known record was achieved in Ypres (1317-1318), when two million el cloth were woven; in 1356, however, they produced only

791,000 el. During peak production, the quantities reserved for export must have been twenty to thirty times greater than what was produced for the local market. These figures dwarf the 40,000 pieces England produced for export in 1400. At the same time, they reveal the vulnerability of the textile industry in the Low Countries. The supply of unprocessed English wool was not always reliable; wool stock moved between Bruges and Antwerp numerous times in the first half of the fourteenth century, and was finally housed in Calais after 1353. The lack of English wool was only one of many political and economic troubles that could precipitate massive unemployment. Brabantine success, therefore, mostly came at the expense of the Flemish textile industry, as regional economic activity shifted to take advantage of the more favorable conditions in Brabant.

The economy in Brabant was also stimulated by the proximity of France, which served as an enormous market for its goods. The annual fairs of Champagne and Châlons, not to mention the distribution net around Paris, were particularly important. The Brabantines exploited Flanders's political troubles with France and its trade quarrels with England (manifest after 1270), by seizing shares in markets once belonging to the Flemish. In fact, Brabantine merchants made deep inroads into these markets by buying wool and selling cloth. With this new business, the city of Antwerp introduced a second fair in the two weeks following Pentecost, while the older fair, following the Nativity of the Virgin on 8 September, was extended to the end of the month. The yearly cycle of trade fairs was further expanded in 1330 with the establishment of two annual fairs in Bergen op Zoom, a convenient harbor on the East Scheldt. These four annual fairs formed the basis of the phenomenal commercial expansion of Brabant in the sixteenth century.

In both Brabant and Flanders the textile industry partially shifted from the cities to the towns and villages. By the end of the fourteenth century, the Florentine firm Alberti purchased all the cloth produced in Wervik, a Flemish town, and the German Hanseatic League sold cloth made in the villages around Mechelen and in the Kempen region. These products were cheaper than the urban variant, since rural wages were lower, the quality of domestic wool was lower than English wool, and the regulations for manufacture were less stringent. Brabantine villages also used fuller mills, which saved a good deal of gritty labor but which were forbidden in the cities because of the rough quality they produced. Aided by a more capacious transportation system, these cheaper goods reached a large European market of artisans and merchants who had previously found foreign cloth too expensive.

Crisis or Reorientation?

Older historical works tended to describe the economic reorientation described above as a "crisis." On closer examination, it would be more accurate to say that crisis (or decline) in some areas was accompanied by economic growth in others. Economic activities and labor markets were displaced from region to region, a mobility that was consistent with the capitalist mode of production already well-developed by the great merchants of the day. Vigilantly watching for the most favorable combination of economic factors, they pounced quickly on new market opportunities. While the large guilds and crafts often sought protectionist regulations, entrepreneurial merchants established contracts with smaller, independent artisans, adapting quickly and efficiently to the fast-changing market forces. Economic "crisis," therefore, was not as significant a phenomenon in the fourteenth century as the rise of merchant capitalism, an important economic dynamic which would greatly affect subsequent developments in the Low Countries.

The Breakthrough of Bourgeois Culture

Urban Architecture

Throughout much of Europe, ecclesiastical institutions and the court life of the nobility determined the whole tenor of cultural life. In the Low Countries, however, the large cities exuded their own political and cultural confidence, a confidence they often expressed in stone. The

City scene as depicted in a fifteenth-century illumination by Jan de Tavernier.
(Koninklijke Bibliotheek, Brussels.)

most quintessential bourgeois monuments, found almost exclusively in Flanders, were the bell towers. These towers served various functions; watchmen were able to scan the surrounding countryside from their heights, and they housed the large city bells used to sound an alarm and summon the artisans to work. The bell towers also contained a fortified chamber housing city charters and privileges. Prestige was another justification for their erection: a high and sturdy bell tower often became the symbol of a city. It dominated the landscape and allowed the city to be identified from near and far.

In Bruges, Ghent, Ypres, and Kortrijk, the bell towers were attached to the great cloth halls, the centers of the regional economy. In Aalst, however, the bell tower was part of the city hall, dating from the early thirteenth century, and Douai followed this example in the fifteenth century. Like the bell towers, both cloth halls and city halls were ambitious monuments, designed to demonstrate the wealth and power of the cities. The cloth hall of Ypres is the most arresting example: begun in the early thirteenth century and not finished until 1307, the hall stretched some 140 meters and included a bell tower seventy meters tall. The vast size of the hall far exceeded its counterparts in Ghent and Bruges, and may have been built to compensate for Ypres's smaller size. In any event, Ypres's textile trade went into decline shortly after its completion (as described above), and it soon became clear that the city's ambitious construction exceeded its economic means. Bruges built a very spacious cloth hall, complete with bell tower, on the Great Market over the course of the thirteenth century; in 1284, artisans started construction of the so-called water hall on another side of the square where ships could be loaded and unloaded. This building, long gone, must have been about ninety meters long and twenty-two meters wide, and featured sixteen pointed arches on the ground level, which guaranteed optimal accessibility. Completed in the 1360s after three phases of construction, the building featured a bluish natural stone on the first level, but in the fourteenth century the builders switched to brick, which could now be produced in large quantities by the city's own brick ovens.

Other public buildings also began to dominate the city landscape, like the large meat hall of Ghent, built at the beginning of the fifteenth century. All of the cities constructed hospitals in the late Middle Ages; the architecture of Saint John's in Bruges and the Bijloke in Ghent are remarkably fine examples. Churches, of course, were also built, rebuilt, and enlarged, but it was the new importance of the bourgeoisie's public architecture that gave an additional dimension to the city skyline.

Literary Life

The blossoming bourgeois culture was no less multifaceted in its literary accomplishments. It should be noted that diverse genres of Dutch literature sprouted throughout the Low Countries, inspired by the famous and able poets of the late thirteenth century. Yet fourteenth century Brabant stimulated a richer literary life than Flanders. Brabantine dukes and their courts spoke Dutch, while the Flemish counts spoke French, and this may account for part of the difference. Several literary genres appear earlier and more decisively in Brabant, particularly his-

torical chronicles, which either played up the valiant deeds of the Brabantine dukes or assigned them a central role in world history.

This kind of chronicling was evident in Louis van Velthem's early
fourteenth century translation of the *Historical Mirror*. Van Velthem
extended the book's original time frame beyond 1256, making use of
John of Heelu's *Rijmkroniek*, which had been written for the court. Both
books are invaluable sources for the events taking place around 1300.
The dukes also received praise in the form poetry, including the *Wapen-
lied van Jan III*, possibly written in 1334. Court heralds, trained to recognize the shield insignia of the nobility, carefully painted the various
coats of arms in their heraldic registers, replete with flattering poetry
for the respective lords and ladies. The herald of Guelders (ca. 1400),
first active at the court of Guelders and later in Holland, created both
beautiful registers and useful historical chronicles. Histories were
not confined to the noble courts, however. A magistrate's clerk from
Antwerp, John of Boendale, was commissioned by his superiors to
write a history of the Brabantine dukes, the first volume of which
appeared in 1317. It was precisely at this time that the Brabantine cities
were exercising authority in the name of the duke, so Boendale's work
gives important insights into a bourgeois political vision of the early
fourteenth century. Incidentally, Boendale also wrote several didactic
works for a Brabantine nobleman.

The bulk of Dutch-language books were translations of French
works; there are both Brabantine and West Flemish translations of the
famous *Roman de la Rose* (the West Flemish version was heavily edited
to make it more realistic). In Flanders, lyric poetry long continued to be
sung in French; the earliest surviving Flemish texts in this genre, dating
from 1390, are the 147 love poems emanating from Bruges (the so-called
Gruuthuse Manuscript). These poems probably stemmed from a group
of troubadours, since many of the songs included material dating from
the twelfth and thirteenth centuries. Other famous narratives were
translated from the German, including the travel saga of the Irish monk
Saint Brandon, who, through wonders and visions, learns many spiritual truths. *Beatrijs*, a high point in the spiritual genre of the period,
recounts the story of a nun who succumbs to worldly love. After many
bitter travels in which Beatrice's temporal love fades, she returns to her
convent, where she discovers that the Virgin herself had replaced her in
her absence. The mystical tradition begun by Hadewijch (see Chapter
Two) continued in the person of John of Ruusbroec, a Brussels chaplain,
who established a community in the Groenendaal cloister in 1343. His
tracts outline the basis for the "common life," in which he tries to unify
mundane work with an inner sense of godly joy. Through his contemporary, Geert Groote, and the *devotio moderna*, Ruusbroec exercised considerable influence on the European spirituality of the period.

Very few secular plays from the fourteenth century have survived, but those still existent predate famous mystery and miracle
plays like *Mariken van Nieumeghen* and *Everyman* (*Elckerlyc*) by half
a century. Secular works often consisted of epic tales and stories of
courtly love, genres practiced throughout Europe. Although many
works must have been lost, surviving works like *Lancelot*, *Esmoreit*, and

Gloriant, all about the tragedy of courtly love, are of a dramatically high caliber. By 1400, these plays were performed in eastern Brabant before a seated public. They were adapted translations from models circulating throughout Europe. Farces, usually featuring a cuckolded spouse, were also performed.

Analyses of Dutch-language texts of the fourteenth century reveal a richly variegated mix, influenced by international trends but also possessing unmistakably original components. Brabant is better represented than Flanders because of the common language of the cities, nobility, and court. Flemish illumination paintings and book production, however, continued to be of international quality, inspired as they were by French examples.

Nothing has yet been said of the northern regions. Albrecht of Bavaria's rule as count of Holland and Zeeland, begun in 1358, transformed his residence at The Hague into a center for musical and artistic creativity. Of the numerous poets, singers, and musicians who visited Albrecht's court, William of Hildegaersberch is the most acclaimed. Although he established a reputation for moralizing verse, his more irreverent and farcical poetry indicates that he was no less gifted in these genres. The herald of Bavaria was also active, singing of the nobility's martial feats as if their incursions against the Frisians were a virtuous crusade. The court chaplain, Dirc of Delft, wrote sophisticated sermons for Albrecht, employing complicated symbolism. Illumination also reached new heights of artistry by 1400, as clerics painted remarkably expressive fringes on the books which they presented to the countess. The best of these artists and writers were emancipated intellectuals, conscious that their own talents had enhanced their status. As such, they did not regard their service to the count as reason to avoid criticizing the court and the social elites. In this way, the new bourgeois confidence of the fourteenth century came even to permeate court life.

2. The Burgundian Century (1385-1477)

Dynastic Strategies

The Low Countries of the late fourteenth century hardly constituted a unified whole, and only the most prescient seer could have predicted the subsequent political events which welded the region together. But the princes of Europe continued energetically to expand their own territories. They had no qualms about ruling over far-flung realms which had little in common with each other. Bavaria and Holland, or Burgundy and Flanders, were separated by some seven hundred kilometers, but were respectively "united" under one prince. The nobility regarded such combinations as trumps which could be played at the right moment in a high-stakes game: territories could be expanded or traded for holdings adjacent to the nobility's own centers of power. Since territories were united and redistributed in accordance with the principles of private law, dynastic chance – births and deaths – could both wreck ambition or give unexpected opportunities for territorial advancement. There were, moreover, always plenty of princely pretenders, often with their own armies, who were willing to take advantage of every opportunity to fuel their own ambition. This made the complex games of action and reaction even more unpredictable.

It is tempting to interpret the unification of the Low Countries as a logical, even inevitable, sequence of events. Previous generations of nationally minded historians took precisely this view, interpreting the rise of their respective state – whether the Netherlands, Belgium, Germany or France – as the natural course of history. All of these historians imposed a unity on the past that they wished to see in their own time. Contemporary historians, however, discount the notion that there was any collective "Netherlandic" identity in 1400; allegiance to the principalities themselves remained weak, at least in the absence of acute external threats. People thought of themselves as citizens of a city, or members of a village community, and any wider sense of loyalty remained restricted to the persons of ruling princes or to the leaders of political factions.

The House of Bavaria

In 1400, the House of Bavaria controlled more principalities in the Low Countries than any other dynasty: Albrecht was duke of Straubing (in Lower Bavaria) and count of Hainaut, Holland, and Zeeland; his brother John was the bishop-elect of Liège (chosen but not consecrated). Their sisters also occupied high positions: Isabella was the queen of France and Margaret was the future duchess of Burgundy. In 1385, the Houses of Bavaria and Burgundy literally wedded their fortunes together in a double marriage, in which a female and male from both houses were represented. This cemented a political alliance between the two families. But it also increased the potential for competing claims within this extended family, which was later evident in Philip the Good's demands on Jacoba, countess of Hainaut, Holland and Zeeland in the 1420s.

The long reign of duke Albrecht (1358-1404) initially brought peace to Holland after a decade of party conflicts. In 1392, however, old rivalries resurfaced with full intensity when followers of William, the heir apparent, fought supporters of John VI of Arkel, the exchequer and leader of the Kabeljauw party (see previous section). William VI (1404-1417) made no secret of his sympathies for the Hoeken. Costly wars against the Frisians (1396-1401) and on the southern frontier near Arkel (1401-1412) also placed a heavy financial yoke on the cities with few compensatory gains (some commercial restrictions were loosened), fomenting urban discontent. As a result of these tensions, politics in Holland, Zeeland, and Hainaut became increasingly vulnerable to outside influences, which were eager to exploit the country's internal divisions.

Burgundy

The second greatest dynastic power in the region was the House of Burgundy. The 1369 marriage of the Burgundian duke, Philip the Bold, to Margaret of Male, heir apparent of Flanders, gave the Burgundian duke rights to rule not only Flanders, but Artois, the small northern French counties of Nevers and Rethel, and the Franche-Comté, adjacent to Burgundy. Moreover, Philip managed to secure a promise from the French throne to return French Flanders (Lille, Douai, and Orchies), lands that had been wrested from Flanders in 1312.

It remained to be seen whether the Burgundian dukes would remain dependent vassals of the French king or emerge as a new, independent dynasty. A long-term crisis surrounding the French crown prevented this question from being definitely answered until well into the fifteenth century. King Charles VI ruled as a minor from 1380 to 1388, and by 1392 showed signs of insanity. Charles's weakness gave his rival uncles free rein to pursue their own ambitions, and the English invasion of France further eroded central authority. Given this situation, it is hardly surprising that Philip and his son, John the Fearless, riveted their attention on Paris, where they built up their patronage and used the royal treasury for their own purposes. It is not impossible that Philip himself cultivated ambitions of becoming king. In any event, for the time being the Burgundians remained preoccupied with French politics.

Brabant

The third largest power in the Low Countries was Brabant, where the childless Joanna became the focus of innumerable intrigues. Her first marriage to Count William IV of Holland might have led to the formation of a central Netherlandic union, but William's untimely death in 1345, in a campaign against the Frisians, precluded this. Her second husband, Wenceslas of Luxembourg, might have compensated for this loss, but he, too, died prematurely, leaving her childless. Joanna's decision to surrender her lands to the House of Burgundy after her death was due both to Philip's diplomatic initiatives and to his marriage to Margaret, a niece of Joanna. In 1396, she turned over the little duchy of Limburg to them and chose their second son Anthony as her successor in Brabant. Their oldest son, John the Fearless, had been passed over because the States of Brabant expressed their collective displeasure at the prospect of being ruled by a duke who spent all of his time outside the duchy. They were also too attached to their own institutions to let a French prince like John absorb them into a heterogenous conglomerate of domains that largely belonged to the kingdom of France. Brabant was, after all, still a part of the Holy Roman Empire. Anthony's selection, however, did no harm to the Burgundian cause in the Low Countries; it only created new options for the future.

Guelders

The fourth power, the duchy of Guelders, was often at war with its neighbors Holland and Brabant. Guelders and Holland were locked in a particularly intense struggle for control of the tiny but strategic principality of Arkel, which bordered all three regional powers. Holland eventually won Arkel in 1412, but meanwhile the duke of Guelders had been accumulating power elsewhere. The personal union in 1393 with the duchy of Gulik (see last section) was only the first step; the dukes of Guelders soon attained considerable influence in Utrecht and asserted themselves in the Oversticht (now present day Overijssel and Drenthe), Friesland, and Groningen. In these areas, there was little central authority – only local control by prominent landowners – and the dukes saw a golden opportunity to expand their power. Their ambitions came to nought, however. The dukes of Guelders were childless, and as a result, the personal union between Guelders and Gulik was broken in 1423. Guelders was reduced to its original size, and was soon threatened by surrounding powers, including Brabant and (after 1430) Holland. Furthermore, the political administration of Guelders was weak; local autonomy was considerable, a tradition strengthened by the fragmentation and the extensive size of the duchy. Moreover, the economic development of its river region lagged behind those of the surrounding powers (including the bishopric of Cologne).

Under these conditions, Guelders was easily subject to the influence of its more powerful neighbors. Both the Burgundians and the king of France, for example, used the internal divisions of the duchy to present their own ducal pretenders. Guelders's proximity to the Lower Rhine meant that it also had nemeses outside the Netherlands. Yet even the great regional powers – the Burgundians and the Habsburgs – found it difficult to rule Guelders, since the duchy's numerous factions always conspired to undermine whoever was in power. It was not until 1543 that the Habsburgs finally put Guelders under their control.

The Bishoprics

By 1400, the bishops of Utrecht and Liège saw little opportunity to expand their territories, and the largely futile efforts of the bishop of Utrecht to extend his influence to the northeast was the only notable exception. Rather, the bishops were the targets of surrounding dynasties, who were eager to place their favorites or family members in a bishop's chair. Dynastic political influence was manifested in the selection of John of Bavaria as bishop of Liège and Frederick of Blankenheim (supported by the duke of Guelders) as bishop of Utrecht. The duke of Burgundy managed to appoint his followers to the bishoprics of Arras, Cambrai, Tournai, and other such cities. These strategies may smack of power and corruption, but few dukes and counts ever forgot that their own ability to control the future was very limited, and they accordingly pursued every means possible to even the odds. In the Low Countries, they also learned never to underestimate the power of their own subjects, although they took increasingly systematic steps to repress their ambitions.

Renewed efforts by the ruling princes to deal with their troublesome subjects became apparent in the Liège crisis of 1408, which signalled a new phase in their efforts to restrict the freedoms of the population. The bishop, John of Bavaria, proved unable to contain a rebellion of artisans and a portion of the nobility who were supported by the duke of Orléans, then the most influential regent in France. John the Fearless, duke of Burgundy and the archrival of Orléans, came to the bishop's rescue, using his political alliances with Brabant and Hainaut-Holland to keep Liège out of the French sphere of influence. In a campaign which culminated in the Battle of Othée, the armies of John, William VI of Holland, and Anthony of Brabant crushed the rebellion in Liège, ending a challenge to their dynastic power. As victor and as the formal mediator in the negotiations, John the Fearless exacted a heavy fine from the vanquished and diminished the political role of the guilds. His triumph was later expressed on a great walled carpet hung at the Burgundian court, designed to imbue all visitors with the glory of his dynasty. In hindsight, Othée was just the first in a series of defeats for urban autonomy in general and the rights of the guilds in particular. Both the Burgundians and Habsburgs would prove adept at undermining the local privileges of the Low Countries.

Burgundian Domination

The death of William VI of Hainaut-Holland in 1417 triggered a new and particularly ferocious party conflict when two pretenders, each representing a complex coalition of rival forces in Holland, laid claim to the vacant throne. Jacoba was the designated, legal and recognized heir, but her uncle John, bishop of Liège (who still refused to be consecrated as a priest), saw William's passing as an opportunity to fulfill his own worldly ambitions. He resigned as bishop and secured the support of the king of the Romans, Sigismund, who was anxious to demonstrate that he, and he alone, would determine the lines of succession within the Empire. Sigismund formally granted Hainaut, Holland, and Zeeland to John as fiefs, and arranged his marriage to the duchess of Luxembourg, Elizabeth of Görlitz. He also contested Jacoba's marriage to her second cousin John IV of Brabant to both the pope and the Council of Constance, on the grounds that Jacoba and her husband were both grandchildren of Philip the Bold. Sigismund thus hoped that Hainaut, Holland and Zeeland – through a personal union with Luxembourg – would be saved for the Empire instead of falling into the hands of the Burgundians.

The subsequent developments of this conflict are quite complex and full of fortuitous twists and turns. The struggle for succession in the House of Bavaria also coincided with the Hundred Years' War, so that both France and England had a high stake in its outcome. But the marriages of both the ex-bishop John and Elizabeth, and of Jacoba and John IV were to be childless, John IV of Brabant was politically inept, and both Johns died prematurely. The combination of these factors offered Philip the Good of Burgundy (1419-1467), as neighbor to and as a relative of all the parties, a golden opportunity to gain the disputed lands for himself. Philip took action soon after John of Bavaria died on 6 January 1425. Legally, Hainaut, Holland, and Zeeland reverted to Jacoba and John IV (or to one of them), but the first was isolated in Hainaut and the second was not inclined to fight for his rights. Even in Holland, Jacoba's support among the Hoeken was too weak to fend off the diplomatic initiatives of Philip the Good, who also laid claim to Hainaut when John IV died in 1427. By 1428, Philip's steady military pressure, combined with his successful wooing of the cities of Holland, compelled Jacoba to surrender. But Philip's eventual victory over Sigismund was also due to more predictable factors: in contrast to the emperor, whose nominal authority vastly exceeded his real power, Philip's more centralized administration allowed him to move quickly and effectively. Thus the Burgundian duke triumphed after a decade of diplomatic machinations and open conflict, and his success proved to be an important turning point in the history of Low Countries: much of the region became subject to a single ruler.

In the Peace of Delft of July 1428, Jacoba recognized Philip as her successor and her stadholder, with the right to appoint six of the county's nine councilors and the right to a corresponding share of its income. No longer would she be permitted to marry without his permission, and when, in 1433, she disregarded this restriction and married Frank of Borselen, Philip forced her to renounce all of her remaining rights. The cities and the nobility backed the Peace of Delft, which, in an effort to quiet the region, stipulated that all posts in Holland and Zeeland would be evenly distributed between the Hoeken and the Kabeljauwen. Further conflict between the two parties was forbidden.

Nor was this the end of Philip's acquisitions. In 1429, the last count of Namur died without an heir. Philip had already paid the substantial sum of 132,000 gold crowns in 1428 for the privilege of ruling this small but strategically located county, and had ensured that the States of Namur would recognize him. In the following year, 1430, the Brabantine branch of the Burgundians also died out and Philip became the new duke of Brabant. Misgivings in the States of Brabant and by the emperor about Philip's latest windfall could not stop the duke, but Philip was forced, in his inaugural act of *Blijde inkomst*, to yield many concessions to Brabantine self-determination: Brabant retained its own autonomous institutions, a sovereign council as its highest legal body, its own exchequer (known as the *Rekenkamer* or *Chambre des Comptes*), and the right to its own administrators. In this way, Brabant kept more of its autonomy than (for instance) either Flanders or Holland, where Philip respectively appointed reliable Burgundian and Flemish officials to oversee his interests. For decades to come, the Burgundian stadholders of Holland and Zeeland were French-speaking Walloon nobility, like De Lalaing and De Lannoy, who – more than local officials – could be trusted to represent the interests of the Burgundian dukes.

Detachment from France

The 1420s were thus an important watershed for the Low Countries; although the House of Burgundy's ambitions in Paris were stymied, it managed to pick up no less than three principalities in the Low Countries. The counts of Guelders also died out in 1423, but there were limits even to Philip's influence. It is clear that most of the initiative for the creation of larger political entities lay with the dukes and counts themselves, not only because they directly stood to gain or lose from dynastic marriage and death, but because they usually commanded the armies necessary to achieve this end. Philip the Good's considerable diplomatic skills also served him well in gaining the acceptance of his new subjects, an objective for which he negotiated extensively with the various States. But Philip's bid for power could not have succeeded without the wealthy base that Flanders and Artois provided him in the first place.

Although Burgundy was long an integral part of France, Philip and his successor, Charles the Bold, gradually oriented themselves toward the Empire. This development was due in no small measure to the new principalities Philip had accumulated, which, without exception, formally belonged to the Empire. Thus the Burgundian's reorientation toward the Empire did not stem from fear of the emperor's power (which remained weak) but from the fact that Burgundy – with two duchies and five counties – was now the most powerful force within the Empire. The three principalities the Burgundians retained in France were simply no longer as important to the dukes' interests. Distancing themselves from France was not only a possibility for the Burgundian dukes, but politically advantageous.

Burgundy's Territorial Limits

By 1435, the formation of the enlarged Burgundian Netherlands had been achieved. In the French-Burgundian peace treaty of that year, which nullified the old Anglo-Burgundian alliance against France, Philip received Picardy and many smaller dominions from the French crown. He now ruled over a large, mostly contiguous area which included some of the wealthiest parts of Europe, empowering him to act independently of both the French king and emperor. Although his greatest gains now lay in the past, Philip continued to accumulate additional territories. In 1441, Philip had his aunt, Elizabeth of Görlitz, recognize him as her heir to the duchy of Luxembourg, hence taking advantage of the fifth dynastic house to become extinct in the Low Countries. Philip took the city of Luxembourg by force and in 1443 bought off his rival to the duchy, the duke of Saxony, who had been backed by the emperor. Elizabeth did not die until 1451, and it was only then that Philip became duke of Luxembourg. The local nobility, accustomed to considerable autonomy, resisted Philip's efforts to assert his ducal prerogatives. But Luxembourg was neither demographically nor economically vital to Philip. The duke attained another success in Utrecht, where the canons had selected Gijsbrecht van Brederode of the Hoeken party in 1455. The Burgundians, pressuring the pope and flexing military muscle, persuaded Gijsbrecht – for a tidy sum – to withdraw as bishop, and Philip's illegitimate son David was invested as bishop of Utrecht. Apart from these relatively modest territorial acquisitions, Burgundian policy after 1435 primarily aimed at the internal consolidation of its government.

Philip's ambitions could be checked, however. The English were none too pleased with Philip's abandonment of their alliance, and he soon had to contend with English raids and attempts to damage the economy of his maritime territories, which had long been dependent on England. Philip's reaction to these developments was unfortunate; in July 1436, he laid siege to English-held Calais, where English wool exports were centered. To do so, he ordered a fleet to be sent from Holland and Zeeland and mobilized artisan militias from the Flemish cities. These troops proved singularly unmotivated to fight their most important trading partner, and Philip blamed the artisans when they decided, after waiting a month for the fleet to blockade the city by sea, to go home. Philip's relations with the Flemish cities deteriorated further during the prolonged absence of English wool, a commodity of immense economic importance to the clothmakers of Flanders, Brabant, and Holland. Ghent and Bruges revolted, further disturbing domestic peace and sharply demonstrating the limits of dynastic ambitions.

A New State?

Internal Consolidation

With the sizable territorial acquisitions of 1425 to 1435 now behind him, with Franco-Burgundian peace attained, and with a series of truces keeping the peace with England, Philip began to concentrate on the internal consolidation of his holdings. Each of the principalities under his rule had its own legal traditions, so that his lands hardly constituted a unitary state. It was more like a personal union where domains far away from, and having little in common with each other, were ruled by the same prince. Philip was well-acquainted with the centralized construction of the French state and he regarded it as a model for his own lands. To conform his dominions to French statecraft, the duke employed three methods which built on each other. First, he built a number of overarching structures which had authority over all his possessions, or all his possessions in the Low Countries. Second, he standardized the administration of the various principalities. Last, he attempted to break local resistance to his rule by offering attractive incentives to regional elites – and by crushing them by armed force if they refused. As a result of these measures, the period from 1435 to 1476 witnessed the rise of a powerful monarchical state in the Burgundian principalities.

At the same time, the methods of centralization were often so heavy-handed that they fomented widespread resentment, which reached across many sectors of the population and across all of the Burgundian domains. Regional revolts popped up as disaffected subjects seized the opportunity to rebel – and some of them succeeded in rolling back Burgundian power. In particular, the events of 1476 and 1477 would give rise to new protests against the repressive state and its high-handed functionaries.

In any event, the new standard of administrative unity imposed by the Burgundian dukes should not be compared to the contemporary understandings of bureaucratic efficiency. In Holland, for example, Dordrecht refused to support Amsterdam in its struggle to force the Hanseatic League to cede Baltic trading and shipping rights, nor did Dordrecht derive much sympathy from the rest of Holland in its efforts to keep its staple (its rights as a trading center) on river goods. In 1444, Dordrecht was condemned by Burgundian officials for rebellion and contempt for authority, and shorn of its staple, which was now divided among the other cities of Holland. The city steadfastly refused, however, to pay its taxes to Holland. In order to end the old party conflicts that had plagued Holland, the duke installed councils of eighty, forty, and twenty-four prominent persons, who were to nominate candidates, two for every position, to the magistracy. In doing so, he hoped that the stadholder and Council of Holland, the highest legal and administrative organ in the county, would consist of only moderate Hoeken and Kabeljauwen. This arrangement functioned until 1472,

Detail from The Wise and Foolish Virgins, *in the style of Pieter Brueghel, showing women engaged in the textile industry. (Koninklijke Bibliotheek, Brussels.)*

when duke Charles the Bold decided – for financial reasons – to appoint all the magistrates himself. This led to a preponderance of Hoeken, and a resurgence of the old party conflicts. History seemed to repeat itself as Holland once again became subject to power intrigues and the banishment of adversaries.

Financial Reforms

Meanwhile, the dukes of Burgundy hoped that reforming institutions from the center would lead to greater administrative unity and efficiency throughout their dominions. In 1433, there were three exchequers: one in Dijon for Burgundy and adjacent lands; one in Lille for Flanders, Artois, Hainaut, and Picardy; and one in Brussels for Brabant, Limburg, and (later) Luxembourg. Another one in The Hague was added for Holland and Zeeland in 1447. However, regional and local authorities maintained their own bookkeeping systems, making it difficult to determine actual revenues and expenses. When the court did not have the funds on hand to pay its expenses, it often sent creditors directly to local sources of revenue, further complicating the financial picture.

In 1445, a special commission set up by the central authority determined that 46 percent of all state revenues were spent regionally and locally, with only 54 percent reaching the central Burgundian treasury. The revenues that the duke earned as lord of his domains, such as fines, tolls, and minting rights, varied substantially from district to district, discrepancies which increased in the process of sending revenues to the central treasury. The duchy of Burgundy and the Franche-Comté made relatively heavy contributions to the central authority, but when its adjacent dependencies are also included, Burgundy contributed only about one quarter of the duke's income. Flanders made the single greatest contribution to the Burgundian treasury – no other region even came close – but Picardy (acquired only in 1435) also delivered handsome returns. In contrast, ducal revenues in Holland-Zeeland and Brabant-Limburg were relatively small. Another striking comparison is the difference between the gross income of the whole county of Namur, which totaled 16,000 pounds, and the tolls collected at Gravelines alone, which came to 26,000 pounds, the result of taxes assessed on English wool arriving from Calais. The Burgundian dukes, therefore, were most interested in the wealthy coastal areas, but it was there that their search for financial advantage led them into direct conflict with the well-organized trading and artisanal interests.

The Burgundian administration also derived a portion of its income from grants from the respective States. After 1471, the central administration requested one grant from the entire Burgundian Low Countries, so that a proportional system of taxation had to be developed. Flanders, Brabant-Limburg and Holland-Zeeland were each required to pay a quarter of the total – Hainaut 7 percent, Artois 6 percent and Namur 1 percent. However, this arrangement did not rest on a solid knowledge of what each region could financially contribute, since the Burgundians lacked a system for determining the real wealth of each territory. Proposals to count hearths as a way of determining taxes ran afoul of local officials, especially in Ghent and Bruges, who refused to cooperate. For this reason, the per capita tax rate assessed by the central administration varied considerably from region to region: from 1444 to 1467, Holland's per capita rate was ten times higher than in Picardy, three times higher than in Hainaut, and nearly twice the rate assessed in Brabant and Flanders. These inequities were felt all the more keenly by 1480, when taxes were twice as high as they had been a half century earlier. In particular, the seizure of power by Charles the Bold in 1465 led to a series of wars which resulted in nearly unalleviated tax increases.

Domain Incomes per Region, 1445		
	Gross percentage	*Net percentage*
Burgundy[1]	26.0	33.7
Flanders	24.0	18.9
Picardy	11.8	15.9
Artois	10.6	2.8
Holland-Zeeland	9.5	8.0
Brabant-Limburg	7.9	10.7
Hainaut	7.6	7.1
Namur	2.6	2.9

[1]And adjacent lands.

Burgundian Administration and Justice

Administrative and judicial centralization followed financial central-ization. Territorial expansion meant that the duke's councilors became overburdened. Between 1435 and 1445 a special judicial body – eventu-ally called the Great Council – grew out of the duke of Burgundy's council and gradually assumed the powers of a central high court. The Burgundians clearly intended to develop a unitary system in which their own legal decisions would take precedence over all local and regional interests. The Great Council, which ultimately consisted of six-teen councilors and sixteen secretaries, expanded its authority as the realm's highest court; it developed its own registry, and appointed a public prosecutor in 1449 and (later) a special receiver. In its early period, the Great Council did not sit in a permanent location; like the Burgundian court itself, it moved from place to place.

The Great Council chiefly concerned itself with matters pertaining to ducal laws and administration, but disputing parties could also ask the Council to amend judgments rendered by local magistrates or regional councils. Following his takeover of Holland and Zeeland in 1428, Philip reformed the "Court of Holland" into an important regional judicial council that in subsequent years developed sophis-ticated procedures which justified its intervention in an increasing number of legal and administrative cases. When, in 1462, the duke pre-scribed further professionalization, half of the judges and all the plead-ing lawyers possessed a law degree. Principles of Roman Law, such as the concept of lese majesty, were systematically introduced by the pub-lic prosecutor, the *avocat fiscal*, to impose the court's authority over the unruly nobility. The Burgundian dukes also sought to promote admin-istrative centralization by giving both parties engaged in litigation the right to bypass local courts altogether and present their case directly to the regional organs or to the Great Council itself. This generated a lot of potential for jurisdictional disputes, as local officials rightly perceived that their powers were being undermined by the higher courts. Even the judges of the regional councils, appointed by the duke himself, sometimes felt bypassed. The worst conflicts were evident in urban and rural districts where local elites – including increasing numbers of uni-versity-trained jurists – judged cases according to local charters and common law. These traditions contrasted sharply with the decisions of the ducal judges, who determined cases from the standpoint of the cen-tralized administration, a system in which they hoped, incidentally, to make a career.

The centralization of the Burgundian state was also evident in other areas. In 1433, the duke issued a new coin, "the fourlander" (*vier-lander*), which could be used throughout the Burgundian territories. In 1437, Philip called upon the States of Brabant, Flanders, Hainaut, Hol-land, Zeeland, Namur, and Mechelen to negotiate together on a com-mon currency. In 1438, their representatives met again (this time without delegates from Holland and Zeeland), as they would in 1441 and 1461 (these times with delegates from Holland and Zeeland). Issues like coinage, tolls, English wool exports, and protectionist policies against English cloth were all on the agendas of innumerable gatherings of cities throughout the Burgundian realm. The intraregional scale of these negotiations and their intensification over time paralleled the rise of uniform laws and regulations, which stimulated authorities to tackle problems not only on a local, but also on a regional level. This new kind of cooperation made it more difficult for foreign trading partners, like the English or the German Hanseatic League, to play the Flemish, Brabantines and Hollanders against each other. After 1464, the duke ordered that the States of each principality no longer meet separately but together, in a body called the States-General after 1477. In this way, too, the regions of Burgundy increasingly interacted with each other.

Bureaucratic Growth

The expansion and strengthening of central and regional organs required new functionaries to run them, functionaries who often supplanted the powers of local authorities, particularly the urban magistracy. This new officialdom became a special class; no longer tied to their place of origin, they moved from place to place as their careers directed. Local officials strongly objected to this rootless officialdom; they preferred local talent. But since loyalty to the duke was the chief purpose of the new officialdom, the dukes often appointed "foreign" functionaries (those from another principality) because they were more likely to serve the Burgundian state than local interests. The dukes also preferred administrators from Burgundy itself, since they formed a loyal core which could be deployed anywhere. In Brabant, the *Blijde Inkomst* agreements still assured that only Brabantines were appointed to local positions – but elsewhere the dukes' aim of a centralized bureaucracy overruled local preferences.

A large majority of this bureaucracy spoke French, which served as the administrative language throughout the Burgundian realms – despite the fact that most of the Low Countries was populated by Dutch-speaking inhabitants. The investigation commission assigned in 1457 to root out bureaucratic mismanagement throughout the territories consisted of five Francophones and one Dutch-speaking Brabantine. The *Chambre des Comptes* in Lille – which also oversaw Flemish finances – operated exclusively in French. The bookkeeping of the Council of Flanders (which met in Ghent) was also in French, although legal proceedings were kept in the language of the litigants. The Great Council only heard cases in French. Accordingly, some bureaucrats from Flanders, Brabant, and Holland changed their language and their own names to French, to the detriment of their Dutch-speaking subjects. In Holland and Brabant the councils and *Rekenkamers* still used Dutch – they had come under Burgundian control later than Flanders – but their correspondence with the Burgundian center was in French.

At the head of this new bureaucracy was the chancellor of Burgundy. Nicholas Rolin, serving in the post from 1422 to 1457, built up a considerable base of power for himself, including a noble title and a large income. Rolin's power remained limited; he was unable to bypass the duke on important decisions and was eventually dismissed in a power struggle with the Croy family. But his power and influence was

Jan van Eyck, The Holy Virgin
with Chancellor Rolin, *1425.*
(Musée du Louvre, Paris.)

considerable while it lasted. He also had the means to commission a
large altarpiece by Jan van Eyck and to establish the beautiful Hospital
of Beaune, which included Rogier van der Weyden's impressive trip-
tych, *The Last Judgment.* To this day, Rolin's initials and those of his wife
adorn the walls, girders, and glass windows of the hospital. Rolin's
exceedingly successful, if unhappily terminated, career is illustrative of
the ambitions of Burgundian administrators, who sought after personal
enrichment and increased status. University-trained jurists with a bourgeois background, including Rolin, were as well represented in the
Burgundian hierarchy as nobility and high clergy – a remarkably egalitarian attainment by fifteenth-century standards. Expertise had triumphed over heredity at the Burgundian court, but the duke (and not
only the duke) still considered it necessary to ennoble Rolin, so that he
might stand on equal social terms with his noble peers.

As the Burgundian state expanded, it attracted increasing numbers of mandarins who had a stake in its health and growth. At the
same time, the chasm between the Burgundian bureaucracy and their
subjects – who continued to think strongly in local and regional terms –
continued to widen.

Resistance against Integration

The formation of states in Europe occurred over a long period of time,
from the eleventh to the nineteenth centuries, with England and Germany forming the best-known extremes, and the Netherlands roughly
occupying a middle position in this chronology. The parameters of these

consolidated states depended, however, on already existent structures and institutions. Rulers could unite administrative principalities, but real integration was contingent on the weakness of local and regional power. The greatest resistance to Burgundian centralization manifested itself in Flanders, where the tradition of urban autonomy was strongest. Repeated jurisdictional conflicts between the sovereign-bailiff, the highest public prosecutor in the county, and the Flemish cities occurred whenever the former arrested one of their citizens; according to the city charters, only city magistrates could try one of their own. In 1401, after a serious escalation of recriminations, the Ghentenars finally succeeded in getting the sovereign-bailiff, Jacob van Lichtervelde, dismissed and sent to the Holy Land as a penitential pilgrim. After a similar altercation in 1436, Bruges banished the sovereign-bailiff, Colard van der Clyte and the captain of Sluis, Roeland van Uitkerke, from Flanders for fifty years, even though both were noblemen and functionaries of the count.

Revolt in Bruges

The Bruges Revolt of 1436 to 1438 did not end well for the proud city. In March of 1438, Philip the Good called the States of Flanders, Artois, and Hainaut to Arras to witness his judgment against the defeated Bruges. Bruges's defeat was magnified by the location of the proceedings; Arras's location outside of Flanders was intended as a humiliation of the city. In addition to other symbolic punishments, Bruges lost control over its outpost at Sluis and over surrounding lands in western Flanders, and was obliged to pay the enormous indemnity of 480,000 pounds. The sheer size of the amount becomes clear when it is compared to the 280,000 pounds that all of Flanders paid as annual subsidy in 1440, or the portion of this (24,000 pounds, or 15.7 percent) which Bruges was slated to pay. The Burgundian administration intended Bruges's humiliation as a warning to all potential rebels. Moreover, Bruges's financial prostration and political decline served the interests of the duke, since the city could no longer function as a regional opponent to his rule. The Council of Flanders now replaced the magistrates of Bruges as the court to which residents of Bruges had to go when in litigation with other Flemings.

Philip had not sought conflict with Bruges in 1436; indeed, the squabble with England had made the revolt quite inconvenient for him. But the city's rejection of his early efforts to achieve a peaceful solution, and a battle in March 1437 which put his own life and the lives of his court in danger, turned the rift with Bruges into an matter of prestige for Philip. Not only did his splendid triumph over the rebellious metropolis do much to restore his image after the Calais fiasco, it also gave Philip the opportunity to increase the prerogatives of his judges and administrators. Thus Bruges became, after Liège in 1408, the second major city to be stripped of its privileges and hegemony over its hinterland.

The Salt Tax

In 1447, the Burgundian administration made an important decision designed to increase central authority. Following the example of France, the duke decided to levy a permanent consumption tax on salt, a product not only indispensable for eating but also for food preservation. Since salt could be produced at only a few locales, its taxation would be relatively easy. For Burgundian policy makers, the salt tax was a well-considered plan. It would guarantee the state a fixed income, make negotiations with the cities difficult, render the various States superfluous, and replace the uncertain financial grants and subsidies on which the central administration had relied. As an indirect tax, it would be collected automatically. Moreover, it was an unbiased method of raising taxes, since it could be uniformly applied in all regions. Salt consumption could even be used to assess the incomes of each province, an improvement on the cumbersome technique of counting hearths.

The French king's steady income from the salt tax (the *gabelle*) and the English king's tolls on wool exports would not have escaped Philip's notice; he dreamed of having the same kind of automatic revenues. The duke found it increasingly unacceptable that his subjects could demand an account of his spending before surrendering funds to him, or that they could deny, reduce, or delay the funds he had requested. This was also precisely the reason why his subjects opposed the salt tax: their acceptance of it would undermine their negotiating position and reduce their influence in the administration of the country.

The proposal for the salt tax was first introduced to the Broad Council of Ghent, the hundred-man association which represented the guilds in the largest city of the Low Countries. If they agreed, the rest of Flanders would follow, and with Flanders, the rest of the principalities – or so Philip thought. To his surprise, the Broad Council refused to ratify the proposal. Was the Council moved by the consideration that the tax was regressive (harder on the poor than the rich), that it would lose bargaining power if it passed, or both? Whatever the case, the duke left Ghent with bitter feelings. A few months later, he tried to pass the tax in Bruges, but with no more success. As a result, the salt tax was never implemented, and resistance to consumption taxes remained so strong in the Low Countries that the duke of Alba's infamous "tenth penny" tax, more than a century later, ran into immediate and vigorous resistance.

The Subjugation of Ghent

Relations between Philip and Ghent had been damaged badly by the salt tax issue, and they only worsened during annual city elections when the duke tried to prevent his opponents from regaining their magistrates' seats. When the Burgundian judiciary harassed prominent burghers of Ghent, it only made it clearer that Philip now intended to provoke a crisis that would undermine Ghent's power. In contrast to Bruges, the city still enjoyed the broad privileges that it had received in the fourteenth century. In 1450, the duke presented his grievances against Ghent to the bewildered States of Flanders and increased the pressure by violating Ghentenar privileges and recalling his bailiff, which put a halt to all legal proceedings in Ghent. Angered, the Ghentenar guilds went on strike and issued a call to arms in October 1451. Attempts to mediate the dispute failed in the face of Philip's determination to reduce Ghentenar power, and by the summer of 1452, Ghent was surrounded by a military

blockade. However, the decisive battle did not take place until July 1453, at Gavere, when Ghentenar militias panicked after one of their own gunpowder depots accidentally exploded.

Ghentenars surrender to Philip the Good (1453) in this fifteenth-century illumination. (Kunsthistoriches Museum, Vienna.)

Philip took full advantage of his victory, just as he had in 1438. The indemnity of 480,000 pounds was identical to the amount exacted on Bruges, and though the duke later forgave 168,000 pounds, the remainder was still equal to what all of Flanders paid as grants between 1440 and 1443. The Ghentenar magistracy's legal power beyond the city gates was dramatically curtailed, and their judgments were now subject to appeal by the Council of Flanders. The influence of guild leaders in the city administration was eliminated, and the guilds were obliged to surrender their proud banners. Philip carefully orchestrated the symbolism of Ghent's defeat: magistrates and guild leaders had to pros-

trate themselves before the duke, bareheaded, barefoot, and in penitential garments, offering the guild banners to the victorious Philip.

Philip intended his subjugation of Bruges and Ghent – the Low
Countries's largest cities – as cautionary tales for the remaining ones.
The new fear of ducal power was most telling in Brabant. The Brabantine cities had also complained about the infringements of their rights
as the regional Council of Brabant, like its counterparts elsewhere,
expanded its prerogatives and operated within the traditional jurisdiction of the city magistrates. In 1459, the duke used the conflict between
Brussels and the duke's legal officer, the *amman*, to void an important
privilege of 1421. In that year, the States of Brabant had suspended duke
John IV for countless violations of the *Blijde Inkomst* and for mismanagement, and had instated his younger brother as regent; the younger
man recognized their grievances and accepted the principle that all
ducal councilors were to be held accountable to the States. Now this
early expression of popular sovereignty and ministerial responsibility
was easily swept aside by the Burgundian duke. The powerful monarchical state was clearly in ascendance.

Burgundy's Internal Weaknesses

At the same time, the Burgundian state exhibited remarkable weaknesses. Its enormous bureaucracy was inefficient. Officers of justice
turned over only a small percentage of the fines they collected to
regional receivers, who themselves proved just as susceptible to corruption as the local tax collectors, stewards, clerks of court, and
chancery officials. Because of lax controls, officials on all levels were
able to divert state property to personal ends. As a result of the struggle
of power between the Croy family and chancellor Nicholas Rolin, the
duke ordered a full-scale investigation of administrative irregularities
in 1457. The investigation found massive violations, and Rolin and the
chairman of the Great Council, Bishop Jean Chevrot of Tournai, were
forced to vacate their positions. However, the investigation soon ended
when the Four Members of Flanders and large Brabantine cities spontaneously offered a grant to the duke if he would end it. A close network
of interests apparently existed between local elites and Burgundian
administrators: they belonged to the same families and to the same
patronage system, and both groups were unquestionably tainted by the
shady transactions they made with each other. Mid-sized cities like
Saint-Omer and Lille cultivated exclusive contacts with top Burgundian administrators and dignitaries as a way of pressing their interests
at the Burgundian court. One good turn deserved another, and those
with power used it to build patronage. Commitments to "public service" were not deeply rooted in the administrative apparatus, and per-
sonalistic views of power were too pervasive for bureaucratic ethics, as
understood in the modern sense, to develop. Thus, despite the state
machinery's formal commitment to "the common good," its administrators enriched themselves at the state's expense, leaving the Burgundian state in a chronic financial crisis.

The state's troubled finances provided further incentives for graft.
The state did not pay its civil servants well, and they resorted to bribery

to supplement their income. To raise money, the administration leased many of its positions to interested persons. Merit hardly played a role in a system that often sold offices to the highest bidders - men who sought a handsome return on the capital they had invested in their office. The common people who funded these none-too-subtle machinations could only look on with dismay. Only bribes could secure the services of bureaucrats, and abuses of power were widespread and open. The fault lines of resistance were no longer between the cities and their noble rulers; instead, powerful groups within the cities began to oppose the cliques of city administrators and Burgundian bureaucrats who owed their loyalty to the duke.

The first large-scale protests erupted during the entry ceremonies of duke Charles the Bold in 1467, as riots broke out in various cities in opposition to duty increases. In Ghent the people demanded a repeal of the humiliating terms of 1453, such as the closing of some city gates, and the duke himself was barely able to escape the crowd. Charles responded by teaching his Ghentenar subjects a lesson. In January 1468, Charles summoned their guild leaders and magistrates to Brussels (again, outside of Flanders to underscore their defeat) to hear his judgment. After waiting several hours in the snow, they heard the verdict: the guilds were to surrender their banners and were stripped of their say in the appointment of magistrates; from now on, the duke himself would choose the magistrates. The riots in Ghent had only precipitated the further abasement of the city.

Charles the Bold seriously considered even heavier sanctions against the sullen cities. In 1465, using military pressure, Charles persuaded the States of Liège to recognize him as hereditary prince, relegating the city's bishop to the spiritual realm. The cities revolted several months later to protest this act, and when Charles heard that he had been ridiculed in Dinant, he reacted by razing the city. Serious resistance and ugly fighting continued through 1467 and 1468, and when the Burgundian army camp was hit by a surprise attack near Liège, the duke gave his soldiers free rein to plunder, kill, and burn in the episcopal city.

The Power of the State

If we want to understand how state power grew to the extent of the extravagances mentioned above, then we need to consider several crucial factors. The expansion of Burgundian territory worked to the advantage of the duke and against each principality and city. Rebellions were usually local and isolated; the dukes' subjects seldom made concerted attempts to oppose him, and this meant that the duke could bring the preponderance of his power to bear on hopelessly inferior forces. In fact, it is striking how loyal most of the duke's principalities remained when a local rebellion broke out. In 1452 and 1453, for instance, Philip was able to count on support from all his other subjects when he marched on Ghent. In this case, the lack of national or regional identity only helped the duke. The development of cannons also made it easier for princes to pulverize the walls of defiant cities. The city militias, so effective a military force in the fourteenth century, were now no match for the professional armies of the great rulers. Resistance was also weakened by the Burgundian state's positive legacy, which included the period of peace and relative prosperity lasting from roughly 1440 to 1475, opportunities for lucrative careers, the promotion of international trade, and even the chances for smaller cities to escape the domination of their larger counterparts and the power of feudal potentates.

The combination of these factors gave the Burgundian state a decisive edge over the once hegemonic cities, which had now been effectively straitjacketed by the duke. The conspicuous subjugation of cities in Flanders, Liège, and of Utrecht (1455-1456) was designed to instill fear in the other cities. Pressure was softer in Holland and Brabant, but the Burgundian drive for greater control seldom slackened.

Burgundy's Golden Age

Plagues did not disappear from the Low Countries in the wake of the fourteenth century's demographic crisis, but epidemics became less extensive and less frequent. Serious plagues swept the region from 1437 to 1438, 1457 to 1459 and, in a series of local outbreaks, from 1480 to 1492, but they did not prevent a gradual increase in population. With most of Europe enjoying demographic growth, merchants of the Low Countries found expanding markets for their exports. Between 1400 and 1475, trade volume in the Low Countries doubled, and economic growth was especially marked in northern Brabant, where the annual fairs at Antwerp and Bergen op Zoom generated much activity. Furthermore, shipping in Zeeland and Holland underwent a significant expansion, and Dutch skippers were prominent in the trade with England and along the Baltic and Atlantic coasts.

For these reasons, wages could at least remain stable throughout the fifteenth century, despite the increase in population. In 1440, wages for the construction industry in Bruges rose 10 percent above the wages that had been in place since 1400. Opportunities for employment must have been good in many sectors of the economy, especially in international trade. The coopers' guild in Bruges registered 668 new master coopers between 1375 and 1500, an average of 5.3 per year. Only 21 percent of these masters were following in their father's footsteps, suggesting that this guild, so important for transportation and trade, remained an attractive employment option.

High purchasing power, domestic peace, controlled tax pressures, a stable currency, rising trade volume – all of these factors made the Low Countries prosperous in the three decades after 1440. These prosperous years were the halcyon days of Burgundian culture and would not soon be replicated. Not only would the workers of the mid-fifteenth century know a standard of living higher than either their parents or children, they would enjoy an abundance that would not be seen again, at least not in the southern Low Countries, until the early nineteenth century.

The Trading Metropolis of Bruges

Between 1380 and 1480, Bruges was unquestionably the most important trading city in northwestern Europe, the center of an international economic system in which the rest of the Low Countries played a significant but secondary role. The system included countries providing raw mate-

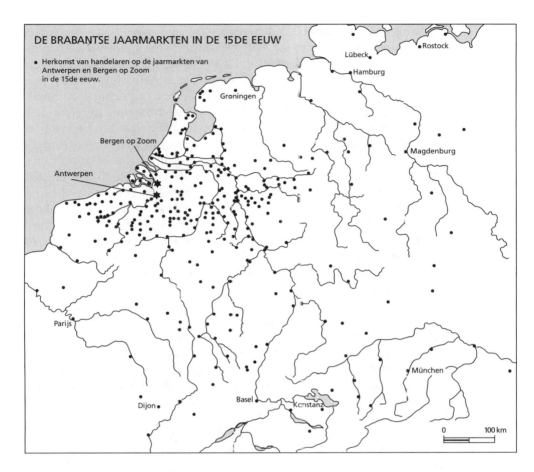

Brabantine Annual Fairs in the Fifteenth Century

rials like England, Scotland, Castile, and Prussia, as well as the markets for these materials in northern, central, and southern Europe. The interdependence of the system meant that developments in one sector quickly had system-wide consequences. The rising price of English wool and the growth of cloth production on the island reduced wool exports from England, giving the Castelan sheep farmers new economic opportunities. The Low Countries' growing trade with Spain also introduced new products which could be shipped easily together, like unfinished leather. In Bruges an important guild, the Corduaniers, was established to process this leather (they named themselves after the Spanish city of Córdoba, an old Arabic center whose styles were eagerly imitated in northern Europe). Spain also delivered tropical fruits, intermittent shipments of grain, frequent loads of ore, and increasing amounts of colonial goods, like ivory and sugar cane originating from the Azores, where the Despars family of Bruges also invested in plantations. Bruges and other southern Netherlandic cities also began to specialize in artistic crafts which produced fashionable luxury goods for foreign and domestic elites looking for ways to spend their newfound wealth.

Over the course of the fifteenth century several other regions began to seriously expand their own economic activities in the shadow of Bruges. The Island of Walcheren in Zeeland served as a secondary harbor and winter haven for Antwerp through the sixteenth century, as vessels originating in Bordeaux, La Rochelle, Brittany, England, and Scotland frequently anchored off the town of Arnemuiden. Skippers from the Baltic, on their way to southern France or Portugal, routinely spent their winters in Zeeland, where they used the time to refine their cargo of rough Atlantic salt. Arnemuiden functioned as an outpost both for Antwerp and Bruges: for the former because of its distance from the coast, for the latter because of serious silting in the Zwin Estuary. Antwerp benefitted from a series of floods between 1375 and 1424 which turned the West Scheldt into a navigable river capable of carrying two-hundred-ton ships. We know that later in the century about four hundred skippers operated out of Antwerp, together amassing a fleet totaling some six thousand tons, including twenty-four hundred tons suitable for sea travel. Much of their freight went to England, often in the service of Cologne merchants, but their vessels could be found along many European coasts, from Norway to Italy. During the fifteenth century, Antwerp generated so much economic growth that it also stimulated the surrounding regions. Cities like 's-Hertogenbosch, Lier, Mechelen, and Herentals all benefitted from a strong surge in inland shipping, which continued to grow until 1550. The two annual fairs in Bergen op Zoom, on the East Scheldt, remained an important source of economic activity, as did the two in Antwerp. Foreign traders stationed in Bruges traveled in large numbers to Antwerp during the fairs, and even purchased residences and warehouses near Antwerp's Great Market. Clearly, economic growth in both Zeeland and northern Brabant was associated with the metropolitan role that Bruges played throughout the region.

Holland and the Sea Trade

The expansion of the sea trade in Holland was no less impressive. We have explained above how the Dutch, thanks to their competitive position in relation to the German Hanseatic League and the southern Low Countries, managed to become important maritime traders. It is plausible to argue that the political unity of the Low Countries under the Burgundians prevented trade wars among Holland, Brabant, and Flanders; after 1433, the central administration initiated negotiations between the cities of these regions in an effort to coordinate and regulate their collective markets. Currency rates and protectionism against cheap English cloth were important items on the agenda.

Conflict with the Hanseatic League, however, now seemed inevitable: ships from Holland routinely made forays into the Baltic, a sea which the Germans regarded as their own preserve. Lübeck in particular actively resisted Dutch competition, since the Dutch escaped all of the regulations and restrictions that were imposed on League members. After numerous acts of piracy, a hundred-ship fleet from Holland and Zeeland captured twenty-two vessels of a Prussian salt fleet off the coast of Brest in 1438. This, of course, precipitated retaliation, and soon a real trade war broke out. In 1441, a Dutch fleet forced the opening of the Danish straits to Dutch traffic, and in the truce that followed, the

Danish king was paid to safely escort ships through this strategic passage to the Baltic.

The truce was extended every ten years and lasted until 1471, when new negotiations granted the skippers from Holland and Zeeland an important extension of their rights in the Peace of Utrecht of 1473 – a victory due in no small measure to the support they received from Charles the Bold. Dutch traders would no longer be obliged to send their Baltic cargoes to the Hanseatic staple in Bruges before exporting them elsewhere. Furthermore, the sheer size of the Dutch fleet in the Baltic meant that the Hanseatic League was no longer able to restrict their trade. This breakthrough for the Dutch, which would remain in effect for several centuries, was also helped by the deep divisions within the League itself - between the Wendish cities (led by Lübeck) and the Prussian cities. The latter, as frequent traders with the Dutch, had a considerable interest in maintaining good relations with Holland. The Peace of Utrecht was the death knell of a protectionist system that had worked to the advantage of both the Hanseatic League and Flanders, and it opened the way for free trade in the Baltic.

This economic system was characterized in the Low Countries by the pivotal role of the cities on the coast and at the mouths of the great rivers; these cities bought raw materials from afar, processed them into high-quality goods, and then exported them all over Europe. Only Northern Italy was economically stronger, and in many areas, such as trade financing and the organization of long-distance trade with the Levant, the Low Countries remained dependent on the Italian cities. However, for Western Europe, Bruges and Antwerp had become the "core" of economic activity. Interior, agrarian regions like Hainaut, Artois, Namur, and Luxembourg formed a "periphery" which functioned within the system by delivering raw materials and buying the processed goods produced in the cities.

Demographic Centers of Gravity

The economic importance of each region can also be seen in population figures. Although documents of the time often give incomplete or indirect information, there are well-organized fiscal records, dating from around 1470 for most regions – a legacy of the Burgundians's efforts to create a proportional tax system. For Holland, however, the oldest overview dates only from 1514, for Friesland 1511, and we can make only rough estimates for Zeeland, Utrecht, Groningen, and Drenthe. Given that the records only count families, historians must factor in a multiplier to derive approximately how many individuals were living at the time. There is relatively little information on which to base this multiplier, so generalizations can lead to distortions. But on the basis of census figures for Ypres in the fifteenth century and Leiden in 1574, some historians have pegged the average urban family at four members (it used to be counted at 4.5) and the average rural family at five. Using these multipliers, we estimate that the Low Countries had 2,776,000 inhabitants at the turn of the sixteenth century; excluding Picardy (which reverted to France), the population was over 2.5 million people. Of the latter estimate, 27 percent of the total (705,000) lived in Flanders and 16 percent in Brabant – together mustering 43 percent of the population. Holland was a distant third, with 10 percent. Not surprisingly, the coastal areas and (to a lesser extent) the great rivers show the largest concentration of people and the highest level of urbanization; 30 percent of the population in Flanders, Brabant, and Hainaut, and a full 44 percent of Holland's people lived in cities. The northeast and southeast regions of the Low Countries were the most sparsely populated.

Taken as a whole, population density in the Low Countries was higher than in surrounding regions; there were seventy-two persons per square kilometer in Flanders, sixty-three in Holland, forty-four in Hainaut, and forty in Brabant, with an average for the whole region estimated at fifty-three persons per square kilometer. In contrast, sixteenth century Italy had forty-four, France thirty-four, and the Empire twenty-eight persons per square kilometer; and England's population in 1500 could not have totaled more than four million people.

Ecclesiastical Life

Given the high density of the Low Countries it is amazing that only one bishop's see – Utrecht – lay in Dutch-language territory. The remaining bishoprics, far to the south and east (Tournai, Arras, Cambrai, Thérouanne, and Liège), had been established in the early Middle Ages, and only in 1559 did church organization catch up with demographic developments by establishing more bishoprics in the north. This shortcoming did not prevent the church from penetrating almost all aspects of faith and life. Poor relief functioned via the parochial churches and according to the ecclesiastical calendar, with so-called Dishes of the Holy Spirit. Charity was distributed in or in front of the church following Sunday Mass and feast days, or according to the pious wishes of departed souls who perhaps reckoned that their last-minute gifts might boost their spiritual standing in the afterlife. Various brotherhoods were also active on the parochial level, in which the laity sought to honor particular saints or practice specific form of Marian devotion. Like the guilds, the brotherhoods maintained countless chapels within the urban parochial churches, for which expensively painted and polychromated wood altarpieces were specially designed. Guilds, brotherhoods, cities, and noble families all organized processions on the feast day of their respective saints. The ecclesiastical calendar gave so many opportunities for veneration – several dozen a year – that the number of annual work days in the years before the Reformation could not have been more than 270.

In this context, artists still devoted most of their energies to creations with religious functions or themes. Portraiture did become more common over the course of the fifteenth century, and works of art, including religious ones, became increasingly realistic. Painters of the southern Netherlands, unduly known as the "Flemish primitives," excelled in extremely detailed depictions of reality which formed the basis of their religious compositions. Hundreds of identifiable plants, a wide range of precious fabrics and jewels, a glistening fountain, and the beautiful naked bodies of Adam and Eve could all be found in Hubert and Jan van Eyck's famous altarpiece, *The Mystic Lamb* (1432), which demonstrated the brothers' commitment to a colorful portrayal of reality and to religious motifs. The magistrate from Ghent, Jacob Veyt, and his wife Elizabeth Borluut, who commissioned the work, made sure that they, too, were realistically portrayed in the piece. The prominent canon Van der Paele (certainly no Adonis), chancellor Rolin, and many others had themselves painted into religious works, appearing in the same size as – and only barely below – the Virgin and Child. Devotion to Mary was the primary purpose of this art but much of the background had a worldly content.

Increasing worldliness is not, in fact, an inappropriate description of trends within the institutional church of the late Middle Ages. Cardinals and parish priests alike had difficulty concentrating exclusively on their spiritual callings, since their positions a so had political significance. The Burgundian dukes interfered in the appointments of top church dignitaries just as the nobility had done for centuries. They saw to it that loyal followers were named to one or more important ecclesiastical positions with considerable sources of income. In return, the dukes expected financial and spiritual support. In 1515, Pope Leo X solemnly recognized what had long been the practice throughout Western Europe: princes were officially permitted a say in the naming of bishops and abbots in their principalities, and allowed to dispense scores of other lucrative benefices such as canons and deans. Officeholders often tried to collect additional ecclesiastical positions as a way of increasing their influence and income. Some clerics used their position to steep themselves in the humanist thought of their time and accumulated impressive libraries; two of Philip the Good's sons, David of Burgundy (bishop of Utrecht) and Raphaël de Mercatel (abbot of Saint Bavon's, near Ghent) distinguished themselves in this way. Other clerics served as important functionaries to the dukes; in the fifteenth century, almost all of the bishops of Tournai chaired the Burgundian Great Council. In these kinds of appointments, prestige, influence, and money figured more prominently than pastoral care or solitary prayer, and they contributed to an enormous rate of absenteeism among clerics, who relegated the duties of their church offices to unqualified proxies. It is revealing that the Dutch Augustinian monk Aurelius praised Pope Nicholas V (1447-1455) in his *Divisiekroniek* (1517) because "he was not tainted with the sin of simony, offering benefices, high office and prelacies in exchange for gifts, which is a common practice nowadays."

The lay faithful reacted to this in different ways. First, there was the highly popular and very emotional devotion of certain saints, especially Mary, who were ascribed mediating powers. There was also a very formal devotional life in which pious prayers, deeds, gifts, and foundations were "traded" for sins. This practice was stimulated by the trade in indulgences, in which the church collected money from people in exchange for a reduction of time in purgatory (where souls paid the price for earthly sins). Originally introduced during the "holy years" of 1300, 1400, 1450, 1475, and so on, indulgences were later extended to support the construction of church buildings like the cathedral of Utrecht, which became the target of reformers who strongly opposed this quantitative piety. Monastic life grew stricter in reaction to these developments in the late fifteenth and early sixteenth centuries, a trend that was financially supported by spiritually minded women in the nobility. The *devotio moderna* movement, with its strict observance of monastic rule and emphasis on simplicity, individual prayer, and personal devotion, was part of this trend toward greater spirituality. It was inspired by Geert Groote (1340-1384), who as a deacon in Deventer preached fiery sermons against priests taking concubines and monks accumulating worldly goods. Monasteries and convents which transferred their allegiance to the Brothers and Sisters of the Common Life (organized as the Congregation of Windesheim) played an active role in the production of small and sober devotional books, all of them in the vernacular. These books included biblical fragments, saints' lives, and texts from the Church Fathers. The thousands of surviving examples indicate that they were widely read by men and a good number of women. This religious pursuit certainly met the needs of many laity, but it was not enough to restore lay confidence in the established clergy. The far-reaching worldly orientation of the ecclesiastical hierarchy led them away from their primary tasks and undermined their credibility; it also reduced the élan necessary for church reform.

Burgundian Patronage of the Arts

The Trappings of Power

Duke Philip the Bold of Burgundy (1384-1404) of made many efforts to add artistic luster to his young dynasty, following in the tradition set by the French royal House of Valois. The dukes of Burgundy spent more resources on exalting their reputations through artistic creation than most rulers in Western Europe, efforts aimed as much at rival princes as their own subjects. Because the Burgundians had only recently established themselves, the status-conscious dukes deemed it especially important to underscore the importance of their many titles with ornate beauty. By the mid-fifteenth century, Philip the Good felt that he had become worthy of kingship and tried to compensate for his lowly ducal status through the exceptional splendor of his court. Philip the Good intended to show the world his true greatness, and filled all his ceremonial events with fanfare and great luxury. He called the best artists of the Low Countries – Klaas Sluter, Jacob de Baerze, and Klaas van de Werve – to Dijon to sculpt figures for the ducal mausoleum in the Carthusian cloister of Champmol. The Maelwael brothers painted illuminated texts for him, using a strikingly beautiful script. Philip's successors would continue this trend, though the growing wealth and importance of the Low Countries meant that its artists increasingly found customers at home.

To express their power and greatness, the dukes could draw on an inexhaustible supply of world-class artists from the Low Countries. The artists' patronage sprang up, therefore, to a large extent from the initiatives, inspiration, and motives of the Burgundian dukes. At the same time, the dukes were able to rely upon the traditional artistic centers in the Low Countries which had been stimulated by the urban bourgeoisie, and which were already well-known and respected throughout Europe. This intersection of ducal initiative and artistic tradition unleashed a new energy in all of the arts. Some artistic activity from this time has been inaccurately labeled; for example, the "Flemish primitives," "Brabantine gothic," or "Flemish polyphony," in which four generations of artists in a number of centers form supposed categories. Production was so great that much of it could be exported, especially in artistic crafts: jewelry, expensive clothing, painted panels, and carved objects. Musicians, too, traveled from one princely court to another, where they performed as the most famous singers and composers of their time.

The dukes of Burgundy set a trend which the elites of society soon followed: court nobility, clergy, city administrators, rich merchants, and the well-endowed abbeys all became enthusiastic patrons of the arts. None of the famous artists of the Burgundian and Habsburg periods worked exclusively for the ruling princes; there were always other clients who, like the dukes, were eager to demonstrate their own power and prestige.

The flowering of artistic life in the Low Countries largely corresponded with the period (described above) of political stability, peace, and welfare. This correspondence is, of course, not an absolute one: the region's talented and important painters like Robert Campin of Tournai flourished before the Burgundian dukes patronized the arts. In the fourteenth century all of the large cities of the southern Low Countries produced impressive architecture, paintings, and manuscript illumination. The point here is that the dukes gave a new impetus to existing traditions and stimulated artists, at least in several centers, to new heights of creativity. Campin's brilliant student, Rogier van der Weyden, left the Tournai workshop of his master for Brussels, where the ducal court and the burghers alike eagerly commissioned his services.

The only real court painter of Philip the Good was Jan van Eyck. Serving at the court from 1425 until his death in 1441, his office was listed as *valet de chambre*. This humble title did not prevent him from being sought out by many luminaries in Ghent and Bruges, who wanted him to create spectacular altarpieces for them. The duke also retained miniaturists, mostly from Artois and Hainaut. The master builder for the court was the Brabantine Jan van Ruisbroek. He expanded the various residences of the duke, especially the palace at the Coudenberg in Brussels. Musicians were also on hand at the court and were primarily responsible for church services. The divide between church and secular music was not wide, however, and the known works of singer-composers like Giles Binchois, Antoine Busnois, and Guillaume Dufay consist of several musical genres.

Tapestries

The Burgundian court did not rely exclusively on its own artists but routinely solicited the services of workshops in the

Portrait of Philip the Good by Rogier van der Weyden.

*The 1473 session of the Order of the Golden Fleece is
the subject of this fifteenth-century illumination.
(Kunsthistorisches Museum, Vienna.)*

large cities. The most striking creations
are the tapestries, mostly manufactured
in Arras and Tournai, whose great size
and high price truly made them princely
gifts; a beautiful series of twelve tapestries, each containing episodes of
the Trojan War, cost the equivalent of 120 years' wages for a skilled
laborer. The high cost was due not only to the materials – which included
threads of wool, silk, gold, and silver – but also to the wages necessary to
sustain highly qualified weavers over a number of years. Because of both
their size and rarity, these tapestries made a deep impression on all those
who saw them. It was no coincidence that the dukes hung these tapestries in their reception halls, especially during ceremonies.

When duke Charles the Bold married Margaret of York at Bruges
in 1468, the wedding guests were treated to a series of tapestries documenting the victory of John the Fearless over Liège in 1408. The chronicler Jean de Haynin also reports that other tapestries were present,
including ones depicting the history of Gideon and the fleece, a whole
series on the great deeds of Chlodowech, and one devoted to King Ahasuerus, who ruled over 127 provinces. All of the tapestries clearly

played to the triumphalism of the Burgundians. Philip the Good had been only slightly more circumspect when he commissioned of tapestries on Alexander the Great, but symbols of power were evident in other works, such as the so-called Thousand Flower tapestry, in which the duke's shield and motto is placed alongside other dynastic symbols like the Cross of Saint Andrew and the flint. The tapestry devoted to Gideon was not incidental, either; it conjured up the story of the Golden Fleece, the chief symbol of the Burgundian dynasty.

Tapestries were pointedly aimed at the denizens and visitors of the court. Through these tapestries, they were steeped in the themes of rulership so cherished and promoted by the Burgundian dukes. But the Burgundians's patronage of church art had a still greater impact, since many more people had occasion to see them. The great tombs at Champmol and the Carthusian convent at Montereau, which Philip the Good had built in 1435 so that prayers could be continuously offered for the benefit of his murdered father, are examples of their patronage. The Burgundians' most noteworthy legacy was stained windows and altarpieces, although most of these works were commissioned not by the dukes but by their top functionaries.

The dukes showed a special interest in books and paid for countless Latin works to be translated into French; many of them were chronicles of their newly won territories, histories of the world, and stories of the heroic deeds of persons such as Alexander the Great and Charlemagne. Not surprisingly, these histories tended to justify the political world that the Burgundians had wrought. This tendency was most manifest in the works of the court chroniclers like Enguerrand de Monstrelet and Georges Chastellain, who were responsible for describing events of the recent past.

The Burgundians were particularly eager to retell the old Greek myth of Jason and the Argonauts, since the Golden Fleece served as their own symbol. They also appropriated the Brabantine literary tradition, in place since the thirteenth century, of recounting the history of Troy and hailing the dukes as direct descendants of the Greek heroes, a line which was ostensibly traceable through Charlemagne. Both myths were used to illustrate the ideals of knighthood propagated at the Burgundian court; in 1430, duke Philip used the occasion of his third marriage to establish the Order of the Golden Fleece. Founding a knightly order was usually reserved for kings, but Philip used the impressive symbolism of the order to bind the highest nobility of his diverse dominions – some only just acquired – and his princely allies to him.

Manuscripts

It should be said that if the Burgundians commissioned many beautiful manuscripts to reflect their glories, they also supported purely literary, theological, and philosophical works. Whatever the genre, they showed a particular interest in its aesthetic qualities. It is no coincidence, for instance, that a number of illumination manuscripts depict an illumination workshop when it is being visited by duke Philip or the young Charles the Bold. Many books include a solemn scene in which the duke, surrounded by high nobility and functionaries, is offered a new manuscript. The dukes' emphasis on ceremonial presentation explains why they so highly valued costly and beautiful manuscripts. As patrons they were visible in the texts and images of their manuscripts, via their coat of arms, symbols, mottoes, and depictions of such ceremonial presentations.

It seems plausible that when chief courtiers caught a glimpse of these ornate works they decided to accumulate some for themselves. Louis van Gruuthuse, knight of the Golden Fleece and stadholder of Holland and Zeeland, was a well-known bibliophile, amassing an impressive collection of manuscripts in his Bruges palace. King Edward IV of England was so moved by the collection during his temporary exile that he ordered twenty-four of his own copies in 1471. A love for beautiful handwriting, now a fad among elites, led to a wider production and distribution of books – and of their intellectual message.

Popular Entertainment

Among the common people, however, the Burgundians made their biggest splash through their lavish public ceremonies. When entering their cities, or in weddings, burials, diplomatic journeys or receptions at the court, the Burgundians made each ceremony a masterpiece of theatrical production. In ceremonies which lasted for days, commoners were allowed to feast their eyes on the court in all its glory: the beautiful robes, expensive jewelry, and the stately bearing of its courtiers. Banners and musical instruments added further color to the event. In 1454, a year after his triumph over Ghent, and only a few months before his "Pheasant Banquet," in which he and his court solemnly pledged to retake Constantinople from the Turks, Philip the Good set off on an international tour, participating, as the Empire's most important prince, in the imperial diet *(Reichstag)* at Regensburg. Although Philip gained no tangible results from his presence, the splendor of the Burgundian company made an impression on their poorer Swabian and Bavarian hosts, and elevated Philip's reputation considerably. However, in the long run, Philip's orientation toward the Empire had more than symbolic results; it would result in the marriage of the Burgundian crown princess to the emperor's heir Maximilian in 1477.

The duke's subjects also played their own role in many of these ceremonies. When Philip visited Ghent in 1458 for the first time since the city's revolt, its inhabitants celebrated for days. Paintings and tapestries, plays, poems, and music were presented to the duke along his procession route. The city fathers gave silver scales with the city's coat of arms to those citizens with the best decorations and the best performance. Biblical themes, stories from antiquity, images of saints, and heraldic symbols were all portrayed in a myriad of ways. The high point consisted of a *tableau vivant* which featured the Mystic Lamb – a reference both to the Golden Fleece and the famous Ghent altarpiece of Philip's court painter. Bourgeois culture and court culture were never separate from each other; they carried on a continuous dialogue.

In Bruges during the wedding feasts of Charles the Bold in 1468, tournaments were held in which great warriors demonstrated their prowess before astonished crowds of commoners. Sluis (the port of arrival for Charles's English bride), Damme, and Bruges all held festivities for a week, including fireworks on two of the evenings. After the marriage ceremony in Damme, the wedding party headed for Bruges, where they were met by a pageant of clerics (including the bishops of Cambrai and Utrecht, two half-brothers of Charles), the local guilds, and dozens of "nations" or associations of foreign traders, including Hanseatic Germans, Italians, Catalans, English, and many others. The highlights of the celebration were the banquets, followed by intervals with special effects, dancing, and games. Scores of artists were charged with the architectural design and decoration of the feast halls, including the young Ghentenar Hugo van der Goes.

The effects of the Burgundian dukes' patronage were much greater than the commissions they directly gave to artists. These amounted to no more than 3 percent of the budget, including palace construction in Dijon, Arras, Lille, Bruges, Ghent, and Brussels, the most expensive patronage projects. Rather, the extravagant and public display of court life, which appealed to the people of the fifteenth century, would prove a more important legacy of the Burgundians. Not only did court chroniclers record this glory; foreign observers spread news of the splendor of the court to the four winds. The populace, too, imitated the dukes' grand style, both in their elegant and expensive manner of clothing and in their purchase of art works. Burgundian cultural life bloomed precisely because it was not confined to the court; the wealthy elites of the great Flemish and Brabantine cities were eager to increase their standing among the common people by donating altarpieces of their own. The urban culture of the bourgeoisie, in place since the fourteenth century, now found new forms of expression in its interactions with the Burgundian court, as the social ambitions of the burghers intersected with the calculated splendor of the dukes.

3. The Habsburg Century (1477-1588)

The Low Countries and the Habsburg Empire

Duke Charles the Bold died in 1477. With the marriage of his only heir, Mary of Burgundy, to the archduke Maximilian of Habsburg, the Low Countries and the Franche-Comté formally came under a new dynasty – a dynasty that would rule the southern part of the Low Countries until 1794. At first, little changed; the young prince Maximilian, unaccustomed to the highly developed and urbanized society of the Low Countries, required time for acclimation. Moreover, the Burgundian state machinery had by then become so deep-rooted that the arrival of an Austrian nobleman and a few courtiers did not have much of an impact. Maximilian's elevation to the position of King of the Romans in 1486 and his departure from the Low Countries would, however, have significant consequences. The genealogical vicissitudes which had brought the Low Countries under the same dynasty would, in subsequent decades, make the Low Countries a part of Spain's far-flung empire.

The Burgundian and Habsburg Dynasties in the Low Countries.

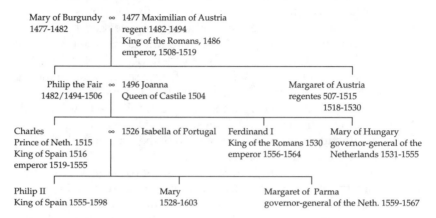

In 1495, Maximilian arranged the double marriage of his children, Philip and Margaret, to Joanna and Juan of Castile. A classic alliance between two powerful dynasties, it had the effect of surrounding the Habsburg's old enemy of France on three sides. Spain was rapidly becoming an important power; in 1492, the "Catholic kings," Ferdinand of Aragon and Isabella of Castile, had taken Grenada, the last Muslim bulwark in Iberia, and had sent Columbus on his way to the Americas. (No one in 1495 could, of course, fully assess the importance of either event, and to many the former was more impressive than the latter.) The Spanish dynasty, however, suffered from chronic bad health. The heir-apparent Juan died five months after his marriage; his sister Isabella, married to the king of Portugal, died a year later, and their son followed her in 1500. In this way, Joanna of Castile became the only heir to Spain and all its colonies – which meant that her husband Philip the Fair now ruled over Spain in her name. However, he died unexpectedly during his entry into Burgos (Spain) in 1506, leaving behind his wife Joanna "the Mad," who had become mentally ill. In time, their son Charles, born in Ghent in 1500, succeeded them, becoming king of Spain in 1518. In 1515, he was recognized as lord over the Low Countries, and in 1519, he was chosen to succeed his grandfather Maximilian as King of the Romans, becoming Charles V. Raised in the Low Countries, Charles was long distrusted as an outsider in Spain, especially since he brought numerous councilors and artists from the Low Countries with him when he became king. In Charles's huge empire, the Low Countries still occupied an important and strategic position, but now it would be ruled from a distance.

Under the Habsburgs, the tension between the long tradition of autonomy in the Low Countries and the tendency toward a centralized monarchical administration would rise over the course of the sixteenth century, culminating in a crisis. Would it be possible to keep the most economically advanced portion of Europe within the confines of Europe's most powerful and increasingly coercive monarchy? This was the central question in the ensuing dramas.

Maximilian of Habsburg; engraving by Lucas van Leyden. (Rijksmuseum, Amsterdam.)

War and Domestic Tensions

In the 1470s, Charles the Bold negotiated with the emperor about a marriage between their respective heirs after it became clear to him that he would produce no male successors and that his dynasty would die with him. He tried to strengthen his bargaining position by increasing his power within the Holy Roman Empire. He put the prince-bishopric of Liège under his temporal authority in 1468, received various privileges in Alsace, and in 1473, annexed Guelders through a combination of force and intrigue. In an effort to assert his influence within the archbishopric of Cologne, Charles squandered an entire year in the unsuccessful siege of Neuss, and in Lorraine he temporarily expelled the lawful duke.

Charles's military ambitions had far-reaching results, both internationally and domestically. The duke's wartime absence caused him to ignore his subjects and their concerns; the personality of princes like Charles could have a great effect on the people they ruled. The wars also absorbed increasing amounts of money, and taxes nearly tripled in several years; in Flanders, taxes rose from an average of 78,500 pounds per annum (1466-1471) to an average of 223,500 pounds (1472-1476).

The state's hunger for money was so great that an increasing number of administrative positions were sold to the highest bidder, without the least guarantee of the officeholder's competence. Surrounding states also reacted to Charles's drastic moves; King Louis IX of France exploited the duke's problems in the east and invaded Picardy and Artois. The Swiss Confederation, threatened by Charles's adventures, sealed an alliance with Lorraine, Savoy, and France and defeated Charles's armies three times, driving him out of Lorraine in 1476. Finally, the monomaniacal duke himself was killed at the Battle of Nancy on 5 January 1477. Charles the Bold had failed to win a royal crown for himself, and his territorial possessions came, via his daughter's betrothal, under the rule of the Habsburg dynasty, which was then turning the German kingdom into their hereditary possession.

The great powers soon filled in the vacuum that had been created by Charles's unexpected demise. France annexed Burgundy, Picardy and Artois, the first two territories for good. Liège and Guelders regained their freedom. Meanwhile, in a number of cities, Charles's angry subjects rebelled against the administrators' ever-present abuse of power. Some functionaries, like the chancellor Hugonet, the governor Humbercourt, and a dozen-odd magistrates, paid with their lives; they were sentenced to death under pressure from the infuriated masses of Ghent. The inexperienced duchess, Charles's daughter Mary, had no choice but to accede to all the demands put upon her by the States-General. In the concessions of 1477, she undid much of the centralizing arrangements that were begun under Philip the Good and intensified under Charles. The large cities, duchies, and counties thus regained many of the legal, fiscal, and other prerogatives that they had lost to the centralized Burgundian state.

It is striking that in this critical phase the States-General never thought of choosing another dynasty to rule over them, even though one possible candidate, the French king, demanded the return of his fiefs, Artois and Flanders, because there was no male heir to rule over them. It is also striking that the respective States of the Low Countries opted to remain a union of principalities. The only exceptions were Liège and Guelders, which had been seized illegally by Charles; and Luxembourg, where a large part of the nobility preferred to be ruled by the duke of Saxony or the king of Bohemia and Hungary (a position they maintained until 1480). The core regions of the Low Countries, however, had reached such a level of political integration that they desired to maintain their mutual ties. Their "Great Privilege," which was twenty articles long, established the consensually derived conditions on which the new union would be based. In hindsight, it might be called the first common constitution of those principalities of the Low Countries which had remained under Burgundian rule.

Territoriality and Centralization

Charles the Bold had made every effort to centralize and expand the authority of the Burgundians. His sudden demise had triggered a strong reaction from his oppressed subjects, who succeeded in slowing much – though hardly all – of the centralizing impetus initiated by the

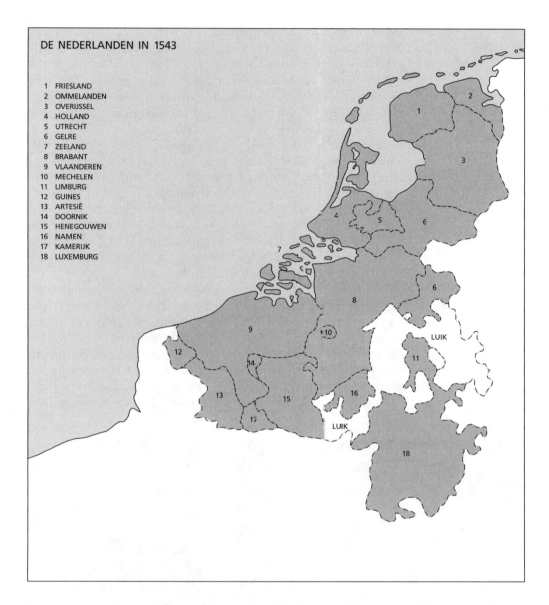

DE NEDERLANDEN IN 1543

1 FRIESLAND
2 OMMELANDEN
3 OVERIJSSEL
4 HOLLAND
5 UTRECHT
6 GELRE
7 ZEELAND
8 BRABANT
9 VLAANDEREN
10 MECHELEN
11 LIMBURG
12 GUINES
13 ARTESIË
14 DOORNIK
15 HENEGOUWEN
16 NAMEN
17 KAMERIJK
18 LUXEMBURG

The Low Countries in 1543   Burgundian duke. The logic of Charles's policy, however, would continue to serve as the leitmotif of his sixteenth-century successors. The aim of centralized control remained the same, but its realization depended on favorable circumstances, and even the great Habsburg empire was subject to the vicissitudes of historical fortune.

Antagonism toward France formed much of the basis of Habsburg foreign policy; until 1559, Europe's two greatest monarchies were routinely at war with each other, a long-term conflict with ruinous effects on both sides. In the Peace of Cambrai (1529) – which ended hostilities for nine years – King Francis I of France was forced to permanently abjure his claims to Flanders and Artois, while Charles V renounced his claims to Burgundy, which had been in French hands since 1477. At the same time, good relations with England remained the cornerstone of

Habsburg diplomacy, both for economic reasons and for the pursuance of anti-French policy. Under the Habsburgs, the Low Countries's tie with the Empire became more important – a logical extension of the "Burgundian" territories feudal dependence to the Empire. The Low Countries' tie to the Empire was formally expressed in the "Burgundian Kreis" (or Circle) of 1548, which functioned as the regional government for the "Seventeen Provinces" of the Low Countries.

Emperor Charles V consolidated his territories following the pattern established by his Burgundian predecessors. He repudiated the temporal powers of the bishops of Tournai (1521) and Utrecht (1528). Like many of his predecessors, Charles also built a sphere of influence in the northeastern Netherlands. In 1523, he began to extend his influence to Groningen (the Ommelanden), Friesland, and Drenthe, but ran into fierce resistance from Charles of Egmond, duke of Guelders. In 1536, however, the emperor defeated his rival, and in 1543 he forced the last duke of Guelders, William of Gulik, to abdicate.

It is remarkable how much effort both the Burgundians and the Habsburgs were forced to expend in order put these northeastern hinterlands under their control. Their distance from the centers of power and their lack of internal political cohesion certainly played a role in this. Moreover, the expansionist dukes of Guelders benefitted from all domestic and foreign resistance to Burgundian and Habsburg rule. France in particular supported Guelders as a useful ally against its archenemy. At the same time, the Spanish-oriented Habsburgs often had

A detail from Pieter Brueghel's Census of Bethlehem *(1566). Brueghel is also depicting the paying of the tenth penny tax in his own time. (Koninklijke Museum voor de Schone Kunsten, Brussels.)*

other, more pressing priorities than using their immense power against the northeastern provinces of the Netherlands. Thus the rhythm of power politics in the Low Countries depended on dynastic concerns, which often had little to do with the Low Countries themselves.

After consolidating their territories, the Habsburg princes, like the Burgundians before them, turned toward the task of unifying and centralizing their administration. In doing so, they encountered the resistance of local authorities, who represented the cities, the guilds, and the lesser nobility. These authorities stubbornly clung to their prerogatives, which essentially consisted of legal and fiscal powers – their resistance was already evident in their rejection of the uniform salt tax in 1447. And, as in the days of the Burgundians, local revolts would give the Habsburgs sufficient pretext to reduce the power of local authorities.

The Means of the State: Taxes

In 1521, the Habsburg administration asked for exceedingly high taxes to finance their war against France. Set at 500,000 pounds in 1521 and 600,000 in 1522, these taxes were nearly three times higher than the peak tax years of 1472-1476. The States of Flanders, Brabant, Holland, and Zeeland granted the request only on the condition that they outfit and pay the troops themselves. In order to ensure military victory – and to compensate the States for the heavy taxes – the emperor was forced to make far-reaching administrative concessions to regional and local authorities. The same cycle recurred in 1542, when the Habsburgs went to war with France and Guelders. In order to finance the war, the administration wanted a direct tax of 10 percent (the so-called tenth penny) on income derived from stationary goods and from the profits derived from trade, and an indirect tax of 1 percent on exports. The States agreed to these taxes only for limited periods of time, ending the tenth penny tax in 1545 and the indirect tax in 1554. The States refused to surrender their authority to pass *temporary* spending measures or their right to approve Habsburg goals requiring their money. In this way, they continued to hold considerable leverage with the Habsburg administration.

After 1523, Habsburg functionaries increasingly avoided asking for new taxes from the States-General, which represented the Low Countries as a whole. They found so much resistance to their high tax proposals that the only way they could achieve their aims was to give away favors to regions and cities whose support they sought for the taxes. As a result, Flanders paid one-third less tax than it was formally assessed, and Holland sometimes paid 40 percent less than its official tax burden. This helped lead to significant shifts in levels of taxation in the respective Seventeen Provinces that would form the United Netherlands. In the 1540s, Flanders and Brabant in particular paid a heavier share than they had in 1473, while the tax burden of Holland and Zeeland had lightened considerably. The taxes imposed on the core territories of Low Countries (Flanders, Brabant, and Holland) increased from nearly 78 percent in 1473 to 83.5 percent between 1540 and 1548. These figures, in fact, downplay the economic importance of lands seized by Charles V between 1521 and 1543. It is possible that his administration attempted to soften their forced incorporation through the imposition of only light taxes. This would help explain why these regions did not play prominent roles in the Dutch Revolt and only became a part of the Dutch Republic during the military conquest of the 1590s.

Share of Taxes Paid to the Central Administration by Province		
	1473	1540-1548
Flanders	25.4	33.8
Brabant and Mechelen	22.3	29.3
Holland and Zeeland	27.0	12.7 + 4.4 = 17.1
Hainaut Valenciennes	7.1	5.5
Artois	6.2	5.6
Walloon Flanders	2.9	3.3
Guelders		1.1
Toumai		0.93
Namur	1.3	0.90
Friesland		0.59
Overijssel		0.55
Luxembourg	2.4	0.38
Limburg	2.0	0.30
Utrecht		0.28
Groningen and Ommelanden	0.26	
Picardy	3.1	

As mentioned above, the state lacked any impartial method to distribute the tax burden; even its functionaries proposed proportional and direct taxes as a way of making the tax system more efficient. It was precisely the States, however, who opposed such a system since it would undermine their own role in setting taxes. Thus the political tug of war between regional authorities and the central administration – and among themselves – created a very unequal tax burden that worked to the disadvantage of Holland and Zeeland in the fifteenth century and to their advantage in the sixteenth. The increasingly favorable tax burden served to stimulate economic growth in these provinces, a subject we shall take up later.

State Power

Did the Low Countries gradually integrate under the personal unions that ruled over them between 1384 and 1543? The ruling princes made many efforts to unify what had been exceedingly diverse administrative and legal traditions among their provinces. In the first place, they tried to eliminate any influence from foreign sources of authority. The French king's renunciation of claims to Flanders and Artois in 1529, for instance, removed any threat that the Parlement of Paris could exercise any judicial power in these territories. Similarly, an accord with the papacy in 1515 stipulated that ecclesiastical courts outside the Low Countries could only intervene with the permission of the Habsburg administration. (Only Luxembourg remained under the direct ecclesi-astical authority of the archbishop of Trier.) This process of state inter-vention in church affairs was completed in 1559, when bishoprics were redrawn to coincide with political boundaries. The unification of the Low Countries found its most significant expression with the formation of the seventeen-province "Burgundian Kreis" (1548) within the con-fines of the Empire, and with the standardization of the rules of suc-cession in the Circle (1549), in which Philip (II) was uniformly recognized as heir to Charles V. (As it happened, the Dutch Revolt ensured that Philip would be the only sovereign to benefit from this tidy arrangement.)

It is unclear what geographical or political identity the Burgun-dian Kreis represented, other than that it consisted of the four duchies, seven counties and ten lordships. Only in the mid-sixteenth century did people attempt to give a name to these Seventeen Provinces: *Nederland* or *Nederlanden* in Dutch and *Païs Bas* in French, or *Belgique(s)* from the Latin. What is clear is that the central administration worked hard to transform these old principalities into provinces of a unitary state. In fact, the term "province" pointed back to the Roman imperium, an imperium that seemed, more than ever, to have been restored by Charles V. The "provincialization" of the Low Countries was acceler-ated when Charles converted Brussels into a major administrative cen-ter. In 1531, Brussels replaced Mechelen, where the governor-general, Margaret of Austria, as Charles's aunt, had represented him during his minority and during his near constant absences; and where her council and the high judicial court, the Great Council, had sat.

The development of an administrative apparatus in Brussels reflects the centralizing ambitions of the regime, a goal largely carried out through the division and specialization of the royal court. In 1473, for example, Charles the Bold created a high court and a High Council for Finances in Mechelen that were given a separate and independent existence from the ducal court. This tripartite division of powers con-tinued, despite many changes, until 1531, when it was reorganized into political and administrative sections. The first section was organized under what became known as the Council of State, to which the emperor named high nobility. The Privy Council, consisting chiefly of jurists, primarily concerned itself with administrative matters, but also functioned as a kind of supreme court. It also possessed new powers that attest to Habsburg aims: court verdicts in Brabant, Guelders, and Hainaut, which were not subject to review by the Great Council, could now, on procedural grounds, be overturned by the Privy Council. Lastly, central fiscal administration was placed in the hands of the Council for Finance. These three so-called collateral councils cooper-ated closely – and often informally – with each other, and many of the important decisions were made outside the official plenary sessions.

The governors-general, appointed for the Low Countries to rule for the absent monarchs, played a central role in this administrative apparatus. But they were also completely dependent on Charles V, who was determined to place his personal stamp on policy; and later they were at the mercy of Philip II, who exceeded even his father's zealousness in this regard. From 1507 to 1567, the task of governor-general fell to the widowed daughters of the reigning monarchs; these daughters enjoyed both an independent status and, as close blood relatives of the ruling princes, were reliable representatives of the Habsburg monarchs. Philip II's decision to break with this tradition by appointing the duke of Alba as governor-general would serve as an additional source of public irritation to his autocratic rule.

The Standardization of Law

In 1531, the administration also ordered the codification of all common law, which had formed the basis of civil law. Common law had hundreds of local variations, and the codification was designed not only to ensure justice for the emperor's subjects but to promote greater legal standardization throughout the Low Countries. The writing down of the common laws of cities, villages, and rural areas was intended to give the central administration the opportunity to supplement or correct local common law with a well-defined body of Roman law. Only with these corrections would common law be formally recognized by the higher courts. Local administrators were hardly enthusiastic about this reform – which undermined their own legal authority – and they made every effort to delay the integration of local jurisprudence with a centralizing vision derived from Roman law. As a result, only a score of local common laws had received Privy Council approval by 1579, according to the central government; most, therefore, did not possess full legal force. Criminal law in the Low Countries was no more uniform; the central administration issued a large number of ad hoc ordinances which dealt with specific problems, and it was only in 1570 that the duke of Alba's Criminal Ordinances gave a systematic coherence to penal law.

The central administration issued laws that limited the prerogatives of local magistrates by issuing universal and mandatory guidelines for dealing with certain legal problems. New cultural manifestations, like the printing press, secular theater performances, and "heresy" were frequently the topics of Habsburg ordinances; the administration's concern about public order is also evident in their many regulations regarding innkeeping and vagrancy. New beliefs and ideas could be more quickly transmitted through new methods of mass communication, and the Habsburg regime, like their counterparts throughout Europe, tried to halt this perceived threat by demanding a stricter code of behavior from its subjects – a trend known in international social scientific literature as *Sozialdisziplinierung*. Common law and the power of local magistrates were also undermined by the increasingly intrusive judicial review of higher courts. Centralization did not only bring new or higher judicial courts; it also placed these courts in a hierarchy over existing courts. Parties who were unhappy with verdicts in local courts could now appeal to the central high courts in the hope of reversing adverse decisions. After 1531, these higher courts did not restrict themselves to ruling according to local common law; they often used Roman law to clarify or rectify problems they saw in the local laws. Local magistrates knew that bad decisions could be overturned by higher benches, and this alone provided a powerful incentive to conform to the new legal standards.

The new authority of the central courts like the Great Council of Mechelen or the Privy Council is evident in their increasing caseload. Between 1500 and 1504, the Great Council issued an average of 39 verdicts per year; between 1546 and 1550, the number had risen to some 135 per year - and this does not include the annual average of 39 verdicts issued by the Privy Council. A striking number of verdicts - 40 - pertained to cases from Holland, compared to Flanders (41), Brabant and Mechelen (22), Artois (14), and Zeeland (12). Considering that many other appeals were settled out of court or terminated for other reasons, these numbers make a convincing case that the higher courts had become an important means of centralizing state authority.

Economic Growth and Financial Innovation

Demographic and economic growth occurred throughout northwestern Europe from the late fifteenth century until around 1565. In some areas of the Low Countries, annual growth reached 1 percent a year, and by the mid-sixteenth century, Brabant and Holland again attained the high population densities of 1300. This growth was not evenly distributed; in Flanders, the most densely inhabited region, it was slower. The Flemish suffered particularly from the economic stagnation of the 1530s, which was triggered in part by serious food shortages. But in all of the core region – Flanders, Brabant, and Holland – the export trade formed the basis of economic growth in this period.

Textile exports enjoyed a particularly strong resurgence, particularly from the rural areas of southwest Flanders, which specialized in making light fabrics for the European market. In the 1560s, the town of Hondschoote alone produced 100,000 serge pieces from Spanish and domestic wool. Cloth weaving also expanded enormously in the countryside of southeastern Flanders, Hainaut, northern Brabant, and near the city of Haarlem in Holland. The cloth industry in Leiden declined, but Amsterdam became an important harbor for exports from Holland, and numbered 30,000 inhabitants by 1560. The level of Dutch trade in the Baltic can be measured by the toll registers of the Danish kings; the number of voyages made by Dutch ships entering the Baltic in the 1580s was three-and-a-half times greater than what it had been in the 1530s. Ships from the Low Countries accounted for about half of all registered ships, and Holland alone provided roughly 80 percent of the shipping found in all of the Low Countries. This growth is remarkable, but it is important to add that Dutch volume through the Danish straits remained proportionately stable; other countries were growing just as fast.

Antwerp's rapid rate of growth was the most striking economic phenomenon of the sixteenth century, and made it the most populous city in the Low Countries. In 1480, the city still numbered only 33,000 residents; by 1526, it boasted 55,000 inhabitants; and by 1568, more than 100,000, which put Antwerp among the very largest cities of Europe. Migration can be the only explanation for this stupendous growth, a trend evident in the economic stagnation and depopulation of eastern Brabant and Flanders. For these migrants, Antwerp seemed to offer unlimited opportunities for trade and commerce. The basis for their hopes was the system of annual fairs in Brabant, which were particularly important in the years before 1530. During these four annual fairs, which lasted from four to six weeks each, the opportunities of free trade – in contrast to the Flemish protectionist regulations – became evident to thousands of enterprising people, who now, in increasing numbers, flocked to the commercial mecca of Antwerp.

Antwerp's free trade policies also made the city the favorite of English traders, since Flemish cities like Bruges were closed to English cloth for protectionist reasons. In contrast, Antwerpians developed an industry which specialized in the finishing, dyeing, and selling of rough English cloth. Antwerp's annual fairs could count on the whole Low Countries as their hinterland, and it was through the demand at these fairs that regional producers, both urban and rural, determined their supply. The German Hanseatic League was also an important trading partner. Although they moved their office from Bruges to Antwerp only in 1553, they accepted a house on the Antwerp Corn Market from the city council in 1468. From this it seems clear that Prussian grain imports became an important part of trade in the fast-growing city. Cologne and the South German cities, particularly the commercial magnet of Frankfurt, were other important partners; and the Portuguese, with spices and sugar, offered new links with the newly "discovered" worlds of Asia and America. With satellite harbors cities on the nearby island of Walcheren, Antwerp received some 2,500 ships or 250,000 tons in a good year, four times the volume of London's harbor.

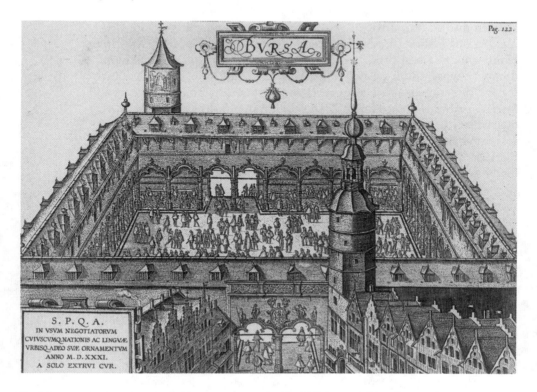

The Antwerp exchange; engraving by Pieter van der Borcht. (Stedelijk Prentencabinet, Antwerp.)

In 1532, Antwerp opened a new stock exchange, the first of its kind, which was designed to organize the mushrooming business of trading money and securities. Until then, debts were settled at the conclusion of the yearly fairs, as bills were exchanged or surrendered to third parties. The new exchange offered the opportunity to do this on a daily basis through the sale of securities, speculation, and financial exchanges. State debt soon provided a strong impetus to the development of the Antwerp money market. Since capital streamed to Antwerp from the great South German and Genoan merchant-bankers, not to mention from Castelan traders, agents of the emperor were permanently stationed in Antwerp after 1520 to negotiate loans for the Habsburg administration. The pressures on the Antwerp money market, combined with the spectacular growth of the metropolis, led to a series of innovations in trading techniques. These innovations formed a bridge between the Italians' leading financial role in the Middle Ages and the important changes introduced by the Bank of England at the end of the seventeenth century.

The first innovation created the legal right to trade in commercial debt. Around 1500, creditors could transfer their bills to others, who were now entitled to press the same claims against the debtors. This promoted quick settlement of trading debts through the use of commercial papers which did not require the use of cash. To add security to this arrangement, traders later added the requirement that all debtors remained co-responsible for the payments made by the debtor they had designated to assume their debts. In order to ensure accountability, people assuming the debt literally signed their names on the backs of the original debtors; this endorsement could be repeated again and again, to remind all parties where the ultimate responsibility of the debt lay. Other trading cities adopted these measures, and they became law throughout the Low Countries in the imperial ordinances of 1537 and 1541. This system was further refined in the late sixteenth century, and when Protestant Antwerpians fled the city in the 1580s, they brought these innovations to the exchange in Amsterdam, where many of them took up residence. A third innovation was the acquisition by third parties of bills of exchange, which were purchased at less than their face value and before their expiration dates. This practice originated at the exchange, where cashiers kept and transferred accounts, acted as brokers and took advances (*disconto*) on the principle. This gave traders the advantage of disposing of cash whenever they found it convenient to do so. The earliest report of this practice dates from 1536, but it was limited for decades to times when money was especially scarce. By 1600, this Antwerpian technique would be more broadly applied to the beginnings of a modern exchange and banking system.

The Culture of the Renaissance

Given both the centuries-old traditions of artistry in the Low Countries and the region's increasingly central role in sixteenth century Europe, it cannot be surprising that Dutch cultural expression was at its most brilliant during the late Renaissance. Painting, sculpture and architecture were all at the vanguard of European artistic developments. The exuberant late Gothic style reached its apex in the early sixteenth century with the completion of the Antwerp cathedral; and Antwerp's city hall, completed in 1565, is a grandiose prototype of Renaissance architecture in the Low Countries. Governor-General Margaret of Austria (1507-1530) continued the tradition of the Burgundian patronage of the arts at her court in Mechelen, as evidenced by her court chapel. Many regional musicians and composers left the Low Countries for foreign patrons, including the most famous of them, Orlandus Lassus (ca. 1532-1594), who became choirmaster in Rome and Munich. (The fame of his works was partly thanks to his contacts with the Antwerpian music publisher, Tielman Susato.) It is interesting that music from the Low Countries played such a leading role in the European music scene between the fifteenth and seventeenth century but has not succeeded in doing so ever since.

Books and Culture

Every artistic guild, especially those in Antwerp, had its own first-rate practitioners who sold their work to the wealthy, both foreign and domestic. Consider the art of making books: by 1500, some urban printers were actively hunting down ancient vernacular texts, from chronicles to plays to descriptions of unusual events. We know of a snow figurine contest, held in Brussels in 1511, because a rhymed description of it was published by an amateur poet. Local poets also wrote of more formal ceremonies, including an extensive – and published – account of Charles V's *Blijde Inkomst* into Bruges in 1515. The art of rhetoric – which could include anything from doggerel verse to real theater – found scores of practitioners in all the cities of the Low Countries. They grouped themselves in chambers, of which the larger cities had several each. These chambers of rhetoric competed among each other for the approval of the public and the support of the city administration or other notables. But they also fought for honor, holding contests to see who would be acclaimed "the jewel of the land." Such competitions took place in Ghent (1539) and in Antwerp (1561). Theater troupes added color to life by performing plays, often for days at a time, for a broad public. Many poets did not refrain from poking fun at the clergy or expressing Protestant sentiments, which sometimes prompted crackdowns from the central government. What can be said about all of this is that the public's broad interest in these literary manifestations served to make the Dutch language an increasingly important link between the various regions of the Low Countries.

Christopher Plantijn's establishment of a publishing house in 1555 turned Antwerp into the most important center of activity for printers. Plantijn's printing techniques and dissemination of texts of learning and high culture were unrivaled in northwest Europe. His most shining achievement was the publication of an eight-volume edition of the Bible in five languages: Latin, Greek, Hebrew, Syriac, and Aramaic. This work earned Plantijn the special protection and patronage of Philip II, who awarded him a contract for all the liturgical books to be used in Spain. In 1575, Plantijn employed eighty assistants and owned sixteen presses. Like many Antwerpian products, a good share of Plantijn's business was

Title page of a 1584 orthodox Catholic edition of H. Jansen, Beelden en figuren uit de Bijbel *(Images and Figures from the Bible), published by Christopher Plantijn. (Museum Plantin-Moretus, Antwerp.)*

foreign; in 1566, 46 percent of his business came from the Low Countries, 25 percent from the Empire, 21 percent from France, and 6.5 percent from England.

Later Spain became an important source of business because of the patronage Philip had given him. Over the course of thirty-four years in the business, Plantijn managed to publish some 1,887 books and 563 loose pages. One-third of the books were religious in content, another third humanist or didactic. Sixteen percent were academic works and 13 percent consisted of ordinances and pamphlets. Plantijn published little in the vernacular; he considered the risks, in a time of religious turmoil, too great. As a result of this turmoil, Plantijn established a Leiden branch in 1583, where he transferred an important part of his Greek and Hebrew lettertypes. There they served as the foundation for the famous orientalist editions published in Leiden. In any event, the presence of printer-publishers stimulated the spread of new ideas, whether religious or political. Ten thousand pamphlets were published in the Low Countries during the sixteenth century, especially in Flanders and Brabant, where they were often illustrated with woodwork or copper engravings. These pamphlets must have substantially influenced the opinions of the middle classes, and thus played a key role in the Dutch Revolt.

Erasmus

A publishing house like Plantijn's was both a business and an intellectual center, where learned humanists carefully read the proofs of their works. By the early sixteenth century, contacts existed among scholars, civil servants, and printers interested in humanism. In 1509, Erasmus

(1469-1536) dedicated his most famous work *The Praise of Folly* to Thomas More. When, in 1515, More arrived in Bruges to represent the interests of English merchants, the two great humanists met each other. (At the time, More was working on his most famous work, *Utopia*, a vision for an ideal society; and one of their mutual friends, Jeroom Buysleden, councillor in the Great Council of Mechelen, was to write an introduction for it.) Erasmus's *Praise of Folly* used the theme of the world turned upside down to openly vent satirical criticism of all social roles, not least that of the clergy. Originally a monk from Stein (near Gouda) and formed by the lettered traditions of the *devotio moderna*, Erasmus was well on his way to becoming the symbolic leader of European humanism. For the future emperor Charles he wrote a "princely mirror" and several works on war and peace, but Erasmus considered his new two-language publication of the New Testament and the writings of the church father Saint Jerome far more important; both were based on his critical study of the ancient Greek and Latin texts. At the University of Leuven – then the only university in the Low Countries since its establishment in 1425 – Erasmus founded the Collegium Trilingue on the inheritance bequeathed by Buysleden. Here scholars studied the Hebrew, Greek, and Latin sources of the Christian faith. Despite his caustic polemics with Luther and other theologians, Erasmus shared their critique of religious formalism and the worldliness of the church. But he refused to break with the Catholic church, even though he had no patience with the war-making popes of his day. His independent, critical stance made it impossible for him to function at Leuven, and drove him far away from his parochial monastery in Holland to the custody of powerful friends who would protect him. Erasmus's innumerable sharp insights and arguments, especially his *Colloquia* (which soon became a part of any classical education due to its beautiful Latin), exercised a considerable influence on the intellectual elite of his age. Nurtured by his critical writings, they would take up new and more radical positions in the late sixteenth century than their master could, or would, have taken.

Pieter Brueghel

Of all the great sixteenth century artists the Low Countries produced, Pieter Brueghel (ca. 1528-1569) might be the most representative. His paintings reflect not only the general tendency toward more worldly topics, but also express what we would now call popular culture: games, fairs, carnivals, popular sayings, weddings, and rural life. The carnivalesque component of his work is still a source of inspiration for a certain cultural style in southern parts of the Low Countries. Brueghel was also a sharp social critic and fulminated, in his own way, against the consequences of growing social tensions - consequences which were most poignantly depicted, perhaps, by the blind and the crippled leading each other into the abyss. He also painted Protestant open-air services (held at the edge of the city) where half of the public watches pigeons rather than listening to the sermons. Brueghel created disturbing works on subjects like the slaughter of the innocent in Bethlehem by soldiers with a strong resemblance to Philip II's Spanish troops, as well as painting the horrible scenes of death and destruction which came with the Spanish efforts to repress the Dutch Revolt in 1567. If it is true that art follows money, and that art is most expressive in times of sharp social conflicts, then the Low Countries, particularly Flanders and Brabant, must have been a rich breeding ground for artistic creativity in the sixteenth century.

The Dutch Revolt

The last thirty years of the sixteenth century did not only signal the deepest crisis in the history of the Low Countries; they also proved to be an important chapter in world history. The stakes were high: the Spanish global empire was confronted with a revolt from the most important economic region of the world. From the earliest days of the Reformation, new and diverse religious movements had found support in the large Brabantine and Flemish cities, and the effort by the Spanish administration to root out religious dissent was antithetical to the open mentality which existed in these cities. The growing absolutist tendencies of Spanish authority were also a major source of resentment among local nobility and burghers who cherished their autonomy. Thus one could argue that the conflict was essentially between two fundamentally opposed civilizations, between the Castelan nobility, steeped in the spirit of the *reconquista* and colonial acquisition, and the progressive world of trade and commerce which nourished the many new cultural impulses of the Renaissance.

The personality of King Philip II also unquestionably contributed to the sharpening of the conflict. In his view, Protestants were heretics and the proponents of representative government were rebels. He refused to negotiate with such people, and as a result, peaceful solutions – despite the many efforts to find them – invariably ran afoul of Philip's refusal to compromise.

Time Difference

The great geographical distance between Philip II – who left the Low Countries for good in 1559 – and the complex society who rebelled against his authority in the 1560s added to the depth and seemingly unavoidable tragedy of the coming conflict. The king wanted to personally manage all the affairs of state, but his capacity to do so was undermined by slow communications and the filtered information that came from his distant provinces. He also needed to weigh the divergent interests within his empire – such as its growing rivalry with the Ottoman Empire in the Mediterranean, or with England in the Atlantic – before he considered how he could maintain his authority in the Low Countries. Moreover, Philip had difficulty making up his mind, and he routinely let months of indecision undermine his control over situations. At crucial moments, indecision in Madrid produced a power vacuum in the Low Countries, which the opponents of the king used to full effect. During the long periods of confusion in Spain, the States of Brabant, Flanders and Holland were able to take decisive steps in formulating their own sovereignty. When Philip did decide to act, his orders took one month to reach their destination. Perhaps most important, Philip never completely understood that his own empire was shifting and evolving, and that old solutions were inadequate for new circumstances.

Thus it is possible to speak of a cultural divide – widened by physical distance – between the stubborn and narrow monarch with his centralizing vision for a world empire, and the dynamic, pluriform society of the Low Countries, which Spanish courtiers could hardly imagine. This divide would prove to be a strategic advantage for the rebels; they got the opportunity to work out, step by step, political solutions that rose from the conflict between the king and his subjects. In this way, moderates – who as late as 1575 founded Leiden University in the name of the king – could evolve into revolutionary republicans who by 1588 had lost a taste for royal rule.

Core and Periphery

This explanation cannot alone account for the Revolt, however. Past historians have all too often been satisfied with one-sided theses of the Revolt; for some, the religious zeal of the Calvinists was decisive, for others it was the self-confidence of the local nobility, the moderation of regional Catholics, the growing class-consciousness of the artisans, or the Dutch love of freedom. All of them identified an authentic part of the puzzle, but not the whole picture. We certainly also wish to avoid the impression that the revolt pertained only to "the North," which became the Dutch Republic, or that the rebels all shared the same political objectives. Between 1566, the year of the iconoclastic riots, and 1588, the year that the Republic was formally established, a gradual radical-

Philip II, in an anonymous painting from 1546. (Museum voor de Schone Kunsten, Brussels.)

ization took place as moderate options, long supported by a majority, became unviable.

When, in 1581, the ultimate question rose as to whether the Low Countries should break with the Spanish king, its inhabitants were divided into three camps. Groningen and the Walloon (French-speaking) districts (with the exception of Tournai) had already reconciled themselves with Philip. In sharp contrast, Flanders, Brabant, Holland, Zeeland, and Friesland declared the king deposed from his princely right to rule. Somewhere in the middle were Guelders, Utrecht, and Overijssel, which refused to adopt either position. These divisions did not fall out of the sky; this chapter has repeatedly underscored the fact that the southern and eastern provinces like Artois, Hainaut, Namur, and Luxembourg – those areas least committed to the revolt – were relatively thinly populated, more agrarian, less commercialized, and lightly taxed. Only recently incorporated into the Habsburg empire, they were the most strongly oriented toward other regions. The original fault lines were thus not between "the North" and "the South," but between core areas, consisting primarily of the wealthy and urban coastal provinces, and the periphery, stretching from Groningen south to Luxembourg and Artois. The permanent division of the Low Countries between north and south could not, therefore, be foreseen in 1581.

Church and State

Without descending into economic determinism, it is still clear that urban areas, including the French-speaking cities of Tournai and Valenciennes, were most open to the "new religion," that is, to the many variations of Protestantism. Antwerp soon became the center for the Protestant faith; as early as 1523, two monks had been burned at the stake there for preaching Lutheran ideas. In contrast, the agrarian population, the most prominent burghers, and the nobility remained overwhelmingly and staunchly Catholic. Peasants with side businesses in textile manufacturing and wool weaving, however, were exceedingly receptive to the preaching of Anabaptists and (later) Calvinists. Extensive social research has shown that during the Spanish siege of Antwerp from 1584 to 1585 – when the Protestant tide was already ebbing – one third of the population identified themselves as Protestants, and most of them as Calvinists. One third of the city was Catholic, and the remaining third refrained, in those "evil times," from overtly expressing religious sympathies. This pattern was repeated, to a lesser extent, in all of the other cities of the core region: a minority of conscious Protestants, of which the Calvinists were the most dominant group after 1580, a minority of decided Catholics, and an equally large number of undecided souls, who, if not Protestant, were no longer loyal to Rome. It is interesting to note that Protestants in Flanders and Brabant largely came from the more or less propertied middle classes (46 percent) and from wage earners, who represented over half of the total. Why did they – rather than other social groups – opt for the new faith?

There are, of course, any number of considerations which made Protestantism attractive to various categories of people, not to mention individual convictions which also motivated many people. At any rate, sympathy for the Reformation meant a rejection of the status quo, which was embodied by the close relationship between the absolutist state and the Catholic church. This relationship was predicated on the notion that the monarchy had been established by God, and that the king was obliged to safeguard true worship. No one embodied this increasingly distrusted ideal more than Antoine Cardinal Granvelle, archbishop of Mechelen and the first councillor of state under Governor-General Margaret of Parma. Sharp critique of Granvelle by the other high nobility in the Council of State forced Margaret to ask Philip II to transfer him from the Low Countries. The realignment of bishoprics to reflect political boundaries and the advent of the Inquisition in the Low Countries were other striking examples of this cooperation between church and state: the emperor forbade heresy, the ecclesiastical courts prosecuted and convicted, and the state punished. With this close relationship, it was easy for people with economic grievances, either because authorities wronged them or because they faced a decline in their standard of living, to be automatically branded as "heretics."

The attraction of the Protestant reformers lay foremost in their sincere inspiration, in the authenticity and hope of their message, and in the strong sense of spiritual responsibility they placed on each individual. They brought their message in a new and simple form, and it made Catholic ritual seem like empty formalism. But for the simple farmer-weavers from western Flanders and for the petit bourgeoisie who faced a decline in prosperity, Protestantism was less about choosing a new faith than about enthusiasm for a salvific message that blamed all their misery on the guardians of church and state. Since it was the state that fought the Reformation as heresy, these discontented groups found it natural to oppose both the church *and* the state.

William of Orange's leadership of the Revolt began in 1564, when, as a member of the Council of State, he led the legal opposition to Philip's policies until the spring of 1566. Born into the high nobility, William was raised in the court of Brussels. His land holdings, although mostly in Brabant, were diverse, but as the prince of Orange he was considered a sovereign ruler. As stadholder for the king in Holland and Zeeland, William possessed important legitimate authority, but it was his position within the high nobility which entitled him to influence policy in the Council of State. The Council, chafing under Philip's authoritarian style of rulership, demanded a greater say in the formation of policy, and William of Orange also urged the king to soften the ordinances against heresy, since religious reforms were taking place in all of the neighboring countries. The authorities' repressive measures would not reconcile people to the Catholic church, whose spiritual decay, William thought, must be evident to all. William remained Catholic until 1566, but even as a Catholic he rejected the notion that princes could rule over the consciences of their subjects. His tolerant position, inspired by the humanistic Christianity of Erasmus, went a long way in meeting the demands of the Protestants. The Council of State sent one of its members, the count of Egmond, to the king in January 1565 with this message. Philip sent the representative back empty-handed and later communicated to the Council that heretics must not be tolerated. In this way, Philip made it impossible for moderates either to oppose his policies or to obey him, and the king's stance created a groundswell of support for the repeal of the antiheresy laws.

The Escalation of Violence

Despite the ordinances against heretics that had been issued since Charles V, the Reformation spread rapidly in the Low Countries after 1550. At the same time, however, the Inquisition redoubled its efforts to combat heresy; between 1521 and 1550, an average of thirteen persons were tried annually by these ecclesiastical courts. By the 1550s, the average was sixty per year, and between 1561 and 1565 it was 264. By the early 1560s, serious shocks in the economy had undermined the standard of living of many social groups. In the first place, the debt of the Spanish state increased from two million guilders in 1544 to seven million in 1556, a deficit too large for the silver fleets from America to cover. In 1557, Philip responded by declaring a moratorium on state interest payments to service its debts. This measure, the first in a series of so-called state bankruptcies of the Spanish government, financially ruined both the South German bankers and the host of small investors who had bought state bonds on the Antwerp exchange. In the second place, the departure of the English cloth staple from Antwerp in 1563 not only meant massive unemployment for the urban and rural processors of English cloth, but also for all the traders who sold these processed goods. Last, an awful harvest after the severe winter of 1564-1565 drove up food prices, and despite increased shipping through the Danish straits, bread and grain prices reached the highest levels of the century, triggering widespread hunger in the region.

It was in this context that a number of nobility, bound together by the now famous Oath of the Nobles, urged the governor-general in April 1566 to soften the laws against heresy. Local and regional rulers feared riots in the climate of economic crisis if the Inquisition continued its work. The governor-general sympathized with their petition, although the count of Berlaymont, head of the Council for Finances, scoffed that these lower nobility were mere "beggars" – an expression of contempt which later became the badge of honor for the rebels. The governor-general decided to send two of the noblemen, the marquis of Bergen-op-Zoom and the lord of Montigny, to Madrid to inform the king of the situation; they were executed as "rebels." Later concessions by the king to the nobility's request, and efforts by the governor-general to maintain as much tolerance as she could, would prove inadequate to prevent subsequent events.

On 10 August 1566, a fervent Calvinist sermon in the village of Steenvoorde, then a rural textile center in western Flanders, prompted the congregation to violently purge the local monastic church of all "papist idolatry." This purely religious act soon became the symbol of defiance to Spanish rule, as crowds in many locales turned to smashing statues and stained-glass windows as an expression of their deep-seated discontent. Within a week, "idols" were wrecked throughout western Flanders, including the cities of Belle, Poperinge, Menen,

An iconoclastic riot in the Low Countries.
(Bibliothèque Nationale, Paris.)

Ypres, and Dixmude. By 20 August, the "Protestant fury" had reached Antwerp, and from there it spread to Ghent, Mechelen, Breda, Middelburg, and 's-Hertogenbosch. By the third week, images were being destroyed in Tournai and Valenciennes, Amsterdam, Utrecht, Delft, Leiden, The Hague, and Brielle. The movement continued to spread north and east in September, but by then it had gradually taken on a more organized character.

This assault on the church deeply shocked the Spanish king. An American silver fleet had just arrived, and Philip now used the money to send an army to restore order in his restive provinces. The designated troops, however, could not cross the Alps from Italy until April 1567, and they did not arrive in the Low Countries until August – a year after the unrest began. By then, peace and order had returned, and the governor-general asked the king to countermand the invasion. But the king rejected her request. When, on 22 August 1567, the duke of Alba quartered 10,000 foreign soldiers in the large Flemish and Brabantine cities, the invasion no longer had the effect of restoring order; rather, the populace regarded it as a provocation.

At this point, a tolerant approach from the authorities still could have soothed the growing resentment. Moderate members of the Council of State like William of Orange and the counts van Egmond and Hoogstraten had reached a compromise with members of the Oath of the Nobles to tolerate Protestant services at the edge of settlements, while insisting that Catholic worship also be respected. Contrary to the intent of the moderates this compromise had the effect of increasing Protestant following, and precipitated Calvinist coups in Valenciennes, Tournai, and 's-Hertogenbosch. This in turn only fostered Catholic resentment and fears.

The Duke of Alba

The decision of the Spanish royal council to send the duke of Alba to maintain a hard line against heretics came precisely at the time when local authorities had become more tolerant toward Protestant preaching, and it led to the sharp polarization of positions. Alba's immediate installation of the Council of Blood (or Council of Troubles), headed by two Spanish judges and empowered to punish "serious offenses against God and the crown," confounded the sense of justice most inhabitants of the Low Countries shared. This extraordinary court, with its secret proceedings, went against the traditions and rights to which the population had become accustomed. Even the counts of Egmond and Horne were arrested after a meeting with the unsuspecting governor-general – despite their recent oaths of loyalty to the king In violation of the counts' right to be tried, as Knights of the Golden Fleece, by their noble peers, the Council of Blood convicted and beheaded them for lese majesty because, as stadholders, they had been too tolerant of Protestants. Their fate soon became a symbol of Spanish oppression. The Council also summoned William of Orange as a defendant, but he had left the Low Countries in April 1567. He had lost his faith in the king, and had therefore, unlike Egmond and Horne, refused to renew his oath of fealty to Philip. He would now lead the opposition from his German possessions, out of the reach of the Spanish king.

The Council of Blood issued 1,071 death sentences and banished 11,136 persons, confiscating their property. Its actions triggered a wholesale flight to France, England, and western Germany. Some of the banished formed bands of "beggars" who, through guerilla warfare or piracy, tried to destroy Spanish authority in the Low Countries. The conflict escalated further in October 1568 when William of Orange risked an invasion of Brabant, in a military move that is traditionally considered the beginning of the Eighty Years' War. The campaign was unsuccessful, however, as expected popular support failed to materialize and as William lacked the money needed to sustain a long-term campaign.

Philip appointed Alba as governor-general in December 1567, and the duke immediately used his authority to rationalize and reorganize the affairs of state. Alba systematized the penal code into the Criminal Ordinances. More importantly, the duke developed a new system of taxes that would reduce the regional government's dependence on both Spanish subsidies and the unreliable States. Alba designed a 1 percent tax on assets, a 5 percent property tax, and a 10 percent sales tax. The chief advantage of this system was that it gave government functionaries permanent and automatic sources of revenue; it even gave the population an even distribution of the tax burden. The States-General assembly of 1569, meeting for the first time in a decade, strongly opposed these taxes, since they effectively eliminated their say over tax policy – and their influence in the government. Antwerp and Amsterdam complained that the taxes would be ruinous to their trade. Nevertheless, Alba used threats to pass the 1 percent tax, and made two substantial concessions to the assembly to pass the 10 percent sales tax. Hesitation in administrative circles delayed the intro-

Emblematic depiction of Alba's tyranny. Hundreds of prints and pamphlets circulated during the revolt, each championing its party's cause. (Atlas van Stolk, Rotterdam.)

duction of the sales tax until 1571, when opposition to it was so widespread that officials decided to repeal the tax in 1572. The hard-line posture of Alba's government had helped ensure that the population violently opposed its tax system, even though it had never been implemented.

The "Sea Beggars'" successful raid on Brielle on 1 April 1572 – and the willingness of several cities in Holland and Zeeland to harbor them – stemmed to a large degree from growing resistance to a government that practiced arbitrary rule, encouraged the Inquisition, extorted money and was directed from abroad. By 1572, twenty-six city councils backed the revolt William had initiated in 1568 and of which he had become the natural leader. This widespread political opposition led to the first "free" meeting of the States of Holland, which assembled on their own authority. Twelve cities participated; Amsterdam did not. The States' decision to call William back as stadholder and to declare freedom of religion were in themselves acts of rebellion, and the States provided the nucleus of political and financial authority that was necessary to sustain the resistance to Spanish rule.

All of this spurred Alba to muster his army – numbering 67,000 men in 1572 and 86,000 in 1574 – for a campaign. The pro-Orange cities of Mechelen, Zutphen and Naarden were thoroughly ransacked by his forces. Alba's military operations in Holland, however, were much more difficult, owing to the abundance of water in low-lying districts, which the rebels could flood to their advantage. Moreover, the rebels possessed a conviction and motivation which came from fighting for their own just cause, and William of Orange's inspiring words, more than his organizational abilities, provided an important source of morale for the resistance. His considerable influence, however, was not without limits; his insistence that Catholic services be respected in the cities of the Revolt was ignored, as repression against Catholics – and against priests and monks in particular – increased.

The Spanish army managed to take Haarlem after seven months, but Alkmaar and Leiden withstood the sieges of 1574, and Middelburg went over to the rebels. Thus Alba's six-year tenure as governor-general ended in failure: all of his major administrative and military efforts had come to nought, and Spain was still obliged to pay for half of his army. The whole region had unified in resistance to the king's policies – particularly the resentful provinces of Brabant and Flanders – and the open military insurgency in Holland and Zeeland could not be defeated. Alba's heavy-handed policies had further undermined the legitimacy of Spanish authority, and if many still formally recognized Philip as their sovereign, many others were searching for alternatives.

Attempts at Peace

Spanish military expenditures in the Low Countries – and against the Turks – led in 1575 to the second moratorium of interest payments on the state debt. The badly paid soldiers mutinied and deserted, pillaging the countryside as roving bands of robbers. Talks launched in Breda by the new, moderate governor-general, Don Luis de Requesens, to restore Spanish authority foundered under the demands of the rebels, which included a guaranteed role for the States in political decision making, the departure of foreign soldiers and functionaries, the end of religious persecution and an amnesty. Requesens's sudden death in March 1576 precipitated another power vacuum which lasted for months. The States of Brabant, Flanders, and Guelders made use of the time to make an accord with the States of Holland and Zeeland. The demands made by the rebels at Breda now found a broad base of political support, and when the States-General, at the request of Brabant, convened in October 1576, it approved these demands. On 28 October the representatives of Brabant, Guelders, Flanders, Holland, and Zeeland agreed upon the terms on which they would accept peace, and publicly issued these conditions in the so-called Pacification of Ghent on 8 November 1576. In light of the apparent powerlessness of the crown – its mutinous troops killed 8,000 Antwerpians and destroyed six hundred houses in the so-called Spanish Fury of 4 November – provincial representatives took the initiative by making tough demands of the Spanish king.

The representatives of the eastern provinces, from Groningen to Luxembourg, expressed reservations about the Pacification. Protestantism was much weaker in these provinces, and Spanish rule accordingly less severe. This did not deter the more rebellious provinces from developing new terms of governance designed to protect them from future arbitrary rule. In a series of charters, the members of the respective States worked out a new government, which was based on respect for local and regional rights and traditions, as well as on local and regional say in the central government, and which bound the monarch to constitutional limitations. Ignoring these limits could lead, if the States decided, to deposition of the monarch, and to the selection of another prince. These constitutional experiments, which gradually

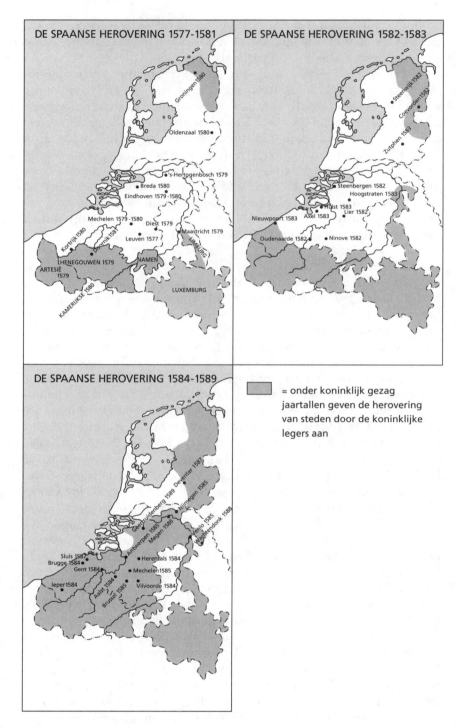

Military developments, 1577-1589.

formed the basis of the future Dutch Republic, were primarily inspired by the Brabanders and the Flemings. The former could point to the acts of *Blijde Inkomst*, which Philip had sworn to uphold in 1549. They were also acquainted with useful historical precedents, such as the temporary suspension of John IV of Brabant and his replacement by his brother from 1420 to 1421. As a member of the noble estate in the States of Brabant, William of Orange could personally draw on these constitutional traditions. For the other provinces, however, where political rights were not as well-established, the justification for their own revolutionary acts required more imagination.

Radicalization

In the course of 1577, the guilds of Brussels, Antwerp and Ghent took the initiative and formed revolutionary committees. Tired of the slow pace taken by the States, the middle classes seized power in these cities and installed pro-Calvinist city councils, and most Flemish and Brabantine cities followed suit. The so-called Calvinist Republic of Ghent has always received the most attention because of the city's political radicalism and the precedent of the fourteenth-century republic. But perhaps the most striking feature of the Calvinist Republic of Ghent was its high intellectual tone. We know that in the short period from 1578 to 1584, at least thirty highly learned Calvinist pastors were active in the city. Protestant teachers, including many talented exiles who had returned to Ghent, replaced Catholic instructors at the city's grammar school. The Ghentenar Peter Datheen came back from Heidelberg to take charge of the Theological Athenaeum, which soon won international fame as a Calvinist seminary and surpassed Leiden University as a theological center. The Frenchman Lambert Daneau, who had studied under Calvin, also came, as did Alexander Ratlo, who moved from Leiden to teach philosophy, ethics, and physics. Two other professors, one from Heidelberg and one from Leiden, also joined them. This interesting academic experiment ended when the Spanish conquered Ghent in 1584, but its legacy left its mark in the northern Low Countries. Many exiles from Ghent fled to the north, bringing with them the strict variant of Calvinism they had cultivated in the south.

It was based on a proposal made by Ghent's city leaders (and adopted by the stadholder of Guelders, John of Nassau) that Brabant, Flanders, Tournai, Holland, Zeeland, and Guelders agreed to seek a closer union. They pledged not to make a separate peace with Philip II, to collectively defend their rights and privileges, and to assent to arbitration when differences rose among them. This agreement was proclaimed on 23 January 1579 as the Union of Utrecht. Although other provinces could join, reactions in the northeastern Netherlands remained cool – and the French-speaking provinces responded with outright hostility. The king's new governor-general, Alexander Farnese, duke of Parma, had seen a new opportunity in the growing aversion of the Walloon nobility and clergy to Calvinist radicalization in Flanders and Brabant. These traditional powers had retained much more influence in the Walloon districts, with Tournai as an obvious exception. Parma easily gained their support when he promised them the restora-

Portrait of William of Orange, painted by A.T. Key around 1580. (Mauritshuis, The Hague.)

tion of their privileges and the removal of foreign troops. The Union of Arras, signed on 6 January 1579, now firmly arrayed Artois, Hainaut, Namur, Luxembourg and Limburg against the revolt.

Still, hopes for a brokered peace had not yet dissipated. In talks that took place in Cologne between May and December 1579, Emperor Rudolph II mediated between representatives of Philip II and the Dutch-language provinces. These high-level negotiations always got stuck on the same issue: the king's steadfast and principled refusal to grant any kind of religious toleration. That William of Orange's Act of Toleration in Antwerp (1566) and his policy in Holland had seemed to foment persecution of "papists" only confirmed Philip's mistrust of the insurgents, and the rebels were certainly no more trusting of Philip.

At this point, the process of radicalization reached its natural end, as the rebels decided to make a complete break with the king. In the summer of 1580, Philip II declared William of Orange an outlaw. The prince reacted by compiling a very extensive *Apology*, in which he stressed that it was the king himself who had broken faith with his vassals, that it was Philip who had committed crimes against divine and temporal laws, and that it was he who had violated the same rights he had sworn to uphold. The king, moreover, had refused to recognize his errors despite his subjects' many reproaches. Philip had become a tyrant, and no one was obliged to obey a tyrant. William began negotiations to find another ruler for the Seventeen Provinces, and settled upon the younger son of the French king, the Catholic duke of Anjou. The States-General was open to the proposal, but insisted, in line with their earlier pronouncements, that Anjou, too, could lose his right to rule if he violated his oath to defend their rights. Assured of this, Brabant, Flanders, Holland, Zeeland, and Friesland signed an accord in January 1581 recognizing the duke; Guelders, Utrecht, and Overijssel, however, held off from formally joining them.

The Act of Abjuration in July was the next logical step. In a comprehensive explanation that echoed William's *Apology*, the States-General outlined which promises Philip II had broken in the contract that he had made with his subjects at the beginning of his reign. Philip had also violated natural law, existing rights like the Brabantine *Blijde Inkomst* and the Great Privilege of 1477, and had repeatedly scorned many other customs and laws. He had treated his subjects in the Low Countries arbitrarily, as if they were colonial natives. He had even sought to rule over their consciences. This tyranny did not need to be obeyed, since the king had himself broken the ties with his subjects. For these reasons, Philip was no longer fit to rule over them, and the States-General would choose and crown a more deserving prince.

Unlike the suspension of John IV of Brabant in 1420, the Act of 1581 permanently severed Philip from his right to rule. The step was, of course, a very serious one; the rebels could not easily dispense with the most powerful sovereign in Europe. For this reason, the States had long delayed such a decision, and it also explains why their argument for the break was closely and carefully argued. What had happened, however, was more than just an exchange of ruling princes; it was a revolution. A popular movement had precipitated a widespread revolt which had overthrown a whole political and ideological system, replacing it with a new arrangement in which the middle classes would become the central players.

No longer was sovereignty conceived in terms of the divine right of kings; rather, supreme authority rested in the collective will of representatives whose mandate was provisional and temporary. They remained responsible to local communities who could always hold them accountable. It was only during the Revolt that these concepts were systematically worked out, but they had long existed in the political traditions of the Low Countries; for centuries, representative government, especially in the cities, had given form to this practice. The States-General now applied the principle of representative government to themselves. It was a principle that would, over the course of time, find emulation in England and the United States.

The Weapons Speak

The choice of Anjou proved to be an unfortunate one. He was distrusted for his Catholicism, the French military support he had been expected to bring failed to materialize, and he found it difficult, despite his promises, to work with the States-General. After his January 1583 coup in Antwerp failed, the duke slunk back to France. By 1582, Parma, both a great strategist and an expert diplomat, could again enjoy the full financial backing of Philip, who had just concluded a long-term truce with the Ottoman sultan. Parma besieged the Flemish and Brabantine cities one by one, cutting off their supply routes and starving them into surrender. Ghent fell in September 1584, Brussels in March 1585, and Antwerp succumbed, after a seven-month siege, on 17 August 1585. William of Orange, murdered by a Catholic on 10 July 1584, no longer led the rebels, and their cause now seemed in peril.

Parma's terms of surrender dictated that "heretics" must leave their cities within two years. 200,000 persons did so, including a number of Walloons, substantially increasing the flow of exiles that had begun under Alba in 1567. By 1589, the population of Antwerp had been reduced to 42,000, less than half of what it had been in the 1560s. Although tens of thousands left for England or the Empire (with concentrations in Frankenland and the city of Altona, near Hamburg) some 150,000 refugees fled, directly or indirectly, to the northern Netherlands. Their motives must have been a combination of religious conviction, economic considerations, and a desire for freedom. In any event, their migration was an enormous boon to the northern provinces, since the refugees were very often skilled craftspeople, traders, intellectuals, and artists. Nor were their numbers insignificant; even in big cities like Leiden and Amsterdam, Brabantines and Flemings together constituted one third of the population at the end of the sixteenth century. Their strong faith, which had prompted them to leave their homes, would also serve as an important factor in the rise of Calvinism in the north.

The States of Holland now sought help in England, but English military aid remained quite limited. The English did prove willing to offer the earl of Leicester as a replacement to the duke of Anjou. Although Leicester converted to radical Calvinism, he never managed to build a relationship of mutual trust with the States. When in 1587 he, too, made the blunder of planning a military coup against several cities in Holland, his legitimacy vanished and he returned to England. In 1588, the States proclaimed a republic. Driven more by negative experiences than a consistent theory, the States-General no longer sought a sovereign to rule over them. They would now simply appropriate that role for themselves.

The Great Assembly of the States-General, meeting in 1651 at the Binnenhof's *Great Hall in The Hague; painting by Dirck van Delen. (Rijksmuseum, Amsterdam.)*

4 The Dutch Republic, 1588-1780

A.T. van Deursen

By the late sixteenth century, the northern portion of the Low Countries had successfully resisted the formidable power of the Spanish empire. Supported by England and France, the rebellious provinces won crucial military victories over the Spanish, in part because Philip II concentrated his forces against France. A wide range of the local population supported the revolt, but with the cessation of hostilities in the Twelve Years' Truce (1609-1621), the Dutch Republic became badly divided along religious lines, and this led to political turmoil. The Dutch Republic's political will to retake the southern provinces from Spain declined for various reasons, and a permanent division between north and south was largely a fact by 1609, although this boundary was not formally recognized until the Peace of Münster in 1648

The Dutch Republic underwent explosive economic growth during the first half of the seventeenth century, benefitting from the domestic problems which beset its potential trading rivals, France and England. The Republic's wealth also fostered a cultural life that reached unprecedented heights of achievement.

Dutch power declined in the face of a resurgent England and France, and by the mid-eighteenth century the Republic had become a small power which sought to avoid military conflicts. Its economy, too, contracted and only a small elite managed to retain their wealth. The Dutch Republic, led by the stadholders from the House of Orange, became an oligarchy. Increasingly, the Republic's economic woes and the policies of the oligarchy fostered resentment among the middle classes, prompting them increasingly to challenge the Republic's ailing institutions.

1. The First Ten Years of the Republic (1588-1598)

The Success of the Revolt

1588: We have now arrived at the point where the paths diverge. The dream of one great country is past, and the seventeen provinces fall into two groups. The temporary reunion that occurred some two and quarter centuries later would last only fifteen years. After 1588, the history of the Low Countries can no longer be told as one story. If the Fleming had been nearly synonymous until then with the "Netherlander," the Hollander now took over this dominant position in the northern provinces, becoming the embodiment of a new, northern Netherlandic identity.

All of this is, of course, no more than the wisdom of hindsight. Only an optimist could have predicted that a couple of rebellious provinces in the northwest would be capable of winning their precarious bid for independence. Only a pessimist could have thought that the rebel provinces would eventually cut their ties with the southern region. For William of Orange, the Revolt had been in the collective interest of all the Low Countries; he scarcely would have been able to imagine an independent state without the inclusion of Brabant and Flanders. From the vantage point of 1588, the permanent division of the Low Countries was not yet inalterable; the formal and definitive split came only with the peace treaty of 1648. In 1588, the split still seemed highly unlikely; in 1648, people regarded the division as both natural and inevitable. It was in these sixty years that the Republic of the northern Netherlands developed its own new identity.

What did the Dutch need to create a viable state? The first priority, of course, was winning the war for independence. In the eyes of Spain, Holland and its allies did not constitute a sovereign state; they were a band of rebels in a little corner of the Habsburg empire. Defeat for the Dutch meant, therefore, not a reduction of their power, but the complete destruction of their already cherished independence. Thus it was absolutely essential for them that they win a clear victory over the Spanish. However, Spain was then the greatest power in Europe, and for that reason the Dutch were forced to find allies to support their cause. To find them, the Dutch first needed to prove their own ability to resist. This naturally included financial resources, since money is the nerve of war. But it also included a firm sense of cause, since no resistance can continue for long if people are not committed to more than their lives and their property. Finally, the Dutch needed strong leadership with much energy and organizational talent – essential assets in this time of danger. In a word, foreign assistance, financial muscle, a high sense of purpose, and uncommon leadership were all of vital importance in 1588.

We begin our story in 1588, and it was precisely in 1588 and 1589 that international changes conspired to give the Dutch foreign help. In the summer of 1588, Philip II dispatched his famous Armada not only to quell the Revolt but also to drive the Protestant Queen Elizabeth from the English throne. The Armada failed in both aims, and this had important consequences. First, the English realized that they, too, were directly threatened and that they had the same enemy as the Dutch. Second, the Armada's defeat gave the English a new confidence that they were strong enough to resist Spain. The alliance between England and the Dutch Republic from 1588 onward was never a particularly enthusiastic one, but both parties recognized that they had a common cause against Spain.

Developments in France were of even greater import. Henry III, the last king of the House of Valois, was assassinated in 1589. His closest male relative was Henry Bourbon, king of Navarre, who became King Henry IV. As a Protestant, he was unacceptable to many French, and when the Catholic party resisted this Huguenot pretender, it received help from Spain. Philip II accordingly ordered Parma, the governor-general, to send the bulk of his forces in the Low Countries to France. It was a decision with far-reaching consequences. Parma had resubjugated Brabant and Flanders to Spanish rule, and his military campaigns in Gelderland (Guelders) and Overijssel were making good progress. It was only a matter of time, it seemed, before Parma's sizable army would invade Holland and other centers of the Revolt, putting an end to the rebellion.

It is not impossible that through this order Philip unwittingly saved the Republic. In any event, the immediate danger posed by Parma's force disappeared, and the French king and the Dutch Republic were driven to form an alliance against Spain in 1589. It was an alliance that would know many crises and periodically be inactive, but it would not be terminated until the Peace of Münster.

Prosperity in Holland

Thus the young Republic was able to find allies. In this respect, the diplomatic initiatives of the Republic's new leader, Johan van Oldenbarnevelt, were more successful than those of William of Orange. Both men were superb diplomats, but Oldenbarnevelt had more to offer. Holland's considerable wealth, not yet apparent in 1588, attracted international interest before the end of the century, and demonstrated that Holland possessed its own power: money.

The Low Countries had long grown wealthy from a highly diversified system of trade and flourishing commercial markets. Although this wealth was not evenly distributed across the region, it was not restricted to just a few cities or provinces. Before the Revolt, Antwerp had functioned as the dominant center of this wealth. After the Revolt, the structure remained the same: relatively well-distributed wealth, with Amsterdam now functioning as the center of activity. Despite this continuity, the Revolt also precipitated an even more important change: although the Spanish-controlled areas were hardly pauperized, most of the economic impetus now moved to the rebellious provinces. Antwerp did not become a giant poorhouse, but Amsterdam had clearly replaced it as the commercial capital of Europe.

This shift did not occur by magic. The process dates back to 1585, when Parma succeeded in taking Antwerp. And though the States-General still controlled garrisons in Sluis, Ostend, and Bergen op Zoom, the fall of Antwerp meant that the Revolt had effectively lost its base in the southern Low Countries. Migration from south to north, a trend apparent before 1585, now substantially increased in scope, as labor, talent, and capital sought their development in Holland and Zeeland. The choice of these regions was not arbitrary or coincidental. It was here in the northwest that the possibilities for prosperity, previously shared by all the western provinces, could be found.

The Republic also benefitted from shifting commercial patterns. The sixteenth century witnessed the rise of a truly global economy. Intercontinental trade existed in the Mediterranean before 1500, but it was only in the course of the sixteenth century that East Asia, West Africa, and the Americas were integrated into the European economy. Trade volume within Europe itself also intensified, as the trading regions centered in the Baltic, Mediterranean and North Seas, and the Atlantic Ocean oriented their respective products toward each other. The quality of sea-going vessels improved, and skippers traveled greater distances to deliver their cargoes. At the same time, the risks inherent in the sea trade increased: not just wind and rain, pirates and privateers, but especially in this context, the financial risks skippers faced in purchasing products at local markets. It was difficult to calculate precise times of arrival over long distances, and even if skippers could accurately calculate this, they still could not know if the goods they sought were available in the markets in sufficient quantity or at affordable prices. The best solution for this problem lay in the creation of one centrally located market, where goods from throughout Europe could be housed and sold. In this way, traders could be assured of constant supplies, stable, acceptable prices, and permanent demand. The Low Countries' location made it the ideal place for the creation of such a central market, such a staple market.

This was a gift of fate, but people must also seize an opportunity when it presents itself. For centuries, Hollanders had been exceedingly active in trade and shipping, and by 1585 their ships transported bulk goods like lumber and grain throughout Europe. Profit margins were never very large in this business, and traders were obliged to trim costs, preferring simply constructed ships designed for maximum bulk and requiring a minimal crew. Shipping remained cheap in this way, but those unfortunate enough to lose a rye-laden vessel to stormy weather or war, for example, could be ruined overnight. For this reason, ships from Holland often had multiple owners; an ordinary cargo ship could have thirty, forty, or even a hundred owners who shared their profits and their losses. This system also made it possible for small investors to put their money into ships; this provided additional capital for the growth of the shipping industry.

In this way, the Hollanders succeeded in moving a high volume at a low cost, and became the dominant players in the transport of bulk goods. But grain and lumber were by themselves hardly the basis for a staple market. Local specialties helped the Hollanders expand their trade: cloth from Leiden and linen from Haarlem, both of whose industries were powerfully stimulated by the labor and capital arriving from the southern provinces. Agriculture, too, was an indispensable link in the chain. Grain imports from the Baltic regions made it possible for farmers in Holland, Friesland, and Zeeland to specialize in export products like butter, cheese, and the cultivation of "industrial" crops like rapeseed and flax. The war actually helped the economy in the northern provinces, since the Republic blocked the Flemish harbors and closed the Scheldt, Antwerp's avenue to the sea. This alone prompted many Antwerp merchants to set up shop in the north, bringing with them not only money, but their expertise and their connections with the trade centers of the Mediterranean. Through them, Holland gained a share in the trade of high quality goods, a vital component in a truly comprehensive staple market.

Note the bleaching fields in this View of Haarlem *by Jacob van Ruisdael. (Mauritshuis, The Hague.)*

In summary, we can see how the conjunction of an unusually propitious set of circumstances had a cumulative effect on Holland's prosperity. Its growth did not rest on trade and shipping alone, however largely these two words may be written. Commerce, agriculture, and stockbreeding were all indispensable as well. The well-being of the city dwellers increased, but those living in the countryside fared no worse. And just as merchants and peasants both did their part to boost their collective welfare, so too did native-born Hollanders and southern emigres work side by side to create the economic wonder of the Dutch Republic.

Money flowed into the country. It did not necessarily follow, however, that the state itself was solvent. In the sixteenth century, large and powerful countries like Spain and France went bankrupt several times. The most important reason for state bankruptcies was the inability of an administration to develop a good tax system, in which a proportional burden was placed on the population. The rich had money, but they also had influence, and had to be spared. Thus the poorer segments of the populace were often taxed beyond their means, requiring coercive – and expensive – means of collection that substantially reduced anticipated revenues.

And how did the Republic manage their finances, particularly in the face of their war with Spain? One of Holland's most notable features was that its wealth was widely distributed. This made for a relatively broad tax base, and enabled the population to meet their tax obligations without ruinous effects. The tax revolts which racked France throughout the seventeenth century were not replicated in Holland, where such rebellions remained limited in size, scope, and duration. The tax system in Holland was also extraordinarily well-suited to collect maximum revenues in a country where the large majority of people were neither rich nor poor, yet were pleased with their modest prosperity. In contrast to France, taxes were not primarily assessed on total household income. This tax did exist, but it usually did not exceed more than a few guilders per household. Rather, authorities found indirect taxes on goods more profitable. These taxes made all merchandise slightly more expensive, but prices were never exorbitant. In this way, consumers fulfilled their tax obligations with every purchase, and their copper *stuivers* and *duiten* turned into the millions of guilders that flooded the Republic's treasury. For the state, too, Holland's prosperity was worth its weight in gold.

The Republic's Political Structure

An administration with sufficient money can forge energetic policies – provided it is well-organized. The Republic, however, never attained this state. It remained a federation of autonomous provinces – seven in number after the Republic's seizure of Groningen in 1594. The duchy of Gelderland retained its first rank in the official pecking order, followed by the county of Holland, and then Zeeland, Utrecht, Friesland, Overijssel and Groningen. An eighth province, Drenthe, was granted self-rule but enjoyed no representation in the States-General, the Republic's legislative body. Drenthe, therefore, did not experience the same fate as the so-called Generality Lands – conquered portions of Brabant and Flanders, which were ruled directly by The Hague. In principle, the seven ruling provinces were given an equal share of power, and equal authority to block important decisions with their veto. It seems a certain formula for disorder and indecision, yet the Republic became a great power under this arrangement. Thus it might be helpful to inquire if the system's obvious shortcomings were not compensated by some hidden virtues.

The Union of Utrecht (1579) had united the rebellious regions "as though they were one province." This kind of unity was necessary since the participants collectively waged war against Spain. To achieve this goal, they had one leader, William of Orange, and one governing body, the States-General. At the same time, however, the war was being waged to protect the freedoms and privileges of the respective provinces. In other words, the ends of the war were to preserve the independence of each province, and their close cooperation was a necessary means to this end. If the end itself was given too much priority, then each province would give disproportionate attention to its own interests; if the means overshadowed the aim, regional autonomy was threatened. Statesmanship in the Dutch Republic thus usually consisted of trying to find a middle way between two ideals that were, ultimately, incompatible with each other. Maintaining this balance through coercion or violence was futile, since each province was free. Only negotiation, compromise, and consensus building offered a way of making policies on divisive issues. This art was called *"persuasie."* Without mastering it, no one could rule the Republic.

Those proficient in this art could be given a leading place in the Republic, and some of them exercised their role forcefully and energetically. But they could never become dictators. The whole structure of the Republic made it very difficult for one individual to concentrate power. This was true on all levels. The juridical equality of the seven provinces was the clearest expression of this. But the same was true at the next level down, with the nobility, cities and the district councils in each province. In order to get something done in the States of Overijssel, for example, one had to cultivate good relations not only with the *burgemeesters* of Kampen, but also with the bailiff of Salland. On the level above the provinces, in the central administrative organs in and around The Hague, the same wide distribution of power is evident through the range of important deliberative organs: the States-General, the Council of State, the Admiralty Councils, the Generality's auditor, quartermaster-generals of the mint, and so on. There is little point in describing or delineating their respective prerogatives. What is important to note is their collective characteristic: meeting in council. It was normal to give authority not to a person, but to a council.

This did not prevent all arbitrary use of power, of course, but it did limit it. To change a council's policy through persuasion usually meant that one had to give attention to the interests of more than one person, and more than one province. Persuasion, therefore, was not the same thing as manipulation. The eventual decisions of the council were typically backed by a considerable majority, which gave a broad base of support to the policies of the States-General and eased the implementation of decisions. And given the strong political position of the commercial elite in Holland, there was a reasonably strong guarantee that the Republic's policies would often serve the interests of those who provided the country with its prosperity.

Amidst these councils of consensus stood the solitary figure of the stadholder. Actually, there were two of them, one residing in Holland and the other in Friesland. But both were unique. They could be stadholders in more than their own provinces – the stadholder of Friesland often held the same title in Groningen and Drenthe, and the stadholder of Holland always held this title in the remaining provinces – but they possessed no formal authority outside of their own provinces. Stadholders shared their power with no one. This was determined when the position was established. William of Orange had held the title of stadholder. But the essence of his task after 1572 was not what the word stad-holder, lieutenant, connote. He no longer stood in stead of another, as he had for the king of Spain. He was the leader of a rebellion, with all the authority which necessity demanded. The need for leadership continued after his death, and it became necessary to create a new "stad-holder" who would possess enough prestige to make his leadership acceptable to all.

In the sixteenth century, prestige was almost inextricably linked with birth, and no one in the rebellious provinces was more highly born than William's son, Prince Maurits of Nassau, who succeeded his father. But in a state where public authority is not tightly defined, the content of high office is usually dependent on the qualities of the person hold-ing the office. Maurits seemed eminently capable of military leadership, but did not exercise much political ambition. Thus despite his title he did not become the country's functioning political leader, as his father had been. Instead, this task fell to Johan van Oldenbarnevelt.

Oldenbarnevelt was then officially the Advocate, or (to use a later title) the Pensionary of Holland. It meant that after the stadholder he was the highest functionary in the province of Holland. He served as chairman of the regional States' assemblies, wrote the official corre-spondence to domestic and foreign officials, and led Holland's delega-tion at meetings of the States-General. For a man of his talent and ambition, this was basis enough to accumulate power and influence. Thus the pensionary was usually one of the most influential persons in the Republic. The power of the pensionaries should not be overesti-mated, however, by seeing them as eternal rivals of the stadholders. The pensionaries could not successfully compete with the stadholders, for reasons outlined below.

In the first place, the Pensionary of Holland represented only one province of the Republic. What was good for Holland was not neces-sarily good for the other provinces. Thus the other provinces regarded

Maurits, Prince of Orange (1567-1625).   *Johan van Oldenbarnevelt.*

the pensionary, much more than the stadholder, as the representative of Holland's particular interests. Second, there was an enormous difference in status between the two offices, despite the fact that they were both, officially, administrative positions. The pensionary received status *through* his office; the stadholder received his office *because* of his status. The names of Pieter Steyn and Johannes Hoornbeek are known today because these men became Pensionaries; the princes of Orange already enjoyed a name, and it was precisely this name that lent prestige to the stadholder's office. Third, the stadholder was always the commander of the army and the navy. He was not authorized to use them for purposes other than serving the Republic. But if the interests of the Republic were defined differently by parties implacably opposed to each other, then the stadholder could use military coercion to force the parties to accept his opinion. No power in the Republic could prevent him from choosing his own course, if he so desired.

The Place of the Church

Sober spectators of the situation in 1588 might theoretically have conceived these political possibilities. But they could not have imagined any confrontation between Maurits and Oldenbarnevelt, since both were working together toward the same goal. That unity of purpose was true of all who supported the Dutch Revolt. Historians sometimes have been engaged in learned debate about which had first priority: politics or faith, the struggle for civil freedom, or for the church. Posed this way, the question is a false dilemma. When Hollanders negotiated with the Spanish governor-general Requesens for the protection of their old privileges, he countered by saying that they themselves should begin by restoring the Catholic church to its former status. From his perspective, he had made a telling point; what greater privilege could the Dutch people have than to belong the Roman Catholic church? But the ideal of freedom held by the rebels lost its purpose without freedom of thought, and this was incompatible with late sixteenth-century Catholicism. For that reason, the church in the free Netherlands would have to be Protestant.

The nature of this Protestant church remained a matter of dispute, as is often the case among Protestants. There were those who placed great emphasis on the word freedom. The church must be open to all, without regard to their particular opinions. The purest form of this ideal was the so-called libertine church which operated in the city of Utrecht during the last decades of the sixteenth century. This church offered its preaching, baptism and communion to all, without distinction. Oversight and control were absent; the church gave its services to everyone, and asked nothing in return. From this perspective, the church is, in a sense, coextensive with the people; everyone is welcome, and there are no conditions for membership. On the other hand, no one need attach themselves to the church. Church attendance and communion are optional and the church can make no demands of anyone. Seen this way, the church consists only of clergy. Such a church is thus at once quite broad and quite narrow. It does not need to be sustained by congregational life, but is rather a public service, funded by public sources. It is the state which has the leading interest in such a church, and it is the state which accordingly exercises responsibility over the qualitative and quantitative level of the services. Utrecht alone ever had such a church, and after several decades it became clear that this arrangement was unworkable. Still, the Utrecht model corresponded closely to the ideal that many political elites held, especially in the province of Holland.

But another model also sprang from the churches, one that might best be labeled "Calvinist." It had little in common with the libertine church model. In the first place, the Calvinists opposed full doctrinal freedom, insisting that there be complete agreement on the essential articles of faith. They desired that everyone, without distinction, sub-scribe to the confessions which the church had formulated. Second, they strove for a tightly structured church government, organized on local, regional, and national levels. Local congregations were united in regional units (classes), which in turn were united in provincial and national organs (synods). This kind of organization lent itself to a mutual theological supervision which would guarantee purity of doc-trine, but it was especially supposed to ensure that church members lived sober and upright lives. Ecclesiastical discipline, therefore, was one of the essential marks of the Calvinist church. In contrast to the lib-ertine model, membership was not without its obligations. At the same time, however, the church was a voluntary organization; no one would be forced to join, or even pressured to do so. But those who did choose to become members – and partake of Holy Communion – were expected to understand the seriousness of their commitment.

The Calvinist model was implemented nearly everywhere in the rebellious provinces. In its confessions, in its organization, and in its day-to-day practice, the church became Calvinistic. This unquestion-ably slowed the growth of the church. One did not become a member by birth, but by choice. And since the choice was a serious one with seri-ous consequences, many declined to join out of fear, laziness, or indif-ference. There were others who consciously rejected the Calvinist model; it was not the Reformation of which they had dreamed. Ten-sions, therefore, continued to surround the church. As long as the war with Spain required full attention, these tensions were largely dormant. But the differences were too great to simply disappear over time. In fact, two different spiritual impulses could be found in the church throughout the history of the Republic: the so-called precisianists, who insisted that faith and life conform to the church's standards, and the latitudinarians, who preferred a looser and broadly based church. It is not quite right to call them parties; they were two different, often opposed mentalities. The clergy would typically lead the precisianists; many regents could be found among the latitudinarians.

The Course of the War

The great Dutch historian Robert Fruin finished his famous *Ten Years from the Eighty Years' War* in 1857, in which he characterizes the period lasting from 1588 to 1598 as the time when the young Republic secured its independence and established a firm basis for the future. The outline of the Republic's successes have already been sketched, and there is no further need to delve into the specifics of its military campaigns. We have already noted that the Republic was greatly helped by Spain's decision to allocate most of its resources to the French and away from the Dutch front. Maurits and Oldenbarnevelt made maximum use of the decision, however. Oldenbarnevelt was adept at steering policy making in The Hague, ensuring agreement among the provinces – and securing their willingness to shoulder the costs of the war. Maurits made the provinces' financial sacrifice easier to bear with the magnificent military results he achieved on the field. If the 1580s was the decade when the southern provinces were permanently lost to the Revolt, then the 1590s formed the period when the eastern and northern provinces were definitely won for the Republic. It was then that the inclusion of Groningen, Nijmegen, and Coevorden into the Republic was decided – and that the Netherlandic cities of Bruges and Antwerp would remain under Habsburg rule.

This was the course of events, but at the time, this shift was neither intended nor realized. Maurits conducted the war in consultation with his cousin, the Frisian stadholder William Louis of Nassau. The northern Nassaus, descendants of William the Silent's brother John, often became rivals and adversaries of their western cousins, but Maurits and William Louis remained on excellent terms. Maurits had a sympathetic ear for the priorities of his Frisian relative, and this certainly played a role in the Republic's efforts in retaking northern and eastern cities like Groningen, Steenwijk, Delfzijl, and Coevorden. Thus the provinces of Friesland, Drenthe, and Groningen (the Ommelanden) were freed from enemy extortion, and able to contribute fully to the financial cost of the war. The same was true of Gelderland and Overijssel, where the Spanish were obliged to abandon their last military fortresses. By the end of the 1590s, the whole area north of the Maas and the Scheldt Rivers lay in the hands of the Republic. This was an important milestone, but it was not the ultimate military aim of the Republic's leaders. They still planned on carrying the fight into Brabant and Flanders, the old center of the Low Countries.

2. The Question of War and Peace (1598-1609)

Uncertainty over War Aims

The old prejudice that history consists only of the dates of battles will never wholly disappear. A repudiation of this view is hardly necessary, since almost every history book, including this one, demonstrates this is not true. Battles often say very little, and they say even less about the Eighty Years' War. Those wishing to compile a chronology of the conflict will find a whole series of sieges, not battles. On both sides, land forces consisted chiefly of garrisons. Only a relatively small portion of troops – constituting a field army – had the special task of capturing fortresses. The defense could respond in several ways to the enemy's field army. In the first place, it could try to make its fortresses as strong as possible. In the second place, it could lay siege to one of the enemy's cities, in order to compensate for any losses of its own. There was also a third method: attempting to knock out the enemy by using one field army to directly attack another. Then, and only then, would there be a battle. But the value of a pitched battle remained limited: it did not lead to the seizure of territory, since the garrisoned fortresses of the enemy remained intact. It could, however, buy time, since the losing field army would be unable to conduct new operations until the following year. But as long as the loser possessed money, military defeat could always be recouped by a fresh supply of soldiers, and as long as Germany remained a poor country with a surplus labor supply, there would always be enough mercenary soldiers.

Thus there were few battles in the struggle against Spain, and they had little impact on the course of the war. But it is striking that in the period we are describing, one of these rare battles took place: it was in 1600, near the small Flemish city of Nieuwpoort. There was a time when every Dutch girl and boy learned that date in school, and when its importance in Dutch history was assumed. But the Battle of Nieuwpoort is, when well-considered, a very strange red-letter date in the history of the Fatherland. Prince Maurits's chief characteristic in waging war was his cautiousness. He always preferred certainty, even if small risks might bring him substantial gains. Maurits never subjected his forces to dangers that could be avoided; he was no Napoleon or Charles XII of Sweden, whose armies roamed foreign fields hundreds of miles from home. Seldom did the prince venture farther than a day's journey from The Hague, allowing him to quickly return in the event of a political emergency. And yet it was the same Prince Maurits who in 1600 was present at the Battle of Nieuwpoort.

By 1598, the war had entered a new phase. The Republic's seizure of the eastern Netherlands was complete. All cities in the seven provinces were free of Spanish troops. As a result, the Republic's leaders began to plan new conquests to the south. Maurits himself supported this endeavor, but from the borderlands, a strategy which was subsequently evident when he besieged Grave and Sluis. In 1600, however, the government aimed at taking a greater prize: Dunkirk, the regional base for Spanish privateering. Oldenbarnevelt wanted to capture it, and for understandable reasons: the privateers of Dunkirk did thousands of guilders damage each year to Dutch shipping. The seizure of the city, therefore, was worth risking something. But what? If it was only a matter of money, then it was an affair the States-General could decide. But it also pertained to people – a force of 15,000 men, nearly half of the Republic's army. These soldiers would be required to march deep into enemy territory, without the possibility of an orderly retreat if they were attacked and unable to withstand the assault.

Maurits fought at Nieuwpoort, and won. But it brought no results. Maurits's name was magnified as a consequence of the victory, but it was the kind of glory for which he cared little: much bloodshed, much heroism, without so much as a square foot gained. It was just the kind of useless glory that can give a general a bad name in future generations. But even if an event yields no results, people can still draw lessons from it. Nieuwpoort taught the Dutch two things. First, it showed them that the war could not be quickly decided. Daring action and brilliant victory could not determine the course of the war. The only other option was patience – a policy long preferred by Maurits, whose carefully calculated strategy has brought solid results, but results which worked only slowly and cost a good deal of money. Second, it showed that hopes for the Flemish population's support for the Republic's army were illusory. The Nieuwpoort campaign had not triggered a popular rebellion against Spain, as the occupation of Brielle had done in 1572. Thus it became increasingly clear that the South could not be liberated with local support, but instead would have to be conquered.

In 1600, these insights were not yet universally shared. Many immigrants to the Republic regarded themselves as temporary residents; Holland was their refuge, not their new fatherland. Thus they continued to hope that the gates of Ghent and Bruges would again be open to them. Year after year, these refugees continued to earn their bread in the large cities of the western provinces, and the most successful among them lived very well. As a group, they generated a powerful impetus for trade and commerce; they led the way in the arts and sciences, and provided the Reformed church with many pastors and elders. But they lacked political influence; administration and policy-making remained in the hands of the native Hollanders. On the one hand, this situation fostered a certain political detachment among the immigrants and strengthened their desire to return to their native land. On the other hand, since the immigrants could not determine the political direction of the Republic, they were unable to make the conquest of the southern provinces a high political and military priority. Instead, it was Holland's political leadership, headed by Oldenbarnevelt, who would decide these priorities.

But did they desire to retake the South? Some people began to regard the Republic as a completed whole, prosperous and powerful enough to stand by itself, without the southern provinces. From this perspective, territorial expansion only meant greater military burdens without any clear material advantage. Indeed, many of Holland's political leaders began to show signs of self-satisfied complacency. They attributed the success of the Dutch Revolt to themselves, and ascribed the loss of Brabant and Flanders to the natives of those provinces. They interpreted the natural resentment of the disadvantaged immigrants as fanaticism and misplaced pride. Oldenbarnevelt's first political opponents, the supporters of the Earl of Leicester in the 1580s, stemmed almost exclusively from the southern provinces. His ecclesiastical adversaries during the Arminian disputes (see below) were not solely from the South, but Oldenbarnevelt himself believed that his enemies were chiefly southerners. Certainly Oldenbarnevelt – and many other prominent figures in Holland – did not regard the conquest of Brabant and Flanders as an integral and natural part of their war aims. It is illuminating that although some parts of Flanders and Brabant eventually came under the Republic's control, they were denied representation in the States-General – even though these provinces had once sent delegations to it. These conquered territories, called the Generality Lands, were administered directly by The Hague, and were denied their own States and hence the right to decide their own regional affairs.

Perhaps their attitude toward the conquest of the South would have been different if the prospects of war had been better. But France had made peace with Spain in 1598, and England followed suit in 1604. King Henry IV of France continued to support the Republic, but Spain was now able to pool all of its military resources against the seven provinces. Moreover, the new Spanish commander, Spinola, proved to be more than Maurits's equal. With the recapture of Groenlo and Oldenzaal, Spinola created new Spanish enclaves within the boundaries of the Republic. Maurits was unable to turn the tide; Spain had succeeded in taking the military initiative from the Republic.

Despite their successes, however, the Spanish could not deliver a knock-out blow to their foe. Realists in Madrid or Brussels (the capital of the Spanish Netherlands) were forced to recognize that the war could not be won. Spain was no longer the great power it had been under Philip II, and the rebellious coastal region of 1572 had blossomed into a Republic with seven provinces. Neither party had the means to decisively defeat the other, and the time seemed ripe for negotiations.

Peace or Truce?

Negotiations were successfully concluded in the Twelve Years' Truce of 1609. It was not intended as a permanent peace. Nor did hostilities entirely cease during the Truce; outside of Europe, the war simply continued, especially in the East Indies (present-day Indonesia), which Dutch merchants had reached by the end of the sixteenth century. This led to the establishment of the United East India Company in 1602, but we shall return to this later. More directly relevant is the fact that there was also conflict in Europe. There have been times in European history when people thought war was imminent; international tensions were so strongly felt that armed conflict seemed the only option. Many people believed this during the 1950s, for instance, when the Cold War was at its iciest. These tensions were also present in Europe at the beginning of the seventeenth century. And just as in the case of the Cold War, people interpreted all problems and tensions in the light of one all-encompassing ideology.

Unlike the Cold War, however, the ideology was not about economic or political systems; it was about religion. The opposition between Rome and the Reformation could not be reconciled, and Christian Europe was divided into two camps – one Catholic, one Protestant. But many people, especially many Protestants, did not believe that this uneasy coexistence would last. Protestants had not forgotten the Armada of 1588, and saw it as evidence that Spain still sought hegemony over a wholly Catholic Europe. The struggle between the two opposing forces could be seen everywhere: in the Dutch fight for independence, in the war between Lutheran Sweden and Catholic Poland, in the mounting tensions within the German Empire between the Catholic League and the Protestant Union. And it was in Germany that the great conflict would eventually erupt, dragging all of Europe's great powers (with the exception of England) into war.

For this reason, it was a truce and not a peace that was concluded in 1609; in subsequent years, both sides would send their troops eastward to fight in Germany. Distrust of Spain was simply too great in the Dutch Republic for real peace to be desired. Spain in turn held grievances of its own: Dutch merchants would have to leave the Indies, the Scheldt would have to be opened for shipping traffic to Antwerp, and Catholics would have to be allowed to freely exercise their religion. The Republic refused to make any concessions on these points.

We shall take up the matter of the Indies later. The Dutch decision to close the Scheldt to traffic is understandable for economic reasons; Holland benefitted from the European trading patterns that stemmed in part from the decline of Antwerp as a major port. From its perspective, the southern regions would just have to accept that Amsterdam had surpassed Antwerp. The matter of the Catholics in the Netherlands was a separate issue. The Republic considered its cause as the Protestant cause. Given the international nature of the religious conflict, its leaders could have regarded Dutch Catholics as a Trojan horse, an enemy within the walls, who had to be suppressed with hard measures. But generally, the Republic refrained from treating Catholics as traitors and subversives.

On this matter, in fact, the Republic could afford to be mild, because Dutch Catholics showed little interest in taking up arms against their government. They, too, knew that Spain fought for the complete restoration of the old church. If they lived in cities which had switched hands, such as Oldenzaal or Grol, they might welcome the return of Spanish Catholic rule. But they did not attempt to bring about restoration themselves. Catholics sometimes voiced their resentments against Protestant rule, but their discontent remained a matter of words. Parma's seizure of Brabant and Flanders in the 1580s had prompted Protestants to flee in droves, but Maurits's successful campaigns in the eastern provinces triggered no such response; Catholics stayed in the Republic. If people left Overijssel or Drenthe in search of a better life, they did not go to Brussels, but to Amsterdam – even if they were Catholic. Refugees from the South were hardly all Calvinists; many had been drawn to the North by economic opportunity. Similarly, many Catholics —whether in Holland or the East – knew their best chance at prosperity lay within the confines of the Republic, and were willing to accept the religious preferences of Holland's leaders.

The authorities reacted to the Catholic presence in an accommodating fashion, at least in Holland. In other provinces, the level of tolerance might have been a degree lower, but in Holland officials soon worked out a stable arrangement. On the one hand, they insisted on the Protestant character of the state and the privileged position of the Reformed church; on the other hand, the authorities thought it best not to provoke the region's many Catholics, who kept quiet as long as they were not subjected to extreme indignities. The official position was that everyone had freedom of conscience, but not everyone had the freedom of public worship. In practice, of course, no church can accept this distinction; worship is an intrinsic part of religious duty, not a privilege granted by a benevolent state. Authorities more or less recognized this, and were prepared to make the necessary concessions. They gave Catholics the minimum freedom necessary for the practice of their faith, but officially forbade Catholic worship as a way of ensuring that Catholics never took more than the minimum that they had been granted. In this way, the Republic preserved domestic peace as it waged war against Europe's great Catholic power.

Dutch tolerance, now so famed, thus included a fair amount of opportunism – which was precisely the reason for its success. For the Dutch authorities, tolerance was no theoretical construction, borne out of the study of closely reasoned but abstract considerations. It was rather a typical product of the pragmatic culture of Holland. Still, Dutch tolerance did contain a principled component, which could be traced back to the old instinctual dislike of coercing conscience. Toleration, therefore, did not extend only to Roman Catholics; Lutherans, Mennonites, and (later) Remonstrants profited even more from this freedom, and the relatively early end to the prosecution of witches resulted from this same conviction. Also, the Republic's Jewish community, especially in Amsterdam, received more generous terms to practice their faith and life than its counterparts did in other European states. In the long run, this tolerance substantially influenced and changed Dutch society. In the short run, however, it was seriously challenged by the religious disputes of the Twelve Years' Truce.

3. The Disputes of the Twelve Years' Truce (1609-1625)

Political Divisions

The usual fate of truces is to be broken. This, however, was not the case with the Truce of 1609. Both Spain and the Republic had good reason to keep the temporary peace, and both sides made an effort to keep hostilities from breaking out – even in the face of increasing international tensions. But the Twelve Years' Truce was not extended; in the end, European tensions made a renewal of the conflict inevitable.

After 1609, in fact, we can see that the conflict between Catholics and Protestants was internationalized. Until the Truce, the most serious conflict in Europe was fought between Spain and the Republic. The advent of the Thirty Years' War (1618-1648), however, largely shifted the conflagration to Germany, and the reopening of hostilities between the Dutch Republic and Spain in 1621 must be seen in the light of the German war. But how did the Dutch themselves make the connection between international developments and their own struggle against Spain? The domestic disputes within the Republic during the Twelve Years' Truce stemmed in part from how to interpret international developments.

Christian Europe straddled two major fault lines: it lay between both Rome and the Reformation, and between France and the Habsburgs, Europe's most powerful royal house. Under Charles V and Philip II, the Habsburgs had tried to dominate Europe. France was the chief opponent of their ambitions, and all principalities threatened by the Habsburgs sought succor from France. The Republic, in fact, had itself received much help from France. At the same time, France was a Catholic country. Those Dutch who regarded religious differences as the basis for international alliances would never, therefore, be fully able to trust the French. Maurits was wary of the French for this reason; Oldenbarnevelt was not. Herein lay the principle difference between the two men.

The Dutch pensionary had always been committed to the alliance with France, believing that French interests would always compel it to pursue policies favorable to the Dutch Republic. Situated between Habsburg Spain and the Habsburg Netherlands, France would always be locked in conflict with Spain to ensure that it did not become a Habsburg satellite. This had also been the view of William of Orange. But it was not a view that contributed to his popularity. His brother, John of Nassau, had unsuccessfully tried to find a Protestant alternative to the French by gaining the active support of the German princes. It is also no coincidence that after William's death in 1584, it was the English whom the Dutch wooed for aid. For those who thought in primarily Protestant terms, England was the most natural ally. Maurits himself became increasingly sympathetic to the view that the war was an essentially religious conflict, and that Protestant England was therefore the best ally. For this reason, he opposed a truce or a peace treaty with Spain. The conflict between Protestants and Catholics had to be fought and won. In Maurits's judgment, therefore, the Twelve Years' Truce only postponed a successful resolution of the struggle.

When the Truce began, it first looked like it might last only twelve months, instead of twelve years. In 1609, the childless duke of Gulik died. When several candidates made claims to succeed him, King Henry IV of France openly backed the Protestant pretenders Brandenburg and Palatinate-Neuburg; and a great European war seemed inevitable. But at just this moment, Henry was assassinated by a Catholic fanatic. Was it the action of a loner? The supporters of an international Protestant alliance doubted it; they regarded the murder as the heinous act of a Catholic conspiracy, encouraged by Spain and the pope. Their suspicion hardly diminished when the new French administration took a more cautious course and tried to arrange a double marriage between the French and Spanish dynasties. The end of France's alliance with the Republic seemed imminent.

Oldenbarnevelt's faith in the French alliance was not swayed, however, by these developments. Although the influence of the pro-Spanish faction had now visibly increased, he believed that political reality would prevent the French from forsaking the Republic in favor of Spain. He proved to be right; France continued to support the Republic after 1621, and in 1635, it even went to war against Spain. But if the future vindicated Oldenbarnevelt's views, they were not widely accepted at the time. Those Protestants who were convinced that France had switched sides had difficulty making the distinction between a pro-French and pro-Spanish position. For them, statesmen like Oldenbarnevelt, who supported the French alliance through thick and thin, could only raise suspicions. Were they not secret friends of Spain?

These rising suspicions against Oldenbarnevelt, while serious, need not have led to fatal consequences for the pensionary. Time would tell who was right. But another reason for distrusting Oldenbarnevelt, which surfaced during the religious disputes of the Twelve Years' Truce, would strengthen these initial suspicions and seal his fate.

Religious Divisions

The religious disputes within the Republic had, as such, nothing to do with international politics. They stemmed from changes in the Reformed church, which had become increasingly Calvinistic since its formation in 1572. The church's doctrinal unity was one of the most important aims of the Calvinists; they desired that all Reformed pastors support Reformed doctrinal statements, namely the Heidelberg Catechism (1563) and the Belgic Confession (1561). This occasionally created local problems, especially when city authorities regarded these demands as infringing on their own prerogatives. But it seemed that this problem might disappear over time, as the older generation, who had been raised in a time of greater doctrinal freedom, died out. Calvinism seemed established enough to ensure that every new minister would have to support the Reformed confessions.

These expectations, however, were not met. A new critic within the Reformed church, the theologian Jacobus Arminius, began to raise questions about the truth of Reformed doctrines. At his initiative, the discussion was reopened, particularly in regard to its most controversial belief – Calvin's doctrine of election (God choosing people for eternal salvation) and reprobation (God choosing people for eternal damnation). Calvinism was premised on the belief that human beings had lost their capacity to do good ever since Adam and Eve had sinned in the Garden of Eden. They were inclined by nature to hate God and their neighbors. They had lost the power to resist evil. Thus their only hope of salvation was through God's grace. Some received this grace, others did not. For reasons of his own, God himself determined who would be saved. But those who were elected (chosen) by God could have every confidence that they would see eternal life.

This doctrine was striking because it was a radical break with the old notion that religion is really just another name for virtue, in which the believer tries to be good in order to attain salvation. For Calvinism, virtue was not a precondition for salvation, but its effect. The saved would live out their lives in thankfulness and in obedience to God's commandments. The doctrine can also be called biblical, because it has its basis in the New Testament, particularly in Paul's Epistle to the Romans. But it was not a logical doctrine: if people can only be saved by God's own electing grace, are they guilty of the sins they are helpless to prevent? Why is one person saved and another doomed?

Paul himself was content to let the dilemma stand, and so were the Calvinists. The doctrine does not solve the tension between divine election and personal responsibility, but insists that both are true. Election is grace, and yet damnation is based on guilt. It was on this point that Arminius had his reservations, and he attempted to develop another doctrine of election: the saved were those people who God knew would believe. For Arminius, therefore, God's decision to choose (election) stemmed from a person's decision to believe. For his Calvinist opponents, however, faith was a gift, given to those God had chosen to save. The difference between these two views was not only crystal clear, but easy to understand. Pastors could explain the issue from the pulpit, enabling every church member in the Republic to choose sides in this theological debate.

This was the last thing Holland's leaders wanted. Their own ideal for the church was still the open, libertine model of the late sixteenth century. For them, it was obvious that there must be room in the church for both opinions. But it soon became apparent that the governing bodies of the Reformed church tended to oppose Arminius's position, and to close church offices to his supporters. When Arminians complained of this situation to the States of Holland in their "Remonstrance" of 1610, they found a sympathetic ear. The conflict between the Remonstrants, named after their statement of beliefs, and their foes the Contra-Remonstrants, soon came to a head.

The Reformed church was now badly divided This was not the last conflict to afflict the church during the Republic, but it was the last to result in a church split, not least because authorities made sure it would never happen again. But what happened in the 1610s was another story, one closely linked to the foreign policy of the Republic. Oldenbarnevelt was at once both the great champion of the alliance with France and the great protector of the Remonstrant minority in the Reformed church. For the Calvinists, Arminianism was a serious heresy. What if the one sin were the consequence of the other? And Oldenbarnevelt not only wanted Arminians to be tolerated but to be given a position of equality within the church. Was this perhaps a sign that he was moving toward a kind of toleration which would ultimately include even the Catholics? But if Catholics gained their religious freedom, then the great barrier to peace with Spain would be removed. As a result, Rome and Spain would soon be masters of the Republic. For many Calvinists, a secret plan to surrender the Republic could be the only explanation for Oldenbarnevelt's otherwise inexplicable indulgence toward the Remonstrant heresy.

Not everybody took this twisted reasoning to its extreme logical conclusion, but there were many who could find no noble motive in Oldenbarnevelt's ecclesiastical policy. Led by him, the States of Holland wanted both parties to be completely reconciled to each other. It was not enough for the States to maintain a purely formal ecclesiastical unity, in which Remonstrants and Contra-Remonstrants would, in effect, set up two separate churches within the Reformed church, each with its own buildings and pastors. Instead the States wanted both parties to sit in church next to each other, listen to each others' sermons and partake of Holy Communion together. In substance, what they wanted was a reorganization of the church into the old libertine model. The Calvinists had fought hard to create a church which monitored and guided the doctrines and life of church members. But Oldenbarnevelt wanted them to leave the determination of what was true and false doctrine to the secular authorities: the States, not the church, would decide what was acceptable doctrine and behavior. Under this arrangement, the church would be forced to allow persons whom it judged unworthy to sit at the Lord's Table to partake in Holy Communion.

Many Calvinists found this completely unacceptable, and it led to splits in numerous locales. In Alkmaar, Gouda, Brielle, Rotterdam, Schoonhoven, and The Hague, Contra-Remonstrants refused to attend Reformed services. They attended church in nearby villages, or called their own gatherings in barns and warehouses. It became apparent that the States had saddled the church with a burden that it was unwilling to bear. The States of Holland, therefore, had two options. First, it could admit its defeat and let the church decide its own affairs. But this option was rejected by Oldenbarnevelt and his supporters; for them, the state's authority over the church was a principle that could not be surrendered. Second, if the church refused to bow before state authority, the only option was coercion – using violence if necessary.

The States chose this solution, both willingly and unwillingly. On the one hand, they believed they had the right to force a solution. The church was simply too important to leave to the clergy. The state had to have the authority to determine the parameters of the church. Of course, this also meant that it was obligated to maintain and defend these parameters. The government would use its own means to do this, including the meting out of punishment to those who resisted its authority. On the other hand, the States recognized the problem of using secular authority and law to restore order in the church. It smacked too much of violating people's freedom of conscience and was at variance with their own cherished principles of tolerance. But if the church was not itself willing to be tolerant, then the state would have to violate its own principles. It would have to force the church to be tolerant.

In the so-called Sharp Resolution of August 1617, the States accordingly directed that cities be free to enlist soldiers to suppress any ecclesiastical disturbances. Local garrisons could also be used for this purpose, and their commanders were ordered to unconditionally obey the wishes of the local magistrates.

This resolution moved Maurits to action. Now there would have to be a split in the state, just

The execution of Oldenbarnevelt, 13 May 1619.
(Atlas van Stolk, Rotterdam.)

IVSTITIE AEN IAN VAN OLDENBARNEVELT GESCHIET,

as there was in the church, he wrote Willem Lodewijk. He was particularly distressed that soldiers would be forced to repress the Reformed citizenry. It seemed unbelievable, but the Sharp Resolution fit neatly into a policy which aimed at surrendering the Republic to Spain. For Maurits, therefore, the resolution was a confirmation of his worst fears. He could no longer trust Oldenbarnevelt.

The summer of 1617 was the turning point in the religious disputes. From then on, Maurits actively sought to support the Contra-Remonstrants and to bring about the downfall of Oldenbarnevelt's party. He did this with the same caution and slowness that marked his military career. He gradually reduced Oldenbarnevelt's influence in the States-General of the Republic, and eventually in the States of Holland. In doing so, Maurits could count on popular opinion, on Oldenbarnevelt's political foes, and on the English ambassador and his sovereign King James I, who were deeply suspicious of the pensionary's pro-French policy. But most of all, Maurits could rely on the fact that the army was first and foremost loyal to him, its captain-general, and not to the city magistrates or the States of Holland. With this all-important advantage, Maurits could prevent the civil war that some feared; the very threat of force was enough to create a new government in The Hague, as the councils of state were occupied by new majorities that were supportive of Maurits and the Contra-Remonstrants. Maurits's efforts reached a successful conclusion in August 1618, when he had himself instructed by the States-General to place Oldenbarnevelt and his closest associates in detention. The prince had brought a decisive end to the conflict.

A New Arrangement

The victors faced two challenges. They had to create a new political and ecclesiastical order, and they had to decide the fate of their prisoners. Their solution to the second problem has taken the fancy of historians, and with some merit. It is difficult to imagine a statesman who served the Dutch Republic with greater distinction than Oldenbarnevelt, and yet he is the only one to have been publicly executed. His death sentence can only be understood in the light of the deep suspicions that we have sketched above. His accusers were unable to see that their charges against him lacked any basis in fact. At the same time, it is fair to say that Oldenbarnevelt pursued a dead-end policy in the last years of his life, defying the expressed will of the majority. Even in countries with no democratic systems of government, such a course usually ends in failure, since the government needs to rely on coercion and violence to achieve its aims. The government can only succeed in this if its ability to coerce is nearly limitless. In Holland in particular, and the Republic in general, the state lacked the means to coerce the majority. Oldenbarnevelt overstepped the boundaries and paid the price with his life.

The pensionary based his defense on the fact that he was the appointed administrator of Holland and that his policies had enjoyed the support of the States of Holland. As such, he owed his loyalty to the States of Holland, not to the States-General of the Republic. His argument was, from a legal standpoint, very strong, even indisputable. Oldenbarnevelt, a schooled jurist, fully realized that he could wish for no better defense. It was in his interest to represent the conflict as a struggle between Holland and the Generality, in which he presented himself as the principled defender of regional sovereignty. In reality, the pragmatic politician Oldenbarnevelt had cared little about such principles. He did what was best for Holland, and if another province behaved in a manner incompatible with Holland's interest, he did not hesitate in using the Generality to force that province to redirect its course. His influence was so great both in Holland and the States-General that it was in fact the pensionary who gave direction to the power of the States-General. This instrument, however, slipped from his hands during the Truce, when the majority of Their High Mightinesses turned against him. From this time on, Oldenbarnevelt pursued his policies from within Holland, not out of principle, but because he had no choice. That Holland had a formal right to determine its own course was merely a propitious circumstance which Oldenbarnevelt fully exploited during his trial. But this hardly made Oldenbarnevelt the champion of a great political principle. He was an ingenious opportunist who took every advantage which fate accorded him.

There was no political reform in the Republic after 1618. Even if Oldenbarnevelt's successors, men of considerably lesser ability, had been able to bring about such change, no one would have felt the need for it. It was enough to solve practical problems – especially those pertaining to the church.

In 1618, a national synod (church council) convened at Dordrecht to deal with the divisions within the church. As expected, the Synod of Dordrecht (or Dordt) condemned the Remonstrants, excising them from the Reformed church. The Remonstrants founded their own church which was initially vulnerable to persecution but which, in the course of ten or fifteen years, received public recognition as a legitimate church. The triumph of the Contra-Remonstrants, meanwhile, had the full backing of the secular authorities. In this respect, the new leaders of the Republic differed from Oldenbarnevelt. But they, too, were opposed to an independent church which determined its own course without state oversight. It would be wrong, therefore, to regard 1618 as the year that the church triumphed over the state. Still, the change was significant: Oldenbarnevelt's successors enjoyed the confidence of the church, and they were, accordingly, better suited to keep order and peace in the church. They were prepared to accept the triumph of the Calvinists over the libertines. The authorities did not, however, put an end to the conflict between these two groups. The more liberal latitudinarians and more orthodox precisianists would continue to battle each other, with the authorities often siding with the former.

But in 1618 this was not yet the case. The authorities in The Hague were now expected to orient their foreign policy toward Protestant England and away from Catholic France. The French deeply regretted Oldenbarnevelt's fall from power, while the English had always supported Maurits. But efforts to change the course of the Republic's foreign policy quickly foundered. While the French and Dutch were still tied together by a common enemy, English and Dutch interests hardly coin-

cided. The Republic, for instance, wanted to
lend aid to the Protestant princes in Germany when the Thirty Years' War broke out

The Synod of Dordrecht, 13 November 1618.
(Atlas van Stolk, Rotterdam.)

in 1618; its leaders recognized that what happened in Germany was
crucial to their own future. But King James I of England was too indifferent to continental conflicts to offer anything but verbal support. On
the other hand, the English were very interested in the Republic's economic power, which threatened their own commercial ambitions, and
the English government hoped that the new regime in The Hague
might address their economic grievances. Their hopes proved idle:
Contra-Remonstrants proved just as unwilling to negotiate on the cloth
trade, fishing, and commerce with the Indies as their Remonstrant predecessors had been.

The fate of the Indies was the most spectacular point of difference between the English and the Dutch. By the time of the Truce, the United East India Company had begun to demonstrate its potential and responsibilities. Dutch merchants had formed this company in 1602 in order to reduce the risks of Asian trade, which were too great for individuals or small groups to bear. In the first place, a voyage to the Indies took months, and merchants had to wait a couple of years before they saw a return on their investment – a lag time far in excess of any other commercial venture. In the second place, ships bound for the Indies traveled through waters claimed by the Spanish, requiring that investors adequately provide for the defense of their vessels. Fitting these ships with sufficient manpower and guns cost more than was necessary for ordinary maritime ventures. In the third place, the shipper needed to be assured of a safe harbor where his ships could anchor undisturbed until they were loaded and ready to sail home. Because they could not predict their time of arrival, shippers could not count on arriving in the right season. For this reason, it was advantageous for these harbors to include warehouses where the desired cargo could be stored out of season until the ships arrived. All of this required a strong organization and a larger infrastructure than even the richest merchant could afford.

The construction of this infrastructure took years to develop. The Dutch side of the organization began in 1602, when the company was established with five chambers, each from the most important trading cities, and a central board of directors called the Heren XVII (Seventeen Gentlemen) who lived in Amsterdam. Soon, however, it became evident that a directory was also needed in the Indies. The company accordingly created the grandiose-sounding position of governor-general, charged with leading the company posts in the Indies. The first governor-general ensconced himself at the start in the Moluccas, since the spice trade was the most lucrative for the company. But it soon became desirable to find a new location that was closer to the travel routes. Governor-General Jan Pietersz. Coen chose the city of Jocatra on Java, which he seized by force and renamed Batavia, in honor of the Germanic tribe that the Dutch considered their ancestors. It would remain the administrative center of the Dutch East Indies until the 1940s.

In doing so, Coen followed his own instincts more than the instructions of the company, which had no interest in establishing a permanent Dutch colony in the Indies. They were strictly interested in trade, and wanted no further entanglements. But the men charged with expanding trade in the Indies did not always see a way to increase profit without violence. Coen himself had no qualms in using force, and his most accomplished successors followed his violent example. They could not see how to conduct trade in this strange world, far away from home, without using force. They thought it necessary to coerce Asian princes and merchants to keep to their contracts; and other Europeans, too, needed to be persuaded that they were best off buying Moluccan goods at the Amsterdam stock exchange instead of venturing to the Indies themselves. For Coen, European competitors needed to be scared away; it made little difference to him whether the vessels he attacked belonged to the Spanish enemy or to the English ally. Despite instructions to the contrary from the homeland, Coen saw it as his task to keep the company's monopoly intact by keeping all rival ships out of the East Indies.

Thus even during the Synod of Dordrecht, which was backed by the English king and represented a high point in Anglo-Dutch relations, shadows were darkening the alliance. They deepened in 1621 when the Republic resumed the war against Spain. James I was willing to negotiate an end to the war in Germany, but it soon became clear that he was not going to help the Protestants there —even though his son-in-law, the elector of the Palatinate, was now the leader of the German Protestant cause. James thus proved unwilling to share the costs of war with the Seven Provinces, and the Republic's own war effort was hardly helped by the English position.

Maurits's last years were not his most successful. His own energy had diminished, and his reputation was tarnished by the execution of Oldenbarnevelt. The head of the House of Orange was the symbol of national unity, but Maurits could no longer unify the country – he would never be able to regain the confidence of those he had defeated. A failed attempt by Remonstrants to assassinate him in 1623 is evidence enough of this, and only his death in 1625 made reconciliation possible.

4. The Gold of the Golden Age (1625-1648)

Consolidation

The Golden Age is Paradise Lost: the time in which all people were happy. At least that is what people once believed – that an idyllic Golden Age existed before the present age of injustice, violence, hunger and poverty. Peace and prosperity made daily life a pleasure in that blessed but bygone age.

This notion of a Golden Age has a religious quality to it, and because of this it harbors a certain recklessness, crowning a normal piece of history as an epoch of unsurpassable excellence. The Golden Age of the Republic was a time of growth and prosperity, but it was hardly an age of peace and unity, and happiness was just as elusive then as it has been since. If we must speak of a Golden Age, it must be by comparison with other periods: at no other time in Dutch history was there such a rich concentration of human achievement. The land of Rembrandt and Hals was also the land of the poets Vondel and Hooft, the scholars Grotius and Vossius, and the engineers Beeckman and Stevin. The political might of the Republic expanded as Dutch trade and shipping reached global proportions. And if it is true that Dutch political power has seldom been equal to the economic and cultural significance of the Netherlands, then this part of the seventeenth century is certainly an exception to this rule.

It is a striking exception, to be sure, but is it surprising? The Republic at the time Maurits's successor Frederik Hendrik was certainly far different from the rebellious provinces which had declared themselves a republic in 1588. At that time, their future seemed very much in doubt. Within a decade, however, it became clear that the new

Map of Amsterdam dating from 1645.
(Gemeentearchief, Amsterdam.)

state would survive; it possessed the resources and potential to gain a permanent place among the established European states. It was this same potential that transformed the Republic, over the course of the seventeenth century, into a great power.

In 1588, international conditions were favorable for the young state as it was able to rely upon both French and English support. The Republic's dependence on these powers was evident in the first decade of the seventeenth century; when compelled to fight Spain alone, the Republic clearly lost the initiative. Spain was also able to press its advantage after the opening of hostilities in 1621. By the 1620s, the Republic's fortunes were tied to the vicissitudes of the war in Germany, and there was a good deal of concern in The Hague about the Catholic victories achieved there. In general, however, the Republic benefitted from the extension of the war into Germany, especially because it ensured French intervention on the side of the Protestants. By 1635, France and the Seven Provinces concluded a formal alliance. By that time, Frederik Hendrik had proven his mettle, capturing 's-Hertogenbosch in 1629 and, after his campaign down the Maas, Maastricht in 1632. The latter city pushed the permanent boundaries of the Republic far to the south, and from these new positions, the alliance with France seem to promise new opportunities to seize southern territory.

If anyone could bring such a military campaign to its successful conclusion, it was Frederik Hendrik. As a military leader, he was equal to his older brother Maurits; as a political leader, he far surpassed him. In particular, Frederik Hendrik had the knack of getting people to work together in harmony, and this gift ensured that he – more than any other Orange – encountered little opposition to his rule. Under him, the prestige of the stadholder increased, both inside the country and out.

England remained aloof of the war in Europe, increasingly consumed by its own growing domestic troubles. The conflict between the king and Parliament, exploding into civil war in 1542, diverted English attention from continental developments. Civil strife in England hardly hurt the Dutch; on the contrary. It is no coincidence that it was precisely during the first half of the seventeenth century that the Republic was able develop into a great economic power. The English, consumed as they were with their own internal problems, were in no position to fully pursue their economic rivalry with the Dutch. France, too, experienced serious internal tensions until the 1650s, including open rebellion and civil war. That, too, gave the Republic every opportunity to consolidate its enviable economic position.

The Republic was itself engaged in war, but that formed no hindrance to the further expansion of trade and shipping. Many merchants, in fact, looked forward to the end of the Truce in 1621, because they believed war would be good for business. The East India Company had proven itself a profitable venture. Would a West Indian company be less so? The government had prohibited the creation of such an entity during the Truce, fearful that a Dutch commercial presence in the Americas would provoke the Spanish to break the cease-fire. With the recommencement of war, however, there was every reason to encourage a West India Company, and it was granted a charter in 1621.

The fortunes of East and West India Companies diverged sharply from each other. The United East India Company was an enterprise which regarded the seizure of territory as a means to an end, and which – despite this initial strategy – laid the basis for what became one of the largest colonial empires in the world. The West India Company, on the other hand, aimed explicitly at colonizing territories. Unfortunately for the company, its most important possessions, Brazil and the North American colony of New Netherlands, were respectively seized by the Portuguese and English within a few decades. Surinam and the Netherlands Antilles were the only possessions in the Western Hemisphere to remain under Dutch rule over the long run. As a result, the West India Company won neither large colonies nor substantial profits for the Dutch. Its only moment of glory was a feat of arms: Piet Heyn's capture of the Spanish silver fleet in 1628, and even this accomplishment would have sunk into oblivion had not J.P. Heye written a popular song about Heyn in the nineteenth century. Heyn and the exploits of the West India Company have their place among the heroics of the seventeenth century. But the company barely contributed to the commercial growth of the period.

The Dutch made most of their profits in their own hemisphere. Their skippers were ubiquitous, sailing to all harbors in and around

Europe, from Aleppo to Archangel. Their techniques and methods were much the same as they had been in the sixteenth century, but the demand for their own products, both agricultural and industrial, had increased. Dutch merchants, however, seldom made phenomenal profits. Getting rich quick – and its attendant risks – was not the Dutch way. An exception was the "mad tulip trade" of the 1630s, when tulip bulbs were sold for fantastic prices and speculation was rampant. By 1637, the craze was over. The great merchants were little affected by the speculation, preferring as they did safer investments and more evenly distributed risk. Dutch trade and shipping continued to rest on the broad financial basis that had been established in the late sixteenth century.

Because there were so many participants in trade, a wide spectrum of the population, both the wealthy and not-so-wealthy, could make a modest profit in the country's prosperity. This in turn stimulated greater demand for products beyond people's basic needs. Inventories taken of the farmhouses and townhouses of the middle classes often included silver spoons, silver buckles, and silver locks for their family Bibles. For persons of modest income, there was no Golden Age, but there was, at least, a little bit of silver. For persons of sizable income, the possibilities were greater, and it was primarily their material and artistic consumption which gave the Republic of the seventeenth century its reputation as a place where great art and culture flourished.

The Nature of "Dutch" Culture

We associate this exceptional concentration of human achievement with a time and with a country: seventeenth century Dutch art and culture. The seventeenth-century designation is relatively easy to justify: although great artistry popped up before and after the century, the heavy concentration of talent was unique to the 1600s. The "Dutch" label is more difficult to explain. In the first place, it must be used in its post-Burgundian sense: it refers only to the Republic, not to Antwerp or Brussels. But it can hardly be denied that some of the greatest names in this Dutch culture belonged to southern refugees of the first and second generations. Is it really possible that these men brought nothing but their own Flemish, Walloon, and Brabantine names from the cultural inheritance which the southern provinces had produced? The culture they helped form was no less "Dutch" because of their contributions. But it was a culture with a debt to the inhabitants of the old Seventeen Provinces, and not just from the new seven.

There is a second problem with the term "Dutch." The British historian Charles Wilson has pointed out that the seventeenth-century Dutch were exceedingly adept at applying and devising innovations developed elsewhere. Every large textbook of European history mentions the Amsterdam Exchange Bank, which could supply its customers with a wide variety of foreign coins, lend credit to large and (in certain circumstances) small clients, and introduce its depositors to the ease of transferring money across accounts without using cash. As an institution, it deserved the world fame it received. But the whole idea of an exchange bank was Italian, just as it had been the Italians who developed marine insurance and the double ledger. The same might be said of the new fortress building that began in the late sixteenth century. Maurits's right hand man, the engineer Simon Stevin, was without equal in the Republic, but on a European scale, he was only one of many men who contributed to the new science of engineering.

Dutch culture was at its most innovative when it altered European developments to fit local needs. Local is the right word here, because it indicates that the Dutch of that time possessed a highly developed ability to innovate according to the needs of their own region. No matter where the discovery or invention was made, they made use of it by adopting it to their own peculiar circumstances. This is true of fortress building and the organization of trade, and it is no less true of cartography and water management. Dutch techniques profited from what had begun elsewhere. But what is more Dutch than a Blaeu atlas or a North Holland polder landscape?

Culture, however, is not merely innovation. It is always built on existing traditions. There has been considerable dispute whether Dutch culture of the seventeenth century was Erasmian – inspired by the tolerant humanism of the great scholar – or Calvinist. It is a discussion that undoubtedly could continue through eternity, but it is like arguing over what matters most for a good grain harvest: the climate, the land, or the farmer. To pit Erasmus against Calvin is to introduce a false dilemma. European culture of the seventeenth century rested on two pillars: Christianity and the classics of Graeco-Roman antiquity. They were inseparable, not because they cannot be separated, but because European history had bound them together.

Both Erasmus and Calvin illustrate this point. Take away Christianity, and Erasmus is no longer himself. Separate Calvin from classical traditions, and he is unrecognizable. Both elements, the classical, brought to new heights by Erasmus; and the Christian, as influenced by John Calvin, were visible in seventeenth-century Dutch culture. But both were broader and more multifaceted than this pair of names suggests. The classical tradition encompassed more than the concerns of Erasmus, and the Christian reflected the high degree of religious tolerance in the Republic too much to be associated with only one denomination, even one so important as the Calvinism of the Reformed church.

The intersections of these two traditions differed, of course, from person to person, and had different effects on the art and science produced in the period. But the differences are hard to pick up in the work produced. For example, it is impossible to tell, on the basis of observing the art alone, which Dutch painters belonged to which churches. In literature it is easier, but those without prejudice will also have to admit serious difficulties. How "Catholic" are the rhymed psalms of the Catholic Vondel, the Republic's greatest poet? How Calvinistic is the moralizing verse of his counterpart Cats – who was also read in the Southern Netherlands? One might wonder if their seventeenth century readers had finer intuitions than we – or whether they bothered with the question at all. Whatever the case, most consumers of Dutch culture were themselves schooled in Europe's classical-Christian civilization. They thereby had access to everything that was built on these traditions, and even if they were unfamiliar with the rules normally followed by Dutch authors and artists, they understood the basic aim of the work.

Seventeenth-century literature intended to carry a message to the reader. Poetry ought not merely be the expression of an individual emotion, but a striking expression of universal truth. And because that truth was universal, poets could appeal to all people, regardless of their particular religious beliefs. Literature and poetry that was oriented toward the more particular needs of a specific faith did exist, but it was often of lesser quality. The countless Mennonite hymnals of the seventeenth century, for instance, testify to a vibrant spiritual life, but not to great artistic power. They sprang directly from the Mennonite congregations and were written by ordinary members of the church. The harmony of content and form, sought by the true poet, was beyond their ability.

The search for harmony was implicit in all the arts and sciences. The noblest idea must be presented in the most sublime form. "A word fitly spoken is like apples of gold in a setting of silver." The denizens of the seventeenth century would not only have recognized this maxim as a verse from the Proverbs of Solomon, but would have subscribed to it as an expression of their own ideal. How this maxim helped give form to harmony, however, is not immediately evident. What seventeenth-century culture aspired to become is perhaps made most clear through the help of two men who enjoyed very high standing in that century but who resonated much less among later generations: Jacob Cats and Daniël Heinsius.

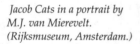

Jacob Cats in a portrait by M.J. van Mierevelt. (Rijksmuseum, Amsterdam.)

It is true that Cats's name is still known in the Netherlands, but is hardly well-regarded. This in itself says little, since today's average readers have read as much of Cats as they have of the more highly acclaimed Vondel and Huygens: nothing. But those who have read Cats will not remember many poetic high points. He was neither eloquent nor profound. And yet neither was he superficial or weak. Every line had to have twelve metrical feet, and each pair of lines had to rhyme with each other. These rules did not enhance the literary quality of his expression. But Cats did know that he must reach his readers, and that he had to say things in a way that would keep their attention. That meant that he had to amuse them. Cats sought a large public, and hence avoided overly subtle jokes. He penned none of the hidden double entendres or the ingenious wordplays invented by the much more gifted, but much less accessible Constantijn Huygens. Cats wanted to instruct his readers through moral lessons, and was thus constrained from doing anything adventurous. Those who desired something more erotically tinted would have to learn Italian. Cats did not want to be a rhymed variant of Boccaccio or Aretino; he preferred easygoing humor, in an earthy style with no shame for the body or its functions.

All of this explains why Cats was widely read; it does not explain why he was praised as a poet. That answer is easy: he was a master of harmony. Cats's name was established with his *Love Images* of 1618. It is a collection of emblemata, that is, of prints with explanatory texts. This genre, too, had Italian origins, but was particularly popular in the Dutch Republic. People could look at the print to learn a lesson taken from every-day life, or to discover the symbol of love in the print, or to find a religious application for what they saw and read. Cats labored hard to give each picture three different levels of meaning: for the young, there was an amorous element; for the middle-aged, a social message; and for the old, a spiritual component. Cats was recognized for his skill in harmonizing word and image. Displays of virtuosity do not make a poet great, and Cats would never become great. But his work conformed to the taste of his times.

Daniël Heinsius, too, was a virtuoso. A professor in Leiden of classical letters, Heinsius cultivated a great acquaintance of ancient texts, allowing him to imitate the style of the ancient Greeks and Romans. This was as people believed it should be; the ancients were thought to have attained a harmony of form and content which had not been replicated since. Reading their works could be inspirational, but it could also be discouraging. Who could possibly hope to follow their stunning example? Heinsius could – and even exceeded their accomplishments. His own culture was not only classical, but also Christian, and thus comprehended truth at a higher level than Graeco-Roman antiquity itself had been able to grasp. Heinsius's first substantial work was a Christian tragedy, written in Seneca's style. It was widely praised for its pure Latin – but also because it offered more spiritually than the pagan philosopher could have. The great harmony of classical tragedy had been brought to a higher level of perfection by Heinsius.

The Latin dramas of Heinsius are forgotten. Only learned scholars read him now, and they make the effort in order to better understand

Daniël Heinsius; engraving by
W. Swanenburg.
(Iconographisch Bureau, The Hague.)

the seventeenth century. No one today would think to read Heinsius for truth and beauty. But let us keep that key word in mind: harmony. The culture of the seventeenth century was suffused with it.

Dutch Painting

The degree of harmony attained by the seventeenth century creators of cultural products was not, however, decisive in determining their reputation for posterity. For that reason, we cannot say that seventeenth-century Dutch painting – the most enduring branch of Dutch art – exhibited the purest form of harmony. The permanence of this genre is, of course, relative; the historian A.M. van der Woude estimates that there must have been literally millions of paintings, of which only a fraction have survived. The buyers of these paintings, presumably, had little notion that they were worth more than the few guilders they had paid for them. Still, the sheer number of these art works is instructive; it suggests that most painters did not set out to satisfy the refined taste of an erudite connoisseur. Rather, paintings were a mass product, containing simple meanings that were accessible to large numbers of people.

This does not mean that Dutch painting was merely simple imitation of observed reality. We no longer classify Dutch painting of the seventeenth century, as people used to, as "realist." We now have more of an eye for its parallel with the emblematic. An emblem introduced an idea that could be expressed in words by a poet. A painting, however, could also give a wordless interpretation of an idea, enabling the beholder to grasp a higher moral truth. Paintings of the period frequently served in this capacity. A painting spoke its own language; its meaning was not superficially transparent, but its message was clear to the initiated. Such a painting demanded ingenuity and knowledge, like one of Huygens's epigrams. His readers attain their full reward only after investing much mental acuity. Those who wish to study Cats in the same manner run the danger of turning his plodding phrases into a deep wisdom which never sprang from within him, or of discovering furtive wordplays which would have made him blush.

The same can be said of many Dutch painters. Their language of forms has recently been redeciphered by the Utrecht historian E. de Jongh and other contemporary scholars, giving us a fuller understanding of the real intentions of seventeenth-century artists. At the same time, we should not forget that these scholars warn us to exercise great caution in interpreting their works. A rose may be the symbol of love, or may – like other flowers – depict the fleeting nature of life. The correct interpretation may depend on the presence of other symbols, like a skull, for example. And it is entirely possible that a painting has no deeper meaning at all, especially those paintings intended for the mass market. Paintings had to find buyers. The skipper from Westgraftdijk, the baker from Delfshaven, or the farmer from Purmerland purchased paintings, but they were unschooled in detecting the hidden significance of painting. Many paintings, therefore, carried little more than the obvious meaning, to be understood to anyone viewing them.

These introductory remarks are important if we wish to develop a coherent picture of a given period. They give us a better sense of the period's art works, making it easier to judge their nature and their place. Usually, these insights are most useful in understanding minor and mediocre talent. Those with the least originality, and hence those

Rembrandt van Rijn, Self-Portrait as the Apostle Paul, *1661. (Rijksmuseum, Amsterdam.)*

with the greatest debt to others, give the sharpest profiles of their age. The truly great, however, cannot be measured in this way. Knowledge of their historical context is vital if we want to plumb the depths of their life and work, but such study is seldom a prerequisite for admiring their accomplishments. Reading Shakespeare while knowing nothing of Elizabethan England may have its disadvantages, but it will not prevent the reader from recognizing a great spirit. So it is with the man whose name is most deeply attached to the Republic's Golden Age: Rembrandt Harmensz. van Rijn.

Those searching for what made Rembrandt such an extraordinary painter, especially those who follow the art critics, will easily feel a sense of helplessness. Rembrandt's work, we read, is expressive and powerful, natural and harmonious, with the subtlety of a virtuoso. Describing Rembrandt's work seems to require superlatives. But this does not serve as an explanation of his genius. Constantijn Huygens was not only one of the first people to be struck by Rembrandt's greatness, but one of the first to attempt to capture it in words, after seeing the painting in which Judas returns the thirty pieces of silver to the high priests:

> I wish to use the painting of the remorseful Judas, bringing back the silver coins to the high priest which had been the price for the guiltless Lord, to exemplify his work. Let all Italy and the earliest Antiquity try to match it with something as impressive and worthy of admiration. The gesture of that one despairing Judas – not to mention the many other noteworthy figures on this cloth – I repeat, of that one Judas, who raves, moans, begging for forgiveness but without hope, or whose countenance yet expresses hope; his wild face, the pulled hairs, the torn clothing, the wrung arms, the hands tied together so tightly that they bleed, falling to his knees in a blind surge, while his whole body writhes in a savage lament, this figure I would measure against every graceful work of art that the centuries have brought forth.

Huygens's words have been cited often, but they are particularly useful to us in demonstrating the significance of Rembrandt. Huygens saw with seventeenth-century eyes, and what he and his contemporaries most admired in a painter was his ability to give an emotional intensity to a dramatic scene through the gestures and expressions of its participants. He found this in Rembrandt's *Judas*: a masterwork of expression and harmony. Huygens was also a good representative of the seventeenth century in that he knew his Bible. He had formed his own impression of Judas's person and character, and knew the role he had played in the history of salvation. That made his confrontation with the canvas all the more intense; the man was no stranger to him. Conversely, the painting made the Bible story more alive to him, since Rembrandt had enabled him to more fully understand the figure of Judas.

Huygens saw Rembrandt's Judas, the fallen apostle, with all the depth of his own unique betrayal and remorse. But Huygens also saw a person in despair, a person from his own time, a person of any age. This timeless quality has made Rembrandt comprehensible through the centuries. The vital, the subtle, the harmonious, and (especially in his later works) the monumental are the means by which he causes us to see. But each generation sees Rembrandt in a another way; they see new images

and discover new interpretations which enrich our understanding of him. This is true of all the greats, including Hals
and Vermeer. Vermeer's young women and Hals's small
children remain with us because we still encounter them
daily. And how many names could we add if we just
restricted ourselves to only the best known: Jan Steen,

Rembrandt van Rijn, Judas
Returns the Thirty Pieces
of Silver to the High
Priests and the Elders,
*1629. (National Portrait
Gallery, London.)*

Gerard Dou, Adriaen van Ostade ... But even then we do an injustice to
the painters of the seventeenth century. Various works once ascribed to
Hals are actually the creations of Pieter Claesz. Soutman, whose name
is but a footnote in art history surveys. Still, the hosts of artists and the
wealth of accomplishment cannot prevent the history of Dutch culture
in the seventeenth century from being described, first and foremost, as
the land of Rembrandt.

Freedom and Restraint

Both painting and literature served more than one public. The drive to
attain harmony in form and content, in Christian and classical, in word
and image, was especially intense in the highest levels of creative
accomplishment. Was the same true for scholarship? Was harmony considered central to that enterprise? We must be careful in constructing a
response. In one sense, the answer is unambiguously in the affirmative;
Daniël Heinsius has just taught us that. But we must not only think of
harmony as the happy union of the classical and Christian traditions.
Both art and scholarship need to have significance – in the fullest sense
of that word. If a poem or painting contains a message, then it has a
practical effect. It does something for everyone who understands the

Hugo de Groot (Grotius), portrait by M.J. van Mierevelt, 1631. (Rijksmuseum, Amsterdam.)

given work. In this sense, we can say that seventeenth-century scholarship, too, wanted to accomplish something. It wanted to produce something that would have practical application.

Let us use the example of one of the most famous scholars of the seventeenth century: Hugo Grotius. If we call him a scholar, it is because we wish to avoid a tighter definition which would limit his importance. Grotius is best known as a jurist, but he may also be included as an important historian, and he himself may have considered his theological work as the most important contribution of his life. With Grotius, too, harmony is at work: the true scholar cannot be confined to one discipline but must be master of them all, fruitful in all fields of knowledge. Grotius understood this ideal like no other. But he could do more – he knew how to use his scholarship as a political instrument.

Accordingly, most of his books aim at achieving a practical goal. His erudite Latin titles, therefore, must not lead us into thinking otherwise. Grotius's *Liber de Antiquitate et Statu Reipublicae Batavae* is a political treatise. Using historical arguments, he sought to prove that the supreme power in Holland belonged to the States – not to the prince, or to the people. His *Ordinum Hollandiae ac Westfrisiae Pietas* is a defense of the church policy of Oldenbarnevelt, of whom he was a close and trusted associate. And his famous *Mare Liberum* defended the right to free trade on the open seas vis-à-vis other states, whose established or growing interests were threatened by Dutch shipping.

Grotius was thus no scholar of the ivory tower. For expressing his views he was imprisoned in the castle of Loevestein, as if to remind scholarship that it cannot serve politics unpunished. For three years he endured imprisonment until he fittingly escaped from Loevestein in a chest of books, a witness to the respect enjoyed by the freedom of the press. In Holland, much could be said or printed that could not reach the light of day in other European countries. Unlimited freedom, however, did not exist even in the United Netherlands. From a distance, the infringements on liberty seem arbitrary, but a close examination of prosecutions reveals a pattern. Once authorities had determined which policy they would pursue, they regarded divergent opinions as unacceptable. As long as politicians themselves argued over policy in The Hague, the press could join the debate – the question of negotiations with Spain, for instance, always generated a lot of heated argument. Thus in matters where the deputies of the States were themselves in disagreement, free discussion went unhindered. Once, however, the States had decided upon a course, an open exchange of ideas would only be tolerated if government authority was fully respected. Criticism of what the States might do was permitted; criticism of what the States actually did was best left unexpressed.

This was the rule that bound those who wrote and spoke. But the only ones in the Republic with access to address a large assembly were the pastors of the Reformed church. A village minister typically delivered one hundred to one hundred and fifty sermons per year. A city minister preached less, but his audience was also larger. But what is preaching exactly? The apostle Paul called it the ministry of reconciliation, and that is what preachers do: they call upon their listeners to reconcile themselves with God. They must, therefore, also exhort the congregation to put aside all things that prevent that reconciliation, so that they might henceforth live in accordance with God's commandments. In a word, preachers taught their congregations to discern good from evil.

This is precisely what any government does through its own laws, and a Christian government like the Dutch Republic set its compass toward Christian moral law. But all governments tend to compromise moral principles, since politics is the art of the possible. God's law, on the other hand, demands what is humanly impossible. For this reason, there could never be complete peace between church and state. What can be said is that the relation between the two was seldom better than in the decades following the Synod of Dordrecht. Peace had been restored to the church along the lines desired by the Calvinists. They were, accordingly, well-disposed toward the government which had delivered their victory. In any event, the political and spiritual orders could not be indifferent to each other. The Reformed church was not a state church (not everyone was forced to belong), but as a "public" church it enjoyed great privileges, and as such, it necessarily cooperated with the state.

The richest fruit of this cooperation was a new translation of the Bible, organized by the Synod and financed by the States – hence its name as the "States translation." In itself, its appearance in 1637 barely changed the lives of seventeenth-century people. They were already acquainted with the Bible. But the new translation did increase the book's clarity and utility; Dutch culture now had a translation equal in reliability and expressiveness to the best foreign translations (such as the King James Version of 1611).

It is a commonplace to say that the Bible is the most widely read book. It was nonetheless true of the Dutch Republic in the seventeenth century, and hence it is no surprise that the "States translation" had an obvious effect on the development of the Dutch language. Regardless of the city or village whose inventories we choose to examine, the Bible easily takes first place among the books owned. The Bible and the prayer book were not the only printed works to be found outside of the cultural elite, but other books were rarely owned by people of the lower classes. Nor did every household have a Bible. Roughly half of Holland's population belonged to the Reformed church in the mid-seventeenth century, and perhaps this statistic is true for all the provinces, although it is difficult to establish this with certainty. But of the Reformed half, we can say that Christianity played a large part in the culture of the common people. They read the Bible, sang psalms, listened to sermons, and were educated by the Reformed schoolmaster, who read Scripture and led the singing in church on Sundays. They were also baptized in the church, their marriages were blessed by it, and they were buried in it, that is, if they weren't menfolk who died at sea.

How much the church influenced the common people cannot be measured. But sources from Holland suggest that the life of rural inhabitants corresponded little to the popular culture of, for example, seventeenth-century France. What is particularly absent in Holland is the role male youths played, through *charivari* and other more or less draconian methods, in enforcing village traditions. This difference need not necessarily be attributed to the Reformed church; it could also have been caused by the social and economic developments which sent young men to sea, causing them to be separated from their villages for months or even years. In the coastal provinces, in fact, a large portion a working-age men labored as fishermen or sailors. This is one of the chief reasons why the street and village images of the seventeenth century prominently featured women – the men were often away. The notion that women only did housework or found salvation in the scrubbing of their doorsteps was never less true than in seventeenth-century Holland. Women were necessarily burdened with the lion's share of work in households with seafaring men; they struggled to earn money and head the household in addition to acting as housewives and mothers.

Life in the interior regions could be different – even totally different, since interregional communications between rural areas were quite limited. As a result, the particular morals and customs of each village and region could easily be maintained. The higher one's class, however, the greater contact one had with other regions. Through these higher classes, Holland's cultural influence moved east and north into other areas of the Republic. The country's elites shared a single culture, and even if it was less developed in the east, it was still part of the same culture. This unquestionably made negotiations among regional leaders easier as they met in high political council to determine the course of the Republic. Within these circles there was the perception that they belonged to the same state, something most villagers in the east and the west of the country had barely begun to comprehend.

From War to Peace

The sense of national unity developed during the war with Spain. Before the Revolt, no one would have construed those Seven Provinces as a whole, with a collective identity. But their common cause and – no less important – the joy of success had brought the seven closer together and strengthened their confidence. The Dutch could be proud of what they had achieved and could be assured that Spain would never again pose a serious danger to the Republic. If the Seven Provinces had fought the war to ensure their freedom, Frederik Hendrik had fully achieved this aim. Was it not then time to consider ending the war and making an honorable peace?

Two developments strengthened the desire for peace. The first was the course of the war in Germany, where the danger of Catholic victory had been averted. Solidarity with the Protestant cause, therefore, no longer required continuing the war. The second factor pertained to the alliance with France. Its entry into the war had broken the balance of power between the warring sides, and the advantage was now invariably on the side of the allies. In the long run, this situation could open the way to the invasion of the Southern Netherlands. But its provinces would no longer fall to the Republic as liberated territory; they would be divided among the allied victors. This posed a greater danger to the Republic, since its southern border would no longer be shared with the far-flung possessions of a declining empire like Spain, but with a victorious France which had emerged from the conflict strong enough to make its own bid for European domination. France's presence in the Southern Netherlands would not really serve the best interests of the Republic. Even if seizure of the Spanish Netherlands would give the Seven Provinces more territory, what advantage would that bring? If Antwerp became part of the Republic, then the Dutch would have to open the Scheldt to shipping and Amsterdam would gain a formidable trading rival. And if Flanders and Brabant were restored to their territorial integrity and admitted to the Republic, then The Hague's control over the Generality Lands would end. Moreover, Holland's leading position in the States-General would be challenged by the new provinces. These reasons added to the impetus for peace in the Republic, especially in Holland.

Peace was concluded in 1648, at Münster. The provisions were much the same as in 1609, only they were now made permanent. Spain formally recognized the Republic, allowing it to trade freely with the Indies, acceded to the closure of the Scheldt, and did not insist on privileges for Dutch Catholics. With such terms, the Republic could regard itself as a victor. At the same time, however, the Peace of Münster confirmed that the Republic of the Seven United Provinces would never add to its number. The Seven Provinces' common history with the southern regions was now a closed chapter.

5. The "True Freedom" (1648-1672)

William II and the European Balance of Power

The Bible tells us twice that spring was the time when kings went on campaigns. This single sentence conjures up an image of a society in

GRENZEN VAN DE REPUBLIEK IN 1648

het grondgebied van
de Republiek der
Zeven Verenigde
Nederlanden

Stad en Lande

Friesland

Drenthe

Overijssel

Hølland

Utrecht

Gelderland

Zeeland

Gelder

Vlaanderen

Brabant

Prinsbisdom
Luik

Limburg

Henegouwen

Namen

Boundaries of the Republic in 1648.   which warfare is perennial. So it was in the Netherlands during the Eighty Years' War. In winter, provi-
sioning an army was so difficult that the fighting usually ceased. But
with the coming of spring and passable roads, hostilities could begin
again. The Peace of Westphalia broke this pattern, or better: it ended it
altogether. This time it was not a temporary cease-fire but a permanent
peace. It also extended beyond the boundaries of Spain and the
Republic; the same peace conference that concluded the Eighty Years'
War with the Peace of Münster ended the Thirty Years' War with the
Peace of Westphalia. To a certain extent, the conference succeeded in
its aims. Since then, war has often been waged in Germany and in
the Netherlands, but never again over the same issues. After 1648, the

equality between Protestants and Catholics, the autonomy of the German princes, and the independence of the Republic were no longer points of contention.

And yet the kings did march on new campaigns in the spring of 1648. The old Catholic-Protestant conflict had receded, since neither side saw any chance to win a decisive victory. But the older conflict between the Habsburgs and France continued. The French believed they could score significant gains against their weakened rival, gains they ultimately sealed with the Peace of the Pyrenees in 1659. Those assessing the results of European wars since the beginning of the century had to conclude that France was the biggest winner. Habsburg dreams to dominate Europe had been irreversibly shattered, and France was the country with both the power and – as soon became evident – the ambition to use the situation to its advantage.

If France's position was much improved, the same could be said of England. In the first half of the seventeenth century, it had played no international role; preoccupied by domestic unrest and revolution, it remained aloof of European conflicts. By the end of the 1640s, however, England's civil war came to an end when Oliver Cromwell's republic replaced the Stuart monarchy, and King Charles I was condemned to death and beheaded in 1649. The new masters of England, powerful and confident, were determined to gain as great a place among the nations of Europe as they had the power to achieve.

The Republic was compelled to reevaluate its own position in this changing constellation of power. It could not be all too carefree in doing so. The Seven Provinces had made tremendous gains since the sixteenth century – more than either France or England. But the base on which the Republic's prosperity and power rested was much less solid. Its territory was small – comparable to a larger French province – but had long boundaries which, in the case of the eastern border, were difficult to defend. Its population remained under two million. Great Britain's population was nearly four times as large, France ten times. The Dutch Republic had achieved wealth and an important position because of its trade and shipping which was conducted all over the world. But it was not able to outfit its hundreds of ships with the guns and manpower needed to secure the republic's protection from enemies on the high seas. If the French and English wished to increase their own share of trade at the expense of the Dutch, it would not be easy for the Republic to prevent them from doing so. Holland had greatly profited during the years when France, and especially England, had been absorbed in their own affairs. But now it would be tested. It would have to defend its lead against two countries, both of which were stronger than the Republic.

In these circumstances the Seven Provinces had to pursue exactly the right course in international politics in order to attain their ends. The search for such a course soon brought them into peril. The Republic was at peace, but the peace was already under pressure. Frederik Hendrik had died in 1647 and was succeeded by his son, the young William II. The new stadholder inherited all the positions his father had held, but the offices of the Republic were always very malleable; the officeholder had to make an office authoritative through the exercise of his own personal qualities. New men always had to demonstrate that they were capable enough to be worthy of the office they possessed. We shall never know if William would have succeeded in proving his mettle had he lived longer. But his three years as stadholder did not show particular promise.

In the first place, William wanted to renew the war against Spain. He believed – or at least he argued – that the alliance with France demanded it. That belief, if it was sincere, demonstrated a high moral sense. But a recommencement of the war would increase the power of France, and thus went contrary to the concrete interests of the Republic. William's international ambitions went further than this, however. His wife, Mary Stuart, was the daughter of the English king Charles I. William felt honor-bound to support his in-laws in the House of Stuart, and wanted the Republic to back them by overthrowing Cromwell's republican regime. It is not clear if the stadholder wanted all of this to happen at once. But it is clear that implementing his plans would have cost the Republic a good deal of money without bringing it direct advantage.

Prince William II and Mary Stuart in a painting by Gerard van Honthorst. (Gemeentemuseum, The Hague.)

It could not be expected that this expensive, risky, and vaguely defined policy would find general support. Holland, which had always carried the main burden of war, believed that peace should have financial consequences and wanted to reduce the Republic's armed forces. When the States-General proved unable to come to a speedy decision on this issue, Holland took matters into its own hands by telling a number of army companies that it would no longer pay them. This gesture was in itself not new; other provinces, too, had acted unilaterally when they believed that they had been saddled unfairly with financial burdens. In such cases, the companies were paid with loans, until an agreement had been reached with the recalcitrant province.

Every province had their occasional difficulties with the Generality, but Holland was not just another province. If Utrecht and Overijssel decided to temporarily close their purses, it caused some discomfort; if Holland did so, the Republic was in grave danger. Officially, Holland paid more than 58 percent of the national tax burden, and it often gave more. In short, the Republic could not survive without Holland, and the Generality was prepared to give the province a large say in the affairs of the Republic. Holland and the other six provinces seldom failed to reach agreement on the main points of policy. But a serious crisis did erupt when they were unable to do so, since the Republic's political system lacked the forms to resolve such a conflict. Consensus was necessary for important decisions, and if a small province insisted on dissenting, it was simply ignored by the other six. Holland, however, could not be ignored, since it held the keys to the Republic's treasury. If Holland stood firm against the six, then there were only two solutions: the six would have to accept defeat with gnashed teeth, or resolve the crisis with violence. Force had been used in 1618, and it would be used again in 1650.

William II's behavior in 1650, in fact, shows similarities with his uncle Maurits's course of action in 1618. The stadholder arrested six of Holland's prominent regents and marched with a sizable army on Amsterdam, the city that was his primary opponent in the States of Holland. He failed to enter the city, but the threat of violence was enough to compel a change in policy; Holland gave up its plans to reduce the size of the military. Again, the captain-general had won, just as in 1618.

Yet the differences between 1618 and 1650 are more significant than the similarities. Maurits intervened only after he was assured that a change of course had sufficient political backing; he knew that there would be a broad, governing consensus after he had neutralized the opposing majority in the States of Holland. William II's support was much more limited; the States-General opposed Holland's arbitrary decision to downsize the military, but they resisted the stadholder's efforts to renew the war. When William introduced plans to resume it in the autumn of 1650, the States-General balked, precipitating a new crisis. This time, however, the crisis was not about a dispute between Holland and the Generality, but about the power of the stadholder. Had he now attained so many princely trappings that his political will was decisive – even against the expressed will of the Republic's government? No one shall ever know, for the prince died after a short illness, in November 1650, only twenty-four years old.

The Regents of Holland

William's death opened the way for an entirely new solution to the constitutional problem. Holland dispensed with the problem of the stadholder's role by simply abolishing the position. This rather radical turn was made easier by that fact that William's son, born after his father's death, was too young to assume the duties of that office. The provinces could have appointed the Frisian stadholder, Willem Frederik, to serve as guardian for the infant prince, but none of them did. The Frisian did succeed his relative William II as stadholder in Groningen and Drenthe, but the other provinces, accustomed to sharing their stadholder with Holland, left the position vacant. This shows how little confidence William II enjoyed at the time of his death; his efforts to increase his own power had found no substantial support among the Republic's leaders, even outside Holland.

Thus began the period in Dutch history which we call (with our apologies to the northern provinces) the First Stadholderless Era. The name points to an absence, as if there should have been a stadholder. This can be contested, of course, and it was. Opponents of the stadholder understandably believed that the position was not needed in the Seven United Provinces. Through the seventeenth century, no other republics had had stadholders, nor have there been any others since. And yet the designation "stadholderless" is not entirely inappropriate. A country may not need a stadholder, but it does need a government, and someone needs to head that government. The Dutch Republic now lacked a constitutional head of state, a position once filled by the stadholder.

It was natural enough, then, that the other high official in Holland would now fill in the vacuum. In 1653, the office of the Pensionary of Holland fell to the very young but unusually competent Johan de Witt, the son of a prominent Dordrecht family. For nearly twenty years he functioned as the Republic's real chief, a position he owed to his rare talents, the weight of his office, and the dominance of Holland. Every coin, however, has two sides. De Witt had many gifts, but he remained a paid employee of the States of Holland. He held high office, but the masters of Holland were not about to subordinate themselves to their servant. Holland may have dominated the Republic, but the other provinces' sovereignty could not be compromised, and Holland needed their votes in the States-General. With these limitations, De Witt always had to act with circumspection. He could never, through the weight of his office, insist on obedience; rather, he had to persuade his opponents. If interests sufficiently coincided, De Witt was the one to achieve a consensus; if arguments were not enough, then he was compelled to use other means to achieve consensus. Those means, too, were part of the game of persuasion, and even an utterly upright person like De Witt had to play the game. For nearly two decades, he largely succeeded in satisfying both his masters in Holland and in finding enough support among the six other provinces. But De Witt never became a dictator, and his position remained precarious.

The First Stadholderless Era can be characterized by two developments. Domestically, it was marked by the increased dominion of the regents – the country's ruling patrician class – under so-called "True

Johan de Witt in a portrait by Adriaen Hanneman. (Museum Boymans-Van Beuningen, Rotterdam.)

Freedom." Internationally, it was the age of the trade wars. Both were inseparably linked to each other.

True Freedom was the right of the regents to be masters of their own lands and their own cities. This freedom was no longer limited by the stadholder, and it would no longer be subordinate to the higher unity of the Union. Proponents of True Freedom preferred, in fact, not to speak of a Republic; the regents referred to seven independent republics, since every province was fully sovereign. Holland's interests were best served in this conception, since the weaker the central authority, the better the position for a strong regional power like Holland. But for most regents, such questions of statecraft remained a theoretical abstraction. Although a small group of leading figures dealt with these issues in the governing councils of The Hague, a much larger group had little involvement with national or international concerns. The typical regent was a local administrator whose life and career was confined within the walls of his own residence.

What exactly was a Dutch regent of the seventeenth century? A person of such status had to meet a number of minimum requirements. In the first place, a regent was highly born. He was not nobility, but belonged to the very highest ranks of the bourgeoisie. From the perspective of that time, it seemed natural that birth should determine one's office or profession. The son of a shoemaker or a goldsmith had the best chance to follow his father, and he was trained to do so; why would it be different for the sons of the regents?

A second prerequisite was access to substantial assets. This was as important as the first, since both status and money are needed to reinforce each other. Without money, no one can maintain their high status. But there was another reason: wealth provided a check on corruption. Money played no role for a regent, as long as he possessed enough to be carefree. Only then could he resist the temptation to dishonestly enrich himself. What we call corruption was normal in the seventeenth century, but it was not regarded as moral or desirable behavior. People of the time valued honesty and incorruptibility in their judges and governors as virtues. They were well enough acquainted with human nature, however, to understand that temptation was inherent in the office. The richer the regent, the more resistance he would have against the enticements of money. From this perspective, the public interest was best served by men who were financially well endowed.

There is a third characteristic of the regent – not a prerequisite, but nonetheless a tendency among the regent class: they belonged to a common culture. They went to Latin school as boys and many of them had spent several years at a university. They spoke enough French to ridicule any member of their class insufficiently acquainted with the language. They knew the history of Greece and Rome, and also knew something of Dutch history, especially pertaining to Holland. They cherished art and literature, and decorated their rooms with paintings and other attractive objects.

Most of them only appreciated the fine arts; they served society better by acquiring a tasteful collection than by developing their own creative spirits. Their education, moreover, did not train them in painting or sculpture. But in science, literature, and music several of them were able to reveal their talents. Johan de Witt himself translated tragedies and wrote mathematical treatises. Without the name De Witt, the former accomplishments would have sunk even further into the oblivion they deserve, but the mathematician De Witt has his own reputation today, independent of his high political office. It is true that his mathematical skills served him well in that office. His study of annuities and mortgage rates had practical applications: in determining which manner it was most advantageous for the government to borrow money, and how much interest it should pay. The same practical orientation we observed in seventeenth-century culture was also evident among the regents of Holland. Mayor Johannes Hudde of Amsterdam made his own study of water management, and his fellow Amsterdammer and colleague Nicolaas Witsen was knowledgeable in shipbuilding. Perhaps the pensionary Jacob Cats belongs here as well, with his long, moralizing verse dedicated to the support of Christian marriage, so that the fatherland might have more virtuous citizens and more obedient subjects.

That culture was more than the ornamental side of a carefree existence was taken for granted by these persons. It had to have norms, and it had to offer a choice between good and evil. But it is also true that the tradition of tolerance had become second nature to the regents, and thus we can include a tolerant attitude as the fourth and last characteristic of their collective portrait. Tradition can become brittle when yesterday's truths turn into today's rules and regulations. If a tolerant tradition does this, it is in conflict with itself, since it cannot condone anything that is really new. From this perspective, it was the Jewish philosopher Baruch de Spinoza who most sharply challenged the principles of this tolerant tradition. The seventeenth-century Republic had its share of free spirits, but there were none like Spinoza, who dared to break with the foundations upon which all of Christian culture rested. His denial that the Bible was the word of God made him a lonely exception among the great figures of his day. Since people could not understand, let alone appreciate his views of the Bible, they felt he had nothing to say to them. In the 1670s, in fact, his writings were forbidden in Holland. Evidently people had come to think that he had exceeded the limits of tolerance. During his own lifetime, however, he was not prevented from expressing himself.

Religion and Politics in the Age of the Regents

For Spinoza, the True Freedom of the Dutch regents brought much liberty of thought and action. But the limits of tolerance were more evident on the right end of the religious spectrum than on the left. The French philosopher Descartes, for instance, was given more latitude in the Netherlands for his controversial views than he would have been given in his Catholic homeland, and many of his followers succeeded in attaining teaching posts at Dutch universities. Even a Spinoza, as we have noted, could lead a quiet life under the rule of the regents. No freethinking sage was ever summoned to leave his city within twenty-four hours. But several Reformed pastors were forced to do just such a thing.

Everyone learns the lessons of history in his own way. One could regard the Synod of Dordrecht as the triumph of orthodox Calvinism. For many Calvinists, the establishment of right doctrine formed the basis for further improvement in church and society. The reform of doctrine now required another reformation: to bring the Christian life into conformity with biblical norms. This was the aim of theologians and pastors like Gisbertus Voetius, William Teellinck, and Abraham van de Velde, with Utrecht forming the center of this movement, which was best known as the Further Reformation.

The regents, however, interpreted the lessons of history differently. They saw to what extent church conflicts could disturb the peace of the country and were determined to prevent it from happening again. The Synod of Dordrecht only confirmed their conviction that good ecclesiastical policy must have the preservation of peace and order as its principal goal. The regents accordingly imposed two ground rules on the church. First, they prevented the church from making new doctrinal pronouncements. If differences of opinion again divided the church, there would be no more synods to decide the issue. When the Leiden professor Cocceius and his Utrecht counterpart Voetius engaged in sharp dispute over a number of theological issues, the authorities prevented any church body from choosing sides. In the orthodox seventeenth century, this policy did not change the essential character of the Reformed church. If this policy were continued, however, it would mean that the church would no longer adhere to its doctrinal confessions. Second, the regents were equally insistent that the church not promote political divisions. A minister who criticized the authorities' deeds and intentions from the pulpit faced disciplinary measures, which included, in extreme cases, banishment from his city or province.

The kind of preaching that got ministers into trouble with authorities was a result of various motivations. Sometimes ministers made a defense of a controversial theological position that was too fiery for authorities. Sometimes, their emphases on Christian piety and lifestyle went further than local authorities found acceptable. In a few cases, the preaching carried an undesirable political message, although this was not the most common reason pastors were punished. But it is true that Reformed ministers did not offer much support for the regents. Their sympathies lay instead with the House of Orange, and their political preference was the restoration of the stadholder. If political parties had existed in the Republic, they would have allied with the Orangist cause.

But such parties did not exist. It would be incorrect, moreover, to understand the history of the Republic essentially as the conflict between the Orangists and the regents. There simply was no constant political polarization which offered a clear choice between the Orangists and the States' party, as the True Freedom group was often called. The average regent, after all, was primarily concerned with furthering the interests of his own family within his own city. For the sake of these interests, he tried to expand his personal power, by advancing the careers of other members of the local elite on the basis of services rendered and received. Under these circumstances, groups that were bound by common interests, and which are now commonly called factions, could form under various regents within a given city. They did not, however, rest on an ideological basis, and their composition could change if new marriages or collective economic activities made another combination seem more fruitful.

But although there were no political parties as such, the two sides continued to oppose each other. A good number of people did not concern themselves with this political conflict, including many regents. It is a truth for every age: between black and white there is a large gray area where most people choose to dwell. They might have a slight preference for one side or the other, but it is not a pressing issue for them. For that reason, both black and white can hope for victory. Those in power may count on the docility of the masses, and are able to keep the small number of opponents at bay. The opposition, however, knows that the rulers cannot rely on broad support. A palace revolution may be enough to turn the tables.

The Trade Wars

For this reason, political opposition was continually present during the First Stadholderless Era, although it was not always an active opposition. Still, the tension never disappeared, not least because the government of Johan de Witt repeatedly confronted the United Provinces with the necessity of a political choice. If this period has just been described as the high tide of the regents, it may now be characterized as the age of the trading wars. These wars, too, prompted people to make political decisions.

The Republic had attained great prosperity, thanks to its trading and shipping. Its overseas companies controlled their own ports in Asia, Africa, North and South America. Dutch ships traversed the Mediterranean and Baltic in large numbers, and Dutch fishermen found employment in the North Sea and North Atlantic Within Europe, the Dutch played so dominant a role in shipping freight that a large share of French, German, and English goods were carried by Dutch skippers. One of the smallest countries of Europe transported more goods than any other competitor.

It could not be expected that the Republic would enjoy this happy state of affairs forever. Sooner or later, competition would emerge. After the Peace of Münster, the English and (later) the French governments adopted new economic policies designed to promote and protect their own economic interests. The strengthening of both countries' positions, however, could come only at the expense of the Republic. The English Navigation Act of 1651 was the first measure which threatened Dutch commercial primacy. It stipulated that foreign ships could only import goods if these vessels originated in their own country. This was clearly directed against the Republic, since most "foreign' ships were Dutch. The Navigation Act was, in effect, an economic declaration of war on the Republic, and it made armed conflict imminent. In 1652, the First Anglo-Dutch War broke out.

The Republic attained few glorious triumphs during the war. Its navy did have good leadership, including admirals Maerten Harpertsz. Tromp and Michiel Adriaensz. de Ruyter, who acquired international reputations as seafighters. But it was unprepared to fight a naval war and lacked the right equipment to successfully engage the English. In the Peace of Westminster, signed in 1654, the Navigation Act was kept in force. The English also demanded a concession from the Dutch which had played no role in the original reason for going to war: permanently excluding the prince of Orange from the stadholderate. This wish was understandable enough. The republican government of Oliver Cromwell wanted to prevent a grandson of executed king Charles I from leading the Seven Provinces (stadholder William II had married Charles's daughter Mary Stuart). The Dutch did not see it this way, however. In their view, the young William III was not primarily the grandson of Charles, but of Frederik Hendrik. The States-General, therefore, refused to accept this English demand, and it was not adopted in the final peace accord. But England secretly reached an agreement with Holland (the so-called Act of Exclusion), in which Holland pledged to prevent the office of stadholder from ever falling to William III or his descendants.

For De Witt, the agreement was no sacrifice. But it certainly was offensive, letting a foreign government dictate who could and could not attain high office in the land. It was, moreover, an unholy mixture of national and factional interest. The Act of Exclusion would only serve to strengthen the ties between the followers of the House of Orange and the banished House of Stuart. For this reason, it is exceedingly difficult to separate the trading wars and Dutch foreign policy from the conflict between the stadholder's supporters and the so-called States party.

Dutch intervention in the Northern War (1658-1660) between Denmark and Sweden had relatively little to do with this continuing conflict, however. Trade in the Baltic was then of vital interest to all the great powers of Europe. Swedish lumber was particularly indispensable for shipping, and as a result, every country which desired economic power required it. Eastern European grain, too, had become an indispensable food supplement for almost all areas of Western and Southern Europe. All of this needed to be transported through the Sont strait between Denmark and Sweden. Closing the Sont in the seventeenth century had an equivalent effect on Europe as an oil embargo would today. The Republic in particular had a overwhelming share in the Baltic trade, and was thus compelled to maintain friendly ties with the masters of the strait – or force them to accept its friendship. When, in 1658, the balance of power between Sweden and Denmark threatened to become permanently disrupted, the Republic entered the conflict on the side of the weaker Denmark, forcing Sweden to accept terms of peace which secured Dutch interests.

De Witt's efforts to give the Republic a formidable fleet had yielded a handsome dividend in northern waters. The true proof of his success, however, would come through a war with England, which would have to be resumed sooner or later. The Stuart monarchy had been restored, effectively killing the Act of Exclusion, but relations between the two countries did not improve with the advent of Charles II. Outside of Europe, the two countries treated each other as enemies, and, in 1665, war was officially resumed – the Second Anglo-Dutch War. This time, the Republic was much better prepared. At sea, it proved more than an equal match for England. The Dutch surrendered New Netherlands (New York) in the Peace of Breda (1667), but they received Surinam in return.

The peace was hastened by developments on the European continent. French armies invaded the Southern Netherlands in 1667; Spain, unable to offer strong resistance, faced the possibility of total defeat. This was neither in the interests of England nor of the Republic. Together with Sweden, they formed a triple alliance in 1668 to maintain the status quo. King Louis XIV of France was obliged to end his offensive and had to content himself with a small territorial gain for the time being.

Louis XIV was not a man who could be content with a modest prize when there was a chance for more, however. The forced peace only increased his hostility toward the Republic. Relations between the countries were already under considerable pressure as a result of France's aggressive economic policy. Louis's minister, Colbert, wanted France to be a rich and prosperous country, and he worked to make France economically independent. He believed that the country should no longer be dependent on other nations for its prosperity – and certainly not on the Republic, whose share of international trade was far greater than it deserved. If the Dutch wished to trade with France, then they would have to pay for the privilege. Colbert substantially increased tariffs, hoping to force Dutch shipping to surrender its French trade to French shipping.

Admiral De Ruyter defeating the English in the "Four Days" Battle, June 1666. The painting is by Willem van de Velde de Jonge. (Rijksmuseum, Amsterdam.)

Thus the Republic faced two great enemies, one with Europe's largest fleet, the other with Europe's largest army. In order to successfully resist both, the Republic would need to assemble more soldiers than France, and more ships than England. It was thus confronted with a problem that it could not solve by itself. The Republic was simply not a great power like England or France. But the Dutch did, of course, wish to enjoy the fruits of their past attainments as long as possible. They tried to do this by playing one dangerous neighbor off against the other. It would hurt France if the Republic became a satellite of England, and it would harm England if the Seven Provinces became a French vassal. This was a very sensible policy – as long as the French and the English themselves clearly understood their own strategic interests. This was central to De Witt's foreign policy. He assumed that the French and the English governments would objectively assess the international situation. In any event, it is difficult to imagine De Witt doing anything else. Even if the Republic could have been made impregnable to Anglo-French attack, De Witt would never have found the provinces prepared to pay the heavy taxes such a defense required.

Thus the Republic was not only unprepared when war broke out against England and France in 1672 (including its allies the elector of Cologne and bishop of Münster), there was no possibility it could have been. De Witt might have survived this severe threat if it were not, as in 1618, for a complicating factor. By 1672, the young son of William II was a grown man. His mettle was known to but a few, and certainly no one yet had a full appreciation for it. But everyone realized that it would be impossible to exclude him from the Republic's

The horribly mutilated bodies of the De Witt brothers on a strappado. Engraving by R. Roghman. (Museum Mr. Simon van Gijn, Dordrecht.)

political life forever. The Orangist cry had already been heard in the streets during the Second Anglo-Dutch War. Now, with enemy armies making rapid and seemingly irresistible inroads into the eastern and central parts of the Republic, the cry became a chorus.

William's elevation to stadholder became inevitable, and he assumed office in July 1672. De Witt asked for and received his own dismissal. Unlike Oldenbarnevelt in 1618, he faced no criminal charges. But he did not escape vigilante justice; together with his brother Cornelis, he was murdered by a mob in The Hague on 20 August 1672. William III never punished the perpetrators.

6. The Republic under William III (1672-1702)

The War of 1672

The murder of the De Witt brothers is a low point in Dutch history. It is a deed which defies empathy or justification. On that day, authority failed in its duty, and the participants in the brothers' deaths lost their humanity. This is a judgment that is not peculiar to our own century. If we say that every contemporary of Oldenbarnevelt should have condemned his execution, then we have removed ourselves from the time in which it took place. If we condemn the actions of the East India Company in the Moluccan islands, then we apply moral considerations unknown to the perpetrators. But in 1672 there was no question of a tragic misunderstanding, or of a harshness, which those then living regretted but deemed a sad necessity. The murders were a completely indefensible crime, executed with repulsive cruelty.

The event, however, is explainable, meaning no more than that the motives of the killers can be traced. In Dutch history, 1672 has often been called "the year of disaster." Why it was so described can best be explained if we look back to the long years of struggle against Spain. In those days, enemy armies occasionally penetrated deep into the Republic, and villages and the countryside in the way were at the mercy of these armies. But fortresses could only be taken after a lengthy siege, and a country with many such walled cities (like the Republic) was considered militarily very strong. It was a great achievement to take three of these fortified cities in the course of one year, as Frederik Hendrik had done in 1632. Given this history, the course of the war in 1672 was nothing less than shocking. Not three cities but three provinces fell into enemy hands within a few weeks. No one had thought this possible. In April, the citizenry had still merrily danced to the tune, "The king of France, with one hundred thousand men." On 12 June, the French marshall Condé crossed the Rhine, and within nine days he was master of Utrecht. People had never experienced this kind of war, and it was not long before they blamed the government for a gross dereliction of duty – or worse. Fury, shame, disbelief, and fear made it impossible to give a positive assessment of De Witt's foreign policy, and people regarded him as personally responsible for the disaster of 1672.

Many regents, too, were demoralized by July 1672. A total defeat seemed inevitable. In hindsight, it is less striking that a large part of the Republic was so quickly taken than that the Republic survived so severe a threat. There is no single explanation for the Republic's escape. Certainly the French must have later regretted that, after seizing Utrecht and the Gooi, they did not immediately attack the so-called "water-line," which the Dutch had not yet adequately prepared for defense. Capitulation seemed so near that the French may have thought active military measures were unnecessary. But this assessment proved premature.

Cautiousness may have played a role, too, in French failure to follow up on their initial success, or perhaps they were compelled to stop their drive. The French armies had taken so many cities that a large part of their strength went into garrisons. The king of France, therefore, no longer had one hundred thousand men to deploy against the province of Holland. Finally, the French may have hoped that the English would soon land on the coast of Holland, saving them the trouble of assaulting William's fortresses. At sea, however, the anti-Dutch alliance failed to gain ascendancy; instead, the Dutch fleet under Michiel de Ruyter effectively prevented a coastal invasion.

William III had no influence over any of these developments. The French were led by their own considerations, and if De Ruyter had to share the credit of his success with anyone, it was Johan de Witt, who had always championed a strong navy. And yet it is possible to argue that William's actions, too, were of decisive significance. There is an unmistakable parallel between the role this Orange played in the summer of 1672 and the actions taken by his great-grandfather a century earlier. The well-known saying that one does not have to succeed to persevere has been attributed to both, and both could have said it. Both Williams knew, through their resolute fortitude, how to embody the inspiring leadership which gave others the courage to continue their efforts in defense of an uncertain cause. Only a few Dutch cities, particularly Amsterdam, energetically backed William III. But it was he who personally ensured that defeatism was kept out of the negotiations with France and England.

There was, however, one major difference between William III and William I. The first Orange knew how to win peoples' favor; William III lacked that art. Even if we keep in mind that William's long exclusion from high office during De Witt's rule could have had no positive effect on his character, coolness, aloofness, and cynicism remained the basis of his personality. He commanded respect, but little sympathy. He was even more successful than William I, however, in finding the means to attain his ends, and in 1672, those ends were winning the war. In subsequent years, William would aim at preventing a repetition of 1672, an aim which became the cornerstone of both his domestic and foreign policy.

William's foreign policy sought to mobilize all possible European allies into a coalition against French hegemony. After the Peace of Westphalia, France had become the most powerful country in Europe, and under Louis XIV it actively attempted to dominate the continent. It was prepared to use all of its military, diplomatic, and financial assets to gain this position and to keep it. William III regarded it as his life's mission to resist the French threat. In war and in peace, the struggle against France was always in William's thoughts, and he constantly searched for allies who shared his concern. This was necessarily the case in 1672, when William had no choice but to find allies. It was a matter of life and death, and survival was not possible without allies. Thus in 1673, the first coalition was formed through the so-called Quadruple Alliance, which included the Habsburg emperor, Spain, Lorraine, and the Dutch Republic.

The war took a positive turn that year. At the end of 1673, Louis's forces retreated from the occupied Dutch provinces. Coalition forces seized Bonn in Germany, a major supply center for French operations, and Louis feared that the army of occupation would be isolated. Around the same time, the anti-French party in England gained the upper hand, and Parliament refused to give Charles II the finances to pursue the war against the Republic. In February 1674, the two countries officially made peace. The anti-Dutch coalition of Louis XIV had been broken, and the Republic had succeeded in forming an anti-French coalition.

The United Provinces, in fact, became the backbone of this alliance. It was vital that all the provinces back William's efforts, and for this rea-

The Glorious Assault on Maastricht, *a French print celebrating the seizure of Maastricht by Louis XIV's army on 13 June 1673. (Bibliothèque Nationale, Paris.)*

son, William strengthened his grip on the Republic's administration. Coming to power in a time of crisis, William eagerly took advantage of the power vacuum he found. The Pensionary of Holland had always functioned as the Republic's foreign minister. With De Witt gone, William now appropriated this task for himself. Official ambassadors and envoys continued to manage routine diplomatic affairs, but William established a network of trusted confidants who quietly determined the course of foreign policy according to the stadholder's instructions.

William also strengthened his grip on the States-General. Gelderland, Utrecht, and Overijssel, freed from French occupation, could again send their representatives to the councils of The Hague. But there they met with a hostile reception. There was a strong current of feeling in Holland that these provinces should be denied a place in the States-General, since they had done too little in 1672 to resist the French. They should now be annexed into the Republic, as conquered territory, without the right to decide common policy. William III prevented this plan from being carried out, but did so in such a way as to ensure that the three provinces would henceforth be loyal to him. The formal status of these provinces was not altered, but their position was changed by a new set of statutes. In particular, the stadholder was given, from 1674 on, the responsibility of naming appointments to the three provinces' most important posts. This ensured that the stadholder would always have three votes in the States-General. Moreover, Zeeland had always been politically controlled by the stadholder, giving William a fourth vote. In this way, William III came closer to full control of the Republic than any of his predecessors.

Nonetheless, the Union remained an alliance of seven unequal provinces. Those wanting real control the Republic had to be master of Holland. When William was appointed stadholder, he was also given the latitude to purge local magistrates in Holland. He again received the authority to choose new functionaries from a list of two candidates presented by any given city. William thus gained adherents in every city – adherents who could also make their voice heard in the States of Holland. But he had one weak point: Amsterdam, which retained the right of appointment for itself. Amsterdam played a role in the States of Holland similar to the position Holland played in the States-General; as it was impossible to decide national policy without the consent of Holland, so it was impossible, at least in the long run, to rule Holland against the wishes and interests of Amsterdam. In 1672, Amsterdam had strongly backed William, but when the danger receded and the war against France made little headway, Amsterdam became increasingly interested in peace. Despite William's resistance, a peace party gained the upper hand, and in 1678, the Peace of Nijmegen put an end to the first great coalition's war against France.

William III versus Louis XIV

William could not regard this peace as more than a truce, since French ambitions for European domination had hardly been vanquished at Nijmegen. Louis XIV soon enough gave evidence of this. Although peace formally lasted for a decade, Louis made few efforts to hide his quest for power. Even during peacetime, he demonstrated little respect for the boundaries of the Southern Netherlands or (as was more often the case) the German Empire, using far-fetched arguments to claim territory that had never belonged to France, but which perhaps centuries before had ties with cities or counties now lying in France. In this manner, Luxembourg and Strasbourg fell without a fight to the French. The other European powers, including the Republic, followed these developments with concern. But Amsterdam resisted war, and reprisals against France remained limited to the conference table.

The turning point came in 1685. Two events of that year brought about a change in European politics: the revocation of the Edict of Nantes and the coronation of the English king James II. Since 1598, the Protestants in France had been a legally protected minority. It was not religious equality; the French king retained the title *Sa Majesté très Catholique* and was crowned in the Rheims cathedral. The Edict of Nantes was thus a fragile thing, a concession to a feared minority, granted to them after six religious wars. The Protestant minority lost its power during the seventeenth century as the great nobility, once its principal source of support, returned to the mother church. At that point, the Protestants underwent the fate of all weak minorities. They were the objects of distrust and discrimination, and they gradually lost their rights as their standing declined. The revocation of the Edict of Toleration was, therefore, no more than the last step in a policy Louis XIV's government had long pursued. France was now officially a wholly Catholic country. But the consequences were not restricted to France. In the first place, French refugees now streamed to the Dutch Republic, Switzerland, Brandenburg, and other Protestant countries. In the second place, Louis had given Europe a taste of what French hegemony would mean: not only French culture and a French-dominated economy, but a French church with a French faith.

The second event was the death of Charles II, who was succeeded by his Catholic brother James II. Catholics constituted a small minority in England, smaller even than the Protestants in France, but they were universally distrusted. When James began his reign with an edict of religious tolerance and the opening of government posts to all Christians, regardless of creedal affiliation, most English regarded the move as a measure designed to favor Catholics. At first, they comforted themselves with the idea that James would not last forever, and that in a few years the throne would go to his Protestant daughter Mary, who was married to William III. The birth of a male heir to James in June 1688, however, dashed this hope. The temporary discomfort of a Catholic king was now magnified into the disaster of a Catholic dynasty.

Such a dynasty could have far-reaching effects on the balance of power – not least for the Dutch Republic. A Catholic king of England would find his most natural ally in the king of France, and then the coincidental Anglo-French alliance of 1672 might return for good. Under these circumstances, William III had to accept the English opposition's invitation to come across the Channel and drive his father-in-law from the throne. The States were willing to accept the risk of war, and even Amsterdam dropped its opposition, impressed by the religious persecution in France. The expedition to London, launched in the fall of 1688, went extraordinarily well – almost no resistance was offered. Together with his spouse Mary, William was crowned king. James II, the friend and coreligionist of Louis XIV, had been replaced by Louis's most bitter foe, William III.

This triggered a war that, excepting a few brief pauses, lasted twenty-five years. As king of England, William could now form an ideal coalition, which included the German emperor, Spain, England, the Republic, and a number of German princes. Even with so great a number of allies, the coalition struggled to hold its own against France. The Peace of Rijswijk, concluded in 1697, was not particularly disadvantageous to Louis. But no one regarded the peace as definitive. Everyone knew that Charles II of Spain would soon die childless and that Louis would demand the succession for his own grandson. A new war, therefore, was certain, and William diligently prepared for it. The War of Spanish Succession began in May 1702. William did not live to see it, however, having died in March. In France, his death was spontaneously celebrated as a holiday.

Those describing this period of Dutch history must necessarily emphasize political and military developments. In those years, the

Republic had to carry its responsibility as a great power and make its contribution to a new balance of power in Europe which could form the basis for a lasting peace. At William's behest, the Republic accomplished this task and paid for it dearly. During the War of Spanish of Succession, it would become clear that the Republic was living beyond its means. During the 1690s there was yet little indication of this. But the first signs eventually did appear which suggested that the Republic's glory days were over. Trading and shipping were not in decline, but, instead of growth, there was economic stagnation and retrenchment. The Republic had to accept the fact that its international competitors, backed by stronger governments and possessing greater potential, were breaking open the Dutch lock on trade. Furthermore, the military expenditures it was forced to spend in order to maintain its position were costing the country more than it could recoup on the world markets. Not only politically, but economically, the Republic would have to accept its status as a second-rate power.

Amsterdam merchants, typically full of self-confidence, were aware of the importance that their activities had for the development of the arts and sciences. Indeed, the links between economics and art are hard to deny. We find the greatest painters, poets, and architects in the first half of the century, when Dutch trade was at its height. The gener-

Johannes Vermeer, View of Delft. *(Mauritshuis, The Hague.)*

ations of Rembrandt and Hals, Vondel and Hooft, were not followed by artists of equal accomplishment. Johannes Vermeer, active later in the century, belongs among the greats, but he was not highly known or regarded in his own time. The philosopher Spinoza can also be reckoned among them, but he, too, did not achieve wide recognition during his life. The same can be said of another denizen of the late seventeenth century, who has since achieved fame in European cultural history: the Amsterdam pastor Balthasar Bekker.

Much of Bekker's life has been romanticized. He is presented as a courageous crusader against superstition, maligned and misunderstood by the church. It is true that Bekker vigorously contested seventeenth-century demonology. But it is no less true that witchcraft prosecutions had ceased long before Bekker's day, and that no one wanted to reintroduce them. If many pens wrote against Bekker, it was not because he was a lone hero defending the persecuted witches of his day. Internationally, he may have played such a role, particularly in countries still burning witches at the stake in the late seventeenth century. Within the Republic, however, Bekker's *Enchanted World* created a commotion as another volley in a prolonged series of theological disputes which lasted throughout the seventeenth century and which, incidentally, did not disappear after 1700. Only theologians discussed Bekker's ideas, and the topic of witches played a very modest role in their discussions. Opponents were more likely to criticize Bekker for his method, which seemed to undermine biblical authority by placing reason above revelation. Seen this way, Bekker was indeed a man ahead of his time. He was not so much the man who fought against old superstitions as the one who, in his exegesis, paved the way for the rationalism of the eighteenth century.

7. A Great Power in Decline (1702-1751)

Political Decline

In the course of the first half of the eighteenth century, the Republic was reduced to one of Europe's small powers. In 1702, it was still counted among the great powers, and it played a substantial role in the last war against Louis XIV. The vicissitudes of this war have their place in the history of the Southern Netherlands, but to those in the north, the great battles at Ramillies and Malplaquet are largely unknown. For the Republic, they had significance only insofar as they brought it closer to financial prostration. The Peace of Utrecht in 1713 gave the country but very modest compensation for the years of war: the southeastern city of Venlo. Two years later, the Republic attempted to increase its security by reaching an agreement with the new Austrian masters of the Southern Netherlands, in which the Seven Provinces attained the right to station garrisons in a number of fortress cities along the French border. The so-called Barrier Treaty would ostensibly guarantee the Republic's security against a new French attack.

The treaty signalled a reorientation of The Hague's foreign policy, which became increasingly defensive in nature. In one sense, it continued a longer tradition; Johan de Witt, too, had attempted to protect the Republic and especially Dutch trade through defensive treaties. But such alliances are a guarantee for peace only if their signatories are prepared, when necessity dictates, to go to war. The Republic, however, lacked the will to fight and when, in 1747, the country could no longer avoid war, it was in no condition to wage it.

The Republic's military weakness, which suddenly became manifest in 1747, was quite remarkable. The country had lived in peace for thirty-four years, much longer than ever before. It might be expected that years of saving would have ensured that the Dutch defenses would be in good shape. However, this was not the case, on the contrary. The War of Spanish Succession had cost the Republic so much money that it never recovered from it. The States of Holland noted in 1728 that it was a war in which, more than any other, people had insufficiently weighed the war's justification against the war's cost. Its financial legacy had long-lasting effects on Dutch life, and when war broke out in 1747, the States was still wrestling with the old war debts. This debt, it should be added, dated further back than 1713. Since 1672, the country had fought three lengthy wars against France, and during the intermittent lulls, the Dutch still needed to be vigilant, keeping a large force under arms. It is hardly an exaggeration to speak of a forty-year French war, and when it ended in 1713 a large portion of the bill still needed to be paid.

The war debt was so high that the States of Holland was forced to spend 70 percent of its income in the years after 1713 paying interest. Under these circumstances, it was a heavy burden to deploy even a small army to man the fortress cities, and the thought of financing additional troops for an offensive war was inconceivable. It is difficult to say if the other provinces fared better financially than Holland. We know less about finances in Holland than we would like to know, and our knowledge from the other provinces is even more limited. The tax burden of the other provinces was presumably lighter, but none of them had the financial means of a city like Amsterdam, either. Moreover, the level of commitment to national affairs was lower outside of Holland than inside it. In Haarlem or Rotterdam, people could discuss war and peace in light of their own economic interests. But what relevance did French economic rivalry and French tariffs have for the citizenry of eastern towns like Deventer and Doesburg? If military preparedness was important for Holland, then Holland would have to pay for it.

As long as the war lasted, all the provinces were nonetheless willing to share its burden. Peace, however, removed the incentive for unity, and the slogan "everyone for himself" increasingly defined political life in the course of the eighteenth century. Everyone, of course, was forced to be frugal, since an empty treasury makes for poor policy, but the will to refill the common purse was clearly even weaker than it had been in the seventeenth century.

There were no real prospects for recovery. Materially, the Dutch did not suffer directly, but they had the wind against them. When the Republic defended free passage in the Sont during the Northern War in the 1650s, they fought to maintain their predominant economic position. Around 1660, 63 percent of Sont traffic was Dutch; sixty years later, it was 50 percent. The decline was not disastrous, but it was a foreboding trend. Most serious, perhaps, was the fact that the Dutch were not being replaced in the Baltic trade by one large power, but by a number of countries. They no longer purchased their wheat and wood in the staple markets of Amsterdam, but sent their ships to the source itself. This change began in the late seventeenth century, and was especially encouraged by the English and French governments. It became increasingly clear that the Dutch could not regard foreign competition as a temporary irritation; they would have to live with its long-term effects. Dutch merchants retained a considerable percentage of international trade, but the good years of growth were long past, and there was nothing they could do to improve the situation.

So we could say that the Second Stadholderless Era (which began after the death of William III in 1702) is a period in which the government lacked well-defined aims. To be sure, it sought to maintain the peace, and supported every peace initiative emanating from London, Paris, or Vienna. It was also more or less oriented toward England. But the Republic's desire for peace did not rest on a position of strength, from which it could resort to more forceful measures if its sincere hope for peace were obstructed. The Republic was fortunate that, in the thirty years following the Peace of Utrecht, the English – and especially the French – refrained from pursuing an aggressive foreign policy. These decades of peace also hid the Republic's weakness, and as a quasi-great power it was always included in diplomatic consultations. The Republic's lack of strength was finally unmasked in 1747, and then for good.

If a country has no great ambitions and must content itself with a quiet existence, then there can be little objection to leaving its administration in the hands of a small group of experts. They need not be persons of extraordinary ability as long as they are familiar with the affairs of state and possess the skills to get along with their fellow human beings. Those with greater gifts, in fact, run the risk of frustration, chafing that their talents are not being used for the greater service of the community. After the death of the pensionary Anthonie Heinsius, who steered the country through the War of Spanish Succession, the Second Stadholderless Era produced only one statesman of the first rank: Simon van Slingelandt. Historians who chose to make him the subject of a biography will be rewarded by his deep insight into the Republic's governmental institutions, of which Slingelandt was an uncommonly incisive critic. They will also have to put up with the pensionary's perpetual whining, for there have been few people with such long and rapidly advancing careers who have struggled more, from their youth onward, with feelings of being misunderstood than Simon van Slingelandt. But it is true that his qualities would have permitted him to do far more than he ever achieved. He could have given the Republic energetic leadership and brought about reforms in its administration. But his age had little use for such talents.

Domestic Administration

Slingelandt experienced this frustration in national government. But it was just as true of the provinces and the cities – at least once basic issues of political control had been settled. The death of William III, as we have noted, had ushered in a new stadholderless period, since the regents had grown thoroughly tired of William's intrusions. In the short term, the shift brought about a political crisis, especially in those provinces where the stadholder's power was strongest: primarily Zeeland and the three provinces subject to the new regulations of 1674. In various cities there was social unrest, particularly persistent in Gelderland, and even some bloodshed. These disputes have gone into history as the conflict between the "New Crew" and the "Old Crew." The New Crew essentially favored change; it stemmed in part from the initiative of regent families shut out of power by William III, and in part from the result of discontent among the middle classes who had no say in the political process. These middle class groups scarcely benefitted from their protest; once their support had brought a new faction of regents into power, the burghers were thanked for their help, and the regents ran the country as they had before.

The regents have gained a bad reputation because of this, both among their contemporaries and with posterity. The resentments of the former will be described below. Posterity has since begun to understand that the infamy of the eighteenth-century regents was not completely their own fault. How could they achieve renown if the Republic were not called to great things? And were not their administrative skills necessary to keep the Republic out of dangerous adventures? The United Provinces of the Second Stadholderless Era was a state on the night watch. The only requirement asked of the its administrators was that they remain awake. Given the modest task set before them, the regents did not do so badly, although it can hardly be denied that they had their faults. If the government has no program, and if administrators pliantly and routinely attend to whatever matters are at hand, then it becomes more likely that the exercise of public power will become an end in itself. A government post gives prestige and income, two nice perquisites. Its pleasures should not be lost for future generations, thought the regents, and a good father should try his best to ensure that his children, too, share in its fruits. There was every chance a regent would succeed in this, provided he had enough friends sitting with him on the council – friends who knew how to give and take. Informal arrangements would determine how to apportion the city's share of administrators. And if someone should happen to land a high position beyond his abilities, no matter: administrative and legal decisions were decided by whole councils, where an occasional incompetent could not undermine the quality. In quiet times, this kind of arrangement can keep peace and order for a long while.

There were those who wanted to disturb this peace and order. During the First Stadholderless Era, there had always been an Orangist undercurrent, and many believed that in the long run it would be impossible to deprive the Republic of a stadholder and to keep the House of Orange from power. After 1702, that undercurrent was much weaker. There was a candidate to succeed the childless William III: his Frisian relative Johan Willem Friso. He, however, was only fifteen, and in 1702 his stadholderate in Friesland was still ruled by his guardian and mother, Henriëtte Amalia von Anhalt-Dessau. The States of Holland saw no reason why they should be supervised by this mother-son combination. Matters eventually might have taken another turn if Johan Willem Friso had not drowned in 1711. But with his death there was no longer an Orange with much influence in The Hague. As in the case of 1650, the stadholder did have a son, born after his death, but he grew up in faraway Leeuwarden and remained practically unknown in Holland.

Concerning the issue of the stadholder, it depended, as always, on Holland. The young prince, later known as William IV, became stadholder of Friesland at his birth, stadholder of Groningen in 1718, and of Gelderland in 1722. He also assumed that office in Drenthe, which governed itself but had no representation in the States-General. By 1722, then, half the Republic had a stadholder, but that counted for little more than nothing as long as Holland belonged to the other half. Furthermore, William had difficulty making further political inroads. In the first place, there was no real Orange party. It is true that there were people, including some regents, who desired the restoration of the stadholderate, but nowhere, either on the national or provincial level, was there a political grouping that expressly aimed at this change in government. The ideal may have lived with some, but it did not inspire them to take organized action. In the second place, William's Frisian court lacked the money and the political clout to bolster the Orangist cause. If one wanted to motivate regents, influence their votes, and move them toward a collective stand, then one needed to offer them something, preferably high office. But those with little power also have little to give. Thus William IV and his friends were able to accomplish very little. They could only hope for a dramatic turn of fate, a repetition of 1672.

That dramatic turn came in 1747. This time, too, it involved a war with France and its invasion of the United Netherlands. French forces did not make it as far as they had in 1672, but the Barrier had not been able to stop them, and they soon controlled Dutch territory south of the great rivers. These developments happened more gradually than in 1672, so that panic and confusion did not return in the same measure. But Orangist cries were heard again, and again they proved irresistible. In this crisis, William IV accepted the stadholderate for all the United Provinces.

This was not merely a restoration of the old position. William IV would differ from his predecessors in two important respects. In the first place, none of them had ever held the stadholderate over all seven provinces. William IV was thus the first to hold sway over the whole country. In the second place, the stadholderate was now made a hereditary position, to be inherited either by male or female descendants of William IV. The mood was so favorable toward a more forceful administration that the inexperienced William IV was able to attain even more power than William III had ever possessed. In effect, the Republic became a monarchy in 1747. The title of stadholder was maintained, but it was little more than a memory of the past, since it had lost all semblance of dependence. The States had lost their freedom to have, or not to have, a stadholder.

Skirmish on the Dam, Amsterdam, during the riots of 1747. (Atlas van Stolk, Rotterdam.)

Democratic Opposition

William IV would need to use his new powers. The revolution of 1747 had been made possible by the external military threat. But it was intensified by a growing unhappiness among broad sections of the middle classes, discontent with how the Republic was administered. The Republic had always been a country in which a relatively large number of people engaged in political discussion – much larger than the small number of regents actually formulating policy. Freedom of the press was not unlimited, but it was free enough to publish any information of real significance to the public. There was also a fair degree of room for opposing viewpoints. By the seventeenth century, people had begun to form their own political opinions about which policies the Republic should pursue. The broad public had no direct say in the affairs of state, but the ruling regents, like any other government, could hardly show complete indifference to their opinion.

This remained the case during the eighteenth century, but a new factor very slowly began to assert itself. The exchange of ideas was no longer restricted to the direction of policy, but began to include discussions about the very political institutions of the Republic. The first sign of this was in 1672, and the conflicts between the Old and New Crews raised the question again. A further intensification of the issue began after William IV took office. This trend was not yet apparent in 1747, when a popular movement backed the Prince of Orange without giving much thought to a political program for structural reform. In part this was because the level of reflection had not yet reached this point, and in part because they trusted that the new strongman would have the solution. When William proved unable to meet these expectations, a second wave of unrest swept over the United Provinces.

That the war was not going well was the least of the public's concerns, although resounding victories might have distracted them from their grievances. But negative reports from the front confirmed the general sense of unhappiness. Taxes were high, especially in Holland. We have seen why these taxes were necessary: the province had a high rate of debt. The population had to bear the burden, year in, year out, without any spectacular successes on either the foreign or domestic fronts. For them, the heavy taxes seemed to serve no purpose.

Moreover, Holland's tax collection system did not exactly promote a sense of common purpose. Most taxes were gathered, not by officials, but by private parties who leased the right to do so from the state. These parties were obligated to pay a predetermined annual amount to the government, since the government had given them the authority to collect a certain tax. They paid the agreed upon sum directly to the government. Anything above this amount first had to go toward covering their administrative costs, and what remained was their own private profit. The system was not without merit. It spared the state from taking on a sizable bureaucracy, and it limited the possibilities for tax fraud. Civil servants could be corruptible, but tax leaseholders were far less likely to be so, since a high tax return was in their best interest. The chief weakness of the tax lease system was that it provided no moral encouragement for people to pay their taxes. Those paying less than they owed did not have to feel guilty about undermining the common good. Rather, they were only reducing the profits of the leaseholder, who, regardless of revenue, was obliged to turn over the predetermined sum to the government. Certainly no one had any sympathy for the tax collector, on the contrary. Complaints about high taxes were all directed at him. He was the exploiter who enriched himself with the sweat of the common people. In 1748, political activists took up the reform of this tax system as part of their program.

The center of these efforts could be found in Amsterdam. This is where the name most commonly associated with the movement arose: the *Doelisten*, named after the militia target halls where they typically congregated. But the name is more than coincidental. The bourgeois city militias, charged with keeping peace and order in their city, consisted of burghers who were wealthy enough to pay for the cost of their own military equipment. Their officers belonged to the regent class, but the soldiery represented a much broader group of the urban population. Militiamen often had their own businesses, so that they acutely felt the bite of high taxes. Moreover, they were educated enough to possess political judgments that went beyond personal prejudice; they read newspapers and pamphlets. Accordingly, these *Doelisten* thought that they, too, should have a share of political power.

In Amsterdam, middle-class power was thus expressed through the militias. In other locales, other kinds of organizations that were based on local traditions would play a similar role. In some places, for instance, the call went up to restore the old guilds' political influence. These phenomena should make clear that in 1748 there was as yet no national program with a unified set of demands. But we can point to two main aims of this widely divergent movement. The first was the abolition of the tax lease system, the second was a broadening of the basis for political participation. No one spoke of throwing out the regents, only (in this initial phase) of a modest increase in the political say of groups which had, hitherto, been completely shut out of power.

William IV was supposed to be the leader of this movement, a man of the hour who would give concrete expression to its desires. He had the political winds at his back, for even the regents had worked to give him an unprecedented lock on power. He would usher in a new political order to the cheers of the whole bourgeoisie, whose support would only increase William's already substantial power. But the stadholder did not live up to expectations. It is easier to read history than it is to read the future, and William IV based his actions on what the past had established as precedent. His predecessor William III had ruled with the help of the regents by keeping them under pressure and thus ensuring that they did his bidding, and this is what William IV attempted to do. He was not a visionary who understood that the future belonged to the middle classes. It is also not clear if he would have benefitted from concessions to the middle classes. Moreover, the old system was not that fragile; it would take more than forty years before the regents finally fell from power. It is possible, therefore, that William IV took the wisest course – even if his wisdom was nothing more than an unimaginative and superficial conservatism.

That William paid a price for his lack of imagination is something he hardly would have perceived, and perhaps there were only a few who were profoundly aware of his missed chance. But 1748 is not an unimportant year in Dutch history. A nascent reform movement sought support from the stadholder and was ignored. Orangism had rebuffed political reform, and it was the last time political reformers would seek help from the stadholder.

The *Doelisten* movement was in itself a passing phenomenon. It provided no direct inspiration for the following generation, and it brought no political discussion groups into existence. But it was a sign of coming political change. The Dutch middle classes began to express themselves more vocally, and authorities could no longer count on their unconditional loyalty. In the seventeenth century, regents associated rebellion with the mob. They believed that the mob sometimes acted spontaneously, and that it was sometimes provoked by higher personages. It was never completely reliable. In contrast, the middle classes were considered reasonable. It was their militias, after all, which were charged with reigning in unrest in the cities. In 1748, however, this old pattern had broken down. A new age had dawned.

Cultural and Church Life

The new temperament would develop only gradually over the course of the eighteenth century. Ultimately, it strongly influenced the country's politics, and was expressed in its culture. In the Second Stadholderless

Era, however, there was still little sign of it. Dutch culture of the early eighteenth century was not especially distinguished. It lacked the great figures of the seventeenth century and hence did not possess the ability to express a unique artistic or literary vision. For this vision it had also become too sensitive to the influences of the dominant French culture.

Growing attraction to things French need not be an artistic disadvantage. The poets of the seventeenth century had also worked with internationally accepted rules and forms. Vondel and Huygens were the recognizable contemporaries of Milton and Donne, all of them drinking deeply from the same spiritual sources. But the carriers of Dutch culture in the early eighteenth century added little of their own to the foreign examples they imitated. Instead, they became thoroughly enmeshed in French culture. It was precisely the most creative Dutch spirits of the eighteenth century who insisted on using French whenever they said anything important. The philosopher Frans Hemsterhuis wrote exclusively in French, and Belle van Zuylen opted for French long before she left the country. Can it surprise us that the family archives of the regents include many letters in French, exchanged between the great ladies and gentlemen of Holland? The Englishman James Boswell went to study at Utrecht in 1763 because he thought it would be good for his French. The elite culture of the Republic, presumably, was in danger of losing its Dutch moorings.

The most important developments in the country's spiritual life of the time took place in the ecclesiastical realm. Not in the middle, where the Reformed church was still sturdily planted, but at the great fringe areas where the less fortunate took their more modest places. Dutch Catholics occupied a considerable portion of this space. Insofar as their lives bore the stamp of their faith, they functioned at the edges of public life. It was scarcely all peace and rest at these edges. On the one hand, Dutch Catholics faced the same questions that confronted their church internationally. Jansenism, that branch of Catholicism inspired by Augustine (and described more fully in Chapter Five), also had its influences on the Republic. On the other hand, many priests serving in the Republic became irritated that the Dutch church was treated by Rome as a mission area (i.e., without its own church hierarchy) and that it remained subject to the papal nuncio in Brussels. Religious orders like the Jesuits felt this less keenly, but the secular clergy chafed under this treatment.

Open conflict broke out in 1723. Catholic opponents of papal policy elected their own archbishop of Utrecht. Rome refused to accept this act of emancipation and excommunicated the new archbishop. The result was a schism in which the nationally based "Old Catholic church" challenged the church of Rome. It did not get the broad support which its leaders hoped for, and the overwhelming majority of Catholics remained faithful to the mother church. Meanwhile, immigration from the German borderlands increased the Catholic population of the Republic. But these immigrants had no political influence and very little culturally.

As we have noted, the culture of the early 1700s was as undistinguished as its politics. In his classic sketch of Dutch culture in the seventeenth century, Johan Huizinga rejected its characterization as the "Golden Age," saying this term was more appropriate to the eighteenth. Wood and iron, pitch and tar, daring and energy – these are the catchwords for Rembrandt's age. The external glitter and ostentation of imported luxuries – these were the identifying marks of the eighteenth century, a truly "golden" age. Perhaps the problem of this period is best defined by the vague and much maligned notion of "an age of transition." The Republic was still rich and prosperous, internationally respected, with its administration in the hands of the same class of men who had so ably guided it in the seventeenth century. The old solutions seemed to work so well that new ones were scarcely considered. And yet a great power had become a small one, and the center of international trade had moved to London. Culturally, the classical tradition lost its dominant position to German scholarship and French reason. Tradition was no longer the last word but an object of critical analysis. The Dutch, too, would have to find new answers to new problems.

8. The Crisis Nears (1751-1780)

Economic and Political Problems

In recent years, looming European unification has sparked a discussion about Dutch national identity. Dutch people went searching for the country's historical roots, uncovering the origins of the Republic, reevaluating the roles of Erasmus and Calvin, and attempting to identify the traditions behind Dutch tolerance. In the end, however, they could not recognize themselves in the Dutch of the seventeenth century. The average Dutch man or woman of the late twentieth century has nearly as much difficulty identifying him or herself with Jacob Cats and Jan Pietersz. Coen as they do with the old Germanic tribes or with the *Hoeken* and *Kabeljauwen* of the Middle Ages. Nevertheless, all of these figures indisputably belong to their past, and all of them, in one way or another, contributed to the creation of today's society. But if the contemporary Dutch wish to find historical subjects resembling themselves, then they will first find them in the second half of the eighteenth century.

Historians appear to have realized this somewhat earlier than the general public. Since the 1960s, they have given growing attention to the Patriots and the Batavian Republic, which replaced the old Dutch Republic in 1795. If historians used to regard the Patriots and the Republic of 1795 as an unhappy interlude of foreign domination, they now have more of an eye for how Patriotism and the French Revolution paved the way for the Dutch liberalism of the nineteenth century. If old liberal historians like H.T. Colenbrander once repudiated their Batavian ancestors, scholars are now more likely to regard the revolutionaries of 1795 as important forerunners to the constitutional monarchy. The reforms of the Dutch state did not begin in 1813 with the return of the Prince of Orange, as was once supposed. Rather, they had their beginning with the Patriots, and first found expression in the constitutions of the Batavian Republic.

Beggar, in a drawing from 1772.

This chapter will end in 1780. We must not run ahead of the events, but we must see them in the light of that future. This does not mean that the judgment of the present generation is decisive, since it may be mistaken in its rising appreciation of the late eighteenth century. Many insignificant developments have been trumpeted in the textbooks with great fanfare; might not the reform movement of the eighteenth century be such an example? In any event, the self-confidence and optimism of the current generation are native to the period itself. On the one hand, people were aware of the shortcomings of the Republic's government and concerned about the decline in prosperity. On the other hand, they shared the expectation that they, as people living in the modern eighteenth century, would be able not only to critically analyze the problems, but also to find solutions for them.

Those problems were sizable enough. The economic descent of the eighteenth-century Republic is a well-established theme in the history books. Although no longer described in highly dramatic terms, the fact of the decline remains intact. In absolute figures, trade and shipping volume from 1750 to 1800 do not fare badly. But these figures do not reveal that the Republic's share of international trade declined significantly during the period. Amsterdam's harbor remained an important center for shipping, and its financial institutions still dominated European capital. But it lost ground to Hamburg, and much more to London.

Positive developments in agriculture and fishing could not reverse Dutch fortunes.

At least the Dutch of the eighteenth century had become well aware of the darker side of economic developments. They certainly professed to see them. In Holland, wages in the seventeenth century had been relatively high. In the eighteenth century, they remained at the same level, but the cost of living declined, increasing real wages. After 1750, however, this happy situation was reversed. Historical demography informs us that the population of Europe rose sharply in the last half of the eighteenth century. This had happened before, around 1500, and the consequences were not dissimilar: more people, accordingly more demand for food, and a substantial increase in the cost of basic necessities. This trend became particularly evident in the 1770s. Wage earners were compelled to spend more of their income on food, and less of their income on other items, like clothing and household goods. This prompted a decline in industrial production, and with it, a decline in employment. Many people now became dependent on public charity, and a growing number of beggars appeared in the streets, appealing to the kindness of more fortunate citizens.

International developments were hardly rosy, either. Great powers come and go, a truth to which the history of eighteenth-century Europe fully attests. The Republic's best days were over, and Spain and Sweden, too, were spent powers. In contrast, Prussian ascendancy became fully evident under the forceful Frederick the Great, and Russia was emerging from its isolation to play a role in European politics which was more in line with its great potential. Together with France, England, and Austria, Prussia and Russia formed the five great powers of Europe, and international politics would now be determined by how these powers measured their interests. European politics shifted to new priorities, since Prussian and Russian interests had become more important, and Spanish and Dutch interests less so. Relations among the great powers were themselves subject to much flux. The centuries-old enmity between France and the Habsburgs was no longer a fixture of the diplomatic landscape, and new combinations of alliances, even temporary ones, were possible whenever mutual interest dictated them.

All of this naturally had effects for the Republic as well. In the Seven Years' War, begun in 1756, the Habsburgs made an alliance with France for the first time in history, fighting against England and Prussia. The new alliance between the emperor and the French king meant that the Austrian Netherlands was no longer a buffer between France and the Republic. The barrier fortresses the Dutch maintained at the French border now hardly served a purpose. For this reason, it is understandable that the Republic did not wish to risk war against this Franco-Austrian alliance. At the same time, however, the Dutch had friendly ties with England, whose government let it be known that it was counting on the Republic's friendship. When the Republic decided to remain neutral, its old friendship with England was diminished. Energetically diligent in undermining the enemy's capacity to trade, the British navy, then dominant on the seas, captured numerous Dutch merchant ships and declared their cargoes contraband.

The dilemma of Dutch foreign policy became manifest during the Seven Years' War. If the Republic wished to defend itself against a land attack, then it would need a strong army – especially now that the Barrier had lost its strategic significance. If they wished to protect their trade against English chicanery, then they would need a fleet equal to His Majesty's navy. Both options cost a good deal of money, and the Republic simply was not powerful enough to adequately meet both challenges. If it divided its resources between the army and navy, the paltry results would impress neither the French nor the English. If it made a clear choice for one or the other, the Republic would be permanently tied to one of the great powers. Giving a priority to rebuilding the fleet would mean friendship with France; beefing up the army would mean an alliance with England. And it was precisely England and France which were routinely at war with each other. Even if after an alliance the Republic should still wish to remain neutral, it would no longer be in a position to maintain its independence alone. It would need to rely on its foreign ally.

The Dutch were divided on what to do. Since the days of William III, the Republic had always tried to attain a balance of power in Europe. Now that this balance was achieved, the Republic became its victim. As long as French domination remained a threat, the Dutch could agree, more or less, on foreign policy. Consensus was not always easy to reach, but in 1688 and 1702 every Dutch statesman realized that the only responsible course was to resist France. By the second half of the eighteenth century, however, no European power loomed so large that all other dangers seemed tiny in comparison. The choice between France and England, therefore, could become a matter of discussion. In Holland, for instance, trade was the central issue. Many people in that province did not want to be dependent on their English rival, but wanted the Republic to give the priority to a naval defense. This would lead, of course, to a pro-French foreign policy. The Republic's interior provinces, on the other hand, were more anxious about the threat of enemy armies; they preferred that most of the money be spent on strengthening the country's land forces. This would mean, in effect, a pro-English policy. This preference was strengthened by the traditions within the House of Orange. On three successive occasions, the head of that house had married an English princess: both William II and William III had married a Mary Stuart, and William IV had married Anne of Hanover. The Oranges had numerous friends and relatives at the English court. For them, a French-oriented foreign policy was hardly an option, and they fostered the traditional ties between the two sea powers.

Orange rule, however, had itself become a problem. William IV died in 1751, only forty years old. Inaugurated with high expectations and showered with power after power, he failed to achieve anything of consequence. Nor was his successor immediately prepared to do anything more; in 1751, William V was only three years old. He did become stadholder upon his father's death, in compliance with the hereditary statute of the position. But he remained for the time being under the guardianship of his mother, Anne of Hanover. The eighteenth century produced great women rulers like Maria Theresa of Austria and Catherine II of Russia. Anne, however, was no such figure. She attended to the interests of the House of Orange, but gave the Republic no political leadership, and none of her advisors had sufficient skill or prestige to offer it themselves. When she died in 1759, the guardianship fell to the provincial States. Duke Ludwig Ernst of Brunswick-Wolfenbüttel became captain-general of the armed forces, but was explicitly denied a political role.

It was not likely, however, that the duke would refrain from playing this role. As long as rebuilding the navy or the army remained a burning issue, the position of captain-general could hardly remain apolitical. It was, after all, the duke's duty to guard the stadholder's interests until an Orange could assume power. William IV had managed to procure considerable influence over appointments to government posts. During his rule, the system existent under William III returned. In every province, the seventeenth century stadholder had installed trusted allies who advised him on who should fill each office. And because there were a number of good positions to give away, William III had been able to increase his grip on the Republic's administration by making the stadholder's favor a prerequisite for a successful governmental career. William IV reintroduced this system and had accumulated much influence through the parceling out of government posts. After his death, both Anne and Brunswick did their very best to keep the system in place.

In 1766, William V reached majority, assuming his duties as stadholder. He was not the first Orange to assume so heavy a task at so young an age. Youth had not prevented his predecessors from acting resolutely in the affairs of state, but William V did not act with the same decisiveness. He remained dependent on the duke of Brunswick, and they even made a secret accord with each other: Brunswick obligated himself to further advise the prince, and William promised that the duke would never be held accountable for his advice. It was a strange contract, in which neither party had much recourse if the other party should be unwilling to follow it. And they were strange characters, too, who would think their interests furthered by such an arrangement. At least as long as the so-called Act of Consultancy remained secret it could do little harm. When it was revealed many years later, however, at the height of factional infighting, it would cost Brunswick his position.

It was this same William who now officially led the Republic. He was the head of its patronage system and could staff the governing councils with his clients and cronies. He had the power, and he would have to use it to keep the Republic's fortunes afloat. His legacy is not impressive. If we ask why he failed, we would first have to say that his influence over the provinces was uneven. In Friesland and especially the large cities of Holland, local authorities had managed to circumvent William's patronage, establishing their own spheres of influence. With the exception of a rare military coup, conducting policy against Holland had always been doomed to failure. These are the established facts, but they do not wholly explain William V's failure. Political tensions reached crisis levels under his rule, but he never attempted a coup d'état. He refused to do what Maurits and William II are so often blamed for, but his reputation is none the better for his restraint. If William II had too much decisiveness, William V had too little. He could not easily make decisions, and yet he did not want others to make them for him, either. He did not trust others' judgments, but trusted his own even less. He wanted to carry the responsibility alone, but could not assert himself as the leader of the nation. He possessed a well-developed patronage system, but he did not use it to initiate forceful and energetic policy.

Cultural and Political Reform

Political malaise, economic decline, growing poverty, pauperism: all of these suggest an age of decay. One need not subscribe to Marxist determinism in order to expect little from the culture of this period in Dutch history. The period cultivated no great spirits. Neither the arts nor the sciences produced any dizzyingly high achievements. Its people were mediocre and so were their accomplishments. The best of them, however, were able to produce work of fine, if not the highest, quality.

A typical representative of this period is the historian Jan Wagenaar. His twenty-one volume *History of the Fatherland* was a significant achievement. Wagenaar's history, as he himself admitted, pertained only to Holland, not the Republic. But those who keep this limitation in mind (as opposed to many of his later readers, who equated Holland with the Republic) must admit a certain admiration for how Wagenaar managed to complete a project of such size. Without a precedent on which to model his work, he organized it by his own lights, finding sources and developing his own method to analyze them critically. He

Jan Wagenaar (Stichting Icono-graphisch Bureau, The Hague.)

managed to pen a history that was used for generations and even now is not entirely outdated. And yet despite its merits, *History of the Fatherland* has two shortcomings which are not only particular to Wagenaar, but typical of his age. In the first place, it lacks style. Those who manage to read a hundred pages of Wagenaar without falling asleep will have learned a great number of facts, but will have encountered no arresting turn of phrase. In the second place, Wagenaar is not above party spirit. It is not that Wagenaar was a dishonest historian; he tried to be objective and to do justice to the motives of his subjects, and these efforts strengthened his authority as a scholar. That his personal preferences are nevertheless clearly visible can be forgiven him. But they did affect his representation of Dutch history, and thereby contributed to the politicization of the past, a trend all too evident in the party conflicts of the late eighteenth century.

Wagenaar has received additional attention here because his work is a mirror of eighteenth century culture. Though no longer possessing the luster of the seventeenth century, it was still capable of energy and accomplishment. It had inherited the seventeenth-century spirit, but was no longer identical to it. We can say of the seventeenth century that it wanted to preserve the harmony between Christian and classical civilization. Those who wish to harmonize the dissimilar, however, will often have to give priority to one or the other. The overwhelming majority of seventeenth-century lights chose, when pressed, to side with the Christian tradition. For that reason, their culture was and remained primarily Christian, regardless of how many Greek and Roman values had crept into it.

Thus an important change began during the eighteenth century, with the advent of the European Enlightenment. It came slowly to the Republic, and the universities in particular remained long wedded to the older intellectual tradition. The Enlightenment is only very vaguely discernible in Wagenaar, for example. By the last quarter of the eighteenth century, however, it attained a dominant intellectual place. The alliance between Christianity and the classical tradition gave way to a new one between Christianity and Enlightenment. The goal, though, remained the same: full harmony between the two. Both had their own contributions to make which the other needed to respect. The Enlightenment preached the message of progress, which could be attained through educating children in the light of reason, and in applying human knowledge to the service of humanity and of society. Christianity brought divine revelation, contained in Holy Scripture, and taught that God is the Supreme Architect of the universe, and that he leads all things toward a friendly, harmonious social order. In the eighteenth century, this form of optimistic Christianity and a Christian-based Enlightenment managed to maintain harmony with each other. But there can only be one master in a house, and from now on, reason would play that role.

This is at least true of the main currents of thought which determined Dutch culture. The rise of the Enlightenment, of course, also generated resistance, namely within the Reformed church. Not everybody believed in the new harmony between Enlightenment and Christianity,

and a number of Reformed pastors took issue with the increasing rationalism they encountered. They did not find much sympathy for their
concern, however. The dominant culture was not open to their opinions, and the new ideas eventually made inroads within the Reformed
church. Traditional Calvinism was thus pushed toward the margins,
both in church and society. The old truths were now especially held by
simple souls and those with small incomes. They did not break with the
church but had lost their confidence in its institutions. Worshipping in
unofficial conventicles, they formed the basis of a new movement which
would, in the nineteenth century, lead to new church denominations.

But they had little influence in a dominant culture which was
enlightened, Christian, optimistic, and full of enthusiasm for building a
better world – starting with the Republic of the Seven United Netherlands. Denizens of the new culture recognized the problems of their
age, but their belief in progress inspired them to find solutions, both for
the stagnant economy and the political impasse. Their optimism is most
clearly evident in the attempts to restore national prosperity undertaken by the so-called Economic Patriots. From an organizational standpoint, they excelled at their endeavor. The second half of the eighteenth
century was, incidentally, generally a time when people had a good
sense of organization. In a host of places, societies were set up to promote art and science in order to increase the happiness of the common
people. These societies were not necessarily tied ideologically to efforts
at political reform. But both the political and nonpolitical organizations
are signs of the same trend: the attempt by the middle classes to assert
their own role in public life.

One such society, the Holland Society of Sciences, provided a
national forum for discussion on economic issues when, in 1777, it
established a special section, the Economic Branch, to deal with such
issues. The society was (and still is) established in Haarlem. But the
Economic Branch had chapters throughout the country, and thus had
good access to a whole variety of information. The men of the Branch
well understood that the future was not just about Holland, but about
all the provinces; not just about trade, but also about agriculture and
commerce. But if they possessed a breadth of vision, they lacked an
analytical ability. They never did discover the real reasons for the economic decline. They attributed it to a lack of moral spirit and national
will. The optimism of the Enlightenment provided them with a solution: an improved education would teach people the old virtues of hard
work and frugality. This was looking back, nor forward. It is no coincidence that these reformers spoke so often of restoration. They were,
therefore, not yet real revolutionaries, since they searched the past for
an answer to their questions.

For the same reason, the political opposition of the 1770s was still
vague and inchoate. In the States-General and the States of Holland, a
feeling of discontent with the stadholderate system and a rejection of its
pro-English direction were the principal points uniting those who
wanted change. Democratically minded reformers were not usually
found in these high political circles. But despite their different motives,
both the democrats and the States party of the regents were brought

together by their opposition to the stadholder. The American Revolution enjoyed the heartfelt ideological support of the democratic party. The regents of Holland, particularly those in Amsterdam, had little interest in the theoretical underpinnings of the new United States, but they were interested in how Holland's trade might find new outlets in a country that was fighting a bitter war of independence against England. A pro-American, anti-Orange party thus emerged in the States of Holland under the leadership of several Pensionaries who would later be identified among the Patriots, but who were driven by much different ideals.

Further conflicts would cause the democrats and the regents' party to go their separate ways. The 1780s, and especially the Batavian Revolution, would bring a clarity to the political arena, long absent during the rule of William V. But this goes beyond the purview of this chapter. A eulogy for the Republic of the Seven United Netherlands cannot yet be given, for the Republic would not meet its death until 1795, and no one in 1780 could yet predict the circumstances of its demise. Nor was it yet clear that the reformers would triumph. For the time being, they would be strongly assailed in politics and the press by their opponents. But they had confidence in the future, and time would tell if their optimism was justified.

Ball at the court of Albrecht and Isabella, as depicted in a painting by F. Francken de Jonge, ca. 1611-1616. (Mauritshuis, The Hague.)

5 The Spanish and Austrian Netherlands, 1585-1780

C. Bruneel

The Habsburgs continued their efforts at centralizing their administration and tightening dynastic control over the Southern Netherlands. Attempts to make its administration more Spanish were part of their policy. The high nobility of the region, dismayed by their declining influence and the disastrous war against the North, unsuccessfully hatched a plot against the Spanish authorities. The South suffered greatly due to the effects of the war and an economic decline which was deepened by protectionism and mass migration from the South to the Dutch Republic. In the last half of the seventeenth century, the Southern Netherlands suffered again under the wars launched by the great powers, in particular those instigated by the ambitions of the French king Louis XIV.

The Austrian Habsburgs assumed control of the Southern Netherlands in 1713. After the end of the War of Austrian Succession (1748), peace and prosperity returned under Empress Maria Theresa as a result of the so-called Theresian Compromise: a large degree of self-rule in exchange for higher taxes and increased opportunities for Vienna to direct central policy in the region. The economy expanded as a result of government stimuli. Rising production in agriculture and rural population increases led to a decrease of land per capita and a labor surplus, making proto-industrialization possible.

Under the Spanish Habsburgs, the Southern Netherlands became the bulwark of the Catholic Counter Reformation. Religious life was especially influenced by the Jansenist controversy in the late seventeenth century. Beginning with Maria Theresa, relations between church and state became more adversarial. The empress resisted the Ultramontanists (who desired more papal influence in state and society) and strengthened her control over the clergy, policies which would be pursued even more forcefully by her son and successor, Joseph II.

The period begins with an unexpected development: the creation of a new state in the northern provinces, the result of their successful rebellion against Spain. Yet many in the South continued to feel a certain sense of kinship with the North, at least until 1625 or so, when the feeling largely disappeared and southerners developed a completely negative image of the Dutch Republic. Various factors widened the chasm: the religious divide, the South's economic dependence on the North, and the increasing cultural differences between them.

By virtue of its location, the Spanish Netherlands became vulnerable to attack by Spain's enemies. Bound to Spain and without its own allies, the region paid the price of Spanish defeats with its territory. Later, the great powers used the region as a "barrier" between France and the United Provinces. Eventually, the Southern Netherlands enjoyed a certain neutrality, a special status which was accorded to the region by the great nations of Europe as a way to keep the balance of power. The region was viewed as a sort of satellite state, a chess piece in the dynastic strategy of the Habsburgs.

The monarchs ruling over the Southern Netherlands saw their authority stymied by regional privileges, and all of them sought to impose a greater measure of centralized absolutism. Finding the right people to further this aim was obviously very important. The central government depended on jurists and administrators who themselves favored increased centralized authority. They could use their professions to weaken the various forms of personal authority and local power of their opponents. Thus the nobility slowly lost their prerogatives to these functionaries. The central government's fight against local power and privilege was clearly manifest in the towns and provinces. The ruling princes used their right to oversee local finances as the pretext to intervene in municipalities and increase their supervision over local affairs. They were only too eager, moreover, to make use of their right to appoint the magistracy in certain cities. In this way, they had indirect influence over who they would face in future negotiations, since these magistrates appointed representatives to the third estate of the States.

Although not democratically elected in the current sense of the word, the States were the representative body of every province, and were the principal opponents of the centralizing ambitions of the Spanish kings and (later) the Austrian emperors. Their traditional line of defense lay in threatening to withhold the grants (*bede*) sought by the sovereign. The ruling monarchs made every effort to reduce the States' financial power, but by and large failed to make much headway. The States, however, did routinely accede to their sovereign's financial requests. After 1600, the States agreed to the monarch's annual request for grants, after only formal deliberation of each petition. This pattern did not preclude short outbreaks of resistance, however, as when Hainaut and Brabant protested against the financial requests of Joseph II in the 1780s.

For a long time, the spirit of the Counter Reformation united church and state, and left its imprint on art and literature. At first, the Counter Reformation stimulated a spiritual energy and elan, but its long-term effects were stifling and finally led to antiecclesiastical reaction. After 1750, secular authorities began to resist the Ultramontanists, who believed in the personal infallibility of the pope and his direct jurisdiction over the local church. Instead, they became open to the Enlightenment and French classicism, using its ideas to justify government efforts to reduce the power of the church in the political realm.

Political developments, both in and outside the country, had obvious and important effects on the economy. After a relatively prosperous period in the early seventeenth century, economic activity suffered a downturn until the middle of the eighteenth century. The economic policies of Maria Theresa then freed the Southern Netherlands to a large degree from foreign dependence, stimulating the region's economic potential. Real industrial centers sprung up, providing the basis for the Industrial Revolution.

1. A Permanent Separation (1585-1648)

From the North-South Division to a Brief and Uncertain Independence

After the Spanish capture of Ghent and the surrender of Mechelen, Antwerp capitulated on 17 August 1585. This resounding Spanish victory put the region's governor-general, Alexander Farnese, duke of Parma, at the pinnacle of his career. His most difficult task, however, lay before him: reconquest of the North, which, surrounded by water, constituted a formidable fortress. Philip II's decisions, however, prevented him from launching a full-fledged attack on the North. First, Parma was forced to lend assistance to the construction of the supposedly invincible Armada against England; later, he was obliged to support France's Catholic League to ensure a Catholic monarch in Paris. Philip's desire to control these two powerful countries relegated the problem in the Netherlands to a secondary priority. Moreover, the Spanish king reckoned that success in England and France would in itself stop their support of the northern "rebels."

Philip's decisions had fateful consequences for the shifting boundaries between the Southern Netherlands and the United Provinces, as Spanish forces lost ground during the military operations of the 1590s. But Philip's military priorities were not the only dubious aspect of his administration of the Spanish Netherlands. Like many other sovereigns of his time, he regarded his lands as patrimonial possessions, to be used for his own good pleasure. His efforts to turn the Netherlands into a centralized monarchy, and later to offer it as an object of exchange, had no other objective than the promotion of his own royal interests. When Philip signed the Act of Abdication (1598), leaving the Netherlands to his daughter and son-in-law, the archdukes Isabella and Albrecht, he had only one thing in mind: putting an end to the financial and military hemorrhage which was weakening the power of the Spanish crown. Formally separating the Netherlands from Spain was supposed to ease the crown's troubles. In this way, Isabella and Albrecht inherited a restored Burgundian state, which (to the disappointment of the two) was not elevated to a kingdom. In any event, this reform came too late

The archdukes Albrecht and Isabella in a copper engraving dating from about 1600. (Universiteitsbibliotheek, Leuven.)

to reunite the Northern and Southern Netherlands. Representatives of the States-General in Brussels had hoped to discuss the various provisions of the new state in 1598. But they were left out of the process, and only asked to approve it when it was unveiled by Richardot, head chairman of the Privy Council. At most, the representatives were able to express a few wishes, without the hope that they would be granted. Meanwhile, the seats representing the northern provinces remained vacant. The slim hopes of reconciliation had been dashed.

Philip's cession of the Netherlands to his daughter Isabella and her husband contained strict conditions. The territory would revert to Spain in the event of either spouse's death, if they had produced no heirs. Given the age of the archduchess, this was a distinct possibility. If they did bear an heir, the Spanish king had the right to approve his or her marriage. Furthermore, the archdukes were obliged to swear their unwavering allegiance to the Catholic faith; they would lose their right to rule if the pope should ever accuse them of heresy. Economically, the Netherlands was also prohibited from trading in the Indies. The secret provisions of the Act were even stricter: the young archdukes promised to do whatever Philip II instructed them to do. They pledged to prosecute heretics and under no circumstances allow them in public service. The Spanish king also retained full rights over a number of strongly fortified fortresses, as well as the right to appoint their governors.

The continued presence of Spanish troops throughout the country also considerably restricted the archdukes' independence. When the war and subsequent negotiations went badly in the struggle against the United Provinces, the new government lost any authority it had in the court at Madrid. Philip III regarded the Act of Abdication as a last attempt by his father to restore peace to the Netherlands and treated his brother-in-law Albrecht as just another governor. Philip gave military leadership in the region to Ambrosio Spinola, but an acute lack of money – followed by mutinies – forced an end to his operations. The development of new alliances among Europe's great powers, a new receptiveness to negotiations in the Dutch Republic, and the good offices of the French and English ambassadors presented the Spanish with a solution. On 9 April 1609, the Twelve Years' Truce was signed in Antwerp. Philip III and the archdukes recognized the United Provinces as "free lands, states and provinces over whom they had no authority." As long as the Truce lasted, the boundaries between the Republic and the Spanish Netherlands would remain the same. The Scheldt remained closed, as it had been since 1585, when Holland's fleet had tried in vain to relieve Antwerp. The city remained closed to seagoing vessels, who were now compelled to unload their cargoes in Holland's harbors, where barges would take them upstream into Antwerp.

Absolutism Strengthened

The Spanish crown introduced a new political course in the Southern Netherlands after the moderate Duke of Parma died in 1592. It aimed at strengthening the Spanish king's absolutism by turning the Netherlands's governing apparatus over to the Spanish state bureaucracy. After the departure of Italian mercenaries in the wake of Parma's death, and during Philip II's intervention on behalf of the Catholic party in France, Spanish functionaries flooded Brussels. The Council of State, which consisted of local nobility, lost more and more of its powers to make foreign policy, and despite its protests, was no longer consulted on matters of war. The new governor-general surrounded himself almost exclusively with Spanish advisors, the most of important of whom was the secretary of state and war. This functionary – doubling as the governor-general's personal secretary – cosigned the army's orders and changed the official correspondence to Spanish, particularly for secret and coded letters. None of this changed when the Netherlands received nominal independence under Isabella and Albrecht. After all, they too were Spanish, the former by birth, the second by education.

Thus by the beginning of the seventeenth century, Spanish influence in the southern regions was at least as great as it had been under the duke of Alba. Three men set the tone for this phase of Spanish rule: general Spinola, the father confessor, who was also the political confidant of Archduke Albrecht, and the secretary of state and war, all three of whom were directly appointed by the Spanish king. Only one native found favor in the eyes of Madrid: Jean Richardot, chairman of the Privy Council. A friend of the humanist Justus Lipsius and the painter-diplomat Pieter Paul Rubens, Richardot was an ambitious man, an Hispanophile (which he readily admitted) – and a fervent proponent of royal absolutism. Absolutism, he believed, could be imposed on the Netherlands, as long as one was realistic about the circumstances and avoided breaking with too many regional traditions. Richardot ardently defended Philip's act of provisional independence before the States-General in 1598, and when that same body took months to deliberate over a grant to the archdukes in 1600, he declared in the name of the archdukes that a grant of 3.6 million guilders had been approved, and sent the representatives home.

Meanwhile Spanish juntas, composed of high Spanish administrators and military officers, further eased the Council of State out of its traditional duties in diplomacy and war. Domestic policy was left in the hands of the Privy Council, comprising largely of jurists. With Richardot's death in 1609, the Council was left with no great personality to lead it. Still, it continued its task of unifying the region's law and jurisprudence. In 1606 it issued an edict declaring that customary law needed to be reviewed and codified by the central government if it were to remain in force. The Privy Council tried to bring both the civil and criminal law of the various provinces into greater uniformity; the Eternal Edict of 1611 was a first step in achieving this.

The formal independence of the Southern Netherlands did not last long, and its reannexation to Spain occurred in two phases. In 1616, the Act of Abdication was effectively repealed when Philip III again demanded that the southern provinces take an oath of allegiance to him, confirming the rest of Europe's doubts about the sovereignty of the archdukes. When Albrecht died in 1621, his wife was demoted to the level of governor-general. The second step, which took place in the same year, was the resumption of the war which followed the end of the Twelve Years' Truce. Philip III (who also died in 1621) had decided to renew the war to oppose Holland's expansion in the Far East. The pope, too, favored the war to prevent Catholicism from disappearing in the United Provinces. In declaring war and mobilizing his forces in the region, the king ended the last illusion that the Southern Netherlands was independent.

The Truce changed nothing in the Spanish government's attitude toward its subjects in the Netherlands, and the military defeats that the Spanish armies suffered only intensified the bitterness of the region's own leaders. The Council of State lost still more of its power to govern, and the affairs of state were decided by a commission, which could find only two natives loyal enough to be included. Even the Hispanophile nobility complained about this unhappy state of affairs.

Eventually their discontent with the prevailing system led to the so-called Conspiracy of Nobles. Secretly encouraged by France's Cardinal Richelieu, a group of nobles planned to overthrow the regional government with the military assistance of France and the United Provinces. But the plotting nobles did not realize that they were being used by Richelieu, who wanted to weaken Spanish authority in the Netherlands without a French military invasion. The nobles were thus abandoned to their fate. The conspiracy also fizzled because unforeseen peace initiatives toward the United Provinces undermined the already very limited support for their cause. In order to raise the heavy taxes required to pay the soldiery, Isabella was forced, under pressure from the whole country, to call the States-General together in 1632 (for the last time, as it turned out). The archduchess agreed to the States' demands for direct negotiations with the United Provinces, with peace, or at least a truce, as its goal. The resulting initiatives proved to be the fatal blow for the conspirators. Arrests, a few executions, and a general amnesty in 1634 put an end to the plot.

The Spanish authorities were now even less inclined to regard the local nobility with any favor, and the nobility made no further efforts to increase their political participation until the early eighteenth century. Meanwhile, the new chairman of the Privy Council, Pieter Roose, profited from the death of Isabella in December 1633. He quietly undermined the South's negotiations with the Republic, which was not difficult to do, given the hostility to peace talks both on the part of the North and on the part of Philip IV. Having failed, the States-General was dissolved, never to meet again under Spanish authority.

Through the wars and diplomatic intrigues of the early seventeenth century, foreign statesmen began conceiving of a new role for the Southern Netherlands. Instead of conquering or dividing the region, they began to see it as a buffer state between France and the United Provinces. Richelieu first expressed this view during the Franco-Dutch alliance of 1635, and Mazarin, his successor under the young king Louis XIV, would take up the idea again in 1658. The proposal also gained currency in the Republic. Spain – despite the continued fighting – remained, as always, prepared to negotiate on the region's future, given its increasingly exposed position in the Southern Netherlands. The opening of the peace conference at Münster permitted emissaries to intensely negotiate this issue. The Peace of Münster, signed by Spain and the United Provinces on 30 January 1648, confirmed the provisions of the Twelve Years' Truce, this time for good. Spain again formally recognized the Republic as a fully sovereign state, abandoning any claim to it. The boundary between the two countries was established, and free trade between them began – although the Scheldt remained closed. Moreover, the Peace finalized the territorial losses of the Spanish Netherlands: northern portions of Flanders and Brabant would remain under the Republic, although the final boundary across Flanders would not be established until 1664.

Internally, the absolutist offensive of the Spanish crown continued its momentum, evident in the decline of three regional forces: the diminishing role of the Council of State, the virtual disappearance of the States-General, and the waning political role of the high nobility, which now showed more interest in the glamour of the Brussels court. Spanish royal authority was still obliged to tread with care around local and provincial privileges, but the process of centralization nevertheless continued.

On the provincial level, the evolution of two institutions symbolized the rise of centralized power. The old provincial high courts had traditionally enjoyed priority over the provincial States. They directly represented the prince, while the States were only representatives of the king's subjects. The organization of the high courts, their composition and their prerogatives, had been established in detail under

Charles V and eventually under the archdukes. These "courts" did not just have judicial powers, as they do today, although judicial appeals were an important part of their task. They also had powers to legislate and implement laws. In most provinces, a governor headed these courts; he was usually a member of the great nobility with proven military or diplomatic abilities. These governors pledged their service to the ruling prince – but as vassals, not as bureaucratic functionaries. However, the governors' potential for independence led the monarchs of the seventeenth and eighteenth centuries to push for the abolition of the post of governor whenever possible, and they gradually succeeded in doing so, with a few exceptions. The high court's chairman increasingly supplanted the governor before he eventually assumed his position altogether. As a trusted confidant of Brussels, the chairman could be counted upon to further administrative centralization. Accordingly, chairmen were increasingly chosen for their political, rather than juridical skills. They were expected to counteract the influence of the provincial States, which remained too politically unreliable for Brussels's taste.

The centralizing process was also noticeable in the other influential post in the high courts: the fiscal officer, a function largely established by an edict of 1603. The fiscal officer also inherited a good deal of authority once belonging to the provincial governor. He was closely associated with, and responsible to, the Privy Council. Judicially, his specific tasks made him the chief defender of the prince's rights and prerogatives; politically, he was the eye and the arm of the central authority.

Most members of the courts and councils were jurists. But the class background of its members varied considerably; some councils contained a high percentage of "*de courte robe*" (nobility) and some included high-ranking churchmen. But in general, the number of nobility and their influence in these organs declined precipitously during the seventeenth century. Although the provincial high court stood in the monarch's service, it was not merely a blind instrument of central authority. The old provincial privileges had stated that the provincial high court was also supposed to be "the depository and guardian of the provincial laws." It was therefore required to determine whether new royal ordinances were in accord with each province's respective laws.

The provincial States were, by their very nature, the strongest defenders of local privilege against centralized authority. By the seventeenth century they had lost their offensive role, but they proved more than willing to obstruct or slow new royal demands on their power. Each "States" included the three "estates" of society, but not all three were invariably represented when the States of the various provinces met. The First Estate, the clergy, was often only represented by the abbots of the large abbeys; the lower secular clergy, serving the parishes, hardly ever played a role. The nobility (the Second Estate) had its own rules for determining its representatives, if it was not, as in the case of Flanders, politically irrelevant. The Third Estate, representing the commoners, usually only included representatives of the large cities, whose administrations were heavily influenced by the guilds. Important sections of the population, therefore, had no representation whatsoever in the formation of the States' policies.

The first task of the States was to reach a constitutional agreement with the new ruling sovereign. Each province had its own ceremonies to welcome the new ruling prince, each province concluded its own agreement with the sovereign, and each prince swore, through an emissary, to honor its privileges. Then the States swore an oath of loyalty to the sovereign on behalf of the subjects. Even royal jurists recognized the value of such a reciprocal agreement, and the prince had no choice but to acquiesce. The developing modern state required ever increasing sums of money, and so the sovereign ruler was obliged to call the States together with increasing frequency. Without the ruler's command, they could not convene, nor could they dissolve themselves. After they were dismissed, day-to-day policy was carried out by the States' Permanent Deputation. It included members of the three estates and was present in nearly all southern provinces in 1600. The Permanent Deputation worked together with the pensionary, who was the legal advisor and head of the province's administration.

After Richardot's political intervention of 1600, the various States routinely gave the king the grants he wanted, although they maintained the formalities of request and consideration. Sometimes they dragged out the procedure, and the formal approval of funds took a year. Sometimes the king also asked for special grants, or, in unusual circumstances, outright gifts. In these cases, passage by the States could hardly be taken for granted. Whatever the case, the mechanisms for decision making were quite variable and complex. In Brabant, for example, the opposition of one representative of the three cities represented in the States could delay or complicate collection of a tax – even if the rest of the province had approved it. The official record of the States usually included appendices of both complaints and positive proposals which were penned by regional interests. The States also decided how the grants would be funded – that is, how they would be taxed. Usually, it involved property and excise taxes, which were collected by the States themselves.

Economics and Society

The Economics of War

The war and its dislocations naturally had an effect on the region's demography, and regional analyses permit us to sketch the broad contours of population shifts. One shift was particularly dramatic in the second half of the sixteenth century, when a mass migration, otherwise unheard-of in modern times, shook Brabant and Flanders. Between 1540 and 1630, some 150,000 persons left for the United Provinces, most of them between 1577 and 1589. They were not only ordinary wage earners; they were especially the highly skilled artisans and the intellectual elites of the region. The migration of their expertise, therefore, gave the North a great advantage. The reason for their exodus was chiefly religious, but economic motivations were also a root cause. Whatever the motivation, the Spanish gave the inhabitants of Antwerp two options after the city fell: to stay – if they became Catholic – or to emigrate. Given this choice, the metropolis declined in population from around 80,000 people to only 42,000 in 1589.

Another, more long lasting cause of demographic bloodletting was the epidemics of disease. "*A peste, fame, et bello libera nos, Domine*" ("From pestilence, famine and war, save us, O Lord") was the prayer recited in the churches. This ugly trio constituted the great evils of the time, and they were closely related. The plague recurred – although fortunately with diminishing force – from the end of the sixteenth century to its last outbreak in 1669 and 1670. Under the general names of "dysentery" and "fevers," many other sicknesses also left their effects. Wars were particularly effective in spreading disease, and fewer people died on the battlefield than succumbed to the epidemics introduced by soldiers during their campaigns. Once caught from the soldiery, villagers would spread a disease among themselves.

The third plague, famine, was less connected to the other two, since climatic changes and bad weather were the chief reasons for hunger. Bread was the staple food of the population and a bad harvest meant catastrophe. But war also had its direct and indirect effects. It could lead to the destruction of crops, or disruptions in the transportation of food. Hunger, in turn, provided the right conditions for epidemics.

In spite of its own persistent rhythms, the economy was hard hit by the war. The 1580s in particular had dealt it deep wounds. Economic activity, which declined sharply in Antwerp, was evident in, among other things, the rental prices of homes. Declines in tithing, as documented by the church, point to a virtual standstill in agricultural production. Forges and weaving mills were abandoned. Once peace returned, however, there were some signs of recovery.

Here we must make a clear distinction between the countryside and the cities. Restoring urban economic vitality is a slow and difficult process, while in the countryside people need only, in a manner of speaking, take up their shovels in order to produce a crop. Even between cities there were large differences. Antwerp, for instance, was much harder hit than Ghent, and there is no doubt that Antwerp's prosperity was already waning before 1585. By 1595 there were signs of a tentative – but hardly sustained – recovery. And in the mid-seventeenth century, like many other cities in Europe, Antwerp would experience another economic blow, made worse by a new war in the Southern Netherlands.

The Recovery of Antwerp

Still, Antwerp managed to reorient its economy, and its sure, if slow, recovery after 1600 rested on a number of pillars. Maritime trade was not destroyed, although it suffered heavily in the war. Economic links over land continued with Germany, Italy, and France, despite a decline in transportation. Trade from Antwerp also developed a new character. If countless families emigrated to the United Provinces and Germany, there were also many others which left for Venice, Naples, Messina, Cadiz, Seville, and Lisbon. There they created Flemish "nations," which formed a trading network with Antwerp as its center. Antwerp provided the finances for this trade, which could be done without the goods ever passing through the city itself. Until 1650, this network consisted largely of family businesses; later, it was done through the temporary union of small and middle-sized merchant enterprises, a fore-shadowing of the modern corporation.

The Scheldt city also remained the most important financial center of the Spanish Netherlands. Antwerp became the pivot in a great exchange market, as an intermediary between the Protestant North and the Catholic South, precisely at the moment that the North's commercial interest in the Mediterranean was growing. The city hosted a stock exchange where hosts of brokers and bankers (who were also often traders) met each other. Antwerp, moreover, was the place where the States, cities, and private parties borrowed money – even after Brussels and Ghent also became important financial centers in the eighteenth century. The city also retained a place in the insurance markets.

The last pillar of Antwerp's economic reconversion was its industry, which specialized in the production of art works and luxury goods. They were exported to Italy, Vienna, parts of Central Europe, and the Iberian peninsula. The Moretus family, successors to Plantijn, used their printing firm for the massive distribution of Spanish religious books throughout Catholic Europe – and the Spanish colonies. Likewise, Antwerp had a near monopoly on the production of devotional prints. In the textile sector, silk production flourished. In addition, numerous factories were set up to refine sugar and salt, and to produce glass and soap. After 1635, the city also became the most important center of copper processing.

The Rest of the Country

The story of Antwerp's recovery cannot adequately summarize economic developments in the rest of the Spanish Netherlands. Textiles

Frans Francken II's The Painting Cabinet of Sebastiaan Leerse *shows the curiosa chamber of a wealthy family at the beginning of the seventeenth century. (Koninklijk Museum voor de Schone Kunsten, Antwerp.)*

remained the most important commercial sector, but during the crisis of the late sixteenth century the demise of the cloth industry in the large Flemish and Brabantine cities could no longer be prevented – efforts at protectionism notwithstanding. Rivals in Verviers and the surrounding region superseded the traditional centers of cloth manufacturing, winning international fame for their own lighter cloth, which was now preferred over the heavier product that the larger cities produced. The linen sector recovered earlier than the wool industry, although it was not until 1650 that output equalled that of 1570. Clearly, the Flemish and Brabantine cities were no longer the economic powerhouses they once had been, and the countryside enjoyed more economic advantages than it had before. Cities like Ghent and Bruges were only able to compete with the rural districts, where handicrafts were cheaper, by specializing in highly finished products.

By the beginning of the seventeenth century, the tapestry industry began to grow again, as did all the artistic guilds. The enthusiasm for reconstruction after wartime, which went hand in hand with the élan of the Counter Reformation, demanded a new decorative style for church buildings. Gold and coppersmiths enjoyed a resurgence in places like Dinant, Bouvignes, and Liège. North of Luxembourg and along the Sambre and Maas Rivers the economic recovery after 1600 was driven by iron production, since these districts possessed enough water power and wood to engage in coal production. Luxembourg profited from the renaissance of metallurgy in Liège, and it exported iron to the city in return, where it was turned into nails and spikes. The prince-bishopric of Liège, neutral in the conflicts between Spain and the Republic since 1577, found a market for its iron goods in the shipyards of the Dutch Republic. Its neutrality also allowed it to specialize in the weapons industry.

The Truce of 1609 brought relative prosperity to the Southern Netherlands. The archdukes protected the national industry with mercantilist zeal. The guilds enjoyed a resurgence, and many people regarded them as a form of protection against the anarchy of past times. They would protect local markets from outside competition and free, unorganized labor. People of this period were completely oblivious to the risks this stifling kind of protectionism entailed.

Prices and wages remained relatively stable, but broad segments of the population experienced a decline in their standard of living. Many families could not count on a living wage. Borrowing money was a necessity for many people, who became easy prey for usurers. To prevent excesses, the archdukes supported the creation of fifteen "Mountains of Charity" between 1618 and 1633. Inspired by the Italian model, these institutions were supposed to end the demand for private lending banks which charged their customers interest rates of 20 to 30 percent. The Mountains lent money at much lower rates, in exchange for pawned goods.

Pauperism

If one had to choose an image that would characterize the society of this period, then it would be the beggar or the vagabond. Their familiar presence haunted rulers, townspeople, and countryfolk alike. Sometimes these threatening figures also took on the role of deserters, since the many wars, roving soldiery, and irregularly paid armies only made vagabondage worse. The Twelve Years' Truce certainly brought no relief to this situation. The countryside was rife with danger, and when the farmer gathered his harvest, he literally did so with a musket strapped over his shoulder. On the other hand, the anonymity of the city also proved attractive to many shady characters.

Even during years of peace, the bulk of the population lived on the edge of pauperism. There were many charitable institutions, the result of private initiatives, but there was a distressing lack of coordination among them, which limited the efficiency of such efforts. Under Charles V, several attempts, none of long duration, were taken by the state to address pauperism more systematically. But after his abdication in 1555, the central authority largely counted on the church to alleviate suffering. It also left the problem to local administrative councils – one way in which the central authority benefitted from honoring provincial and local autonomy. The ruling sovereign did issue laws designed to control and punish begging and vagabondage. The host of ordinances, the frequency in which they were reissued, and the escalation of punishments – including being sent to the galleys – all point to the seriousness of the problem. But the economic cause of pauperism, namely involuntary unemployment, was all too often ignored by contemporary observers. In 1615, however, master artisans in Brussels were instructed to only take as many apprentices as they could afford to compensate – lest the boys become beggars. But generally speaking, all people physically capable of labor but who did not work were considered loafers and were subject to the punitive ordinances.

European societies obstinately continued to cultivate the image of the work-shirking loafer, who had to be taught and forced to work. Following the example of England, Germany and especially the United Provinces, several cities in the Southern Netherlands opened houses of correction in the first half of the seventeenth century. This approach proved inefficient: in addition to the usual problems with forced labor, the lack of space in these institutions soon provided another limitation; it could not meet the scope of the problem. The cities, moreover, lacked the will to finance these houses with sufficient funds only making the situation more complicated.

The Counter Reformation

Parma's victories led to the complete restoration of Catholicism. Rejecting religious pluralism, the Catholic church and the Spanish king expressed their desire for a homogenous Catholic society. No Protestants were tolerated. The conditions of the Twelve Years' Truce and the Peace of Münster guaranteed that Protestant citizens of the Dutch Republic could travel freely in the Spanish Netherlands, but they were forbidden from establishing residence. The official position against Jews was even more hostile.

Recatholicizing the Southern Netherlands was not very difficult, since Catholicism was already the deeply anchored faith of most inhabitants of the region. Moreover, the religious climate under the archdukes was well-suited to this effort; deeply religious and very pious, Isabella and Albrecht backed recatholicization with all the means at their disposal. Under them, the Southern Netherlands became a bastion of the Counter Reformation. At the center of a religiously divided Europe, the region became a haven for English and Irish Catholics seeking refuge, and the secret Catholic missionaries who were sent to Holland, chiefly under the Jesuits, are one example of the area's militant Catholicism. The papal nunciate in Brussels, established in 1596, quickly became an important diplomatic post.

The Counter Reformation employed three strategies to recatholicize the country: educational formation, theological uniformity, and clerical oversight. These were just as much applied to the lower clergy as they were to the laity. The bishops saw it as their task to implement the decrees of the Council of Trent, which had established the agenda for the Counter Reformation. By 1613, most bishops had established seminaries for instructing priests and had issued numerous directives designed to restore both priestly authority and competence. Deans, the representatives of the bishops, now visited local parishes with increasing frequency, ascertaining their moral and spiritual condition and evaluating the performance of the clergy under their supervision.

Schools – and they varied considerably in quality from the cities to the countryside, where they were open only in winter – were first and foremost a place for Christian education. Religious education was more important than profane learning, which chiefly consisted of learning to read and – only in the case of the best students – learning to write and do sums. Usually instruction was left to clerics, but it was invariably under the oversight of the church. In the cities, Sunday schools educated children who were obliged to work during the week, but such schooling differed little in content from the instruction offered elsewhere. The poor who removed their children from this compulsory education risked losing their public assistance.

Adult piety was encouraged through memberships in brotherhoods, Jesuit sodalities, and participation in pilgrimages. The local pastor was supposed to oversee the religious practices of his flock, and did so through a *status animarum*, which kept accounts of his parishioners per family. He had the responsibility of maintaining the baptismal, marriage, and burial records, which were recognized by the state as legal documents. The priest also made sure that every family performed its Easter duties and reported violators to the dean, who in turn passed the names on to the ecclesiastical courts. The same could happen to public sinners and suspicious persons. This was, incidentally, the age of witchhunts, particularly between 1592 and 1625.

The Counter Reformation was no less reliant on the religious orders, of whom the Jesuits were the most ardently committed (they even produced their own canonized saint, Jan Berchmans). Parma's and the archdukes' patronage and protection of the Jesuits eased their expansion into the Spanish Netherlands, and within thirty years they had quadrupled in size. In 1626, they counted nearly 1,600 members and headed thirty-four colleges. Through the quality of their education and superb pedagogy, they gained the favor of the intellectual and social elites, as well as the support of municipal authorities. The Jesuits were also very active pastorally; they exerted much influence on the consciences of the laity as catechists (educating the faithful), and as preachers and confessors (forgiving their transgressions). Absolving sins gave the orders the opportunity to become influential in state affairs, a role which they sought with increasing transparency. Jesuits were also present in the countryside through their missions, and in the army as chaplains.

Both men and women contributed to the blossoming of the religious orders, expressing themselves through active piety and social engagement: charity, care of the sick, medical assistance, and education. For laity, the spiritual ideal was set forth in the *Introduction to the Devout Life* by Francis de Sales, bishop of Geneva. The prince-bishopric of Liège also experienced a Catholic reawakening, primarily under Bishop Ferdinand of Bavaria. Here, too, the Jesuits played a dominant role.

After 1640, the Southern Netherlands was rocked by the Jansenist controversy. Initially a theological dispute, the controversy eventually spilled over into morality and politics, dividing the whole country into pro- and anti-Jansenist camps. Catholic theologians were in fundamental disagreement with the conclusions of Cornelius Jansen, former professor of the university of Leuven and bishop of Ypres. His book *Augustinus*, published at Leuven in 1640, was part of a debate that went back to the Council of Trent in the 1560s. One side emphasized the rational capacity and the freedom of human beings; the other, influenced by Augustinianism, emphasized the moral weakness of human beings since the Fall and their complete dependence on God's grace. Jansen

Cornelius Jansen van Leerdam, the man who unintentionally gave his name to Jansenism. (Universiteitsbibliotheek Leuven.)

took the Augustinian line, and his ideas were spread by the secular priests teaching in Leuven. The bishop also decried the indulgent humanism of the Jesuits and urged his flock to live a rigorously moral and spiritual life.

The pope condemned Jansen's ideas in 1642, but this only triggered more opposition. Pieter Roose, chairman of the Privy Council and a friend of Jansen, resisted Rome's intervention in the name of the ruling prince. In doing so, he became the mortal enemy of the Jesuits. Various bishops also refused to publish the papal bull. King Philip IV's efforts to end the dispute also failed, and the archbishop of Mechelen and the bishop of Ghent – now supported by the Council of Brabant – refused to back down from their Jansenist convictions. The pope ultimately punished these prelates with interdicts and suspensions, and in 1653 they capitulated. By this time, the controversy had spread among the whole clergy, which was divided between Jansen's supporters – including many of Leuven's theologians – and opponents, led by the Society of Jesus. In a country where politics and religion were so closely intertwined, the Jansenist controversy would not be restricted to the church.

The Triumph of Catholicism in the Arts and Letters

Intellectual life in the Southern Netherlands was heavily influenced by the relations between the church and the state. The Counter Reformation, with the express consent of the state, expressed itself in all culture and art of the period. A return to tradition was the prominent motif, with the Jesuits (again) playing a decisive role.

Naturally, education, as the first mould for young spirits, was considered very important. By the end of the late sixteenth-century crisis, higher education had become strictly regulated. In 1587, Philip II renewed the prohibition on studying abroad that he had first issued in 1570. The University of Leuven received a new governing statute in 1617, after civil and religious authorities had subjected it to a lengthy inspection and given the university its seal of approval. The statute would, despite later amendments, remain in force until the end of the ancien régime. The Jesuits tried to compete with the universities by offering public courses in philosophy, but they did not really succeed in this. They persisted, however, in their efforts to influence the educational system and secured a very important role in secondary education.

In the first half of the seventeenth century, scientific and literary production was dominated by members of the Society of Jesus, both quantitatively and qualitatively. The work of the Jesuit Bollandists has best survived the test of time. Father Jean Bolland undertook the titanic task of creating a critical edition of hagiographic sources, the *Acta Sanctorum*. Outside of the Jesuits, the name of the philologist and neo-Stoic philosopher Justus Lipsius deserves mention. In 1592, he returned to the Catholic faith after renouncing Protestantism, and reestablished himself at Leuven. René-François de Sluse was a renowned mathematician who maintained a regular correspondence with Pascal, Huygens, and Descartes. The philosophy of Descartes was condemned by the theological faculty of Leuven, at the behest of the internuncio, but Cartesianism continued to deeply influence philosophy and the sciences at the university.

FRONTISPICIVM DOMVS PROFESSÆ. SOCIETATIS IESV ANTVERPIENSIS.

Intellectuals knew that the mind is inspired by the power of the word and through the ideas spread by books. But illiteracy was widespread, and the Catholic church knew that the common people

The baroque façade of the Carolus Borromeus Church in Antwerp, designed by the Jesuits Peter Huyssens and Franciscus Aguillon (1614-1624). Etching by Christianus van Lom from 1717. (Universiteitsbibliotheek Leuven.)

were particularly open to the power of the image. Images were thus the chief medium of the Counter Reformation, and architects, painters, sculptors, and goldsmiths united their talents to turn the church into the palace of God. The eyes and the senses were supposed to feel the victory of the church triumphant, and the gold, the altars' white and black marble, the richly ornamented pulpits, and confessional booths all had to exude divine beauty and radiance. The church's front façade itself looked like a heavily laden and richly decorated altar.

The Flemish baroque churches were the result of old and new elements. Many constructions preserved the Gothic structure with its vertical orientation, but its exterior was newly dressed with Italian influences. The stylistic infiltration, applied hesitantly at first, came to full fruition in the Jesuits' many churches. The Carolus Borromeus Church in Antwerp is the most beautiful example of this trend. Not all architects, incidentally, were Jesuits. Lay architects like Jacques Francart were also accomplished; Francart demonstrated the multifaceted interests of his contemporaries by uniting his engineering skills with his talent for painting. His *Book of Architecture* (1616) helped spread the principles of the new art throughout the Southern Netherlands. Pieter Paul Rubens also brought numerous façade sketches and blueprints of patrician homes from his stays in Genoa and Mantua. The distribution of these drawings gave the elegant circles a knowledge of – and taste for – the new architectural style. Although some homes also showed Italianate influences, most of the architectural energy of the period remained religious in orientation.

Rubens dominated the painting of the period. Influenced by his extended stay in Italy, he powerfully unified the older and newer tenors of the art and put his brush to the service of the church. His work is characterized by pomp and splendor, the power and passion of movement, and the severity of his colors. Yet he was not contemptuous of profane realities. His mythological scenes abound with vitality and health; they are odes to the female body with its curves and forms. Rubens was court painter to the archdukes, but he was also well-read and served, as occasion dictated, as a diplomat. His prolific artistic pro-

Pieter Paul Rubens, Adoration of the Magi. *(Museo del Prado, Madrid.)*

Pieter Paul Rubens, Self-Portrait. *(Kunsthistorisches Museum, Vienna.)*

duction was largely thanks to the efficient distribution of work in his studio, where many apprentices studied under him and specialized in their own genres. Rubens would complete their paintings, asserting his own personality on the nearly finished canvasses. His best pupils managed to retain their own styles, although they were clearly under the influence of their mentor. Anton van Dyck specialized in patrician portraits, and became court painter of the English royal family. Jacob Jordaens continued the folksy realism of the sixteenth century. The glow of his *Feasts of the Epiphany*, where the king is drinking, is more reminiscent of bourgeois circles than of royalty.

Sculpture, too, was open to Italianate influences. Sculptors were anxious to show the style's élan and compete with the painters, despite the limitations of their medium. The influence of Rubens is also present in sculpture. Most sculptors worked in families, of whom the Duquesnoys are one of the most famous examples.

The court of the archdukes developed its own worldly style. Itinerant troupes of comedians gave performances around the country. Grand theater productions, pompous and didactic, were also performed at Jesuit colleges. Chambers of rhetoric continued to play a role in more popular culture. Their activities were regarded with suspicion by the bishops' censors, who were extremely alert to the dangers of the theater.

2. Despondency and Crisis in the Age of War (1648-1713)

Consequences of the European Wars in Domestic Politics

The end of hostilities with the Republic in 1648 did not end the conflict with France. Spain concluded the Peace of the Pyrenees with France only in 1659, and the French threat was hardly eliminated by this brief and fragile peace. Indeed, the dark clouds of war forecast stormy weather for the Southern Netherlands throughout the late seventeenth century. In particular, the battlefield triumphs of Louis XIV spelled serious territorial losses for Spanish Netherlands, as they chipped away at its southern borders. Dunkirk, Lille, Douai, and all of Artois were annexed by France in 1667, and the duchy of Bouillon was forcibly transferred to the De la Tour d'Auvergne family in 1678. It now became a sovereign state within the French sphere of influence, despite the bishop of Liège's protests, who did not refrain from condemning the transfer as "usurpation".

The Treaty of Rijswijk (1697) forced Louis XIV, for the first time, to make concessions to the European alliance arrayed against him. But the imminent fight for the Spanish throne soon threatened the stability and peace of Europe. The childless Spanish monarch, Charles II, expired on 1 November 1700, leaving his kingdom to Philip V of Anjou, grandson of Louis XIV. The Austrian Habsburg emperor Leopold, however, preferred see his own youngest son, the archduke Charles, inherit the Spanish crown. The Spanish governor-general of the Southern Netherlands, Maximilian Emanuel of Bavaria, sided with Anjou and received the help of French troops. In 1701, England, the United Provinces, and Austria concluded an alliance in The Hague, in which they supported the Austrian emperor's claims to the Spanish crown. English and Dutch support for Austrian claims had much to do with strengthening their own positions and securing their trading empires.

Maximilian Emanuel was forced to abandon Brabant after his defeat by the English general Marlborough at Ramillies in 1706. The victors asked the representatives of the conquered regions to accept the son of the Austrian emperor as King Charles III. The new monarch pledged to honor their privileges and to make no changes in the religious settlement. The States of Brabant accepted this offer, and was quickly followed by the States of Flanders.

This success did not ensure amicable relations within the alliance. Holland's leaders distrusted their Austrian ally; they had not taken up arms to establish another Habsburg dynasty in the region but to achieve the old dream of setting up a military barrier against France. This goal was explicitly stated in the Great Alliance of 1701, and in the Peace of Utrecht in 1713 the Republic was given all of Louis XIV's possessions in the Southern Netherlands. The treaty stipulated that the Republic would surrender these territories to the Austrian Habsburgs as soon as they reached agreement with the Republic's States-General on the construction of the anti-French barrier.

The uncertain political situation, the eruption of new wars, the disastrous financial situation, and the bad behavior of the irregularly paid soldiery all led to a political change of direction in Brussels. The governors-general, beset by pressing problems, no longer showed much interest in domestic matters, as long as the respective States approved the requested grants. Most governors-general, in fact, remained unacquainted with the region's affairs, preferring to look for more attractive posts elsewhere. Between Isabella's death in 1633 and the turn of the century, the Southern Netherlands was governed by no less than fifteen governors-general, who served for an average of five years.

The Hispanophile tendency diminished greatly in influence during the late 1660s. The absolutist drive, too, had weakened, but that did not means its effects were no longer felt, even at the local level. The revised statutes for a number of cities, implemented during this period, indicate absolutism's continued presence. Cities in the Spanish Netherlands were subject to high taxes, and the central administration proved unable – or unwilling – to relieve the high debts of these cities. The fundamental causes for this unfortunate situation stemmed from the wars of the sixteenth century, and for the same reason, these debts only increased in the seventeenth. The king would ask the cities for very substantial financial help before, during, and after each conflict. In a short space of time, he asked for large grants which were used for (among other things) the maintenance of urban garrisons or fortress repair. Usually, cities could only pay for these taxes by borrowing money. When a city's debt became too high to pay, the central authorities cited the incompetence of local officials as a pretext to assert their own influence locally. The central government then altered the city's administration: the composition of the magistracy was changed, with the king's authorities now naming their own appointees to fill key positions in the cities. The central government also attempted to reduce the influence of guilds in the cities' administration. These changes sometimes provoked popular riots, as in Brussels during 1698, when mobs agitated for a return of the old privileges and a reduction in taxes. These outbursts, however, only increased the resolve of the government to maintain a hard line.

A similar reaction to the same kind of urban protest movements was evident in the prince-bishopric of Liège. There the traditional autonomy of the cities declined further after 1650, a trend highlighted by a new restrictive statute imposed on the capital city of Liège in 1684. Gradually, various cities were subjected to the stern guardianship of the central authority, a process which continued during the eighteenth century. Cities were now ruled by administrative organs, which took on an increasingly oligarchic character. Reliable administrators were recruited by coopting them from their past allegiances, and the representatives of the guilds and trades declined in these governing bodies.

The public administration of the Southern Netherlands was corrupted by the selling of offices. The sale of government posts, by monarchs or their administrators, was hardly new nor restricted to the region. From the sixteenth century on, however, this practice was gradually codified. Philip IV's edict of 2 May 1626, which prohibited private parties from selling offices, was presumably issued to preserve his own monopoly on the practice. A financial crisis in the mid-seventeenth century introduced the Spanish "medianate" system for all but military offices. Any candidate for a position would be required, before his appointment, to offer a loan to the treasury, theoretically equal to a half year's salary. Actually this amounted to a tax, since the sum was never repaid. Every new appointee to the state administration was obliged to pay this fee. This was a handy source of income for the king, but it also led to ever more overt forms of office buying. Originally, the least qualified candidates could remain in contention for positions by offering additional loans at a low interest rate of 5 or 6 percent or even with no interest at all. Better candidates, however, soon felt the pressure to do the same, and eventually government positions simply went to the highest bidder. Selling offices proved so lucrative for the kings that they ultimately created completely extraneous positions, simply to fill their treasuries. Loans made were seldom paid back on time, if they were paid back at all. In time, a government post became the effectual property of its holder and part of his familial assets. This helps to explain why noble families dominated some sectors of the royal administration, and why complex family ties allowed a very few noble families to keep the highest state positions for themselves.

The careless increase of government posts – and the revenues needed to sustain their salaries – resulted in a heavier financial burden for the state in the long run. But it was precisely these treasury deficits which made a short-term solution like selling offices look so attractive. If one considers the other sources of income upon which the king had to rely, one might have some empathy for his position. The provincial States only approved grants that would be used for purposes to which they had agreed. The king had also traditionally relied on his personal domains to give him income. But now (with the official approval of the States) he pawned or directly sold his principalities, lands, and rights to gain more money. This obviously had short-term benefits but long-term disadvantages for the monarch. In any event, the king found eager buyers of his property among the merchant class, who used these opportunities to enrich themselves and buy offices. By combining government service with the titles they had purchased from the king, many wealthy middle class families gradually ascended to the lesser nobility.

Under the short reign of Philip V of Anjou, the centralization process, implemented according to the French model, resumed in high gear. In 1702, a Royal Council replaced the three old Collateral Councils (the Council of State, the Privy Council, and the Council of Finances), but because of the war, the Royal Council functioned more like a government of military occupation. The most important position in the new council belonged to Jan van Brouchoven, Count of Bergeyck, who served as superintendant of finances. Intendants were also sent to each province to act as representatives of the central government. This system, well-established in France, was not entirely new to the Spanish Netherlands. A form of it had been introduced in 1668, but it was diluted after protests from the Council of State. Although Bergeyck wanted to make it a permanent position, the position of intendant remained limited in this period, restricted largely to assisting the military effort by overseeing police and financial affairs, and to consulting with army leaders. Meanwhile, the war heightened the need for both money and men. When unable to assemble enough volunteers for the army, the regime introduced conscription by lottery, with men being allowed to find replacements for themselves. The government also tried to increase its revenues, by making it mandatory, for instance, to use stamped, taxed paper on all public documents.

Most of the Southern Netherlands fell under the collective authority of England and the Dutch Republic as a result of the anti-French alliance's military successes between 1702 and 1706. The reforms of Philip V were abolished, and a body of English and Dutch emissaries governed the land via the Council of State, which now consisted of the country's most important nobles. In contrast to Philip V, these emissaries encouraged local autonomy, which increased local participation in financing the war against the French. The Dutch and the English had nothing to lose by encouraging regional autonomy, since their administration of the country was temporary. From their standpoint, it made good strategic sense to let the Austrian Habsburgs struggle to build a strong monarchy on a territory where local privilege had so recently been reinforced.

Trade Protectionism and Economic Depression

Industry in the Southern Netherlands suffered stagnation – perhaps even decline – in the last quarter of the seventeenth century, the victim of war and the international economic situation. Already, in 1660, the French finance minister, Colbert, had increased the tariffs on imported luxury goods, a measure which directly hit the region's industry. The subsequent economic crisis only increased pressure on the government to take a protectionist posture to save what was left of these enterprises.

Originally, the government's tax on trade was inspired by fiscal considerations. This was the reason for the creation of "licenses" conceived during the war against the Republic. Since the state was unable to prevent trade with the enemy, it imposed taxes on these imported goods and issued permits to trade in them. Duties were not yet based on the assessed weight or worth of the shipment, but these regulations may still be considered the beginning of a customs system, which was permanently established in 1654. The ruling sovereign obtained significant income from custom duties – especially since he was not required to share the proceeds with the provincial States. He alone set the tariffs on import-export rights. To be sure, he could not be blind to the needs of his subjects, especially in hard times, or to the complaints of manufacturers. The sovereign was always compelled to weigh the balance of opposing interests in what was usually a complicated financial picture.

The European powers fighting in the Southern Netherlands also restricted the freedom of the ruling monarch. The region remained, for example, under the customs duties of 1670 and 1680 until the middle of the eighteenth century. These taxes were implemented precisely at the beginning of the long recession that lasted until 1725 to 1730. The rather heavy duties of 1670 were in force along the border with France; the duties of 1680, influenced by Antwerp's business circles, applied to trade with the prince-bishopric of Liège and the United Provinces. These fees were much lower than along the southern border, and stimulated imports from England and Holland.

Meanwhile, protectionism exacted a heavy toll on the prosperity of various industrial sectors. Light draperies suffered under the adverse economic circumstances, and linens, while continuing to grow in the 1670s and 1680s, eventually also succumbed to hard times, languishing away during the first quarter of the eighteenth century. Later, the linen industry would be the only sector to truly recover from this serious slump. It was a largely agrarian activity, and was concentrated in the Land of Waas and the fief of Kortrijk (Courtrai). Ghent would serve as a pivot for the international linen trade and (later) as the region's cotton center.

The rich natural resources of the southern districts of the country explain the importance of the two other industrial branches, namely the iron and coal industries. Starting in the seventeenth century, coal became increasingly important both as a source of heating and industrial production. The iron and coal industries were centered in the Borinage and in the areas around Charleroi and Liège. Economic expansion of these sectors, however, ended as a result of the wars of Louis XIV, the presence of cheap English imports made possible by the duties of 1680, and because of technical difficulties.

The Jansenist Controversy and the Mediocrity of Intellectual Life

Once the most important aims of the Counter Reformation had been attained, it was inevitable that cultural creativity and energy would slow down. This trend was apparent in the Southern Netherlands during the late seventeenth century. The Jansenist controversy continued to cause a high level of unrest in the country's spiritual and intellectual life. Despite the pope's condemnation of *Augustinus*, Jansen's ideas continued to be widely read, both at Leuven and among clergy and laity. This development is partly explained by French religious influence, particularly by the *Messieurs* of Port-Royal, a group of French clerics and intellectuals who advocated fundamental reforms in religious life. In the Southern Netherlands, Jansenism was no longer only a matter of theological debate, but increasingly concerned its moral consequences. The arrival of the French Jansenist exiles Arnauld (in 1679) and Quesnel (in 1685) rekindled the flames of this controversy, and the whole country was divided between proponents and detractors. The Spanish king retained a hostile posture toward Jansenism, but the provincial high courts supported the movement, making it difficult for the governor-generals to implement the king's anti-Jansenist instructions. In 1690, the archbishop of Mechelen led a powerful offensive against Jansenism, a course also taken by his contemporary in Liège, Joseph Clement of Bavaria. Still, Jansenism seemed to have triumphed by the beginning of the eighteenth century; despite strict countermeasures issued by Philip V of Anjou, it thrived in a climate of tension and unrest.

The state's official position toward other faiths did not change in the wake of this dispute; Catholicism remained the state religion. But a certain pragmatism did evolve among the region's leading classes, which contrasted sharply with the rigorous Catholicism of Madrid. The financial disaster of the 1650s prompted some officials, for example, to consider a proposal by Amsterdam Jews to pay for a colony in Vilvoorde, and Antwerp's city administration negotiated the construction of a synagogue in Borgerhout. The pope, warned by the nuncio in Brussels of these plans, protested against these proposals, and Philip IV put an end to them.

The deep poverty of the region's intellectual and artistic life echoed the region's economic decline. Catholic restoration had been solidly established, most obviously manifest through the overwhelming influence of the Jesuits. The country's souls were decidedly catholi-

David Teniers de Jonge, Village Wedding *(1652).*

cized, making religious zealotry unnecessary. The church-building craze came to an end. Baroque remained the leading style, and insofar as new churches were constructed, they were only variations on this theme. One of the high points of lay architecture in the period are the guild halls of the *Grand Place* in Brussels, reconstructed after the bombardment of 1695. Gradually, French styles gained in influence; although religious architecture remained baroque, the Louis XIV style could be discerned in secular construction. Mediocrity was the chief suit of painters in the period; many of them worked on painting series documenting daily life, which were destined for the interiors of bourgeois homes. The only great name among them is David Teniers de Jonge. Sculpture also found a great artist in Jean Delcour of Liège. Many of his colleagues from the Southern Netherlands found work in France, in the service and to the greater glory of the Sun King Louis XIV. But the protectionist policies of surrounding countries contributed to the decline of artistic production within the region itself.

3. Early Austrian Rule amidst Disillusionment and Decline (1713-1748)

The Barrier

Because the Austrian emperor was in no condition to wage war alone against France, he accepted the Dutch Republic's conditions (stipulated in the Peace of Utrecht) for an anti-French barrier in 1714. Negotiations in Antwerp led to the third and definitive Barrier Treaty of 1715. The treaty's first article recognized the emperor's possessions in the Southern Netherlands as a single entity, indivisible from his other Habsburg lands in Germany. Furthermore, the agreement stipulated that a number of cities in the region would be occupied by garrisons of 30,000 to 35,000 men, three-fifths of whom were to be Austrian, two-fifths Dutch. The maintenance costs for these troops, amounting to 500,000 écus, would essentially fall on the population of the Southern Netherlands. Religiously speaking, Catholicism remained the only legal faith, with the exception of the Dutch Barrier garrisons. The treaty reconfirmed the closing of the Scheldt. In the final days before the signing, England and the Republic also managed to ensure that the import duties in the Austrian Netherlands were readjusted to benefit themselves; they were to remain in force until the parties concluded a new agreement. No such agreement was ever forthcoming, since the Dutch and English had no incentive to negotiate.

The new arrangement generated much dismay in the Southern Netherlands, which was now effectively – at least in terms of trade – at the mercy of the Dutch Republic. Public resistance to the treaty increased when France, ill at ease with the Barrier, proposed to the Republic that the Barrier be scrapped in favor of neutrality for the Austrian Netherlands, to be guaranteed by the great powers. In 1716, the States of Flanders and Brabant sent a delegation to the Austrian emperor outlining their complaints. The emperor accordingly sent the Marquis de Prié to renegotiate the treaty, and after two years of diplomatic effort, several clauses injurious to the Southern Netherlands were deleted from the Barrier Treaty.

In 1713, Emperor Charles VI established the rules of succession for his lands in the Pragmatic Sanction, which, after it was approved by all the States, was solemnly publicized in the Southern Netherlands in 1725. The great European powers were supposed to guarantee that the

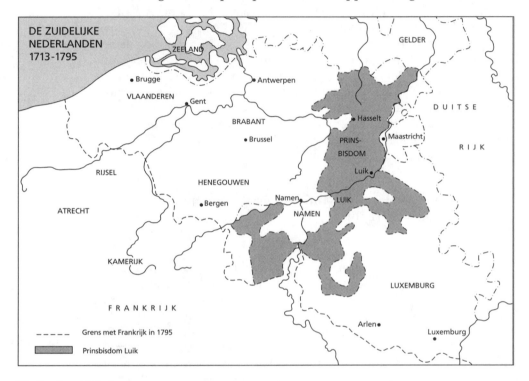

The Southern Netherlands, 1713-1795.

sanction be put into effect when Charles died. However, when his daughter Maria Theresa succeeded him upon his death on 20 October 1740, in accordance with the sanction, the War of Austrian Succession immediately broke out. Austria was attacked by France, Spain, Prussia, the elector of Bavaria, and Poland. In 1744, France declared war on England, which had sided with Maria Theresa. In moving against Austria and England, Louis XV did not hesitate to attack Flanders, and the Dutch Barrier garrisons offered only weak resistance. The victory of Maurice of Saxony at Fontenoy (1746) opened the way for French occupation of the Austrian Netherlands. Under the Treaty of Aix-la-Chapelle (Aachen) in 1748, however, the old status (as stipulated by the Treaty of Westphalia and subsequent agreements) was restored, and Austria resumed control over the Southern Netherlands.

Another Surge of Absolutism

All rulers put their own mark on the institutions of government, although they are always limited, of course, by circumstances. Charles VI was indecisive, searching long and hard for the best method by which to rule. He was hardly averse in principle to imposing French-style abso-

Governor-general Maria Elizabeth. The inset at right is the Coudenberg Palace, the Brussels residence of the region's governors-general until 1731. Copper engraving by Christianus van Lom, 1716. (Universiteitsbibliotheek Leuven.)

lutism on his subjects, but he was also bound by international treaty to respect the privileges of each province. Still, as the successor to the Spanish Charles II, he was concerned about governmental continuity. For this reason, he established the High Council for the Netherlands in Vienna in 1717, a more active successor to the Council for the Netherlands and Burgundy which had once functioned in Madrid.

Since the emperor resided far from the Netherlands, he was officially represented by the governor-general. The absence of Governor-General Eugene of Savoy, who was off fighting the Turks, led to the introduction of a new permanent function, the minister plenipotentiary. Officially, this functionary was empowered to execute the government's policies while remaining subordinate to the governor-general. He was a highly placed diplomat, serving, in effect, as the confidant of the emperor, who reserved the right to give him direct orders – without consulting the governor-general. The minister was also empowered to correspond directly with the emperor, if he judged it necessary to do so. Herein lay the origins of a governmental dualism, which potentially pitted the minister plenipotentiary and the governor-general against each other.

In 1718, the idea of a single administrative organ for the Southern Netherlands was reintroduced. The plan was to collapse the three Collateral Councils into the Council of State, a proposal primarily intended to reduce costs. Vienna also wanted to put an end to the interminable jurisdictional fights between the three councils. The plan gave the emperor an opportunity to side with the old nobility and to introduce French-style intendants. The emperor was encouraged by the support he received in the High Council for the Netherlands and was especially enthusiastic about the introduction of intendants. But it was precisely this last measure which generated so much opposition within the Austrian Netherlands, although intendants would regularly reemerge in reform proposals until the mid-eighteenth century.

Friction with his minister plenipotentiary, the Marquis de Prié, against whom local resistance was so fierce it bordered on outright rebellion, and problems with a nobility unwilling to subordinate themselves to a mere advisory role, forced Charles VI to change course. Prié was forced to resign, and in 1725 the emperor put his sister in charge of the Austrian Netherlands. Archduchess Maria Elizabeth was forty years old, sensible and energetic, and very pious. She was heavily influenced by her father confessor, the Jesuit Amiot, and regarded the presence of a minister plenipotentiary as an intrusion on her prerogatives. For this reason, she ordered the grandmaster of the Brussels court to ensure that the minister would not act independently of her.

Charles VI's rule was marked by hesitancy and indecisiveness. His administration's accomplishments were quite meager, and evident only after 1730. In place of the more powerful intendants, the government eventually decided to send commissioners, entrusted only with very specific assignments, to instruct local governing bodies. If the emperor gave in on this point, it was not due to a change of principles but to the great success of an agreement reached with Ghent in 1734, following the central government's audit of the town's finances. Instead of insisting heavyhandedly on reform, the central government resorted to an age-old regional tradition. This time the audit was not formal and meaningless, as was typical of the past. Rather, the audit, well-managed by an able functionary, led to a well-ordered new statute for Ghent. The Ghent case was convincing; the way to control local and provincial finances had been found, and the case of Ghent would serve as inspiration for the following administration under Maria Theresa.

Charles VI was confronted with the Austrian Netherlands's heavy public debt, which amounted to 15 million guilders in 1715 – and a yearly interest of 737,000 guilders. Despite economic efforts to improve this situation, the state's annual deficit was just as bad in 1733 as it had been in 1721. Military expenditures swallowed anywhere from 50 to 70 percent of government revenues. The shortage of capital limited the emperor's options for political action. Selling offices, of course, was an easy means to raise money, and the principle was increasingly applied to local and city offices. But the disastrous condition of the treasury hardly bolstered Charles's absolutist aspirations, since he now had to beg the States to give him additional grants or gifts. Charles was fortunate in that he could count upon the good credit rating of his subjects, which was better than his own. He was able to pay his debts to the United Provinces, for example, thanks to the capital that the States of Brabant had been able to borrow at lower interest. But Charles was compelled to make concessions for these favors; in this case, the States of Brabant was given direct access to a portion of the custom duties. Financial necessity, therefore, often forced the emperor to cut some kind of deal with his subjects, undermining his plans to impose a centralized and absolutist government.

Social and Economic Stagnation

Regional industry experienced somber times, caught between the custom laws of 1670 and 1680. The textile sector was badly affected in particular, but the tapestry trade, once so dynamic, also lay moribund. The linen industry, too, was at a low point. Yet between 1725 and 1730 a few bright spots gave glimmers of hope in this bleak economic situation.

Already before 1725, a group of astute and wealthy merchants had done their part to expand their own economic opportunities. After 1714 or 1715 these traders from Ostend, Ghent, Bruges, and Antwerp became interested in making profits from trade with the Indies. At the time, Charles VI was approving other trading companies within his empire (such as Trieste's Levant Company in 1719), giving these merchants inspiration for their own venture. In 1722, the emperor lent his protection, through the patron saint Charles, to the Imperial and Royal India Company of the Netherlands, better known as the Ostend Company. It received a thirty-year charter, granting it a monopoly on trade with Africa, and the East and West Indies. The company's promising start raised the hackles of the great powers, however, and Charles, anxious to secure their cooperation in his daughter's future succession to the throne, squashed his subjects' trading hopes by terminating the company in 1731.

Poverty and the problem of public assistance remained constant factors. The grain crises of the early 1690s, which witnessed spectacular price increases, the famine of 1693 to 1694, the "great winter" of 1709-1710 and the "long winter" of 1740 with their scarcity and their epidemics, and the frequent military campaigns were dark chapters which took their heavy toll on the physical and spiritual well-being of the common people. The Austrian regime, no less than the Spanish, was confronted with the gigantic problem of poverty. At the beginning of his reign, Charles issued a landmark ordinance against beggary and vagrancy. The idea of imprisoning loafers and teaching them to work resurfaced around 1720; taking their cue from Holland, the French-speaking city of Mons opened a "house of correction.' But again, these efforts were without much success because they were only stopgap efforts. The generosity of Governor-General Maria Elizabeth allowed Brussels to establish workhouses in 1734, where unemployed women and men might keep body and soul together. But here, as in the past, there was insufficient will to maintain these institutions, and they disappeared within several years.

Their disappearance left only Charles's criminal penalties to discourage people from beggary and vagrancy. Pillories, floggings, and temporary or life-long banishment (which included brandings for repeat offenders) were all used to discourage these practices. Whether through persuasion or force, this solution to the problem created a vicious circle, in which undesired fugitives and exiles roamed from district to district – sometimes even across borders. Indeed, foreign beggars were especially badly treated, and often they were forced to return to the place where they had a right to draw on public assistance.

Temporary disasters were not the basic root of this poverty; it had causes which had remained constant over the centuries. Workers could never be certain of their future: their loans were too low and remained the same for decades despite the rising cost of living. They received no pay for days not worked, whether holidays or sick days. Moreover, workers had to face the threat of seasonal unemployment, or simply a lack of work – not to mention the possibility of accidents. Pay in the textile sector hardly covered the most basic needs like housing and food. In addition to the men's income, families were in dire need of the money women could bring in – and even on the few copper coins earned by children, who were sent to work at an early age.

The End of Jansenism

The advent of Austrian rule did not put an end to the close association between religion and politics. As a result of the Barrier Treaty, foreign troops were stationed in the Southern Netherlands – including Calvinist (Reformed) soldiers and their families. Their army chaplains made vigorous efforts to convert the local population, and Catholic bishops blamed their presence for the expansion of Protestantism in the Southern Netherlands. Yet their efforts should not be exaggerated; their activities remained restricted to a few old rural centers in Flanders, Hainaut, and the duchy of Luxembourg. Cities like Antwerp, Brussels, and Ghent had long contained small numbers of Protestants. At any rate, by the early eighteenth century, authorities offered a certain measure of religious toleration; Protestants were allowed to worship together in private, as long as they did not provoke a public scandal. Most of the population, however, remained solidly Catholic in their faith and in their prejudices.

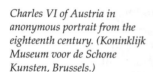

Charles VI of Austria in anonymous portrait from the eighteenth century. (Koninklijk Museum voor de Schone Kunsten, Brussels.)

Meanwhile, the Catholic church continued to be undermined internally by the Jansenist controversy. The bishops' struggle against Jansenism suffered a setback during the War of Spanish Succession, when a number of bishops' sees remained vacant for longer than usual. Such was the situation when Clement XI published the papal bull *Unigenitus* in 1713, which condemned 101 theses found in the Jansenist Quesnel's *Moral Reflections*. The bishops of the Southern Netherlands charged the faithful to make the pope's condemnation a rule of faith and life, and the bull proved effective in combatting Jansenism. Resistance in the Southern Netherlands to the bull was less than it was in France, and it seems that the bishops' long efforts to combat Jansenism among the clergy and the theological faculty at the University of Leuven had paid off. And yet it was a professor of canon law at Leuven, Bernard van Espen, who came to symbolize further Jansenist resistance. Jansenists demanded that the pope's decision be subject to a general church council, and appealed for the help of the state, which, they supposed, was also threatened by the pontiff. They argued that the bull had not been subject to royal approval, without which it had no legal force in the Southern Netherlands. For matters of church dogma, however, no such approval was needed. The Council of State and the provincial high courts, themselves defending the prerogatives of the state against the claims of the Ultramontanists, intervened on behalf of the Jansenists. Charles VI unsuccessfully proposed a compromise solution in 1723, and it was only the arrival of Governor-General Maria Elizabeth two years later that brought a new, and final, phase to the controversy. Distancing herself from the emperor's instructions and adhering to the advice of her father confessor, she moved forcefully against the Jansenists. Van Espen was forced to leave for the Republic (where he soon headed the Old Catholic seminary in Amersfoort), and in 1730 the University of Leuven obliged all of its students to swear an anti-Jansenist oath and give explicit allegiance to *Unigenitus* and a doctrinal form issued by Pope Alexander VII. The struggle had been decided. Georges Louis de Berghes fought for a similar outcome in the prince-bishopric of Liège, although it would take until 1740 before the Jansenists there were completely defeated. The anti-Jansenist victory meant that the Roman Catholic church in the Southern Netherlands became solidly Ultramontanist, fully supporting the pope and his cause.

4. The Theresian Compromise and an Era of Peace and Prosperity (1748-1780)

Centralization with a Human Face

The Peace of Aix-la-Chapelle (1748) put an end to the Austrian War of Succession. Representing Austria at the peace conference was Wenzel Anton, Count von Kaunitz, the former minister plenipotentiary, and the acting governor-general in Brussels. Kaunitz assumed the leading role in Austrian politics after a brilliant diplomatic career in Paris; while there, he had succeeded in pulling off a total "reversal of the alliances" by persuading the French to end their anti-Austrian alliance with Prussia – and to join Austria instead. In 1753, Maria Theresa named him chancellor of court and state. Gifted with unmistakable political talent, Kaunitz was both an efficient and flexible administrator when it came to advancing Habsburg absolutism, and his personality dominated Austrian politics throughout the period. In 1757, he succeeded in abolishing the High Councils of the Netherlands and of Italy which had been centered in Vienna. Instead, the chancellor himself would make all decisions pertaining to the Southern Netherlands – with the authority to override all regional officials.

All of Kaunitz's decisions were to be presented to Maria Theresa for final approval. Her own decisions must be understood within the context of what later became known as the "Theresian Compromise." Maria Theresa remained firmly committed to absolutism, but proved willing to accommodate this aim to local conditions and customs. She was prepared to delay a decision if a region did yet not appear ready to accept it. By her reasoning, however, this was only postponement – not cancellation – of herains, to be tried again in better times. She never lost sight of her course but realized that compromise was sometimes necessary. Maria Theresa demonstrated a wisdom and tactfulness which contrasted sharply with the hatchet approach preferred by her son Joseph II, who wished to impose uniformity on the basis of pure reason. Both, however, were committed to the same absolutist course.

The Austrian rulers reentered in the Southern Netherlands in early 1749. They were accepted by the population without resentment;

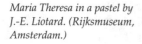

Maria Theresa in a pastel by J.-E. Liotard. (Rijksmuseum, Amsterdam.)

French occupation forces had not only exerted a hard financial burden but had shown themselves unwilling to respect traditional privileges. The Austrian government also used the occasion of their return to assert their full sovereignty over the Southern Netherlands. Maria Theresa, unimpressed with the Dutch military resistance at the Barrier in 1747, unilaterally decided not to pay for their presence, despite protests from the United Provinces.

The forced inactivity of the Austrian bureaucracy, chased out of the Southern Netherlands during the war of Austrian Succession, now proved a boon for reform. Financial changes were especially urgent. City and regional governments had incurred heavy debts as a result of the demands and tax increases of the French. More important, Vienna realized that its unwieldy administrative structure needed to be streamlined. The success of such a reform depends completely on the quality of the people charged with undertaking it, and in this case, fortunately, the right people were found.

An important development took place in the top echelons of government, a development which reached its climax under the government of Joseph II. Gradually, the governor-general was reduced to a figurehead, while the real power was put into the hands of the minister plenipotentiary. Vienna realized that administrators, even ones so highly placed, were easier to dismiss than members of the imperial family, and hence more likely to follow instructions. Ministerial personalities and styles varied, but the political course remained the same. It was not easy, however, to deprive the governor-general of his power. Charles of Lorraine, for example, attempted to exercise real power during his first years as governor-general. In the course of time, however, Charles was dissuaded from this course by the empress' entourage, and he turned into a carefree Francophile who cared little for the affairs of state. Good-natured, moderate, and loved by the people, Charles occasionally used his popularity to confound Vienna's policies. The States realized that they could exploit the increasingly open rivalry between the minister and governor-general in Brussels. They knew how to flatter Charles in order to obtain concessions from him which the minister plenipotentiary would never countenance. The secretary of state and war, who was of foreign origin as well, also increased his influence over the affairs of the Austrian Netherlands. Nominally under the command of the governor-general, he was in reality the right hand man of the minister plenipotentiary. He functioned as the chief of the minister's cabinet, and replaced the minister when necessary. Joseph II alleged that it was this gray eminence who really ruled the country, provided his memory, information, and relations with his two superiors were sufficiently good.

The Council of State, following the example of its Austrian counterpart, was reduced to a largely ceremonial function. Membership in this organ was now honorific, given to hard-working functionaries who had served the regime well. The Privy Council, meanwhile, was enjoying its glory days under the leadership of Patrice-François de Neny, who headed the council for twenty-five years before his dismissal in 1783. Open to the ideas of the Enlightenment, he was also anticlerical, as was the minister plenipotentiary Cobenzl. Neny was a proponent of a national Catholic church with a Jansenist cast, largely independent of Rome. Moreover, unlike Cobenzl, he was a firm defender of regional privileges, the chief issue which separated the two men. Neny also took it upon himself to write the *Mémories historiques et politiques des Pays-Bas autrichiens* (*Retrospective of the History and Politics of the Austrian Netherlands*), a history designed to instruct the future emperor Joseph II.

Finances

The central government often possessed no adequate overview of provincial and local finances. In 1748, the old system of commissioners was expanded into a junta. This specialized, temporary commission, based on the Spanish model, was supposed to give the government such a financial overview. The commission's work resulted in demands for a more permanent oversight organ, and in 1764 the Junta of Administration and Grants was established. The new commission's name rightly suggests that the junta's original powers had been broadened; no longer restricted to auditing and reforming local finance, the central government now intended the junta to exercise more active control over provincial and local administrative bodies. But this was no easy task, since the junta's efforts faced much prejudice and resistance.

The primary fiscal aim of the empress' administration was to ensure both the permanence and reliability of taxation, minimize the restrictions on the revenues, and improve the efficiency of collection. To do so, it was more or less necessary to reform the respective States, and this naturally required the utmost tact, with careful attention to domestic and international factors. At first this task was complicated by the War of Austrian Succession, which required the government to ask the States for large sums of money.

In 1754, however, the central government won a substantial victory in Flanders. In the eighteenth century, Ghent and Bruges dominated the States of Flanders and its Permanent Committee. Smaller cities and fiefs began demanding their full say in the States, and the central government supported their bid – for a price. From now on, the central government, with the support of the smaller municipalities, asked the States to pay a regular fixed sum, plus a portion of the costs incurred by the imperial court and a proportional share of a special grant that the States had just refused to give the emperor. The governor-general, with Vienna's approval, announced this reform, but it still needed to be ratified by the States of Flanders. Exercising subtle coercion, Cobenzl succeeded in preventing resistance in the First Estate (the clergy), a body which had recognized that this reform would be the deathknell of the States' traditional powers. Cobenzl let the clergy know that refusal would mean that the government would rigorously implement a tax on church buildings and grounds – traditionally exempt from taxes – in order to compensate for losses in fiscal revenues from the States.

In other provinces, the central government failed to achieve this degree of power over its respective States. The empress' agents, however, did their best to undermine regional privileges by introducing a new theory of governance. The agents recognized that the States had the right to determine to what extent taxes should be raised in order to meet revenue needs, but they maintained that the States did not have the right as such to refuse the empress' request for grants. Moreover, the empress herself made calculated use of her right to appoint administrators in many cities. These administrators formed part of the Third Estate in the provincial States, and so it was in the best interest of the central government to find local officials who would be sympathetic to her policy.

In any event, the central government succeeded in establishing a stable source of income from all the provinces of the Austrian Netherlands – a net revenue of 3,850,000 guilders annually. Flanders and Brabant, the most densely populated areas, paid about two thirds of this. In addition to this sum, the States also offered the empress additional gifts to cover extra costs; between the War of Polish Succession (1733) and the War of Bavarian Succession (1778-1779), this amounted to 37,000,000 guilders. Between 1733 and 1779, the cumulative total of annual gifts and subsidies came to around 165,000,000 guilders, with an additional 84,000,000 given in loans. The Austrian Habsburgs believed that their subjects in the Southern Netherlands had a natural duty to lend this level of financial support to their policies.

Throughout the eighteenth century, the costs and benefits of the tax burden imposed on the Austrian Netherlands were a matter of dispute: Brussels called the region's contribution "a friendly settlement," whereas Vienna criticized this attitude as excessively indulgent. Kaunitz himself thought that the respective States were getting off far too easily. The financial stakes, of course, were enormous; in 1780, grants and subsidies from the States amounted to 45.5 percent of imperial income from the Southern Netherlands, compared to 18 percent from domain usage and nearly 37 percent from import duties. In all of this, the aim of the empress was not to cripple the States, but to remold them in line with her own priorities. Their activities had to conform to one central principle: regional self-rule under the direction of the empress and her ministers.

Population Growth in the Countryside

Epidemics, famine, and war: these three scourges dominated life in the Southern Netherlands between the late sixteenth and early eighteenth centuries. After 1740, however, epidemics became less frequent (at least until 1790), and hunger no longer had the same deadly results, in part because of growing potato consumption.

This fundamental difference between the periods before and after 1740 explain the population pattern. One can speak of an "accordion" demography in the seventeenth century: sledgehammer mortality rates made it impossible for the population to rise above a certain level. The high rate of births in the 1600s made it theoretically possible to recoup the population lost to plagues within five or ten years, but the frequency of other disasters prevented this from happening. But after 1700, and certainly after 1740, the decline of plagues meant that few factors stood in the way of substantial population increase.

Still, infant and children's mortality rates remained high. This was especially true of infants, and their death rates would have been even higher had it not been for the practice of breastfeeding them for a very long time. Smallpox was probably the leading cause of death for children over a year old. But social standing and wealth also determined whose children would survive. 726 out of every thousand children born to the nobility in Brussels during the 1750s would live to see their tenth birthday, but among traders and artisans it was 581, and among the poor only 393. In comparison, 679 out of every thousand children born in the Brabantine countryside survived to age ten.

The cause of these deaths (at least during normal times) was a lack of hygiene, both private and public, and of how children were brought up. Dirty hands and polluted water exposed the whole society to sickness, and the poor and lower classes in particular were vulnerable to epidemics. Assistance to the poor remained largely a matter of private charity and was first and foremost the responsibility of the church. The state was usually concerned about poverty only insofar as it affected public order. This changed in time as the new scientific insights of the Enlightenment began to make an impact in the Austrian Netherlands. Their practical effects remained modest, however: they included debates over better education for midwives and surgeon-barbers, over inoculation against smallpox, and over prohibitions against burials in churches, which were to be replaced by cemeteries outside the city walls.

By the mid-eighteenth century, the countryside was a veritable population reservoir. In areas where industrialization began, people married younger and produced more children. Part of this labor pool left for the city, putting a halt to urban depopulation and, in some cases, contributing to population increases. Urban population concentrations lay well above the Sambre and Maas Rivers. Antwerp, the largest city of the sixteenth-century Netherlands, still only counted 43,000 inhabitants in 1755, but by 1784, it numbered 51,000 inhabitants. Brussels could thank its own population surge to the presence of the governors-general and their courts, and in 1784, it mustered nearly 75,000 people. Liège (still a capital city) and Ghent both had between 50,000 and 55,000 thousand inhabitants. They were followed by Bruges (31,000), Tournai (26,000), and by Mechelen, Leuven, and Mons (roughly 20,000 each). By the standards of Europe's largest cities, however, these centers were still small; Amsterdam had a population of 200,000; Paris 550,000; and London some 650,000. Statistically, the Austrian Netherlands remained a primarily agrarian region despite high urban density in a few areas.

The still relatively decentralized structure of the state makes it difficult to make even a rough estimate of the population before 1784. In that year, there were between 2,400,000 and 2,650,000 people living in the Austrian Netherlands and the prince-bishopric of Liège. About one quarter of them lived in cities – it was still a largely rural society, but had a relatively high degree of urbanization by European standards of the day. Population density averaged eighty-two inhabitants per square kilometer, but there were wide variations from district to district. Historians estimate that in the 1780s, 62.5 percent of the population in the Austrian Netherlands spoke Dutch (unlike today, Brussels in the 1780s had a population that was 90 percent Dutch-speaking), 31 percent spoke French, and 6.5 percent German.

Economic Politics: In the Service of Trade and Commerce

After 1748, Maria Theresa's economic policy took a radical turn, leading to an upturn in the economy and, by the 1770s, sustained growth. The Treaty of Aix-la-Chapelle had removed former trade restrictions imposed by the Southern Netherlands's neighbors, although the Scheldt remained closed. Accordingly, on 27 January 1749 the Austrian government introduced much higher import duties, to the dismay of England and the United Provinces. Customs duties would now also be regulated by a number of special ordinances aimed at one product or region. These duties would be easier to collect, but they were especially preferred because they had a smaller psychological impact on the public. The Directory Bureau, which considered the implications for international trade, gave the government advice on customs duties. From 1759 on, it kept general statistics on trade volume. This gave the government a better grasp of the economic situation, and improved its ability to make sound political decisions. The Austrian administration also began to use statistical surveys for political purposes.

Minting money was a royal right, and Maria Theresa, resuming a tradition that had been abandoned since the time of the archdukes, ordered the minting of silver currency. The Austrians, much to Kaunitz's disappointment, were compelled to use a private bank for state transactions, since the Southern Netherlands possessed no public bank.

Another innovation was the government's active effort to improve the transit trade through the Austrian Netherlands, whose favorable geographical location potentially made it an important crossroads in Europe. Continuing an initiative begun in the 1730s, the empress sought to make the transit trade more attractive by easing transit taxes and administrative formalities. She also provided for an expansion of the infrastructure, such as the harbor improvements in Ostend, the deepening of the canal to Ghent, and the construction of customs warehouses. Mechelen and especially Leuven became transportation centers, connected by many roads and waterways. In the seventeenth century, goods were transported by water, and in the eighteenth century, the canalization of the Dender River and the digging of the Leuven-Mechelen Canal demonstrated that waterways were still vital to economic life. But most efforts were now directed toward ameliorating the road system, a priority which had already begun under Philip V in 1704, primarily for military reasons. Unimproved roads, virtually impassable during rainy periods, were paved with cobblestones. It should be stressed that the Austrian government was not intimately involved in all aspects of road construction. It restricted itself to the technical aspects of the project, to the writing out of permits, and to the arrangements of loans. Actual road-building initiatives were left to the States, to the cities, and even to wealthy property owners who saw road improvement as a way to increase the value of their own estates. Together, these efforts created some 2,850 kilometers of paved roads in the Austrian Netherlands.

Coal mine in Wallonia. Painting by Léonard
Defrance. (Musée de l'Art Wallon, Liège.)

Spain, with its immense colonial market, remained the Southern Netherlands most important trading partner in the eighteenth century, just as it had been the century before. The balance of trade was strongly tilted in favor of the Austrian Netherlands. Importing its wool from Spain (in the eighteenth century, largely via the Republic), the Austrian Netherlands exported a variety of goods, of which light textiles were the most important. Trade with the United Provinces was also vital, since the Dutch were middlemen in the importation of a host of foreign products. Exports to Holland, on the other hand, were insignificant and led to a large trade imbalance. Trade deficits with England lasted throughout the eighteenth century, although after 1750 their negative consequences were softened by the growing transit trade that the Austrian Netherlands provided for English goods. France exported wine, alcohol, and fashionable clothing to the region, but also continued the policies of Colbert, protecting its factories from outside products. The Austrians' own protectionist policies, however, had at least one important effect on the regional economy: they stimulated the establishment of officially sanctioned companies, thus encouraging commerce throughout the Austrian Netherlands.

The textile sector grew strongly. Before mid-century, cotton became widely popular, whether in full cotton or blended fabrics. A taste for the exotic certainly contributed to cotton's success. The tremendous rise in cotton production – at the expense of wool, linen, or silk – was plainly evident throughout the last half of the eighteenth century, as factories for pressed cotton sprang from the ground. As a result of its declining market in Holland, the wool cloth industry in the eastern regions of Limburg and Verviers was forced to find new buyers at the German annual fairs.

The development of the coal industry was hampered by technical difficulties. Exploring promising coal veins, for example, was hindered by engineers' inability to pump ground water out of the mines. Technical skills were good enough in the Liège region to avoid a number of problems, but it was only with the advent of Newcomen's steam engine in the early 1720s that an efficient method to pump out the ground water was found. Improvements in the transportation system and a more protectionist customs policy stimulated the advent of the Charleroi industrial basin by 1760 and perhaps as early as the 1740s. Glass production was also facilitated by the nascent coal industry, and its base expanded beyond its traditional center in the prince-bishopric of Liège. After 1770, iron from Luxembourg was shipped in high volume to the factories and nail forges of the Charleroi region. By the early nineteenth century, both Charleroi and Liège would serve as important centers of the Industrial Revolution.

The construction of houses, roads, and dikes, not to mention the remodeling and repair of noble estates, abbeys, and churches, increased the demand for stone. Rising demand stemmed in part from new laws which prevented religious communities from investing their income in new real estate. In addition to this domestic demand for stone, Hainaut and Walloon Brabant exported much of their stone to the United Provinces. The production of finely glazed earthenware and porcelain also prospered during the second half of the eighteenth century, and the factory *Manufacture de Tournai* achieved an international reputation.

In the food sector, beer was unquestionably the most important industry, providing some cities with nearly half of their tax revenues. In the countryside, it was brewed for individual use. After the decline of the beer industry in the Flemish cities, Brabantine beers were the only ones that enjoyed a broad reputation. Wherever beer was produced, however, it was mostly destined for domestic markets. The distillation of grain alcohol depended on harvest levels. During a severe grain shortage, such distillation was forbidden, and in times of abundance and low grain prices, it was encouraged, since it provided an extra source of income to farmers. The draff and waste water of beer brewing also served to fatten local herds. In this way distilleries multiplied throughout the countryside during the Austrian period. Sugar and salt refineries also increased after 1765, thanks to changes in the customs laws.

As the economic sectors expanded, their products became more diversified. Gray and white lace were products of an expanding cottage industry and were widely exported. Women, whether young or old, beguine or nun, all spun lace, but the highest quality work was done by specialized female workers. They worked in the service of an agent who supplied their designs and thread and who marketed their products. In the same manner, enterprising middlemen traipsed throughout the countryside in search of cottage-made textiles, which they then offered to traders in the cities. These traders in turn sold their wares in an interregional market of buyers.

This labor pattern could also be found in other sectors. The country's high volume in nail production was due to the large number of forges – as ironworking constituted an extra source of income for many farmers. They often transported the cast iron they made, or the charcoal they produced, from nearby woods to regional forges. Conversely, many miners, smelters, and other industrial workers earned extra income from small-scale farming.

In the cities, the guilds anxiously held on to their monopolies. It was increasingly difficult to become a master, and in some cases the position became hereditary, open only to sons of masters. The system confirmed the dominance of these masters over the rest of the artisans, who did not have the slightest possibility of gaining access to the guilds' hierarchies. It also hindered economic development. New sectors of the economy could largely evade the stranglehold of the guilds, but in some trades, like metalworking, the boundaries were hard to draw. This lack of clarity often precipitated lengthy and ruinous legal processes to determine which parties had rights and privileges. The central government, particularly under Joseph II, used these court fights as an excuse to limit the power of the guilds. But like Turgot's efforts in France, Joseph's attempts were defeated. The guilds were so politically influential in the cities that they were almost impregnable to attack.

Farmers bring their products to market in E. van Siclers, The Coulter of Ghent in 1763.

Still, it must be said that the great textile workshops that formed the basis for future factories operated in a sector traditionally controlled by the textile guilds. The same development can be seen in the glassworks and tobacco industries, as well as in the glazed earthenware and porcelain sectors. By the late 1700s, the number of workers employed at one site could equal several hundred. But to a large degree, the system of production still relied on a combination of labor: partly from the urban workshops, partly from the putting-out system in the countryside. Urban workers complained that cheaper rural workers gave them unfair competition, and throughout the eighteenth century, the magistracy of the smaller cities demanded that rural workers be restricted to agricultural production only.

The Expansion of Agriculture

The size of farms varied considerably across the Southern Netherlands. The small-scale size of Flemish agriculture, with few large estates, was admired in Europe in the seventeenth century. Influenced by the Flemish example, the Austrian government proposed to dismantle the large estates found elsewhere, particularly in Walloon Brabant, Namur, and Hainaut. This government policy really only succeeded after 1755 in Hainaut, where the size of farms was limited to roughly seventy hectares.

In Flanders, even small parcels of land (between one and five hectares) were capable, if intensely cultivated, of sustaining a whole family. The earth was broken with a spade and liberally treated with manure, urban waste, and peat ashes imported from Holland. As land use became more intensive, new crops were now harvested between the traditional ones. But it was a life of subsistence, and farmers, faced with more mouths to feed, increasingly abandoned the old practice of leaving some fields fallow as a conservation effort. The absence of fallowed fields also compelled Flemish farmers to build stalls for their animals in order to replace the fallow lands which had provided grazing meadows. This made manure collection easier, but it also meant that more feed would have to be found for the cattle. At this point, the system began to break down: the ground was not fertile enough, nor techniques productive enough, to ensure a greater supply of feed. Unable to expand their land to accommodate their growing size, farmer families increasingly looked for supplemental sources of income. They often became spinners or weavers, contributing to the process of proto-industrialization in Flanders.

Cattle or wheat? In most regions, the answer was both. But there were exceptions. Until the sixteenth century, the Land of Herve had been able to sell its grain to neighboring countries, but in the seventeenth century, prohibitions on grain exports threatened the district with ruin. By early in the seventeenth century, most local farmers were forced to switch to cattle, and nearly 80 percent of the land was eventually earmarked for grazing. From then on, the Land of Herve specialized in selling fattened cattle, butter and cheese at the market of Aubel, near Maastricht.

Stock raising declined in the Austrian Netherlands around 1770, partly as a result of higher grain prices. Moreover, the three waves of epidemics of the eighteenth century, particularly the third one, had made people suspicious of animal herds. In order to contain this last plague, the government ordered the slaughter of every infected or suspected animal. But the keeping of some animals remained indispensable for farming, not only because of their manure, but also (at least for smaller farmers) because cattle were needed for plowing (some farmers relied on a cattle pool for this purpose). Moreover, meat was always a welcome supplement to a farmer's diet.

Bread remained the chief staple, but via the army, the potato was introduced; its use spread from Flanders and Luxembourg after 1710.

Potatoes initially were used as cattle fodder, but it soon became the staple of the poor, particularly during grain crises. By 1770, this pattern had been fully established, both in the city and the countryside. Rye was the grain most widely used for bread, but wheat was grown on the best soil. In the less productive lands of the southern districts, farmers increasingly specialized in bearded wheat and buckwheat (the latter could also be found in the Kempen).

Until the mid-eighteenth century, the population remained dependent on grain imports from the Baltic. By mid-century, however, the Austrian Netherlands was able to export limited amounts of agricultural products, mostly to Holland, which continued to control the grain markets. Certainly the active interest of the government played a role in this shift, as did rising prices – and profits. When productivity stopped increasing, the government encouraged the development of new agricultural lands, to be shared as a "commons" by villagers. The results were mixed. Usually these lands were not settled or cultivated, but the poor were able to use the meadows to graze their animals.

The physiocrats, with their view that agriculture was the only true source of wealth, held sway for a brief time in the late 1750s, but they did not really change policy in Brussels, which continued to follow a pragmatic economic course, as circumstance dictated. The government ultimately showed greater interest in the success of the industrial sector, and subordinated agricultural interests to it. Unwilling to shield agriculture from foreign competition, they increasingly nurtured and protected the region's industries. Even agricultural goods with industrial significance, like flax and rape, were more strictly controlled than other farm products.

The Persistent Problem of Pauperism

By the eighteenth century, poverty was worse than ever. Real wages for the working classes generally declined after 1720, although there were substantial differences between the countryside and the cities, as well as among regions. Flanders, for example, fared better than many other regions, owing to the strength of its proto-industrialization. But a wide chasm between rich and poor was no less visible in Flanders. Landowners and leasers gained the most from rising flax prices, while day laborers – who could be found working even on the smaller farms – had to work 50 percent more to earn the same real wage as their fathers. There was no easy way out, since the population increase had led to a labor surplus.

The surge in unemployment prompted Maria Theresa in 1765 to reissue the antivagrancy edict of 12 January 1734. Her text refers explicitly to the substantial increase of beggars and vagrants. She ordered guards and patrols to be strengthened in order to arrest these "criminals." The growing number of abandoned children was other evidence of rising poverty.

Confronted with the futility of repressing the destitute in this way, philanthropists began developing their own ideas with which to combat the problem, largely borrowing ideas from abroad. In 1764, Beccaria's *Dei delitti e delle pene* (*Of Crimes and Punishments*) appeared. As it was quickly translated into French, jurists in the Austrian Netherlands soon became acquainted with it; and on the basis of its conclusions, the central government twice proposed that torture in judicial proceedings be abolished. The provincial high courts, mostly very conservative, strongly resisted this "dangerous innovation," and only a few people favored an outright abolition of physical punishment. Influenced by Enlightenment thinking, Burggrave Vilain XIIII urged that criminals and loafers be treated more humanely, and managed to convince the States of Flanders to build a reformatory in Ghent for criminals and the unemployed. Brabant would follow this example by establishing a similar institution in Vilvoorde. The autonomy of each province – and the costs that each would have to incur – prevented this kind of penal reform from being nationally applied. Vilain XIIII eventually made the distinction between forced labor for criminals, and public workhouses for the unemployed; and under the influence of the Ath magistrate Taintenier, poor relief and crime were regarded as separate problems, to be reformed in different ways. In penal law, physical punishment was replaced, when feasible, with imprisonment in penitentiaries. As for poor relief, reformers tried to centralize a highly fragmented system which rested on the charity of the church and private parties. Some cities' administrators established "general chambers for the poor," an echo of their predecessors' efforts under Charles V, who had also tried to set up a general fund to assist the poor.

Church and State

The relationship between church and state began to change by the late eighteenth century. The state gradually began to view its seventeenth-century alliance with Rome as a form of subservience. Indeed, the Ultramontanists had become quite influential under Maria Elizabeth, giving Rome a good deal of say in the affairs of state. The correspondence between Maria Theresa and Charles of Lorraine indicates their concern about this situation, and the government adopted a new church policy. From now on, it attempted to set up a national church, which could be directed by the state rather than by Rome. The state's efforts to insist on its own authority within the church were neither infrequent nor unsubtle, and were sometimes conducted in a petty manner. After 1753, the government issued laws aimed primarily at preventing the church from owning more real estate. Interestingly, the government increased the use of the legally binding *placet* to declare the decisions of the church the laws of the land, since it was often in the interest of the state to do so.

The government's changing attitude toward censorship also reveals this shift. Censorship had been tightened during the religious disputes under Charles V and was again strengthened during the Jansenist controversy. The guidelines established in 1616 (under the archdukes) and 1729 (under Maria Elizabeth) gave most of the power of censure to the church. Ecclesiastical censors, as representatives of the bishops, had the right to review all publications, while the government censor was no more than a figurehead. Maria Theresa ended this arrangement, introducing measures which effectively broke church power in this area. For example, the Index, a list of books condemned by Rome as heretical, no longer carried legal weight. The state would no longer ban books attacked by the church if secular authorities thought they were useful, and government censors were far more tolerant of new philosophical ideas than were their ecclesiastical counterparts.

Other measures pertained to the regular clergy of the Austrian Netherlands. Maria Theresa wanted them to become less dependent on foreign influences. She also set definite limits on the dowry and entrance age of novices. She was, incidentally, quite eager to obey the papal orders of 21 July 1773 abolishing the Jesuit order; this ended their long domination in the Southern Netherlands.

The Advent of the Enlightenment and French Influence

Secular authorities found in the Enlightenment an ideological basis for their fight against Ultramontanism. It is not that the state favored full freedom of expression, however; it continued to permit only those ideas which coincided with its own aims.

The government's new direction was evident in their educational policy. It wanted to transform the University of Leuven into a state university, according to the Viennese model, and in 1754, in order to achieve this end, Patrice-François de Neny was appointed royal commissioner of the university. However, his initiatives were too tactful and moderate for Vienna's tastes. The University of Leuven, like most universities in Catholic Europe, suffered from a general lethargy, and its loyalty to Rome hardly encouraged state financial support. The end of the Jesuit order did give the state a new opportunity to intervene in the humanities education at secondary institutions, when the measures against the Jesuits led to the closing of the seventeen (out of sixty) secondary schools ("colleges") they administered. In their place, fifteen royal "colleges" were opened in 1777. The new state education of these colleges introduced a new curriculum. Without abandoning the old literary emphases, the curriculum put more emphasis on the sciences, mathematics, geography, and modern history. The new curriculum was not hostile to religion, but the circumstances under which these colleges had been reorganized triggered resistance of a part of the clergy and caused a good deal of bad feeling. Most parents preferred to entrust their children to the Augustinians, Oratorians, Franciscans, and Dominicans, and in 1778-1779, the new royal colleges received only 27 percent of all humanities students in secondary education.

To stimulate the intellectual climate, Cobenzl established a Brussels literary society in 1769, where professors from Leuven could meet each other. In 1772, it became known as the Imperial and Royal Academy for Science and Belles Lettres. Kaunitz and Cobenzl steered the Academy toward the solution of practical problems at the expense of more speculative enterprises. In Liège, the *Société d'Emulation* was set up, under the protection of the prince-bishop Velbruck. Through state intervention, the Austrian Netherlands and the prince-bishopric of Liège regained a measure of the intellectual luster it once possessed.

Cartography had been a specialty of the region in the sixteenth century, but had since entirely disappeared. Between 1771 and 1778, Count Joseph de Ferraris had the whole country surveyed, culminating in the so-called Cabinet Map of the Austrian Netherlands. Colored and highly detailed, only three exemplars were printed. The map was restricted to government use and supplemented with detailed explanations. But an amended edition, excised of "state secrets," was made available to the public in order to defray the costs of the survey.

The Enlightenment fascinated Governor-General Charles of Lorraine and his entourage. His library, as well as the books collected by statesmen like Cobenzl and Neny, attest to this fascination. The size of this circle must not be overestimated, however, as it was limited to a few prominent nobility and influential government officials. Outside of Brussels, proponents of the Enlightenment could also be found in several small but robust groups. Masonic lodges, where comraderie went hand in hand with ritual banquets, played an important role in the spread of Enlightenment ideas. Traces of their existence go back only to the 1740s, and the Freemasons remained, for the time being, at the edges of institutional life. Only in 1764 did the marquis of Gage, François-Bonaventure du Mont, attempt to unite them under his authority, and they later enjoyed the support of prince-bishop Velbruck of Liège.

Books were the ideal medium for spreading French ideas, since they could easily travel from Paris to Brussels or Liège. After 1750, the latter city was particularly open to the ideas of the Encyclopedists, important advocates of the French Enlightenment. The city's presses specialized in reprinting their works, and cheap copies were secretly distributed across the Southern Netherlands. Works approved by the censors were announced with small advertisements in the press. The arrival of French immigrants in Brussels around 1760 prompted various "gazettes" to be established, often of short duration. A new, more stable wave of "gazettes" began in 1772, and for some smaller cities like Leuven and Mechelen they became the basis for their first local newspapers. Intellectual discussions were also conducted in *journaux*, comparable to today's magazines. Intellectual activity was not absent in the Dutch-speaking provinces, either; from 1779, the *Flemish Indicator of Sciences and the Free Arts* offered its readers syntheses of over sixty European periodicals. All of these literary periodicals, however, remained subject to the censors. Pierre Rousseau, originally from Toulouse, at first managed to publish his *Journal encyclopédique* in Liège. The synod of the prince-bishopric, however, asked the theological faculty of Leuven to render a judgment of Rousseau's publication, and they condemned it in 1759. Rousseau then decided to move his presses to Bouillon.

The success of French ideas also increased the stature of the French language. The military occupation of the 1740s and its many traveling theater troupes, the flourishing court life after the war, and the governor-general's French circle all glorified Parisian taste and fashion. This was part of a much longer trend, and it was only strengthened by the widespread French influence in the Europe of the Enlightenment. At every rung of the social ladder, the ability to express oneself in French was considered elevating. Officially, French and Dutch remained on equal footing in the Southern Netherlands. Even in dual-language regions, all persons had a legal right to address the provincial administration or the central government in their own language. Still, some people were occasionally coerced to speak French, violating the country's established privileges. French was both the language of the court and of the central government.

Most of the population of the Southern Netherlands tended to express themselves visually rather than through literary forms. This was certainly the case among the lower and middle classes, where illiteracy was still widespread. One survey conducted throughout the provinces in 1779 found that 39 percent of all men and 63 percent of all women were unable to write their names. Inventories of the deceased's estates included numerous images (statues, pictures) but very few books; only half of the estates inventoried in Brussels between 1750 and 1796 listed any books at all. One in five of those who did own books possessed no more than ten, many of them manuals. Prayer books were the most common item.

The reestablishment of academies in the cities, occurring between 1765 and 1775, gave the arts new opportunities. In Liège, Léonard Defrance, who was heavily influenced by the Encyclopedists, gave much attention to the themes of the Enlightenment. Laurent Delvaux of Nivelles dominated sculpture of the period. Beginning with a baroque style with affinities for the rococo, Delvaux later advocated the simplicity of classicism. The influence of French taste was noticeable in the façades of the Louis XV and Louis XVI hotels constructed in Antwerp, Ghent, Mons, and Liège. Churches increasingly took the form of a Graeco-Roman temple, crowned with a three-cornered pediment. The new neighborhood constructed around Brussels's City Park and the Royal Square is also a monument to French classicism in the Southern Netherlands. Both French and native architects worked on these projects. The most famous of them is Laurent Benoît Dewez, who played an essential role in spreading the new style and who specialized in the redesign of many abbeys.

No one can study this last period of the Southern Netherlands without noticing the central role of empress Maria Theresa. In his eulogy given years later, Bishop Nelis of Antwerp said that she was the first ruler who possessed both distinction and dignity. For forty years she served the House of Habsburg, but she also, to a certain extent, served the interests of the Southern Netherlands. Her subjects paid high taxes for this privilege, to be sure, taxes the empress regarded as the normal duty of all commoners. But in defending her own independence against Europe's great powers, she also defended the region's independence, strengthening its political and economic systems. If her economic policies did not always succeed in this regard, they nonetheless did much to stimulate the Southern Netherlands's trade and industry. At the same time, she remained committed to absolutism and centralized government, despite her willingness to soften her position, for tactical reasons, from time to time. Her government, strengthened by Enlightenment ideals, had also firmly resisted Ultramontanism. Her son and successor, Joseph II, would pursue the same goals, but his direct and less careful approach would trigger much more resistance.

Cossacks take Utrecht in 1813, as depicted in this painting by Pieter Gerardus van Os. The French have evacuated the city and the Russians are hailed at the gates as liberators. (Centraal Museum, Utrecht.)

6 Revolution in the North and South, 1780-1830

J. Roegiers and N.C.F. van Sas

The Dutch Republic teetered at the edge of civil war in the years
between 1780 and 1795. Foreign powers intervened twice to affect
the outcome: Prussia in 1787 to bolster the conservative forces, and
the French Republic in 1795 to support the revolutionary Patriots.
In that year, the newly proclaimed Batavian Republic became a
French satellite state. In 1806, Napoleon made his brother king of
Holland before annexing the whole country into the French Empire
a few years later.

Unrest spread through the Austrian Netherlands when Emperor
Joseph II attempted to push through the same administrative, legal,
and ecclesiastical reforms that he had introduced elsewhere. To
prevent this, the region's political and church leaders declared the
Republic of the United Belgian States in 1790. Although the great
powers of Europe ensured that the republic's existence was short-
lived, the Austrians did not long enjoy their return to power. In
1794, French armies invaded the Southern Netherlands, and in the
following year, annexed it to France.

After the fall of Napoleon, the great European powers merged the
North and South into one United Kingdom, under the Dutch king
William I. Influenced by the Enlightenment, the king jealously
guarded his royal prerogatives. His policies rejuvenated the
economy, but his authoritarian style alienated liberals, and in the
South, a coalition of liberals and Catholics began to resist his
policies. That their grievances led to the Belgian Revolt of 1830 did
not stem from their intentions; rather, the revolt's cause – and
consequences – had more to do with William I's own actions.

1. The North (1780-1813)

The Patriots' Era

England unexpectedly declared war on the Dutch Republic in the last days of 1780, bringing an end to more than a century of "natural" alliance between these two sea powers. London initiated the Fourth Anglo-Dutch War because it believed that Hollanders had long neglected the responsibilities of their alliance with England. Holland, with only a modicum of its seventeenth-century power left, assiduously sought to steer clear of conflicts with both Britain and France and – in the best merchant tradition – to earn profits through trade with all warring parties. It greatly irritated the English to see that the rebellious American colonies, which had just declared independence, could rely on Dutch shipping to supply them via the Caribbean "golden rock" of Saint Eustatius. The last straw was the Republic's decision to join the League of Armed Neutrality, initiated by Catherine the Great of Russia, which sought to preserve the rights of neutral maritime nations and which, in practice, was aimed chiefly at England.

The war had dramatic consequences for the Republic. Within a few weeks, hundreds of Dutch merchant ships, laden with cargoes worth tens of millions of guilders, were seized by the English. Trade practically stopped, and the already so vulnerable economy received a blow from which it could not recover. For some time, the Dutch had lost ground in relative economic terms to England and France, but now they experienced losses in absolute numbers, triggering an economic decline unknown in the history of the Republic.

The consequences of this decline were as drastic as they were unpredictable. The war politicized a portion of the population, initiating new political conflicts which came to an end only with the Prussian intervention of 1787. Indeed, during the Patriots' Era (1780-1787), the Dutch developed their own version of the revolutionary movements which swept through Europe at the close of the eighteenth century. The changes in the state which the Dutch began, however, would find their culmination only in 1848, when Thorbecke's constitutional revolution completed the transformation of the Dutch political system.

The Dutch Enlightenment

The politicization of the Patriots' Era can only be understood in the context of the Dutch Enlightenment, itself a variation on a much wider European phenomenon. The Enlightenment played an important mediating role in the international Republic of Letters in the first half of the century, and after 1750, its cosmopolitan (and essentially French) ideas became more internalized as various Dutch writers and speakers sought to introduce these ideas to their own publics. In religion, for example, reason took a prominent place alongside divine revelation. Reading material also became far more diverse, supplementing the iron repertoire of the Bible, printed sermons, and morally uplifting books. It is not so much that more people began to read, but that the same well-educated public – amounting perhaps to 5 percent of the population – developed a different and broader orientation. Popular magazines, modeled on Addison and Steele's *Spectator*, instructed middle class people on how they should act in a society which – thanks to Enlightenment insights – could be better and happier than ever before. They also taught them to be satisfied with their established position in society, that is, under the regents yet above the people. The Enlightenment hardly preached social revolution.

The Enlightenment's emphasis on virtue, knowledge, and happiness led people to conclude that society was malleable – that it could be improved, even perfected. This obviously had an appeal in a country which – as many Dutch supposed – was in a state of decay, militarily, economically, and (not least) morally. The themes of decline (as the problem) and Enlightenment (as the solution) were so prominent in the 1760s and 1770s that one of can speak of an enlightened "cult of the Fatherland." Countless societies and associations based on the new ideal of sociability, which held that human beings reach their full potential through cooperation with others, were dedicated to the restoration of the Fatherland, whether to its economic, moral, social, or literary health. These efforts to bring about national regeneration united the smallest poetry society with larger undertakings such as the *Oeconomische Tak* (Economic Branch, 1777) and *Maatschappij tot Nut van 't Algemeen* (Society for Public Welfare, 1784). The latter organization aimed both at stimulating self-cultivation among the middle classes and educating the common people.

The economic decline of the Republic became increasingly apparent during the last of half of the century. The economy also became more one-sided: the financial sector flourished, and agriculture and a few industries, such as the Dutch *jenever* distilleries, did well enough. But trade, shipping, fishing, and small businesses all fared poorly, throwing many Dutch into misery. The chasm between rich and poor became more noticeable, and the Republic's wealth, still considerable, became less evenly distributed. The negative consequences of this trend – structural unemployment and distressing pauperism – were especially evident after 1770.

The Patriots

The shock of the Anglo-Dutch war threw the Republic into a crisis of authority that would last until 1787. The "cult of the Fatherland," so active in the 1760s and 1770s, was now transformed into a fierce and aggressive nationalism that its proponents called "patriotism." The new nationalism made good use of the media created by the Enlightenment: in addition to pamphleteering, which long had accompanied the Republic's political crises, it could count on a political press such as *De Post van den Neder-Rhijn* and the *Politieke Kruyer* (*The Political Porter*), which were modeled after the old moral "spectators" but with much more explosive content.

The war revealed how deeply the Republic had sunk. The Patriots blazed with activist zeal in an effort to remedy the situation, but possessed little power to do much about it. Their powerlessness only increased their invective against the status quo, and they soon (unjustly) blamed stadholder William V for the Republic's military weakness, even accusing him of "treason." The new nationalists viewed England as their foreign archenemy and the stadholder and his entourage as their chief domestic foes. Within a few years, their attacks on the stadholder contributed to William's subsequent loss of prestige, seriously undermining his political position.

The stadholder's power in the 1780s was a mix of formal prerogatives and informal practices. Officially, he remained (despite the hereditary nature of the position since the 1740s) in the service of the seven provincial States. By virtue of local and provincial statutes, however, his control over the state apparatus was formidable, not least because of his influence in the selection of city councils. The stadholder's powers were implemented (and interpreted) by an informal network of confidants throughout the Republic, who gave a national cohesion to the stadholder's policies. One of the Patriots' chief aims was to disrupt this network, and in doing so they could rely upon regents who longed to regain the power they had once enjoyed in the stadholderless periods.

In the 1780s, "Patriot" was a catchall word to describe everyone who favored regeneration of the Republic, opposed England – and thus supported France – in foreign affairs, and resisted the stadholder and his associates at home. The term also immediately became associated with the desire of many educated and enlightened citizens to have a greater say and influence in local government. But Patriots came in all shapes and sizes, and their collective profile resembles a crosssection of the population: rural nobility (including Joan Derk van der Capellen, the only truly national leader the Patriots produced), urban regents (certainly in Holland), the middle class and – in various locales – the common people. Local and regional conditions played an important role in determining the size and composition of the movement. Nonetheless, the Patriots' ideology had national pretensions which united a movement that, in a highly decentralized Republic, was necessarily fragmented in nature.

Roughly speaking, the Patriots' program rested on three goals: power (that is, recovery of the Republic's once enviable international position), participation (by the middle class in local government), and moral rearmament (reintroduction of the Fatherland's old virtues, as reinterpreted by the Enlightenment). The first goal was a valiant but futile effort, given the powerlessness of the Republic. The second aim, however, became increasingly important as antistadholderate regents, in word and in deed, continued to undermine William V's power. In many places, reform movements sprang up, developing slowly and accumulating a wide range of demands. The reforms were oriented toward the local situation, but they fit well into the national program which had been well-publicized by the reform-minded press.

The watchword of the Patriots was "constitutional restoration": restoration of all the rights and privileges which had been lost over the course of years or even centuries. They maintained that ordinary citizens, the cities (or rather, their regent classes), and the provinces had lost their independence to the stadholder. In reality, the watchword served as an umbrella for a whole range of concerns, some of them quite old, but some of them quite new, including those inspired by the natural

rights theories of the Enlightenment. The call for "restoration," therefore, did not necessarily mean that all Patriots wanted a return to the
way things once were.

By the mid-1780s, politicization had led to polarization, as demands
for reform sharpened. Some regents began to fear the consequences of the
very reform movement they had once encouraged. Changes in local government, in fact, often led to the growing power of the middle class at the
expense of the regents, preventing them from regaining the lock on
power they had enjoyed in the stadholderless periods. The regents may
have shaken off the stadholder, but they were now forced to reckon with,
and be held accountable to, the urban middle class.

Patriots, in all their variations, were not the only ones to fill the
political spectrum. Their opponents, the Orangists, were hardly politically inactive, but they were clearly on the defensive and were relatively unsuccessful precisely among the enlightened middle class, the
group most supportive of the Patriots' movement. Incisive and erudite
Orangists like Adriaan Kluit, Elie Luzac, and Rijklof Michaël van Goens
offered a counterprogram that went far beyond merely assailing the
hollowness of Patriotic aspirations; they articulated a principled, even
thoughtful conservatism. Through them, politicized citizens knew that
they had a choice between two different ideological systems, and the
presence of such a clear political choice may mark the 1780s as the
decade in which modern politics was "invented "

This choice was not restricted to reading through political programs; the politicization of the 1780s also included rich opportunities
for political activism and organization. Old and new forms flowed sur-
reptitiously together, and the Patriots were particularly good at adapting old means to suit new ends. Their organizers energetically
introduced petitions, which they employed on a massive scale. Public
opinion was shaped by countless pamphlets and (in a more systematic
fashion) by periodicals. The most striking form of political action was
the new civic militias, the Free Corps. Thousands of middle-class men
joined the Free Corps drills, inspired by the classical republican ideal
which said that any citizen worthy of the name must be prepared to
defend his house and home, city and country The Free Corps also
sought to rejuvenate the old civic militias, themselves merely shadows
of what they once were, and it introduced a new democratic innovation:
militiamen now elected their own officers. Militias, therefore, did not
merely appeal to men's desire for martial glory: they were expressions
of middle class will, democratic ambition, and political activism. After
military drilling, in fact, many militiamen attended political readings
and debates (which not infrequently included drinking).

Even the most radical Patriots did not favor a radical overturn of
the social order. Gradualism was their motto and, for the most part,
their practice. Although many wanted a thorough reorganization of the
political system, no one wanted a social revolution. The Patriots' principle of popular sovereignty (in which final authority rests with the
people) was not necessarily revolutionary, and in practical terms it
always meant, as they maintained, a "government by the people
through representation," never a full democracy.

The Patriots often have been criticized for their failure to move beyond uncoordinated local actions, and for a lack of unity and effective organization that proved fatal to their cause. But this is to judge them from a more recent standpoint; the Patriots did not function in the same centralized, unitary state that the Batavians developed after 1795. In almost the same breath, the Patriots have been blamed both for fomenting revolution and not being revolutionary enough. The Republic's political organization made it necessary, in fact, for the first reforms to take place on the local level. The cities, after all, were the primary centers of power in the Republic. The Patriots hoped that their new influence in the cities would next reach the provincial level and finally the States-General. In this way, the whole political system would gradually but effectively be reorganized. So if it is true – as historians often maintain – that the Patriots failed because they restricted themselves to local actions, then it is also true that their successes stemmed from the same localism.

These Patriots successes varied considerably from place to place. The movement achieved its greatest victory in Utrecht, where in 1786 several years of activity led to a general reform of the municipal administration and the replacement of most regents. The Patriots were also strong in a number of Holland's cities, and it seems certain that, if the Prussians had not intervened, they would have triumphed there as well. By 1786, tensions between the Patriots and Orangists had become so high that the country verged on civil war. This struggle for power was still undecided when Princess Wilhelmina, the resolute wife of the indecisive William V, tried to break the impasse by returning to The Hague from Nijmegen (Nimwegen), where she and the stadholder had resided during the recent unrest. Her detention by the Gouda Free Corps at Goejanverwellesluis ultimately led to the Prussian invasion of September 1787.

Princess Wilhelmina detained at Goejanverwellesluis, 28 June 1787; engraving by G.B. Probst. (Atlas van Stolk, Rotterdam.)

The years of politicization between 1780 and 1787 sealed the fate of the ancien régime. The old order was restored in 1787, but only with foreign help, namely from Prussia and England. The political culture of the Dutch Republic had undergone a revolution in the 1780s, and the outcome would prove impossible to reverse.

Restoration of the Oranges

The Patriots offered almost no resistance to the professional Prussian army of some 25,000 men. They had hoped for assistance from their French ally, but Parisian promises of support failed to materialize. The tottering government of Louis XVI did not lack the will to intervene but the means. Its inability to act, incidentally, did not go unnoticed in France, and contributed to the monarchy's loss of prestige on the eve of the French Revolution.

Orangist restoration came with all the signs of pure political reaction, including plundering and the use of terror against opponents. Patriot functionaries were dismissed and replaced by Orangemen. Paradoxically, a number of the new appointees themselves came out of the middle class, adding fresh blood (as had been the case in 1747 and 1748) to the political system, further accentuating the break with the ancien régime. Fearing retribution, thousands of Patriots fled their cities, provinces, or the Republic itself. Most returned after a short absence, but several thousand remained in the Southern Netherlands or France, returning only after 1795.

Orangist triumph was not fully secure, however, and moderate Orangists like the new grand pensionary of Holland, Laurens Pieter van de Spiegel, realized this. The stadholder's government was artificially sustained by England and Prussia, and it soon proved incapable of introducing reforms which might have reduced the country's political pressures. The Patriot movement continued to function underground, and even began to reassert itself openly once the wave of reaction had ebbed. Patriots did so, for example, through reading associations, which were sometimes simply the continuation of the old patriotic societies. And instead of emphasizing local and provincial reforms through "constitutional restoration," many Patriots now began advocating more radical political changes (a trend also evident in enlightened Orangist circles).

Meanwhile, the great revolution taking place in France after 1789 inspired both admiration and revulsion in the Dutch Republic. The revolution came perilously close in 1793, when French armies exported revolutionary ideals by marching as far as North Brabant. They soon retreated, but in 1794 they retook the Southern Netherlands, threatening the Republic again. When the Republic's great rivers froze in the winter of 1795, the last great barrier to French invasion was neutralized, and when the French general Pichegru marched into the Republic, he encountered no military resistance. The Orangist regime had not been able to rehabilitate itself after the restoration, but waited in powerlessness as its demise neared. As the French armies approached, William V fled to England, and the Patriots achieved their greatest success in the "velvet revolution" of 1795.

The Batavian Revolution

The Batavian Revolution was the mirror image of the 1787 restoration: in both cases, Dutch politics was turned on its head because of foreign intervention. The French armies, incidentally, were a calming presence as the Patriots took control of the government; by this time, the Directory in Paris had clearly distanced itself from the revolutionary excesses committed during the Reign of Terror (1793-1794). The revolution in the Netherlands was orderly, accomplished through cooperation between the Patriots who had returned to the country with the French armies and those who remained at home – including those who (through the reading associations) had further developed their political ideals. General Daendels, returning from exile, urged that the Patriots free themselves from Orangist rule in order to prevent the appearance of French invasion. When French armies neared a city, local Patriots (now called Batavians, in honor of their ancestors from Roman times) took over the municipal administration and welcomed their French comrades into the city. The French decided to play along with this game for several reasons. In the first place, they sincerely sought to further the ideals of the Revolution by offering brotherhood to all oppressed peoples. Second, the French feared that poor treatment of the Batavians would cause the country's still considerable riches to disappear.

Internationally speaking, the new Batavian Republic was no more than a French satellite, a pawn in France's power game. This would remain the case until 1813, when the international balance of power was again turned on its head. The French also saw to it that they were handsomely reimbursed for their roles as liberators and protectors; in the Treaty of The Hague (1795), which confirmed the Republic's satellite status, the Dutch pledged to pay them 100 million guilders.

On the other hand, the leaders of the French and Batavian republics tried to maintain at least the appearance of equality between the two countries. The French respected the Netherlands as an historic nation and regarded the Batavian Republic as France's most important "sister republic," an indispensable ally against England. And in domestic affairs, the Batavians were free for a number of years to prove their own revolutionary mettle. One of the first acts of the new regime was to proclaim, in various forms, the "Rights of Man and the Citizen," thus participating in the great revolutionary movement then shaking the Western world. This included, among other rights, the equality of all Christian denominations before the law. Regional administration also underwent big changes, to be finalized in a new constitution: the provincial States were abolished and replaced with Provisional Representatives. The States-General continued to exist for the time being, but now included delegates from Drenthe and North Brabant, provinces never before represented in that body.

The most important task facing the Batavians was reforming the state, and they deliberated on this issue for three years without reaching an agreement. On this important constitutional question the Batavians were roughly divided into three parties (although we cannot speak of parties in the modern sense of that word): unitarists, who favored a centralized state; federalists, who wanted to keep a measure of provincial

Meeting of the National Assembly, the Netherlands's first democratically-chosen body, in March 1796. (Atlas van Stolk, Rotterdam.)

sovereignty; and moderates, pragmatists who were also generally committed to a unitary state. These divisions applied only to the issue of what form the state should take, and in reality, the political dynamics were more complicated. In the late 1790s, it was not uncommon to make a distinction between "revolutionaries" and "moderates," terms which usually indicated tactics and methods rather than political content. Also, proponents of the unitary state usually wanted a reform of state finances that would consolidate provincial debt into a single national debt (the *amalgama*) and would introduce a system of general taxation.

The framing of a new constitution was the most important task facing the States-General's successor, the National Assembly, when it met in March 1796. For the first time, the Netherlands had a democratically elected legislature, indirectly chosen by universal male suffrage. Relatively few men were barred from voting: those on public assistance, Jews and, of course, those who refused to accept the new order. The National Assembly engaged in both detailed and elevated debates about the future of the Fatherland. These constitutional discussions did not lead, however, to a satisfactory arrangement. The "fat book" constitution, finally presented to the citizenry in 1797, looked so much like an untidy compromise that it was rejected by a decisive majority of the electorate.

The Constitution of 1798

The inability of the Batavians to produce an effective constitution was one of the factors that encouraged a group of radical Batavians, with the blessing of the French ambassador and the help of the French and Dutch armies, to overthrow the government in January 1798. At stake was more than the constitution, however. For the coup plotters, the impasse at the Assembly was symptomatic of a nation adrift, a nation which badly needed radical intervention to revitalize a revolution that was already three years old. Within a short time, the new government wrote a constitution in which the unitary principle was consistently applied (including in the area of state finance) and in which a new vision for society was outlined. Unity of law, separation of church and state, abolition of the guilds, educational reform and, last but not least, the duty of the state to instill love of the Fatherland were all part of the new constitution. In its programmatic optimism, the constitution was a typical product of the Dutch Enlightenment. Sometimes truly visionary, the Constitution of 1798 also included many articles which were unenforceable and remained on the level of good intentions.

The Netherlands's first constitution was characterized by a form of democratic centralism. In the name of national unity, local democratic experiments of the past three years, themselves outcroppings of the old Republic's decentralized nature, came to an end. Political directives would now be sent from the top, and policy was not to be slowed or obstructed by endless deliberations from below. Government policy was determined by an executive administration consisting of five directors, who were assisted by eight ministers or "agents." The old provinces were dissolved and replaced by eight departments which, after the French example, were given geographical names.

The new radical regime was certainly not very popular. But the fact that it had broken through the constitutional impasse was much appreciated throughout the country. Many moderates were so thankful for this contribution that they would have willingly supported the radicals if their revolution had only been more "national," that is, been more concerned with national cooperation and reconciliation. But instead of seeking unity among all Batavians and finding a broad base of support for its constitution, the government preferred to operate more exclusively, with a smaller (and presumably more reliable) base of support. Their purge of functionaries and voters created a good deal of resistance. Moreover, some of the new leaders gave the impression that they were more concerned about their own interests than those of the country. Within six months of having seized power, the radicals were themselves victims of a coup in June 1798. The new government, consisting of the "agents" (heads of the administrative departments) of the overthrown regime, kept the new unitary constitution. But it sidelined the radicals and endeavored to create a broader "national" basis for the revolution.

Insofar as it produced a unitary constitution (and the centralization of state debt), 1798 was a red-letter year in Dutch state building. But it was a low point in nation building. The coups and purges of that year permanently alienated many Batavians from politics. and within a few years, Dutch society had become entirely depoliticized. Disenchantment also stemmed from the worsening economic situation which now swept over the nation. Agriculture escaped decline, but trade, shipping, and fishing received heavy blows from the nearly constant wars with England. Attempts to punish this old archenemy foundered at the Battle of Camperdown (1797), in which the Dutch navy suffered an ignominious defeat. Dutch colonies, too, were lost to the English, although it would take until 1811 before Java, the country's most important overseas possession, was finally seized by British forces.

National Reconciliation

Political disillusionment did not necessarily translate into an active desire to return the Oranges to power. A Russo-English invasion of North Holland during 1799 failed in part when its effort to trigger an Orangist counterrevolution was unsuccessful. William V and his family remained in English exile and became increasingly detached from the affairs in their own country. For many Dutch, the role of the Oranges in national politics seemed a thing of the past.

The widespread disenchantment did lead to the long-desired "nationalization" of the revolution around 1800. Old Orangists could again participate in public life. Another coup in 1801, masterminded by the French, brought about a change in personnel and reforms in the governmental structure, as the country's new leaders struggled to find a new equilibrium both between the executive and legislative branches, as well as between local and national governments. The new State Administration of 1801 was at once less democratic and less centralized than the Constitution of 1798, which was now abolished. The old Orangist regents were reappointed to government office – they worked side by side with the Batavians – and the names of the old provinces were restored.

The "nationalization" of the Batavian Revolution stimulated new feeling for the Fatherland, evident in the period between 1800 and 1813. It found its roots in the Cult of the Fatherland, popular before 1780, but it utterly lacked the cult's (naive) optimism – conditions had deteriorated too much for that. Nor was the new love of the Fatherland political in orientation; instead, it emphasized the cultural qualities of the nation and its historical development. Poets like Helmers, Loots, and Tollens gave expression to these concerns by demonstrating an active interest in Dutch language and speech. The history of the old Dutch Republic was now regarded as a closed chapter, but precisely for this reason received much interest. Practitioners of not only literature but also painting – in a break with the past – devoted increasing attention to historical themes. The Dutch school of painting of the seventeenth century was now praised as the embodiment of Dutch "national taste." This rather melancholy interest in the Fatherland was briefly abandoned during the Peace of Amiens (1802-1803), which gave the Dutch new hope. Trade and shipping rebounded – only to be squashed again when the war with England resumed.

As the Dutch reconciled themselves to one another, the French began to behave less like liberators and more like occupiers. Although

Dutch disillusionment with politics continued, the French continued to experiment with the country's system of government. The bloodless coup of 1801 did not give the French the administrative and political reforms they expected, and in 1805 they demanded a new system of government. The powers of the twelve-man council were now concentrated in a kind of presidential position with the old title of grand pensionary, a position Napoleon had specially created for the able moderate, Rutger Jan Schimmelpenninck.

The grand pensionary's administration lasted only a year, but it made important and enduring contributions. Schimmelpenninck handpicked a number of gifted ministers who succeeded in quickly implementing many of the reforms that had been on the table for years. This was particularly true of Gogel's tax reforms: they replaced the oppressive excise taxes with a general tax, which attempted to assess the heaviest burden of taxes on those who could most afford to pay them. The School Law of Van den Ende further developed Dutch elementary education, expanding the initiatives begun by Van der Palm in 1801. In the long run, Batavian educational reform, which regulated both school inspections and teacher competency, unquestionably enjoyed as great an influence as the far-reaching state and tax reforms. Some observers have even regarded the School Law as the essence of the Batavian Revolution, and it received widespread praise far into the nineteenth century.

In 1806 the Netherlands became a monarchy when Grand Pensionary Schimmelpenninck was dismissed and replaced by Napoleon's brother, Louis Bonaparte. "Good King Louis" continued to follow the course outlined during the Schimmelpenninck administration. In 1808 his government finally abolished the guilds, those quintessential relics of the ancien régime. But even Louis did not perform well enough for his brother the emperor. Rather than primarily serving French interests, Louis attempted to identify with his Dutch subjects. He was lax, for example, in enforcing the Continental System, Napoleon's rigorous plan to prevent European trade with England, which in effect asked the Dutch to blockade their own trade. Napoleon thus annexed the Netherlands into the French Empire in 1810, accomplishing this in two stages.

Despite the Netherlands's loss of independence, the French still treated the Dutch with some deference, and, after Paris and Rome, Amsterdam became the third capital of their empire. But the country hardly benefitted economically (as the Southern Netherlands had for years) from its potential access to the immense French domestic market, since the tariff wall remained in place until October 1812. This so-called *tiërcering* also had severe effects: only one third of the interest on the state debt would now be paid, wreaking havoc on charitable institutions, which had often put their assets into state bonds.

Annexation to France may have been of short duration (it continued only until 1813), but it constituted a critical break with the past, sharper in some respects than the various coups and constitutions that punctuated Dutch history between 1795 and 1810. In addition to the loss of independence, the annexation introduced French law into the Netherlands, which – though replaced by Dutch law at a much later date – has continued to exert lasting influence. Napoleonic efforts to attain admin-

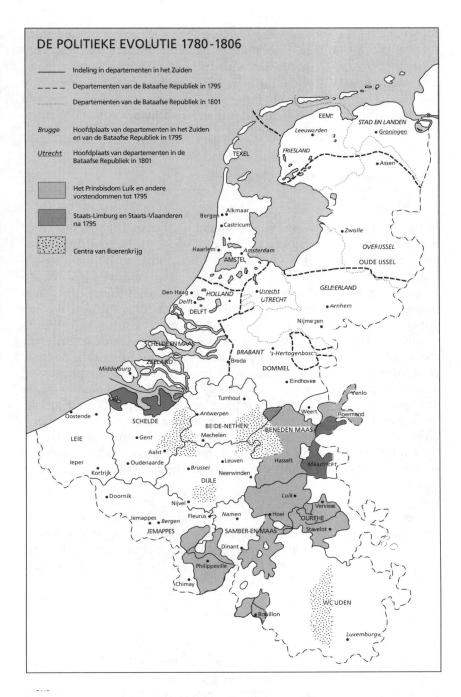

DE POLITIEKE EVOLUTIE 1780-1806

———	Indeling in departementen in het Zuiden
– – –	Departementen van de Bataafse Republiek in 1795
··········	Departementen van de Bataafse Republiek in 1801
Brugge	Hoofdplaats van departementen in het Zuiden en van de Bataafse Republiek in 1795
Utrecht	Hoofdplaats van departementen in de Bataafse Republiek in 1801
▨	Het Prinsbisdom Luik en andere vorstendommen tot 1795
▨	Staats-Limburg en Staats-Vlaanderen na 1795
⋮⋮⋮	Centra van Boerenkrijg

Political evolution in the Low Countries, 1780-1806.

istrative uniformity also affected the country; changes included the judicial system and the introduction of the civil registrar and the land registry. In these ways, the annexation cut the country's ties with the former Dutch Republic and established the foundations for the nineteenth century.

Meanwhile, French occupation became increasingly repressive. Customs officials strictly enforced the Continental System, and the proliferation of spies and censors gave even this quiet corner of the French Empire the appearance of a police state. When Paris introduced conscription to supply its armies with troops, anti-French resentment increased, especially when the sons of the Dutch elites were forced to join the so-called Guards of Honor. This resentment did not lead to a political form of nationalism, but it intensified Dutch cultural identity which had been growing since 1800.

2. The South (1780-1814)

Joseph II's Reforms

In June and July of 1781, great excitement hit the Austrian Netherlands when the new emperor, Joseph II, arrived for a visit. The reactions to his presence were strongly divergent, however. Some felt honored by the interest the emperor paid them – more than two centuries had passed since any of his predecessors had deigned to visit the region. They praised his accessibility: he accepted thousands of his subjects' written appeals. But local authorities were disappointed because the emperor, traveling incognito, forbade all forms of civic celebration. In Brussels, too, functionaries of the central government worried about the possible motives of the sovereign. Some of their number had been questioned and criticized by the emperor, and many feared that the emperor might put an end to the Theresian Compromise (see Chapter Five). Catholic bishops were the most concerned, however. Cardinal Franckenberg, archbishop of Mechelen, offered his objections to Joseph's plan to introduce religious toleration. He also weighed in against the government's suspension of anti-Jansenist measures and the state's lax censorship of dangerous books.

The cardinal's written appeal was not well received by the emperor. It only fortified the emperor's conviction that the Austrian Netherlands was a country with a confused administrative structure, a slow and unreliable justice system, a meddling church hierarchy, and little taste for modern culture and science. Its economic health was crippled by the closed Scheldt and the guild-infested cities; and politically it remained neutralized by the Barrier Treaty. At first, the emperor resolved to rid himself of this odd and far-flung region. Negotiations to trade the Austrian Netherlands for Bavaria were resumed but came to nought when the other great powers failed to offer the necessary support. Joseph did, however, succeed in terminating the Barrier Treaty, and troops from the Dutch Republic left their fortresses in 1782. Two years later, however, he failed in his attempt to force the Dutch to open the Scheldt. The Treaty of Fontainebleau (8 November 1785) resolved the differences between the emperor and the Republic which had nearly led to war.

Since he could not be rid of the region, Joseph II decided to subject the Austrian Netherlands to a rigorous program of reform. His aims were clear: the new administrative science, cameralism, taught him that the prosperity and well-being of his people constituted the power of the state. The Austrian Netherlands, therefore, like all the other Habsburg

Emperor Joseph II, ruler of the Southern Netherlands, in an anonymous eighteenth century portrait. (Koninklijk Museum voor de Schone Kunsten, Brussels.)

lands, must contribute to the welfare and security of the whole. To achieve this, it was essential that the Viennese authorities be able to direct the region's public life through a strongly centralized administration in Brussels. Obviously, far-reaching reforms needed to be implemented before this would become reality.

During his inspection tour of 1781, the rather peculiar emperor was all ears when it concerned reform proposals suggested by government officials, and he attempted to enact them whenever he judged them practicable and commensurate with his goals. His futile effort to open the Scheldt stemmed from these proposals, as did his decision to declare Ostend a duty-free harbor, which, incidentally, achieved quick and happy results during the Anglo-Dutch war of the early 1780s. Joseph's ecclesiastical reforms, too, had long been in the drawer of the Privy Council, including plans to break the monasteries' ties with their foreign superiors, to rid theological education of Ultramontanist tenets, to strengthen civil authority over marriage, to hold the country's innumerable church fairs on one day, to move graveyards from the churches to the countryside, and so on.

In fact, relatively few of the enacted reforms stemmed from the personal initiative of Joseph II himself. The most important of these was the Declaration of Tolerance (12 November 1781), which gave first Protestants and then Jews the full rights of citizenship and limited freedom of worship. The significance of this measure was largely symbolic, since hardly any Protestants lived in the Austrian Netherlands. But many people felt the decree was a great change, in which the centuries-old alliance between church and state – the Counter Reformation ideal – had been sundered. For them, the whole Catholic nature of the country now seemed threatened. But the emperor saw no reason to exempt the Austrian Netherlands from a policy that had worked well elsewhere, including in Austria itself. Indeed, the situation in Austria was foremost on Joseph's mind when, in 1783, he began to bring about the end of "useless" (that is, contemplative) monasteries and developed plans for the abolition of "superfluous" monastic institutions. In raising revenues through these measures, he hoped to finance reforms in parish life.

It is telling that regional officials, like those in the Privy Council, attempted to limit the effects of the emperor's tolerance measures; and Joseph himself was well aware that he needed new people, sympathetic with his political ideals, to implement his radical reforms. Joseph's governor-generals, his sister Maria Christina, and her husband, Albert of Saxony-Teschen, had to content themselves with a purely ceremonial role. No longer finding pleasure in his work, the minister plenipotentiary Starhemberg was forced out in 1783 and replaced by Count Barbiano di Belgiojoso, who was an unconditional Josephist. P.F. de Neny, president-chief of the Privy Council, also resigned in 1783. Although bad health contributed to his departure, Neny also resented the emperor's slight regard for his early efforts at reform. He would not be replaced until the administration had completed its reorganization of the central government.

In 1784 the impatient emperor judged the time ripe for definitive, radical, and wide-ranging reforms. His government had already devoted a couple of years to accumulate the necessary statistics and reports for an overview of the situation. Using this documentation, the government now introduced reforms in rapid succession. Economic policy was the most cautious of these reforms. Since ascending the throne, Joseph had attempted to break the power and monopolies of the urban guilds, but the greatest sign of economic liberalization came in the decree of 11 December 1786 which removed all duties and restrictions on the grain trade. Under pressure from vested interests, however, the government was soon forced to repeal this measure; and during the economic slump of the late 1780s, protectionism remained the center of economic policy. The emperor's social policies were more innovative; he set out to more evenly distribute the wealth and cast poor relief in a new mould. Joseph replaced all charitable brotherhoods and foundations with a single Brotherhood of Active Charity (8 April 1786). Hygiene and public health were also given greater attention, and elementary education was improved through a new inspection system and the introduction of a normal school.

The emperor's truly radical measures were reserved for the Roman Catholic church. The bishops unanimously protested the edict of 28 September 1784 which essentially made marriage a civil, and not a religious, function, thereby robbing the church of a segment of life over which it had enjoyed nearly exclusive jurisdiction. But the real storm broke loose after the government established a General Seminary in Leuven (16 October 1786), with a branch in Luxembourg. Would-be priests were prohibited from attending the old training centers, whether they were the bishops' seminaries, the universities, or the monastic schools. Instead, all seminarians were to be sent to the General Seminary, where they would be schooled according to the Josephist ideal of a true shepherd: free of Ultramontanist thinking, tolerant, the very model of active charity, and full of commitment to the common good. Within a month the seminarians revolted against the strict discipline and the "heretical" anti-Ultramontanist education of this improvised organization. The bishops steadfastly maintained that the formation of the clergy was their task, not the state's. Soon an avalanche of pamphlets swept over the country as the new church policy was hotly defended and attacked.

The government faced serious trouble when the church found sympathy among other groups who felt equally threatened by the Josephist reforms – especially government functionaries. In early 1787, two decrees (dated 1 January but published at the beginning of March) introduced sweeping administrative and judicial reforms. In the first decree, the secretary and state and war and the three Collateral Councils (including the Privy Council) – which had existed since the days of Charles V – were replaced with a single General Governing Council, under the chairmanship of the minister plenipotentiary. The region was reorganized into nine "circles" under the leadership of an intendant. Unlike earlier intendants, who primarily served as representatives of the central government, these new functionaries also received additional administrative powers from the provincial high courts, and even from the provincial States. At the same time, the delegations of the States to the central government were reduced to one deputy each.

The second decree abolished all existing law courts, replacing them with a streamlined and rationalized system of justice already in place in Austria. The colorful quilt of manorial jurisdictions, magistracies, provincial high courts, ecclesiastical courts and other privileged judicial organs all had to give way to one Sovereign Council of Justice in Brussels, two courts of appeal (Brussels and Luxembourg), and forty district courts.

The "Small" and Brabantine Revolutions

These two decrees cost countless people their positions or their provincial or local base of power. Resistance centered in the provincial States, first in Hainaut, then Brabant and Flanders, but outcries came from all manner of councils and courts. Riots erupted in many locales. Civilian militias were called out to restore order, but in reality they functioned more like their predecessors in the North, the Patriotic Free Corps. The States of Brabant called upon the successful Brussels lawyer, Henri van der Noot, to defend its interests. In a long memorandum, Van der Noot showed how the rights of the nation had been violated by the reforms. Regarding the Brabantine charter, the *Blijde Inkomst* (see Chapter Three), as the basis on the region's law, Van der Noot and the States charged that this "constitution" had been attacked. Moreover, Joseph II had promised, when he became their sovereign lord, to respect this charter.

Hendrik van der Noot; engraving by
E. Scott, 1790. (Koninklijke Bibliotheek,
Brussels.)

The States assembly did not reject all of the emperor's reforms out of hand, but they did demand that as a contracting party they be given a say in the process.

The governors-general, alarmed by the scope of the protest, suspended all the reforms on 30 May 1787 – without consulting the emperor. In addition, they invited everyone who felt their rights had been violated to express their grievances on paper. These concessions, as it turned out, added fuel to the fire; the triumph over imperial centralization was loudly celebrated in many places. Joseph II, surprised and furious, summoned the governors-general, representatives of the States, and the cardinal of Mechelen, both to dress them down and assure them of his good intentions. Minister plenipotentiary Belgiojoso was dismissed. The emperor proved willing to repeal his judicial reforms and the establishment of the intendancies, as long as his ecclesiastical reforms would remain in place. It is clear that he hoped to divide the opposition by making his weakest opponent, the church, the scapegoat for all that had transpired.

Meanwhile, the emperor appointed a new minister and a reliable army commander to restore imperial order, which they achieved to a reasonable degree by early 1788. The "Small Revolution" of 1787 had been defeated. Open opposition continued only in a few locales, such as the University of Leuven. The diocesan seminaries in Antwerp and Mechelen were forcibly evacuated, resulting in dozens of deaths among the citizens of Antwerp. Van der Noot left the country for fear of reprisals, and with the knowledge of a portion of the States, urged officials in The Hague, London, and Berlin to drive the Austrians out of the Southern Netherlands. The lawyer proposed that his country be united in some form with the Dutch Republic. His plans were received with polite suspicion by these governments, and they took no action.

By 1789, however, the government was losing its control over the situation, despite its increasingly punitive measures. When the States of Hainaut refused to cooperate with the reforms, Brussels revoked provincial privileges on 30 January. The same fate awaited the duchy of Brabant, where the guilds of Brussels – Van der Noot's circle – formed the core of anti-Austrian resistance. The emperor abolished the *Blijde Inkomst* and the whole Brabantine political system on 18 June 1789. Ecclesiastical resistance reached its highpoint on 26 June when Cardinal Franckenberg formally condemned the emperor's General Seminary; the emperor was now regarded by his Catholic opponents as a perjured and condemned heretic. Through all of this, the underground and exiled opposition enjoyed new support. Even the urban bourgeoisie and professional classes, whose Enlightenment ideas had originally led them to sympathize with imperial reforms, were now repulsed by the government's "tyrannical" policy, which had not shirked from the spilling of blood. They formed clubs for political discussion, and read, spread, and wrote clandestine pamphlets. Moreover, they forged plans to overthrow the coercive regime.

A group, formed around the Brussels lawyers J.F. Vonck and J.B.C. Verlooy, established a secret society in April and May of 1789. Called *"Pro Aris et Focis"* ("For Altar and Hearth"), the society planned an armed popular uprising to throw the Austrians out of the country. Clerics saw to the collection of funds. On 30 August, they resolved to trust the leadership of the army of national liberation to a retired military man, J.A. Vandermeersch. When Vonck sought contact with Van der Noot, the latter opposed the plan; he had more confidence in foreign intervention, possibly through another European war than in domestic rebellion. The members of *Pro Aris et Focis*, in contrast, preferred to trust in their own power, and by late summer had mobilized a large pool of men ready to fight. Most of them gathered across the Dutch border in the North Brabantine city of Breda, where, thanks to the mediation of exiled clerics, they were joined the Van der Noot group in a committee of national liberation. In October 1789, members of the States of Brabant, the Antwerp canon P.S. van Eupen (long active in clandestine opposition through the Ultramontanist and anti-Josephist movement), Van der Noot, "General" Vandermeersch, Vonck, and most of the leaders *Pro Aris et Focis* decided to go into action.

On 24 October, a 2,800-man army of liberation invaded the Kempen. *The Manifesto of the Brabantine People*, proclaimed from Hoogstraten's city hall, declared that the perjured duke Joseph of Brabant had lost his right to rule. On 27 October, the Austrians attacked the army in Turnhout and suffered a shameful defeat – in part because of the population's support of the rebels. By 16 November, the liberation army had taken Ghent, the last obstacle before it swept over the countryside. Brussels fell to the patriots on 12 December, as Austrian soldiers and imperial functionaries hastily left the country. By 22 December, all of the provinces, with the exception of Luxembourg, had been freed.

The United Belgian States

The Committee of Breda, as the rebel government became known, was led by Van der Noot, who took the title of minister, and Father Van Eupen, the state secretary. They represented the provincial leaders in the States and the Ultramontanist clergy, groups long hostile to Joseph II and the forces behind the "Small Revolution" of 1787. They had also financed the revolt which had driven out the Austrians. Now they denied newcomers like Vonck and Verlooy a place in the reorganized government. At the invitation of the States of Brabant, the States-General of the Southern Netherlands convened at Brussels in 1790 – the first such assembly since 1632. In the early morning of 11 January it passed the Act of Union, which had been prepared by the indefatigable Van Eupen. It established the United Belgian States (*Etats Belgiques Unis*), the first time, incidentally, that a government designated itself as "Belgian."

The new republic was to be a loose confederacy. Final sovereignty rested with each of the provincial States, which would appoint its representatives to the States-General, the highest organ of the union. A new body, the Sovereign Congress, would run the day-to-day affairs that the States had entrusted to the union: foreign affairs, defense, coinage, administration of common assets, and mediating interprovincial conflicts. In practice, the government was led by Minister Van der Noot and State Secretary Van Eupen. They firmly resisted any tinkering with the three-class system of the States, convinced that if people were to scorn this age-old and highly respected institution, everything would be up for grabs and the country would be subjected to the same revolutionary situation then taking place in France. Such a situation would, above all, bring the position of the church into danger.

Vonck and his friends, as well as other self-described "democrats," fundamentally disagreed. They agitated for a more or less radical reform of the States in order to make them more representative, so that the urban middle classes and eventually the rural population would enjoy a greater say in Brussels. Many of them wanted a national assembly of the kind then meeting in Paris. In response, the government, supported by the bishops, launched an uncharitable campaign against the "Vonckists," accusing them of all kinds of foul motives. This led to a rash of assaults against their persons and looting of their property in March 1790; and some of their number wound up in prison or fled to France. In the meantime, peasants in southern Flanders revolted against the new government. Joseph II had promised to improve their lot by reducing the power of the great landowners and tax collectors who now sat in the States. Their rebellion, too, was bloodily suppressed.

Van der Noot's government did not succeed, however, in securing promised foreign support. On the contrary, when the recently established Triple Alliance of the Dutch Republic, Prussia, and Great Britain sought closer ties with their Austrian opponent, the young republic's fate was sealed. The Reichenbach Convention reached an agreement on 27 July 1790 between the Triple Alliance and the new Austrian emperor Leopold II (Joseph II had died in February). They permitted him to reconquer the Southern Netherlands as long as he would respect its traditional institutions. When Austrian troops marched into the region in November they encountered very little resistance.

The "revolution from above" that Joseph II had tried to force on his subjects failed because the emperor had made a number of miscalculations. Political self-consciousness, inside and outside the States, was too great in the Southern Netherlands for its citizens simply to roll over and accept Joseph's policy of uniformity. The wealth and power of important social groups were simply too considerable to tolerate the danger that Joseph's reforms presented them. The highly Ultramontanist clergy were far too entrenched in society for Joseph to dismiss them so lightly. Moreover, a wide segment of the population was not so backward as to be unfamiliar with the new language of freedom that was hardly restricted to France.

The Brabantine Revolution of 1789 was no "revolution from below." Rather, it was the result of a compromise in which many parties voiced their grievances, but in which the clergy and the traditional provincial power brokers enjoyed the greatest say. It was an essentially conservative endeavor. These "revolutionaries" had much to regain and much to defend, and most had little interest in attaining new triumphs or making new contributions. If this experiment had been allowed to continue, political evolution, of course, would have produced change over time. The far-reaching effects of the French Revolution, after all, also began with the revolt of the nobility. But international developments put a premature end to this experiment in the Southern Netherlands.

The most important consequence of the events of the 1780s was certainly the political mobilization of broad segments of the population. In the battle between Joseph II and his foes, then between the States and their opponents, public opinion diverged into Josephists, Vonckists, and defenders of the States. Through both political action and government repression, people had learned how to detest each other. The importance of religious issues and the role the clergy played in the events would have a lasting effect on the nation's political composition, as the opposition between the clericals and the anticlericals became the deepest divide in national politics.

Austrian Restoration and French "Liberation"

Representatives of the emperor, Prussia, Great Britain, and the Dutch Republic met in The Hague on 10 December 1790 to sign a convention stipulating the conditions in which Austrian rule would be reestablished in the Southern Netherlands. By and large, the convention determined that all of Joseph II's ecclesiastical, administrative, and judicial reforms would be rolled back.

But it was no easy task restoring domestic tranquillity to the Austrian Netherlands. Both Josephists and democrats took vengeance on the government in a new wave of pamphlets. They especially blamed the clerics for the unhappy end of the revolution. Although the new

Austrian government proved willing to reimplement some reforms, many proponents of Joseph's lost reforms lamented that the Austrians was far too lenient toward the rebels – almost all of whom had retained their positions. No one seemed happy with the new arrangement, and the death of Leopold II on 1 March 1792 only increased the malaise.

The most radical of the political activists continued their exile in revolutionary France. There they conspired with their compatriots from Liège, who had driven out their own prince-bishop in 1789 but were forced to flee when foreign armies restored the bishop to power. In late 1791 they formed the Committee of United Belgians and Liégeois, and pledged themselves to liberate the Fatherland and establish a republic. With the French troops of General Dumouriez, they invaded the Southern Netherlands and defeated the Austrians at Jemappes (6 November 1792). In towns of any consequence they established a "Club of the Friends of Freedom and Equality" and attempted to put the local administration under their control. Finally, they favored incorporation of the Southern Netherlands into the French Republic. General Dumouriez, however, preferred that the Austrian Netherlands keep a measure of self-government and permitted the conservative leaders of 1790 to stay in power after they won local elections. The radical Jacobin republicans reacted to this with the decree of 15 December 1792 which declared the region a protectorate of the French Republic. They installed their own local governments and law courts, and initiated a fierce smear campaign against the Austrians and the church. After the rigged elections of March 1793, the republican government asked for admission to the French Republic, and the annexation was proclaimed by decree.

In the Battle of Neerwinden (18 March 1793), however, the French were defeated by the troops of the Austrian emperor Francis II, and the republican army and thousands of Jacobins fled the country. This second restoration of Austrian rule was considerably different than the arrangement in effect between 1790 and 1792. Instead of opposing each other, the Austrian government and the country's conservative majority realized they had a common enemy in the French republicans. In exchange for financial support to continue the war against France, the emperor was willing to give the conservatives free rein in domestic matters. These traditional power brokers, however, continued to make more demands of the emperor, and their grudging surrender of funds for the Austrian army were too little, too late.

The French reversed their defeat at the Battle of Fleurus on 26 June 1794, enabling them to retake the Austrian Netherlands and the prince-bishopric of Liège. The last Austrian fortress in the region, Luxembourg, would fall in June 1795. This time, the emperor's troops and administration left the country for the last time. Meanwhile, French victory struck panic into the civilian population, who remembered the first French occupation and who had heard of the Reign of Terror in France. Nobility, clerics, wealthy burghers, and countless institutions sent their most valuable possessions to safety in Germany. Those persons who had most to lose headed eastward with the Austrian functionaries, some to reside permanently or for long periods of time in Austria, Hungary or Bohemia. Most, however, did not get farther than the Rhineland or Westphalia and returned in 1795 when the worst seemed to be over.

The first fifteen months of French rule in the southern Netherlands were a nightmare. The French allowed most of the region's institutions to continue, but only so that they could plunder them. This time they did not treat the Southern Netherlands as a friendly nation to be freed from oppression but as a conquered area that would have to pay for the heavy wartime losses incurred by the French in 1793 and 1794, especially in northern France. Only a minority of the population, particularly old Vonckists and disappointed Josephists, proved willing to cooperate with the new government. The former provinces were each accorded a General Administration, to be overseen by the Central High Administration of Belgium. Native Belgians constituted a majority in all of these organs, but since local and regional governments possessed neither the means nor the freedom to pursue any of their own goals, many public officials quit in frustration. In time, increasing numbers of inhabitants, starting with the propertied classes, became convinced that the only way to stop systematic French looting was to be annexed to France itself. Representatives of countless cities and groups appealed to the Convention of Paris, and on 1 October 1795, the Convention decreed that the former Austrian Netherlands, the prince-bishopric of Liège, and the duchy of Bouillon would become integral parts of the French Republic. From now on, these three regions – separate entities for a thousand years – were politically fused together, a development which continued even after French rule.

Until mid-1797, these new regions of France were ruled by interim governments which quickly moved to assimilate the "annexed departments" into the rest of the country. The region was divided into nine departments roughly corresponding to the current provinces of Belgium. Their first task was to abolish the "feudal" structures of the ancien régime, such as the tithe, the guilds and internal tolls. The French Republic's law went into effect at the beginning of 1797. It proved quite difficult to find suitable administrators to run the new departments and even more difficult to find good cantonal commissioners to preside over local governments. This was no less true in the government's search for judges; many capable men refused their appointments, and others who dared to use their authority to prevent republican or military abuse of power were dismissed. The civic registry, designed to replace the church's parochial records, was implemented on 17 June 1796, but faced a silent boycott in the countryside for years. In the fall of 1796, all monasteries and abbeys were closed, their property assessed, and the greatest part sold to the public. Those who purchased these "black goods" earned the disapproval of countless fellow citizens. Around the same time, the French revolutionary calendar was imposed; it replaced the Christian one and featured new republican holidays largely devoted to the "cult of the law." Only a few functionaries and profiteers observed these holidays. Most clergymen refused to swear loyalty to the laws of the French Republic, which they were obliged to do after the spring of 1797. They believed that in doing so, they would give approval to all republican measures, even the most anti-religious statutes.

The general elections of March and April of 1797, open to all tax-paying males and designed to replace the provisional government, resulted in the victory of anti-French candidates in nearly every locale. The "Belgian" deputies sent to the Legislative Corps in Paris formed a united front, urging the French government to meet the grievances of their constituents, particularly through the repeal of the anti-church laws. By this time, the government in Paris had become noticeably laxer in the enforcement of these laws. But hopes for a full turn in policy were dashed by the coup of 18 Fructidor (in the new calendar, 4 September 1797) and the Peace of Campo Formio (17 October 1797) between France and Austria, which caused many inhabitants to despair of ever returning to Habsburg rule. The new French government quickly ended the loosening of republican policy. A good number of the conservative delegates were purged and replaced by radical republicans.

The law of 19 Fructidor – passed one day after the coup – required all clergymen to swear an oath of hatred against the monarchy and an oath of loyalty to the constitution. Altogether, some 585 priests were deported for their refusal to do so, and hundreds more were imprisoned. Some were shipped to Cayenne in French Guiana, and of these only a handful ever returned alive. On 25 October 1797, the University of Leuven was abolished, its last rector dying in Cayenne. Priests who had not sworn the oath tried to practice their calling in secret; those clergymen who had taken the oath – less out of opportunism than a desire to prevent greater evil – were often shunned by their parishioners. Polemics over the acceptability of the oath thus caused a schism among the clergy themselves. Meanwhile, the lay faithful were deeply shocked by the French imprisonment of Pope Pius VI in January 1798. Would the Republic bring about the very end of the church?

Public discontent swelled to its highest point when the Law of 5 September 1798 introduced conscription for young men between the ages of twenty and twenty-five. The new law sparked serious revolts in many districts, known collectively as the Peasants' War, and lasted a number of months. This new resistance was able to build on a political

Peasants revolt against the French in this drawing by P.A. Goetbloets from 1796. (Koninklijke Bibliotheek, Brussels.)

tradition now more than ten years old, which originated in the Patriot Corps of 1787 and the Brabantine Revolution of 1789. Religious, political, and social motives were closely intertwined in this revolt. The uprising of these "brigands," however, was soon doomed; their training, weapons, and coordination were no match for French troops, and hoped-for international intervention never came. In most places, the rebellion was quickly put down. Rebels held on for nearly two months in the area between the Scheldt and the Rupel, in the Kempen and the Hageland, and in the German-speaking part of Luxembourg before succumbing in December 1798. French repression was extraordinarily violent, and once again the clergy were the ones who paid most dearly for the uprising. Despite the level of repression, repeated incidents persisted throughout 1799. French authority was never more unpopular.

Consulate, Concordat, and Empire

The coup of 18 Brumaire, Year VII (9 November 1797) brought the so-called Consulate to power in France. Originally a triumvirate, it was soon dominated by General Napoleon Bonaparte. The restoration of law, order, and unity were its chief priorities, to be accomplished through strict government measures. Gradually, Bonaparte succeeded in securing the cooperation of the propertied bourgeoisie and a large portion of the nobility – groups traditionally hostile to the French Republic. Still, it took some time before the inhabitants of France's Belgian departments realized how much France's new leader was changing the Republic's course. Few of them were interested in the grand politics of the French capital, and it is hence no wonder that the region was underrepresented in the new government organs: the Senate, the Legislative Corps, and the Tribunate. The prefects in charge of each of the Belgian departments were also all of French origin, although it was now easier to fill local government and courts with native Belgians. On the diplomatic front, the Treaties of Lunéville (15 October 1801) and Amiens (25 March 1802) provided Bonaparte with official Austrian and British recognition of the Southern Netherlands as a "permanent" part of France.

The church also won a reprieve under the Consulate, but it was not until Bonaparte signed a concordat with the Holy See on 15 July 1801 that people fully saw the government's shift in church policy. The church was allowed to reorganize, but the French head of state would continue to exercise much influence in ecclesiastical affairs. The pope succeeded in persuading the two remaining bishops to resign, opening the way for Bonaparte to appoint French bishops to the region's bishoprics (the number of which was reduced from five to eight, as Ypres, Bruges, and Antwerp lost their sees). The priests who had sworn the oath of hatred against the monarchy renounced their error and were integrated in the new ecclesiastical system. This concordat – more than any other measure – reconciled a large majority of the region's population to the French regime, at least for the time being.

But there were also more material reasons to hope for the future. The first years following the French invasion had disrupted the country to the point of ruin, as the economy broke down. Rentiers who had invested their money in state bonds or in the Bank of Vienna lost nearly all of it. The massive sale of "black goods" taken from the church had made many rich, but had also contributed to the collapse of real estate prices. Under the Consulate, however, the economy rebounded. The opening of the Scheldt, improvements in the infrastructure, and the integration of the Belgian departments into the large French market created conditions that were favorable to recovery. The state's good credit was restored. New economic initiatives were encouraged, including the cotton trade in Ghent, wool processing in Verviers, metallurgy in Liège, the glass industry in Namur, and the mines in Hainaut. The government also attempted to reorganize poor relief, which had been thrown into chaos with the liquidation of the ancien régime. It also devoted more attention to education – one of the chief victims of radical efforts to destroy the old institutions – although the results were meager. For these reasons, First Consul Bonaparte was festively received when he visited his Belgian departments in the summer of 1803. Belgians did this not only out of politeness or opportunism, but also in many places out of genuine thankfulness for the regime's accomplishments.

Bonaparte, elected consul-for-life in 1802, had himself declared Napoleon, emperor of the French, in 1804. It was only one part of a sweeping reform that turned France into an absolutist state. After the disappointments with democracy in the past fifteen years, few people held the new absolutism against him. Napoleon used his office to strengthen the rule of law, introducing a new legal code that is justly hailed as a milestone in jurisprudence – and which continues to form the basis of the Belgian legal system. The empire now sought the services of a class of conservative administrators who had not compromised themselves during the radical Jacobin regimes of the 1790s, including some who had even served under Austrian rule. The emperor was particularly keen to capture the loyalty of the old nobility, and their role as great landowners was no longer assailed; some of their confiscated lands, in fact, were restored to them. Napoleon also created new nobility. Through all of this, it seemed that the "good old times" had returned, even though the Southern Netherlands was no longer a separate entity but a provincial backwater of Europe's largest and strongest nation.

The new imperial government also sought to revive education, science, and culture, although with the same enlightened-absolutist and centralizing spirit. Primary education remained neglected, but with the creation of four lyceums (which replaced the departmental central schools introduced during the Directory), secondary education received a new structure. The most success was enjoyed by the many community secondary schools (in reality very Catholic institutions) and the ubiquitous private boarding schools. The well-behaved clergy were now allowed to open their own minor seminaries. Medical students were able to take classes organized in Brussels, Ghent, Antwerp, and Liège. In 1806, a law school was established in Brussels that was supposed to train administrators, lawyers, and magistrates. When, in 1806, higher education was integrated into a single Imperial University, Brussels became the seat of an "academy" which united the medical schools in

Ghent and Liège with the faculty of law in Brussels, as well as with faculties of letters and the sciences.

In order to stimulate intellectual and artistic life, agriculture and industry, most municipalities founded learned societies. In those instances where they were privately established, they were subject to strict controls. Artistically, the whole region soon became part of the French cultural climate. The republican period left little artistic legacy, but now the imperial style in architecture and the decorative arts, and the most severe classicism in the beaux arts and literature, monopolized artistic expression. Particularism and provincialism, which had so typified the cultural and social life of the region in the eighteenth century, gave way to an enlightened and cosmopolitan breadth of artistic life in the French Empire.

When Napoleon visited his Belgian departments again in 1810, he was at the height of his power. He discovered, however, that more enthusiasm was expressed toward his wife, the young empress Maria Louisa, than to himself. She was an Austrian Habsburg, and reminded his subjects of a past age. By this time, too, the French regime had become more repressive, generating new resentments. In 1805, a long series of Napoleonic wars broke out. The worst consequence was the increasingly heavy conscription, followed by the loss of countless young lives.

Systematic efforts to promote the French language were particularly disliked by the lower classes. In the eighteenth century, Francophone tendencies were part of a spontaneous process of social and cultural assimilation. After 1794, however, Paris made this trend government policy. From 1804 on, all public acts had to be published in French in order to gain legal status, and in 1810, the prefect of Antwerp severely restricted Dutch-language publications. When, in 1813, the *Bulletin des Lois* abandoned its Dutch translations, the most-used language of the region had been driven entirely from public life. Dutch (and German) was now only used in primary education and in the pulpit.

The emperor's new ecclesiastical policies ended the public euphoria that had followed the Concordat of 1801. Napoleon's insistence on a single Catholic catechism for the whole empire found widespread resistance, since the catechism promoted a loyalty to the French state many people found hard to stomach. The French detention of Pius VII in 1809 also caused unrest in many places. The new discontent was expressed in the National Council, which Napoleon called together in 1811 as a way for the French Catholic church to reorganize itself without meddling from the pope. Bishops Hirn of Tournai and De Broglie of Ghent were among the chief opponents of government church policy at the Council, and the emperor punished them and their councilors with imprisonment and exile. He forced them to resign and installed new candidate-bishops. In Ghent, where the clergy was strongly Ultramontanist, this precipitated a fierce reaction. Seminarians who refused to recognize the "intruder" were conscripted into the army, and many scores of them lost their lives in this adventure. Meanwhile, many dioceses were managed by vicars who had themselves gone underground. Napoleon's efforts to gain favor by restoring the bishopric of 's-Hertogenbosch met with little success; there, too, his candidate was not accepted by the majority of the people and the clergy.

By 1813, only very repressive measures by the ever present police and increasingly stringent censorship of the press kept the government in control. When Napoleon's armies suffered successive defeats in 1813 and 1814, the French were obliged to gradually abandon the Southern Netherlands, and in the first months of 1814, armies of the anti-Napoleonic allies, mostly Russian Cossacks and Prussian soldiers, swept across the region. Only Antwerp, defended by Carnot, offered any real resistance.

The European powers treated the Southern Netherlands as conquered territory and officially chastised the Belgians for not taking up arms against Napoleon like the rest of Europe. In reality, though, allied leaders had dissuaded them from this course. It was all too clear that such a revolt was doomed to disaster in a country where most young men had been taken away by conscription and where the threat of bloody French reprisals was still very real. The allies also forbade Orangist agitation in the Southern Netherlands; they had decided to give the region to William of Orange, but on allied terms, not through Dutch invasion or propaganda.

The Belgians themselves suffered from a serious lack of leadership; almost all of the country's political elites had been too tarnished by their associations with past regimes – a total of eight in the previous

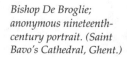

Bishop De Broglie; anonymous nineteenth-century portrait. (Saint Bavo's Cathedral, Ghent.)

twenty-five years – to be generally acceptable to the allied powers. The Austrians, no longer interested in reasserting their authority in the region, also offered no leadership. The provisional government set up by the allies consisted primarily of the old nobility and other figures who had served under Austria or even (especially at the local level) the Van der Noot government of 1790. The liberal bourgeoisie, the newly rich, the buyers of "black goods," ex-Jacobins, and former Bonapartists found no one to defend their interests in the new government. Bishop De Broglie, speaking for a larger constituency, preferred to see the region remain part of France – which now, since the defeat of Napoleon, was under the restored and staunchly Catholic House of Bourbon.

The provisional government itself allowed aspects of the ancien régime to be systematically restored, particularly in regard to the church. Nuns and monks, absent from public life for almost twenty years, reorganized themselves, put on their habits, and demanded their old buildings and possessions be returned. The clergy soon expanded the educational system, and a group of former professors urged the pope, the Austrian emperor, Cardinal Consalvi, the Congress of Vienna, and William of Orange to reestablish the old University of Leuven. Many people in the Southern Netherlands hoped that the days like those before the French Revolution would return. This hope was not realistic, and not only because the allies had decided otherwise. The whole social and political edifice of the ancien régime had largely disappeared, making restoration impossible.

The Southern Netherlands had been a part of a large and fast-evolving nation for twenty years, a period which effectively ended the region's cultural isolation. At the same time, all the ties which once united its inhabitants had been broken, and when William I entered Brussels on 31 July 1814 to become their sovereign, he inherited a deeply divided and uncertain people.

3. The United Kingdom (1815-1830)

Liberation

The year 1813 has an almost mythical ring in Dutch history. Renewed independence and the return of the House of Orange together gave the nation a new start, as it were, and marked the real beginning of the nineteenth century. Recent historiography has tended to downplay 1813 as a radical break, however. It is true that the year restored autonomy to the Netherlands and gave the country a role in the new international order that was designed to keep France in check. At the same time, the country continued to move in the course set during the Batavian-French period, and its administrative apparatus remained largely intact. For these reasons, it is better to regard 1813 as an admittedly important moment in the long-term transformation of the Dutch state, a process which began in the last quarter of the eighteenth century.

The liberation of 1813 was as much a bloodless "velvet revolution" as the Batavian Revolution of 1795. The French, demoralized by the setbacks of their Russian campaign and their defeat at Leipzig, retreated of

Arrival of the Prince of Orange in Scheveningen on 30 November 1813. Engraving by Reinier Vinkeles, after a painting by Jan Willem Pieneman. (Rijksprentenkabinet, Amsterdam.)

their own accord from the Netherlands, creating a vacuum which the Dutch were free to fill. It was not particularly easy, however, to find persons ready to take the lead at this important moment. But the few who did move decisively to mobilize the Dutch, like A.R. Falck in Amsterdam and G.K. van Hogendorp in The Hague, were crucial in determining not only the conditions for independence, now in the hands of the Dutch themselves, but also in supporting of the much more ambitious plan that envisaged uniting the Southern Netherlands with the North. The name Van Hogendorp, in particular, gave the Dutch an international reputation which added weight to their position at the conference table.

William's return to the Netherlands seemed a foregone conclusion by late 1813, although only a few years before links between the House of Orange and the country appeared broken for good. William, the son of stadholder William V who had died an exiled man in 1806, found the age of revolution a hard taskmaster. His fight for the House of Orange's dynastic future had determined the course of his life for years. After kneeling before Napoleon and enlisting the aid of the Prussian king, William wound up again in England, the only country able and willing to assist his dynasty. The terms of his kingship found quick consensus among those most directly involved: the great European powers, the Dutch political elite, and William himself.

Actually, the new king-to-be, named William I, was the least sure of what was expected of him; in such a precarious predicament, he was afraid to ask too much or to do anything that might threaten a restoration of the House of Orange. In any event, the key to the resumption of Orangist power was to "forgive and forget," a theme which Van Hogendorp, in his famous proclamation of November 1813, pledged would be the basis for the new order. In the Netherlands, that meant that the "nationalization" of the revolution would continue, but now under Orangist leadership. William I himself made clear that he would become sovereign only if his authority was guarded by a "wise" constitution, and when he officially became the Dutch monarch (with the title of sovereign prince) in December, it was clear to all that there was an implicit contract between the prince and his people. Several years later, when William's position was secure, William would insist that his sovereignty preceded (that is, superseded) the constitution – a stance which carried obvious and far-reaching political consequences.

The laws which were most closely tied to French rule were dismantled: the customs union with France, censorship of the press, and the state tobacco monopoly. The rest largely remained the same, both in the structure of government and the content of policy. It has been said of William I (not unjustly) that he had fallen asleep in the bed of Napoleon and that at the same time he had become a "Patriot." This meant that he had, in effect, accepted the legacy of the nationalized Batavian Revolution, and that he continued the policy of concentrating and centralizing power begun by the Batavians and the French. Van Hogendorp's *Sketch of a New Constitution* tried to reintroduce the decentralized forms of the old Republic, but these forms were so adjusted to the centralizing principle that their resemblance to the past was more in name than in reality.

The Unification of the North and South

The establishment of the new order was soon overshadowed by a portentous event which dramatically altered the face of the new state: its unification with the Southern Netherlands. From the start William was determined to expand the confines of his country to include this orphaned region (diplomats correctly assumed that Austria did not want it back). In this desire, the Prince of Orange was powerfully backed by Van Hogendorp, who had personified Dutch national resistance to the French. England's position on this issue was crucial, since it had long regarded the Low Countries as its most important sphere of influence on the European continent. Fortunately for William, the British government wanted the Netherlands to serve as a military check to France on its northern border. The exact redivision of national boundaries had not yet been determined, but London did want to see the Northern Netherlands strengthened. This is why William's and Van Hogendorp's detailed plans for unification, with which they deluged the British, were of such vital importance in the unification of the North and South. This crucial decision was certainly made without consulting the people of the South, but northerners, too, barely had a say in the matter.

Publicly the unification was explicitly presented as a "task" assigned by the great powers, designed to keep the French contained on their northern border. Also, the constitutional construction of the new state, described as a *union intime et complète*, was understood as a component of the country's security role. The Eight Articles of London (21 June 1814), in which the European powers established the terms of the new state, was largely inspired by the Dutch themselves. It was chiefly penned by William I's closest confidant, Falck, himself an enthusiast of the old Burgundian ideal of a great Netherlands. The creation of this new state was undoubtedly to the advantage of William I's future position, which – since it was an entirely novel arrangement – made him less beholden to the past of the Dutch Republic and to the title of stadholder held by his forebearers.

The great powers of Europe tried their best to do justice to both parts of the new state in the Eight Articles – especially when it became clear that the Belgians were hardly enthusiastic about the arrangements which had been made for them. The idea of unification with the North was, to be sure, not an entirely new idea; Van der Noot had articulated it in 1789, and the Anglo-Russian expedition of 1799 had given a new impetus to it. In 1814 many members of the old States party in the South were not unsympathetic to the idea, as long as certain conditions were met. They wanted to ensure that Catholics would be treated as equals under a Protestant sovereign (a condition already established in the North by the Batavian Revolution), and that *both* parts of the state would have sufficient influence. Whatever else happened, the Belgians would now be joined to a state with a great past, and this meant that they, too, would have to repay the state debts of the old Dutch Republic.

In the summer of 1814 England returned most of the colonies that it had seized from the Dutch. However, the English did retain Ceylon (which had already been formally surrendered in the Peace of Amiens) and the Cape Colony of southern Africa. The British also kept (after strong pressure from British traders) Demerary, Essequibo, and Berbice (British Guiana) – territories whose wealth was vastly overrated by both the English and the Dutch. London expeditiously returned the Dutch East Indies to William I, including Java. The islands would become the jewel of his colonial crown and their loss was deeply regretted by an expert like the British empire builder Thomas Stamford Raffles.

Napoleon had gone into exile in 1814, but his return to southern France on 1 March 1815 posed a mortal threat to the European order that was being established by the Congress of Vienna. Within three weeks, he made a triumphant entry into Paris, forcing the only recently crowned Louis XVIII to find shelter in Ghent. William reacted without hesitation, proclaiming himself king of the United Kingdom of the Netherlands on 16 March 1815 and calling the population of the North and South to arms in an effort to repulse the Napoleonic threat.

Fear of reannexation to France put an end to the wait-and-see posture that characterized the posture of many Belgians toward the new government. The bishops, who initially regarded the Protestant king with great suspicion, now sung a Te Deum for the new monarch and permitted public prayers to be said for the success of the allied armies. William's army of 25,000, together with the English under Wellington and the Prussians under Blücher, formed the northern front of the ring that the Congress of Vienna wanted to close around Napoleon. The

French emperor now moved against them. As he marched into the Southern Netherlands, he expected, as a "liberator," a warmer reception than he received, but William had been there before him, traveling across his southern provinces in a successful effort to secure their loyalty. While anxiety reigned in Brussels and Ghent about the results of the impending conflict, the decisive battle was won at Waterloo on Sunday, 18 June 1815.

The allied victory over Napoleon, due in part to the efforts of national troops and the bravery of the future William II (the crown prince was wounded in the shoulder during the battle) contributed to the triumphant and unified spirit in the kingdom that summer. In the national mythology of the new kingdom, Waterloo gained a place of great honor. Under the House of Orange, the North and South had fought together for freedom. In the meantime, politicians from the South were quick to capitalize on the gains the victory had made possible. They succeeded in reannexing territories that had remained part of France in 1814 and forced the French to return the art treasures which they had taken from the Southern Netherlands between 1794 and 1814. Rubens's paintings were returned to Antwerp with the greatest of fanfare.

The Political System

After consultations with the Belgians, unification led to several changes in the kingdom's political system. A bicameral legislature was introduced (the North had only one legislature under the Constitution of 1814), which included a First Chamber so stacked with royal appointments that it became known as "the king's menagerie." The States-General received important lawmaking and financial powers but did not always choose to exercise them. Its budgetary powers remained limited, since normal expenditures were funded for ten years at a time. Despite the real powers of the States-General, the new system was not a "parliamentary" one; government ministers remained responsible to the king, not to the States-General.

But William's original willingness to place his kingship within a constitutional framework is in itself enough to make him significantly different from the "enlightened despots" of the eighteenth century, with whom he is often too easily identified. His regime was more constitutional than either his Belgian opponents or Dutch liberals later charged. If the Second Chamber of the States-General really wanted to bare its teeth, it could; and it did so during the deep political crisis of the late 1820s. The constitution itself, moreover, was embedded enough in the political culture to serve as a springboard for the opposition. One of the weakest parts of the new system was the voting system, a highly complicated arrangement with an indirect voting structure, open only to those men who paid enough taxes and expressed in prerevolutionary language. It was hardly effective in stimulating political interest – or including most segments of the population in the political process.

In 1815, the king sent the altered constitution to the States-General, still representing only the northern provinces, for approval, and to 1,604 "notables" of the South – prominent citizens selected by the king to represent the Belgians. To William's great surprise, a number of these notables, led by Ghent's bishop M. de Broglie, launched a veritable crusade against the constitution. The Ultramontanist clergy continued to demand that the Catholic character of the South be constitutionally guaranteed, and they rejected the statute which promised equal legal status for all churches. The call of the bishops to reject the constitution led a majority of the Belgian notables to vote against it. The king, however, could not retreat from his position; the Eight Articles, underwritten by the great powers in 1814, had insisted on the equal protection of all creeds. After an ingenious manipulation of the voting – the infamous *arithmétique hollandaise* – the constitution was duly passed and implemented.

The rear-guard action of Bishop De Broglie and his supporters must be seen as a continuation of the Ultramontanist cause, which for nearly forty years had fought to maintain the Catholic church's important role in society. Under Joseph II, the Directory, and Napoleon, the Ultramontanists had gained the crowns of martyrdom. De Broglie, easily influenced and possessing a somewhat effusive personality, let himself be led by more militant Ultramontanists and proponents of the Bourbon restoration in France; they wanted to go back to a time when the Catholic church and the Catholic state had worked together, each enjoying a monopoly of power in their respective spheres of influence. Even after passage of the constitution, De Broglie continued his resistance and declared that an oath of loyalty to it was unacceptable for all Catholics. The state and its judicial apparatus rather clumsily attempted to silence him by sentencing him, in 1817, to two years in prison. Once again a martyr for the cause, De Broglie managed to make a timely escape to France.

Other members of the Catholic clergy proved to be more flexible. The last prince-bishop of Liège, De Méan, swore an oath of constitutional loyalty when he entered the First Chamber, and the king rewarded him by appointing him archbishop of Mechelen. It was some time, however, before his interpretation of the oath was accepted by Rome – or before all Catholics were free to follow his example. It was primarily through the mediating role of clergymen in the North, particularly the North Brabantine priests, that Catholics came to accept the idea of tolerance. These clergymen had been just as Ultramontanist as their friends in the South, but had also experienced the advantages of religious freedom in the Batavian era. They had come to regard governmental interference, a problem which privileged churches often faced, as a far greater danger. By 1821 it appeared that the Catholic church throughout the Low Countries had accepted the right of everyone to religious freedom.

William's autocratic governing style, influenced by Enlightenment precepts, has drawn more attention from historians than the Dutch constitutional system itself. He preferred to rule through executive resolutions than through laws, and sometimes simply bypassed the States-General when making important decisions, particularly in the financing of large-scale projects. His ruling style was obstinate, activist and authoritarian – and thus subject to all manner of political pitfalls. Not interested in creating a political consensus for his policies, William I made himself very vulnerable politically in the long run, a problem evident by the end of the 1820s. At that point the king, who personally knew and arranged everything himself, could do little to deny his personal responsibility for government policy. William's insistence that he, and he alone, exercise the responsibilities of the kingdom is not entirely incomprehensible. He understood all too well that the success of the *union intime et complète* – a union which he himself had established – rested largely on his shoulders. For that reason, too, he forcefully pushed policies which would strengthen both the state and the nation. His policy was based on the belief that society could be reshaped, with the state playing a guiding and omnipresent role in its transformation. In order to achieve that great and (in his eyes) good end, it was necessary to concentrate more power into his own hands. In this, William was assisted by government ministers like one of the "new men" of the Batavian era, C.F. van Maanen, the king's chief instrument in the government's centralized bureaucracy.

William's effort to build a nation-state was one of trial and error, searching for – and often not finding – the right formula. Rather, fortunate coincidences played a large role in whatever success the union of the North and South enjoyed. The relationship between the two regions, which had not sought union with each other, was often very problematic in the years after 1815. Nor was the rear-guard clerical fight of bishop De Broglie the only important source of tension; economically, too, the regions had different priorities. The North hoped that at least a measure of the old prosperity would return through the revival of trade and shipping. It therefore wanted low customs duties. In contrast, the South wanted high tariffs to protect its young industries. Then the most advanced on the European continent, the factories of the South had thrived under Napoleon's Continental System precisely because cheap English goods had been kept out. It took until 1821 and 1822 before a taxation and tariff system was found that both parties could accept.

Constructing a Nation-State

William's efforts to weld a nation and state together became evident in the early 1820s through the emergence of a clear economic policy. He believed that in pursuing national prosperity the government could transform the strong points of both regional economies – industry and maritime trading – into a source of unity. The colonies would serve this aim, too; Belgian industrial goods would be transported there by Dutch ships, which in turn would bring colonial wares back to the Low Countries. Nor was this policy restricted to the Dutch colonies; Belgian goods and Dutch shipping were supposed to traverse "the whole globe," as the Netherlands Trading Society (NHM) expressed it in their statement of purpose. For William I, this would not only generate prosperity but power. He intended the United Kingdom of the Netherlands to become an economic giant that would transform the country – as in the seventeenth century – into one of the world's great powers.

Between 1821 and 1824, a number of new institutions appeared that – though no one knew precisely how – were supposed to economically integrate the two portions of the country: the Fund for the Encouragement of National Industry (*Fonds ten aanmoediging der Nationale*

King William I in a 1819
painting by J. Padinck.

Nijverheid, 1821), the *Société Génerale*, which would develop as a modern industrial bank, a government syndicate for the liquidation of state debt (1822); and the crowning achievement of these efforts, the Netherlands Trading Society (*Nederlandsche Handel-Maatschappij* or NHM, 1824). The NHM most clearly reveals the chief aim of William's national prosperity policy. It was a semi-governmental organization which was given multiple tasks: it functioned as an import-export organ, gave economic information on the domestic and international economies, and advised the government on relevant issues. The NHM was supposed to become the motor of the country's economy, and enjoyed influence that went beyond shipping and trading, to industry, agriculture, and fishing. Its workplace, as has been said, was the world.

On balance, William I's national prosperity policy did not succeed, but one cannot say that it failed, either. It did not have enough time to prove itself before the kingdom became unglued in 1830. The NHM's ambitious economic plan was just then under way, and it was in the North, not the South, that its close association with the government generated the most criticism. The NHM would find a stable role for itself only after the split between the South and North in the more limited capacity as an East Indies trading association. Meanwhile, the government syndicate accumulated more debts than it liquidated, although William is less to blame for this problem than his critics charged. The *Société Génerale*, on the other hand, was so successful as a bank that the Belgians were able to use it to finance their revolution against its founder, William I; and it continued to prosper under Belgian independence. The Dutch king did a good deal more to improve the economic potential of his country, such as improving the infrastructure through the construction of roads and canals. It should also not be forgotten that the economic structure of both the North and South remained overwhelmingly agrarian under William I. Some of his projects took account of rural life, such as the Society of Benevolence (*Maatschappij van Weldadigheid*), which tried to combat dismal poverty by enabling city paupers to farm the countryside of Drenthe.

In education and intellectual life, too, the king sought reform through a centralized and self-consciously enlightened approach. In the North, the king was able to build on the far-reaching reforms established under the Batavians, but in the South, French annexation had had disastrous consequences for the educational system. For the purpose of national unity, the South, too, was introduced to the Batavians' education law of 1806, with its ideal of an enlightened, moralistic education. The government succeeded in building many new primary schools throughout the southern provinces, in improving the quality of teachers through better training and more inspections, and in introducing classical education. Although the South's new educational system remained suffused with a Catholic spirit, some clergy remained suspicious of these state-sponsored initiatives.

Secondary education – the privilege of relatively few students – remained committed, by and large, to the transmission of the Graeco-Roman tradition. In the North, however, the curriculum of Latin schools did begin to include a modicum of modern languages, geography, and history. In the South, the government set up its own institutions, the *athenea,* and in so doing strengthened its grip on urban high schools – at the expense of the Catholic clergy and their schools. It also attempted to put the bishops' own educational institutions under its control. A royal resolution of 14 June 1825 demanded that all secondary education be approved by the state, and resulted in the closing of the minor seminaries, thirteen high schools, and a number of other private institutions. Catholics reacted with indignation, and in 1829 and 1830 the government was forced to retreat, again permitting the existence of church-sponsored education such as the kind found in the minor seminaries.

The same centralizing and "enlightened" impulse could be found in higher education. The three remaining universities of the North (Leiden, Utrecht, and Groningen) received a new statute in 1815, in which their boards of trustees lost their autonomy and were absorbed into an administrative pyramid with the king himself at the top. A good year later, the same model was used in the South to establish three new universities: Ghent, Leuven, and Liège. Later, all of these universities were given a hand in teachers' and higher technical education. The government met with much resistance when it decided to introduce a *Collegium Philosophicum* at the University of Leuven, which all candidates for the Catholic priesthood were obliged to attend for a couple of years *before* they could continue their studies. The intention behind this reform – to raise the intellectual level of the Catholic clergy – was sincere, but its direct imposition on the church was too provocatively anti-Ultramontanist to prevent a storm of protest and the bishops' decision to completely boycott the new *Collegium*. Even the government's chosen site for the new institution – the former Pope's College – was unfortunate; it was the same one which housed the hated General Seminary forty years before.

Most of the great learned societies, established in the eighteenth-century Republic by private initiative, continued to exist. The exciting cultural and political debates which had once animated their halls no longer took place, but the calmer atmosphere was itself proof of these societies' acceptance into the scientific community. The Society for Public Welfare, the most important of the reform-minded associations, sponsored a whole range of activities designed to promote a "national" culture. The Society was also active in the South, where the priesthood actively combatted it as an initial attempt to protestantize the Southern Netherlands. The South had few equivalent societies of its own, since most state-sponsored or subsidized associations from the French period had quietly expired. In order to replace them, the government reintroduced the centralized model once employed by the Austrian administration. In 1816, for example, a royal resolution reestablished the *Académie des Sciences et Belles-Lettres* of Brussels which had existed until the French occupation. There the surviving members of this Theresian institution mixed with the best scholars the country could boast, from both the South and the North.

The establishment of the *Collegium* in Leuven shows how much William I regarded the churches, Catholic and Protestant, as *public* institutions, which were to instruct the people in right living and thinking. Louis Napoleon had established a department of religious affairs, and William divided this government bureau into two, one for Protestants and one for Catholics. Through these departments, the churches were supposed to support the king's enlightened ideal for a better society. Already in 1816, William gave the Dutch Reformed church a new centralized organization which sharply diverged from the Calvinist model on which it had been based, and effectively made it an arm of the state. By the 1830s, this new organization would prove a stumbling block to the various forms of religious revival which were to influence the Protestant world.

The king wanted to rearrange the Catholic church along the same lines, but ran into the resistance of Rome and the regional clergy. When discussions about the Concordat of 1801 (was it still valid?) and a constitutional place for the Catholic church were not resolved, William simply went ahead with a new church organization for the whole country, a synthesis of the French model (where kings largely chose their own bishops), the older traditions of the Southern Netherlands, and the new "enlightened" church-state arrangements recently implemented in Germany. In 1827, William finally concluded a new concordat with the Holy See. The king was much resented for his subsequent failure to live up to the concordat, despite the interventions of the flexible papal nuncio, F. Capaccini, to encourage his compliance. Nor was this the only issue on which William offended his Catholic subjects. His educational policies, mentioned above, obviously did not please them, nor did his refusal to restore the monasteries. Only those orders committed to primary education (particularly for girls) and tending the sick received permission to take on new members. From 1825 on, Catholic publicists and members of parliament, like the militant J.G. le Sage ten Broek, used the constitution in their resistance against the king's church policy; they argued that freedom of education, (real) freedom of the press, and freedom of association were all natural effects of the constitutionally guaranteed right to freedom of expression. This new generation of liberal Catholics (who emphasized individual liberties) now replaced the old-style Ultramontanists in leading Catholic opposition to royal policy.

William's efforts at "language coercion" now alienated the liberal bourgeoisie of the South, who were anticlerical enough to applaud his moves against the Catholic church. With Napoleon's defeat, French was no longer imposed on the populace as the country's official language, but within a few years William decided that, in order to promote national unity, use of the Dutch language should be encouraged. On 15 September 1819, he issued his famous language resolution, which stipulated that within three years Dutch would be the only language permitted for official business. Sparing the predominantly French-speaking areas, the resolution applied to the largely Dutch-speaking provinces of East and West Flanders, Antwerp, and Limburg, and in 1822, the statute was also applied to the districts of Brussels and Leuven. In 1823, the government gradually increased Dutch language use in the primary and secondary schools of these areas. This policy was not relevant to the universities; Latin retained its monopoly there. Even in French- and German-speaking regions, the government encouraged people to learn the "national language," and those who spoke only French were largely shut out of the national bureaucracy. In pursuing these policies, however, William I had greatly underestimated the degree to which the upper levels of society, throughout the Dutch-speaking regions of Belgium but especially in Brussels, now spoke French. In fact, the petition movements of 1828 and particularly those of 1829 made William's "language coercion" one of their chief grievances.

Crisis, Revolt, and Separation

In the middle of the 1820s, William could devote his full attention to his constructive policy of raising national prosperity. After 1827, however, he was forced to devote increasing effort to solving serious domestic

L'armée hollandaise prenant ses quartiers d'hiver

The Dutch army in winter quarters. *This caricature portrays the Dutch army departing Belgium and seeking refuge in an Edam cheese. (Atlas van Stolk, Rotterdam.)*

problems. He now faced the consequences of his stubborn and – in some cases – unconstitutional – course. In other words, he would now have to pay the price for building the Dutch nation-state without having solicited the support of society in general or the politically active segment of the population in particular. By the late 1820s, William faced resistance from many corners, for many reasons, although he fared best in those circles which had benefitted from his most creative policies – those involving the economy. William's various foes now found common cause, denouncing the concentration of royal power and the manner in which the king had exercised his authority.

By 1828 and 1829, the tensions and unresolved conflicts within the kingdom – which were far more complex than just the differences between the North and South – had turned into a deep crisis of authority. This crisis was not unique to the Netherlands; it could be found elsewhere on the continent, as a new generation of liberals increasingly opposed the authoritarian practices of the "restoration" regimes established in the wake of Napoleon's defeat. The crisis of the United Kingdom of the Netherlands, therefore, was more than a collision between the South and the North; it was fundamentally a crisis between liberals and conservatives, centering on the modernization of the political system and (at least in hindsight) pointing to the eventual construction of the modern liberal state.

The divisions between the North and South were, given the rising level of tensions, certainly higher than they had once been, but people did not yet regard a break as imminent. Many of those persons most sharply critical of William's system did not intend to break up the kingdom, if only because they supposed that the great powers would insist on its indivisibility. Rather, the king's opponents made modernization of the system their collective endeavor, whether they were southern liberals or Catholics (who wanted the same freedom as liberals for their church and educational efforts). In this they were joined by (usually more quiet) northerners, who resented the king's autocratic meddling, either because it undermined the old Dutch traditions of local self-government, or because it flew in the face of constitutional government (liberals were not confined to the South). Together, they demanded that the power shift from the king to the States-General by making government ministers responsible to the parliament. They also wanted a more public (less secretive) administration, better parliamentary oversight (certainly in financial matters), reform of the electoral system, judicial independence from the executive branch, and freedom of the press and education. In addition to these demands, southerners also added their grievance (which could hardly be disputed) against northern domination in the state bureaucracy and in the officer corps. Already in 1828, the Union of the Opposition was established in the South, in which liberal Catholics and young liberals together demanded greater freedom.

The crisis of authority that afflicted the Kingdom of the Netherlands after 1828 led – though hardly inevitably – to the Belgian Revolt of August 1830. The revolt broke out only after the July Revolution of 1830 in France, and was successful only because of changes in the European balance of power. Riots in Brussels at the end of August triggered additional unrest as the situation in the Belgian provinces developed its own dynamic. Various groups had various aims, and the chief cause that united them was their demand that their grievances be addressed. In this rather volatile and unpredictable situation, a vanguard of young militant liberals found that events were going their way. They knew, better than anyone else, what they wanted: a modern liberal state and (before much time had lapsed) an independent Belgium. For his part, William I contributed much to the success of the rebellion. Although this threat to his kingdom clearly demanded a decisive response, William dithered and a fatal paralysis seized his government. Other governments – in particular the four great powers that had established the Dutch kingdom – expected that William would himself restore order. But the military campaign that he finally ordered to march on Brussels at the end of September was symptomatic of his ambivalence; the bloodshed it brought stiffened Belgian resistance, and William refused to do anything more.

In the North, public opinion strongly favored inflicting punishment on the mutinous Belgians, but also thought it good riddance to lose them. When William proved incapable of solving the crisis himself, he appealed to the European powers to do it for him. When the Conference of London met in November, the five great powers were primarily concerned about managing the serious domestic upheavals of that year and avoiding a European war. As a result, they were soon prepared to accept Belgian independence, and on 20 December 1830, they formally decided – after bypassing William – to permit the establishment of an independent Belgium. One month later, the great powers also determined that Belgium should be neutral, each of them pledging to guarantee that neutrality.

For these European powers, the establishment of an independent Belgian state was a negative choice; they acceded to it only to prevent war. No one actually expected the new arrangement to last. France would have preferred to reannex Belgium; both England and Prussia would have preferred the restoration of Dutch authority but acquiesced out of pragmatic considerations. After these three powers had come to accept Belgian independence, Austria and Russia had little choice but to concur.

The great powers' decision to let Belgium break with the Kingdom of the Netherlands did not resolve which "terms of separation" should be implemented. William was prepared to accept the terms proposed in January 1831, but the Belgians were not. They were ready to endorse the Eighteen Articles of June 1831 – which made it possible for Leopold of Saxe-Coburg to become their king – but William was not. The Dutch king shocked everyone by reacting to this proposal with the Ten-Day Campaign, a surprisingly successful military action against the Belgians. But it came too late to alter his fortunes. The Dutch king did get better terms, the Twenty-four Articles, but these, too, he rejected. No more hostilities took place after 1832, but it took until 1838 before William resigned himself to the Twenty-four Articles, and another year before his government became a signatory to them. William had obstinately waited for changing circumstances, such as the outbreak of a general European war, to swing in his favor. In this hope he was initially supported by northerners, who – if not desiring a return of the United Kingdom – at least wanted a restoration of their national honor. As far as William was concerned, his motives were purely Machiavellian, determined by dynastic considerations. Nor would it be fair to say he was unrealistic; the international situation was still unstable, and William was probably not incorrect if he thought that tiny, vulnerable Belgium would not survive a European war.

Leopold I becomes the first king of the Belgians on 21 July 1831, depicted in this water-color painting by J.P. Madou and P. Lauters. (Koninklijk Legermuseum, Brussels.)

7 Belgium since 1830

E. Lamberts

The unionism that held liberals and Catholics together in the 1830s fell apart once the Belgians had securely established their independence. The ideological and religious differences between them soon defined the contours of public life, particularly in the struggle over the nation's schools. At first, liberals enjoyed the upper hand, but over time the Catholic bloc expanded its power. As Catholics extended their control, Belgian society became "pillarized," that is, it was subdivided into separate ideological segments. This development gave a more anti-liberal content to the state.

Social tensions at the end of the nineteenth century contributed to the rise of the socialists, and to an important Christian Democratic movement. These social movements, initially sharp in their criticism of the status quo, were largely integrated into bourgeois society by the eve of the Second World War, leading to a democratic and social consensus which manifested itself in a "neo-corporatist" model of government.

By this time, rivalry between the Dutch- and French-speaking segments of the population became the country's most divisive issue. The Flemish movement, in its long-running confrontation with the Francophone elites, worked to ensure that Dutch language and culture gradually replaced French in the public life of Flanders. After 1970, Francophone Walloon nationalists also helped turn Belgium into a decentralized federal state, in which the country's feuding regions became largely autonomous. This parceling out of the Belgian nation-state was intensified by the fact that after the Second World War the government was transferring more and more of its powers to supranational organizations like the European Union and NATO (the North Atlantic Treaty Organization).

1. The Liberal State (1830-1890)

The basis for the consolidation of the new state was established soon after the Revolution of September 1830 and the Belgian declaration of independence. The Conference of London determined the terms under which Belgium broke with the Kingdom of the Netherlands, terms which finally crystallized in the Treaty of Twenty-four Articles. Meanwhile, Belgians elected their own constituent assembly, the National Congress, which adopted a model liberal constitution and created a constitutional monarchy. Belgium's "unionists," who had fiercely opposed the "despotic" policies of the Dutch king William I, had developed a clear political program which they were now free to implement in the wake of independence. They reduced royal power to ensure the primacy of parliament, gave local government greater autonomy, and granted the citizenry and opinion groups more civil and political rights.

The Belgian Revolution was the work of a coalition of intellectuals, the middle class, the nobility, and the Catholic clergy; and the new constitution they wrote may be considered a balanced compromise of the sometimes divergent interests of these social groups. It did not, however, satisfy the more "radical" republican and democratic groups that had played a decisive role in the revolutionary days of 1830. Indeed, the new, essentially bourgeois state was effectively insulated from a thoroughgoing democratization which would have included less wealthy segments of the population. Thus the urban bourgeoisie would come to dominate the Belgian state, especially after 1848. The middle class itself had a broad consensus of support for the liberal parliamentary system, but increasing conflicts between liberals and Catholics, soon the chief source of friction in Belgian political life, would give a more anti-liberal content to the state. Other conflicts, ethnic and social, would engraft themselves onto this ideological confrontation and would lead to substantial changes in Belgium's political structures in the long run.

A Dutch engraving makes fun of the Belgian Revolution's leadership, showing them dancing around a liberty tree. (Koninklijk Legermuseum, Brussels.)

The Making of the Belgian State

Belgium became a constitutional state with civil and political rights for its citizens, which were to be protected by an independent judiciary and a directly elected parliament. The freedoms of opinion, religion, press, education, and association gave many opportunities to individual Belgian citizens, but also to a wide range of associations and societies with an interest in public life. For example, the new climate of freedom had important consequences for the Catholic church, which was now freed from all state supervision by a constitution which implicitly separated church and state. Freedom of education gave the church the authority to develop an educational system on all levels, from primary school to university, and freedom of association allowed religious orders and various church associations to organize themselves. The church would soon take advantage of these freedoms to compensate for its loss of state support.

The constitution also assumed that final sovereignty lay with the Belgian people. Parliament was supposed to express the public will, and was divided between the Chamber of Deputies, dominated by the middle class, and the aristocratic Senate, to which men of only the highest incomes could belong. Not surprisingly, the Senate consisted chiefly of large landowners, and it would often use its authority to check democratic and "socialist" tendencies in Belgian national politics. The constitution stipulated that only men who paid a certain amount of direct taxes – first set at a minimum of 42.32 francs – were eligible to vote for parliament. Soon a law introduced a differential poll tax that took account of income differences across the country, with lower taxes for rural voters than for townsmen. Under this arrangement, 55,000 men, amounting to one-seventieth of the entire population, were granted the franchise. Election law also established a winner-take-all district system, making it difficult for minorities to find political representation.

After some difficulty, the National Congress finally selected an acceptable compromise candidate as king, Leopold of Saxe-Coburg, who was the widower of the English crown princess Charlotte. He would guarantee a policy sympathetic to both the capitalist bourgeoisie on the one hand and the nobility and the church on the other. On 4 June 1831, a large majority of the congress acclaimed him king of the Belgians. He would do much to strengthen the authority of the monarchy, although always within the limits of the constitution.

The Unionist Government

The Revolution of 1830 had been made possible by a "unionist" coalition of liberals and Catholics, and the cooperation between these two camps continued after independence, for both ideological and practical reasons. Many progressive unionists were convinced that religion would no longer play a significant role in political life, now that the church had been given full freedom of action. For them, a further democratization of the Belgian state should now be the top priority. More conservative unionists, however, perceived the tensions between Catholics and liberals as fundamental, but they remained committed to the unionist coalition in the 1830s, not only because of William I's continued hostility to Belgian independence, but also to preserve a united front against the government's domestic enemies. Among these enemies were the so-called reunionists, who wanted a return to French rule. After the reunionist coup failed in June 1831, however, they quickly abandoned their efforts. The Orangists, who wanted a return to the United Kingdom of the Netherlands, were more dangerous opponents, since they included a minority of the great nobility and an important segment of the entrepreneurial class in the industrial cities and trade centers. In the spring of 1831, they managed to incite riots in Ghent and Antwerp. Efforts to topple the regime failed, however, and after another aborted effort in 1834, the Orangists gradually diminished in power. Nevertheless, it was not until 1839, when the Netherlands accepted the Treaty of Twenty-four Articles, that the deathknell sounded for the Orangist cause in Belgium.

Thus unionists felt obliged to cooperate with each other at least until Dutch recognition of Belgium had been secured. As a result, no discernible political parties formed in the Belgian parliament during the 1830s. There was, nevertheless, a vague but discernible field of tension between more democratically oriented deputies, *les verts*, and the more conservative *les mûrs*. The electoral law in fact strengthened the power of conservatives, who could rely on the lower electoral requirements for the more traditional countryside. Parliament did little to contest government policy in the 1830s, in part because nearly 40 percent of all parliamentarians were themselves civil servants or magistrates, people unlikely to criticize their peers in the executive branch. In these years, Leopold I himself determined a large measure of government policy. While not assailing the liberal foundations of the Belgian state, the king sought to increase his own royal authority and to support the conservative forces in the country. To do so, he counted on the support of the nobility, the country's financial circles and the church. To his great surprise, the country's Catholic leaders offered a good deal of resistance to his policies. Liberal Catholics, who had increased their influence during the revolution and who were now supported to an important degree by most Belgian bishops, wanted to keep their distance from both the government and from the king's conservative policies. The king called upon the conservative pope Gregory XVI to pressure the Belgian church into a more conservative stance. Rome responded by reestablishing a nuncio in Brussels and appointing conservative, Ultramontanist bishops to the country. The new bishops obliged the local clergy to actively support the unionist government, especially during elections. This development would have far-reaching effects, since it again intertwined the interests of the church with the interests of the government. It therefore became inevitable that political parties would be formed along clerical and anticlerical lines. At the same time, the church again became strongly associated with political and social conservatism, losing its connection with the more progressive forces in Belgian society.

The first unionist governments were still strongly influenced by the middle class, and their economic policies were committed to developing the country's industry, as well as its financial and transportation systems. After 1834, the landed nobility became more prominent, and the De Theux government reoriented its economic policy toward agricultural interests and the traditional linen industry. It also attempted, through the Provincial and Local Government Acts, to increase the power of the king and the central government at the expense of local organs. It was inclined, moreover, to recognize an important role for the Catholic church in Belgian society, and on several issues gave the church preferential treatment. Relations between church and state, separated by the constitution, were again growing closer.

Liberalism's Breakthrough

Liberal bourgeois circles were unhappy with these developments. The revolution for which they had fought now appeared to have served the interests of the conservatives. Once Belgian independence had been guaranteed by international statute in 1839, these liberals openly took the political offensive. The ranks of anti-Catholic resistance soon grew, including the ex-Orangists, again willing to participate in national politics, and the radicals, whose position became especially strong in the urban centers. The most decisive reaction came from the Freemasons; explicitly condemned by the Belgian bishops in 1837, they now became increasingly politicized. Together, these liberals established their own electoral societies, first on the local and then on the district levels; and their efforts paid off as they strengthened their positions in the municipal administrations and (later) in parliament itself.

The liberals increasingly departed from the unionist consensus, which they now regarded as a cover for the naked power exercised by the nobility and the clergy. They staunchly defended urban interests and the independence of civil authority from church influence. On other issues they were less united, and from the very beginning of their offensive, the liberals divided into factions. The "doctrinaires," including most of the ex-Orangists, represented the propertied middle class. They were socially conservative and unabashedly nationalistic and statist, that is, firm believers in the ability of the state to transform society. The radicals, on the other hand, found their support among intellectuals and the lower middle class. They were more democratic in orientation, socially progressive, and were chiefly active outside the halls of parliament. It was they who took the initiative in convening a national congress of liberals at Brussels on 14 June 1846. The congress forged a platform which would inspire the liberal party for decades: a civil society free from the influence of the church, a gradual extension of the voting franchise, and an improvement in the standard of living among the working class. The congress failed to lay the basis for a liberal party organization, and it would be many years before such a congress again convened. But it provided the liberals with a vision for the future, turned anticlericalism into a common cause uniting both doctrinaires and radicals, and made Belgian liberalism open to further democratization.

Soon the liberal juggernaut seemed unstoppable. In 1847, they won the parliamentary elections and were able to form – despite the severe displeasure of the king – a completely liberal cabinet under

Charles Rogier. Announcing a "new policy," the government attempted to gradually implement the liberal party platform. The February Revolution of 1848 in France, which took place soon after Rogier's government was installed, prompted many frightened European governments to liberalize themselves, and in Belgium, it served to further accentuate the government's liberal character. A new electoral law of March 1848 lowered the voting requirements to their constitutional minimum and abolished the "differential" poll tax that had favored rural voters. The number of eligible voters rose 71 percent, to 79,000 persons, out of a population of 4,300,000. The extension of the voting franchise particularly benefitted the urban bourgeoisie. The stamp tax imposed on daily newspapers was abolished, fostering the creation of a vast – and inexpensive – political press. Under a new law, civil servants and magistrates were banned from parliament, which now became more independent of the executive branch. These reforms laid the basis for a bourgeois and genuinely parliamentary regime. At the same time, the liberals kept Belgium free of the revolutionary turmoil that swept through much of Europe in 1848, and in doing so, many Belgians looked to them as the embodiment of the Belgian political system. This also led to better relations with Leopold I and to a landslide electoral victory in June 1848 – which opened the way for the liberal party program, especially responsive to the demands of the urban bourgeoisie, to be fully implemented.

The Shift Toward an Urban, Industrialized Society

The political rise of the middle class had much to do with economic developments that had been visible since the beginning of the century. In the early nineteenth century, the provinces of Hainaut and Liège boasted advanced coal and iron industries, and Ghent prospered as the center of the cotton-processing industry. Antwerp's harbor also indirectly benefitted from these developments.

At first, the Belgian Revolution had dampened prospects for the new nation's economy, since its exports to the Netherlands and the Dutch East Indies were now cut off. Moreover, the Dutch hindered navigation on the Scheldt until 1839, which inflicted heavy damage on Antwerp's economy. These economic deprivations, in fact, stimulated the Orangist bourgeoisie to oppose the new state. But successive Belgian governments attempted to improve this situation. They encouraged quick construction of a railroad system after 1835, which increased Antwerp's transit trade. In an age of widespread protectionism, the government concluded advantageous trade treaties with France and the German Customs Union (Zollverein). They stimulated industry through their support of investment banks, helping to establish an axis between Walloon industry and the banks of Brussels. All of this led to qualitative improvements of Belgian heavy industry. These improvements did not immediately lead to substantial industrial growth, since the markets for Belgian products remained limited. By the 1850s, however, growing international commitment to free trade – and a new surge in the global economy – would especially improve the fortunes of Walloon industry.

The Flemish (Dutch-speaking) provinces fared less well; Ghent's cotton factories constituted the only modern, mechanized industry in the region, and they recovered only with difficulty after the loss of their markets in the Netherlands and the Dutch East Indies. More dramatic was the collapse of traditional flax-spinning and linen-weaving during the 1840s, cottage industries which employed one-third of the working population in East and West Flanders. These cottage industries simply could not compete with England's mechanized linen industry, which was able to flood the market with fashionable and inexpensive fabrics. Unionist governments attempted in vain to save these cottage industries through premiums and protectionist measures. To make matters worse, the Flemish countryside was afflicted with severe crop failures; between 1844 and 1846, the grain and potato harvests failed, depriving many cottage workers of their supplementary incomes. Famine and epidemics swept the region. By the end of the 1840s, East and West Flanders, which under Dutch rule were still prosperous provinces, were reduced to poverty.

Under these circumstances, the economic balance between the Dutch- and French-speaking parts of Belgium came to an end. Flanders, for centuries the economic center of the Southern Netherlands, now became "poor Flanders," a condition which had negative consequences, incidentally, for its once vibrant cultural life. Ghent was the only city with a large and modern industry, and it remained economically vulnerable. Antwerp did grow slowly as it developed a labor-intensive service sector. Through all of this, the Flemish economy retained a strongly agrarian character; in 1846, 52.5 percent of the working population was engaged in agriculture, com-

Le Grand Hornu, a major Belgian industrial site in the mid-nineteenth century, is depicted in this 1846 print. (KADOC, Leuven.)

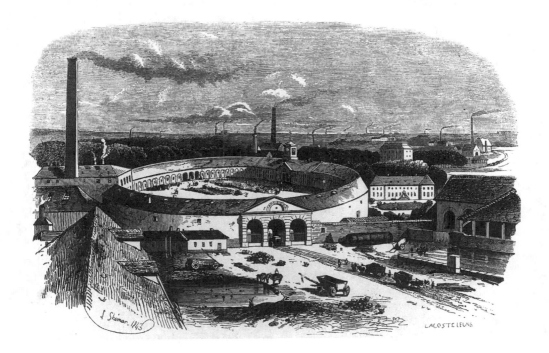

pared to only 23 percent in the Walloon provinces of Hainaut and Liège. Between 1846 and 1880, the Dutch-speaking provinces share in the country's industry declined from 41 to 29 percent, while the French-speaking provinces' share increased from 47 to 62 percent. In search of work, many Flemish migrants moved south to the industrial centers of Wallonia and northern France.

Thus Flanders and Wallonia clearly showed two sharply contrasting patterns of development – and two contrasting social patterns. Overwhelmingly agrarian Flanders remained, to a large extent, dominated by the landed nobility and the church, and was thus politically and socially more conservative than Wallonia. It was the business class of Wallonia and Brussels, on the other hand, who formed the backbone of doctrinaire liberalism. Moreover, it was only in the Walloon industrial cities where there was a significant potential for working class radicalism. Ghent formed the only Flemish exception to this rule.

The economic boom, begun around 1850, lasted until 1873. Cheap grain imports from North America and Eastern Europe brought a collapse in grain prices during the 1870s, and a grave crisis once again buffeted the Flemish countryside. Peasants abandoned the land in droves, and in Flanders, the share of peasants and agricultural workers declined to 36.5 percent by 1896. But they could find little work in the cities because industry, too, faced hard times caused by the decline of exports. The Belgian metal industry, particularly reliant on international markets, was hit by a structural crisis and adjusted with difficulty from iron to steel manufacturing. All in all, Belgian heavy industry was subject to repeated and sudden shocks from the world economy during the 1870s and 1880s. The sustained depression after 1873 contributed to social unrest and would lead, by the late 1880s, to important economic and social changes. For the time being, however, middle- class domination was not threatened, and under most of its rule, Belgium enjoyed an increase in prosperity.

Sharp Social Contrasts

But it was primarily the propertied business class which reaped the fruits of economic expansion. In 1846, they possessed half of the country's real income, and by 1880, their portion had climbed to two-thirds. Throughout the nineteenth century, this class comprised about 10 percent of the Belgian population, which substantially increased from roughly four million in 1846 to six-and-a-half million fifty years later. The very top of the bourgeoisie was able, through royal recognition of its services and standing, to rise to the peerage or to marry into noble families. The nobility itself grew numerically between 1840 and 1914, although as a percentage of the total population it remained static (2.5 families per 10,000 inhabitants). In contrast, the number of the lower middle class (the *middenstand*) swelled, thanks largely to a spectacular expansion of the service sector, discussed further below. The increase of the lower middle class would, in the long run, have important social and political consequences.

On the other side of the social spectrum lay the small landowners and tenant farmers, who formed the overwhelming majority of those engaged in agriculture. They suffered greatly under the string of agrarian crises that racked nineteenth century Belgium. Next to them were wage earners of all kinds, who constituted some 63 percent of the working population in 1846. The largest portion worked in agriculture (42.5 percent), followed by crafts and trades (25 percent), cottage industries (16 percent) and mechanized industry (16 percent). Over time, the number of agricultural laborers and outworkers decreased as the number of industrial workers increased.

The living conditions of factory workers before 1850 were abysmal. The first industrial business survey of 1846 revealed that an average cotton worker earned 656.08 francs a year, while the minimum cost of living amounted to 742.56 francs. In 1853 and 1854, the first scientific survey was undertaken to examine the budgets of industrial workers. It revealed that only the best-paid workers, miners, and metalworkers, were better off materially than Belgian convicts. At the same time, factory workers labored twelve to fourteen hours a day, or about eighty hours a week. Women and children were particularly common in textile factories, but they were also employed in the mining and metal industries. Women, and especially children, were paid far less than men. After 1850, economic prosperity helped improve the situation somewhat; the index for real wages rose from 100 in 1853 to 149 in 1875. Still, a large segment of the working population remained mired in mis-

Mine Gas Explosion in Frameries, 130 Deaths *is the title of this 1879 print. Not only were housing conditions wretched for factory workers, their working conditions were also hard and dangerous. Serious accidents were a part of daily life. (KADOC, Leuven.)*

ery, providing the basis for the militant socialist movement that became increasingly important during the late nineteenth century.

Liberals in Power

For the time being, however, the wealthy liberal bourgeoisie set the political tone of the country. Belgian liberalism showed greater cohesion than its Dutch counterpart, but the differences between the doctrinaires and the radicals remained. The anticlericalism that united them became increasingly more militant, especially among the radicals. A number of liberal intellectuals sought solace in Protestantism, while others became anti-religious. Again, the Freemasons played an important role in this development. After the prohibition on political activities within Masonic lodges was lifted in October 1854, the Freemasons became increasingly involved in partisan conflict and formed the vanguard in the struggle against clericalism. As the conflict with the Catholic church sharpened, many lodge members moved toward agnosticism or unbelief. The advent of a rationalist free-thinking movement, which found resonance chiefly among the lower middle class, artisans, students, and intellectuals, further contributed to the spread of anti-religious sentiment.

The Masonic lodges formed the center of liberal organizational life, which aimed at offering alternatives to the growing number of Catholic organizations in the country. Liberals created their own social and cultural societies and stimulated the development of a liberal press. Liberal domination of the press, in fact, partly compensated for Catholic domination of the country's educational system.

As a result of these efforts, middle class liberals managed to build a culture of their own which clearly contrasted with its Catholic counterpart. In general, liberals were more open to modern intellectual and artistic trends than were Catholics. The difference can be seen, for example, in architecture; liberals opted for neoclassicism, while Catholics had a decisive preference for the "Christian" neo-Gothic. Catholic literature competed with Belgium's liberal-minded literary culture, which reached a highpoint with Charles de Coster's *The Legend of Ulenspiegel*. The dividing line between Catholics and liberals could be drawn for some artistic disciplines as a whole; the opera and (for a long time) the theater were considered exclusively liberal enterprises.

The doctrinaires of this generation of liberals, exemplified by W. Frère-Orban, were largely statist in orientation. They saw the state as an active participant in the country's economic life. They believed that the state should also play a moral role by instructing and elevating the whole population, and encouraging them to better themselves. Public education was the primary tool to this end. The doctrinaire desire to increase the role and authority of the state was an important part of their anticlericalism.

The radicals, in contrast, were less statist, and not committed to centralized government. Rather, they favored less state intervention, more free trade, and more power for provincial and local governments. They were antimilitaristic. Radicals also wanted compulsory education, universal suffrage for literate males, a progressive income tax, and the abolition of all legal discrimination directed against the workers. In many of these issues, they routinely clashed with the doctrinaires in conflicts which impeded liberal efforts to assert their common agenda.

The successive liberal governments which ruled Belgium after 1847 were controlled by doctrinaires who saw to it that the state would play a supporting role in the economy, primarily to the advantage of the middle class. Under these governments, the state contributed to the consolidation of capitalism by lowering duties and levies (such as import and export fees), by reducing the prices of transport and communication, and by establishing public credit institutions.

But the doctrinaire governments were most interested in pursuing an anticlerical policy, as they attempted to roll back the church's influence in public life, which it had won during the 1830s and early 1840s. They imposed restrictive measures on the Catholic church, limiting its property rights, secularizing church graveyards and the church's role in public charities and public education.

The liberal confrontation with the Catholics was particularly sharp in these last two areas, since charities and schools were vital components in society. The anticlericals maintained that the state must guarantee the freedom of all its citizens by creating equal opportunities for non-Catholics in these two areas dominated by the Catholic church. In the 1850s, liberals initiated a heated debate over the character of public charity, and finally succeeded in wresting public poor relief away from the influence of the church.

The struggle for the future of the public schools was much more important, and no issue polarized liberals and Catholics more than the fate of the country's schools. The Belgian constitution guaranteed complete freedom of education, without state supervision. Accordingly, Catholics established their own dense network of schools in the years after 1830. In 1835, for example, they established the Catholic University of Leuven, while the local state university established under William I's rule disappeared. The constitution also created the possibility for public (that is, nonsectarian) education, but with little effect, much to the liberals' annoyance. Nor did existing public schools often escape Catholic influence. In 1842, the government laid the basis for the development of a coherent network of municipal primary education. The Catholics finally backed the plan after successfully insisting that such public education be in fact Catholic. A similar measure could not be secured for secondary schools, however. In 1850 liberals vastly expanded public education in the secondary school system and determined that the clergy could no longer act as an official authority in public *athenea* (high schools). Moreover, religion became an optional course of study in these schools.

This measure led to the first school "war," which ended with a compromise but was, in effect, won by the liberals. Through it, the Catholic church lost much of its influence over public secondary education. Later on, the same happened in the state universities of Ghent and Liège. The church perceived that public education became hostile to its cause and established, even more than before, its own network of Catholic schools. In this way, two opposing school systems were arrayed against each other. Whatever the disadvantages, this arrangement increased the number of schools, reducing illiteracy and raising the level of education. In 1866, 53 percent of the population could neither read nor write, but by 1880, this had been reduced to 30 percent.

An Independent, Neutral Nation

Ideology was of much less importance in determining liberal foreign policy than it was in domestic issues. The monarchy, which was gradually losing its influence over domestic affairs, largely continued to determine the contours of Belgian diplomatic and military policy.

The international statute of 1839 which established Belgian independence also compelled the country to renounce its claims to the largest portion of Limburg and to the German-speaking areas of Luxembourg. In declaring the inviolability of Belgian territory, the great powers also insisted on the nation's perpetual neutrality. Belgian independence, however, was repeatedly threatened by its powerful neighbors throughout the nineteenth century, especially after 1848. By then, the alliance among Europe's conservative powers had fallen apart, disrupting the continental balance of power they had once collectively attempted to maintain. Without this balance of power, smaller nations like Belgium became more vulnerable, and the absorption of tiny states during the unification of Italy and Germany created a sphere of crisis in Brussels. Nor did Napoleon III's expansionist policies allay concerns; by the late 1860s, Belgians feared that, in the event of a Franco-Prussian war, their country would become a battlefield. In view of these dangers, they attempted to strengthen the nation's defenses.

Increasing international tensions also changed the relations between Belgium and the Netherlands; mutually threatened, they reconciled. This did not lead to close cooperation, however, since latent rivalries between them continued, especially over shipping. Belgian governments made repeated overtures for greater economic cooperation, but the Dutch not mistakenly feared Belgian expansionism. Brussels's failed diplomatic bid to absorb the Grand Duchy of Luxembourg in 1867 – then under Dutch rule – only confirmed their fears.

Belgian military policy was closely linked to diplomacy. The monarchy was firmly committed to *armed* neutrality and encouraged the strengthening of the country's defenses, especially in the 1860s when international tensions increased. Antwerp became the center of the country's defensive system and was surrounded by a ring of fortresses. This policy, supported by the doctrinaires, was fiercely assailed by the radicals – and by conservatives who, under pressure from their agrarian electorate, had become increasingly antimilitaristic, despite the strain this put on their relations with the king. Incidentally, the new king Leopold II (1865-1909) had more liberal leanings than his father, but he continued to support the church as a religious institution.

The Advance of Political Conservatism

Liberalism dominated Belgian political life between 1847 and 1870, but it slowly lost its powerful position. A conservative party gradually formed to resist the liberals, finding much of its support from traditional elites and the church. In this way, the church's close association with the conservative forces in Belgian society strengthened after the 1840s.

The conservatives remained true to unionism for some time after 1847. Unlike the liberals, they only slowly set up their own electoral societies, which eventually received the support of Catholic social and cultural organizations in the large cities. In 1878 a nation-wide Federation of Catholic Circles and Conservative Associations was formally established. This organization would slowly increase its influence over both district voting societies and the right wing ("*la droite*") of the Belgian parliament.

Gradually, the conservative party found ways to broaden its base of support. At first, in the 1840s and 1850s, it drew most of its support from the countryside and the smaller cities, making the liberal-conservative rivalry seem synonymous with the conflict between urban and rural interests. Over time, however, conservatives also made inroads in the large cities, where they found some support among the propertied class worried about the social order. They also increasingly recruited from the lower middle class, which was gradually gaining a greater say in Belgian politics. These recruits gave the conservative party a more populist, democratic element by the 1860s, and in 1871, their influence led to the expansion of the voting franchise in local elections. As the conservatives gained more of an urban following, the political opposition between "liberal" cities and the "conservative" countryside receded.

As early as 1870, the conservative party gained control of the government for a few years, but after 1884 it would eclipse the liberals for good. By that time, many conservative, middle class liberals had been alarmed by the virulent anticlericalism and the democratic tendencies of the radicals and the socialists. The economic crisis of the late 1870s, inadequately handled by liberal governments, also strengthened the links between the agrarian population, the lower middle class, and the traditional elites. Between 1884 and 1914, the conservative party enjoyed a virtual lock on the country's government and on national policy.

The ideology of this "conserving" party was characterized by a traditionalism at once romantic and pragmatic. Conservatives demanded respect for the national institutions and social structures that history had given the Belgian people. They recognized the rights of the individual citizen, but they insisted that the individual should be socially integrated in larger units like family, profession, and local community. These natural connections had to be preserved and even strengthened. Conservatives therefore favored a hierarchical and organic society. They also wanted greater decentralization. They were particularly receptive to the role of the church in society, which they believed should be free to exercise its moral mission and socially stabilizing influence.

Conservatives were not of one mind, however, on either the role of the Catholic church or the Catholic nature of their party, and they were divided between liberal Catholics and Ultramontanists. This division, already evident in the 1830s, grew stronger over time. Liberal Catholics, especially strong in the cities and among political elites, possessed a great confidence in Belgium's liberal institutions and the climate of freedom fostered by them. They regarded the conservative party as a constitutional, moderate center party that – for the most part – should respect the religious impartiality of the state, although they believed that the church should play an unfettered role in Belgian society. In contrast, the Ultramontanists enjoyed great support not only among the clergy and the nobility but among the common people as well. They were more anti-liberal and insisted on traditional patterns of authority. They expected that the conservative party would be, first and foremost, a Catholic party, and would make the defense of the church its top priority. Many understood this defense to include a measure of state support for the church. Both the antiliberal politics of the Holy See (particularly under Pius IX) and the anticlerical policies of Belgian liberals served to strengthen the Ultramontanists. As a result, the pressure to transform the conservative party into a real "Catholic" party grew ever greater until the 1880s, when this goal was largely achieved.

The Catholic church in turn served as the single most important supporter of the conservative party. The church had used the freedom granted by the Belgian state to develop its own religious, educational, and charitable activities; and anticlerical measures only steeled Catholic resolve to further develop such organizations. The church also attempted, with a certain insular mentality, to protect the faithful from non-Catholic influences. Catholics were explicitly prohibited, for example, from reading "bad" newspapers. Catholic cultural and recreational societies were set up for the faithful, who moreover were put under heavy pressure to send their children to Catholic schools. The cultural ethos of this Catholic subculture was largely antimodern, with much nostalgia for the Christian Middle Ages, a time which was praised for its ideal society. These themes are discernible in literature (for example, in the poetry of Guido Gezelle), in Catholic social and political thought, neo-Thomistic philosophy, church music, architecture and the arts (with its neo-Gothic proclivities). With an eye toward political mobilization, Catholics established increasing numbers of organizations devoted to moral and educational purposes. Such organizations first aimed at reaching the middle class, but later also the workers. The anti-liberal Ultramontanists, who showed a greater social conscience than liberal Catholics, were especially zealous in establishing popular Catholic organizations. In doing so, they paved the way for a mass political movement with an explicitly Catholic character.

As long as voting remained restricted to the relatively wealthy, popular movements could not exercise direct political influence. Thus the conservative governments between 1870 and 1878, and again after 1884, chiefly appealed to the support of the urban bourgeoisie. These governments cultivated close ties with high finance and the business world, and they pursued an economic policy scarcely different from their liberal predecessors; they kept the revenue structure (which relied heavily on sales taxes) and kept direct taxes low. Despite the economic crisis, these governments remained wedded to the principles of free trade, to the advantage of the middle class that was active in industry and trade. After 1884, however, the government did introduce a few cautious measures to combat the agrarian crisis. Conservative foreign policy, too, did not depart from those pursued by the liberal cabinets, and Leopold II continued to exert his great influence in this area. The king would even be given the opportunity, as we shall see, to pursue his personal colonial policy.

The Beginnings of "Pillarization"

The conservative cabinets of the 1870s were exceedingly careful not to reignite the religious question. They refused to undo the secularizing legislation of the liberals and to give in to the demands of the Ultramontanists. When the liberals again came to power in 1878, they decided – in order to win the masses for liberalism – to end clerical control over primary education once and for all. All municipal schools were put under the control of the state, and religious instruction was scrapped from the curriculum. The Catholic bishops responded by declaring total war on these measures. The "school war" of 1879 to 1884 was the most fiercely fought political conflict in Belgian history, and finally resulted in Catholic triumph. Primary education was again restored to the jurisdiction of the cities and towns. A full return to the pro-Catholic law of 1842, however, did not occur, and religious education would in fact become optional. Liberal school policy after 1850 generally undermined the church's influence in public education, although this was more true in secondary and higher education than in the primary level. Gradually, Catholics themselves recognized that public schools should be religiously neutral, but they compensated by establishing their own comprehensive school network. Later, they would successfully ask the government to subsidize these private schools.

The Law of 1 July 1879 largely removed church influence from primary education. In reaction, Catholics en masse established their own schools, with such effect that the official schools witnessed drastic reductions in their number of pupils. Print from L'Etudiant catholique, *1879. (KADOC, Leuven.)*

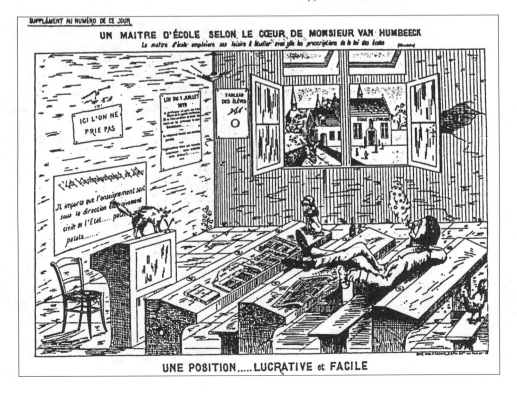

SUPPLÉMENT AU NUMÉRO DE CE JOUR

UN MAITRE D'ÉCOLE SELON LE CŒUR DE MONSIEUR VAN HUMBEECK

UNE POSITION.....LUCRATIVE et FACILE

Through their struggle against the central government's liberal and secularizing policies, many Catholics became strongly anti-statist. Napoleon I, William I, and the Belgian liberals had all used the state apparatus against the church, and Catholics now consistently favored a minimal state which would leave room for free Catholic initiatives. They developed the "subsidarity principle," which held that the state should leave as much as possible to local government and private institutions. They wanted to give their own Catholic organizations, which encompassed a large segment of the population and kept this segment within the church's sphere of influence, the greatest possible opportunity to develop and pursue their own goals.

As a result of these developments, not only Belgian political life but much of society became segmented, that is, divided into distinct subcultures with religion or (in the case of the liberals) political ideology serving as the basis for these subcultures. Catholics developed a powerful web of associations alongside their own political party, as did liberals and (eventually) socialists. Later, social scientists would characterize this process as "pillarization" (*verzuiling*), in reference to the multiple religious or ideological "pillars" that buttressed the political system. A similar development took place in the Netherlands at about the same time. This "pillarized" model of society would be further developed after the turn of the century, when new, popularly based organizations, functioning as intermediate structures between the individual and the state, would become increasingly important in the political system. The age of bourgeois individualism and the unchallenged rule of a small political elite were both coming to an end.

Ethnic Nationalism versus State Nationalism

In the course of the nineteenth century, Belgian conservatism, like its European counterparts, strengthened its electoral appeal by adding nationalism to its ideology. But Belgium is striking in that it produced two forms of nationalism which developed side by side. Belgian "state nationalism," weak as it initially was, had helped lay the basis for the revolt against William I and gained in appeal after independence. This nationalism was largely fed by the memory of the collective past and latent hostility toward Holland. After the revolution, the government actively worked to stimulate Belgian patriotism as a way of ensuring the future of the country. In particular, it stimulated a "national" historiography and oriented cultural life in a "national" direction. As a young nation, Belgium had a need for its own identity and a glorious past. In order to extol the Belgian past, the government commissioned historically minded Romantic painters like G. Wappers and encouraged national literature. Artistic and intellectual life in this period was largely characterized by a quiet romanticism in service of the nation. This Belgian nationalism, which found support both among middle-class liberals and Catholics, did become stronger over time, in turn strengthening the authority of the state itself.

But Flemish ethnic nationalism – which found its base exclusively among the Dutch-language population – also gradually increased in popularity. This form of nationalism resented the culturally French character of the Belgian state, and advocated a dualist system in which Flemish culture and language (understood in its broadest sense) would gain a separate but equal status. Belgians had long been aware of the differences between the Walloon south and the Flemish north, but the new Flemish nationalism gave the difference a political character; and its demand for a dualist arrangement would increasingly determine the future of the new state. At first, however, the Flemish movement was not anti-state or anti-Belgian, on the contrary. Its proponents simply believed that Flemish history and culture were an essential though neglected part of a larger Belgian nation.

The Flemish movement began in the 1830s as a philological and literary movement. Flemish philologists and literary figures began to call for the preservation of the Dutch language, which was threatened by the Francophone trends of the past decades and by the Francophone culture of the new state. The Belgian constitution guaranteed freedom of language, but French had become the only official language. Belgium's new leaders did not regard this as a problem, because the propertied, politically active classes in Flanders had themselves become largely Francophone since French occupation. Proponents of Flemish language preservation began their efforts by establishing a standard written language in 1841. It would be important for the future that they opted for a Flemish spelling that – for all the antipathy toward Holland and strength of regional particularism – differed little from the Dutch language north of the border. In this way, they secured the unity of the Dutch tongue and Netherlandic

The Lion of Flanders *of Hendrik Conscience made an important contribution to strengthening Flemish consciousness. This title page to the book was designed by Gustaf Wappers, an important Romantic historical painter. (Universiteitsbibliotheek, Leuven.)*

DE LEEUW VAN VLAENDREN.

culture. A strongly engaged Flemish literature emerged, which committed itself to "religiousness, morality, and nationality." The work of Hendrik Conscience is illustrative of this trend. His *Lion of Flanders*, a historical novel about Flemish resistance to French annexation during the Middle Ages, did much to foster Flemish national consciousness.

Unionist governments demonstrated a well-intentioned paternalism toward Flemish language and literature, but they were much less receptive of the political demands of Flemish partisans, first formulated in a petition in 1840. The petition asked that the Dutch language be given a modest place next to French in the schools, administration, and courts of Flanders. The Flemish cause, however, rested chiefly on lower middle-class support. Sandwiched between the Francophile higher bourgeoisie and the politically inactive masses, the Flemish initially had little political power of their own.

As this petty bourgeoisie (or *middenstand*) grew in size and gained more political rights in the second half of the nineteenth century, this began to change. After 1848, the Flemish movement made more emphatic political demands. They demanded legislation that would make Dutch, like French, an official language in the administration of the Flemish provinces. In order to achieve their political demands, they were obliged to work within the existing party structure; the district winner-take-all electoral system gave them little opportunity to secure parliamentary representation on their own. For a long time, the Flemish movement tried to remain neutral in the clerical-liberal conflict, holding on to the old unionism. When staying out of the conflagration was no longer possible, the Flemish partisans split, some becoming liberals, other conservatives. It is interesting, though, that both groups joined the progressive wings of their respective parties.

In the 1860s, Flemish agitation reached a new level, strengthening its position by becoming a potent pressure group. It also became more radical. The inability of the French-speaking political establishment to sympathize with their demands prompted many in the Flemish movement to lose their patriotic zeal for the nation-state of Belgium. By the 1870s, they attained their first political successes because the liberals and conservatives, who were locked in a struggle for power, sought allies among minority groups. The first language laws permitted Dutch to be used in courts and in administration on the local and provincial levels. Later, some Dutch instruction was allowed in the curriculum of the Flemish *athenea* and the status of Dutch in the judicial system was expanded. In this way, the role of Dutch in public life increased, and the dual-language system in Flanders was gradually realized. These gains can be attributed to the improved organization of both liberals and Catholics in the Flemish movement, who on occasion worked together. The Flemish cause also received an important impetus from the Flemish student movement (largely Catholic in orientation) which first began in West Flanders under A. Rodenbach and soon spread to the other Dutch-language provinces.

The Advent of the Social Movements

The Flemish movement antedated the workers' movement as a political force, but as a movement its regional and social appeal were relatively weak. In contrast, it would take until 1885 before workers would organize themselves into a significant socialist party, but the party's effects on Belgian politics were immediate, and greater than those of the Flemish movement.

The workers' movement had deep roots. The first labor associations, springing out of the artisan culture of the cities, appeared relatively early by European standards. Most of these associations simply pooled funds in case of sickness or accidents among its members, and were tolerated by the government because of their social utility. The first cooperatives appeared in 1849, but did not last long. The first real labor unions were established in 1857 by Ghent textiles workers, and, though disguised as mutual-aid societies, were in fact socially militant organizations. In various cities, workers established umbrella labor associations. These early organizations were hardly socialist, but they did have contacts with the radical liberals, who helped pass laws ending legal discrimination against workers, particularly when the prohibition on unionization was lifted in 1867.

Early socialism of the French variety made inroads into Belgium, but it was largely restricted to socially engaged intellectuals and members of the bourgeoisie. Moreover, their failed revolutionary activities in 1848, which had prompted a hard government crackdown, also discredited this bourgeois socialism. In the wake of these events most socialists reorganized themselves into secret freethinker lodges, which chiefly recruited members from among the artisans. From now on, these socialists explicitly turned their hostility toward the church which they regarded as an ally of the propertied classes because of their ever tighter association with the conservatives. Most Belgian socialists of this period were strongly attracted to an apolitical anarchism. They demanded structural economic reforms and the elimination of oppressive political structures. The socialist groups joined the First International in the 1860s; their most important international spokesman was César de Paepe, who advocated an anti-authoritarian collectivism based on autonomous communities. After 1867, Belgian socialists, inspired by foreign example, tried to establish more contacts with the existing labor associations.

The defeat of the Paris Commune (1871) and the collapse of the First International led in the early 1870s to the disorientation of the socialist workers' movement. Scattered local groups remained for some time under the influence of anarchism, but after 1875, a new generation began to orient themselves toward German social democracy; and the idea of establishing a labor party began to ripen. Workers in Wallonia were still overwhelmingly opposed to political action, but regional workers' parties were set up in northern Belgium, first in Flanders, then in Brabant. In 1879, these two parties merged into the Belgian Socialist Party. Initially, its popular base of support was quite weak, and most workers' associations remained outside the party. It was only in 1885, with a further extension of the voting franchise on the local level and the pressures of the economic crisis, that these associations abandoned their apolitical mentality. In that year, the Belgian Workers' Party (BWP) was founded in Brussels; it now united many unions, cooperatives and mutual-aid societies. Following the German model, these organizations were integrated into the party. From the beginning, the BWP was rather pragmatic in orientation: it sought universal suffrage, compulsory education, social legislation, collectivism and separation of church and state. In the late 1880s, a more revolutionary form of social-ism, popular especially in Hainaut and led by Dufuisseaux, sprang up, but quickly foundered. By 1890, the socialist workers' movement had regained their unity, and were well-positioned to launch their cam-paign for universal suffrage.

The collectivist and anticlerical – even anti-religious – posture of Belgian socialism, which had been able to coopt most workers' associa-tions in the 1880s, stimulated the growth of an anti-socialist, Christian workers' movement. Catholics had long been sensitive to social issues, although in two different ways. A number of liberal Catholics were committed to the notion of political emancipation for the masses and to social intervention by the state on their behalf (Bartels, Ducpétiaux, and De Jaer). The Ultramontanist wing, which gradually became dominant, was less interested in emancipation and more in a corporatist model. They wanted, above all, social harmony and advocated the concept of an organic society (Périn). This movement enjoyed much influence among popular Catholic organizations. From the 1870s on, they helped found "corporations" or guilds – organizations including both employ-ers and wage earners. This kind of organization would be particularly successful in the countryside and to a certain degree among artisans. In time, Catholics would also establish more progressive types of profes-sional organizations in order to compete with the socialists and their more combative labor unions. Thus the labor movement, like the Flem-ish movement, would be divided along religious and ideological lines. But whether Catholic or socialist, the rise of the workers' movements would leave its mark on Belgian society after the late 1880s.

2. The Integration of the Social Movements (1890-1935)

A new political climate swept over Belgium at the end of the nineteenth century. A violent workers' revolt in March of 1886 in the industrial regions of Wallonia forced the social question to the foreground. The most pressing issue centered on whether the working class – including an important segment with openly revolutionary aims – should be included in the country's bourgeois parliamentary system and recog-nized as an equal player. The answer was in the affirmative, although the political integration process of the working class was gradual, last-ing until the eve of the Second World War. The incorporation of the Bel-gian masses into the existing system was made easier by economic recovery at the turn of the century, a development which improved their standard of living.

A Strong Economic Expansion

The workers' revolt of 1886 was due in part to the long-lasting eco-nomic depression which had persisted since 1873 and brought troubled times upon the Walloon metal industry. Industrialists tried to combat

A socialist caricature from 1900 shows the pyramid of tyranny, lambasting the interests which oppress the proletariat. (KADOC, Leuven.)

LA PYRAMIDE DE LA TYRANNIE

the economic crisis in numerous ways. They improved products through technical innovations, which made a transition from iron- to steel-making possible. A new electrical industry sprang up, with important applications for metals production and for smaller businesses, which could now rely on electrical engines. Gasoline engines were also quickly and widely used in Belgium, and the country boasted many gasoline engine manufacturers. An important chemical industry also developed. Agriculture, too, witnessed important structural shifts, as farmers found that increased livestock production and an emphasis on labor-intensive horticulture gave them lucrative urban markets.

Higher government spending also softened the crisis. The state's share in the Gross National Product rose from 12 percent in 1880 to 18.5 percent in 1910. Increases in state spending had much to do with the government's investments in the transportation and communications sectors. Railroads and waterways came almost exclusively under state control. The telephone industry, too, was taken over by the government in 1893. But the state also spent more money on social programs. Government contributions to public housing and insurances helped

Women working in a Walloon mine, ca. 1920.
(Photo: A. Beeken, Brussels.)

strengthen the domestic market. Moreover, the government made efforts to strengthen exports by helping create markets that would be dependent on Belgian goods. It rendered diplomatic support to Belgian enterprises involved in the development of public works outside the country, such as the construction of rail and tram lines in Russia, China, Egypt, and South America. The colonial politics of Leopold II promoted Belgian investments and construction enterprises in Central Africa. Through these efforts, the Belgian economy became heavily internationalized.

Prosperous times reappeared after 1896 as the economy again took up a rhythm of growth. Domestic markets expanded and so did exports; more than 30 percent of the products made by Belgian heavy industry found foreign buyers. On the other hand, imports also rose. In particular, the depletion of the Walloon mines forced the Belgians to import coal – in addition to the large quantities of semimanufactured products and foodstuffs on which the country would now permanently depend.

Economic growth worked chiefly to the advantage of Wallonia, where Liège gradually replaced Hainaut as the main industrial center. It was Walloon industry which had the largest share in the internationalization of the Belgian economy. The ties between Walloon industry and Brussels banks grew even closer as they formed a cartel with huge capital investments. In particular, the *Société Générale* increasingly developed into a financial powerhouse, strengthening its grip over the Belgian economy.

Flanders also witnessed a gradual upturn in the economy at the turn of the century. In the first place, the Flemish seaports of Ghent, Zeebrugge, and especially Antwerp were all stimulated by Walloon exports. Growing imports, too, were crucial for the Flemish ports. The import of foreign raw materials prompted young industries, partly financed by Brussels banks, to establish themselves near these harbors. Antwerp's service and industrial sectors would give the city the leading role in Flanders's resurgent economy in the twentieth century. Flanders also benefitted from the discovery in 1901 of rich deposits of coal in the province of Limburg, although systematic mining of these deposits would begin only in 1917. Many people shared high hopes that coal would regenerate the economy in largely rural Limburg. Finally, the expansion of the recently modernized Flemish textile sector enhanced the region's economic vigor. The mechanized cotton and flax industries of Ghent grew substantially, helped by the relative decline of the English textile industry. And the revitalized industries did not remain restricted to Ghent; modern factories were also established in Eeklo, St.-Niklaas, Lokeren, and Kortrijk.

On the eve of the First World War, tiny Belgium enjoyed the status of a medium-sized economic power, and its economy now overshadowed that of its neighbor to the north. In 1860, Belgium had been a poorer country than the Netherlands, despite its modern industries. By 1890, however, it could match the Dutch standard of living, and soon surpassed it.

Improved Social Conditions

The fruits of economic growth had positive effects on the total population but were distributed very unevenly. Entrepreneurs and financiers were the chief beneficiaries of industrial expansion. Workers in the industrial sector (whose numbers swelled from 447,000 in 1846 to 934,000 in 1896 and to 1,176,000 in 1910) gained a very modest 4 percent gain in real wages between 1896 and 1910 – despite dramatic increases in labor productivity. Improvements in the workers' standard of living in this period had less to do with rising wages and more to do with changes in the terms of employment and with the advent of nascent social services. Although many abuses persisted, conditions clearly improved during the two decades prior to the First World War. The quality of housing rose, as did sanitary conditions at work. Working hours were reduced to ten or eleven hours a day, and stricter regulations protected women and children in the workplace. By the beginning of the twentieth century, Belgian workers were better fed and better dressed than before, and their savings, as well as their expenditures for social services, had increased.

The economic crisis had considerably thinned the ranks of those once engaged in farming; in the 1880s and 1890s, employment in the agricultural sector declined by one third. Still, small family farms managed to hold on, thanks partly to the Catholic party's agrarian policies and to the efforts of various agricultural associations. After 1896, farmers, too, shared in the fruits of the economic recovery.

The lower middle class also struggled through the economic changes near the turn of the century, but they grew in number and partook of the greater prosperity. In 1900, some 95 percent of all Belgian industrial enterprises consisted of small workshops, employing craftsmen and artisans. The tasks of these skilled workers evolved as industry changed, and some professions switched from the production of goods to their sales or repair. The service sector, which grew from 196,000 persons in 1846 to some 784,000 in 1910, swelled the ranks of the *middenstand*. This included members of the "free professions": engineers, servants, bureaucrats, and salespeople. Together, the lower middle class constituted an important segment of the Belgian population, and though not yet politically organized, they exercised great influence in Belgian society at the turn of the century.

Democratization

Reform of the Electoral System

By the late 1880s, the Belgian government was under great pressure to further democratize the political system. While most neighboring countries had considerably extended the voting franchise, voting eligibility in Belgium still depended on a minimal property requirement, a criterion testifying to the political strength of the Belgian middle class. Extending the franchise was also made more difficult by the fact that doing so would require a change in the constitution. Still, pressure from socialists, radicals, and a number of socially progressive Catholics to change the electoral law only increased. In 1890, the Catholic Beernaert government gave the green light for electoral reform. Proponents began the task of finding the large parliamentary majority necessary to amend the constitution. This required cooperation among the largest political formations, and the Nyssens-Féron Bill, a compromise between Catholics and radicals, emerged as the strongest plan for reform. In September 1893, the franchise became universal for men: all men at least twenty-five years of age were entitled to vote. Extension of the franchise to women was not discussed. The new law also established a "plural" franchise; some men, for reasons of ability, wealth, or family responsibilities, were allowed to cast two or three votes. The rather complex system of voting criteria ensured, in effect, that members of the propertied and educated middle classes received three votes each and members of the lower middle class two, while workers would have to content themselves with one vote each. Middle class dominance was thus assured. Moreover, voting was made compulsory for all eligible

The new system of the General Plural Franchise, in which members of the propertied and intellectual middle classes were given three votes each, ensured bourgeois predominance in Belgian society. Caricature from The Candle is Out, *1912. (KADOC, Leuven.)*

voters, a law which was designed to help the moderate parties. All in all, the new electoral system proved especially advantageous for the Catholics (who racked up 68 percent of the parliamentary seats) but was a disaster for the liberals (who now commanded only 13 percent of the seats). The socialists received their first parliamentary representation under the new law (18 percent).

During the debate over the franchise, a number of socially progressive Catholics and a few radicals, influenced by corporatist thinking, proposed to transform parliament into a chamber where various "interests" in the population would each be guaranteed a voice: the workers, the capitalists, and the intelligentsia. Their idea found little support, but an 1895 municipal election law, designed to keep the socialists out of power, made some attempt to base local representation on class "interests." However, this experiment was never very successful. A more lasting effect of the 1895 law was that it introduced a system of proportional representation, which on the local level and under specific limited terms was supposed to replace the district winner-take-all system.

Gradually, many people began to see the advantage of introducing proportional representation on the national level, since the winner-take-all system was disadvantageous to minorities. The liberal party in particular found it hard to field successful candidates after 1893; in most Flemish districts, they were overwhelmed by the Catholic party, and in most Walloon districts, by the socialist BWP. Their representation in parliament mostly depended on electoral alliances they formed with the socialists, and their future existence was by no means certain. With the liberals in decline, political polarization set in as the country increasingly divided between Catholic Flanders and socialist-liberal Wallonia. For those concerned with the country's political stability, it thus seemed wise to abandon the district system in favor of proportional representation. The conservative faction within the Catholic party resisted the proposed change, but in 1899, proportional representation was implemented at the national level, making Belgium the first European nation to abolish the district winner-take-all system. As expected, this reform helped the liberals, who now no longer depended on the socialists for their political existence. Socially progressive Catholics – now called Christian Democrats – also strengthened their positions in parliament and in the government as well. Because of proportional representation, the Catholic party gradually turned into an organization representing various special interests.

The electoral system was not changed again in the years before World War I, despite efforts by the socialists to abandon plural voting in favor of a universal one-man, one-vote system. Meanwhile, the implemented reforms gradually changed the character of the Belgian political system. Over time, representatives no longer consisted of "notables," chosen from a select voting pool, but increasingly included spokesmen of large interest groups and social movements with ties to the established parties in parliament. These parties now exercised increasing control over who would sit in parliament. All of this was a slow process with important long-term consequences: both the government and especially the king would lose their freedom of movement to the political parties. Leopold II, increasingly deprived of real influence in domestic policies, developed his own personal projects, like urban architecture in Brussels and Ostend, or the colonization of Central Africa (see below).

The Social Movements' Integration into the Political Parties

The political parties began forging close links to the increasingly better-organized social movements. The socialists initiated the linkage between party and mass movement, but the Catholics were to have the most success in applying this innovation, because they managed to integrate diverse movements and interest groups into their party.

The socialist workers' movement, organized under the auspices of the BWP, assigned central committees to head each of the movement's component organizations. Workers' cooperatives, which gave solid financial support to the socialists' political and cultural activities, were especially important to the movement in these early years. The BWP, with much of its electoral support in Wallonia, became a formidable force under the leadership of Emile Vandervelde. The party arrayed itself against the status quo, and would be inspired for decades by the party program of Quaregnon (1894), a mixture of Marxist and anarchist principles. The BWP's ultimate aim was the establishment of a classless society, with the collective organization of labor. Unlike Lenin's future model for Russia, they envisioned a collectivist state which would be decentralized.

Because the future socialist state would be controlled by the workers themselves, the socialists sought further democratic reforms of the country's electoral laws. Despite its collectivist program, the BWP engaged in close cooperation with progressive liberals, a cooperation furthered by the Masonic freethinkers' tradition common to both parties. Over time, moderate, liberal-progressive ideas made their way – almost imperceptibly – into the BWP, turning the socialist party in a reformist direction, which tended toward class reconciliation. The formation of coalitions with the liberals in municipal councils helped push the socialists in this direction. When the strike of April 1902 – designed to force the government to accept a one-man, one-vote system – failed, the BWP forsook street violence as a means to its ends. Striking deep organizational roots into Belgian public life, the socialists were incorporated into society and thus became less of a threat to the existing order. The middle class nevertheless retained a fear and distrust of this presumed revolutionary threat.

The Catholics, too, were busy setting up their social organizations. In contrast to the secularism of the socialist workers, the Christian workers' movement was heavily influenced by Catholic social teaching, as set forth by the papal encyclical *Rerum Novarum* (1891) and by corporatist thought. Catholic social doctrine taught interclass cooperation and social harmony, and for this reason, the bourgeoisie found the Catholic workers' movement easier to accept than its socialist counterpart. The Catholic workers' movement stood for social consensus, legislation to shield and protect workers, and for social insurance. However, they opposed the collectivism of the socialists and were keen to stop the de-christianization of the working class. For the time being, the Christian mutual-aid societies, trade unions, and cooperatives were less successful in recruiting members than the socialist ones. In 1891, these various Catholic organizations united with other popular associations into the Belgian People's League.

Initially, Catholic social organizations were largely directed by the socially engaged bourgeoisie. After 1900, however, the League witnessed increasing internal tensions, as Catholic union leaders exhorted their rank and file to become more assertive in securing greater rights for themselves. Gradually, the impetus grew for a comprehensive class-based national organization, which would increase the fighting spirit and the political influence of Catholic workers. Through their social actions, the Catholics succeeded in keeping a large segment of the working class, particularly in Flanders, within the church's sphere of influence. They would be even more successful among agricultural laborers. In July of 1890, the Catholics established the Belgian Farmers' League (*Boerenbond*) along corporatist lines. Its efforts at introducing cooperatives and various types of insurance lay at the heart of its success. Interestingly, the farmers' guilds were largely integrated into the Catholic church's pastoral work.

The lower middle class proved more difficult to organize than either the workers or the farmers. It was only at the end of the nineteenth century, when its numbers had mushroomed, that the *middenstand* was regarded as a separate social class. Over time, the group's self-image became clearer, particularly as small tradesmen and artisans competed with the large warehouses, cooperatives, and mechanized industry that threatened their livelihoods. On the local level, they established associations primarily designed to defend their occupational interests. It was the Catholics in particular who attempted to organize the *middenstand* on a regional and, finally, on a national level. They believed that artisans, shopkeepers, and salespeople were a necessary buffer between labor and capital, and at the same time the best guarantee for the preservation of traditional values and the institutions of church and family.

The connections between popular Catholic organizations and the Catholic ruling party grew increasingly tight over the years. Catholic leaders knew it was very important that their party, conservative and middle class as it still was, also secure the support of the Catholic working class. When the threat of an independent Christian Democratic workers's party emerged in 1895 (with proposed links to the Belgian People's League), it was quickly nipped in the bud. The Catholic clergy believed that the unity of all Catholics was essential if the church was to retain its influence in society; and the Catholic workers themselves, already heavily committed to other Catholic organizations, proved more or less willing to support the old Catholic party. For the time being, they were resigned to exercising little political power. Only in those instances when the Catholic bourgeoisie showed a particular unwillingness to compromise did Christian Democratic rifts ensue – most famously when Father Daens led a pro-Flemish, Catholic breakaway movement in the southern reaches of East and West Flanders. The

A. Daens (1839-1907) posing for an 1894 photograph. (KADOC, Leuven.)

popular organizations did gradually attempt to assert more influence over the national Catholic party, favoring the transformation of the party into a *standenpartij*, based on different classes, and with guaranteed representation for workers, farmers, and the *middenstand*. They first realized this goal on the local level and did not realize it at the national level until 1921. But already before the First World War, Catholic workers had managed to strengthen their position within the party and the government.

The liberal party, which traditionally relied on intellectuals and the business class, was not a mass party like the socialists and Catholics, who were able to tune in to a broad spectrum of the population. Insofar as the liberals had a more popular base, it came through the radicals, who had set up their own Progressive Party in 1887. After 1890, the Progressives would demand universal male suffrage, and supported many other political and social demands of the socialists, although they rejected socialist collectivism. Increased Progressive cooperation with the BWP during the 1890s, in part out of political necessity, blurred the ideological divisions between them. Once the system of proportional representation had been introduced, however, the differences between the socialists and Progressives sharpened again. By this time, the doctrinaire liberals also proved willing to accept modern democratic tenets. In 1900, the two liberal factions, doctrinaires and Progressives, reconciled at a unification conference, where they strongly supported both the one-man, one-vote principle and compulsory education. Progressivism slowly disappeared as a political force after the merger. But its contributions – leading the liberal middle class toward democracy and helping to integrate socialism into the political system – made the radical-Progressive party an important part of Belgian history.

By 1905 or so, the basis for a more democratic political life in Belgium had been laid. Reformism had replaced revolution in the BWP, and the Catholic workers' movement showed signs of democratization. For the time being, however, both the propertied and lower middle class (including farmers) continued to set the political tone for the country, thanks in part to the electoral strength granted them through the plural voting system.

Catholic Government Policy

A series of successive Catholic governments followed a cautious pro-church policy, which led to the strengthening of social and political pillarization in Belgium along religious and ideological lines. At the same time, the government tried to manage change and to reduce social tensions.

Increased Pillarization

In the 1880s the Catholic party held too small a parliamentary majority to ignore liberal opposition on a range of issues concerning the role of religion in Belgian society. After 1893, however, Catholics politicians enjoyed a much larger majority in parliament and a stronger popular base, and they acted accordingly. The Education Law of 1895 strengthened the place of religious instruction in public primary schools and made state allowances available to all private schools which accepted the state's established curriculum and state inspection. Having achieved this goal, Catholics actively attempted to increase the level of state subsidies to the private (mostly Catholic) primary schools. This proposed reform was closely associated with the move toward compulsory education; in 1900, 16 percent of the population was still illiterate, and socioeconomic considerations made it imperative that illiteracy be eradicated. Compulsory education implied that public education would be free of cost, but Catholic schools without state subsidies could not meet this criterion. In order to make the choice for a Catholic education financially viable for parents, Catholics asked for more state subsidies for private primary education. The anticlericals, however, were resolutely opposed to this measure, and their increased representation in parliament after 1900 prevented the proposal from being enacted until 1914, when compulsory education together with substantial state subsidies to private schools was finally implemented.

In this way, the so-called system of subsidized freedom was established. The same system was applied to the social sector as trade unions, mutual-aid societies, and housing associations were also given a measure of state financial support. This arrangement was based on the Catholic "subsidarity principle," in which important social tasks were left to private initiatives – initiatives which received partial financing from the state. Needless to say, state funding of these "intermediate" institutions, those standing between the state and the individual, only strengthened their social importance.

Funded "intermediate" organizations were mostly pillarized institutions, representing Catholic, socialist, or liberal constituencies. The base of these pillarized institutions was certainly broadened by the advent of the popular social movements, which sought not only material improvements for their members but recreational and educational opportunities as well. The Belgian populace was thus incorporated to an increasing degree into the Catholic, socialist, and liberal subcultures which now determined the social landscape. Although pillarized life began with the mobilization of adult men, women were also integrated into pillarized organizations after 1900. It is striking how easily feminism, which first made its presence felt in Belgium at the turn of the century, was integrated into – and to a large extent neutralized by – the country's pillarized blocs. Meanwhile, the state apparatus and the pillarized organizations worked more and more closely together. The latter's receipt of state funds has already been mentioned. The pillarized organization's close associations with the political parties gave them increasing influence on national policy, and by the early twentieth century, the liberal Belgian state had been given an anti-liberal, corporatist content.

Social Reform at the Turn of the Century

The cornerstone of the Catholic governments' socioeconomic policy was to prevent polarization between workers and the middle class. For that reason, they were committed to improving living conditions for the workers, and enabling them to acquire their own property. At the same time, they wished to prevent the downward mobility of the social middle groups (farmers, shopkeepers, artisans).

Considerable attention was devoted to improving the social conditions of the workers. Following the workers' riots of 1886, a Commission of Labor was established, and it laid the basis for future social legislation. Belgium, in comparison to its neighbors, was far behind in legislation protecting laborers, but this now changed. Labor conditions for women and children in heavy industry were improved (1889), and the first arbitration commissions between workers and employers, inspired by corporatism, were introduced through the industrial and labor councils of 1887. Social insurance became a dominant issue at the turn of the century, and the state created the institutional and legal frameworks for such insurance while contributing financially to private insurance funds. No mandatory insurance program was passed. Catholics feared that this would lead to government insurance, undermining their own insurance associations. Their posture also reveals that Catholic social policy was chiefly aimed at the hard-working, frugal and educated worker, and not the whole proletarian class per se. The Christian Democrats, however, representing the progressive wing of political Catholicism, managed to convince Catholic leaders that compulsory insurance would help the weak in society, and the first modest measures were taken in this direction.

An analysis of Catholic policy toward the workers shows that Catholic governments were led by the "subsidarity principle" and that they sought to forge a harmonious "society of the middle." This was even more obvious in their policies toward the farmers and the *middenstand*. Catholic agricultural policy aimed at keeping the small family farm afloat. After 1893, when electoral reform greatly increased the political clout of the farmers, the parliament devoted much attention to agrarian problems, including protectionist measures (1895), state subsidies for cattle insurance, and savings and loans associations. Government attention to the socioeconomic problems of the lower middle class came later. Only in 1902 did the government establish advisory and administrative organs that concerned themselves with the difficulties facing the self-employed *middenstand*. Shortly thereafter, the government initiated the first protective and supportive measures to assist them. Even more than its agrarian policy, the government's *middenstand* policy supported private initiative. Their motto was: "Help yourself, and the government will help you." It was another variation on the theme of "subsidized freedom."

Nationalist Movements

Nationalism increased throughout Europe in the late nineteenth century, and Belgium was no exception. In contrast to most countries, Belgium possessed three divergent and competing nationalist movements. Belgian and Flemish variations had existed for some time, and now they were joined by a Walloon nationalism as well.

By the turn of the century, the Flemish movement had become broad-based, with a mass appeal, and it accordingly widened its scope. The constitutional changes of 1893 increased the influence of both the lower middle class and the Flemish wing of the Catholic party. Politically strengthened, the Flemish party found a receptive audience among the increasingly powerful Christian Democrats, who gradually committed themselves to the principle that Flemish "emancipation" was a goal equal to the social and political "emancipation" of the working class. Pro-Flemish liberals, on the other hand, lost political influence, but they still made important contributions to the development of the Flemish movement's program. The prewar socialists, in part because of their heavily Walloon constituency, had relatively little interest in the Flemish question.

From 1895 on, the Belgian parliament considered a bill which would make Dutch an official language, to be given the same legal status as French. The Chamber of Deputies accepted the bill, but the Senate made a number of substantial amendments. This triggered a protest movement – the Flemish party's first mass action – that was simply too large for the parliament to ignore. The so-called Equality Law was passed in 1898, making Dutch, along with French, the official language of Belgium. It was a law of great symbolic significance.

The introduction of proportional representation, which strengthened the Catholic party in Wallonia but weakened it in Flanders, proved disadvantageous to the Flemish movement. Only after great effort did it succeed in passing a law which indirectly made the curriculum in private secondary schools bilingual – even though such a law had been passed for public schools as early as 1883. The Catholic bishops, led by Cardinal Mercier, resisted such a coercive measure for a long time on grounds that it violated the freedom of education guaranteed by the constitution. Not surprisingly, the position taken by the country's ecclesiastical hierarchy had a negative effect on their relations with the Flemish movement.

Flemish nationalists eventually came to the conclusion that public life in Flanders needed to be completely rid of Francophone influence, and that Dutch should be the *only* officially recognized language in the north of the country (the so-called territoriality principle). The switch to Dutch

The literary journal Of Now and Later *became the motor for renewing Flemish literature from the 1890s on, particularly through the work of August Vermeylen, Karel van de Woestijne, and Emmanuel de Bom. (Universiteitsbibliotheek, Leuven.)*

in public life was intended to end the language discrimination which stymied the social mobility of Flemish workers, farmers, *middenstanders*, and officials. "Cultural nationalism" aimed at elevating the Flemish people under the leadership of an intellectual elite – a vision sharpened by a conspicuous literary and cultural Flemish renaissance in the 1890s. In order to achieve this, "cultural nationalists" sought to make Dutch the only language used in the regions schools, and they judged Dutch-language higher education, then non-existent, to be of particular importance. Two successive higher education commissions discussed the possibility of converting the University of Ghent, then the only state university in Flanders, into a Dutch-language institution. From 1910 on, this proposal became a matter of intense national debate, although the proposed change was not implemented before the outbreak of the First World War.

On the eve of World War I, a number of Flemish nationalists had become radically anti-Belgian. Part of this antipathy stemmed from the battle for the University of Ghent, but it also had to do with two defeats of the Flemish cause in parliament. The Army Law of 1913 rejected the creation of Flemish regiments, and the Primary School Law of 1914 in turn rejected the territoriality principle Flemish nationalists had sought for their schools. Finally, the Flemish movement was now confronted with both an aggressive Belgian nationalism and the advent of Walloon nationalism. The shock of the First World War would bring about further radicalization of the Flemish movement and rather abruptly raise the question of regional autonomy.

Belgian nationalism, too, had increased in size and significance by the end of the nineteenth century, as the country flowered both economically and culturally. Setting the artistic tone in this period was the progressive intellectual bourgeoisie of Brussels with its strong links to Belgian socialism. It was in this circle that the literary movement "Young Belgium" began. Belgian literature achieved broad international recognition at the turn of the century. Interestingly, it was French-speaking Flemings like Georges Rodenbach, Emile Verhaeren, and Maurice Maeterlinck (who won the Nobel Prize for Literature in 1911) who led the way. These writers were extremely sensitive to social change and broke with conventional bourgeois forms. This was no less true in architecture, where an aesthetic vanguard developed a taste for Art Nouveau; luminaries like Victor Horta and Henry van de Velde sought to achieve a functional beauty in both architecture and the decorative arts. The break with the classical style was most evident in painting, which enjoyed an important revival. French Impressionism also found its adherents in Belgium, but Emile Claus, Rik Wouters, and the First Latem school added their own, more realistic nuances. The country also produced James Ensor, a solitary genius who mercilessly portrayed spiritual chaos and the terrors of a deeper reality.

Belgium's intellectual life showed strong international influences by the turn of the century, and if its cultural life was chiefly inspired by France, its academic life emulated the German model, as Belgian universities and other academic institutions became important centers for scientific research. Despite an important debt to foreign influences, Belgian scientific and artistic achievements around the turn of the century did much to strengthen Belgian national sentiment.

An important contribution to the theoretical basis for Belgian nationalism was given by Edmond Picard, who in 1897 formulated the notion of a "Belgian spirit," which he described as the age-old product of a national "voluntary community." The historian Henri Pirenne let this ideal serve as the basis for his masterful *History of Belgium*, which itself did much to promote national consciousness. The new Belgian nationalism found great popularity among the Francophone bourgeoisie of Brussels. They wanted to demonstrate the greatness of the Belgian nation through (among other things) active foreign and effective defense policies. As expansionists, they also attached great importance to the accumulation of colonies in Africa. But it is also striking that these Belgian patriots increasingly directed their energies against the Flemish movement.

Finally, there was the conflict between the Flemish movement and a nascent Walloon nationalism. Unlike its Flemish counterpart, Walloon nationalism was less about the preservation of French language and culture and more a reaction to the Flemish movement itself, which had attacked the supremacy of the French language in public life. Its first adherents were Francophone civil servants assigned to Brussels or the large Flemish cities, and it initially exhibited a liberal, elitist character. In the 1890s the first Walloon conferences were held, culminating in 1913 with the *"Assemblée wallonne,"* which demanded a separate administration for Wallonia. The demand was not new – it had been requested repeatedly since the 1880s – but it found its most articulate expression in the "Letter to the King on the Separation of Wallonia and Flanders," penned in 1912 by the socialist politician Jules Destrée. The Walloon desire for political autonomy stemmed from the perception that their own region, for all its modern infrastructure and prosperity, was being shut out of the political decision making by Catholic governments that – for the most part – relied on a more conservative and less developed Flanders.

Colonial Expansion

By the turn of the century, rising Belgian nationalism also found expression in imperialism, and the public took an increasing interest in Leopold II's colonization project in Central Africa. Leopold had sought his own African colony since the 1870s, and in 1884 at the Conference of Berlin, his adroit diplomatic moves prompted the great European powers to recognize his sovereignty over the Congo Free State. The Belgian parliament – not very enthusiastically – allowed Leopold to accept kingship over the Congo. Initially, the Congo was not a Belgian colony; rather, it became Leopold's personal possession. The Conference of Berlin stipulated that the Congo must quickly be occupied, however, and for such an immense area this required expensive expeditions. Running into financial difficulties, Leopold II soon made numerous appeals to the Belgian government for financial support, and in this way the Belgian state became increasingly tied to the African enterprise of their king. Belgian Catholic missionaries, too, were sent to the Congo from 1888 on, and Belgian business would soon enter the country to extract its mineral riches.

After 1890, Leopold gradually attained his aim: the occupation and exploitation of the Congolese territory. The area became an enormous source of royal profit, and other business

The White Fathers' mission in Tongres-Sainte-Marie (Lulenga, Upper Congo), ca. 1916-1918. (KADOC, Leuven.)

ventures, insofar as it was possible, were pushed out of the market. The colony finally began to return investments, largely thanks to rubber production. Much of the profit went to the king personally, who spent it in large part on architectural and urbanization projects throughout Belgium. By 1900, however, Leopold's ruthless exploitation of the Congo generated criticism, not only at home by socialists and Progressives but also, and especially, abroad. In 1903, the British government publicly raised its objections to some abuses, and the Congo Reform Association launched a major campaign in Britain to curb Leopold's activities in Africa. An international commission investigated conditions in the Congo, and while nuanced in conclusion, its report criticized Leopold's policy.

The Belgian government, which had already passed up two opportunities to take over the Congo, now succumbed to domestic and international pressure and decided to make it a Belgian colony. Forced by circumstances, Leopold II agreed to transfer his sovereignty in October 1908, after difficult negotiations. The government then set up a highly centralized colonial administration. Though parliament now formally oversaw the Congo, it exercised very little control over colonial policy, which remained to a large degree in the hands of the king and the minister of colonies. In fact, the old alliance between the monarchy, the business world, and the church, so important since the unionist period, was now extended to the Belgian Congo.

The First World War as Catalyst

By the time Belgium had obtained its African colony, its international position had become very precarious. The country's security had long rested on British commitments to Belgium's inviolability, which had been explicitly renewed in 1870. After Britain concluded a defensive alliance with the French in 1904, however, Belgium was no longer secure against possible German attack. Strengthening the country's own defenses became a matter of urgent necessity. Catholic governments, however, were informed by a long-standing antimilitaristic tradition, and it was not until 1908 that they initiated important military reforms. They introduced limited conscription (one man per family), expanded in 1913 as the threat of war increased to a general conscription. The reorganization of the army was at full tilt when the First World War broke out, and Belgium was drawn into the conflict.

Many Belgians fled for the Netherlands during the First World War, where many charitable initiatives were begun on their behalf. This poster, designed by Alfred Ost, dates from 1917.

When the war began in August 1914, the German army relied on the Schlieffen Plan, which aimed at neutralizing French forces by out-flanking them from the north – through Belgium. The Belgian government refused to permit the Germans free entry to execute this plan, and chose to fight when the German army invaded Belgian territory. The government received the support of all the parties, who pledged in a political truce to abandon their differences as long as the war lasted. The socialists, too, joined the national resistance against the Germans after gaining the promise that after the war the principle of "equal sacrifices, equal rights" would be applied.

Between 4 August and 22 November, most of Belgium was occupied by the German army, although much more slowly than the Germans had anticipated – prompting in part the many atrocities the Germans committed during their invasion. By year's end, the Belgian army, led by King Albert I (1909-1934), held only the coastal strip behind the Yser River, and the Belgian government left for the French port of Le Havre, where, functioning under an extraterritorial statute, it continued to exercise authority. Some 600,000 Belgians fled to France, England, and the Netherlands.

Meanwhile, the Belgians who remained under German occupation refrained from guerilla activity. They faced two grave problems: the cutoff of food supplies and the disruption of trade and industry, which triggered much unemployment. With the permission of the Germans, the National Help and Food Committee was set up in October 1914, which, with American assistance, imported and distributed food to the population. The committee was dominated by the Francophone elite of Brussels, especially by the city's high finance circles. It worked together with various political factions, but the spirit of this enterprise was liberal and religiously neutral. The committee demonstrated the considerable power still wielded by the business class in Belgian society. It functioned as a semiofficial government in occupied Belgium and maintained regular contacts with the government in Le Havre. Most important, the committee succeeded, although with great difficulty, in ensuring that the country was supplied with food.

German occupation became increasingly oppressive after 1916. Belgians were required to pay heavy taxes in order to finance the German war effort. The Germans introduced compulsory labor, and more than 120,000 Belgian men were sent to work in Germany. Soon thereafter the Germans began to systematically dismantle Belgian industries. Despite these draconian measures, it cannot be said that the Germans possessed a clear Belgian policy, although maintaining their hegemony over the country was an unquestioned priority. The military and pan-German groups wanted Belgium annexed to Germany, but the government in Berlin sought ways to keep control of the country without either annexing it or paying the heavy costs of occupation.

In order to achieve their goal, the Germans tried to win various segments of the Belgian population over to their side, particularly the Flemings. The war climate had put Flemish nationalism on the defensive vis-à-vis pro-French Belgian patriotism. Some members of the Flemish movement saw the occupation as an opportunity to further their nationalist cause, and they were willing, if necessary, to cooperate with the Germans to achieve this end. The Germans themselves did much to encourage this collaboration movement, and they acceded to Flemish demands, which were at first within the limits of Belgian law, in order to win Flemish support. They soon went further, however. In October of 1916, they made the University of Ghent a Dutch-language institution, thereby fulfilling the most important prewar demand of the Flemish movement. In March 1917 they also divided Flanders and Wallonia along administrative lines. The Flemish wartime activists themselves vigorously pursued their objectives; in February 1917, they established the Council of Flanders, which was supposed to represent Flemish interests in future peace talks. This council, however, was never given any real authority, and these activist plans collapsed once the Germans were defeated in 1918.

Flemish agitation was not limited to the area under German occupation; Flemish soldiers resisting the Germans on the Yser Front also protested against unbearable conditions in the Belgian army. Army leaders were not only Francophone but strongly anti-Flemish, and insisted on giving their orders in French. Most of the Belgian forces consisted of Flemings, and many of them did not understand French. Several intellectuals set up pro-Flemish groups, and when these were forbidden by military authorities in February 1917, the "front movement" operated illegally. These groups increasingly showed radical tendencies, and by May 1917, were demanding self-rule for Flanders. This brought them close to the activists operating in German-controlled territory with whom they sought contact. The Belgian government did almost nothing to address the grievances of the Flemish soldiers, thus further radicalizing them.

Belgian ministers governed from Le Havre through decrees and administrative measures that did not require the approval of parliament, which, under these circumstances, had ceased to operate. The Catholic cabinet saw fit to include a few liberal and socialist ministers, which had the effect of reducing Flemish influence in the government. Tensions did exist within the government precisely over the Flemish question and also over foreign policy. A pressure group of Belgian nationalists wanted to formally join the Allies and to use the country's increased prestige at the future peace talks to expand Belgian territory. King Albert, on the other hand, wished to retain Belgium's formal neutrality and refused to submit the Belgian army to Allied control until August 1918, when he was sure of victory and the restoration of the Belgian state. But the Belgian expansionists would succeed in influencing postwar foreign policy.

World War I revealed both the strength and the weakness of the Belgian political system. Before the war, many Belgians were convinced that the working masses were the weakest link in the chain, because of the socialists' revolutionary noises, their internationalism, and their pacifism. Socialism, however, seemed already well-integrated into Belgian bourgeois democracy, as evidenced by their support of the war effort. In contrast, no one had predicted the revolt of an important segment of the Flemish movement. It now became evident that the political system was less threatened by class conflict than by ethnic and cultural differences. The course of subsequent decades would only confirm this.

A New International Policy

The First World War reoriented Belgian foreign policy. The government, under pressure from Belgian nationalists, asked the Allies for Dutch Limburg and Zeeland-Flanders. These territories were to be taken from the Netherlands, which had remained neutral during the war. It also wanted the Grand Duchy of Luxembourg, which had adopted a rather pro-German position during the war, to be brought within the Belgian sphere of influence. Moreover, it sought to bring some of Germany's African colonies under Belgian administration. But Belgian demands for territory found little sympathy among the Allies; the country's new prestige proved inadequate for a more ambitious foreign policy. Belgium was denied its demands for Dutch territory, and its claims only served to trouble relations with its northern neighbor for years to come. Nor was Belgium any more successful in concluding a political and military union with Luxembourg, although Belgians could be pleased with the Belgian-Luxembourgeois Economic Union (BLEU) of 1921. But the Belgians won territory at the expense of the Germans. The German-speaking region of Eupen-Malmédy on the eastern border was annexed to Belgium, against the wishes of the local population. Belgium was also given administrative control over the German colonies of Rwanda and Burundi, which bordered the Belgian Congo. Moreover, the Allies saw to it that the Belgians received war reparations from Germany. Most important of all, the international agreement of 1839 that kept Belgium neutral was abandoned.

Postwar Belgian efforts at closer ties with Great Britain did not meet with success, but the Belgians were able to cooperate with the French on foreign policy. On 7 September 1920, a Franco-Belgian military pact was signed, which obligated both states to defend the other in the case of an unprovoked German attack; the pact also aimed at countering German rearmament. In 1923 Belgium joined France in occupying the Ruhr in order to enforce the war reparation payments which the Germans had not been making as promised.

Soon domestic resistance to the government's pro-French policy grew, particularly among Flemish Christian Democrats. By 1925 Belgian foreign policy shifted toward the system of collective security offered by the League of Nations. The Rhine Pact, part of the Locarno Treaty between France, Germany, and Belgium, internationally guaranteed the inviolability of the German-Belgian border, and included a treaty of nonaggression between the two countries. Locarno integrated Belgian foreign policy into a larger network of collective security.

Under the influence of the "spirit of Locarno," Belgian relations with the Netherlands also improved. In 1925, difficult negotiations led to a treaty in which the conflicts over shared waterways were resolved, largely in Belgium's favor. For many Dutch, it was an "impossible treaty," and it was rejected by the Dutch First Chamber on 24 March 1927 after a fierce campaign by Dutch nationalists with the backing of commercial interests in Rotterdam and Amsterdam. The defeat of the treaty triggered another downturn in Dutch-Belgian relations.

Economic Revitalization and Depression

The First World War precipitated a sudden break in the development of the Belgian economy. Industrial production plummeted in 1914, and wartime operations, the requisition of raw materials for the war effort, and the partial dismantling of the infrastructure all caused great damage to the economy. The country had lost 12 percent of its prewar wealth – 18 percent if one also counts the loss of Belgian investments in Russia and Central Europe. Belgium's economic edge over the Netherlands, so recently gained, was lost by the war.

Economic recovery after the war was seriously undermined by the persistence of wartime inflation, which successive Belgian governments found impossible to cure. Fortunately, the loss of purchasing power was tempered by a number of social measures. Meanwhile, the government slid into a large deficit because of several factors: the disappointing tax revenues of a hastily implemented progressive income tax in 1919, a number of monetary miscalculations, and the meager German reparation payments, which were less than one third of the expected sum. Only in 1926 did the financier Emile Francqui correct the situation by converting the floating state debt into shares of the newly organized Belgian Railways. At the same time, he devalued the Belgian franc to one-seventh of its prewar value. This made it an undervalued currency, but it greatly stimulated Belgian exports, which had suffered in the inflationary spiral.

Francqui's reorganization helped restore the traditional industrial sectors to prewar levels of production. Technical innovations also helped to restore the economy, especially in the metal industry. Developments in the transportation sector also opened new vistas, such as the foundation of Sabena, Belgium's national airline, in 1923. The flourishing of the Congolese economy – not least the profits of the Union Minière – had additional stimulating effects within Belgium itself.

The Flemish economy followed the same upward course. By 1935 the coal fields of Limburg would account for some 21 percent of total Belgian coal production. The transport of this important commodity was made easier in 1935 by the completion of the Albert Canal between Antwerp and Liège. The Limburg mining industry failed to stimulate other economic sectors, however, and it remained a subsidiary of Walloon heavy industry. On the other hand, Flemish harbors and canals attracted new industries. Antwerp gained from the Congolese trade. The diamond industry became important, and American automakers also established new plants in the region. Of great importance was also the mechanized textile industry, which accounted for much of the increased industrialization throughout East and West Flanders.

Flanders's shift toward an industrial economy was supported by an extension and strengthening of its financial infrastructure. The Flemish developed their own financial network to supplement the traditional Belgian investment banks, the most important examples of which were the General Bank Association (1928), with strong ties to the Agrarian League, and the socialist Labor Bank (1913). The capital of these banks originated from the savings of workers, farmers and the *middenstand*. These people were more prone to invest in budding business enterprises than in the older banks of Brussels.

Workers' real wages increased in the last half of the 1920s. Between 1891 and 1929, their real income had increased an average of 18 percent. The self-employed *middenstand* also benefitted from the economic prosperity; and the income of farmers, who still constituted 17 percent of the working population in 1930, improved as the agricultural sector was mechanized. Saving rates in the countryside skyrocketed and laid the basis for the growth of the General Bank Association and the Agrarian League's Concern, which in 1930 numbered among the largest Belgian enterprises.

In the 1930s the economy seriously deteriorated as a result of the financial crisis that had hit the United States at the end of 1929. In 1931, Belgian exports – the cornerstone of the country's economy – tapered off, and world prices for the country's commodities declined sharply, although production costs remained relatively stable. The collapse of the British pound in September 1931, which sucked other currencies down with it, deepened the troubles. Although the Belgian government adopted a stern deflationary policy designed to lower production costs, Belgian prices remained stubbornly high in comparison with those of its chief trading partners. Exports were further undercut by increasing protectionism throughout the world. By 1936, Belgian export volume was only at 43 percent of 1929 levels, and certain industrial sectors, like the Belgian auto industry had to be given up altogether. The Flemish textile industry received heavy blows, but Walloon manufacturing, through its high degree of mechanization in its diverse economic sectors, withstood the crisis better than its Flemish counterpart. The banks with strong links to industry also encountered difficulties, and the new Flemish banks were the

Economic crisis in the 1930s: Rerum Novarum *march in Ghent, 10 May 1934. (KADOC, Leuven.)*

most vulnerable. The socialist Labor Bank and the Catholic General Bank Association both failed, although their saving accounts were covered by government intervention.

The economic crisis also led to increasing unemployment. In 1930 there were 76,000 persons without employment; by 1932 this number had risen to 340,000. More than a third of all insured workers were either partly or fully unemployed. Women in particular were dismissed in high numbers. As a result, the nominal national income in 1934 was roughly 34 percent less than what it had been in 1930, but thanks to the drop in prices, real wages remained higher than 1913 levels and certainly higher than in the hard years after 1918. Farm incomes also declined, but to a lesser extent, although the Depression certainly cost many farm laborers their livelihoods. The consequences of the economic crisis for the lower middle class are less easy to sketch, but it is clear that the declining purchasing power of Belgian consumers had a negative effect on the retail trade and small industry. Established, self-employed shopkeepers also lost business to large numbers of people who, in this time of great unemployment, tried to establish their own businesses.

Successive governments tried to combat the crisis with a traditional liberal deflationary policy and through a moderate form of protectionism. The results were disappointing, and it gradually became clear that a totally new course was necessary. The impulse for reform came from two different directions. Socialists introduced the Plan of Labor, designed by Hendrik de Man, which presaged the move toward a planned economy. At the same time, Paul van Zeeland, the vice-governor of the National Bank, proposed a policy, inspired by the British economist Keynes and by Franklin Roosevelt's New Deal, which sought reforms in the direction of a mixed economy.

In March of 1935, Van Zeeland took charge of a government which increased state intervention in the economic sector. The new government improved Belgium's export position by devaluating the franc by 28 percent, and reduced unemployment through a comprehensive public works program. It reformed the Belgian banking system which, because of its close ties to industry, had been much harder hit by the Depression than its Dutch counterpart. As a means of fostering greater financial stability, banks were prohibited by law from serving both as investment and savings banks, and the government established a bank commission to regulate the sector. The government also set up other semi-governmental organizations in the financial sector, as well as advisory commissions that were to prepare the way for further state intervention. The economic recovery, apparent after 1935, reduced the urgency of zealously implementing the planned structural reforms, however. All in all, though, Van Zeeland's government had laid a solid basis for the expansion of the mixed economy after the Second World War. From now on, economic policy would be oriented toward achieving full employment and social justice, an effort which was supported by the new social and democratic consensus that was taking shape in the mid-1930s.

Further Institutional Democratization

Electoral Reform

The First World War helped precipitate a further democratization of the Belgian political system. Socialist loyalty simply had to be rewarded, and the Bolshevik Revolution in Russia (1917) made concessions to the working masses a high priority for Western European governments. Already, on 11 November 1918, King Albert and representatives of the National Help and Food Committee came to an agreement at Loppem Castle, which included social reforms and a one-man, one-vote elec-

Catholic election poster from 1932. Socialism is embodied in the person of Emile Vandervelde (left), the "patron" of the socialist party.

WETGEVENDE VERKIEZINGEN 1932

MET SOCIALISME KOMT STEEDS COMMUNISME

STEMT VOOR DE KATHOLIEKEN

toral system. In doing so, they simply bypassed Catholic conservatives, who had hitherto exercised much influence over policy. These conservatives were even forced to accept that the elections of 16 November 1919 for a constituent assembly – called to approve these electoral changes – were already to be conducted on the basis of one-man, one-vote. The conservatives deeply resented the "coup of Loppem" and the technically unconstitutional election, and it was cold comfort to them when they were given greater funds for Catholic primary education in exchange for this crucial concession.

The elections for the constituent assembly brought substantial change in parliamentary composition. Catholics in the Chamber declined from 99 to 73 seats, and the liberals from 45 to 34, while the socialists climbed from 40 to 70. The socialists were now nearly as numerous as the Catholics, and the liberals were hence, as they had hoped, courted by both sides for a parliamentary majority. In 1921 the constituent assembly introduced several important changes to the constitution. Through a number of substantial changes the Senate became more democratic. More important, the one-man, one-vote principle was now passed into law, with all Belgian men over 21 years of age eligible to vote. Women were still prohibited from voting in parliamentary elections but could now vote in local elections. Permitting women to vote for parliament in the future was made easier by a provision that required only an ordinary law with a two-thirds majority. Both the socialists and the liberals were leery of female suffrage, since they feared it would boost the Catholic vote. Unlike in the Netherlands and the Anglo-Saxon countries, feminism was not strong enough in Belgium to force a political breakthrough on women's suffrage.

The constitutional changes had far-reaching consequences. The one-man, one-vote system, combined with proportional representation, substantially changed the political constellation of power. From now on, it would be rare if one party seized the majority in parliament. Thus the age of one-party cabinets passed away, and coalition governments became the rule. These coalition governments could only be formed after negotiations and concessions among all the relevant parties. The new system meant that more political compromises were necessary and that politicians needed to remind themselves that their adversaries in the opposing parties might one day become their coalition partners.

Coalition governments also gave the king a greater opportunity to exercise his influence over policy, and Albert I, whose prestige both at home and abroad had greatly increased because of his wartime leadership, did not let the opportunity slip away. He had close links to the business world and relied especially on the liberal party for his military and foreign policies. Domestically, he assumed both a rather anti-socialist and anti-Flemish posture.

The political parties, as the makers and breakers of governments, also gained in influence as a result of the changes. More than ever, the parties were themselves under pressure from the country's social movements and from interest groups. These pressure groups allowed the various people whom they represented an increasing say in government policy. This happened very gradually, however, since there was still much resistance among the middle class to the full integration of these social movements into the political system.

Social Democratization

Belgium's social movements enjoyed spectacular growth after the war. This was especially true of the socialist trade union movement, which numbered more than half a million members in the 1920s. But they soon had to reckon with increasing competition from the Christian trade union movement, which included 340,000 members in 1939. By this time, Catholic workers had managed to develop their own movement, free from the middle-class paternalism which once had dominated the Christian labor movement. After 1921, their various organizations were united under the Christian Workers' Alliance (ACW). The ACW stood for cooperation between employees and employers and co-management of factories by the workers.

The Belgian Farmers' League also witnessed a substantial expansion. In 1934 it consisted of over 270,000 loyal members, most of them in Flanders and Walloon Brabant. The *middenstand* movement, in contrast, was much less structured, and regional particularism retarded the growth of national umbrella organizations. In the 1930s, right-wing extremists were able to exploit the discontent among the lower middle class. Finally, however, a democratic and Christian *middenstand* organization managed to enjoy the strongest representation among this segment of the population, and in 1945 it would become the National Christian *Middenstand* Alliance. Employers for their part organized in a non-pillarized professional organization, the *Comité Central Industriel*, the forerunner of the Alliance of Belgian Enterprises (1946).

The pillarized movements more or less constituted the electorate of the large political parties with whom they had institutional ties. Thus the growing size of the socialist workers' movement helped the BWP electorally; in 1925, it attained its highest electoral benchmark, 39.43 percent of the vote. The party dominated Wallonia, and in Flanders it grew especially in Antwerp and the southern districts bordering on the Walloon industrial centers. Among the socialists, a certain tension between reformism and revolutionary élan continued, but reformism was further reinforced, largely through the increasing influence of the trade unions. From 1921 on, the BWP had to guard its left flank against the communist party, but communist membership remained small for the time being and was further undercut when Trotskyites abandoned the party in 1928. From the right, the BWP faced middle-class hostility, and for a long time it was unable to counteract it. The party entered a period of malaise, made worse by the crisis in the cooperatives that had been spawned by the failure of the Labor Bank. By 1935, however, the BWP was able to regain unity and inspiration through its campaign to implement the Plan of Labor.

The Catholic party remained Belgium's largest party in the interwar years, although it had lost its majority in parliament. In 1921, it was reorganized as a *standenpartij* with guaranteed representation for each class: the upper middle class, the farmers, the workers, and the *middenstand*. This strengthened democratic forces within the party. The

1930s vintage postcard of the Catholic Flemish Radio Broadcasting Association. (KADOC, Leuven.)

Cliché : Maandschrift "RADIO„

Catholic Union, as the party was called, had no centralized organization. Rather, it was a "constituted party," made up of quasi-autonomous political groups. In Flanders the party possessed a strongly democratic and pro-Flemish wing, while in Wallonia it was more conservative. The Catholic Union defended the church's role in Belgian public life, free education, the family, private property, interclass cooperation, national unity, and the monarchy.

After 1918, liberal representation in parliament shrunk considerably. On average, the party could count on anywhere between 12 and 16 percent of the votes. It was, to a considerable extent, dominated by Brussels intellectuals and businesspeople. The pro-Flemish liberal groups and the handful of liberal mass organizations which had sprung up at the end of the nineteenth century were now wholly marginal in significance. The liberals of the 1920s regarded themselves as Belgium's preeminent national party. They also remained loyal defenders of public education and a classical liberal economy.

The social movements and the political parties, increasingly intertwined, had won their own prominent place in the pillarized landscape of Belgium, which became increasingly varied through a host of women's organizations, youth movements, and sports associations. The press remained highly pillarized, although demand for commercially produced papers increased. As a means to maintain social control over their own people, each religious or ideological pillar also attempted to exercise influence in the new mass media. They were only partially successful in this ambition, and their opponents, the commercial enterprises, were increasingly active in the media and in the larger world of culture and the arts. Radio, of course, was an important new medium of the interwar period, and after 1923 a number of private stations went on the air, including Radio Belgique, which enjoyed close contacts with the Brussels business world and the royal court. The pillars, too, began their own stations. In 1930 the parliament funded a public radio network, the National Institute for Radio (NIR), which was inspired by the example of the British Broadcasting Corporation. Unlike the BBC, however, the NIR was placed under the control of the political parties and was required to allocate air time for "party-affiliated" organizations. Thus the Belgian network, although "public" by statute, was placed under the supervision of the country's religious and ideological pillars.

Belgian film largely escaped pillarization. After World War I, Belgium became the European country with the most movie theaters per capita. There was very little effort to regulate the source or content of films, and the country was soon awash with American movies. The Catholic church attempted to guide the faithful through its own film board, but it never really had much influence over this medium. Thus pillarized organizations managed to exercise only partial control over the new mass media and popular culture.

This was also true of popular sports, such as soccer and bicycling (then considered a lowbrow pastime), which drew increasing numbers of fans after the war. On the other side of the spectrum, high culture with its individualistic ethos was, in general, equally free of pillarized influence. The Belgian art world, though already highly internationalized, became even more so, and now also appropriated American innovations. Expressionism and its complete break with bourgeois realism became an important artistic trend in Belgium, both in literature and painting. Belgian painting, in particular, achieved a high artistic level with the Second Latem school (Servaes, Permeke) and surrealist painters like Paul Delvaux and René Magritte.

From Social Confrontation to Social Consensus

The increasing political weight of the (socialist) workers' movement ran into much resistance from the middle and upper middle classes during the 1920s and 1930s. European politics moved to the right after the Bolshevik Revolution, and Belgium was no exception. The government coalitions in power between 1918 and 1940 reveal the general pattern. There were nine Catholic-liberal-socialist cabinets of national unity, cobbled together during the many economic and political crises of the period. In addition there were six Catholic-liberal cabinets, a single Catholic-socialist, and no socialist-liberal governments at all. Religious and ideological divides lessened as the middle-class parties formed a common front against the socialists. It is also interesting to note that the relatively small liberal party was able to exercise considerable influence on national policy, as did big business. Their influence, to be sure, had much to do with the importance of economic and technical questions in this crisis-ridden period. But their inclusion in government had just as much to do with neutralizing the socialist threat.

Responding to difficult political and economic conditions, the cabinets of national unity between 1918 and 1921 did make fundamental concessions to the workers' movement as outlined by the Loppem Agreement. This included not only the electoral reform described above but also important social legislation. The first postwar governments reduced the working day to eight hours, guaranteed the right to strike, set up the first joint industrial committees (arbitration councils of employers and employees), tied wages to retail prices, and introduced the progressive income tax.

In 1921, however, the middle-class factions were able to push the socialists out of the government. When the BWP won a landslide victory in 1925, their inclusion seemed imperative and after difficult negotiations the first "Roman-Red" cabinet came into existence under the leadership of the Christian Democrat P. Poullet and the socialist Vandervelde. The new government wanted economic recovery while seeking to temper social ills; it was also antimilitaristic. However, it ran afoul of big business, which torpedoed the new government's plans for recovery and forced its resignation. Seen in this light, the end of the Poullet-Vandervelde government signalled a conservative seizure of power and a repudiation of the "coup of Loppem." The conservatives would dominate Belgian politics until 1935.

The bourgeoisie, having shut out the socialists, was required to make concessions to the Flemish nationalists for their support (for the concessions it made, see below). It was also forced to accommodate the ACW, which supported the Catholic-liberal governments via the Catholic Union. As a result, social insurance laws were further developed. The ACW was also a supporter of pro-family policies, and parliament soon allocated state subsidies to families, first for wage earners (1930), then for the self-employed (1937). The Catholic workers' organization saw to it that the subsidarity principle was maintained in the social insurance sector, despite resistance from employers and the left wing of the BWP.

The economic crisis of the 1930s precipitated a crisis of the political system. Parliament was criticized for its inefficiency, and government policy was denounced as too unstable. The close ties between government and business were also attacked. A number of Belgian voters, especially from the middle class, thus abandoned the traditional parties and became attracted to several authoritarian parties with fascist tenets. Responding to this political malaise, the democratic Belgian parties underwent a striking transformation around 1935. A new generation of politicians – who would lead their parties for decades – assumed control over these parties and pledged themselves to a "democratic center." A social and political consensus was forming which would survive the Second World War and provide the backbone of the postwar political system. The social movements now became fully integrated into Belgian society, as bourgeois resistance to them was weakened by right-wing defections to authoritarian and fascist groups.

The Catholic party was given a more democratic structure in 1936, which strengthened the position of the Christian Democrats. The course of the Catholic Bloc, as it was now called, was determined more than before by a political platform. The socialists, for their part, also made important changes. They now resolutely backed Belgium's parliamentary system. Under Hendrik de Man the party abandoned its revolutionary posture; he moved the party to the right, further integrating it into the system. De Man's Plan of Labor, which became a legend in its own time, argued that the Depression could be overcome through the cooperation of workers, farmers, and the *middenstand*. The socialists now wanted to construct a mixed economy, aiming both at full employment and an expansion of the free market. The state would be given considerable new powers to achieve these aims. In drawing up the Plan of Labor, De Man largely departed from the BWP's traditional Marxism, opting instead for a "national socialism" that emphasized words like "order, authority, responsibility" – concepts which made socialism more palatable to the bourgeois parties. As the BWP moved to the right, the communists strengthened their position and now formed a real threat to the party from the left as they exploited the social unrest of the 1930s.

The new orientations of the Catholics and the BWP increased cooperation between them, and together they worked on a policy that would lead to economic recovery. The democratic forces now took belated action against the financial interests which had destroyed the first "Roman-Red" cabinet in 1925: they deprived the banking world of its traditional influence and subjected it to government regulation. The new coalition also activated social reforms, further cutting working hours in a number of economic sectors and introducing paid vacations. They further institutionalized arbitration between employers and the unions, with the government now serving as a third party in the negotiations. In this way, Belgian society was increasingly organized along a neocorporatist model that would be fully realized after 1945; and by the late 1930s, the basis for the postwar political, social, and economic system was already in place. The increasing dangers of Europe's totalitarian movements, fascism and communism, gave Belgium's political parties a powerful incentive to build a democratic and social consensus that would enhance the legitimacy and credibility of the country's institutions. In the elections of April 1939, some 80 percent of all Belgian voters supported the parties that had built the new parliamentary democracy. The most important source of dissonance came from the Flemish nationalists, whose unhappiness with the Belgian state could not be assuaged and who would seek, as in the First World War, more radical methods to realize their aspirations.

Flanders Granted a Dutch-Language Statute

The Flemish movement lost steam after 1918, compromised as it was by the collaboration of the "activists" with the German occupier during the war. It was also faced with the resurgence of Belgian nationalism which had also reduced, for the time being, the appeal of Walloon regionalism. But the long-term potential of the Flemish movement was actually increased by the one-man, one-vote reform (since Flemings accounted for more than half of Belgium's population) and the educational and economic improvements within Flanders during the 1920s. As before the First World War, Flemish militants were represented in all the major parties. Although their presence in the influential liberal party declined considerably, they made inroads in the BWP, especially in the Antwerp federation of Kamiel Huysmans. The most important pro-Flemish group, however, was still centered in the Catholic party, now under Frans van Cauwelaert. These Flemings held themselves to a minimal program, demanding that Dutch become Flanders's only official language. They did not propose changing the unitary, centralized Belgian state. The successors of the World War I activists, however, held that this demand did not go far enough. In 1919, they established their own Flemish nationalist group, the *Frontpartij*, which demanded political self-rule for Flanders. Many also desired closer ties with the Netherlands.

But Flemish militants, whether moderate or radical, made little headway in the anti-Flemish atmosphere following the end of the First World War. To be sure, a 1921 law applied the territoriality principle for the first time to local administration, but it did not prevent growing Francophone influence in the municipal governments in and around Brussels – areas once solidly Flemish. Flemish militants spent most of their efforts after 1921 attempting to make the University of Ghent again a Dutch-language institution, and first had to content themselves with a bizarre compromise in 1923, which pleased no one. The very limited legislative progress of the Flemish nationalists only intensified their anti-Belgian and anti-parliamentarian sentiments. Demands for a decentralized federal system – even separation from Belgium – increased, especially among the young. The institutional crisis of the 1930s only further fueled radical Flemish nationalism; the *Frontpartij*, renamed the Flemish National League (VNV) in 1933, became a rising force in national politics (it won 16 parliamentary seats in 1936).

Flemish nationalist pressure had become so strong by the end of the 1920s that the Catholic-liberal coalition decided it must find a comprehensive solution to the language question. Parliament passed a series of laws implementing the territoriality principle under which each region would have its own official language and which, in effect, ended French as an official language in Belgium's non-Francophone districts. The University of Ghent fully became a Dutch-language institution in 1930, and it was not long before Dutch became the mandatory language in Flemish administration, courts, and schools. A small number of districts – Brussels and a few mixed population areas – remained bilingual. Residents there retained the right to use either French or Dutch in public life. These areas had become increasingly French for decades, a sociological process which was not stopped by the new legislation. But elsewhere the Flemish movement attained the demands they had formulated since the 1890s.

These achievement, however, were not sufficient to placate pro-Flemish circles. There were certain inadequacies in the new language laws; they lacked enforcement measures, for example, and hence were badly implemented. The VNV's call for a more decentralized federal structure found increasing support among Flemings, even moderate ones, especially within the Catholic party. In fact, the Catholic Bloc became a federal party in 1936, with separate Flemish and Walloon divisions. This was the same federal principle that many Flemish militants wished to apply to the Belgian state. Their endeavors, however, would be compromised once more by the collaboration of radical Flemish nationalists with the German occupier during the Second World War.

3. The Partition of the Belgian State (1935-1993)

The democratic and social consensus created in the 1930s was temporarily threatened by the German invasion and occupation during World War II, but it was strong enough to survive the war. Religious and ideological conflicts briefly flared after 1945, but pillarized stability soon returned. The most significant postwar change was that the Belgian state itself lost much of its power, both to supranational European organizations and to increasing regionalism. By the 1990s, the once unitary state was fully federalized.

In the Wake of the "New Order"

Although the democratic consensus grew in the years after 1935, fascist influence was hardly absent in Belgium. Already in the 1920s, right-wing Francophones were attracted to authoritarian groups like the *Action française* in France. The advent of Italian fascism and German Nazism only strengthened these authoritarian tendencies, and by the 1930s, radical Flemish nationalism was increasingly attracted to Nazism. The new Flemish nationalist party, the VNV, developed into an anti-democratic, corporatist party. After 1935 a number of Francophones from the right-wing group Catholic Action joined Léon Degrelle's Rexist movement, which decried Belgium's parliamentary chaos and adopted a number of fascist ideas. It enjoyed a short-lived success, especially in Brussels and Wallonia. But when it became clear that Degrelle wanted a fascist-Rexist dictatorship he lost the trust of the same middle class constituents who had provided the bulk of his support.

It cannot be denied that ideas of the "New Order" found increasing resonance in Belgian society during the 1930s – even within the traditional parties themselves. In the Catholic party, for example, particularly in its Flemish wing, there was a tension between a willingness to defend democracy and a desire to form a right-wing political force with the Flemish nationalists of the VNV. Many Belgians felt that democracy had been too weak, and that the country's problems demanded that the government assume greater power. The new king Leopold III (1934-1950) was himself not unreceptive to this trend. The general right-wing climate also had effects on Belgian foreign policy, which was primarily directed by the king and elitist, conservative circles. They distanced themselves from France, then under the left-wing Popular Front, by terminating the Franco-Belgian military alliance. The

Belgian government was particularly anxious to avoid antagonizing Nazi Germany, now a growing threat to the country, and thus resorted again to a neutral course in October 1936, relying only on Belgium's own resources for its defense.

The new course of independent neutrality did not keep Belgium out of the Second World War. On 10 May 1940, France, the Netherlands, and Belgium were attacked by Germany. The Belgian army resisted for eighteen days before capitulating. King Leopold III, acting more as army chief than as head of state, turned himself in as a prisoner of war – much to the displeasure of the Pierlot cabinet, which (after France had surrendered to the Nazis) fled to London. There the Belgian government-in-exile put whatever resources it had at the disposal of the Allied war cause – in particular the Congo and its natural wealth.

This time, all of Belgium was subject to German occupation. The German military administration kept the Belgian bureaucracy working and pursued relatively moderate domestic policies. The Nazis, displeased with the army's course, introduced a "civil administration" for Belgium in July 1944 – a few months before the liberation of the country – to be headed by an SS *Reichscommissar*.

Belgian businessmen managed to restore the country's economic production after the surrender in May 1940. They did not want to repeat the experiences of the First World War and opted for a limited, managed production – a policy course which at least indirectly helped the German war effort. The Belgian economy was gradually integrated into the German war machine and arranged along corporatist lines. The workers were all brought into one organization, the Union for Manual and Clerical Workers. Businesses were themselves placed under a stringent public organization, and economic relations between employers and workers were closely managed. This form of state corporatism, forced upon the Belgians by the Germans, would have very little influence on postwar socioeconomic developments.

A number of jurists and bourgeois politicians wanted to establish a kind of royal "directory" which would try to preserve Belgian nationhood as much as possible. In this they were encouraged by Leopold's entourage, although the king himself made it known that he, as prisoner of war, was prohibited from any kind of political activity. Still, it was clear that Leopold, like many other Belgians, wanted to keep a modicum of Belgian independence in the face of a possible German victory over the Allies. Leopold requested, and received, a meeting with Hitler at Berchtesgaden in November 1940, in which the king asked the Führer to guarantee Belgian independence. Hitler, however, refused to make any concrete concessions, and the king abandoned further political efforts. Leopold also ignored the Belgian government-in-exile and did nothing to encourage underground resistance against the Germans. His political testament of January 1944 – written when the Germans removed him to Austria – confirmed the king's antipathy toward the government in London and his earlier-held authoritarian views. Leopold's wartime utterances and actions would lead to the crisis of the monarchy after World War II.

At first, Belgium did not suffer greatly under German occupation. Most of the population adopted a wait-and-see attitude. A minority of the BWP, led by De Man, were even willing to collaborate. But it was primarily the authoritarian parties, the VNV, and the Rexists, that actively cooperated with the Germans. The VNV wanted to establish a Flemish state under German domination, and a more radical movement, DEVLAG (an acronym spelling "the Flag") wanted Flanders to be absorbed into a greater German Reich.

As the war turned against Germany, the occupation became more oppressive. From the spring of 1942, the Germans began to requisition Belgian equipment and compulsory labor. They stepped up the executions of hostages and the deportations of Jews and resistance fighters. Belgian public opinion now turned against the Germans, and by the summer of 1942, in the wake of the first deportations, the Committee for the Defense of the Jews was organized. Those going into hiding found a widespread network of support at their disposal, and half the country's Jews avoided deportation by doing so. In 1942, the first organized resistance units also appeared which, while including people of various political persuasions, chiefly consisted of socialists and communists. The resistance increased in scale after the Allied landing in Normandy on 6 June 1944, and it played a role in the liberation of Belgian territory in the autumn of that year. The guerillas' left-wing political aspirations, however, were soon neutralized with the help of Anglo-American military authorities.

The Second World War had consequences analogous to the First. It had a democratizing effect on Belgian society and further integrated the working class into the political system. As in the First World War, it strengthened Belgian patriotism and weakened the Flemish movement. It indirectly contributed to a brief resurgence of religious and ideological tensions evident in the 1950s. But perhaps most important, the war brought, as in the case of the Netherlands, a definite end to the independent neutrality long pursued by Belgian leaders.

Participation in International Structures

In order to better guarantee its security and to support its export economy, Belgium now became committed to working within broader international structures. By the end of 1944, it had already become a member, along with the Netherlands and Luxembourg, of the Benelux system of economic cooperation. Belgium also became a member of the United Nations, although the Cold War soon reduced this body's effectiveness as a vehicle for international peace. Belgium now belonged, like much of Western Europe, to the American sphere of influence, and joined, like many of its neighbors, an increasing number of international organizations. The socialist politician Paul-Henri Spaak, who steered the country's foreign policy between 1944 and 1966, was instrumental in these developments. He played an important role in the creation of a regional defense organization that was expanded into NATO in April 1949. He also supported European unity and became the Council of Europe's first chairman. Belgium also backed the Schuman Plan for the creation of the European Coal and Steel Community (ECSC) in 1951. It is interesting to note that the trade unions supported the proposed Community more than the employers, who were afraid of foreign com-

Paul-Henri Spaak.
(Photo: Levan, Brussels.)

petition and overly intrusive government regulation. Because of their concerns, Belgian diplomats contributed to the weakening of the ECSC's supranational authority.

Some years later, many Belgians harbored suspicions of the supranational, political dimension of the proposed European Defense Community, although a majority of deputies voted for it. Finally, the French killed the plan. All of the Benelux countries made important contributions to the foundation of Euratom, the European Community for Atomic Energy and, above all, the European Economic Community (EEC). In fact, the Spaak Report laid the basis for the Treaty of Rome (25 March 1957) which established the EEC. Brussels became the permanent seat of the European Commission – the executive organ of the EEC – and thus gradually became an important political center in Europe. Brussels' political importance was further strengthened when both NATO's civilian and military headquarters were transferred from Paris to the capital city in 1966.

Belgium consistently supported greater European unity. Together with the Netherlands, it became a vigorous advocate of British membership in the European Community, and in 1967, the country helped stimulate the merger of many already existing European institutions.

The Tindemans Plan, named after the Belgian premier who conceived it during the 1970s, developed a strategy for the creation of a political European Union – a plan which would find partial realization only in the 1990s.

Decolonization

Belgium's Atlanticist and Europeanist policies enhanced the international role of the country, and this, in a certain sense, compensated for the loss of its African colonies. The country would decolonize the Congo, Rwanda, and Burundi very quickly, and with little preparation – a policy which had everything to do with the political insignificance of the colonies in Belgian public life. Colonial policy essentially had been determined by the monarchy, the business world and the church; and the country's political movements, although powerful in domestic affairs, had little say in the administration of the Congo.

Belgian big business and Catholic missions, in fact, largely dominated the Congo in the years after 1908. Congolese education, chiefly consisting of an extensive primary school system, was completely in the hands of the church, which received large government subsidies to this end. They established few secondary schools, and higher education, with the exception of seminary training, did not exist at all until 1954. Christianization of the native population was a great success; 40 percent of all Congolese were nominally Christian in 1960, and some 80 percent of these were Catholic. The Congolese economy was completely dominated by large capitalistic enterprises and especially by a number of subsidiaries

Belgian colonialism in the 1950s: medical care in a Leopoldville (Kinshasa) school. (Photo: J. Mulders.)

of the *Société Générale*. The *Union Minière* and its affiliates, which specialized in the mining of copper, diamonds, gold, and later on uranium, provided one-third of the Congo's income during the 1950s.

At the beginning of the 1950s, many Belgians still hoped that the Congo would remain their colony for a long time to come. They regarded the Congo as a happy oasis in Africa, because its inhabitants enjoyed economic prosperity, good medical care, and primary education. By 1956, however, the first signs of black nationalism appeared and quickly increased as other African countries decolonized. In late 1958, Belgian politicians decided that the Congo, too, must be prepared for independence at some date in the distant future. However, the serious riots in Leopoldville (Kinshasa) which erupted in January 1959 and a civil disobedience campaign by Congolese nationalists immediately challenged this long-term policy. Belgian public opinion, not particularly attached to the colony, clearly rejected use of violence against the African inhabitants. There were, moreover, no forces within the Congo that gravitated against independence; the church remained neutral on the issue, or even supported decolonization, and the white colonists were not politically organized. For these reasons, the Belgian government decided to grant immediate independence to the Congo, hoping that its ties with Belgium would remain close enough to facilitate the construction of an efficient and competent African administration over time. On 30 June 1960, the Congo became independent.

Brussels had drawn up institutions for the new state that closely replicated the Belgian social and political system. But these institutions did not prove suitable for a society as heterogeneous as the Congo. In the absence of strong structures, personalities decided the day, and soon the radical Lumumba faced off against the pro-Western Tshombe and his power base in the Katanga province. In July 1960 – only days after independence – part of the Congolese army rebelled, triggering a tragedy of mass proportions. Whites fled the country and Katanga seceded from the Congo. Both Lumumba and Tshombe were among the thousands killed in the ensuing conflicts. Partly thanks to United Nations intervention, the Congo remained a single state but only at the cost of a military dictatorship headed by Mobutu, which came to power in 1965. Belgian decolonization policy, insufficiently prepared, had failed. It succeeded only marginally better in Rwanda and Burundi, which both became independent on 1 July 1962. The failure was the direct result of decades of paternalistic policies conducted by small, elitist groups. In Belgium, too, these groups saw their power decline in the decades following World War II.

Building a Social Market Economy

In Belgium itself, the great social movements further increased their social and political influence after the defeat of Nazism. The attraction of authoritarian thinking, still evident during the occupation, almost completely disappeared after the war. Commitment to democracy grew, evidenced in part by a 1948 electoral law which gave women the right to vote in national elections. This reform, incidentally, had negligible effects on election results, and there would still be very few women deputies in parliament for some time.

In 1945 many Belgians wanted the country's political system reformed, and some of them founded the Belgian Democratic Union (UDB), a progressive party committed to ending pillarization. But it fared very poorly in the national elections of February 1946 (2 percent of all votes) when the electorate demonstrated its loyalty to the traditional parties. Meanwhile, these parties were already in the process of transforming themselves. The Catholic party continued the restructuring that had begun in 1936. It jettisoned its class-tiered system in favor of an organizational model based on individual membership. It also adopted a progressive, personalist ideology as expressed in the Christmas Program of 1945. The party now called itself the Christian People's Party (CVP), a title which indicated that the Catholic church's direct influence had weakened somewhat. The CVP also abandoned its prewar federal structure as a concession to the new political climate. The old BWP also came to an end; the party had been too compromised by De Man's accommodating attitude toward the Germans. The new Belgian Socialist Party (BSP) also became of party of individual members, and forsook institutional ties with the trade unions, mutual-aid societies, and cooperatives. This allowed the trade union movement to achieve its own merger, the General Belgian Alliance of Unions (ABVV), consisting of the socialist trade unions and the militant communist syndicates. The new BSP, feeling pressure from the communists, rejected reformism and returned to the more radical program of Quaregnon (1894). The communists had won great prestige for their important role in the resistance and scored a great success in the elections of 1946. The Cold War, however, gradually neutralized the party's political significance. Moderates in the BSP also regained control of their party, and in the long run, the socialists continued, rather than repudiated, the reformism of the late 1930s.

Until August 1949, the socialists were a permanent part of the successive coalitions that ruled the country; for most of these years they shared power with the CVP. Thus the socialists and Christian Democrats together gave form to the postwar social market economy. As mentioned above, considerable preparations had already been made in this direction before the war. The Pact of Social Solidarity, signed by a number of prominent employers and union leaders in April of 1944, was also quite important in this context. It introduced structural negotiations between labor and management, as well as pledging higher wages and greater social security.

Constructing a welfare state was the first order of business in postwar Belgium. A decree of 28 December 1944 provided a coherent system of social insurance for wage earners. The most important forms of social insurance were made mandatory, pointing to a statist tendency in the postwar welfare legislation. Still, the subsidarity principle continued to operate; the trade unions and mutual-aid societies remained, to a large degree, responsible for unemployment, illness, and disability insurances. These organizations were now, along with employers, directly involved in the management of the country's social insurance system. In addition, a statutory industrial organization was introduced. Workers, acting via their unions, were assigned a role in determining their company's future through joint industrial committees and labor councils. The economic aspects of this industrial organization were coordinated by the Central Council for Corporate Life (1948), the social aspects by the National Labor Council (1952). This large and complex system of labor-management arbitration was modified from time to time, but did not change substantially.

The social market economy came into existence as a compromise between the socialists and the Christian Democrats, but the form it took most closely resembled the vision long articulated by the Christian workers' movement. The workers' movements substantially increased their influence through collective bargaining and the new social insurance system. They were systematically included in socioeconomic policymaking. The trade unions and the mutual-aid societies in particular were able to increase their influence. Specifically, it was the Christian workers' movement – which surpassed its socialist counterpart in membership from the 1960s onwards – which gained most in the long run from the new arrangements.

The *middenstand* movement, which was particularly well organized within Catholic circles, was integrated, together with the Farmers' League and the employers federation, into the system of labor-management arbitration. One can therefore speak of a neocorporatist state structure, in which large interest groups were ever more closely involved in the country's socioeconomic policies. Needless to say, this influence was also further strengthened by their indirect ties with the political parties.

Renewed Religious and Ideological Conflict

The integration of the great social movements into national life helped consolidate the Belgian political system. The institutional stability that this gave to Belgian public life was obscured by the ideological polarization which took place in the years after World War II between Catholics and Flemings on the one side, and the anticlericals and Walloons on the other. These two alliances now hotly debated the punishment of collaborators, as well as the future of the monarchy and the school issue.

The Punishment of Collaborators

In the wake of the occupation, Belgian authorities moved to purge and punish those who had collaborated with the Germans. Many Flemings became convinced that Catholic Flemish militants bore the brunt of punishment as a means to increase the power of the left-wing parties. Whatever the motivation, the Flemish movement suffered a serious setback through these anti-collaborationist policies. At the same time, the war led to a striking resurgence of the Walloon movement. Wartime resistance groups coalesced into postwar pressure groups, and socialist and populist impulses dominated postwar Walloon nationalism. The "new" Walloons actively sought to redress the alleged second-class status that the Belgian state had accorded the region. They also expressed worries about the condition of the Walloon economy. At the Walloon National Congress of October 1945, nationalists demanded autonomy

Poster supporting the return of King Leopold III, ca. 1949. (KADOC, Leuven.)

for Wallonia and even considered possible annexation with France. The popularity of this nationalism weakened as the economy improved, but the tone had been set for future debate.

The Future of the Monarchy

Catholic Flanders also received another blow: the abdication of Leopold III. Initially all parties were badly divided on the question of whether the king should regain the Belgian throne. The leftist parties made the return of the king contingent on parliamentary approval, a condition which effectively eliminated speedy resolution of the issue. The CVP backed the king, a position which increased its electoral share. It sponsored a nonbinding plebiscite held in early 1950, in which nearly 58 percent of all voters wanted the king's return, while more than 42 percent opposed it. The "yes" vote differed greatly among regions, however; in Flanders it was 72 percent, in Brussels 48 percent, and in Wallonia only 42 percent. In subsequent elections, the CVP won an absolute majority in parliament, and the new Catholic government introduced a motion – accepted by parliament – that Leopold was to no longer be barred from assuming his duties as king. Under extremely tense conditions, the king returned to Brussels on 22 July 1950. In response, the socialists and the communists organized political strikes and riots which were particularly intense in Wallonia. Faced with a revolutionary threat, the government backed down and forced Leopold to abdicate in favor of his son Baudouin in August 1950. By this time, however, the question of the monarchy had poisoned the CVP's relations with the other parties and sharpened Flemish-Walloon tensions. Resistance to Leopold had been strongest in the industrial centers, revealing a class element to the tensions as well. The issue had thus widened all the fissures that divided Belgian society, shaking the country to its very foundations.

The School Issue

The CVP felt greatly humiliated because it had succumbed to the street violence. It would now try to realize the rest of its program in the face of left-wing resistance. Outstanding educational issues and the organization of social insurance soon provided additional sources of conflict between the two sides. Now that many more students were attending secondary schools and (at a more modest rate) higher education, the whole issue of state subsidies to private schools needed to be reconsidered. In order to guarantee continued freedom of education, the Christian Democrats favored increasing the subsidies to cover private secondary and higher education more adequately – generating much resistance among the anticlericals. The Christian Democrats also attempted to make the developing social insurance network less statist in character.

In the elections of 1954, the CVP lost its absolute majority in parliament. The socialists and liberals, bent on revenge, now formed their own cabinet based on their shared anticlericalism. The formation of a liberal-socialist government – unthinkable in the 1920s and 1930s – demonstrated how much tensions between the middle and working classes had diminished. The new left-wing cabinet would now pursue educational and social insurance policies radically different from those of its Catholic predecessor. Subsidies to private education were drastically reduced, and the number of state schools dramatically increased. Catholics protested en masse against these measures, and the Catholic bishops voiced their opposition. In a campaign less visible but no less intense, the Christian labor movement resisted the new government's social welfare policies, which strengthened the state's role in this area.

The anticlerical parties lost the elections in 1958. The CVP again managed to win an absolute majority in the Senate, but not in the Chamber of Deputies. Under these circumstances, left and right proved willing to lay their weapons down. Both sides had attempted to impose their will on their opponents, and both sides had been punished for doing so by an electorate that ostensibly preferred more consensual politics. The school issue was now permanently settled. Freedom of school choice became the central principle of the School Pact (1958). It was guaranteed by a sufficient number of both public and private schools, and by free secondary education for everyone. A similar arrangement was later worked out for higher education.

The issue of social insurance was also amicably settled. The state assumed ultimate financial responsibility, while the social organizations in charge of their insurance schemes continued to exist. This arrangement strengthened the role of the state without undermining pillarized

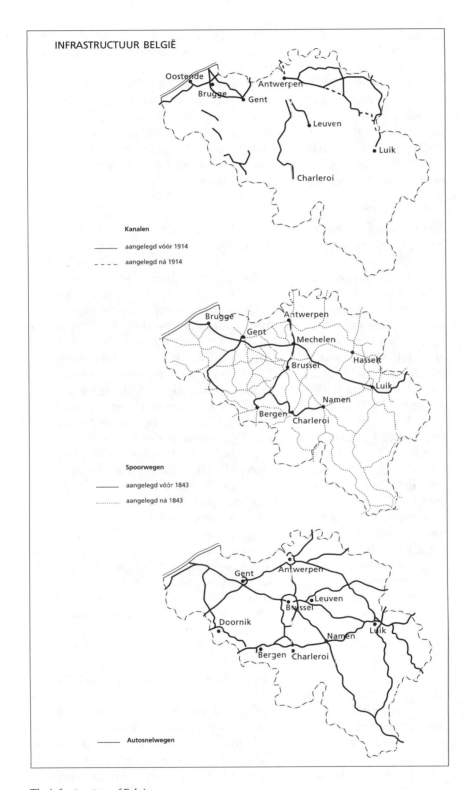

INFRASTRUCTUUR BELGIË

Kanalen

———— aangelegd vóór 1914

- - - - aangelegd ná 1914

Spoorwegen

———— aangelegd vóór 1843

.... aangelegd ná 1843

———— Autosnelwegen

The infrastructure of Belgium.

institutions, as happened in the Netherlands. The Catholics proved willing to soften their anti-statism, as long as the subsidarity principle was not threatened.

The new statutes governing education and social security would end the country's religious and ideological tensions without undermining the country's pillarized structures. On the contrary, the laws only strengthened them. Pillarized educational institutions, trade unions, and mutual-aid societies all flourished with their government subsidies. Not surprisingly, these institutions would exert constant pressure on their parties to keep this system in place.

The Affluent Society

The ideological conflicts of the 1950s masked the economic problems facing Belgium. The country had experienced rapid economic recovery after 1945, in part because the war left its infrastructure relatively undamaged; Antwerp harbor, for instance, had fallen unscathed to Allied forces. The apparent ease with which Belgium recovered proved illusory, however. Its industrial structures and production apparatus were obsolescent, and its recovery rested on the ruins of neighboring countries. But as these countries built brand new infrastructures, Belgium fell behind, and by the 1950s its growth rates were far less impressive than those of other Western European countries. Unemployment was relatively high. The government did little to address these problems, and by 1958 these structural crises had become very apparent.

At this point, the Belgians were blessed with new opportunities. The day of 1 January 1958 marked the beginning of the European Economic Community, opening up new markets. The global economic boom also greatly helped Belgian industries. By 1960, the government, having resolved the politically thorny issues of education and decolonization, became a dynamic force in improving the country's economy. The stagnation of the 1950s had revealed a number of structural weaknesses, each peculiar to the country's regions; heavy industry in Wallonia, light industry in Flanders, and the service sector in Brussels all had their own special problems. The government developed a regionally differentiated economic policy. It managed to attract much foreign investment and stimulated the growth of nuclear energy, the transportation infrastructure (chiefly freeways), and the industrial expansion of the country's harbors (like Zeebrugge). In response to growing economic problems in Walloon coal mining, the government attempted its reorganization in the years after 1958.

The government's activist policies helped Belgium to adapt to the changing structures of the world economy. Petroleum increasingly displaced coal in the energy sector, and petrochemicals in particular enjoyed spectacular growth. Prosperity fostered the growth of the metal industry and the production of durable goods. Industrial plants were increasingly located near the country's harbors in order to facilitate both the easy import of raw materials and the easy export of finished goods.

This evolution mostly benefitted Flanders, where the chemical and metal industries experienced strong growth. The cultural emancipation of the Flemish population helped, moreover, to increase labor

productivity. As a result, the Flemish economy grew faster than the Walloon, so that the per capita product of the former surpassed that of the latter for the first time in 1966.

The Sixties, *a drawing by Gal (the pseudonym of Gerard Alsteens) in Knack, 1988.*

Agriculture also had a part in the economic growth, although to a lesser degree than other sectors. The percentage of the population engaged in agriculture declined drastically, from 12 percent in 1947 to barely 3 percent in 1980. At that time, however, the total value of the country's farm-to-food system still amounted to some 20 percent of national income.

Economic prosperity facilitated a remarkable decline in unemployment; in 1970 only 3 percent of all insured employees were without work. The number of seasonal laborers fell sharply. The number of foreign workers, however, increased, and by 1974 some 8 percent of the population was not of Belgian nationality. Women were increasingly mobilized into the work force; in 1970, they represented 30 percent of the working population, a figure which climbed to 42 percent in 1991.

The demographic structure of the population changed substantially. The average number of births per marriage had been in decline since the nineteenth century in Wallonia and Brussels, but in Flanders the Catholic church's influence had kept the numbers high. Now Flemish birth rates also fell off rapidly. In 1973 contraceptives were legalized, repealing a 1923 law forbidding their sale. Government policy now aimed at family planning. In 1990, abortion was legalized after a difficult political process. Life expectancy further rose, thanks to an excellent health system, from 57 years of age in 1930 to 72 in 1970. From the 1970s on, the Belgian population barely grew; it hovered just under the ten million mark: 57 percent of them were Flemings, 33 percent Walloons, and roughly 10 percent from Brussels.

The Belgian population enjoyed the growing prosperity. The decreasing percentage of family income needed for food reveals this trend: still 65 percent in 1910, it declined to 36 percent in 1961, and 25 percent in 1973. As Belgians took affluence for granted, they began to show more interest in quality of life issues which went beyond purely material concerns.

A longer lifespan, increased prosperity and education, and recreational opportunities all had their effects on cultural life, which now enjoyed greater support than ever before. The breakthrough of the electronic media culture characterized the period. Belgian television programming began in 1953 and quickly became an important component of people's leisure time. Like Belgian radio, television became a public monopoly. By the 1980s, these monopolies were challenged when commercial stations were allowed to broadcast their own programs, first in radio, then in television. The traditional press lost subscriptions as a result of these new media. Newspapers were forced to merge, and after 1975 they received direct government subsidies in order to survive the competition with radio and television.

By the 1960s, a distinct youth culture had sprung up, which expressed itself politically in a host of protest movements. The rise of this youth culture also had much to do with new recreational forms, like rock music, which had a strongly commercial character. Comic strips were another important part of this youth culture, and Belgian artists designed comic strips, such as *Tintin* and *Robbedoes*, with a broader European appeal.

Belgium's more traditional forms of cultural life were further internationalized. This was especially marked by a new orientation toward the Anglo-American world, although Francophone Belgian writers like Marguerite Yourcenar and Georges Simenon cultivated closer ties with French literary circles. Belgian artists were less likely to affiliate themselves with political and social movements than they had been in the past, and became proponents of alternative lifestyles. Perhaps most striking is that the various art forms increasingly influenced each other. Experimental writers like Hugo Claus, for example, were influenced by abstract art and surrealism, and painting and sculpture increasingly used each other's forms.

From a Unitary to a Federal State

The "Community Question" as a Central Issue

The economic developments sketched above had important consequences for Flemish-Walloon relations, which again came to the forefront after the school settlement of 1958. The language issue had already received a broad political dimension in the 1930s, but now it would be extended to socioeconomic life, thanks to Walloon concerns about their economy. From now on, the "language question" was replaced by the "community question," which defined the conflict as one between two different communities with divergent interests.

The Flemish movement, still burdened by the collaboration of its radical wing during the Second World War, made a slow recovery during the 1950s. Both the government's anti-collaborationist policy and Leopold's forced abdication generated resentment among many Flemings whose militancy on the school issue was also a manifestation of their disaffection. By the 1950s, a number of Christian Democrats advocated a strengthening of language homogeneity and a regional economic policy that would end Flanders's lag in economic development. In 1954 a new Flemish national party was founded: the People's Union (*Volksunie*). It distanced itself from the former VNV and understood itself as a democratic, pluralistic party that wanted to turn Belgium into a federal state.

While Flemish self-consciousness slowly grew, the Walloon movement underwent a sudden radicalization. By the early 1950s, Walloon grievances had diminished, but they reappeared at the end of the decade when Wallonia began to lose much of its heavy industry. The once proud coal mining industry, long the region's economic backbone, collapsed, and the Walloon steel industry soon faced the same decline. Pent-up tensions exploded during the campaign against the so-called Unity Law of 1961, which primarily sought to stimulate economic growth but which also raised indirect taxes and trimmed social spending. Strikes in Wallonia soon took on almost revolutionary proportions, and it was the Liège syndicalist André Renard who gave the protests a radically regionalist character as well. The protesters lost the fight, but the communalist polarization did not subside. In March of 1961, Renard established the Walloon Popular Movement (MPW), which wanted the government to bring about both a more federal and a more socialist political system. Later, other small Walloon parties were established, and in 1968 they merged into the *Rassemblement Wallon* (RW), which would play an important political role for the next decade. Meanwhile, French-speaking politicians from Brussels established the Democratic Front of Francophones (FDF) in 1965, which would for a short time become the largest political party in the capital. It cooperated with the *Rassemblement Wallon*.

The Walloons were not alone in their activism. By the 1960s, the Flemish movement took the political initiative, thanks to the electoral success of the People's Union. In 1962 they were able to force through the delineation of language boundaries and of Brussels's city limits, which were still surrounded by Flemish-speaking areas. This included some exchange of territory, which was generally more advantageous to the Walloons than to the Flemish. Some of the boundary changes created tensions that even today have not disappeared; when the Fouron region was transferred from the French-speaking province of Liège to the Dutch-speaking province of Limburg, it sent shocks throughout Wallonia. The 1962 agreement restricted the Brussels region to nineteen municipalities, although Francophones in six adjacent boroughs were allowed their own administrative and educational facilities. Within Brussels itself, a 1963 law strengthened the position of Dutch in the schools and in business. The language homogeneity of Flemish Brabant, which remained vulnerable to Francophone influences, was further aided when the French-speaking part of the University of Leuven left in 1968 to found its own university in Wallonia. The "Leuven question" caused much turmoil throughout the country and precipitated a permanent split in the CVP when its Flemish and Walloon wings established their own parties. Soon, the other older parties divided as well, so that by 1978, no national parties were left.

The Leuven question sealed the fate of the Belgian unitary state, setting in motion the process which would lead to the regionalization and the federalization of the country. A revision of the constitution, passed in December 1970, officially recognized the autonomy of the Flemish, French and also German "cultural communities." At the same time, it established three separate economic regions: Flanders, Wallonia, and Brussels. Neither the administrative and financial powers of these new entities, nor their boundaries, were fixed by the constitutional amendment, but would have to be determined by a subsequent law to be passed by two-thirds of parliament. The constitutional revision explicitly protected the rights of linguistic, religious, and ideological minorities.

These far-reaching changes did not lead to peace between Flemings and Walloons. On the contrary, they only precipitated further heated arguments, especially in regard to the specific powers of each regional authority and the precise boundaries of Brussels. The fate of the Fouron region also routinely dominated these discussions. The Flemings made use of their cultural autonomy in order to strengthen the Dutch-language homogeneity of their own region, while the Walloons concentrated their efforts to bolster the Francophone position in the Fouron region and in Brussels.

It proved impossible to find a two-thirds parliamentary majority to pass a regional government law in the 1970s. In 1977 the national government – which at that moment also included nationalistic parties like the People's Union and the FDF – drew up the Egmont Pact. This agreement outlined the prerogatives of the regional governments, but it also strengthened the position of the Francophones in the areas surrounding Brussels. Thus the Egmont Pact, although backed by the People's Union, generated much resistance in Flanders; and in the end, the pact only led to the fall of the government and a schism within the People's Union. Dissidents within the People's Union founded their own political organization, the Flemish Bloc, which would later turn into a radical right-wing party.

The Economic Recession as Catalyst

Meanwhile, the communalist tensions were complicated by the economic crisis that manifested itself after 1974. Industrial growth slowed considerably. At the same time, some of the negative consequences of the consensus economy came to light. For example, modernization of the industrial system had been undermined by growing government support of endangered businesses. It became apparent that too much investment had gone into obsolescent industries. Moreover, the introduction of a comprehensive collective bargaining system made wages rise at the same rate in weaker economic sectors as in stronger ones. The recession of the 1970s also led to high inflation – 13 percent in 1975 – the result of too large an expansion of the money supply, first in support of Belgian business, and later to pay government expenditures. The inflation was also caused by the rising price of raw materials – especially oil in the fall of 1973 – and the relative increase in labor costs. Many business sectors lost their competitive edge through this inflation, especially because newly industrialized nations were beginning to sell their goods precisely when the volume of world trade was beginning to stagnate. This stagnation was itself caused by instability in the world's financial markets, and by the transfer of purchasing power from oil-importing to oil-exporting countries, triggering a structural shift in world consumption patterns.

The malaise in production went hand in hand with a decline in profits, as well as with the closing of many businesses and growing unemployment (over 8 percent of all insured wage earners in 1976). Clearly, the Belgians needed to find ways to restructure economic activity.

The economic crisis hit the Walloon steel industry hard, and it suffered massive unemployment and gigantic financial losses. The government attempted to revive the steel industry through extensive – and expensive – restructuring plans. Other large industrial sectors – textiles and the garment industry, shipping and (later) the coal mines of Limburg – also encountered difficulties and asked for government assistance. They all received the status of a "national sector," so that every region would receive its share of governmental financial support.

Belgium Becomes a Federal State

The country's economic problems, complicated by the communalist dimension, gave politicians the motivation to reintroduce a law outlining how to regionalize Belgium. This happened through the constitutional changes of 1980. The country's economic regions were given socioeconomic powers. At the same time, the prerogatives of the "cultural communities" were enlarged. They were given charge of portfolios such as health care and welfare. The Flemish decided to merge their economic region with their "cultural community", thus merging two authorities into one. The national government s financing of these eco-

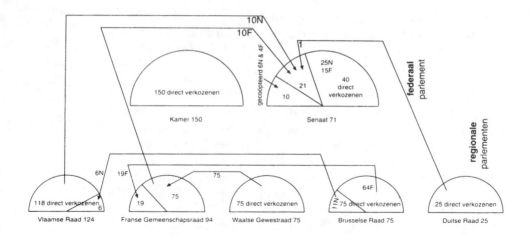

Political structure of Belgium After the Fourth Constitutional Reform, 1992-1993.

nomic regions and communities was organized on the basis of various criteria, and in the future, the regions were to be granted their own power of taxation. Finally, the economic regions and cultural communities – with the exception of Brussels – were given their own regional governments.

These constitutional changes were accompanied by a reconstruction of the economic "national sectors." Government financial support was now equally distributed across regions; supporting the Walloon steel industry, for example, implied that the Flemish textiles, coal industry, and shipbuilding also deserved government money. This was an extremely expensive solution, and the Flemings – who resented that they bore the brunt of the financial burden – increasingly demanded an economic federalism in which each region would pay only for its own projects.

In 1988 a new constitutional change brought Belgium an important step closer in this direction. The authority of economic regions and cultural communities was considerably expanded. Economic policy, including control of the "national sectors," the energy sector, public works, and transportation affairs were all surrendered to the economic regions, and education was turned over to the cultural communities. The Brussels region was finally included in these arrangements, under the condition that its Flemish minority be guaranteed a say in its affairs.

The transformation of the Belgian state was not yet completed, however. Under extremely difficult conditions, a new constitutional change was passed in the spring of 1993. The sixth constitutional change in Belgian history – and the fourth change in the state structure – had far-reaching consequences. It transformed Belgium into a federal state with an asymmetrical construction of "communities" and "regions" which now became states within a state. Four states – the Flemish and the German "communities," and the "regions" of Brussels and Wallonia – would now choose their own parliaments. The powers of these ministates were further increased; they were even authorized to sign international agreements on matters relating to their jurisdiction. The national government and parliament in Brussels were slimmed down; the Chamber of Deputies and the Senate continued to exist, but no longer had the same powers. The Chamber did receive, in addition to its remaining prerogatives, exclusive control over the federal government. The Senate, while retaining limited legislative powers, was now largely reduced to a deliberative assembly, although it was also specifically charged with promoting harmonious relations between the Belgian states. Finally, the 1993 changes abolished the province of Brabant (as of 1 January 1995); it would now be divided among the new provinces of Flemish Brabant and Walloon Brabant.

The Pillarized, Neo-Corporatist State Persists

The federalization of Belgium did little to undermine the pillarized, neo-corporatist character of the social system established at the turn of the century. The same opinions and interest groups which dominated the Belgian state and the country's organizational life for so long now easily readjusted themselves to the new regional structures. They continued to exercise great influence over regional governments via their political parties, especially in the cases of the Christian Democrats and the socialists. The monarchy was no longer an independent and potent political force; Leopold III's abdication, the internationalization of foreign policy, and decolonization all eroded its power base. But Baudouin I (1951-1993) did give the monarchy great moral authority, and under him it remained the most important symbol of Belgian national unity.

The large social movements played a sizable role in determining government policy, which between 1961 and 1931 was almost exclusively in the hands of Christian Democrats and the socialists. In the 1960s, the socialist ABVV and Catholic ACV managed to present a united labor front, and the Christian and socialist mutual-aid societies also began to cooperate with each other. The cooperation of the trade unions and the mutual-aid societies increased their weight in the consensus economy and in government social policy.

The state did not restrict its intervention to socioeconomic issues, but increasingly made initiatives in the country's cultural life, although always in consultation with the dominant religious and ideological organizations. Reforms in the School Pact of 1973 confirmed the de facto division of two state-supported educational networks, one public, one Catholic. Non-Catholics were particularly anxious to protect alternative ideological and philosophical viewpoints, and the Culture Pact (1973) guaranteed such groups access to cultural subsidies. This had the effect of keeping Belgian cultural life pillarized, and strengthened the religious and ideological organizations which already determined the contours of Belgian society.

The pillarized, neocorporatist system remained robust – despite the cultural changes, evident since the 1950s, which might have undermined it. Ideological and religious intolerance – one of the bases for the pillarized edifice – declined in the face of greater mobility, the influence of the new media, increased secularization, and greater openness within the Catholic church. Before the 1950s the church had maintained an antimodern posture, but now it began a dialogue with the modern world. It demonstrated a greater sensitivity to freedom of conscience and more respect for the individual's search for truth than had hitherto been the case. The church's willingness to use political power for religious ends now weakened, and all of these factors contributed to a partial political "depillarization."

The People's Union became the first ideologically pluralist party. In 1961 the liberal party, having lost much of its appeal after the school war subsided, repudiated its traditional anticlerical position. It transformed itself into the Party for Freedom and Progress (PVV), becoming more populist in character, especially in Flanders. The PVV gnawed away at the CVP's right wing, strengthening the relative position of left-wing formations (like the ACW) within the Christian Democratic party. As a result, some Christian Democrats committed themselves to a "progressive front" in 1968 with the socialists. The socialists, however, maintained strong if implicit ties with the anticlerical "freethinking" tradition, and it soon appeared that pillarization was more firmly embedded among the working class than it was in middle class circles. But the Catholic electorate increasingly voted for a whole range of parties as faith became ever less a consideration in electoral behavior. Religion remained a significant factor in political life, however, as Catholics (and others) zealously defended the religious and ideological arrangements already in place. The religious factor manifested continued relevance especially on moral issues like abortion.

Thus one could say that while Belgian voters "depillarized," the pillarized institutions themselves remained intact – much more so than was the case in the Netherlands. Belgium's pillarized organizations retained their privileged connections with the political parties and kept their memberships high through pragmatic changes in their ideology, and through the efficient social services they offered. The country's pillarized institutions were able to persist because they were so closely intertwined with the state apparatus, and because of their services and social usefulness.

This did not stop the new liberal party from attacking the pillarized, neocorporatist system, although not always in a consistent manner. In 1973, for example, they actually supported the Culture Pact, which further pillarized the cultural sector. Still, it must be said that the liberals, with both their libertarian and statist traditions, never enthusiastically supported pillarization. In the late 1980s, they especially proved willing to systematically challenge the system, but even before, neoliberalism had criticized Belgium's neocorporatist system as the chief cause of high government expenditures. It was the liberals who largely led the economic recovery program of the 1980s, which included the reorganization of public finances, cutbacks in government expenditures, and the introduction of a far-reaching scheme to slow wage and income increases. Employment policy, too, was increasingly determined by neoliberal ideas. For some years, the trade unions were forced on the defensive, but they rebounded when better economic times returned around 1986, and when a new "Roman-Red" cabinet took office. Despite the recession, the unions' influence had not been significantly undermined. Liberals were thus compelled to broaden their base of support in order to dismantle the pillarized, neocorporatist system, and in late 1992, Flemish liberals

Jobs da's zoals jongens.
Je neemt niet de eerste de beste.

Ik kies nu de goede studies, want mijn toekomst is mij lief.

In the beginning of the 1990s, the government launched a campaign to break through gender patterns, especially by encouraging young women to pursue "male" occupations and studies.

changed the PVV into the VLD (Flemish Liberals and Democrats) as a way of fostering a wider appeal.

Another threat to the established system came from the new social movements which first appeared in the 1970s. They were, in a certain sense, a product of the youth protests of the 1960s, stressing less overtly material concerns. The environmental movement is perhaps the most obvious example, but there were also the peace and Third World movements – closely allied in Flanders – each with a more international perspective. Interestingly, nuclear energy hardly generated protest in Belgium, and feminism, though enjoying renewed interest and popularity, never attained the same public attention and importance it gained in the Netherlands.

The activism of the Alliance for a Better Environment, established in 1970, succeeded in making the environment an important political issue. The various parties tried to coopt the concerns of the environmentalists but were not able to prevent them from establishing their own political movement. By the late 1970s, environmental activists were ready to enter parliamentary politics, and in 1981 the Flemish AGALEV party (an acronym for "to live differently") won its first seat in parliament – the first time for an environmental party anywhere. Its Francophone counterpart, ECOLO, won some 10 percent of the votes in the 1988 elections for the European parliament, the highest percentage of any Green party in Europe. These parties increasingly showed interest in a wider array of issues than those related to the environment, and became the political expression of other social movements as well. The peace movement in particular, which grew dramatically during the 1980s, was a forum for highlighting the environmentalists' own cause. The Greens quickly collided with the Belgian political system because they favored direct democracy and open public policy – practices far different from the closed, elitist consensus politics long practiced in the country. But as a relatively small opposition party, they could not easily change these practices.

In this way, both neocorporatism and pillarization simply continued as Belgium was transformed from a unitary to a federal state. The electoral success of anti-system parties on 24 November 1991 made it clear that the political status quo was now being questioned by a large segment of the population, and that voters were looking for a new equilibrium in the political system. The ruling parties now realized that measures would have to be undertaken to close the gap between the citizenry and the government, to increase the political interest of the individual, and to foster the political system's autonomy from the large pillarized structures. Thus in the 1990s, Belgians belatedly followed a course of political reform already taken in the Netherlands two decades earlier.

But Belgium had come a long way in its institutional development since 1830. The unitary, liberal state born of the Belgian Revolution, which had enjoyed its halcyon days in the years after 1848, had undergone dramatic changes since the late nineteenth century. Religious and ideological conflicts had given rise to pillarization, and social conflicts had been channeled into a neocorporatist framework. Later, the ethnic and cultural tensions would lead to the federalization of Belgium. Economic and security concerns led Belgians into the European Union and NATO. All of these political developments generated a complex political system characterized by an intricate division of power. The cohesion of this system was assured in the course of the twentieth century by organized interest groups and large social movements, which served as intermediaries between the state and its citizens. It was only at the end of the century that the dominant role of these organizations was seriously put into question.

View of Rotterdam city center. The Germans bombed the city in May 1940 and as a result, new buildings dominate its skyline. Rotterdam's modern look is symbolic of the highly developed nature of Dutch society in the twentieth century.

8 The Netherlands since 1830

J.C.H. Blom

After Belgian independence, the Netherlands – once among the most powerful states in the world as the Republic of the United Netherlands – resigned itself to the status of a small European power. The country did manage to retain an extensive colonial empire for more than a century. The country remained quiet during the revolutions of 1848, but the threat of revolution caused the king to proclaim a relatively modern, liberal constitution. This laid the legal and political basis for the modernization of the country, which was slow at first but which accelerated in the 1870s. Economically, socially, and culturally, the country changed much around the turn of the century. Through all of these changes, the Netherlands became a modern constitutional nation-state with a democratic parliamentary system. The country possessed a varied and relatively prosperous economy, a lively national culture defined by a broad "bourgeois" moral consensus, and a striking social segmentation along religious and ideological lines (pillarization).

The Netherlands suffered under some of the greatest upheavals of the twentieth century: the Depression of the 1930s, German occupation during World War II, decolonization, and the Cold War. These intrusions did not prevent the growth and expansion of the country's pillarized institutions, which enjoyed their heyday between 1920 and 1960. A welfare state emerged from a growing body of social legislation, from the consensus economy, and from increasing state intervention. Major social and cultural shifts accounted for a "cultural revolution" which took the country by storm during the 1960s. Pillarization largely disappeared, and new demands for openness and participation, for personal growth and secularization led to a much more "liberal" set of values. But in many respects Dutch society continued to develop along long-established lines.

Economic stagnation, especially acute in the 1980s, created serious problems, including high unemployment and a financial crisis for the welfare state. These problems persisted, and public confidence in politics waned. The country also faced considerable environmental problems and the consequences of political and cultural internationalization.

1. A Small European Nation-State (1830-1870s)

The North Goes It Alone

The Belgian revolt against William I's United Kingdom of the Netherlands triggered an overwhelmingly patriotic response in the North. The king's efforts to quell the rebellion of the "despicable and mutinous Belgian race" found support everywhere. The naval officer J.C.J. van Speyk, for example, was adulated by the whole nation after February 1831 when he blew up his own gunboat on the Scheldt rather than let the rebels seize it. The Ten-Day Campaign, which William initiated in the summer of 1831 to end the rebellion, also generated much enthusiasm. The Dutch public denounced French infamy when Paris threatened to intervene against the initially successful campaign, and they bitterly complained about the behavior of the great powers, which, despite their earlier promises, essentially abandoned the Dutch. Before long, many of the king's northern subjects wanted to be rid of the South; although Belgium deserved punishment, it had proven more trouble than it was worth.

"Then rather be blown sky high:" J.C.J. van Speyk destroys his own ship. (Atlas van Stolk, Rotterdam.)

Opposition liberals and Catholics in the North, much less powerful than in Belgium, found the Dutch political climate inhospitable in the 1830s, since both liberalism and Catholicism were strongly associated with the revolt. The liberals were effectively silenced for the time being; Dutch Catholics remained loyal, notwithstanding the failure of a few militiamen in Catholic areas to follow their marching orders.

In the end, the king's persistence in holding on to the South gravely tried his loyal subjects. The financial burden of his policy was exceedingly high, and as a result the Dutch desire to fight waned. When in 1839 William finally accepted terms of separation, it came as a relief.

Meanwhile, the kingdom's financial problems had become the basis for a new, although still numerically weak, liberal opposition. However, their rather limited proposals for constitutional change were rebuffed by the king. William's popularity was further undermined both by his uncompromising hostility toward an orthodox Protestant secession from the Dutch Reformed church in 1834 and his petulant attitude toward his Catholic subjects. His plans to marry a Belgian Catholic countess, Henriëtte d'Oultremont, was the last straw in this tradition-ally Protestant country; embittered by the widespread criticism of his person, William abdicated in favor of his son in 1840. William II would rule the country until 1849.

Belgian independence reduced the Kingdom of the Netherlands to roughly the borders of the old Republic of the Seven United Provinces, which had been dominated by Holland. This state had suffered from a chronic economic crisis since the 1780s. With Belgium gone, the Dutch were forced to rethink their country's internal organization and its posi-tion within Europe. It was now clear that William I's ambition to make his kingdom a major international power like the economically mighty Dutch Republic of the seventeenth century would have to be given up. The economic advantage of the Republic had long since dissipated, and the Netherlands was merely a small country, both in size and popula-tion. In 1839, the kingdom could count nearly three million inhabitants, a number which would grow to over three-and-a-half million in 1869 and only a decade later to some four million. Dutch colonial posses-sions, mostly in Asia, did little to increase the country's "smallness." Indeed, some observers came to question whether, as a result of Belgian independence and the economic problems of the 1840s, the country could maintain its independence.

In the arena of practical politics, however, this doubt never played a crucial role. As an independent, well-established state, the Nether-lands would not simply disappear. Despite doubts and difficulties, the romantic nationalism which then swept over Europe did not leave the Netherlands untouched, and the unique nature of the Dutch people and their great national potential received much emphasis. Even if the pros-perous and great era of the Republic would never return, its glory days could remain a powerful source of inspiration for the Dutch nation. The founding in 1839 of the journal *De Gids* (*The Guide*), with E.J. Potgieter as its central figure, was a form of cultural expression which success-fully combined literary criticism and a positive, well-mannered patrio-tism. In art, historical paintings also sought to give expression to national feeling.

But in international politics the Netherlands had to accept the role of a small nation surrounded by large (and stronger) powers. Relations with its new neighbor, Belgium, would remain difficult in the ensuing years. Disappointed by the experiences of the 1830s, the Netherlands detached itself from "the grand politics" of Europe – a response similar to what occurred in the eighteenth-century Republic. For economic rea-sons, too, it seemed prudent to steer clear of international conflicts. Without realizing it, the Dutch thus laid the basis for a policy of neu-trality that they would maintain for another century. Initially, therefore, Dutch neutrality was born of resignation, weakness, and economic calculation; as the years went by, the Dutch developed higher principles to undergird this policy: international law, ethical considerations, and the reasoning that it was in Europe's interest that the important Dutch river delta never fall into the hands of a great power. In this way, neutrality, aloofness, and independence each became, as circumstances dictated, unshakable principles by which the Dutch judged their country's position in the world. It was only after 1945 and the shocking experiences of the Second World War, that the country's neutrality came to be seriously questioned.

This is not to say that the Netherlands shied away from all diplomatic and international developments. In particular, the country had an important interest in its economic relations with other countries. Regulating commercial traffic on the Rhine, for instance, demanded much energy. By the middle of the nineteenth century, the Dutch usually followed a general European tendency toward free trade, since it was advantageous to the Netherlands's open, internationally oriented economy. Sometimes circumstances forced the Dutch to take a stand in foreign entanglements. In 1866 and 1867, the Luxembourg question threatened to involve the Netherlands in the tensions surrounding German unification and growing Franco-German antagonisms. King William I, also Luxembourg's head of state, had considered selling the duchy to France. This generated international problems, including attempts by Belgium to acquire their tiny neighbor to the southeast. A serious international conflict was averted only at the last moment, when Luxembourg and the Dutch province of Limburg, which had belonged to the German Confederation before its dissolution in 1866, formally renounced all ties with Germany. This narrow escape only strengthened Dutch commitment to neutrality.

Economic and Social Relations

The 1830s and especially the 1840s were financially difficult years, chiefly because of William I's expensive policies. The government introduced a financial reorganization aimed at restoring the economy. The pragmatic and moderate Amsterdam banker, F.A. van Hall, played a central role in this policy as the minister of finance. But an agrarian crisis in the 1840s – precipitated by failure of successive potato harvests and the social unrest it generated – only made conditions worse.

Still, the Netherlands during the nineteenth century was one of the richest and most prosperous nations in Europe, and hence the world. It enjoyed a relatively well-developed and diverse economic structure which provided the basis for gradual economic growth through a good part of the century. Although the economic power of the Golden Age had long since vanished, the Netherlands always remained important for its international trade and for being a financial center. The country's infrastructure was excellent and was further improved over the course of the century, first by roads and canals, later by railroads. Moreover, its agrarian sector was both regionally differentiated and highly developed; it enjoyed strong markets, particularly for its dairy products. Throughout the nineteenth century, farm products were of vital importance to the country's economy and were quite possibly the Netherlands's chief source of prosperity. In addition, the Netherlands had long possessed a variegated commercial sector, characterized both by its small-scale operations and its craftsmanship. This sector had lost much of its prominence in the eighteenth century, but it remained an important factor in the country's domestic markets.

The colonies were also of great economic significance. The East Indies produced primarily agricultural goods in international demand, and in 1830 Governor-General J. van den Bosch established a state-controlled "cultivation system" (*Cultuurstelsel*) to exploit the riches of Java. The colonial government, in effect, took over export production, and it obligated the native population to render certain supplies and services. From the colonizer's viewpoint, the new system was a great success. It prompted a substantial increase in Javanese exports, providing strong profits for Dutch trade and shipping. The Dutch state, too, gained a long-lasting and considerable financial advantage; the system provided the government with as much as 30 percent of its total annual revenues. The Netherlands's financial reorganization program and the drive for balanced budgets, not to mention desired improvements in the infrastructure, gave the "profitable supplements" (*"batig slot"*) from the colonies an important role in state finance.

Objections to the *Cultuurstelsel* – that it undermined private initiative, or that it was unjust to the native population and that its implementation encouraged abuses – did not find much public support until

Multatuli, in a nineteenth-century lithograph. (Iconographisch Bureau, The Hague.)

the 1860s. Multatuli's novel *Max Havelaar* is the most celebrated of these protests, but it was not an exception. Liberals like W.R. van Hoëvell and I.D. Fransen van de Putte worked politically to end the system, and succeeded, after much heated debate, in 1870. Exploitation of the Dutch East Indies was now assumed by the private sector.

The Netherlands was not well positioned to take part in the industrialization which had already transformed England and which by the early nineteenth century was beginning to make its mark on the continent, including Belgium. The Netherlands possessed few natural resources, and wages in most parts of the country were high in comparison to other European nations. The relative prosperity of the Netherlands, and the gradual but steady economic growth of the economy did little to inspire the new entrepreneurial habits necessary for industrialization. Thus modern industrialization came late to the Netherlands, "taking off" only at the end of the nineteenth century. The appearance of the country's economy, and hence its social structure, remained determined for a long time by trade capitalism and the small business enterprises of shopkeepers and artisans.

For all the importance of the agricultural sector, the Netherlands was an urbanized country by early nineteenth-century standards. But it did not possess, nor did it develop, any large cities of the scope found elsewhere in Europe. The differences between large villages and small cities were not very great. Furthermore, the countryside had many close ties with the cities, so that the differences between urban and rural culture in many areas were less than those present in other countries. Social status was the decisive factor in nineteenth-century society. There were intensive social contacts between members of the country's various social strata and clear delineations of the rights and responsibilities of each class. Normally, persons were expected to live and die in the same social rank into which they were born, although a modest degree of social advancement did occur.

Dutch social hierarchies were complicated and refined, with subtle nuances making distinctions across the many middle groups of the urban bourgeoisie and the various categories of farmers. Urban elites, descendants of the aristocratic regents of the Republic, and wealthy farmers and landowners, including a small number of nobility, set the tone. At the bottom of the social ladder were a great number of poor, both in the cities and the countryside. They faced a life of subsistence, with little hope of improvement. The lowest strata of the middle groups, as well as the category of educated laborers with more or less permanent employment, were in constant danger of joining the ranks of the poor. The poor did benefit from a great number of philanthropic institutions, which offered them a relatively high level of assistance. It is plausible that the scope and depth of poverty in the Netherlands, however serious, was less than in many other European countries.

The country's traditional economic and social forms, as well as the relatively placid socioeconomic life which accompanied them, have led some scholars to opine that the nineteenth-century Netherlands was a backwards, and by extension, poor country. The lead gained during the Golden Age had turned into an socioeconomic lag. This thesis is credible only if England, which clearly became richer than the Netherlands in the nineteenth century, is taken as the standard. In comparison to the rest of Western Europe, the Netherlands was economically and socially different, but it was neither poorer nor less developed and economically variegated than its neighbors. Certainly one cannot speak of economic stagnation; in many instances, just the opposite was the case.

The Establishment of Parliamentary Government
Constitutional Change

The central political debate after 1839 concerned which form of government was most desirable for the Kingdom of the Netherlands. William I wanted the constitutional changes made necessary by Belgian independence kept to a minimum; he could thus retain the authoritarian form of government which gave him direct political influence. Reformers, on the other hand, wanted to use the opportunity to change the relationship between the king and his ministers, and to reduce royal control over state finances. Principled liberals in the opposition supported making ministers fully responsible to parliament, which would greatly reduce the direct political influence of the king. The monarch would thus become a ceremonial head of state, symbolically representing the unity of the people and the state.

But the liberal opposition – who were the champions of a more powerful parliament – constituted only a very small group. Consequently, the constitutional changes of 1840 did not give ministers full political responsibility. But ministers were now required to cosign all laws and royal decrees, and could be prosecuted if they acted unlawfully. Formally speaking, this amounted to very little. But it had the effect of strengthening the ministers' hand vis-à-vis the king, and intensifying public debate between the ministers and parliament. The initially cooperative attitude of William II, who was also more kindly disposed toward the Catholics than his father, was instrumental in this change. But "the Nine Men" proposal by the liberal opposition in 1844 for a more far-reaching constitutional change was not even taken up by parliament for debate. Fear of "the people's influence" was still too great.

Sweeping constitutional change, however, was not long off. In the early months of 1848, revolutionary movements erupted throughout Europe, threatening to overthrow the established order. In the Netherlands itself there was no revolutionary threat, notwithstanding the social restiveness of the recent agrarian crisis and the appearance of a few radical opposition papers. But William II, who in recent years had adopted a more authoritarian position, feared that the Netherlands, too, might soon be engulfed in revolution. He thus transformed himself from "a conservative to a liberal in one night," as William himself described it. Bypassing his own ministers, the king installed a constitutional reform commission. The commission's most important member was the liberal politician and jurist J.R. Thorbecke, who had already published proposals for a new constitution. The commission was thus able to work quickly, and by the end of the year, a greatly revised and in effect entirely new constitution was proclaimed.

J.F. Thorbecke (Atlas van Stolk, Rotterdam.)

This constitution formulated the principles of the Dutch political system in such a way that it could function, virtually unchanged, for over a century, and even today forms the basis of Dutch government. As it turned out, the Constitution of 1848 also ended the crisis of the Dutch state that had persisted since the 1780s. The new constitution made full ministerial responsibility its cornerstone: "The king is inviolable, the ministers are responsible." Parliament continued to consist of two legislative houses, the more important of which, the Second Chamber, would now, like the city councils and the provincial States, be directly chosen by the electorate. The First Chamber was chosen by the provincial States. The Second Chamber received the rights of amendment, interpellation, and inquiry. Debate in the representative bodies was, in principle, public. Furthermore, the constitution guaranteed freedom of religion, education, the press, and assembly. Church and state were supposed to be strictly separated. The principle question of whether ultimate authority was invested in "the people" or the monarch was not explicitly addressed. But the new constitution clearly gave parliament many new powers at the king's expense.

The Constitution of 1848, just like the Belgian constitution of 1831, was unquestionably liberal in character and was among the most "modern" in Europe. This is not to say that after 1848 liberals and liberal principles invariably dominated the Dutch political landscape. On the contrary, there was much hostility toward the liberals in general and to Thorbecke in particular; he was regarded as extremely radical and was wrongly denounced as a republican. Moreover, much of the Dutch political system in 1848 was as yet unformed. Thorbecke and his first cabinet (1849-1853) took important first steps to order it, and their Provincial and Municipality Laws achieved a good balance between the various administrative bodies – a balance which long had been sought. The cabinet's Electoral Law determined that the directly chosen representatives would be chosen on a district by district basis. Although voter participation was no longer determined by social position, the new one-man, one-vote system was still restricted to the prosperous top levels of society, since only the independent bourgeoisie were judged capable of making their own decisions. Voting requirements ensured that only roughly 10 percent of the adult male population could participate in elections for the Second Chamber.

Parliamentary Developments

Parliamentary life did not yet exhibit organized party politics as presently practiced, and many parliamentarians did not have an expressed political ideology. Others did have a clear political orientation. The most easily recognizable were the liberals, especially the supporters of Thorbecke. Above all, they stood for the systematic application of the new constitutional principles in Dutch public life. Arrayed against them were the conservatives, but they possessed neither a clear political program nor a well-developed ideology. Unlike many other countries in Europe, the Netherlands did not have a powerful feudal tradition, typically represented by the nobility, and this made it much more difficult for a strong conservative party to emerge. The most important cause uniting Dutch conservatives in the 1850s and 1860s was their desire to give the king and the ministers who enjoyed his favor as much power vis-à-vis parliament as possible. They also adumbrated a resistance to social change, but in this they were hardly alone.

Most parliamentarians belonged to neither of these political currents. They occupied a middle position, later called conservative-liberal, but in no sense may they be considered a coherent group. These members of parliament characterized themselves by their moderate and pragmatic posture. Although most of them had not been proponents of the new constitution and were certainly no followers of Thorbecke, they believed the time to resist the liberal innovations had passed. In a certain sense, their grudging acceptance of the changes made them responsible for the new political system, although they opposed every effort to further liberalize the system. The conservative-liberals supported a well-ordered and financially cautious administration, as well as the maintenance of the existing social order. The banker Van Hall, mentioned above, was the most important figure among them, and he was reappointed as minister in the 1850s.

King William III, who succeeded his father in 1849, made a few attempts in the 1850s to return the political system to the pre-1848 status quo. He did not succeed. In the first place, the new king possessed a capricious and moody personality, and he could be exceedingly coarse. He lacked a feel for political strategy and tactics, and the most competent conservatives hesitated in giving their support to his plans. But a more important factor in the king's failure was the position of the conservative-liberals, who, while generally quite conservative and inalterably opposed to radical change, had no interest in overturning the Constitution of 1848. Because a strong reaction to political change did not emerge, the parliamentary system could gradually take deeper root.

But the delineation of powers among the king, government ministers and parliament remained a burning issue.

During the 1860s, in fact, the king precipitated another political crisis by attempting once more to break the power of parliament. In both 1866 and 1867, he personally intervened in the elections and in the disputes between parliament and the cabinet, with the purpose of keeping his cabinet in place. In 1866, he even directly appealed to the electorate with a manifesto printed in the national colors. But parliament prevailed. In 1868, the conservative cabinet was forced to resign when the newly chosen Second Chamber rejected the cabinet's policy for the third time. From this time on, it became an unwritten but important rule that cabinets no longer enjoying the confidence of parliament would have to resign. This rule of thumb implicitly underscored the apolitical nature of the constitutional monarch, despite William III's objections and despite the sometimes considerable informal influence that Dutch monarchs have continued to exercise over their ministers.

One cardinal liberal principle held that the state should only sparingly intervene in the lives of its citizens. Individual opportunity and social progress should develop unfettered, and liberals believed that the implementation of this principle would, on balance, yield favorable results. The advent of the liberal state did not mean that all government intervention came to an end, either in the Netherlands or in the rest of Europe. But the Dutch state after 1848 regulated and directed less than it had under the highly activist William I. This was particularly true of the government's pronounced liberal economic policy, which had free trade as its cornerstone. But the state still faced many tasks, both old and new, some of which were even enumerated in the constitution. Next to the state's obvious responsibilities of providing a national defense, maintaining domestic order, and operating a judicial system, many liberals believed that government involvement was justified both to correct undesired social developments and to create the conditions for further economic growth. For example, building the national infrastructure, helping the poor, and funding education were all included in the role many liberals assigned to government.

The country's infrastructure was both improved and expanded in the course of the nineteenth century. William I already had built a large number of new canals and roads. Later in the century, the improvements in the waterways between the open sea and Amsterdam (the North Sea Canal, opened in 1876), Rotterdam (the New Waterway, opened in 1872), as well as the construction of an extensive rail network, were of particular importance. The Netherlands's first railroad, between Amsterdam and Haarlem, opened in 1839, but it was not until the 1860s that the government began a concerted effort to build railroads, which were then turned over to private companies. These developments presaged what is called "the unification of the Netherlands," in which regional differences lessened as internal communication networks increased. This process was also stimulated by abolishing the high tax on newspapers in 1869. Removal of the tax created the conditions necessary for the advent of the popular press at the end of century.

The issue of poor relief generated heated debate, particularly in the early 1850s. The eventual result was an 1854 law which assigned the primary task of poor relief to private organizations (which in the Dutch case chiefly meant the churches), with the state ostensibly playing only a secondary role. In the nation's schools, these roles were reversed. The constitution, which had guaranteed "free" education, stipulated that education was subject to regulation by law. The state was thus responsible for providing adequate instruction throughout the country. This provision generated acrimonious and long-lasting strife, and the "School Conflict" would remain an important political issue until the early twentieth century. Just as in the debate over poor relief, the fierceness of the School Conflict had much to do with the role of religion and the churches in a society which had long been divided along religious lines. Although church and state were formally separated in 1848, they continued to confront each other in public life as they both struggled to gain influence.

Religious Developments and the "School Conflict"

At mid-century, most Dutch belonged either to the Dutch Reformed church (around 55 percent) or the Roman Catholic church (35 to 40 percent). In addition there were various small Protestant churches, as well as two Jewish denominations. The Reformed church, regulated by royal statute in 1816, was the legal successor to the Calvinistic Reformed church of the Dutch Republic. Its leaders wanted it to become an inclusive national church and hence were committed to minimizing dogmatic distinctives that might cause offense. Theologically, the Groningen school, with P. Hofstede de Groot as its most important figure, initially dominated the church. They believed that faith had been corroded by Enlightenment rationalism, and as an antidote stressed the spiritual inspiration and moral guidance of the Bible in general and of the Gospels in particular. Within these margins they left individuals a good deal of room to decide matters for themselves.

Over the course of the century, the Groningen school increasingly was assaulted from two different directions. Orthodox Calvinists rejected the looseness of Groningen theology. Many of them had already forsaken the official church for their own conventicles, and these partly served as the basis for their *Afscheiding* (secession) from the Reformed church in 1834, under the leadership of the pastors H. de Cock and H.P. Scholte. The separatists wanted to maintain strict adherence, both in letter and spirit, to the church confessions written at the time of the Dutch Revolt. At approximately the same time, the so-called *Reveil* appeared, an orthodox revival movement led mostly by aristocrats. It placed much emphasis on personal religious experience and living life according to Christian principles. This group remained within the Dutch Reformed church. Among their most important representatives was G. Groen van Prinsterer, who worked out, in theory and practice, the political consequences of his religious beliefs. He gave ideological form to what he called the anti-revolutionary or Christian-historical impulse. Anti-revolutionary meant opposition to the principles of the French Revolution, which put humanity rather than God at the center of its thought. Groen also believed that by virtue of its historical development the Netherlands was a Christian (i.e., an orthodox Protestant) nation, and that the country's political leadership ought to pursue policies which reflected this history. Long a solitary voice in political life, in the 1850s Groen became Thorbecke's most formidable and principled opponent in the Second Chamber.

The Groningen school was also challenged by increasing numbers of those who, influenced by the Enlightenment and modern science, strongly emphasized the role of reason, including in matters of faith. Religious modernism, with J.H. Scholten as one of its principal advocates, laid the basis for a number of liberal Protestant currents which began to proliferate both inside and outside the Dutch Reformed church. Modernism also fostered a decreasing interest in church affairs, as well as declines in church attendance and membership. In many

respects, these divergent developments paralleled the patterns which had characterized Dutch Protestantism in the old Republic.

In contrast to the multiplicitous character of Protestantism, Dutch Roman Catholics managed to present a unified face to the outside world, although internally there were many disagreements. The formal equality given to all faiths in the Batavian Republic in 1796 had not invariably led to equal status and equal treatment of everyone. Catholics especially had encountered dif-

1853 caricature of Catholic-liberal cooperation during Thorbecke's first cabinet. Standing around the table are government ministers, the pope, and two bishops. Above the table an angel unfurls a scroll with the text: "Freedom of conscience." Resistance of the April Movement led to the fall of the cabinet. (Atlas van Stolk, Rotterdam.)

ficulty under William I. The official separation of church and state in 1848 finally gave the Dutch Roman Catholic church the opportunity to organize itself as it saw fit. In 1853 – for the first time since the sixteenth century – Rome was able to appoint a church hierarchy to the Netherlands, and established five sees, united under the archbishopric of Utrecht. The Thorbecke cabinet, acting in conformity with the new constitution, did nothing to hinder these efforts. But restoration of Catholic sees triggered a strong protest known as the April Movement. Many Dutch believed that the Protestant character of the nation was now in danger. The April Movement failed to stop the Catholic sees, but it did bring down the Thorbecke government; conservative opponents of Thorbecke used the excitement as an occasion to install a cabinet more to their liking.

The April Movement demonstrated that liberals and Catholics had common interests, and consequently they decided to cooperate with each other. Catholics and liberal cooperation was, by nineteenth century patterns, rather unusual, but it can be compared to the unionist alliance of Catholics and liberals in Belgium in the years after 1830. The Dutch Catholic-liberal alliance, however, would not be of long duration. Once the new Catholic ecclesiastical organization had been securely established, and once Catholics began to perceive their own social and cultural emancipation as primary goals, it became apparent that Catholic interests hardly coincided with the aims of the heavily secularized liberals. Their differences were especially evident on educational issues. In 1868, the Dutch bishops issued a pastoral letter emphasizing that Catholics needed their own schools. This helped make the School Conflict the defining issue in Dutch politics during the late nineteenth century.

The School Conflict

The School Conflict was a complicated issue. Ultimately, it was a battle about the character and content of the nation's educational system. Batavian educational reform supposed that education should transcend religious sectarianism and stress broadly Christian and social virtues. This principle had since been more or less maintained; and in practice it contributed, along with other secularizing forces in Dutch society, to an areligious, or at least undogmatic, atmosphere in the country's schools. Obviously, persons who assigned religion a central place in education could not be pleased with this situation. Orthodox Protestants in particular were quick to register their unhappiness. They wanted their own biblical faith to serve as the foundation of their children's education. The role of religion in the schools of a religiously divided nation was a thorny problem, and Groen tried to solve it by proposing that the state found religious schools to accommodate each of the country's various religious groups. Others found Groen's proposal for "public denominational schools" either politically unattainable or inadequate, and preferred to establish their own private religious schools, a right specifically granted in the Constitution of 1848.

Political and social developments after 1848 proved that the "public denominational schools" were beyond reach. The first School Law under the new constitution, authored by the orthodox Reformed cabinet minister J.J.L. van der Brugghen and passed in 1857, left Groen and other proponents of this proposals deeply dissatisfied. Meanwhile, a new generation of liberals, much less reluctant to use state intervention than Thorbecke and his associates, increasingly regarded education as an important instrument in the shaping of both the individual and society. Education in the first half of the nineteenth century, of course, also pursued social aims, namely the preservation of the social order. But these young liberals believed that society would best be served by a well-educated and enlightened population, and that education would bring progress. Religious education played little or no role in their vision. These ideals were at the heart of the Minister J. Kappeyne van de Coppello's School Law of 1878, a law which both substantially raised the quality of Dutch education and which contained strongly secularizing elements.

In contrast, the advocates of religiously based schools had to make do with establishing and financing their own private schools. By 1860, Groen himself conceded that this was the best that could be done. These proponents also set up a host of coordinating and activist organizations, and launched a spirited campaign against the liberals' educational policy in 1872. They were particularly active against Kappeyne's proposals in the late 1870s. By now the real question was no longer the character of Dutch education but how it would be financed. Public schools (with the exception of schools for the poor) were not free, but they received a lot of government revenue. This money came from taxes raised in part from parents who sent their children to the private religious schools, while private schools had to fend for themselves. Many of these "special" schools thus faced financial difficulties, especially after state quality standards were applied to them. One solution to this problem was to subsidize private education. But liberals opposed this course, regarding private religious schools as narrow-minded, old-fashioned, and of low quality. They also feared that doing so would further divide the nation and maintained that such subsidies would be in conflict with the constitution. Thus by the 1870s, the two hostile parties arrayed against each other showed no signs of compromise on the school issue.

New Organizational Forms in Politics and Society

The School Conflict was also so important because it played a substantial role in the formation of "modern" political parties, whose advent in the 1870s coincided with the increasingly sharp debate over the schools. It is not that ideology or interest was absent from Dutch politics in the years before 1870, but that individuals, rather than groups, expressed these ideologies or interests. Local or regional electoral societies usually played only a subordinate and not very politically minded role. Gradually, cooperation on the basis of shared viewpoints and programs became more important. National politics became more significant, and amorphous political currents and tendencies increasingly coalesced into parties in the stricter sense of the word.

Meanwhile, the conservatives were losing more and more ground. After the parliamentary battles of the mid-1860s and the formulation of a new colonial policy in 1870, they possessed few political issues. The so-called conservative-liberals also disappeared in the course of the 1860s. This left the political firmament to liberals of various stripes, and they used this opportunity to transform the Netherlands, in many respects, into a liberal state and society. The new liberals succeeding Thorbecke (who died in 1872) were not afraid to use the state for what they regarded as beneficent purposes. In addition to Kappeyne (see above), S. van Houten also deserves mention as the author of the country's first social welfare law: the so-called Child Law of 1874, which prohibited children under the age of twelve from working in factories.

Arrayed against the liberals were the religious groups. They sought to give their faith a place in politics, and sooner or later developed their own parties; these became known as confessional parties since their founders regarded church doctrinal confessions as the basis of their own political action. The "confessionals" thus more or less took the place of the conservatives, and they retained many conservative elements in their own thought. Orthodox Protestants and Catholics shared a number of "confessional" concerns, but their theological differences and their sharply divergent views of the nation's past – and thus its present – also led to frequent disagreements between them. Moreover, orthodox Protestants developed a tighter political organization much sooner than did the Catholics.

The mobilization of these opposition movements also fostered the social emancipation of Catholics and orthodox Protestants of the lower classes, "the people behind the voters," who were prevented by the stringent voting requirements from direct political influence. The orthodox Protestants were now led by Abraham Kuyper, successor to Groen (who died in 1876). Kuyper poured boundless energy into the cause, both within the Dutch Reformed church and in the political system, developing a stimulating ideology which would be of considerable influence. Within the Reformed church, Kuyper became the leader of what increasingly became the orthodox "party." The national synod, which tried hard to keep all factions within the church, found it increasingly difficult to do so, especially after the reorganization of 1867, when lay members, now exercising the vote, began to assert their own views. In his campaigns, Kuyper introduced an important innovation: the mass press. Kuyper made *De Heraut* (*The Herald*) his mouthpiece for church issues in 1871, and a year later established *De Standaard* to promote his political views. He also helped establish Protestant schools and was active in organizing petition drives against cabinet policy.

The activities of the League Against the School Law became the direct catalyst in the formation of the country's first national party in 1878: the Anti-Revolutionary Party (ARP). It was Kuyper who authored "Our Program," the new party's platform. The ARP both explicitly and systematically nominated candidates, developed political strategies, and consulted with their members in parliament, who now banded together into a functioning parliamentary party. Through their organization, the orthodox Protestants, long a factor in Dutch public life, had found a new way to defend their interests. They now began to contest the social legacy of the overwhelmingly liberal, progress-oriented, and often religiously indifferent bourgeoisie.

The Catholics also mobilized themselves, although their collective organizational form sometimes varied from the orthodox Protestants. Roman Catholics also rejected the secularizing tendencies of Dutch society. Their concerns went beyond a mere desire to hold fast to old forms and old ideas. Just like the orthodox Protestants, they fought for the social and cultural emancipation of their own people, who felt, not without reason, that they had been discriminated against by the liberal bourgeoisie. To a certain extent, the Catholics sought to exert their own influence on the country's public life, and hence were resistant to the interventions of the "neutral" state and to the host of "neutral" private initiatives. Increasingly, they, like the orthodox Protestants, came to prefer their own organizations.

But Catholics and orthodox Protestants were divided by fundamental religious differences and the role of their faith within Dutch traditions. Whereas orthodox Protestants asserted that the Netherlands was by nature a Protestant country, Catholics took great pains to express their loyalty, arguing that they had as much a right to determine the nation's future as did their Protestant neighbors. Another striking difference lay in the highly diverse organizational life of the orthodox Protestants, made more complex by subtle differences among Protestant groups, and the apparent unity of the Roman Catholic church. Catholics had many differences and disagreements among themselves – between clergy and laity, secular and regular clergy, and between diverse social groups – but their one church and its (frequently) direct ties with other Catholic organizations gave them a single point of reference.

In contrast, orthodox Protestants – despite their common sense of purpose and commitment to same traditions and values – were divided into various factions within the Dutch Reformed church and many, sometimes tiny, denominations, most of which were rooted in the *Afscheiding* of 1834. All of them claimed to be Reformed, but they often differed sharply with each other on theological matters. They were much more united politically, especially during the first phase of the School Conflict, since such unity was necessary to construct a common front against their politically and religiously liberal opponents (many of whom also belonged to the Reformed church). Their common purpose also brought them close to the Catholics, at least for the time being. But no one in 1878 could predict the degree of cooperation that Catholics and orthodox Protestants were ready to accord each other.

The 1870s thus witnessed the advent of new impulses that would transform Dutch society. One of these impulses sprang from the liberal segment of the bourgeoisie, who had decisively defeated the conservatives and began their own optimistic, energetic, and progressive efforts to "modernize" the country. But another stemmed no less from their confessional opponents, who had become more assertive in insisting that their own ideas play a major role in the formation of Dutch society. Both groups increasingly saw the necessity of expanding the opportunities for those who did not belong to the country's privileged classes. This in itself was an important new impulse, precipitating further social ferment – and the potential for new tensions.

The intense political conflicts did not corrode national unity, despite some fear that they would. The nation's indivisibility was widely taken for granted, and it was continually stressed. Virtually all political parties and factions expressed their commitment to the whole nation and its prosperity, and Catholics and orthodox Protestants, however much they attempted to attain their own respective places in Dutch society, were no less committed to this goal. That various opposing groups and traditions could coexist in one society was, moreover, hardly a new experience for the Dutch. The Republic, after all, had contained not only precisianists and libertines within the Reformed church, but Protestant dissenters, Jews, and Catholics as well.

2. The "Modernization" of the Netherlands (1870s-1918)

During the last quarter of the nineteenth and first decade of the twentieth centuries, the Netherlands experienced rapid change. This was true of nearly every aspect of society: demography, infrastructure, economics, politics, religion, and culture. These changes found their basis in the developments that had transpired before the 1870s. All of the changes had their own logic, dynamic, and rhythm, but were clearly related and mutually reinforced each other. Such developments, frequently called "modernization," took place throughout the Western world at some point in the nineteenth and twentieth centuries. By the end of the nineteenth century, the Netherlands increasingly resembled other "modern" nations. It possessed a parliamentary democracy with mass parties as the chief political actors, a government that slowly but surely increased its grip over society, a growing capitalistic economy with a strong international orientation, a secularizing mass culture which encouraged national feeling, and an increased number of elitist scientific and artistic cultures that were marked by a high degree of individualism and by extensive international contacts. But the Netherlands also exhibited its own particular characteristics, the most striking of which was the reorganization of traditional religious communities in an age of secularization and mass politics.

Economic and Social Dynamics

The population of the Netherlands dramatically increased from the last quarter of nineteenth century. From just over four million in 1879, the population numbered well over five million in 1899, and some seven million in 1920. Economic expansion accompanied demographic growth, witnessed by the increased economies of scale, and technical and organizational innovations in all economic sectors. Dutch industry also increased in scale, although its growth was initially slowed by the severe international depression of the 1880s. A decade later, however, industrial activity exploded, contributing substantially to the economic growth and prosperity of the country. The Netherlands thus joined the ranks of industrialized nations. But industry never dominated its economy; agriculture, trade, services, and the colonies remained equally important components of a strongly diversified economy.

The agricultural sector experienced a severe economic depression from the late 1870s until the 1890s, and there was good reason to fear that cheap foreign foodstuffs would lead to its complete collapse. Conditions improved, however, before the turn of the century: new production techniques, use of fertilizers, and better organization (cooperatives, dairies, auctions, etc.) laid the basis for renewed economic health, particularly in dairy farming and horticulture. New business ventures in the Dutch East Indies, capitalizing on the Colonial Law of 1870, expanded the range of products available. Some were indispensable for new forms of industry: oil, tin, and rubber exports played an important role alongside more traditional products like rice, coffee, tea, and sugar.

This economic expansion was both linked to and dependent upon the full development of modern capitalism in the Netherlands, which replaced the hitherto dominant trade capitalism. The new capitalism made much more intensive use of all the means of production (raw material, labor, and capital) than had before been the case. During the years of depression, the new economics only worsened the plight of the lowest classes of the populace. The wretched conditions existent among the country's many poor also became much more obvious with the rise of large factories and fast-growing cities; these developments corroded the traditional social structure and sharpened differences between the working class and the bourgeoisie. At the same time, the upper classes grew more sensitive to the predicament of the lower classes. The standard of living among the lower classes – particularly the urban proletariat – was no longer defined as a problem of poverty (which could be ameliorated with poor relief) but as "the Social Question." Its solution became a central political issue in the years around the turn of the century.

But economic growth also laid the basis for an unprecedented rise in the country's standard of living, although for the time being prosperity lagged behind Belgium and its strongly expanding economy. Naturally, the higher classes, especially the successful entrepreneurs among them, were the first to enjoy the fruits of the new prosperity. But the middle groups also improved their own positions in the wake of economic growth; this further strengthened the already strongly bourgeois character of Dutch society. Since the late eighteenth century, the bourgeoisie had been engaged in a largely successful "civilizing offensive" aimed at reforming Dutch manners and mores. One of the offensive's chief effects was a dominant system of values and norms practiced throughout Dutch society, which expressed itself in a complex set of rules regulating moral behavior. A virtuous, frugal, hard-working, and self-controlled family with the father as provider, the mother as housewife, and the children in a naturally subordinate position was the centerpiece of this morality. Patriotism was encouraged and authority was to be obeyed. Respecting the social order was a cardinal virtue, but one could rise above one's social station through hard work, intelligence, and persistence. Liberal individualism, after all, was just as much a part of the nineteenth-century bourgeois moral world as was deference to the social order. The "civilizing offensive" had long prop-

Pieter Jelles Troelstra speaks to a mass gathering in The Hague in support of the universal franchise. (Internationaal Instituut voor Sociale Geschiedenis, Amsterdam.)

agated these virtues through education and a host of social initiatives, and it now concentrated these efforts on the working classes.

These working classes also profited, usually in the long run, from the general rise in prosperity. In fact, increased purchasing power among wide segments of the population played no small role in the expansion of the economy. Buoyed both by their increasing wealth and better schooling, workers became more confident and followed the middle-class example in asserting their own voice. The most effective way to do this was unquestionably by organizing themselves and using the popular press. Unions and political parties were the most important organizations amidst the host of burgeoning organizations for workers.

A modern workers' movement was thus able to develop. The old tradition of rather directionless, incidental (and occasionally revolutionary) outbursts of social unrest was replaced by a movement that used calculated strategies to improve the plight of the workers. A reform-minded, social democratic wing would become the most important and

"All the rail work shall stand still, if your mighty arm it wills,". Drawing by Albert Hahn on the occasion of the Railway Strike of 1903. (Internationaal Instituut voor Sociale Geschiedenis, Amsterdam.)

by far the largest faction in the Dutch workers' movement, but its triumph was by no means evident in the late nineteenth century. The General Dutch Laborers' Union (ANWV), founded in 1871, with its ties to progressive liberalism was initially the most important labor group. Under the inspirational leadership of Ferdinand Domela Nieuwenhuis, the Social Democratic Alliance (SDB, 1881) developed a revolutionary character and tended, over time, toward anarchism. The Social Democratic Workers Party (SDAP) began as a dissenting faction within the SDB but became an independent party in 1894. The SDAP represented a part of the workers' movement which relied on Marxist theories of historical materialism, but the party was at the same time committed to social reform through parliamentary government.

This contradiction in the SDAP, mirroring a pattern in international social democracy, found its counterpart in the trade union movement. Some unions openly organized themselves for conflict and revolution, relying on the militant sentiments of their members. Other unions were much more cautious, emphasizing the importance of solid organization and well-financed strike funds. They also adopted a long-term perspective on fundamental improvements. The National Workers' Secretariat (NAS), founded in 1893, eventually represented the more revolutionary line with its ideological ties to syndicalism. It wanted trade unions to play a dominant role in a future socialist order. Other important unions, first and foremost the General Dutch Diamond Workers' Alliance, chose a less revolutionary course, and in 1906 these moderate groups merged, becoming the Dutch Alliance of Workers' Unions (NVV). Henri Polak was the driving force behind this movement. Numerically, the NVV would come to dwarf the other socialist unions.

The year 1903 proved decisive in determining the course of the country's various socialist groups. The government attempted to strengthen its hand after a successful railroad strike in that year. When labor groups attempted to counter with a general strike they failed completely, and they were forced to reconsider their position. The SDAP, led by P.J. Troelstra, J.H. Schaper, and W.H. Vliegen, and the nascent NVV now chose more decisively for a gradualist route, working for realizable goals within the existent political system – all the while maintaining their socialist ideology and their vision for a classless society. The party's revolutionary side would play an occasional role in the socialists' political activities, but the more radical elements within the SDAP were purged in 1909. The radicals formed their own Social Democratic Party (SDP), which would later become the Dutch branch of international communism. But the more revolutionary or orthodox Marxist groups, although not entirely without influence in trade unionism and politics, remained small. Despite their appeals to the working class, most workers preferred a less revolutionary strategy.

Marxist theory had assumed that the working class would be attracted en masse to socialism, but even the more moderate socialist organizations were unable to recruit the bulk of Dutch workers to their cause. Their "modern movement" (as it was called) faced stiff competition from religious workers' movements. In part in reaction to a radical and "dangerous" socialism and in part as a religiously inspired response to the Social Question, Catholics and orthodox Protestants established a host of their own workers' associations, which were integrated into the web of Catholic and Protestant organizations. Patrimonium, founded by K. Kater in 1876, was an early orthodox Protestant workers' association. It was originally an offshoot of the ANWV, which in the long run proved unable to compete with socialist or confessional organizations. In the 1890s, the Christian National Workingman's Alliance (CNWB) was established specifically for Dutch Reformed workers. The Roman Catholic People's Alliance and the Roman Catholic Workers' Association (both dating from 1888) were their Catholic counterparts. Like the socialists, the confessionals were deeply divided over which organizations and what kind of activism would be most appropriate. In particular, Catholics, led by priests such as A. Ariëns and H.A. Poels, and laity like P.J.M. Aalberse, were engaged in an acrimonious and extended argument over whether workers should first be organized as workers (and thus have a class-based organization) or according to their profession (and thus belong to a professional organization). Bishops finally imposed a compromise on both sides in 1915.

All of the confessional workers' organizations rejected the notion of class struggle that played so important a role, at least initially, in socialist thought. Instead, they sought harmonious cooperation among the various social groups, with each group performing its own important task. The Christian Social Congress of 1891 (in which Kuyper again played a prominent role) and the papal encyclical *Rerum Novarum* of the same year both provided religious rationales for using political action to improve the plight of the workers. Attempts to establish an interdenominational trade union movement failed to take off, not least because in 1906 and 1912 Catholic bishops expressly forbade their flocks to participate. But partly as a response to the events of 1903, large trade unions like the NVV soon also became dominant in confessional circles. The Christian National Trade Union Alliance was founded by influential Protestants like A.S. Talma in 1909, the same year as the Roman Catholic Trade Union. The latter union changed its name several times: it became the Roman Catholic Workers' Union (RKWV, 1925), the Catholic Workers' Movement (KAB, 1945) and the Dutch Catholic Trade Union (NKV, 1963).

Church and Society

Change did not only impact the country's economic, political and social life but affected religious developments as well. The modernization of Dutch society, accompanied by the triumphs of science, growing urbanization, and material progress, fostered increasing religious indifference. The percentage of Dutch claiming no religious affiliation was further boosted by the increasing habit of those with only casual ties to the institutional church to register themselves as having "no religion." In the census of 1879, only a fraction of 1 percent claimed to be unchurched; by 1920, it was nearly 8 percent. Attempts by religious liberals to reconcile faith and reason in new ways, often through morality or personal experience, appealed only to small numbers of people. Orthodox Protestants and Catholics were more effective in turning the tide of unbelief. Both groups could count on the powerful resurgence of traditional religion, evident throughout the nineteenth century, which showed no signs of dissipating at the century's end. These religious movements did not simply attempt to reverse the secular tide; they exhibited sincere religious enthusiasm and an intense search for spiritual fulfillment. For many Catholics and Protestants of this period, faith was not restricted to church activities but was supposed to serve as the foundation for both personal and public activity.

Building on past achievement and their newfound sense of purpose, the orthodox Protestant and Catholic segments of the population were able to both assert their influence over all of Dutch society and turn their subcultures into well-organized religious bulwarks. Centuries old, religious differences continued to divide these two groups, and efforts to unite the two in a single Christian movement foundered. But they did achieve a measure of cooperation.

The Catholics, constituting roughly 35 percent of the population throughout the period, managed to present a relatively unified front to the outside world, despite the sometimes sharp conflicts among themselves. The Roman Catholic church stood in the center of the Catholic subculture, with its clergy, and particularly its bishops, serving as the subculture's leaders, both publicly and behind the scenes. Catholics placed a high premium on intensifying their religious life. Pilgrimages, acts of piety, and religious brotherhoods all attained great popularity. They also established an exceedingly dense network of Catholic organizations, designed both to improve their standing in society and to create religious esprit de corps. Farmers, horticulturalists, the lower middle classes, and especially the workers (which were regarded as particularly vulnerable to irreligion) all had their own associations. Neo-Thomism became the dominant intellectual strain in Catholicism, not only because it strengthened Catholics' ties to the Middle Ages and Catholic tradition, but because for many Catholics it offered a more or less satisfactory faith that could stand in the modern age. The philosophy, based both on Catholic scholasticism and new insights into the thought of Thomas Aquinas, held that the natural and the supernatural were united in a higher synthesis. This philosophy made it possible for Catholics to participate fully in social and cultural life – in the natural world – without forsaking their faith.

Political Catholicism, which rejected both liberalism and socialism as godless ideologies, only managed to organize itself with difficulty in the Netherlands. This was due in part to the fact that Dutch Catholics were heavily concentrated in the south of the country, making Catholic candidates in these districts virtually unbeatable and seemingly precluding any need for tight organization. Political cohesion, however, did increase over time, especially after *Rerum Novarum*'s appearance in 1891, when a more progressive Christian Democratic ideology began to eclipse the quite conservative patterns of Catholic political practice that had hitherto been dominant. The beginnings of a national Catholic party date from 1896, when the country's Catholic electoral associations finally accepted a common political program written by the priest-politician H. Schaepman back in 1883. It would not be until 1926, however, that the Roman Catholic State Party (RKSP) was officially established. In the meantime, both Schaepman and his successor, the cleric W.H. Nolens, succeeded in getting Catholic parliamentarians to work more closely together.

By the 1880s, tensions within the religiously diverse Dutch Reformed church had reached a crisis point, and in 1886 the tensions led to a new church split, known as the *Doleantie*. Kuyper and many of his orthodox followers left the Reformed church, and in 1892, after difficult negotiations, they merged with the *Afgescheidenen* who had left the Reformed church in 1834. Together, they constituted the Reformed Churches in the Netherlands, which included 7 or 8 percent of the country's population. The new denomination would now function as the core of Calvinist orthodoxy in the Netherlands. But it is important to note that a number of other, very small orthodox denominations continued to exist, and that many orthodox Protestants remained within the Dutch Reformed church, which, they held, still possessed its providential mission to the Dutch nation.

In 1906 most orthodox Protestants remaining in the Dutch Reformed church organized themselves into the Reformed Alliance. Religious liberals did the same, establishing the Association of Reformed Liberals in 1913. Religious liberals were also well represented in some of the smaller religious groups like the Remonstrants, the Mennonites, and the Lutherans. This picture illustrates the deep divisions in Dutch Protestantism, both within the numerically large Dutch Reformed church (almost 55 percent of the population in 1879 and still over 40 percent in 1920) and outside of it, in the smaller denominations.

These divisions frequently stemmed from an intense religious faith and a desire to see that faith put into practice in society. The orthodox Protestant bulwark was particularly active in this regard, and many of its premier institutions were Kuyper's creations: the Anti-Revolutionary Party, the Reformed Churches in the Netherlands, *De Heraut*, *De Standaard*, Patrimonium, orthodox Protestant schools and the Free University, established in 1880 to give the orthodox their own center of higher learning. Kuyper was not only adept at institution building and encouraging orthodox faith, he also developed a theological justification for these activities in a doctrine he called "particular and common grace." Briefly summarized, Kuyper held that God's grace was not restricted to the particular grace he bestowed on those he predestined for salvation, but that he extended a common grace to all of society, thus limiting the ruinous effects of original sin. Kuyper also articulated the notion of "sphere sovereignty," which held that most spheres of human activity do not stem from the state, nor owe their allegiance or their existence to it, but possess their own authority – their own sovereignty. Sphere sovereignty helped explain why many held that the confessionals should be able to establish their own organizations instead of relying on the state's "neutral" interventions. Despite Kuyper's social activism, the orthodox Protestant emphasis on personal religious experience could also lead to a retreat from the world into one's own subculture. This was especially true of the Calvinist pietists, whose communal life was principally devoted to discerning who belonged to God's elect.

Socially, the bulk of orthodox Protestants ostensibly consisted of the lower middle classes – the "common folk," as Kuyper called his followers. But at the same time it found wide support across social classes; many of the ARP's parliamentary representatives, for example, were aristocrats. Geographically, orthodox Protestants could be found throughout the country (except, of course, in the Catholic South) but were especially numerous in the country's diagonal "Bible belt," which stretched from Zeeland in the southwest to Groningen in the northeast.

Orthodox Protestantism was not able to sustain a united political front, and in the 1890s, it split into two separate parties. There were many issues contributing to the break: the degree to which orthodox Protestants should rely only on each other, Kuyper's leadership style, the extent to which party discipline was desirable, and the importance of the Social Question and extension of the voting franchise. It was the last issue which became the final straw. In 1894, a group of Anti-Revolutionaries, led by A.F. de Savornin Lohman, found that the proposals for extending the vote, authored by the liberal minister J.P. Tak van Poortvliet and supported by most Anti-Revolutionaries, went too far, and they left the ARP. This group later merged with several others and in 1908 became the Christian Historical Union (CHU), which relied on an electorate stemming almost exclusively from the Dutch Reformed church. The ARP now increasingly depended on its voter base within the Reformed Churches in the Netherlands.

Political Conflict and Pillarization
"The Same Root of Faith"

By 1900 the Dutch political parties had become expressions of the country's most important developments and contrasts. The emerging political system was now characterized by growing political mobilization (the mass party), the intensification of organization and communication (the mass press), and the inclusion of ever wider segments of the population in the political process (democratization). The liberals, who had come to dominate and "modernize" state and society in the course of the nineteenth century, managed to maintain their grip over social and cultural developments. But politically they were challenged by powerful confessional and (later) socialist movements with their own political agendas. The liberals were forced to better organize themselves, and in 1885 they established the Liberal Union as a national umbrella organization. But the liberals, too, split apart over issues such as the voting franchise and the desired degree of state intervention. The most progressive liberals founded the Liberal Democratic Alliance (VDB) in 1901, while the more conservative group became the Free Liberals in 1905. The winner-take-all district system forced the liberal parties to cooperate, however.

Cooperation was no less important for the opponents of the liberals, who contested the dominant liberal vision for society. But such cooperation was difficult to achieve. A confessional-socialist alliance was still not a possibility, and the confessionals themselves were divided along religious lines. Liberals, socialists, Protestants, and Catholics all remained wary of each other. It was only during the electoral struggle against the liberals that the Catholics and the Anti-Revolutionaries managed, after much difficulty, to cobble an alliance together, which the Christian Historicals later joined. Kuyper and Schaepman were the architects of the alliance, and it was Kuyper the virtuoso who again was able to express the ideological underpinnings of the new entente. The most substantial divide between human beings, Kuyper wrote, was between Christians and "pagans," that is, people he regarded as unbelievers, including liberal Protestants. Kuyper's "antithesis" between believers and unbelievers was to serve as the basis of cooperation between orthodox Protestants and Catholics, who shared "the same root of faith." Together, they could defend their freedoms and principles against the unbelievers who ostensibly opposed them.

The new "coalition" sounded more principled than it actually was. It could be highly successful in elections, and after 1887 – when the voting franchise was extended – the confessionals managed on several occasions to win a majority in the Second Chamber. But their success did not eliminate tensions among them. The coalition only worked because Catholics were prepared to accept Protestant domination in confessional cabinets – even though Catholics were a much larger group. The prime minister of these cabinets was invariably a Protestant (including Kuyper, who served between 1901 and 1905). The political emancipation of Catholics thus remained limited. The role of Catholics in state, society, and culture was much greater than it had been in 1800, but they still had a long way to go. A subtle combination of liberal condescension toward orthodox belief in general and toward Catholic "hocus pocus" in particular, and a Protestant arrogance about Protestantism as "the fundamental tone of the Dutch national character" continued to relegate Catholics to a second-class status.

Despite these tensions, most of the electoral competition in the decades after 1880 was fought between the liberals and the confessionals. The socialists remained weak as long as the restricted franchise excluded many of their supporters from voting. But slowly the franchise was extended, and in 1913 the election of fifteen socialists to parliament prevented both the liberal "concentration" and the confessionals from attaining a majority. The liberal parties, which campaigned on a socially progressive platform, offered the SDAP a place in a prospective cabinet. The liberals' offer presented the socialists with a dilemma: should they accept in order to pass reforms favorable to the workers, or should they refuse to become junior partners in a "bourgeois" government ruling over a "bourgeois" society? After heated internal debate, the SDAP decided to reject the offer – a choice that the party would soon regret.

"Pacification" of the School Conflict

The issues stoking Dutch political life from the 1880s until the First World War were the School Conflict, the franchise, and the Social Question. By this time, the School Conflict was chiefly about subsidies. In the late 1880s, the liberals abandoned the hard-line position which they had successfully asserted in 1878, now saying that they did not find subsidies to private schools at variance with the constitution. In exchange they received badly needed confessional support for the constitutional changes of 1887 that were necessary to widen the franchise.

This liberal concession was a first step toward the denouement of the School Conflict. A small government subsidy for private schools was granted as early as 1889. In subsequent years, the subsidy was increased, leading to the proliferation of private schools. This trend reached its logical conclusion in the School Law of 1917, which, in effect, gave public and private schools equal access to government financing. The Dutch refer to the 1917 law as the "pacification" of the School Conflict. During times of relative political calm, parliament also took measures to both improve and expand the educational system. School was made compulsory in 1901, the capstone of a whole century of educational reform which had begun under the Batavians in 1805.

Aletta Jacobs.

The Struggle for the Franchise

The growing participation of numerous social groups in public life made it clear that the very restricted voting franchise dating from the mid-nineteenth century was no longer adequate. Liberals in particular became convinced that voting rights must be expanded, but Kuyper, too, stood to gain from appealing to, as he had put it, "the people behind the voters." The chief issues were how far, how fast, and on what basis the extension of the franchise should take place. These were difficult and divisive issues, since many politicians found universal suffrage unacceptable. The constitutional change of 1887, sponsored by the liberals, made a further extension of the franchise possible. Ironically, it was the confessionals who benefitted most from the expanded franchise, and they now had the numbers to challenge the liberals head on.

In the 1890s progressive liberals like Tak van Poortvliet proposed a near-universal male franchise, which would exclude only the desti-

1918 propaganda poster of the Society for the Enfranchisement of Women. A woman holds the torch of "womens' insight," and knocks on the door of the polling place, saying "Let me in – I bring new light."

tute. After fierce debate, opponents defeated the proposal in 1894. Nevertheless, the franchise was further extended when, in 1896, parliament passed a bill authored by the liberal minister Van Houten, which now allowed hitherto ineligible men to vote on the basis of their salaries, rents, educations, savings, and so forth. As noted above, the socialists were thus able to strengthen their electoral position. In 1917, another constitutional change made universal male suffrage a reality.

An important component of the franchise debate concerned the nascent women's movement of the late nineteenth century, which demanded that women receive the right to vote. This multifaceted feminist movement, led by women such as Aletta Jaccbs, Mina Kruseman, and Wilhelmina Drucker, was also active in other areas, such as securing equal rights and opportunities for women. The movement was successful in opening the workplace and schools to women, but its influence was too small to secure the voting franchise for women; "universal" suffrage still meant only men, right down to the Electoral Law of 1917. Two years later, however, women were given the right to vote. The long process of attaining women's suffrage symbolizes the difficulties confronting the wide-ranging women's movement in the Netherlands. Other issues usually took political precedence. One may plausibly draw connections between the relatively low priority assigned to women's issues and the housewife's role that was given to women in Dutch bourgeois culture, the relatively small number of working women in the middle and upper classes, and the strong position of the country's confessional groups.

The Social Question

The position of women was also related to the much larger Social Question, but in this context, too, their condition was considered a side issue next to the desperate plight of the urban lower classes. Ethical considerations, social compassion, and the realization that the impoverished constituted a threat to the social order all demanded that the Social Question be solved. Before the 1880s, Van Houten's Child Law of 1874 had been the only piece of social legislation, and without the necessary inspections, it remained toothless. But the great social misery of that decade – and the violent Amsterdam Eel Riot of 1886 – prompted the government to act. Once again, it was the progressive liberals who took the lead in sponsoring reform measures, which were designed to both guarantee the working classes a more decent existence and to integrate them into "bourgeois" society. Between 1890 and 1910, a good deal of social legislation was passed, most notably through "the social justice cabinet" of Pierson-Goeman Borgesius (1897-1901). These new laws would serve as the basis for the growing social welfare state of the twentieth century.

The confessionals also supported this trend and made their own contributions in coalition cabinets with the liberals. In all of this, socialist agitation provided a powerful stimulus for reform. There was sharp disagreement, of course, about the speed, nature, and composition of these laws, and about the role of the state. However, there was enough consensus for passing a series of protective measures around 1900 that would become the foundation of a social insurance. But a universal state pension system – an important goal in both progressive liberal and socialist circles – failed to be enacted. Part of the reason was that the confessionals opposed the state having too great a role, preferring a network of private social service organizations that would allow them to set up their religiously based institutions as desired. From then on, politicians attempted to "solve" the Social Question through educational improvements, through a host of educative activities to ameliorate social problems, and by stimulating consultations between employers and the trade unions.

A Quadripartite Society

Dutch society became increasingly segmented as a result of these changes. The liberal part of the bourgeoisie that had exercised so great an influence over state and society in the nineteenth century now lost much of their power, particularly in the political arena. But because of the disunity of their chief opponents they managed to retain considerable influence, and much of their legacy, such as parliamentary democracy and the free enterprise system, remained intact. Free enterprise, incidentally, was also a central precept of the confessional bourgeoisie, and most Catholic and orthodox Protestant employers did not hesitate to join their liberal colleagues in resisting the growing trade union movement.

The liberals succeeded in keeping their most cherished achievements by avoiding confrontation, making partial concessions, and solving knotty social problems through compromise. In this way, social and political change occurred relatively smoothly. Moreover, most confessionals did not reject many aspects – particularly the morality – of liberal bourgeois society. Social democrats, in turn, were tempted to conclude that coercing reforms for the working class had more tangible benefits than struggling for revolution. For the time being, that revolution seemed doomed to failure, although socialist propaganda continued to proclaim its imminent arrival.

Through all of this, the orthodox Protestant, Catholic, and social democratic population groups each increasingly developed closely knit and easily recognizable subcultures. They established their own organizations everywhere to compete with neutral, or ostensibly neutral, organizations. These subcultures possessed their own practices, their own ethos, and their own variations of the old bourgeois values. Thus Dutch society was increasingly divided into four parts, along the old divisions of religion and class. Years later, the term "pillarization" would be used to describe this arrangement.

National Unity

But this segmentation or even division of Dutch society did not undermine the unity of the nation, state, and society, on the contrary. The constitutional and democratic state increased its role in society and grew stronger rather than weaker. Bourgeois associations, whatever their ideological affiliation, continued to dominate the landscape, and their many shared values contributed to the social cohesion of Dutch society. One could even argue that the growing and increasingly self-evident emphasis on the importance of the nation-state and of national feeling – a trend apparent throughout Europe – forced religious and ideological subcultures to emphasize their own identity. Moreover, the pillars were free to stress their own character precisely because they presented no threat to a basic national unity that was upheld by nearly everyone. Thus pillarized Dutch society exhibited variations of national sentiment and patriotism in each of its subcultures.

In reality, neither pillarization nor a unified national culture held absolute sway in Dutch society. Many of the large ideological "pillars" overlapped; the boundaries between them shifted over time. Furthermore, there were many groups that could not, or would not, fit into these subcultures, and there were always individuals who managed to go their own way. This was especially true in the arts and sciences, which greatly flourished during the period. Some artistic expressions

Vincent van Gogh's Spinning Woman; *water-color from 1884. (Galeria de Arte Theo, Madrid.)*

found their origins in the country's subcultures; architects like P.J.H. Cuypers gave the Catholic-inspired neo-Gothic style a wider application, and his design of the Rijksmuseum in Amsterdam includes various "neo" styles. But most leading Dutch artists found their inspiration in international developments.

Dutch literature was reinvigorated by the Eighty Movement, in which figures like Herman Gorter, Willem Kloos, and Albert Verwey articulated a strongly individualistic style based on the principle of "*l'art pour l'art.*" Their journal, *De Nieuwe Gids* (*The New Guide*), broke with what they perceived as the rigidity of *De Gids*. At the same time, The Hague school was responsible for a new flowering in Dutch art with painters such as G.H. Breitner, Jozef Israels, and the brothers Jacob and Willem Maris. Later, Vincent van Gogh – who spent his most productive years in France – achieved world fame through his connections with the international avant-garde. The Dutch also developed a tradition of high quality musical performance, with the Concertgebouw Orchestra (founded in 1888), and its conductor Willem Mengelberg (appointed in 1895) serving as the standard. Alphons Diepenbrock was perhaps the most prominent among the nation's composers.

After the individualistic tendencies of the 1880s and 1890s, many artists attempted to put their art in the service of society. Not infrequently this prompted them to cultivate ties with the workers' movement, as in the case of the former Eightier Gorter, the poetess Henriëtte Roland Holst, and the architect H.P. Berlage, designer of the famous Amsterdam Produce Exchange. Scholarship was advanced through the expansion of the Dutch universities and their international ties. Dutch scientists were especially prominent in the natural sciences, with many of them winning Nobel prizes. The physicists H.A. Lorentz, H. Kamerlingh Onnes, J.D. van der Waals and P. Zeeman, the chemist J.H. van 't Hoff, and the biologist H. de Vries all achieved great fame, fostering Dutch national pride.

The country's glorious past also fostered this national pride, and many poems were sung and statues erected to commemorate this past. Nationally minded historians like R. Fruin, professor of Dutch history since 1860 and founder of academic history writing in the Netherlands, transformed the country's past into a veritable national epic. P.J. Blok, succeeding Fruin in 1894, soon launched his multivolumed *Geschiedenis van het Nederlandsche Volk* (*History of the Dutch People*). The nationalism of Fruin and Blok, with its liberal and Orangist tendencies, did not satisfy everyone. Many orthodox Protestants preferred more religiously oriented historians like W. Bilderdijk and Groen van Prinsterer, who earlier in the century had stressed the Christian character of the Dutch nation. The Catholics turned to W.J.F. Nuyens, who integrated Catholic history with the national past as their own historian.

Foreign Relations and Colonial Policy

The greatness of the Dutch past dissonated with the Netherlands's politically insignificant international role during the nineteenth century. Participating in the fierce competition of modern imperialism was neither possible nor necessary for the Dutch, and they compensated for their small size by congratulating themselves on their moral superiority. This superiority was chiefly demonstrated in their policy of neutrality, increasingly understood in terms of ethics and international law. The Dutch, including jurists like T.M.C. Asser and C. van Vollenhoven, self-consciously followed in the footsteps of their seventeenth century ancestor Grotius, considered the father of international law. They sponsored two peace conferences in The Hague (1899 and 1907), and the 1913 completion of the Peace Palace in the same city strengthened their self-image as lovers of peace.

The Dutch also assiduously fostered cultural ties with their ethnic cousins. The Boers of South Africa were the descendants of Dutch settlers, and on these grounds the nation enthusiastically supported their war against the British at the turn of the century. An actual political alliance with the Boers and the abandonment of neutrality was never seriously contemplated, however, since such action might prompt the British to seize Dutch colonies. Some Dutch also felt kinship with the Flemish population of Belgium, and the establishment of the General Netherlandic Alliance in 1898 was one expression of the new appreciation for a shared cultural heritage. It appears, however, that such sentiments were not particularly widespread; in any event, the Dutch showed little interest in the political struggles of the Flemish movement. Their lack of interest presumably had its roots in the Netherlands's difficult relationship with the Belgian state, which remained strained for many decades following Belgian independence.

The Netherlands's colonies were also a source of national pride, and by the end of the century, the Dutch took an increased economic and cultural interest in them. The Dutch showed no interest in the race for new colonies during the 1880s and 1890s, but their policy in the Indonesian archipelago exhibited all of the traits attributed to modern imperialism. Specifically, the Dutch increasingly intervened in the islands' politics, administration, and culture, actions which effectively led to a modern colonial administration of the Dutch East Indies. At the same time, business concerns both intensified their economic exploitation of the Indies and vastly expanded their operations into other parts of the archipelago.

Although there could be tensions between colonial policy and business interests, the two frequently supported each other. Dutch authority now expanded to the very edges of the archipelago, since failure to effectively take control of these areas would invite other powers to move in. But Dutch business also served as an impetus for expansion, since it required an effective colonial administration to protect Dutch commerce. This expansion precipitated a series of armed conflicts with the traditional native rulers of these regions, who had been used to a great degree of autonomy. The conflict in Aceh, lasting between 1873 and 1903, was especially bloody before the area was finally "pacified" by J.B. van Heutsz.

On the one hand, the Dutch attempted to preserve the native cultures they encountered, cultures intensely studied by scholars like Van Vollenhoven and C. Snouck Hurgronje (the latter of whom used his knowledge to help subjugate Aceh). On the other hand, they also endeavored to "improve" the native populace, to bring them to a higher level of prosperity and morality. Thus the Dutch systematically encouraged formal education among their colonial subjects. Missionaries, too, were quite active. The colonial government's efforts to "elevate" the population shows parallels with the "civilizing offensive" in the mother country. It was also based on the guilt-ridden conviction that the Dutch had a "debt of honor" to pay for the exploitation they exacted on the Javanese during the *Cultuurstelsel*.

This "Ethical Policy," as it was officially called in 1901, was, in a certain sense, the Dutch variation of modern imperialism. In the Netherlands the policy found broad support; both the liberal C.T. van Deventer and the Anti-Revolutionary A.W.F. Idenburg championed its cause, while social democrats like H.H. van Kol also, in effect, backed it. For proponents of the Ethical Policy, Dutch rule and moral mission were inseparable; no measures intended for the benefit of the Indonesians could be implemented without effective colonial control. The expenses incurred by this policy would be taken directly out of the growing tax revenues received from the colonies' profitable businesses. These businesses in turn would profit from an improved infrastructure and a higher degree of education among the natives. Under these conditions, the number of "Europeans" in the Dutch East Indies – which included the Indo-European population – rose to approximately 300,000 persons in 1940.

Prince Paku Buwono X of Surakarta (left), and W. de Vogel, the colonial government's resident in Surakarta, in an 1897 photo. (Koninklijk Instituut voor de Tropen, Amsterdam.)

The First World War

This period of dynamic growth largely came to an end with the outbreak of the First World War. Although the Dutch feared for their neutrality, particularly after various incidents, the warring powers continued to respect Dutch neutrality. This is not to say, however, that the Netherlands was left untouched by the war. For four years the Dutch army remained mobilized to guard the frontiers. More important the war seriously disrupted the international trade on which the Dutch depended. Although some individuals and groups profited from the situation, the war severely affected the economy. It also triggered serious social problems, especially because sufficient food imports were no longer guaranteed. The government introduced a series of regulations to counter the dislocations and even began a system of food distribution. In 1914 many hundreds of thousands of Belgians fled to the Netherlands from their own war-torn country, and although most of them returned after a short time, a substantial number remained until the end of the war.

The outbreak of war prompted the Dutch to join together in national unity. All of the political parties were quick to proclaim support of the government's decision to mobilize the army in order to maintain the country's neutrality. Even the strongly internationalist

SDAP concurred; its leader Troelstra noted that "the national idea is greater than national differences." Although the cabinet installed in 1913 under the independent liberal P. W.A. Cort van der Linden had already aimed at ending the country's long-running political issues, the war provided an important additional stimulus to quickly resolve them.

The so-called pacification of 1917 was a multifaceted compromise which effectively brought an end to the School Conflict and the debate over the franchise. The confessionals could celebrate that their private schools received funding equal to public schools; socialists and (progressive) liberals could be pleased with the universal male franchise, which had required a change in the constitution. The winner-take-all district system was also replaced by a system of proportional representation in which all citizens would be required to vote. This change would have important effects on Dutch politics. For half a century the new system of proportional representation ensured a rather stable composition of the Second Chamber, based on the various sizes of the country's pillarized subcultures. Moreover, political parties were no longer obliged to cooperate before elections in order to receive parliamentary representation.

The Social Question proved more difficult to "solve." Further social legislation was put on hold as a result of the war, but the cooperation between employers and unions grew. In many municipalities the social democrats became active in government policy, including the social policies most important to their own constituents. Despite the growing participation of the unions and the social democrats, social tensions mounted during the course of the war. The lack of food in particular prompted outbursts of discontent, which groups to the left of the SDAP were able to exploit.

The Russian Revolution of 1917 and the revolutionary turbulence that shook Germany at the end of the First World War caused many Dutch to fear or hope that revolution would not stop at the German border. Many authorities were exceedingly nervous and seemed prepared to make far-reaching concessions. Some social democrats – including Troelstra – believed that the age of the classless society had dawned. Sensing the tensions in the country and hearing that many Rotterdam authorities were prepared to capitulate to the social democrats, Troelstra proclaimed that the working class would now take power. But no one had prepared for such a revolution, however, and the socialist leader was soon forced to back down. Instead of revolution, the crisis ended in a mass demonstration of loyalty to Queen Wilhelmina, who had ascended the throne in 1898 at the age of eighteen. Troelstra's "mistake," as the incident became known, seriously weakened the position of the social democrats, who in 1913 had been invited to take part in the cabinet and who had shown such evident loyalty to the nation during the war. They were now suspect of being disloyal, even though most of the social democratic rank and file had long abandoned their revolutionary orientation.

Dutch society thus escaped the First World War with its bourgeois, pillarized character still largely intact. The question now facing the country was how Europe would recover from the war, and how the Nether-

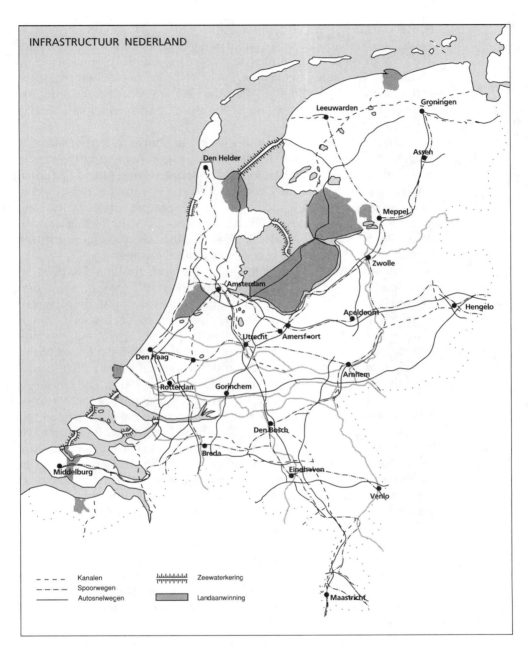

INFRASTRUCTUUR NEDERLAND

Kanalen
Spoorwegen
Autosnelwegen
Zeewaterkering
Landaanwinning

lands, with the important changes of the "pacification of 1917" now behind it, would fare in the postwar world.

Infrastructure of the Netherlands.

3. A Bourgeois and Pillarized Society (1918-1960)

Consolidation in an Age of Catastrophes

The history of Europe from the outbreak of the First World War to the 1960s was characterized by a series of often very violent shocks. The continent plunged into deep economic, political, and spiritual crises. The Western European powers lost their leading global position through the

World Wars to the United States and the USSR, and were forced to decolonize. The Netherlands was a small nation, but it had always been relatively wealthy and was sufficiently tied to global developments to be
affected by the same phenomena. Specifically, the mass unemployment
of the Depression during the 1930s, the German occupation during the
Second World War, and the lost of the Dutch East Indies made a deep
impression on the Dutch.

Despite these upheavals, this period in Dutch history was largely
defined by stability and the further consolidation and expansion of past
achievements. The greatest shocks all emanated from outside national
boundaries; the Netherlands could not escape its consequences, but the
country tried as best it could to reduce its negative effects. In the long
run, it succeeded in doing so. When one compares the Netherlands in
1960 with the way it was in 1920, the similarities and the continuities are
more striking than any far-reaching structural changes.

Economically, for example, the Netherlands continued to develop
along paths already paved in the late nineteenth century, the Great
Depression notwithstanding. The country retained a capitalist economy
in which state intervention eventually reached such levels that it
became a mixed economy. Industrial monopolies, cartels, and the trade
unions also prevented a completely unfettered capitalist system from
coming into existence. Economic growth was an important characteristic of the period, despite the retrenchment of the 1930s. The country's
infrastructure expanded along existing lines. The only obvious exception was the innovation of air travel, particularly the establishment of
Schiphol Airport and the Royal Dutch Airline, KLM. Perhaps most
impressive were the new efforts to reclaim land from the sea, the first
major drainage efforts since the poldering of the Haarlemmermeer in
the mid-nineteenth century. The *Afsluitdijk*, completed in 1932, closed
the Zuyder Zee – now the IJsselmeer (IJssel Lake) – off from the open
sea, and much of it became polderland. After the catastrophic floods of
1953, the Delta Plan was implemented to better protect the islands of
Zeeland and South Holland.

The diversity of the country's economic structure also remained
intact. The well-developed service sector remained of vital importance
for the open, internationally oriented economy. The agrarian sector
underwent a new serious crisis, but a whole range of organizational and
technical improvements helped restore Dutch agriculture after 1950.
The industrial sector continued to grow, especially after a new wave of
industrialization that began in the 1950s. Even before the Second World
War, huge international companies operated from Dutch territory –
most notably Philips, Shell, and Unilever. After Indonesian independence in 1949, the colonial component of the Dutch economy was
largely lost. Contrary to the fearful expectations of many, however, the
Dutch economy more than made up for the difference through remarkable growth in other sectors and through a new orientation toward
European and American markets.

The constitutional monarchy and Dutch parliamentary democracy
easily retained their respective positions. To be sure, there was critique,
some of it fierce, on the way in which politics were conducted in an age

of mass parties. Cabinets were criticized for making weak-kneed compromises instead of acting decisively; others bemoaned the growing state bureaucracy. Dutch parliamentary democracy was also denounced by fascist and communist movements, but they never constituted a serious threat to it. Only the violence of the German invasion of 10 May 1940 was able to put a temporary end to parliamentary democracy. When it returned five years later, its popular support was greater than ever; whatever reservations confessionals and some socialists may once have had for this "liberal" form of government now completely disappeared.

The Pillars

The pillarization of Dutch society was further expanded in the period after the First World War. The liberal wing of the bourgeoisie managed to retain their cultural dominance in many areas through organizations they preferred to present as apolitical, national, general, or neutral. But Catholics, orthodox Protestants, and social democrats developed their own alternate organizational networks, and an increasing number of people found it possible to live completely within their own subculture and its ethos and associations. People found security and a sense of belonging in these subcultural "pillars" – and often a good deal of social control as well.

There were always variations and gradations in the quadripartite division of society among the Catholic, orthodox-Protestant, social democratic, and neutral-liberal subcultures, so that at no point was there ever a complete pillarization of Dutch society. Some areas of life remained relatively unpillarized. Moreover, there were additional smaller groups who held their own ideology, such as national socialism or communism, or their own religious principles, most typically some form of Calvinist theology. The political parties, trade unions, most philanthropic organizations, youth associations and youth work, broadcasting and the press were the most pillarized. The same was true of education, with the important exception of public schools, which typically served children from both social democratic and neutral-liberal homes. In addition, the social democrats did have their own educative and self-improvement societies, and there were a small number of private, nonsectarian schools that often maintained a liberal character.

It is striking how women's organizations also followed the pillarized pattern once female suffrage had been attained. Their number and size grew, but the spirit of female solidarity which had transcended subcultural divides was weaker than before 1919. Indeed, the women's movement was wholly integrated into the pillarized system and made subordinate to it. Thus it may be said that although the women attained notable successes in achieving equal rights, almost all of them were obliged to live according to the prevalent norms of their subcultures. The importance of the woman as housewife and the low number of wage-earning women (in comparison to other countries) were important features of women's existence in the mid-twentieth century.

Sports and recreation, an increasingly significant part of Dutch society, were more weakly pillarized. It is true that there were many Catholic and orthodox Protestant sports clubs, and there were less successful attempts to organize athletics along social democratic lines. But in the long run, the most organized competitions were arranged through national leagues.

With the exception of the pillarized unions and less pillarized employers' associations, it appeared at first glance that economic life was hardly pillarized at all. But people's choice of employees, or choice of shops, could in fact be determined by the subcultures to which they belonged, thus informally extending the influence of the pillars.

The pillars differed considerably in character. Not only were their worldviews different, but their internal relations, their cohesiveness, and their ways of life were as well. The Catholics remained emphatically organized around their church, whose hierarchy both directly and indirectly guided the Catholic pillar. In this way, the Catholics maintained the appearance of remarkable unity, despite continued tensions and disagreements. Next to the church, social organizations played an important role. Corporatist ideas and proposals were introduced to the Netherlands, following international trends within Roman Catholicism. The subsidarity principle (what can be done by a lower organ should not be done by a higher body) was also an important principle in Catholic institutional life. Liberal and socialist ideologies were judged reprehensible because both were godless and based on reason alone. Catholics proposed instead to build an organic society where every social group, in harmonious cooperation with the others, possessed their own tasks, rights, and duties. In practical political terms very little came of this initially, but the Catholic workers' movement and the socially engaged wing of the RKSP employed this ideology to strengthen their position. The papal encyclical *Quadragesimo Anno* (1931), which confirmed the social calling of the church forty years after *Rerum Novarum*, and the social effects of the Depression also fortified this more progressive wing of political Catholicism; in the 1950s they would dominate the new Catholic unity party, the Catholic People's Party (KVP, founded in 1945).

In contrast, ecclesiastical divisions were an important characteristic among the orthodox Protestants, despite many similarities in faith. For example, schisms twice rent the Reformed Churches in the Netherlands, first in 1926, then in 1944. They were politically fragmented as well. Next to the relatively large ARP and CHU, there were also increasingly smaller, highly principled orthodox parties which found representation in parliament. The Anti-Revolutionary Party was itself the center of a highly organized web of associations with close ties to the Reformed Churches in the Netherlands. The Christian Historical Union, with its links to the Dutch Reformed church, played a similar role, although its network was less cohesive and less elaborate. But there was much overlap, and some organizations, like the Protestant trade union movement and the Christian broadcasting association, recruited members across the whole orthodox Protestant spectrum (excepting those very orthodox groups who adamantly opposed radio and television). It should be added that the extensive divisions among orthodox Protestants and the antagonistic feelings they sometimes engendered did little to undermine the recognizability of their pillar to outsiders. To a large extent, there was an ethos that characterized the orthodox Protestant pillar. Social problems also received much attention among orthodox Protestants, but these Protestants were far less active than Catholics in proposing changes in the social order.

For the social democrats, the party, as exponent of their ideology, and the socialist union NVV – by far their largest organization – were central to their subcultural identity, with other pillarized organizations playing an auxiliary role. The social democrats, united in an often difficult alliance, were confronted with how they should reconcile themselves to their minority position in Dutch society.

Propaganda poster for the Plan of Labor, a collective initiative undertaken by the SDAP and NVV. (Internationaal Instituut voor Sociale Geschiedenis, Amsterdam.)

Electoral returns under universal suffrage and proportional representation made it all too clear that the confessionals had succeeded in keeping Christian workers within their folds, and that at least for the time being, the social democrats would have to abandon their hopes for a majority. This forced them to adopt a cooperative posture, a strategy denounced by radical left-wing groups, who repeatedly charged that such cooperation amounted to class treason. Their accusations did little to change the course of the SDAP and NVV, and in time the social democrats' commitment to political consensus, promoting reform and introducing social legislation bore fruit. In response to the capriciousness of the capitalist economy, the social democrats looked for ways to better order the economy and society. Partly under the influence of the Belgian socialists' Plan of Labor, Dutch social democrats moved in the direction of a planned economy, articulated in their own Plan of Labor (1935). It is interesting to note that Dutch Catholics began to develop similar ideas, although their rationales were considerably different.

In this way, the social democratic subculture was slowly but surely integrated into bourgeois society. The interclass foundations of this society, in fact, were explicitly recognized by the SDAP party program of 1937. The SDAP had become, in effect, a bourgeois reform party that tried to appeal to all classes – although its continued concern for social issues revealed its revolutionary past. This fundamental shift resulted in social democrats joining a coalition government in 1939, and its moderate course was confirmed in 1946 when a more inclusive Party of Labor (PvDA) replaced the old SDAP. The new PvDA would serve as a major coalition partner until 1958.

In contrast, the neutral-liberal segment of the population lacked a clear ideological foundation. Certainly political liberalism did not function as such; indeed, liberal political strength continued to decline. Paradoxically, those in the liberal pillar stressed the national and the nonsectarian, rejecting "the spirit of partition" and the pillarization of the country.

Such criticisms of pillarization found fertile ground outside liberal circles as well. In the other pillars, too, there were undercurrents of discontent, frequently critiquing pillarized insularity, the narrow-mindedness it ostensibly fostered, and the lack of national cooperation that resulted from it. These critics would, on occasion, seek each other out, and at the national unity conferences of the 1930s, such encounters took place. Indeed, during and immediately following the German occupation, there was a clear political movement which sought to "break through" the pillarized status quo. But on balance these critical voices were only of secondary importance during the period. The liberal parties proved unable to exploit this discontent; the attitudes and actions of most liberals remained distasteful to the bulk of confessionals and socialists, and the old animus against them was still too strong.

For the reasons mentioned above, liberal circles did not possess anything like a dense network of their own organizations. But because of the dominant position of other pillars, they were compelled to a certain extent to develop their own pillar. Almost against their will, the liberals met each other through their own overlapping organizations and through informal contacts among themselves. Moreover, the liberals shared a common ethos and mentality which kept them together.

The influence of the more or less liberal bourgeoisie of the neutral pillar remained great. Corporate, cultural, and academic life – and in many respects the state bureaucracy – all exuded a liberal ethos. Many areas of life exhibited the secular Enlightenment rationalism and the emphases on personal growth that clearly stemmed from liberal origins; these were so widely accepted that they seemed to be mere common sense. Seen from this perspective, confessional pillarization may be regarded as a "modern," secularized way to keep "traditional" articles of faith in twentieth-century society by forming alternate associations.

The numerical relationships between the pillars remained relatively stable. The population of the Netherlands grew from nearly 7 million in 1920 to almost 11.5 million in 1960. In these forty years, the number of Catholics rose from over 35 to nearly 40 percent of the population. The Calvinist denominations, of which the Reformed Churches in the Netherlands was by far the largest, continued to represent just under 10 percent of the population. (Other smaller denominations seldom constituted more than 1 percent of the population.) Meanwhile, the religiously divided Dutch Reformed church declined markedly, from over 40 percent to just under 30 percent, and the number of those professing no religious allegiance rose from under 10 percent to nearly 20 percent. To a large extent, this striking rise in the number of unchurched simply formalized the attitudes of people who, though nominally church members, had long been inactive or uninterested in religious affairs.

Electorally speaking, the paper exodus out of the Dutch Reformed church hardly disturbed the balance among the pillars. The liberal parties – in the interbellum the VDB and the Freedom Alliance (itself an amalgam of the Liberal Union and the Free Liberals), and after the Second World War the Party of Freedom (1945) and the Party of Freedom and Democracy (VVD, 1948) – found their electoral share slip from 15 to 10 percent, and even well below that during late 1940s. The Catholic party, the RKSP, and its successor the KVP, could count on roughly 30 percent of the vote, and breakaway Catholic parties never amounted to very much. The orthodox Protestant parties, ARP, CHU, and other tiny competitors, garnered on average around 25 percent – a bit higher before the Second World War, a bit under after. The SDAP, too, could count on a quarter of the electorate before the war; in 1946, its successor, the Party of Labor, received nearly 30 percent and increased its share by a few percentage points during the 1950s.

The Pillarized System and the Bourgeois Moral World

Although pillarization is primarily understood as fostering subcultural separation, it also sustained an important degree of cohesion and cooperation within Dutch society. The national whole, not only the pillarized parts, was important. The nature of this cooperation can easily be demonstrated in Dutch political life, but many variations of it could be found in other areas as well. It was the elites of the pillars in particular who were assigned an important role in maintaining this cooperation.

Since none of the pillars possessed a majority (nor hoped to achieve one in the foreseeable future), negotiation – and compromise – were essential. In the long run, an effort was made to include all four pillars in these negotiations. The elites from these pillars would tackle difficult problems – usually behind closed doors – and politically defuse the issues, redefining them as technical problems and unbalanced distribution of services. In most cases, they solved problems by proportionately dividing the resources at their disposal. In other words, the same principle and method which had solved the School Conflict was now routinely practiced.

"Pacification politics" has become a popular phrase to describe this arrangement, and the way Dutch elites solved the radio broadcasting issue is a classic example of how it was done. During the 1920s, radio rapidly became an important means of communication, generating a conflict over who should have access to scarce air time. After intensive negotiations within various commissions, the problem was solved in 1930 by partitioning air time among pillarized groups, all of which were subject to a few government regulations. The four large pillarized organizations each received nearly 25 percent: the General Radio Broadcasting Company (AVRO), the Catholic Radio Broadcasting Company (KRO), the Dutch Christian Radio Association (NCRV), and the social democratic Workers' Association of Radio Amateurs (VARA). Several hours a week were reserved for smaller groups with specific purposes, of which the Liberal Protestants' Radio Broadcasting Company (VPRO) was the most important.

This method of "pacification," however, seldom worked as neatly as it did in the radio issue. When one of the political parties decided to oppose a compromise, perhaps on the grounds of a high ideological principle that their rank and file could not sacrifice, it sometimes precipitated protracted delays in the decision-making process, or even a political crisis. Moreover, it was highly unusual to include all of the

The socialist weekly De Notenkraker *satirizes the political relationship between the Anti-Revolutionary Colijn (left) and the Catholic leader Aalberse in an issue from June 1935. In that year, Aalberse's attempt at cabinet formation had failed because Colijn's ARP had refused to sit in a government including the SDAP.*

large political parties in a cabinet. Since 1918, the confessionals held the keys to parliament, since they invariably received at least half of the seats. Continuation of the confessional coalition thus also seemed the most natural course, and from the 1920s through the 1960s, confessional ministers dominated national cabinets, often enjoying an overwhelming majority in them. But the Catholic-Protestant coalition, initially defined by ballot-box alliances, was not strong enough to ensure long-term, harmonious cooperation. Inter-confessional irritations were too great, and the confessionals did not succeed in developing a well-constructed common program. Thus confessional political domination did not lead to a reorganization of state and society along religious principles, but to the continuation of, as the historian J.J. Woltjer put it, "a liberal inheritance under confessional management."

The position of the RKSP/KVP was of particular importance in this respect. In the first years after 1918, the Catholics hesitatingly opted for the continuation of the confessional coalition, with an occasional liberal minister thrown in. They excluded the SDAP because they judged it insufficiently reliable on issues concerning public order, revolution, the monarchy, and the nation. As a result of the Catholics' prominent electoral position, they compelled their Protestant allies to accept a Catholic premier for the first time; and between 1918 and 1933, C.J.M. Ruys de Beerenbrouck held the position for eleven years. In 1933 he was

ARP leader H. Colijn, a powerful politician with great charisma. Drawing by J. Braakensiek, 1929. (Atlas van Stolk, Rotterdam.)

replaced by the charismatic and politically influential Anti-Revolution-ary, H. Colijn. During his six years as premier, Colijn pursued classic lib-eral socioeconomic policies, prompting him to seek support among the liberals. This course brought him into conflict with the more interven-tionist Catholics, who – after much hesitation and internal strife – decided in 1939 to end their opposition to social democrats in the cabi-net in order to push through more activist social and economic policies. Two SDAP ministers entered the cabinet in that year, but it would not be until after the war that the social democrats reaped the full fruits of recognition. Between 1946 and 1958, the Netherlands was ruled by the so-called Roman-Red coalition, and the PvdA politician W. Drees served as premier for ten of these years. In most of these Roman-Red cabinets, ministers from other parties were also represented, and it was precisely in the late 1940s and 1950s that "pacification democracy" became standard political practice.

This kind of interpillarized relationship placed a premium on an active role for elites and on a relatively passive role for their pillarized constituents. As voters, it was the constituents' task to demonstrate loy-alty to their principles and to otherwise keep quiet. After all, they were, as movements, fighting for great ideas that went far beyond mere polit-ical opinion, and they were expected to close ranks in pursuit of these ideas. In three of the four pillars, socioeconomic equality (already achieved to a large measure) was still an important aim, and this had always required collective discipline and trust in their leaders. For this reason, the pillarized electorates did not object to the role assigned them. But it is highly questionable whether their role was really a pas-sive one. There were many opportunities for active participation within each pillar. Moreover, pillarized cohesion hardly asked people to aban-don their militant commitments or to refrain from testifying to their most cherished principles. Leaders also had to keep the principles of their followers in mind, for any suspicion of betrayal could lead to trou-ble with their constituents.

The connections across pillars were not restricted to the compro-mises made by the elites from each group. They also included the assumption that one's own pillar was an integral part of the indivisible Dutch nation. This widespread commitment to national unity did not primarily express itself as an obtrusive, chauvinistic, or militaristic nationalism – a nationalism hardly realistic, given the international sit-uation. Rather, the Dutch expressed a deep satisfaction in the unique and exemplary qualities of their society, particularly its love for peace and high moral sense. This was sometimes combined with a pathos which touted a glorious past or exhibited pride in the Netherlands's colonial possessions.

National identity was also increasingly associated with the House of Orange. The Netherlands's nineteenth-century kings, particularly through their political ambitions, had generated tensions in Dutch pub-lic life, but their twentieth-century successors – all queens – enjoyed great popularity. Neither Wilhelmina (1898-1948) nor Juliana (1948-1980) attempted to exercise direct political influence. But behind the scenes, they made their opinions known and accordingly exerted influence, all the while respecting their constitutional limitations. Above all, they both – although in different ways – knew how to embody the unity of the Dutch nation.

The near-universal acceptance of similar bourgeois values also unified the Dutch – values which had changed little over the last several generations. To be sure, religion and class introduced their own variations and gradations in this moral pattern, and there were always individuals and groups who deviated from this norm. But in essence these bourgeois values – in which family, order and authority, love of country, diligence, frugality, and self-control were central features – dominated Dutch society, with personal growth as an important corollary. This moral code included a whole range of written and unwritten codes of behavior which were rather rigidly applied in this era of pillarization. Conformity to these rules was fostered by social control within the pillars, as well as by the meddling of philanthropic organizations and institutions which propagated a "better life" through improved hygiene, housekeeping, and infant care.

Actual behavior, of course, did not always conform to moral norms, but it does appear that the continuing "civilizing offensive" achieved notable successes in many areas. For all its diversity, the Dutch nation was generally well-behaved, decent, disciplined, and peaceful. As mentioned above, this was no less true of women and of large groups from the working classes who, thanks to improved social circumstances, became increasingly bourgeois in their sensibilities. The same was true in the countryside; although it retained its own variations, the pattern of values did not substantially deviate from the pattern in the cities. When the hardships of the German occupation seemed have to encouraged moral laxity, both the state and the pillars reacted sharply. They unleashed a new wave of moralizing activities on the population in the late 1940s and 1950s.

Socioeconomic Problems and Increased State Activism

Growing State Intervention

At the turn of the century the political importance of the Social Question had prompted the government to intervene in socioeconomic problems. This trend continued after the First World War. In 1919, for example, the confessional government introduced health insurance and the eight-hour day. Unemployment insurance was expanded. Meanwhile, employers' and employees' organizations increasingly cooperated with each other, initially without government mediation. This did not bring an end to serious social conflict; the textile strikes from 1923 to 1924 and again from 1932 to 1933, the so-called Jordaan Riot in 1934, and the harbor strikes in 1945 and 1946 show that labor friction persisted. Nonetheless, Dutch labor relations were characterized by a high degree of consultation and a low degree of worker unrest. This emphasis on negotiation was, of course, closely connected to the culture of consultation and compromise in Dutch political life. Over time, the government became increasingly involved in labor negotiations as its social policy became intertwined with trade union and corporate policies. Initially, state intervention was restrained and restricted itself to general regula-

Soldiers patrol the Jordaan neighborhood of Amsterdam, July 1934. The Colijn government's decision to reduce unemployment benefits prompted a violent popular uprising in this part of the city, known as the Jordaan Riot.

tions over the pillarized organizations, who implemented government policy and were given proportional state funding to do so.

The restraint of the state was not only based upon the wishes of the pillarized organizations which generally distrusted the neutral state as a liberal institution, but also upon the conviction that the state was limited in its ability to steer social developments. This conviction was strongest in the economic sector, where liberal laissez-faire principles long retained their great influence. But it was precisely instability in the economy that gradually prompted many Dutch to imagine a greater role for the state in society.

The Netherlands suffered acutely as a result of the Depression of the 1930s; at one point, half a million persons were without work (nearly 20 percent of the work force). Moreover, the economic crisis lasted an especially long time; its causes are still debated by historians and economists. The international orientation of the Dutch economy, its domestic performance, and the state's fiscal and monetary policies have all been analyzed. Whatever the reasons, the Colijn cabinets' conservative policies, which intended to adjust the economy to the new circumstances (chiefly through reduced state budgets and the maintenance of a stable currency) drew heavy fire. The state had already expanded its role through limited unemployment assistance and relief to ailing economic sectors (especially agriculture), but calls for a further intensification of this aid now became ever greater. By 1939, the Catholics and the

Looking for work in the 1930s. This man writes that he is willing to do any work, though he is familiar with baking pastries and is a "civilized" and effective salesman.

social democrats were able to agree on an increased measure of state intervention. But the German occupation – in which a foreign government practiced its own powerful intrusions on Dutch society – would delay any new socioeconomic policy until after 1945.

Postwar Neo-Corporatist Tendencies

Reconstruction in the wake of German occupation demanded intensive government action, but this impulse for greater state intervention diminished within a few years. Still, there was no return to the policies of the 1920s and 1930s. By this time, it was widely believed that the state – provided it pursued the right policies – could effectively direct economic and social developments. A 1950 law made room for "public economic organizations," which included elements both from Catholic corporatist thought and social democratic central planning. Some of these new organizations were assigned important roles, particularly the Socioeconomic Council (SER) and the Central Planning Bureau (CPB) under the celebrated economist J. Tinbergen. They were charged with drawing up economic plans and coordinating the roles of the state, business corporations, and trade unions to achieve these plans. The new public industrial organizations never fully implemented their plans, not least because the plans conflicted with the still essentially capitalistic (i.e., liberal) character of the Dutch economy. But the intensive ties between the state and economic life were here to stay. The Dutch state developed neo-corporatist traits, evidenced also in the expansion of both the state and the pillarized bureaucracies. The presence of these dual bureaucracies, incidentally, sometimes caused confusion among Dutch citizens who were entitled to social services.

The most important goals of Dutch socioeconomic policy included full employment, economic growth, and a social security. After a difficult start in the late 1940s, the economy improved markedly in the 1950s. A strongly rebounding international economy was probably the most important factor in this improvement, but U.S. aid in the form of the Marshall Plan, the willingness of the working population (encouraged by the state and pillarized organizations) to accept relatively low wages, and government stimulation of a new wave of industrialization and new technologies were also instrumental. Part of the new prosperity was directed into new investments, and part was used to finance a new wave of social legislation. The population was most impressed with Drees's emergency assistance bill to the elderly (1947), which was expanded a decade later into the General Pension Act (AOW). More than before, the state used its own bureaucracy to implement its laws. The increased role of the state was also apparent in social services, which were still largely dispensed by the pillarized organizations. These organizations increased in number, in scope, and in quality (they "professionalized") because they enjoyed increased state funding for their various services. At the same time, the state expanded both its regulatory role and the administration of its own services – a trend evident in the establishment of the Ministry of Social Work in 1952. The new ministry symbolized the trend toward a more extensive welfare state, which developed under the postwar socialist and confessional leadership.

The economic crisis of the 1930s and the social misery it caused thus further intensified the growth of the state's responsibilities, particularly in the years after 1945.

The Second World War and German Occupation

The great international political crisis that buffeted Europe during the 1930s primarily affected the Netherlands through the Nazi invasion of 1940 and the subsequent German occupation. To be sure, earlier signs of crisis were evident in the advent of Dutch fascist parties, of which Anton Mussert's National Socialist Movement (NSB, founded in 1931) was the most important. At first, the NSB was relatively moderate – stressing nationalist themes and the need for strong authority – and it received nearly 8 percent of the vote in 1935. After that, its message became more radical, and only 4 percent of voters supported it in 1937 and 1939. The NSB's relative lack of success may be attributed to the high degree of pillarization in the Netherlands; the deep ties most voters had with their own pillars went beyond mere party affiliation, and these ties proved a formidable barrier to new parties. The churches and large political parties also opposed national socialism on principle; liberals and social democrats rejected its political ideology and practice, while many confessionals detested its "pagan" character.

But the Dutch army could not withstand the invasion of national socialist Germany in May of 1940, and within five days the Germans were triumphant. For the following five years, the Netherlands was ruled by a Nazi administration under the Austrian *Reichskommissar* A. Seyss-Inquart. This regime had two aims. In the first place, it sought to aid the German war effort and economy through the systematic exploitation of the country. In this aim it succeeded. Voluntarily and involuntarily, the Netherlands's industrial and agricultural firms mass-produced goods for Germany, and a very large number of Dutch were sent to Germany as laborers, most of them against their will. In the first years of the war, this exploitation was conducted in a relatively orderly fashion, and the Dutch could convince themselves that German policy compensated for the complete absence of other trading partners, and that it put an end to unemployment. Later, German exploitation amounted to little more than plundering and kidnapping. By 1945, the Dutch economy had been severely damaged and the population was considerably impoverished.

The occupier's second aim was to Nazify the Netherlands, that is, to convert its people to national socialism, to organize Dutch society along national socialist principles, and to rid the country of all Jews. In this last respect, the Nazis were almost completely successful. Despite protests, such as the February 1941 strike and demonstration in Amsterdam, more than 100,000 Jews – some 75 percent of their total population – were deported and killed in the death camps, especially during 1942 and 1943. The remaining Jews survived by going underground or fleeing the country. In this way, too, the Jews were effectively removed from Dutch society.

The Germans began their reorganization of society by using their power to abolish old institutions and set up new ones. In many areas the old pillarized organizations were replaced by unified organizations, such as the Dutch Labor Front for workers, the *Landstand* for farmers, and the Chamber of Culture for artists. In reality, however, they were empty shells. Most people tried to extricate themselves from these organizations and remained, in effect, loyal to their own pillars. The occupier forbade all political parties except the NSB at the end of 1941, but the Germans generally left the churches alone, preferring to avoid direct conflict with them. Nevertheless, they frequently clashed with individual priests and pastors.

Thus the German effort to Nazify the Dutch population was not realized. A small group of collaborators, motivated by ideology or opportunism, quickly cultivated intensive contacts with the occupier. But the vast majority developed a wait-and-see attitude in 1940, or sought under the new circumstances to achieve their own aims for Dutch society. For instance, the Netherlands Union, established in the summer of 1940, seized on prewar discontent with the pillarized system and strove to give the Dutch nation a unity and cohesion, even if that implicitly meant cooperation with the occupier. The Netherlands Union generated much enthusiasm, but over the course of 1941, it ran afoul of the occupier and was proscribed.

In the course of the war, Seyss-Inquart's regime gradually lost the veneer of accommodation and moderation they had employed to gain support. The harsher the occupier became, the more it alienated the Dutch, and the more they dragged their feet or engaged in active resistance to the Nazis. Some of that resistance took organized form, and many of these illegal groups attempted either directly or indirectly, with or without violence, to undermine the occupier. The most widespread activities of this kind were the publication of illegal newspapers such as *Het Parool*, *Trouw*, *Vrij Nederland*, and *De Waarheid*, and the organization of underground networks for fugitives sought by the occupier.

A second massive expression of aversion to German rule erupted in April and May of 1943, when strikes broke out throughout the country to protest the incarceration of the former Dutch army in Germany. Like the strike of 1941, this one had no direct effect and was repressed. But it signalled a turning point in the already worsening relations between the Dutch and the occupier. In part because of declining German fortunes in the war, the Nazi regime and the Dutch populace were locked in a downward spiral of increased repression and resistance. When in late 1944 the Allies liberated the Netherlands south of the great rivers, and the Dutch government-in-exile ordered a railway strike which disrupted distribution routes, socioeconomic life in the occupied Netherlands was brought to near collapse. Famine swept over the cities, particularly in the west, during the winter of 1945. By the time the Allied armies reached the rest of the country in April and May of 1945 they found chaos, destruction, and an exhausted people.

Breakthrough?

It did not take long, however, for the Dutch to recharge their energy. Relieved by the liberation, a wide segment of the population enthusiastically committed themselves to the renewal of society. They sought not only to rebuild the wrecked infrastructure, but also to construct a better social and political edifice. This commitment to renewal, partly based on the conviction that prewar Dutch society had suffered from serious flaws, had several faces. Some Dutch above all wanted stronger

The Hunger Winter of 1944 meant privation of food and fuel for both young and old. (Nederlands Instituut voor Oorlogsdocumentatie, Amsterdam.)

authority and an autocratically organized state. The prevailing political climate at war's end put a quick end to this impulse. Others wanted radical socialist reform; the elections of 1946 gave the communists 10 percent of the vote (more than ever before, or since), suggesting a measure of radicalization among the population. The Dutch government and Allied authorities – particularly the Americans – were deeply concerned about this development. But social and political conditions for radical change were exceedingly small in the Netherlands, and the communist threat faded.

Initially, it seemed that the more moderate Netherlands People's Movement (NVB) would have more chance for success. The successor to the Netherlands Union, the NVB proposed to break through the pillarized framework, to give Dutch society a new cohesion, and to provide it with a better social and spiritual basis. At first glance, there was every reason to suppose that the NVB would succeed – and that far-reaching social and political change would take place. It seemed logical that the shock of war had forced people to break with their old ways, and that a brand new start could be made. But it soon became apparent that only very limited change would occur. The overwhelming majority of the population simply went back to their trusted pillarized organizations. Most people had not forsaken their subcultures. Moreover, politicians and administrators seldom had the time to devote themselves to grand plans for national renewal; instead, pressing postwar problems like repairing the wreckage, dealing with collaborators, and armed conflict in the Dutch East Indies consumed their attention. Dutch society seemed to require the mobilizing power of the pillarized organizations to encourage the population to exercise the sobriety and restraint necessary to overcome the acute problems facing it If the social and economic importance of the pillars was clear, their political value was even clearer: they could keep the population from communist enticements. Under these conditions, there was no "breakthrough" of pillarization or of the prevailing political system, and changes in the postwar political parties were mostly cosmetic (like changing party names).

Significant change were most likely in those areas where change had already occurred before 1940. In these areas, the German occupation did help to speed change and strengthened the conviction that a break with the past was needed. Indeed, the psychological effects of the occupation should not be underestimated. Many individuals experienced it as a traumatic experience, which divided history between what had happened before and after 1940. The annihilation of the great majority of Dutch Jews was an irreparable loss both to the Jewish community and Dutch society. Furthermore, the war did bring fundamental change to the Netherlands's position in the world: the Dutch abandoned their failed policy of neutrality and were forced out of their East Asian empire.

Foreign Affairs

But it was only *after* the Second World War that neutrality was decisively rejected. Indeed, the apparent success of Dutch neutrality policy during the First World War only strengthened their commitment to it in the years after 1918. The Netherlands's membership in the League of Nations might in one sense have undermined the country's neutrality, but League membership hardly changed the intentions of Dutch foreign policy. The country's long-standing neutrality, incidentally, only intensified Dutch indignation at the German invasion. After the Second World War, the Dutch chose another course, becoming a member not only of the United Nations (the proposed improvement to the League) but of the more restrictive European communities and of NATO. The country's relations with Belgium (and Luxembourg) also improved after a century of irritations. Belgian attempts after the First World War to gain territory at Dutch expense had not improved relations, on the contrary. In 1927 a proposed treaty of cooperation had foundered in the Dutch First Chamber after nationalistic sentiment and economic rivalries reared their heads. A thaw began in the 1930s, especially with the Treaty of Ouchy (1932), which regulated tariffs between the two countries, and in 1944 the two governments-in-exile, both in London, signed the Benelux accords which committed them to further cooperation.

The Netherlands's new activism in foreign affairs was prompted not only by the failure of neutrality, but also by economic considerations and fear of the Soviet Union. In giving aid through the Marshall Plan, the Americans insisted on European cooperation, and in the long run it also seemed desirable to the Dutch to work collectively on Western Europe's economic development. At the same time, many Dutch regarded the Soviet Union as a revolutionary communist danger embodied in an aggressive state. The country must be prevented from seizing Europe as national socialist Germany had been able to do. The internationalism of the communist movement gave their foreign threat a domestic dimension. Thus the Cold War was also fought within the borders of the Netherlands, since Dutch communists had to be prevented from undermining the Netherlands's bourgeois, pillarized society from within. In order to do this, the Dutch needed to close ranks in the national community against the enemy, and this sense of common purpose had a steeling effect on the already rigorous way in which Dutch society enforced standards of morality and decency. The Soviet menace was also an additional argument for increased social legislation, since poverty was regarded as the breeding ground for social unrest and communism.

Loss of the Dutch East Indies

The Japanese had no more trouble invading the Dutch East Indies in 1942 than the Germans did the Netherlands. Their occupation of the East Indies, which for the white population meant extended detention in internment camps, had important political and social effects. A growing Western-style nationalism among the Indonesians was one of the side effects of prewar Dutch colonial development. Initially quite weak, this new nationalism became a potentially potent source of resistance to Dutch rule, alongside traditional indigenous rulers, Islamic movements, and communist agitation. Dutch officials responded by granting the Indonesians certain rights, such as representation in a People's Council with rather limited powers, but at the same time the Dutch repressed resistance to their rule and strictly exercised their authority. The communist revolt of 1926 and 1927 and the mutiny of the largely Indonesian crew aboard the Dutch navy cruiser the *De Zeven Provinciën* in 1933 were important catalysts in the development of Dutch hard-line policy. Dutch defeat and Japanese occupation gave this nationalistic current a strong boost, and on 17 August 1945, two days after Japan's capitulation, the Republic of Indonesia was proclaimed by A. Sukarno (who had worked with the Japanese occupier) and Mohammed Hatta.

The London government-in-exile had expressed its intention to give the Indonesian population a new and equal status within a royal commonwealth. In order to effectively do this, the Dutch believed it necessary to first restore their authority. They wanted nothing to do with the collaborator Sukarno. But when Dutch authorities returned to power under the leadership of Lieutenant Governor-General H.J. van Mook, they encountered armed resistance. Their hopes for reconstructing a new, more independent Dutch East Indies in which natives and colonizers harmoniously cooperated came to nought as both parties became entangled in a complicated diplomatic and military conflict. In the end, the Netherlands, which held fast to its historic and legal rights and to the necessity of restoring authority, order, and peace, lost this conflict. By the end of 1949, they were forced to surrender sovereignty to a federal Indonesian republic, which quickly became a unitary state under Sukarno. Most Dutch and many Indo-Europeans left immediately, or in the course of the 1950s, as repatriates for the Netherlands. They were joined by a considerable number of Moluccans (mostly Ambonese), many of whom had served as soldiers in the Royal Dutch Indies Army. The Moluccans's hopes for a speedy return to Indonesia to establish an independent Republic of the South Moluccas proved illusory.

In hindsight, it is evident that the Dutch government, the Dutch parliament, and the Dutch populace completely misjudged the situation. In particular, they failed to see how popular Indonesian independence was. Furthermore, they proved no more able to perceive how weak international support for the Dutch cause was – especially that the United States would ultimately back Indonesia. The Dutch also did not foresee the huge logistic and financial problems inherent in fielding an army in Asia, and how ineffectual military power could be. The Dutch "police actions" of 1947 and 1948 yielded little military and no political success whatsoever, and through them the Dutch missed a number of potential diplomatic solutions to the crisis. The Netherlands thus suffered a considerable defeat, a defeat repeated in 1963 when the Dutch were coerced to transfer western New Guinea, which was excluded from the 1949 agreement, to the Republic of Indonesia.

In this way, the Dutch empire in Asia was decolonized. But the Netherlands enjoyed a much more placid relationship with its much smaller and economically insignificant "possessions" in South America and the Caribbean: Surinam and the Netherlands Antilles. Surinam became independent in 1975, after a complex series of negotiations and events. The Netherlands Antilles was granted a large measure of autonomy, but its continued status as part of the Kingdom of the Netherlands remains a matter of discussion.

Queen Juliana signs the Transfer of Sovereignty Act in Amsterdam's Royal Palace on 27 December 1949, formally granting independence to the Republic of Indonesia.

Many of those directly involved in the Dutch-Indonesian conflict experienced it as no less traumatic than the Great Depression or the German and Japanese occupations. Loss of the East Indies was also a hard blow to the Dutch economy, but (as noted above) the rising economic fortunes in the 1950s put an end to the country's worst fears.

Dutch Society in the Late 1950s

After more than two decades of crisis and hardship, in which the very independence of the Dutch nation seemed threatened, the prognosis rather suddenly improved at the end of the 1950s. Strong economic growth brought the dawn of unprecedented prosperity. The social legislation of an expanding welfare state gave the Dutch new security, and social stability seemed secured by the close cooperation of the country's subcultures, whose members now felt a certain respect for each other. High moral standards determined social norms and, to a large extent, behavior. Although Dutch society in 1960 differed substantially in some respects from forty years before, many of its characteristics were still the same. It remained a pillarized, bourgeois society, and if anything its foundations were more solid and its networks more intricate than had been the case in 1920.

For the sake of both clarity and nuance it is necessary in this context to point once again to the many exceptions and to the countervailing forces of all kinds, at all levels, that challenged the status quo. Support for pillarization was hardly universal; liberals had always opposed it, social democrats still longed to break through the confessional barriers, and even among the confessionals there were voices who claimed that the social segmentation of the country had gone too far. Bourgeois morality – particularly the rigorous way in which it was often propagated and imposed – was resisted by moderates and by freethinkers who had their own notions of morality, although this tradition had always been quite weak in the Netherlands. This resistance was particularly aimed at the country's rigid sexual morality, to which many people did not conform. The discrepancy between ideal and reality, norm and practice, had grown smaller during the past decades, but in the 1950s it widened again, in part, perhaps, because of the increasing prosperity.

Science and the arts, with their emphases on experimentation and the free exchange of ideas, had never easily accommodated themselves to the bourgeois, pillarized character of Dutch society. By the 1950s, the fast developing social sciences, used by both the state and the pillarized organizations for the formulation and implementation of social policy, also served as a nexus for intellectual exchange across the pillarized divides. Professionalization of the bureaucracy and of pillarized organizations promoted greater homogenization among experts from the various subcultures, and it shifted the emphasis away from enforcing moral norms to professional performance and behavior.

Dutch art of the period partly reflected conventional bourgeois values and the pillarized segmentation of society, but another more artistically significant part of the art world rejected these influences. Dutch avant-garde artists in particular made no attempt to bring their art in line with bourgeois, pillarized values. Instead, most of them were in direct contact with the most important international developments, and they sometimes played an important role in them. The Dutch public had generally had little regard for modern art, including works by artists in the *De Stijl* movement of the 1920s, such as the architects J.P. Oud and Gerrit Rietveld and the painters Theo van Doesburg and Piet Mondriaan. This was no less true of the postwar experimental painters of Cobra, like Karel Appel and Constant, and the poets and writers called "the Fiftiers," such as Lucebert, Gerrit Kouwenaar, and Simon Vinkenoog.

Other writers found wide readership, particularly among the well-educated: Menno ter Braak, E. du Perron, Carry van Bruggen, H. Marsman and J. Slauerhoff before the war; and W.F. Hermans and G.K. van het Reve after 1945. Simon Vestdijk enjoyed popularity throughout the period. Several of these writers' books caused scandals for being "offensive," but in general their work was much praised. However, their books demonstrated no affinity with the dominant bourgeois and pillarized society, and in some instances they explicitly rejected it. Cobra and the Fiftiers, for example, articulated an anarchist-tinted revolutionary dimension which would later inspire self-styled rebels in the 1960s. But in the period between 1918 and 1960 such expressions played no more than a marginal role in Dutch society.

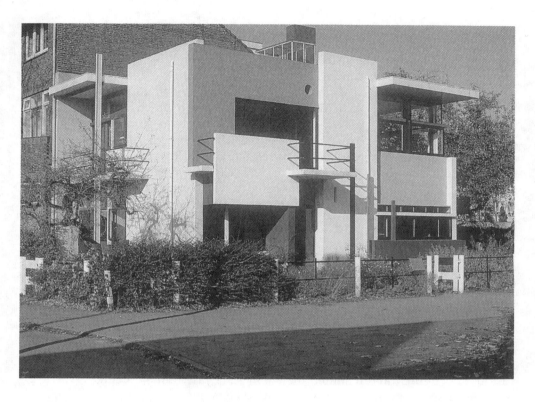

4. Seismic Shifts since the 1960s

The Rietveld-Schröder House on the Prins Hendriklaan in Utrecht, one of the most famous creations of the architect Gerrit Rietveld.

The Renewal Movement of the 1960s

Crown Princess Beatrix celebrated her marriage on 10 March 1966. As her marriage procession made its way through Amsterdam – filmed by the world press – a smoke bomb exploded. For such a quiet, orderly and law-abiding country like the Netherlands, this was a shocking piece of disrespect. The smoke bomb initiated a year of excitement and tumult. Amsterdam in particular became the scene for riots, demonstrations and other public manifestations during 1966. In October the cabinet fell after a long and suspenseful debate – also broadcast on television – in which parliamentary leader of the KVP (Catholic People's Party), N. Schmelzer, introduced a motion of no confidence in the cabinet headed by another KVPer, J. Cals. At the same time, reformers established their own party, Democrats '66, in order to bring about a fundamental "democratization" of the Dutch political system. In the PvdA (Labor Party), young intellectuals mobilized into a "New Left" which sought to give the party a wholly new – and radical – political program.

Outside the established parties, anarchistic, culturally avant-garde, and revolutionary groups, consisting mostly of the young, became active and attracted much attention. Within Roman Catholicism, the New Catechism was only one indication that Dutch Catholics were charting a new spiritual course, which shook the very foundations of their pillar. All of these developments occurred in 1966, and for

10 March 1966: A smoke bomb explodes as the newly-weds Princess Beatrix and Claus van Amsberg ride in a coach through Amsterdam.

that reason the year may be regarded as emblematic of "the Sixties" in the Netherlands, when spectacular events were symptomatic of far-reaching change. Just as at the turn of the century, economic growth and international orientation rapidly gave the country a new face in the 1960s – so much so that people spoke of a "cultural revolution."

It is now clear that such an interpretation was exaggerated. Continuity and stability remained in many respects characteristic of developments within Dutch society. Much of what was new, or was presented as new, had roots in the past, if not the recent past. But it remains incontestable that there was a pervasive sense of change, and that the intensity, scope, and tempo of social, political, and cultural change all markedly increased. Trusted patterns of life and thought were broken, traditional values were now openly questioned. Everything from the past seemed to have no future. The population was no longer willing to follow their leaders as the authorities fell from their pedestals. Personal growth, self-determination, democratization, and "having a say" were the new buzzwords of the 1960s. That decade, incidentally, is difficult to define. Its high point may have been around 1970, with the oil crisis of 1973 bringing the decade to an end. The turbulent year of 1966 may be considered the beginning of the decade, although many of these developments already had been visible for some years.

In any event, it was already apparent in the late 1950s that economic growth was making life easier for the general population. There was a veritable explosion of prosperity, including unprecedented wage increases after 1963, which made goods like household appliances, televisions, automobiles, and foreign vacations, all once considered prohibitively luxurious, accessible to most Dutch. This obviously had effects on both the style of life and on expectations. Material prosperity was soon taken for granted, and by the mid-1960s the Netherlands had become a "consumer society." The assurances of economists and politicians that the economy was under their full control, as well as the discovery of natural gas in Dutch territory, strengthened many Dutch in their conviction that they faced a carefree future. Under these conditions, the two-century long process of secularization intensified. One reason for the decline of the churches' influence stemmed from the expansion of the state's social services, which replaced the old pillarized organizations. Increasingly, social services were implemented by the state, including keystone services like the General Pension Act and the General Assistance Act of 1963. In this way, the nexus between pillarized organizations and the population became less coercive, and people were free to cut their subcultural ties with little material consequence. Thus the pillars' means of social control declined.

In many areas, pillarized institutions retained their functions, and in some sectors they actually expanded during the 1960s. But they faced growing internal problems. Many well-educated and often younger personnel began to believe that professional standards were more important than maintaining the moral and ideological foundations of the pillars they served. They also began to question the value of having separate religious or ideological organizations. In social work, the newest pedagogical and psychological insights won ground; these emphasized personal happiness, personal decision making and personal growth. The value of serving one's subculture or deferring to authority was now made secondary to these new concerns. The sociology and political science of the 1960s also frequently encouraged social service professionals to use their positions to further social reform. This sometimes led to conflict with the pillars' traditional elites.

Already by the 1950s, a richly varied youth culture had sprung up. Unlike many of the old youth movements and service bureaus with their close ties to the adult world, teens in the new youth culture typically distanced themselves from adults. In the early 1950s, "the youth" were widely regarded as a serious problem, and their "rebellious" subcultures were kept at the margins of society. Within a few years, however, the youth cultures broke through this barrier and began to set the cultural tone of Dutch society. There were, of course, important variations among these youth cultures. In the first place, prosperity had

made possible the rise of a highly consumer-ori-
ented clothes and music culture. But there was
also an anti-Establishment culture with connections to older protest currents such as anarchism
and revolutionary socialism. Finally, there was an
"underground" culture which explicitly opted

The 1980s witnessed sharp confrontations between the government and the squatters' movement. Serious riots erupted in October 1982 as police emptied a squatters house in the Jan Luykenstraat of Amsterdam.

out of mainstream society; it had contacts with avant-garde currents in
the arts, which in the 1960s were less marginalized than in the past. The
Cobra artist Karel Appel and the Fiftier Lucebert became celebrities,
and others also profited from their status as iconoclasts. Various artists
and authors like Constant, Simon Vinkenoog, and Harry Mulisch were
quite active in this movement.

In this respect, developments in the Netherlands paralleled those
elsewhere. Indeed, the Dutch frequently looked abroad for inspiration
– particularly to the United States with its hippie culture and its hard-
hitting protests against the Vietnam War. But the Netherlands was also
at the vanguard of the counterculture, especially Amsterdam. There the
Provos, a rather small anarchistic group, received considerable national
and international attention for their public highjinks. The Provos and
similar groups sharply criticized affluent society and consumption-ori-
ented "squares". In their attack on a mentality rather than on a generation, the boundary between old and young began to blur.

"The street" began to play more of a role than it had in past decades:
riots, disturbances, strikes (especially wildcat strikes in the beginning,
as unions lost control over their workers), sit-ins, and demonstrations
all increased in number. The riots of Amsterdam in 1966 have been
mentioned; the occupation of the *Maagdenhuis* in 1969 is another example. Radical students, seeking to democratize the educational system,

staged a sit-in at the administrative offices of the City University of Amsterdam. Nor were actions of this kind without effect. Out of conviction, or by force of circumstance, elites began to make concessions to the protesters' demands. At first, protesters vehemently clashed with the police and other authorities who could not easily reconcile themselves to the changes. After several years, however, authorities learned to employ regulatory rather than repressive strategies, which effectively changed their relationship with the public. At the same time, the well-organized, rather self-congratulatory mass gatherings of the pillarized institutions quickly fell into disuse.

The Netherlands largely escaped the extremely violent terrorism that plagued other countries. The most famous instances of domestic terrorism were conducted by radical South Moluccan youths who demanded an independent South Moluccan republic. They hijacked trains in 1975 and 1977 and staged several other violent actions. Dutch squatters also fought running battles with the police during the 1970s and 1980s. They protested against a lack of adequate, affordable housing by occupying empty dwellings, and some of them believed that their cause justified violence. In particular, police efforts to remove squatters from occupied buildings was likely to provoke sharp confrontation. Moreover, the coronation of Beatrix on 30 April 1980 prompted a large number of sharp street fights between the squatters and the Amsterdam police.

The traditional elite practice of reasonable consultation and sensible compromise behind closed doors was now criticized by a growing chorus of voices calling for greater openness, radicalism, polarization, democratization, and participation of citizens in public life. New concerns and new values became the topics of discussion. Rather than stoutly defending the host of norms and rules with which they had grown up, many Dutch came to the conclusion that everybody should decide for themselves how they wished to behave, thus ushering in the so-called permissive society. Part of the women's movement, influenced by this sea change, abandoned earlier efforts to integrate itself into Dutch society (a strategy increasingly condemned as cooptation), and formulated new demands, built a new constituency, developed new forms, and enjoyed a new élan. In 1968 Joke Kool-Smit helped inspire the activist organization called Man-Woman-Society; in 1970 the radical *Dolle Mina* ("Mad Mina") group appeared. Central to both groups was the demand made by feminists at the end of the nineteenth century: full equality and equal treatment for women as well as men.

One of the most discussed aspects of "the permissive society" was the advent of a new sexual morality, emphasizing sexual freedom. Studies from the 1960s indicate that even before "the new morality" many Dutch had engaged in sexual activities that did not comport with official bourgeois values. Now these practices were no longer kept secret. Homosexuality was no longer a taboo. The introduction of "the pill" in the early 1960s provided an easy way for people to separate sexual intercourse from procreation. A woman's right to an abortion, championed under the slogan "boss of own belly," also became an important political issue.

In reaction to the ostensible passivity of the pillarized life, many Dutch demanded a complete democratization of society, in which citizens would always have a much greater say. They advocated giving all citizens a direct voice in their workplaces, schools, and elsewhere, and putting an end to the paternalism of the old elites. In this way, they hoped to usher in a wholly new society, with new democratic manners and relationships. Many of these reformers found inspiration in Marxist, socialist, and revolutionary ideologies. Others emphasized a much more consistent and more broadly applied democratization.

The royal house did not escape these discussions, and principled opponents of the monarchy were able, for a short time, to lead a public debate about House of Orange's future. But the public was much more interested in the controversial marriage plans of the queen's two eldest daughters. Beatrix wished to marry a German, Claus von Amsberg, and this was not easily accepted, especially among traditionally Orangist circles. The marriage precipitated many reflections on the German occupation, as did the more general debate about the nature and value of authority. Juliana's second daughter, Irene, decided to marry the Carlist pretender to the Spanish throne, Juan de Bourbon Parma. His problematic political position and Irene's decision to become Roman Catholic – her family had ruled over a historically Protestant country for 400 years – presented authorities with a conundrum, which was only solved when Irene repudiated her right to the throne in 1964.

Dutch foreign policy, long supported by a silent consensus, also became the subject of heated public debate. Development aid became an important new theme, which the Dutch saw as a necessary extension of human solidarity. Many new countries, recently decolonized, were poverty-ridden, and most Dutch believed that the West should help ameliorate the situation. Dutch security policy was questioned as resistance to the Cold War and support for disarmament increased. Nuclear weapons in particular were the target of much criticism and protest actions. The activities of (the London-based) Amnesty International and similar groups made human rights' violations the subject of political and diplomatic action. America's prestige as the leader of the Western world was seriously undermined by the Vietnam War, and communist rule in Eastern Europe now seemed less frightening to many Dutch. The idea that states should be formed around nations came under attack, and in the eyes of many Dutch, nationalism and patriotism had become old-fashioned, narrow-minded, and downright dangerous. Universal values would bring all of humanity together. On the face of it, these sentiments provided a fruitful basis for international political cooperation, but many Dutch had become quite critical of the capitalistic character of existing international organizations like NATO and the European Community.

The churches faced both declining adherence and a radicalization and politicization of their members. By 1990 almost half of the Netherlands's 15 million people (a figure up from nearly 11.5 million in 1960) had no affiliation with any religious body. The Dutch Reformed church now represented only 10 to 15 percent of the population; the Reformed Churches in the Netherlands declined to around 5 percent. The Catholic church began to suffer a decline for the first time. In the 1970s and 1980s, the proportion of Catholics went from approximately 40 to under 30 percent. Almost all of the country's denominations experienced an internal radicalization, as traditional beliefs and doctrines were given a political interpretation or made to serve a socially engaged agenda. Liturgy and church organization also underwent a host of changes. The ecumenical movement enjoyed great popularity during these years, although institutional unity remained elusive. It took two decades of cooperation before the Dutch Reformed church and the Reformed Churches in the Netherlands could declare, in 1986, that they were "in a state of union."

The Dutch Roman Catholic church long had been loyal to Rome, and until the 1960s, the Dutch were among the most conservative Catholics in Western Europe. This now changed rapidly. Under the leadership of Cardinal B. Alfrink, the Dutch church attempted to meet the demands of the modern age. In this it was encouraged by the reforms introduced by Pope John XXIII and the Second Vatican Council that he opened in 1962. Dutch Catholics were soon enthusiastically at the vanguard, giving expression to the new open Catholicism. The Latin mass was soon abandoned in favor of the vernacular as the Dutch initiated liturgical innovations. The laity were now consulted on a host of ecclesiastical issues, and the Pastoral Council (1968-1970) gave them ample room to express their thoughts. Catholic morality became much less rigid, for laity and clergy alike, and individual conscience became much more important in determining moral action. As early as 1963, Bishop W. Bekkers declared on television that the individual conscience was important in determining sexual conduct within marriage. Finally, Roman Catholics were given a great deal more freedom in their associations with non-Catholics.

Attempts by more conservative Catholics to stop this process or to reverse it made little headway, at least initially. Later, especially in the 1980s, this began to change as international developments within the Roman Catholic church once again affected the Netherlands. The renewal movement within the Dutch church lost its élan as Rome appointed more conservative bishops, although in most respects the pre-Vatican II status quo did not return. The international Roman Catholic church also put a brake on ecumenical dialogue between Dutch Catholics and non-Catholics, despite an occasional conciliatory gesture.

The mass media played an important part in this atmosphere of radical change and openness. Previously in the hands of the pillarized elites and acting as mouthpieces for the authorities, the media now became independent institutions, committed to hard-hitting investigations of political and social realities – not least behind the scenes. Many politically engaged reporters allied themselves with the reformers who attacked the public and hidden power relations in Dutch society; in doing so, they introduced a new, more confrontational style to Dutch journalism. The intrusiveness of television, with its quick and compelling reporting of current events, was certainly an important factor in this development. Those authorities and other public figures unsure of how to avail themselves of this new medium were now at a strong disadvantage.

It is difficult to distinguish between cause and effect in this complex series of changes. In many respects the causes and effects mutually reinforced each other. Moreover, these developments often had their own dynamic, which also played an important role. An explanation of the these rapid changes may be found in the interaction between a number of new developments that appeared after 1960, as well as the continuation of older, sometimes much older, processes. The shorter term developments included the arrival of material prosperity and the growing international orientation of the general population, partly through the new détente between East and West. The longer term processes, which began to speed up in the 1950s, included the development of the welfare state, the technologization of society, and the professionalization of education, social work, and state administration. Through these changes, the educational level of the population rose – the universities exploded in size during the 1960s – and most people could enjoy more leisure time. Finally, the forces of opposition that had always been an undercurrent in the Netherlands's bourgeois, pillarized society provided points of contact for a new generation of protesters and activists. Discussions among small groups of intellectuals in the 1950s could suddenly take on a mass dimension in the 1960s.

The Results: Depillarization and More Emphasis on Personal Growth

Any conclusions about the protest movements' assault on the Netherlands's bourgeois, pillarized society must be carefully made. It is a mistake, for instance, to suppose that the noisy events of the 1960s necessarily had deep and momentous effects; almost none of the aims sought by the reformers and renewers were completely achieved. Still, important changes took place, changes which might best be summarized as a substantial increase in the rate of secularization. More concretely, this process was characterized by far-reaching depillarization and the increasing importance of personal growth within the dominant set of norms and values.

Depillarization

Depillarization meant first and foremost that most Dutch no longer felt an unquestioned sense of belonging to one of the country's large religious or ideological groups. As this adherence waned, so did many of the specific phenomena characteristic of each pillar. This was especially true, of course, for people who left the churches, but those who stayed also felt freer to choose friends and belong to associations as they themselves saw fit. The social democratic pillar suffered a similar decline.

Dutch electoral results had been roughly the same for fifty years, but depillarization led to greater voting swings and to a serious decline of the confessional parties. Before the 1960s, parties typically lost or gained one or two seats; now losses and gains in a range of five or ten seats became routine. The three large confessional parties, especially the KVP and CHU, lost much of their support between 1963 and 1972, and their collective share of the total vote fell from one half to one third. Necessity prompted them to present a unified program in the elections of 1977, known as the Christian Democratic Appeal (CDA), and in 1980, after years of difficult negotiations, the three parties merged to become the CDA. The ideological foundations of the CDA were no longer "confessional" (that is, they were no longer based on the creeds of any church), and the only remaining evidence of its Christian identity was its general support of the Christian gospel and of Christendom. Perhaps its rather cautious centrist course gave the CDA its new electoral stability; until the early 1990s, it held roughly one third of the seats in parliament. But in 1994, when the popular party leader and prime minister R.F. M. Lubbers retired, the CDA fell back to less than a quarter of the seats.

The PvdA also fell back in the course of the 1960s, but bounced back in the 1970s. In the ups and downs of the 1980s, it managed to retain the support of roughly a third of the electorate. But in 1994 this party, too, had to accept election results which gave them less than a quarter of all votes. The VVD (Party of Freedom and Democracy) appeared to be the big winner in the 1970s (with 20 percent of the vote), but declined somewhat in the 1980s. In the 1994 elections, however, they again scored around 20 percent. Among the new parties only the Democrats '66 (now called D66) managed to hold on, with widely fluctuating electoral results, including a surprisingly high result in 1994 (about 15 percent). The small Communist party also enjoyed something of a resurgence around 1970, but within a decade it was smaller than ever. Toward the end of the 1980s, a number of tiny leftist parties, including the communists, merged into a new one called Green Left. The very small orthodox Protestant parties showed relative stability and made slight electoral gains after the 1960s. Election results also became more unpredictable when compulsory voting was abolished in 1970. Otherwise, the country's political institutions remained intact. The calls by Democrats '66 for a district system, an elected premier, and popular referenda, not to mention subsequent proposals by other reformers, did not lead to structural political change of any significance.

Political parties were not the only victims of depillarization. Many pillarized organizations disappeared, or survived only by fusing with similar organizations. Even though some remained intact, the dense networks of subcultural associations had passed from the scene. Nor was there any longer a common organizational pattern which united these pillarized associations. The confessional parties' decision to form a common party was markedly different, for example, from developments among the trade unions, where the social democratic NVV (Dutch Alliance of Workers' Unions) and its Catholic counterpart, the NKV (Dutch Catholic Trade Union), merged to become the Federation of Dutch Trade Unions (FNV; 1975). The Protestant trade union, the CNV, opted out of the merger. But the differences between the CNV and the new FNV were not so much religious in nature; rather, the CNV followed a more moderate course and recruited members among other professions than the FNV.

Newspapers also cut ties with their pillars, since the new journalistic style did not well serve the construction and defense of pillarized life. A good example of this is *De Volkskrant*, once the highly pillarized paper of Catholic workers. In the 1970s and 1980s, it became a commercial success as an independent and for many years a radical daily. Other newspapers and magazines could not make the transition and disappeared; the social democratic *Het Vrije Volk*, once the Netherlands's largest daily, folded, as did the Catholic dailies *De Tijd* and *De Maasbode*. Two liberal dailies, the *Nieuwe Rotterdamse Courant* and the *Algemeen Handelsblad* merged into the *NRC Handelsblad* with the ambition of becoming the Netherlands's quality newspaper.

The country's broadcasting associations underwent a somewhat different process. The four large associations, the liberal AVRO, the Catholic KRO, the Protestant NCRV, and the social democratic VARA all continued to exist – and even managed to project their own identity and maintain (much looser) ties with the old pillarized world. Only the little VPRO completely changed its character. In 1968 an amorphous group of radicals managed, through a complex series of events, to gain control of this originally liberal Protestant outfit, and took it in a substantially different direction. Over time, the VPRO became the mouthpiece of a cultural avant-garde. New broadcasting associations took their place next to the old ones in the existing system. Two of these, the TROS and Veronica, primarily sought to provide entertainment for mass audiences. The Evangelical Broadcasting Company (EO) was of a different cut altogether, founded by Protestants who considered the NCRV insufficiently orthodox, or Protestant. This company, too, received enough memberships to broadcast on Dutch public television. Technological change in recent years has also made it possible for the Dutch to receive many foreign channels. The government had attempted for a long time to keep commercial broadcasting out of the Netherlands, or to reduce it to short advertising periods between programs. The changes in technology made it impossible to continue this course. The Netherlands currently possesses a dual system, including not only a public system largely subsidized by the government and most of the old broadcasting associations, but also wholly commercial stations now sanctioned by the state.

In education and in health care the pillarized organizations remained strong, but their religious or ideological character became much more difficult to spot, or became less pervasive. Public and private religious schools differed little from each other in content and form, and alternative pedagogical systems (Montessori, Dalton, etc.) appeared in public, Catholic, and Protestant schools. Teachers and students no longer came exclusively, or even mainly, from the subcultures the schools traditionally served; other concerns, such as quality or distance from home, were often more important considerations in choosing a school than its religious, or nonreligious antecedents. Hospitals, clinics, and nursing homes experienced a similar change in their relationship with their patients.

Commitment to Personal Growth

Dutch society was thus no longer pillarized; at most there were the remnants of pillarized life and mentalities. But Dutch society did remain bourgeois in ethos, although here, too, there were important shifts. The most striking – and most enduring – of these shifts was the new importance of "personal growth" as a moral standard. To be sure, this notion had been around for some time as an important liberal principle and a bourgeois characteristic, but its expression was limited by other moral considerations such as family, nation, order, and authority. This now came to an end as the "natural" authority of state, church, employer, association, school, and family disappeared. The decline in authority did not mean, of course, that all individuals were now equally empowered, but such differences were ignored in public discussions and were no longer overtly exploited. Exercise of authority now demanded perennial legitimation, the power of persuasion, and frequent negotiation. The change was most marked in the area of personal manners, which became much more informal.

The importance assigned to personal growth also had far-reaching effects on demographic patterns and on sexual morality. The propaganda of "the permissive society" had considerable success. The social taboo on sexuality disappeared. Homosexuality became much more acceptable in the Netherlands than it had been before. For decades in slow decline, the birth rate plummeted in the 1960s and 1970s. Large families, most typical in Catholic and orthodox Protestant homes, almost completely disappeared, and the average number of children per family dropped as well. A two-children family more or less became the standard, and more couples opted for having no children at all. Divorce, once itself a taboo, became a common phenomenon.

It would go too far, however, to say that Dutch society was no longer bourgeois because of these changes – or that it had jettisoned bourgeois values. Many of the old patterns remained in place. The family, for example, has remained a self-evident and highly respected social institution for an overwhelming majority of the Dutch, even if the value of legal marriage has been relativized. Many Dutch now live together outside of marriage, for short or extended periods of time. Countercultural lifestyles are more easily accepted than before, but they are not commonly practiced – and then only for a short period in one's youth. Indeed, the wide range of consumer choices offered by bourgeois society are more attractive to the great majority of Dutch than any way of life promoted by the critics of capitalism.

Permissive society in the Netherlands actually depends on self-discipline (another cardinal bourgeois virtue) to prevent individualism from going unchecked and creating all kinds of social problems. The Dutch no longer rely on formal codes of behavior, but on subtle, informal rules. To a certain extent, this is also true of law enforcement. The strict maintenance of authority may be gone, but in actuality officials have been quite successful in restoring their authority, after getting over their initial fright in the 1960s. Through more informal and flexible approaches, officials managed to keep the structures of Dutch society intact. A well-ordered and orderly society has remained an important value for many Dutch citizens.

It is thus more appropriate to speak of a sometimes drastic reconfiguration of Dutch bourgeois values rather than of their disappearance. Seen from a broader perspective, it becomes clear that bourgeois society has remained intact in a number of key respects. The economy remains in the hands of entrepreneurs. Politically, the Netherlands

Joop den Uyl, the driven leader of the PvdA and the country's prime minister between 1973 and 1977.

remains a parliamentary democracy. Its constitutional monarchy has easily withstood the republican challenge; after the commotion surrounding the marriages of Irene and Beatrix and the squatters' riots during Beatrix's coronation in 1980, the controversy surrounding the crown died away. Queen Beatrix has, like her mother and grandmother, won much respect from her subjects – partly because she has demonstrated the bourgeois values of competence and devotion to her duties. Perhaps most important, the Netherlands's middle classes, however many variations among them there are, have continued to dominate society. Since the late Middle Ages, the country has not possessed a powerful feudal class, and its aristocracy has always shown many bourgeois traits. None of this has changed. In contrast, distinctive working class cultures and rural communities have either disappeared or conformed to the rest of society.

New Problems in the 1970s and 1980s

At first, the large political parties were not particularly quick-witted in responding to social ferment and the élan for change. But in the 1970s, the PvdA, inspired by the more militantly socialist New Left movement and led by the experienced and driven J.M. den Uyl, presented itself as the party which could bring reform and renewal. After protracted negotiations, Den Uyl managed to form a cabinet in 1973 supported by the PvdA and two new parties, D66 and the PPR (the left-wing Party of Political Radicals); but in order to attain a parliamentary majority he also relied on the toleration of the KVP and ARP (the Anti-Revolutionary Party). Representatives from these two parties also sat in Den Uyl's cabinet with their parties' foreknowledge, but did not formally represent them. Such a complex and difficult arrangement demonstrates just how far Dutch political practice in the 1970s had departed from the pacification model of earlier decades.

Economic Difficulties

The Den Uyl cabinet was strongly committed to bringing about social change, in which "income, knowledge, and power" would be distributed more equitably. This goal was exceedingly difficult to achieve, and the cabinet made only very limited headway. It was difficult to implement effective measures to this end; the parliamentary manoeuvering room of the cabinet was small and the popular surge for social and political change had already crested. To make matters worse, the Netherlands faced an international oil crisis six months into Den Uyl's premiership. In 1973, Arab oil-producing countries, which had already been raising oil prices, decided to cut off all supplies to the United States and the Netherlands because of their pro-Israeli posture during the Yom Kippur War. Their oil boycott generated widespread fears of scarcity and prompted the Dutch to introduce several "carless Sundays." In the end, the boycott proved ineffective, but it did signal a recession in the international economy and thus hampered the cabinet's ambitions for social change. Moreover, the oil crisis also undermined confidence in the government's ability to control economic and social developments.

The economic recession hit the Netherlands hard, particularly psychologically, and it was paired with the retrenchment of the Dutch economy. Much of the country's industry – textiles, shipbuilding, shipping, and important parts of the metallurgic and mining sectors – either fared very poorly or went under. Natural gas, the energy sector, and capital intensive assembly plants (i.e., the least labor intensive industries) remained strong, while dairy production and horticulture in the agricultural sector (which relied on ever fewer personnel) remained a central component of the export economy. The Netherlands retained its vitally important position as a center of international services and distribution. Rotterdam continued to function as one of the world's largest harbors. The further expansion of the Dutch welfare state continued well into the 1970s, giving the Dutch a much greater buffer against economic recession than they had possessed a generation earlier. But it also began to generate financial problems. Entitlement programs, guaranteed by law to all those who met the criteria, had spun out of control. Moreover, the Netherlands suffered under the international inflationary spiral of the 1970s, for which there was no effective remedy.

All of this led to considerable unemployment, especially among unskilled workers – not least the unschooled laborers that the Dutch had recruited first from Spain and Italy, and later from Morocco and Turkey during happier economic times. Unemployment remained high even when better economic conditions obtained during the 1980s. Moreover, the problem was worse than the employment figures suggested, since many Dutch made use of the programs afforded by the welfare state.

Many persons, especially older employees, were sent into the Workers' Disability Act (WAO), a 1966 insurance program which provided government income to those classified unfit for work. It seems, therefore, that fundamental structural changes in the economy have brought not only high productivity (chiefly through a highly trained workforce and advanced technologies) but also low labor participation.

Questioning the Role of Government

As mentioned above, economic difficulties did not stop the Den Uyl cabinet from supporting the many calls for social change that emanated from the 1960s. But in this it was stymied not only by financial but also by practical problems. Government intervention intensified under Den Uyl, and thus the move toward democratization was accompanied by the growth of bureaucracy. Individuals and groups gained a greater say in the governing process, but this hardly improved the efficiency of the state and other organizations. In several instances, government slowness contributed to an increased militancy among activist groups and to violent confrontations, as between squatters and the authorities in the 1970s and 1980s. But in most cases it increased bureaucratization, thus dampening activist interest and fostering public resignation.

There were, however, minor and major exceptions to this trend toward political apathy, including the anti-nuclear weapons movement of the early 1980s, which managed to mobilize huge rallies to protest government policy. Such large-scale opposition forced the government to attempt a high-wire act in which it tried to both appease domestic opinion and maintain its commitments to NATO. Indeed, NATO and European (economic) integration remained the cornerstones of Dutch foreign policy. Development aid also became more important.

The women's movement, too, was highly active and took on many forms. It achieved success insofar as many of its aims (in particular the demand for equal treatment and equal opportunity) became part of official government policy. But as elsewhere, old habits and practices remained resilient, and the position of women changed less than the movement had hoped. The percentage of married women wage earners, for example, remained relatively low.

Another very important issue which stemmed from the renewal movement of the 1960s but which initially received secondary attention was the environment. In 1972 an international group of experts known as the Club of Rome published a report, "The Limits of Growth," which warned that unlimited expansion of the global economy posed serious problems for the environment and would deplete the world's resources. The report prompted a host of activities aimed at protecting the environment. Indeed, there are many places in the Netherlands that are seriously polluted and could, in the long run, be completely ruined. Protest groups and more enduring environmental organizations, in part the descendants of much older nature preservation societies, constantly attempt to draw public attention to these problems. The Dutch government has often proved ready to direct action to remedy such problems, but it has faced several difficulties in doing so. Pollution is a complex problem made more complex by its international dimension. The pollution in Dutch rivers, for instance, largely stems from foreign sources. Moreover, it is difficult to implement regulations and to maintain a balance between adequate environmental protection and keeping a strong Dutch economy.

The state has increasingly intervened in Dutch society while at the same time it has become apparent to many Dutch that government is unable to adequately and adroitly tackle the country's problems. Since the 1970s, the government has had to struggle against this situation. The cabinets (from 1977 to 1982 under the leadership of A.A.M. van Agt, then R.F. Lubbers) were dominated by the CDA (Christian Democratic Appeal) until 1994. Between 1981 and 1982, and 1989 and 1994, the Christian Democrats governed with the PvDA, but for most of the period they shared power with the VVD. The surprising election results of 1994 made history; for the first time since proportional representation was introduced in 1917, the cabinet which emerged did not include confessional (or Christian Democratic) parties. The new constellation of PvDA, VVD, and D66 has been called the "purple coalition," and is presently led by Prime Minister W. Kok of the PvDA.

Since 1977, cabinets have generally been less ambitious in promoting social change and have tried to both trim their budgets and boost the economy, initially with little success, later with more. But all have been relatively powerless in limiting the role of the state, which seems capable of spontaneously expansion. Deregulation and privatization in many instances only displace the problem. Thus the intertwining of state and society (the neo-corporatist state) cannot easily be undone. This problem is clearly complicated by the growth of European institutions, which in practice has often meant even greater bureaucratization. Almost no one doubts the need for international economic and social cooperation, but the bureaucratization that comes with it has raised many questions, and much annoyance.

For the ordinary citizen, government now increasingly appears as a series of anonymous bureaucratic institutions. Cabinets and political parties have had great difficulty in giving voters a clear idea of what political issues matter most and in which direction they are going to find the solutions. Furthermore, the large political parties increasingly seem to differ little from each other; politics often appears to be a string of complex technical questions that are impenetrable to the uninitiated. The parties have thus relied on ephemeral issues and telegenic personalities to set the public political tone instead of principles or a spirited commitment to change.

The social democrats in particular experienced a deep crisis in the late 1980s as a result of the deep doubt about state's ability to solve social problems and fashion an ideal society. The Christian Democrats, who had seemed to regain their confidence under Van Agt and Lubbers, have also found themselves in a serious crisis since their dramatic electoral loss in 1994. Christianity does not appear, in the secularized world, to provide any more of a broad electoral basis for social and political ideals than the socialists can offer. Indeed, the Christian Democrats' absence from the cabinet has made it even more difficult for them to determine a collective course. But throughout Dutch society, political interest has declined since the 1960s and 1970s, and now observers complain about the lack of civic spirit. The degradation of the old communal ties, they reason, has increasingly set citizens in pursuit of their own interests and toward the more materialistic understandings of personal growth that fit so well in a consumerist society. One might ask if this assessment is not somewhat overdramatic, although it is quite clear that the political and administrative system suffers from a certain crisis of legitimacy.

Dutch Identity

Another recent concern pertains to the preservation of national and regional cultures, a concern which originates in two, at first glance quite divergent, phenomena. In the first place, some Dutch believe that their culture is threatened by the presence of a relatively large number of ethnic minorities: foreign workers who have decided to stay in the Netherlands (chiefly Moroccans and Turks, Surinamers and a smaller number of refugees from various countries). In absolute numbers, their presence is modest: less than one million persons. Immigration is also not a new phenomenon for the Netherlands; for centuries, large and small waves of immigrants have been able to stay in the country, and were largely integrated over the course of time. Refugees from the Southern Netherlands at the end of the sixteenth century, Jews and Huguenots during the Republic, and economically motivated migration from Germany throughout the centuries are just a few examples.

It is very much the question, however, whether the new immigrants will integrate as quickly and as flexibly as, say, the Indo-European repatriates who left the new state of Indonesia during the 1950s. The question is complicated by religious differences (in 1990 roughly 3 percent of the population were Muslims and 0.5 percent Hindu) and by the fact that most immigrants have received little or no schooling and thus are in a weak socioeconomic position. There are signs that they are forming a new underclass, with the cultural and political stigmatization that come with it.

In the second place, many fear that Dutch culture will disappear with the increasing Europeanization of economics and politics, and through cultural Americanization – processes that have been underway for decades. In comparison to other nations, the Dutch do not seem especially willing to defend their own language and culture. The depillarization and internationalization which began in the 1960s, and the concomitant decline of once widespread support for the Dutch nation apparently continue to make their effects known. The government has also proven less prepared to foster a sense of nationhood than some of its European counterparts. But it would be premature to speak of an acute threat to Dutch culture.

Thus the Netherlands, like many other Western countries, faces several stubborn problems at the end of the twentieth century that defy easy solution. Still, the country remains one of the world's most prosperous nations, and is certain to remain a full-fledged participant in European affairs. Moreover, the Netherlands maintains a very high level of social services. It is, therefore, a highly stable society which, in a moment of crisis, could certainly rely on the loyalty of an overwhelming number of its citizens. Over the course of centuries – and particularly the last century and a half – growing numbers of groups have been able to exert their own influence in Dutch politics and society. Of course, differences in power have hardly been eliminated. But the Dutch citizenry has received a host of opportunities to participate in public life despite government's increasing demands and regulations upon them. This, too, has given Dutch society a high level of cohesion.

Dutch society at the end of the twentieth century looks completely different from its appearance in 1830. Yet this thorough metamorphosis, evident in nearly every aspect of society, took place with remarkably little violence. However wide the differences, however great the conflicts, and however many the number of confrontations, the Dutch seldom initiated bloodbaths or resorted to extremism. Instead, they consciously maintained their ties to the past. The five years of German occupation formed the only significant exception to this pattern.

Three factors help account for this phenomenon. The Netherlands is a small country that was compelled to forsake international political ambitions. The Dutch were thus obliged to satisfy themselves with their modest status. Furthermore, the Netherlands has been a relatively rich country, which was able to use its wealth to solve its domestic problems. Finally, the Dutch managed, through times of great change, to retain the tradition of compromise. The Netherlands will undoubtedly change much, perhaps drastically, in the future. But it would be highly surprising if the Dutch completely were to sever their ties to centuries of history – and thus eradicate the unique character of Dutch society.

Epilogue

Unity and Diversity in the Low Countries

J.C.H. Blom and E. Lamberts

1. Unity in Diversity

No one attempting to understand the history of the Low Countries can ignore the importance of its geographical features. The region's center lies in the Scheldt, Maas and Rhine Deltas, and at first the Low Countries' swampy landscape kept it a peripheral, sparsely inhabited corner of Europe. The limits of the Roman Empire, the Rhine, cut straight through the region. Under the Carolingians, the Maas region became a core area, but with the rise of new kingdoms, namely Germany and France, the region was once again relegated to the periphery. Even the short-lived existence of Lothar's Middle Francia could not alter this.

The Low Countries were able to attain a central position in Europe only after the sea no longer formed a formidable barrier, once shipping had become an important nexus, and once the inhabitants had developed effective water-control techniques. By the late Middle Ages, the region began to rival Northern Italy economically and culturally.

At the same time, the Low Countries began to coalesce into a political entity, a process evident in the formation of the Burgundian Kreis in 1548. When the northern provinces succeeded in breaking with the Habsburgs during the Dutch Revolt later in the century, military developments largely determined the line between North and South which, with a few exceptions, still determines the border between the Netherlands and Belgium. Similarly, the region's eastern boundaries were largely drawn by dynastic ambitions and military campaigns. The Low Countries' southern border with France did not stabilize until the eighteenth century. Chance played no small role in the formation of these political boundaries.

Economically, socially, and culturally, the horizontal political line that came to separate the South from the North in the late sixteenth century was for a long time less important than the vertical divide which separated the eastern and western parts of the region. The language divide between Dutch and French-speaking areas, evident quite early on, was also incongruent with the political borders. For the most part, the language boundary remained stable except in the southwest, in present-day northern France, where it moved north. Language differences did not often have much political significance until the nineteenth century, when they became a divisive issue in Belgium. The language boundary with Germany in the east initially was not sharply delineated. Indeed, for a long time the change in language was gradual rather than abrupt.

The arbitrary and relative character of the region's political boundary is also illustrated by the Dutch Revolt, which, though it led to the formation of the Republic of the Seven United Provinces in the North, had begun in the South. It was the South, not the North, that possessed the religious, political, and socioeconomic catalysts for the conflict which exploded in the 1560s. It was also from the South, chiefly Flanders and Brabant, that a flourishing economic and cultural life had radiated over the whole region for several centuries, contributing greatly to the region's increasing unity in the fifteenth and sixteenth centuries.

The rise of the Low Countries chiefly rested on the development of a highly varied economy. The region traditionally enjoyed an advanced and innovation-minded agricultural economy. Its cities became magnets of regional and gradually of international trade. They also became centers of flowering and multifaceted artisanal production, and later of protoindustrial commerce. By no later than the thirteenth century, the Low Countries had become a very prosperous region, despite cyclical declines and structural weaknesses.

In the seventeenth century the Republic of the North became – thanks in part to many merchants and entrepreneurs who emigrated from the southern provinces – the uncontested center of world trade. The Republic became the most successful practitioner of the "trade capitalism" of the period, of which colonial trade was an important component. Over time, this position could not be maintained. But generally speaking the Low Countries, both North and South, remained relatively wealthy areas.

The region was also adept at accommodating its economy to the industrial and modern capitalistic innovations of the nineteenth century. Belgium in particular, with its Walloon coal and iron industries, was at the international vanguard of these great changes. The Netherlands, still prosperous, later went in the same direction, and its new industrial sector became an interesting addition to its already diverse economic structure, in which the colonial dimension had also recently become important.

The economic and cultural achievements of the Low Countries during late medieval and early modern times gave the region an important role in international politics. It was the center of gravity for the lands ruled by the Burgundian dukes, and later it was the most developed part of the Habsburg empire. After the decline of Habsburg power, the Republic of the Seven United Provinces became a world power of its own, and was a serious contender for its rivals. This was less true in the eighteenth than in the seventeenth century, but it was not until the nineteenth that the North was relegated to playing a minor role in international politics, as the South had been since the seventeenth century.

That the region's political weakness of the modern period did not lead to a loss of independence – indeed, it did not even prevent the creation of an independent Belgium – had much to do with its geographical position and its economic prosperity. The rivalry among the great powers of Europe caused these states to regularly cast covetous eyes on the region, but this rivalry also prevented the Low Countries from being absorbed by any one of them.

The decline of the great medieval German empire and the weakening of Habsburg power gave France in particular room for expansion on the European continent. French ambition was chiefly resisted by England, and for this reason London – despite continuing economic rivalry with the Dutch Republic – increasingly sought open or tacit alliances with both South and North. The protection this offered the Low Countries was generally efficacious, except during the Napoleonic era and the two World Wars. England had already abandoned its continental aspirations by the eighteenth century. Instead, it endeavored to control the seas and build a large colonial empire while committing itself to maintaining the balance of power on the European continent. Thus England – joined later by the United States – was still committed to the defense of the Low Countries in the twentieth century, first against the hegemonic ambitions of a unified Germany, later against the Soviet threat. It was of vital importance to the English that the strategically situated delta region of the Scheldt, Maas, and Rhine remain free from the control of the great continental powers.

Economic developments in the Low Countries also influenced political institutions and practices. Because the region had long been at the political periphery of Europe, some areas had only weak feudal structures or, as in the case of Friesland, virtually none at all. Moreover, the gradual growth of the cities formed a powerful counterweight to the influence of the nobility. The need for effective water control prompted the rise of small-scale, independent organs in some areas, in which large numbers of commoners, both in the city and the countryside, played an important role. Finally, the conflict between the ruling princes and the (high) nobility was also of lasting significance. Cities acquired more or less natural alliances with these princes against the nobility; in return they received an often large measure of self-rule formally established in charters and "freedoms."

Cities exercised great influence on the policy of dukes and counts in those areas where they had become strong – in Flanders, Brabant, and Holland successively. In these provinces, the political power of the nobility was quite modest, unlike their role in agrarian Guelders or Hainaut. The efforts of the princes themselves to gradually introduce far-reaching centralization were stymied precisely in those regions where powerful cities had already won self-rule. Even in the South, which in the end remained part of the centralized Spanish and Austrian Habsburg empires, a host of more or less representative institutions continued to exercise real power on the regional and local level.

In the Republic, the "old freedoms" became, in many respects, the basis of the new state. The institutions of the Dutch Republic were an exception in an age marked by the rise of royal power in many European countries. The Republic was characterized by a strong traditionalism which constantly appealed to the old rights and practices. This conservative impulse was mingled with new political theories, especially those which underscored the notion that sovereignty lay with the regional States. The Republic was a federation of formally sovereign states in which most power, despite rivalries between all the provinces, was exercised by the rich province of Holland (with Amsterdam as its leading city) and by the stadholders of the House of Orange, an office with its origins in the late Middle Ages.

Despite the appeal to the old privileges, the Republic actually introduced an important innovation. The bourgeoisie (particularly the patrician upper crust) exercised real power, enough, in fact, to monopolize the state administration. Public life was also characterized, partly out of economic considerations, by a wide diffusion of power and a relatively high measure of tolerance. Policy decisions could usually only be made after lengthy negotiations in and between administrative councils, and were thus usually compromises.

Seventeenth-century tolerance was not a matter of principle, although there were some principled pleas in defense of it. In practice, tolerance was granted when those in power found economic or administrative advantage in giving it. Nor did they ever grant it in full measure. In actuality, all inhabitants of the Republic not belonging to the Calvinist regent class and the small group of nobility encountered multiple forms of discrimination. At the same time, the Republic was, by European standards of the day, a veritable oasis of freedom and tolerance.

It is defensible to argue that the central role of the "old freedoms" in the state structure of the Dutch Republic helped prepare the way for the "modern freedoms" of the nineteenth and twentieth centuries. During the *ancien régime* itself, of course, there was neither democracy nor civil rights. The fundamental changes that took place during the tumultuous decades around 1800 should not be underestimated in importance. Conflict in both the South and North reached a feverish pitch in this age of revolution and led to periods of violence. Nevertheless, one can maintain that the transition to parliamentary democracy was accomplished, both in the North and the South, relatively quickly and easily. Both Belgium (1830) and the Netherlands (1848) received modern liberal constitutions which fostered the growth of parliamentary democracy. The fact that both countries had political traditions that allowed the bourgeoisie a voice in government smoothed this transition.

Already by the thirteenth century the urban bourgeoisie had a considerable impact on cultural life. Initially, urban culture developed alongside the dominant cultures of the nobility and the church. In the fifteenth and sixteenth centuries, it had won an equal place among them, and included elements of both. The new culture partly expressed itself in literature and the visual arts – especially painting – and partly in the construction of city halls, cloth halls, and patrician dwellings.

In the Dutch Republic this bourgeois humanist culture, now with a Protestant accent, reached a new apogee. The so-called Golden Age witnessed great achievements in nearly all areas of cultural life. In the South, bourgeois elements certainly did not disappear, but they played a much less prominent role in the baroque culture of the Counter Reformation. Later, in the nineteenth century, bourgeois culture gradually regained ascendancy in Belgium, partly through the early development of industrial capitalism in the country. In the Netherlands, the long-established bourgeois culture enjoyed a renaissance around 1900. The bourgeois cultural domination of the Netherlands and Belgium was made evident over the course of the twentieth century by the advent of a multifaceted popular culture, in which bourgeois elements continued to set the tone.

A certain pragmatism and a focus on succeeding in the sensory aspects of culture have been among the chief features of the bourgeois civilization of the Low Countries. The region has long known a high degree of literacy, and it has produced a number of remarkable philosophers and literary figures. Yet the Low Countries have produced fewer of these figures than the "great" French, German, English or even the "small" Scandinavian cultures. In contrast, the region has excelled in producing many outstanding achievements in the visual arts, particularly painting. The Low Countries have also made important contributions to science and technology, contributions aimed at better controlling nature – and often specifically at controlling water and the sea.

Inhabitants of the Low Countries have long demonstrated great receptivity to foreign cultural influences, a quality which derives from the region's geographical location and the international orientation of its economy. In most phases of the region's history, diverse population groups have shown a cosmopolitan attitude and a relative openness to foreign ideas and practices. The Low Countries have thus often played the role of a cultural mediator, particularly between England and the rest of the continent.

This openness to the foreign and "the other" had something to do with the composition of the population. The delta region had witnessed many great migrations. This was certainly true in the first centuries after Christ, but after a long period of great continuity of human habitation during the Middle Ages, there have been repeated migratory waves through and into the region – up to the present day. The unity of the Low Countries cannot, therefore, be found in collective descent from a homogeneous ethnic group.

Religion has been a very remarkable factor in the history of the Low Countries. Like elsewhere in Europe, the church and the clergy exerted a great influence on culture and everyday life during the Middle Ages. The development of spiritual movements stressing piety and a sober lifestyle is to a certain degree characteristic of the Low Countries, and not unrelated to the region's dominant bourgeois culture. The strength of late medieval mysticism and the *devotio moderna* in the region are two examples of this. Particularly striking is the great success of the Reformation in the sixteenth century and the remarkable number of non-Lutheran Protestants. Anabaptists appeared at the very beginning of the Reformation, and after 1540, Calvinism emerged to become one of the driving forces of the Dutch Revolt.

After 1585, the South again became uniformly Catholic. The Roman Catholic church once more became a central force in the Southern Netherlands, a powerful position, which in the course of time generated sharp anticlericalism. In contrast, a rather unique religious situation developed in the Dutch Republic. There was no official religion or state church, although Calvinist Protestantism did assume a privileged place in Dutch society, and the Reformed church came to be known as the "public church." Within this church, however, there existed a whole range of oppositions, with orthodox Calvinist doctrine and practice at one pole and much more open and lax opinions at the other. Outside the Reformed church, other denominations, including a number of dissenting Protestant bodies, Jews, and Roman Catholics, barely bothered hiding their formally illegal worship services. They were granted freedom of conscience but were subjected to a number of constricting regulations. Nevertheless, a spirit of tolerance existed in the Dutch Republic during the seventeenth century that was unknown elsewhere in Europe.

Even after church and state were formally separated and all religions made legally equal in the nineteenth century, religion continued to make its mark on Dutch society. The same was true in Belgium, where anticlerical forces, much more powerful than in the Netherlands, attempted to reduce the influence of the Catholic church. It is only in the last several decades that secularization in Belgium and the Netherlands has become so pervasive that religion and the churches no longer play a decisive role in culture and society. The indirect influence of the region's religious traditions, however, have by no means disappeared.

2. Diversity in Unity

It is important not to forget that national differences, regional diversity, and divisive forces were no less a part of the Low Countries' history than the features the region had in common. The differences are particularly marked in the area of politics and administration.

The short-lived United Kingdom of William I (1815-1830) is really the only period in which the entire Low Countries constituted one state. It is true that the region showed signs of increasing political unity in the fifteenth century, which culminated in the formation of the Burgundian Kreis in the mid-sixteenth century. But this growing unity had everything to do with dynastic policies which also involved other regions, whether in nearby Burgundy or faraway Spain. The Dutch Revolt ended this process of territorial amalgamation and cohesion. Because the Revolt took place in an age when European states intensely intervened in the religious and ethical lives of their subjects, the division between North and South led to deep cultural differences.

Before Burgundian efforts at territorial conglomeration there was no political cohesion to speak of in the Low Countries. The economic interests and culture of the inhabitants of the Maas, Rhine, and Scheldt delta area diverged considerably at first. Gradually, a number of parallel integrating processes, mutually reinforcing each other, began to change this situation, first in the economic sphere – with the development of trade routes and market systems – and later in politics, as a consequence of dynastic ambitions. In this way, the Low Countries developed close intraregional ties. This growing cohesion was certainly not inevitable; indeed, it is striking that the most successful efforts at dynastic expansion in the region were conducted by outsiders: the Burgundian dukes and the German-Austrian House of Habsburg. The House of Orange-Nassau, which played so central a role in the Dutch Revolt and in the subsequent history of the North, also found its origins outside the Low Countries.

The dynastic politics of the Burgundians fostered feelings of unity across the Low Countries, since they promoted economic and cultural contacts across provincial lines. In the negotiations that followed the death of Charles the Bold in 1477, the representatives of the most important provinces – with the conspicuous exceptions of Liège and Guelders, which had been forcibly annexed by Charles – decided to collectively place themselves under a successor dynasty. Their decision, however, was determined by the necessity of defending their common interests against the ruling prince as much as it was based on any feeling of unity. Attempts by the Habsburgs to improve, standardize, and centralize the administration (in 1531, Brussels became the capital of the region) were embodied in a number of transregional institutions. But resistance to these reforms was considerable, and the provinces used every instrument at their disposal to keep their own unique rights and privileges.

The centralization policy emanating from Brussels – for a long time more tangible than direct control from Madrid – was one of the chief causes of the Dutch Revolt. When the tensions fostered by this policy, exacerbated by economic hard times, collided with the religious divisions which riddled the region, it triggered an eruption with far-reaching consequences that no one could have predicted. Its conclusion was largely determined by military operations and the international priorities of successive Spanish kings. The boundary that came to separate the South from the North did not correspond, as noted above, with the geographical demarcation of the Revolt. But this did not make the boundary less significant in determining subsecuent events.

The North and South thus parted ways in the course of the seventeenth and eighteenth centuries, and the character of both societies became increasingly different over time. The Southern Netherlands remained a not unimportant part of the Habsburg system, with strongly aristocratic traits, a dominant role for the Catholic church, and a baroque culture. In contrast, the traditions of urban autonomy and regional self-rule, often described as typical of the region, continued in the Republic of the Seven United Provinces. In nearly every respect, the Republic surpassed the Southern Netherlands – not least in terms of political power and in its economic and cultural attainments – and in the eighteenth century, the North would even exercise a kind of guardianship over the South. The overwhelmingly Protestant character of the Republic also markedly contrasted with the Catholic South.

Although the Republic distinguished itself from the South, it must be remembered that many of its innovations and most dynamic facets had originated in the southern provinces. To be sure, the institutions of the Republic sprang directly from the particular administrative traditions of the northern provinces, most notably Holland. But it was the southern provinces, especially Flanders and Brabant, which had most fully developed these types of institutions in the years before 1580. It was in the South that the Great Privilege, the Pacification of Ghent, the Eternal Decree, the Union of Utrecht, and the Act of Abjuration had been penned or at least theoretically conceived. It was in the South, too, that Protestantism had been strongest and that trade capitalism had been most developed, and it was there that bourgeois culture had attained its highest accomplishments. But it is also true that forces against these developments were strongest in the South.

After 1585, emigration brought the most energetic and creative practitioners of political, artistic, scholarly, and economic life to the

North. Of course, they faced barriers in the North and were confronted with more moderate political and religious tendencies. For example, the more militant Calvinists – many of them originally from the South – were often checked by libertines in the Reformed church. But their old opponents, the Catholic church and the monarchy, had been swept away. The nobility, moreover, exercised but little influence, especially in the dominant province of Holland. Thus the most dynamic forces in society, previously concentrated in the South, could fully develop in the North during the seventeenth century. In the Southern Netherlands, the emigration had the reverse effect. With the departure of many innovators, the more traditional elements in society could easily set the tone. But these elements also experienced something of a new élan and managed to put their mark on society for several centuries. The polar forces which had struggled with each other in past centuries, particularly in Flanders and Brabant, were now relatively free to develop separately in the North and in the South during the seventeenth and eighteenth centuries.

During the decades around the beginning of the nineteenth century, both North and South followed a somewhat tortuous path toward a modern, constitutional nation-state. This parallel development masks the very different histories of North and South during this period. In the South, conservative forces, not least the Roman Catholic church, were long dominant. Thus the impulse toward more modern ideas and institutions had to come largely from outside the region, first through Joseph II, and later through the French revolutionaries who annexed the Southern Netherlands in 1795. In the North, the forces of reform within the country grew much stronger at the end of the eighteenth century, and were supported by many Catholics who sought to achieve civil equality for themselves. Foreign intervention was also instrumental for developments in the North, itself an indication of the weak international position of the Low Countries. In 1787, the Prussians restored the Oranges to power and thus broke the rising tide of reform. In 1795, however, revolutionary France's invasion of the North ensured the reformers' triumph. Despite the French presence, many of the reforms implemented during the Batavian period were carried out by the Dutch themselves. It was only in 1810 that the North was annexed to the French Empire.

    Given both the diversity and unity of the region, it is a tantalizing, but ultimately unanswerable question whether the United Kingdom of the Netherlands, created after the fall of Napoleon, would have been viable in the long run. It is clear that the union of the North and South was imposed from the outside, by the great powers who believed it necessary to establish a "guardpost" to the north of an expansionist France. Internally, the idea of reunification after more than two centuries of separation was not immediately an attractive one; indeed, many opposed it. The wholly separate paths each region had taken since 1585 and the humiliating Northern guardianship over the South in the eighteenth century both suggest that the enterprise was doomed from the start. However passionately King William I and his lieutenants might have worked for its success, they faced substantial and not easily reconcilable differences and oppositions – politically, religiously, economically, and culturally – which divided the North and South.

Still, it cannot be denied that the king and his associates achieved a great deal in the space of fifteen years. They helped cultivate a modern sense of nationhood that had originated under the ancien régime. But William's ruling style, at once clumsy and authoritarian, and the advent of revolution in Europe during 1830, together proved fatal to the United Kingdom. In their resistance to royal policy, two radically different sources of opposition to the king, liberals and Catholics, found each other. Both were especially active in the South, which had gradually recovered a powerful economic and political dynamic. Although founded on divergent philosophies, Catholic and liberal notions of freedom were sufficiently similar to provide the basis for unionist opposition to the authoritarian policy of William I. Inspired by revolution in Paris, the Belgian opposition was moved to act, and when the great powers failed to back William, the fate of the United Kingdom of the Netherlands was sealed. North and South would again go their separate ways as the Netherlands and Belgium for the rest of the nineteenth and twentieth centuries. National feeling would now coalesce around these two states.

Nevertheless, in the last two centuries both countries have shown greater conformity to general European patterns than had hitherto been the case. Both Belgium and the Netherlands became constitutional states with a bourgeois preponderance of power, and gradually developed into full-fledged democracies. The political struggles and parties of both countries resembled not only each other but also those of other European countries. Political developments in both countries led to the integration of the working classes in a predominantly bourgeois society and to the creation of a modern welfare state with neo-corporatist characteristics.

But even within this general pattern, a number of differences are again apparent. In the first place, it is clear that Belgium was ahead of the Netherlands in nearly all respects during the nineteenth century, especially in terms of economic and political modernization. Moreover, relations between the two countries were spare and cool for a long time. Despite the broad intensification of international commerce, both societies kept political and cultural distance from each other. The traumatic events surrounding Belgian independence explain much of this coolness. But it remains quite striking, for example, just how little interest the Netherlands had in the language conflict raging in Belgium. A common language was an important factor in Dutch national feeling, but it was apparently not strong enough to generate feelings of solidarity with their Dutch-speaking neighbors to the south. "Greater Dutch" sentiments remained relatively weak in the North.

In Belgium, too, national feeling was overwhelmingly defined by the new state. The most prominent proponents of the Flemish movement sought for a long time to attain an equal position within the predominantly Francophone nation-state. As a majority group, they wanted their democratic rights recognized by Belgian state and society. Flemish separatism almost always remained a marginal phenomenon. Flanders's orientation toward the North was stronger than vice versa, but it was chiefly cultural, rather than political, in nature. It was only in the long run that a specifically Flemish "ethnic" nationalism emerged, which was incongruent with both Belgian and Dutch state nationalisms. This situation was further complicated by the advent of Walloon nationalism, which was both a reaction to the Flemish movement and a response to the deteriorating economic position of Wallonia.

The ethnic and cultural tensions dividing Belgium in the last century and a half have given the country a much different history than the Netherlands. These tensions are complex and have caused great problems in Belgian society that persist to the present, and in the last thirty years, they have prompted near-perpetual changes in the Belgian state structure. No such problem exists in the Netherlands. The Frisian movement is too weak to mount a similar challenge to the Dutch system, and is, moreover, a different kind of nationalism.

But religious divisions in the Netherlands complicated matters there in ways similar to the ethnic and cultural conflict in Belgium. Both countries witnessed an opposition between confessional and non-confessional groups, which in Belgium turned into an intense battle between clericals and anticlericals. The religious situation in the Netherlands was made more complex by the divide between Catholics and Protestants, and the many deep differences among the country's Protestants. This had all kinds of social and cultural effects. The really unique religious conditions during the Dutch Republic thus continued, in modified form, into the nineteenth and twentieth centuries. And just as in the age of the United Provinces, the religious situation in the modern Netherlands has had no parallel anywhere in Europe.

The close ties between state, society, and religion in both Belgium and the Netherlands led to the constellation now known as "pillarization." Both countries witnessed a similar segmentation along religious and ideological lines in many areas of society, and thus became characterized by separate, pillarized organizations which were hailed as "an intermediate level between state and society." These organizations, providing a wide spectrum of services to their constituents, also became involved in those sectors that the government considered its responsibility, such as education and social welfare. The state often discharged its responsibilities by regulating and subsidizing these pillarized organizations.

Yet both the structure and functioning of the two pillarized systems also show substantial differences. In Belgium there was no orthodox Protestant pillar. Moreover, the Belgian state lost more of its autonomy as its pillarized organizations took over a large number of functions from the government and at same time made more demands of the state apparatus than was the case in the Netherlands. Partly for this reason, Belgian pillarized organizations better withstood the changes in the 1960s than their counterparts in the Netherlands.

In Belgium, where clientelism had already been strongly developed, pillarized organizations became, to a certain extent, institutions which bound clients to them through the services they rendered. These organizations also largely retained their influence over the state apparatus. But in the Netherlands the pillarized system was essentially dismantled in the 1960s. This encouraged a more open political and cultural climate than existed in Belgium, with more opportunities for individual citizens. Thus one might argue that much older political traditions – the regents' ruling style in the North and the aristocratic and ecclesiastical domination of the South – have continued to exert an influence in recent decades. Their respective views of the state, the exercise of authority, and the relations between government and citizenry help account for the different political cultures of contemporary Belgium and the Netherlands.

In Belgium, differences of wealth and power remained much more obvious, and were from time to time much more fiercely contested than in the Netherlands. The Dutch have attempted, especially since the 1960s, to narrow the differences in status and power. Although the divide has persisted, the Dutch, except for a brief period of conflict around 1970, have tried to minimize the significance of these differences. Dutch manners, too, followed the egalitarian ideal, in which differences in power and status were only subtly evident. All of this suggests that there remains a clear difference of mentality between the North and South.

In the area of foreign policy, too, there are both parallels and striking contrasts. Although Belgium and the Netherlands were only small states, both managed to construct a colonial empire. The Dutch colonial enterprise, which originated in the expansion of trade during the seventeenth century, regained its importance during the nineteenth century. By the end of this century, a Belgian colonial presence had also been established in Central Africa. It is remarkable, though, that there was a greater degree of interaction between Dutch and Indonesian society and culture than ever existed between their Belgian and Congolese counterparts. After the decolonization following the Second World War, the Netherlands's international contacts remained more oriented toward Asia while those of Belgium, for a long time at least, centered on Africa. This pattern was determined by their earlier colonial commitments.

On the European continent, the Netherlands and Belgium were both hemmed in by the great powers of France, Germany, and – though the sea lay between them – Great Britain. Until 1940, both countries largely pursued policies of neutrality. Yet there were clear differences. Dutch neutrality had been born out of disappointment, and was passive and reserved in nature. The country's aloofness toward Belgium fit into this general orientation. Belgium neutrality, in contrast, was much more active. As a newly independent country, it had to fight for a place in the European order. Belgian foreign policy was thus more likely to occasionally diverge from neutrality, certainly after the bitter and traumatic experience of the First World War, which, despite long-standing Belgian neutrality, brought German invasion.

The Second World War substantially changed the foreign policies of both countries. The Benelux agreement was a first step in the growing cooperation between the two countries, and was later supplemented by both countries' participation in NATO and the European Economic Union. Belgian and Dutch interests did not always coincide, of course, but their relations were increasingly characterized by more consultation, greater agreement, and increased collective action.

Indeed, through their deepening participation in a multicultural and increasingly unified Europe, the Netherlands and Belgium have become more aware of their mutual interests and similarities. As small, highly developed states in the northwestern delta region of Europe, both have enjoyed a special relationship with Britain and have shared many interests as they have become involved in the European Union. They both face the danger that Dutch-language culture will be marginalized and internally undermined by increasing European integration. As a result of this threat, a sense of cultural affinity has grown between the Netherlands and Flanders. This rapprochement, although repeatedly slowed by the host of differences between Dutch and Flemish (sub)cultures, has created the modest beginnings of a collective cultural policy within the European Union. The federalization of Belgium has further fostered this development.

Apart from that, it is remarkable that the administrative center of the new Europe, still faced with many challenges to its unity, is in Brussels. In the sixteenth century, the city had been the center of the Habsburgs' ambitious policy that had precipitated the Revolt during the 1560s. Presumably, the history of Brussels is incidental to its present role in the European Union. Still, the city's past may be an instructive reminder that political and administrative ambitions that do not find broad popular support have little chance of succeeding.

The same is true, it seems to us, of cultural policy. If a culture is not sustained by wide popular support, no cultural policy will be able to save it. On the other hand, if a culture enjoys widespread support, then no international or supranational developments will be able to destroy it. That does not alter the fact that an intelligent cultural policy can greatly contribute to a flourishing of arts and literature. At the same time, those committed to a particular culture need not insist it remain the same. Every culture, especially in the highly developed West, is constantly exposed to international influences and changes, which only strengthen its depth and variety. This has been true in the past, and it is no less true of the contemporary culture, or cultures, of the Low Countries.

Recommended Literature

General

A great deal has been written about the history of Belgium and the Netherlands. Only a sampling of this literature, therefore, can be mentioned here. The titles given here yield further bibliographical information, and reviews of new publications may be read in the extended bibliographical section of the history journal, *Bijdragen en Mededelingen betreffende de Geschiedenis der Nederlanden*. There are two multivolumed histories pertaining to the whole region of the Low Countries: J.A. van Houtte and J.F. Niermeyer (eds.), *Algemene Geschiedenis der Nederlanden*, 12 vols. (Utrecht/Antwerp, 1949-1958) and D.P. Blok and W. Prevenier (eds.), *Algemene Geschiedenis der Nederlanden*, 15 vols. (Haarlem, 1977-1983). Both series offer many articles written by specialists familiar with the most recent historiographical developments at the time of publication. Because of differences in accent, approach, and subject matter, it would be useful in some cases to also study the earlier edition. A good three-volume historical summary has been written by J.A. Bornewasser (ed.), and a small number of authors in *Winkler Prins Geschiedenis der Nederlanden* (Amsterdam/Brussels, 1977). E.H. Kossmann *The Low Countries, 1780-1940* (Oxford, 1978), or his more extended version in Dutch, *De Lage Landen, 1780-1980. Twee eeuwen Nederland en België*, 2 vols. (Amsterdam/Brussels, 1986) is an engrossing, informative but highly personal and very readable overview. A survey of twenty centuries of history and culture between the Scheldt and the Rhine Rivers is portrayed by nationally well-known authors in the prestigiously published and richly illustrated *The Drama of the Low Countries* (Antwerp, 1996).

A recent and quite personal synthesis on the problem of nation forming in the Low Countries is L. Wils, *Van Clovis tot Happart. De lange weg van de natie-vorming in de Lage Landen*, (Leuven, 1992). Wils's argumentation is very assertive and his review of recent centuries is devoted almost exclusively to Belgium. One highly interesting piece of older literature is P. Geyl's effort – now generally regarded as a failure – to articulate his Great Netherlandic view of history in the *Geschiedenis van de Nederlandse Stam*, the first volume of which appeared in 1930 (consult the 3rd ed. 6 vols., Amsterdam/Antwerp, 1961-1962). Geyl, incidentally, never got further than 1798, but his *Eenheid en Tweeheid in de Nederlanden* (Antwerp, 1946), includes several essays on the nineteenth century. Of further interest are Geyl's *The Revolt of the Netherlands, 1555-1609*, 2nd ed., (London, 1988), and his *The Netherlands in the Seventeenth Century, 1609-1648*, 3rd ed., (London, 1989), although L.J. Rogier's *Eenheid en Scheiding. Geschiedenis der Nederlanden, 1477-1813*, 2nd ed., (Utrecht/Antwerp, 1980), originally published in 1952, has better stood the test of time. See also the recent comparative study, *A Miracle Mirrored: The Dutch Republic in European Perspective,* (Cambridge/New York, 1995), edited by J. Lucassen and C.A. Davids.

For a handy summary of factual data, H.P.H. Jansen's *Kalendarium. Geschiedenis van de Lage Landen in jaartallen,* 7th ed., (Utrecht, 1988) and H.J.W. Volmuller's *Nijhoffs Geschiedenislexicon Nederland en België,* (The Hague/Antwerp, 1981) are highly suitable. For an introduction to a long and important segment of economic and social history, see J.A. van Houtte, *Economische en sociale geschiedenis van de lage landen, 800-1800,* (Haarlem, 1979). Art history of the whole region is covered by H.E. van Gelder (ed.), *Kunstgeschiedenis der Nederlanden,* 12 vols. (Utrecht/Antwerp, 1963-1965). A good reference work is Sheila D. Muller's *Dutch Art: An Encyclopedia,* (New York, 1996). A literary history of the Low Countries is the subject of a recent and interesting publication consisting of short articles by a hundred-odd authors: M.A. Schenkeveld-Van der Dussen (ed.), *Nederlandse Literatuur. Een Geschiedenis,* (Groningen, 1993). A history of the Dutch theater can be found in R.L. Erenstein et al. (eds.) *Een theatergeschiedenis der Nederlanden. Tien eeuwen drama en theater in Nederland en Vlaanderen,* (Amsterdam, 1996).

The Netherlands

Most historiography, with the exception of more specialized literature dealing with relations between the two countries, focuses on either Belgium or the Netherlands.

For the Netherlands, the classic synthesis of the "history of the Fatherland" is P.J. Blok's *Geschiedenis van het Nederlandsche Volk,* 1st ed., 1892; 3rd ed., 4 vols. (Leiden, 1924-1926). The tenor and other aspects of Blok's oeuvre are dated, but it remains remarkably accessible through its compelling narrative. Another worthwhile and highly readable work, although also obsolescent in some respects, is J. and A. Romein, *De Lage Landen bij de Zee. Een Geschiedenis van het Nederlandse Volk,* 7th ed., 4 vols. (Amsterdam, 1977). The Romeins, husband and wife, also produced *Erflaters van onze beschaving. Nederlandse gestalten uit vier eeuwen,* 11th ed., (Amsterdam, 1977). Both works date from the 1930s.

A recent, three-volume textbook is *Delta, Nederlands verleden in vogelvlucht.* Volume I, *De Middeleeuwen: 300 tot 1500* (Leiden/ Antwerp, 1992) is written by D.E.H. de Boer, M. Boone, and W.A.M. Hessing, Volume II, *De nieuwe Tijd: 1500-1813* (Leiden/Antwerp, 1992) by S. Groenveld and G.J. Schutte; and Volume III, *De Nieuwste Tijd: 1813 tot heden* (Groningen, 1993) by J.T.M. Bank, J.J. Huizinga, and J.T. Minderaa. An interesting and informative book is H. Lademacher, *Geschichte der Niederlande: Politik – Verfassung – Wirtschaft* (Darmstadt, 1983). Lademacher has also authored *Die Niederlande: politische Kultur zwischen Individualität und Anpassung* (Berlin, 1993). Another foreigner who knows the Netherlands well is E. Zahn, whose essay-like book *Das unbekannte Holland. Regenten, Rebellen und Reformatoren* (Munich, 1993) contains highly compelling observations. C. de Voogd, *Histoire des Pays-Bas* (Paris, 1992) is an account stretching from prehistoric times to the present, with an emphasis on the twentieth century. J.I.

Israel's *The Dutch Republic: Its Rise, Greatness, and Fall, 1477-1806* (Oxford, 1995) is at once a comprehensive and highly readable narrative of the Republic.

Of the histories which present an overview of either a particular province or aspect of Dutch history the following are most worthwhile. For the history of several Dutch provinces, consult W.J. Formsma (ed.), *Historie van Groningen* (Groningen, 1976); H. Heringa (ed.), *Geschiedenis van Drenthe* (Assen, 1985); J.J. Kalma et al., *Geschiedenis van Friesland* (Drachten, 1988); and B.H. Slicher van Bath (ed.), *Geschiedenis van Overijssel* (Deventer, 1970). Church and religious history is broadly covered by O.J. de Jong, *Nederlandse kerkgeschiedenis*, 3rd ed. (Nijkerk, 1985) and H. Knippenberg, *De religieuze kaart van Nederland. Omvang en geografische spreiding van de godsdienstige gezindten vanaf de Reformatie tot heden* (Assen, 1992), while many other works focus on specific religious groups. An overview of economic history is given by J.H. van Stuyvenberg (ed.), *De economische geschiedenis van Nederland* (Groningen, 1977). The history of agriculture is specifically dealt with in J. Bieleman, *Geschiedenis van de landbouw in Nederland, 1500-1950. Veranderingen en verscheidenheid* (Meppel, 1992).

An attempt to estimate the size of the Dutch population is found in J. Faber, et al., "Population Changes and Economic Developments in the Netherlands," in *AAG-Bijdragen*, vol. 12 (1965), 47-113; while J.M.W.G. Lucassen and R. Penninx give a brief account of immigration to the Netherlands and its effects in *Nieuwkomers. Immigranten en nakomelingen in Nederland, 1550-1985* (Amsterdam, 1994). J. Lucassen's *Dutch Long Distance Trade Migration: A Concise History, 1600-1900* (Amsterdam, 1991) summarizes Dutch migratory trends over several centuries. The history of the Jewish community has been recently interpreted by J.C.H. Blom, R.G. Fuks-Mansfeld, and I. Schöffer (eds.) in *Geschiedenis van de joden in Nederland* (Amsterdam, 1995).

Biographical sketches of the most historically important members of the House of Orange can be found in C.A. Tamse (ed.), *Nassau en Oranje in de Nederlandse geschiedenis* (Alphen aan den Rijn, 1977). The same author has edited *De monarchie in Nederland* (Amsterdam/Brussels, 1980). A recent overview of colonial history is J. van Goor's *De Nederlandse koloniën. Geschiedenis van de Nederlandse expansie* (The Hague, 1994). W.P. Coolhaas and G.J. Schutte make the extensive literature on this subject more accessible in their *Critical Survey of Studies on Dutch Colonial History*, 2nd ed. (The Hague, 1980). Finally, it is certainly worth the effort to explore the collections of essays written by prominent authors on the Dutch past, including I. Schöffer's *Veelvormig verleden. Zeventien studies in de vaderlandse geschiedenis* (Amsterdam, 1987) E.H. Kossmann's *Politieke theorie en geschiedenis. Verspreide opstellen en voordrachten* (Amsterdam, 1987) and his *Vergankelijkheid en continuïteit opstellen over geschiedenis* (Amsterdam, 1995) include essays with a strongly historiographical orientation and concern many aspects of Dutch history.

Belgium

The standard work of H. Pirenne, *Histoire de Belgique*, 7 vols. (Brussels, 1902-1932) remains a useful source for studying Belgian history, although a much shorter overview can be found in J. Dhondt's *Histoire de la Belgique*, 2nd ed. (Paris, 1968). An informative commemorative volume is A. D'Haenens (ed.), *La Belgique: 150 ans de Culture et de Société* (Brussels, 1980). The history of Flanders is covered by M. Lamberty, ed., *Twintig eeuwen Vlaanderen*, 15 vols. (Hasselt, 1972-1977) and by E. Witte et al., *Histoire de la Flandre, des origines à nos jours* (Brussels, 1983). The medieval period has been dealt with by D. Nicholas, *Medieval Flanders* (London and New York, 1992). For the history of Wallonia, one can consult H. Hasquin (ed.), *La Wallonie. Le pays et les hommes*, 6 vols. (Brussels, 1977-1981). For a history of the Grand Duchy, see G. Trausch, *Le Luxembourg. Emergence d'un Etat et d'une Nation* (Antwerp, 1989).

There are few surveys of more specific aspects of Belgian history. Socioeconomic developments are covered in H. Van der Wee and E. Cauwenberghe (eds.), *Productivity of Land and Agricultural Innovation in the Low Countries (1250-1800)* (Leuven, 1978); A. Morelli (ed.), *Histoire des étrangers et de l'immigration en Belgique de la préhistoire à nos jours* (Brussels, 1992); and C. Vandenbroeke, *Sociale geschiedenis van het Vlaamse volk* (Beveren, 1981). Church history is surveyed in the somewhat outdated but still usable work of E. de Moreau, *Histoire de l'Eglise en Belgique*, 6 vols. (Brussels, 1945-1952). For the field of cultural history, it is worth mentioning H. Liebaers et al., *Flemish Art from the Beginning till Now* (Antwerp, 1985), and J. Stiennon (ed.), *De Roger de la Pasture à Paul Delvaux. Cinq siècles de peinture en Wallonie* (Brussels, 1988).

An extensive and critical overview of the most recent historiography pertaining to the Belgian past can be found in J.A. van Houtte, et al., *Un quart de siècle de recherche historique en Belgique, 1944-1968* (Brussels, 1970) and L. Genicot, et al., *Vingt ans de recherche historique en Belgique, 1969-1988* (Brussels, 1990).

Chapters 1 and 2

In addition to the standard works mentioned above the following studies are very much worth the effort. It is useful to consult A. Lottin (ed.), *Histoire des Provinces françaises du Nord* (Dunkirk, 1988-1989), vols. 1 (J. Desmulliez and L. Milis) and 2 (H. Platelle and D. Clauzel), especially for the (presently French) southern parts of the Low Countries.

W.A. van Es's *De Romeinen in Nederland* (Haarlem, 1981) and A. Wankenne's *La Belgique aux temps de Rome* (Namur, 1979) survey the Roman presence in the Low Countries.

For the history of the migrations and the Merovingian period, see D.P. Blok, *De Franken in Nederland*, 3rd ed. (Bussum, 1979); W.J. De Boone, *De Franken van hun eerste optreden tot de dood van Childeric* (Amsterdam, 1954); G. Faider-Feytmans, *La Belgique à l'époque mérovingienne* (Brussels, 1964); A. Joris, *On the Edge of Two Worlds in the Heart of the New Empire: The Roman Regions of Northern Gaul during the Merovingian Period*

([Lincoln,] Nebraska, 1966); and M. Gysseling and A. Verhulst, *Neder-zettingsnamen en nederzettingsgeschiedenis in de Nederlanden, Noord-Frankrijk en Noordwest Duitsland* (Amsterdam, 1969).

Works on the Carolingian period include F.L. Ganshof, *La Belgique carolingienne* (Brussels, 1958); A. D'Haenens, *Les invasions normandes en Belgique au IXe siècle* (Leuven, 1967) and S. Lebecq, *Marchands et naviga-teurs frisons du haut moyen âge* (Lille, 1983).

The post-Carolingian period and the disintegration of the large principalities are the subjects of U. Nonn, *Pagus und comitatus in Niederlothringen. Untersuchungen zur politischen Raumgliederung im früheren Mittelalter* (Bonn, 1983); J. Dhondt, *Etudes sur la naissance des principautés territoriales en France, IXe-Xe siècles* (Bruges, 1948); W. Mohr, *Die Geschichte des Herzogtums Lothringen*, 3 vols. (Saarbrücken, 1974-1979); and L. Genicot, *Etudes sur les principautés lotharingiennes* (Leuven, 1975).

Aspects of the history of Flanders can be found among other texts in F.L. Ganshof, *La Flandre sous les premiers comtes*, 3rd ed. (Brussels, 1949) and H. van Werveke, *Een Vlaamse graaf van Europees formaat. Filips van de Elzas* (Haarlem, 1976). For Liège, there is J.L. Küpper, *Liège et l'Eglise impériale, IX-XIIe siècles* (Paris, 1981). The book of F.W.N. Hugen-holtz, *Floris V* (Bussum, 1966), deals with Holland, while the history of Brabant is the subject of P. Avonds and J.D. Janssens, *Politiek en liter-atuur. Brabant en de Slag bij Woeringen (1288)* (Brussels, 1989). For the remaining principalities, see J. Baerten, *Het graafschap Loon (11e-14e eeuw)* (Assen, 1969); B.H. Slicher van Bath (ed.), *Geschiedenis van Over-ijssel* (Deventer, 1970); and W. Jappe Alberts, *Geschiedenis van Gelderland tot 1492* (Zutphen, 1978).

The nobility is treated in E. Warlop, *The Flemish Nobility before 1300*, 4 vols. (Kortrijk, 1975-1976; originally in Dutch) and J.M. van Winter, *Ridderschap, ideaal en werkelijkheid*, 4th ed. (Haarlem/Bussum, 1982). The same author penned *Ministerialiteit en ridderschap in Gelre en Zutphen* (Arnhem, 1962). See also L. Genicot, *La noblesse dans l'Occident médiéval* (London, 1982).

The evolution of institutions is analyzed in F.L. Ganshof, *Frankish Institutions under Charlemagne* (New York, 1968) and his classic work, *Qu'est que la féodalité*, 4th ed. (Brussels, 1969). Ganshof has also written "La Flandre," in F. Lot and R. Fawtier, *Histoire des institutions françaises au moyen âge*, vol. 1 (Paris, 1957), 343-426. See also J.P. de Monté Ver-loren, *Hoofdlijnen uit de ontwikkeling der rechterlijke organisatie in de noordelijke Nederlanden tot de Bataafse omwenteling*, 6th ed. (Deventer, 1982); R.C. van Caenegem, "Coutumes et législation en Flandre aux XIe et XIIe siècles," in *Vrijheden in de stad en op het platteland van de XIe tot de XIVe eeuw* (Brussels, 1968), 245-279; L.M. de Gryse, "Some Observations on the Origins of the Flemish Bailiff (*Bailli)*", in *Viator* 7 (1976): 243-294; and B. Lyon and A. Verhulst, *Medieval Finance: A Comparison of Financial Institutions in Northwestern Europe* (Bruges, 1967).

Economic developments are surveyed by W. Jappe Alberts and H.P.H. Jansen in *Welvaart in wording* (The Hague, 1964). A revisionist interpretation of certain aspects of economic life can be found in A. Ver-hulst (ed.), *Le grand domaine aux époques mérovingienne et carolingienne*

(Ghent, 1985); see Verhulst also in "La vie urbaine dans les ancien Pays-Bas avant l'an mil," in *Le Moyen Age* 2, (1986): 185-210. There are also B.H. Slicher van Bath, "The Economic and Social Conditions in the Frisian Districts from 900 to 1500," in *A.A.G. Bijdragen* 13 (1965): 97-133; G.L. Burke, *The Making of Dutch Towns: A Study in Urban Development from the Tenth to the Seventeenth Centuries* (Leiden, 1956); collections such as *Ontstaan en vroegste geschiedenis van de middeleeuwse steden in de Zuidelijke Nederlanden* (Brussels, 1990); and J.M. Duvosquel and A. Dierkens, *Villes et campagnes au moyen âge. Mélanges Georges Despy* (Liège, 1991). The evolution of the landscape is examined in C. Dekker, *Zuid-Beveland. De historische geografie en de instellingen van een Zeeuws eiland in de middeleeuwen* (Assen, 1971); A Verhulst and M.K.E. Gottschalk, *Transgressie en occupatiegeschiedenis in de kustgebieden van Nederland en België* (Ghent, 1980); and A. Verhulst, *Précis d'histoire rurale de la Belgique* (Brussel, 1990). Natural and social history can be found in H. Van Werveke, *De middeleeuwse hongersnood* (Brussels, 1967). The important textile industry is examined from a technical standpoint in G. de Poerck, *La draperie médiévale en Flandre et en Artois*, 3 vols. (Bruges, 1951). For a history of money, see N.J. Mayhew (ed.), *Coinage in the Low Countries (880-1500)* (Oxford, 1979).

In art history, we can point to the general work of H.E. van Gelder (ed.), *Kunstgeschiedenis der Nederlanden*, 4th ed. (Zeist/Antwerp, 1963). A broader history can be found in the two volumes of *Rijn en Maas, Kunst en Cultuur, 800-1400* (Cologne/Brussels, 1972, also in French). L.F. Genicot's *Les églises mosanes du XIe siècle* (Leuven, 1972) and J.J.M. Timmers's two-volume *De kunst van het Maasland* (Assen, 1971-1980) are both very solid studies.

For religious history, E. de Moreau's *Histoire de l'Eglise en Belgique*, 6 vols. plus maps (Brussels, 1945-1952) and R.R. Post, *Kerkgeschiedenis van Nederland in de middeleeuwen*, 2 vols. (Utrecht, 1957) remain essential. Recent studies include P. Bange and A.G. Weiler (eds.), *Willibrord, zijn wereld en zijn werk* (Nijmegen, 1990) and L. Milis (ed.), *De Heidense Middeleeuwen* (Brussels/Rome, 1991). For the secular church, there is C.A. Rutgers (ed.), *De Utrechtse bisschop in de middeleeuwen* (The Hague, 1978); for religious orders, see (among others) P.A. Hendrickx, *De oudste bedelordekloosters in het graafschap Holland en Zeeland* (Dordrecht, 1977) and W. Simons, *Stad en apostolaat. De vestiging van de bedelorden in het graafschap Vlaanderen (ca. 1225-ca.1350)* (Brussels, 1987). Simons has also written "The Beguine Movement in the Southern Low Countries: A Reassessment," in the *Bulletin van het Belgisch Historisch Instituut te Rome* 59 (1989): 63-105; for a source on beguines further north, see F.W.J. Koorn, *Begijnhoven in Holland and Zeeland gedurende de middeleeuwen* (Amsterdam, 1981).

Literature and religion interact in J.D. Janssens (ed.), *Hoofsheid en devotie in de middeleeuwse maatschappij* (Brussels, 1982) and in G. Epiney-Burgard and E. Zum Brunn, *Femmes, troubadours de Dieu* (Turnhout, 1988), the latter of which focuses on female religiosity. F. de Schutter, *Het verhaal van de Nederlandse literatuur*, vol. 1 (Antwerp, 1992) is a useful survey of literary history.

Chapter 3

Volumes 2 through 6 of the previously mentioned *Algemene Geschiedenis der Nederlanden* (Haarlem, 1979-1982) cover the fourteenth through sixteenth centuries. With its detailed information, extensive bibliography, and orientation toward original sources, it is the necessary point of departure for deeper historical study. The works listed below are the most recent and most representative of certain historiographical issues that cover the fourteenth, fifteenth, and sixteenth centuries, respectively.

Political developments of the fourteenth century varied enormously from principality to principality. For Flanders, see J.F. Verbruggen, *De Slag der Gulden Sporen. Bijdrage tot de geschiedenis van Vlaanderens vrijheidsoorlog, 1297-1305* (Brussels, 1952) and D. Nicholas, *Medieval Flanders* (London/New York, 1992). For Brabant, there is P. Avonds, *Brabant tijdens de regering van hertog Jan III (1312-1356)*, 2 vols. (Brussels, 1984, 1991) and A. Uyttebrouck, *Le gouvernement du duché de Brabant au bas moyen âge (1355-1430)*, 2 vols. (Brussels, 1975). For Holland: H.M. Brokken, *Het ontstaan van de Hoekse en Kabeljauwse twisten* (Zutphen, 1982) and A. Janse, *Grenzen aan macht. De Friese oorlog van de graven van Holland omstreeks 1400* (Hilversum, 1993).

Several books have determined the course of recent scholarship on cultural life: F.P. van Oostrom, *Court and culture: Dutch literature 1350-1450* (Los Angeles, 1992); W. van Anrooij, *Spiegel van ridderschap. Heraut Gelre en zijn ereredes* (Amsterdam, 1990); and the exhibition catalogue of H.L.M. Defour, A.J. Korteweg and W.C.M. Wüstefeld, *The Golden Age of Dutch Manuscript Painting* (Stuttgart/Zürich, 1989).

Political unification is central to political developments of the fifteenth and sixteenth centuries. An easily accessible introduction to this topic is W. Blockmans and W. Prevenier, *The Low Countries under Burgundian Rule* (Philadelphia, 1998). The connections between diverse social and cultural tendencies are examined in the richly illustrated W. Prevenier and W. Blockmans, *The Burgundian Netherlands* (New York, 1986). R. Vaughan uses both political detail and extensive citations from original sources in political histories centered around the four dukes of Burgundy: *Philip the Bold: The Formation of the Burgundian State* (London/New York, 1979); *John the Fearless: The Growth of Burgundian Power* (London/New York, 1979); *Philip the Good: The Apogee of Burgundy* (London/New York, 1970); and *Charles the Bold: The Last Valois Duke of Burgundy* (London/New York, 1973).

Aspects of state formation are examined indepth by A. van Nieuwenhuysen, *Les finances du duc de Bourgogne Philippe le Hardi (1384-1404). Economie et politique. Le Montant des ressources*, 2 vols., (Brussels, 1984 and 1990); M.R. Thielemans, *Bourgogne et Angleterre. Relations politiques et économiques entre les Pays-Bas bourguignons et l'Angleterre, 1435-1467* (Brussels, 1966); J. van Rompaey, *De Grote Raad van de hertogen van Boergondië en het Parlement van Mechelen* (Brussels, 1973); R. Wellens, *Les états généraux des Pays-Bas des origines à la fin du regné de Philippe le Beau (1464-1506)* (Heule, 1974); and W.P. Blockmans (ed.), *1477. Le privilège général et les privilège régionaux de Marie de Bourgogne pour les Pays Bas* (Kortrijk, 1985).

Several tone-setting regional studies include J.A.M.Y. Bos-Rops, *Graven op zoek naar geld. De inkomsten van de graven van Holland, 1358-1433* (Hilversum, 1993); M.J. van Gent, *"Partielicke saecken". Hoeken en Kabeljauwen in Holland en Zeeland tijdens de Bourgondisch-Oostenrijkse tijd* (The Hague, 1994); H. Kokken, *Steden en Staten. Dagvaarten van steden en staten van Holland onder Maria van Bourgondië en het eerste regentschap van Maximiliaan van Oostenrijk (1477-1494)* (The Hague, 1991); W.P. Blockmans, *De volksvertegenwoordiging in Vlaanderen in de overgang van de middeleeuwen naar nieuwe tijden (1384-1506)* (Brussels, 1978); M. Boone, *Gent en de Bourgondische hertogen ca.1384-ca.1453. Een sociaal-politieke studie van een staatsvormingsproces* (Brussels, 1990), and his *Geld en macht. De Gentse stadsfinanciën en de Bourgondische staatsvorming (1384-1453)* (Ghent, 1990); R. Stein, *Politiek en historiografie. Brabantse kronieken van de eerste helft van de vijftiende eeuw in hun context* (Leuven, 1994); J.M. Cauchies, *La légalisation princière pour le comté de Hainaut. Ducs de Bourgogne et premiers Habsbourgs (1427-1506)* (Brussels, 1982); and P. Stabel, *Dwarfs Among Giants: The Flemish Urban Network in the Late Middle Ages* (Leuven-Apeldoorn, 1997).

An excellent introduction to the socioeconomic history of the period can be found in R. van Uytven, "Oudheid en Middeleeuwen," in J.H. Van Stuijvenberg (ed.), *De economische geschiedenis van Nederland* (Groningen, 1977), 1-48. For trade, see J.H. Munro, *Wool, Cloth and Gold: The Struggle for Bullion in Anglo-Burgundian Trade, 1340-1478* (Brussels/Toronto, 1973); R. de Roover, *Money, Banking and Credit in Medieval Bruges* (Cambridge [Massachusetts], 1948); and H. van der Wee, *The Growth of the Antwerp Market and the European Economy (Fourteenth to Sixteenth Centuries)*, 3 vols. (Leuven/The Hague, 1963).

The following remain classic studies of the urban economy: N.W. Posthumus, *Geschiedenis van de Leidsche lakenindustrie. I. De Middeleeuwen, veertiende tot zestiende eeuw* (The Hague, 1908) and R. van Uytven, *Stadsfinanciën en stadseconomie te Leuven van de XIIe tot het einde der XVIe eeuw* (Brussels, 1961). Important historiographical revisions in agrarian history have been introduced by A.M. van der Woude, *Het Noorderkwartier. Een regionaal historisch onderzoek in de demografische en economische geschiedenis van westelijk Nederland van de late middeleeuwen tot het begin van de negentiende eeuw*, 3 vols. (Wageningen, 1972); P.C.M. Hoppenbrouwers, *Een middeleeuwse samenleving: het land van Heusden (ca.1350-ca.1515)* (Wageningen, 1992); and E. Thoen, *Landbouwekonomie en bevolking in Vlaanderen gedurende de late Middeleeuwen en het begin van de Moderne Tijd. Testregio: de kasselrijen Oudenaarde en Aalst (einde 13de-1ste helft 15de eeuw)*, 2 vols. (Ghent, 1988).

H. de Schepper offers a nice institutional approach in *"Belgium Nostrum," 1500-1650. Over integratie en desintegratie van het Nederland* (Antwerp, 1987). A recent political study is J.D. Tracy's *Holland Under Habsburg Rule, 1506-1566. The Formation of a Body Politic* (Berkeley/Los Angeles/Oxford, 1990). An easily accessible survey of the beginning phase of the Dutch Revolt is G. Parker's *The Dutch Revolt* (Harmondsworth, 1979) and A.T. van Deursen and H. de Schepper, *Willem van Oranje. Een strijd voor vrijheid en verdraagzaamheid* (Weesp/Tielt, 1984). An essential article on this subject remains J.J. Woltjer, "De Vrede-makers," reprinted in S. Groenveld and H.L.P. Leeuwenberg (eds.), *De Unie van Utrecht* (The Hague, 1979), 56-87. More narrowly framed but landmark studies include M. Baelde, *De Collaterale Raden onder Karel V en Filips II (1531-1578)* (Brussels, 1965) and M. van Gelderen, *The Political Thought of the Dutch Revolt, 1555-1590* (Cambridge, 1992).

For regional studies, see J. Decavele, *De dageraad van de Reformatie in Vlaanderen (1520-1565)* (Brussels, 1975); H.F.K. van Nierop, *Van ridders tot regenten. De Hollandse adel in de zestiende eeuw en de eerste helft van de zeventiende eeuw* (The Hague, 1984); J.W. Koopmans, *De Staten van Holland en de Opstand. De ontwikkeling van hun functies en organisatie in de periode 1544-1588* (The Hague, 1990); G. Janssens, *Brabant in het verweer* (Kortrijk-Heule, 1988); G. Marnef, *Het Calvinistisch Bewind te Mechelen (1580-1585)* (Kortrijk-Heule, 1988); and his *Antwerp in the Age of Reformation: Underground Protestantism in a Commercial Metropolis* (Baltimore, 1996).

On culture there are C. Augustijn's works: *Erasmus* (Baarn, 1986) and *Het godsdienstig leven in de tweede helft van de 16de eeuw* (Utrecht, 1986); H. Pleij, *De sneeuwpoppen van 1511. Literatuur en stadscultuur tussen Middeleeuwen en Moderne Tijd* (Amsterdam/Leuven, 1988); B.A.M. Ramakers, *Spelen en Figuren. Toneelkunst en processiecultuur in Oudenaarde tussen Middeleeuwen en Moderne Tijd* (Amsterdam, 1996); J. Sterk, *Philips van Bourgondië (1465-1524), bisschop van Utrecht, als protagonist van de Renaissance; zijn leven en mecenaat* (Zutphen, 1980); and L. Voet, *The Golden Compasses: A History and Evaluation of the Printing and Publishing Activities of the Officina Plantiniana at Antwerp*, 2 vols. (Amsterdam/New York/London, 1969-1972). For art, the two-volume work of E. Panofsky, *Early Netherlandish Painting: Its Origins and Character* (New York, 1971) remains the standard of reference.

Chapter 4

The period between 1588 and 1795 is not usually treated as a whole in historical works. This is especially true of cultural history, where the seventeenth and eighteenth centuries have been cleft in two. The former has received much attention. Dutch historiography is not rich in classic works with lasting appeal to successive generations. Two such classics, however, do treat the cultural history of the seventeenth century: C. Busken Huet, *Het land van Rembrandt* (Haarlem, 1886) and J. Huizinga, *Dutch Civilisation in the Seventeenth Century* (London, 1968). Those looking for a modern treatment of the theme may consult the previously mentioned J.I. Israel, *The Dutch Republic: Its Rise, Greatness, and Fall, 1477-1806* (Oxford, 1995) or J.L. Price, *Culture and Society in the Dutch Republic during the Seventeenth Century* (London, 1974). Price's book is better thought through and substantiated than the provocative but superficial *Embarrassment of Riches: An Interpretation of Dutch Culture in the Golden Age* (Berkeley, 1986) by S. Schama.

No such studies exist for the eighteenth century. The most general orientation is given by H.H. Zwager, *Nederland en de Verlichting*, 2nd ed. (Haarlem, 1980). As a book on the Enlightenment, it emphasizes innovations and reforms that are not, incidentally, highly regarded by the author. On the transmission and the quality of Enlightenment thought, see W.W. Mijnhardt, *Tot heil van 't menschdom. Culturele genootschappen in Nederland, 1750-1815* (Amsterdam, 1988).

Painting assumed a dominant position in seventeenth-century culture. J. Rosenberg, S. Slive, and E.H. ter Kuile, *Dutch Art and Architecture, 1600-1800* (The Pelican History of Art 27; Harmondsworth, 1977) offers a handy overview of the most important Dutch painters and genres from the Golden Age to 1800. The most recent survey is given by B. Haak, *The Golden Age: Dutch Painters of the Seventeenth Century* (New York, 1984). Publications since then include the important catalogue of the 1991 Rembrandt exhibition in Amsterdam: C. Brown, C.J. Kelch, and P. van Thiel, *Rembrandt: de meester en zijn werkplaats* (Amsterdam, 1991).

For economic history J. de Vries and A. van der Woude's *The First Modern Economy: Success, Failure and Perseverance of the Dutch Economy, 1500-1815* (New York, 1995) is the most important and most recent survey. J.G. van Dillen's work provides an overview of the whole period: *Van rijkdom en regenten. Handboek tot de economische en sociale geschiedenis van Nederland tijdens de Republiek* (The Hague, 1970). J.I. Israel offers more than a new survey of old information in a book initially based on his own research: *Dutch Primacy in World Trade, 1585-1740* (Oxford, 1990). Trade with the Indonesian islands through the East India Company has always most strongly captured the imagination of the Dutch. The organization and methods of the company have been sketched by F.S. Gaastra, *De geschiedenis van de VOC*, 2nd ed. (Zutphen, 1991). A lively description of all overseas enterprises has been given by C.R. Boxer, *The Dutch Seaborne Empire, 1600-1800* (London, 1965). J. van Goor's *Trading Companies in Asia, 1600-1830* (Utrecht, 1986) is also a valuable English-language contribution.

A social history of the Republic is not available. In the above-mentioned textbook by Van Dillen, it plays only a marginal role. The higher classes have received much attention in recent years, especially for the eighteenth century. A summary of the results of this research has been made by J. de Jong, *Een deftig bestaan. Het dagelijks leven van regenten in de 17de en 18e eeuw* (Utrecht, 1987). For the lower classes, there is A.T. van Deursen, *Plain Lives in a Golden Age* (Cambridge, 1991). The immigration from the southern provinces is dealt with by J. Briels, *Zuid-Nederlanders in de Republiek, 1572-1630. Een demografische en cultuurhistorische studie* (St.-Niklaas, 1985), a book which tends to overestimate the size of the migration.

Political history of the period is chiefly examined in works devoted to a wide range of specific topics. Although many of them are of good quality, it goes beyond the scope of this bibliography to name them all. The two great pensionaries of the seventeenth century are both memorialized with in-depth biographies: J. den Tex, *Oldenbarnevelt*, 5 vols. (Haarlem, 1960-1972) or the abridged English-language version of the same book, 2 vols. (Cambridge, 1973), and H.H. Rowen, *John de Witt: Grand Pensionary of Holland, 1625-1672* (Princeton, 1978).

The stadholders fare less well, with relatively recent biographies available only for Frederik Hendrik and William III, namely, J.J. Poelhekke, *Frederik Hendrik, prins van Oranje. Een biografisch drieluik* (Zutphen, 1978) and S.B. Baxter, *William III* (London, 1966).

For a good understanding of the period it is necessary to have some knowledge of state institutions and how they functioned. The reference work for all the formal arrangements remains R. Fruin and H.T. Colenbrander, *Geschiedenis der staatsinstellingen in Nederland tot den val der Republiek*, 3rd ed. (1980). The actual functioning of these institutions is for the most part examined by authors working at the boundary of politics and state institutions. D.J. Roorda's *Partij en factie. De oproeren van 1672 in de steden van Holland en Zeeland. Een krachtmeting tussen partijen en facties* (Groningen, 1961) has demonstrated the relativity of the concept of "party" formation. G. de Bruin's *Geheimhouding en verraad. De geheimhouding van staatszaken ten tijde van de Republiek (1600-1750)* (The Hague, 1991) clarifies the way in which the States-General and the provincial States functioned. A.C.J.M. Gabriels' *De heren als dienaren en de dienaar als heer. Het stadhouderlijk stelsel in de tweede helft van de achttiende eeuw* (The Hague, 1990) shows how the stadholderate's administration under William V was organized.

For information on how war was waged, the dissertation of J.W. Wijn, *Het krijgswezen in den tijd van prins Maurits* (Utrecht, 1934) remains indispensable. P. Knevel describes the development of town militias in *Burgers in het geweer: de schutterijen in Holland, 1550-1700* (Hilversum, 1994). The problems facing the Spanish military leadership come to light in the excellent study by G. Parker, *The Army of Flanders and the Spanish Road* (Cambridge, 1972).

The Catholic past is extensively described by L.J. Rogier, *Geschiedenis van het katholicisme in Noord-Nederland in de 16de en 17de eeuw*, 3 vols., 2nd ed. (Amsterdam, 1947). For the Reformed, especially in the time of the religious disputes of the Twelve-Year Truce, there is A.T. van Deursen, *Bavianen en slijkgeuzen. Kerk en kerkvolk ten tijde van Maurits en Oldenbarnevelt*, 2nd ed. (Franeker, 1991).

Chapter 5

Again, the broad developments of the period are described in both editions of the *Algemene Geschiedenis der Nederlanden* (Utrecht, 1949-1958 and Haarlem, 1977-1983). For the eighteenth century, there is *La Belgique autrichienne, 1713-1794: les Pays-Bas méridionaux sous les Habsburg d'Autriche* (Brussels, 1987). For Flanders, consult E. Witte (ed.), *Geschiedenis van Vlaanderen van de oorsprong tot heden* (Brussels, 1983). Selective bibliographical insights can be found in *België in de 18de eeuw, kritische bibliografie* (Brussels, 1983) and L. Genicot (ed.), *Vingt ans de recherche historique en Belgique (1969-1988)* (Brussels, 1990).

On the formation of the region's boundaries or of its extraordinary institutions there is, among others, N. Girard D'Albissin, *Genèse de la frontière franco-belge. Les variations des limites septentrionales de la France de 1659 à 1789* (Paris, 1970); C.H. Carter, "Belgian 'Autonomy' under the Archdukes, 1598-1621," in *Journal of Modern History*, 36 (1964): 245-259; and J. Craeybeckx, F. Daelemans, F.G. Scheelings (eds.), "*1585: op gescheiden wegen.*" *Handelingen van het colloquium over de scheiding der Nederlanden, gehouden 22-23 november 1985 te Brussel* (Leuven, 1988). For the history of regional institutions, see E. Aerts, M. Baelde, H. Coppens, *Les institutions du gouvernement central des Pays-Bas habsbourgeois, 1482-1795*, 2 vols. (Brussels, 1995); P. Lenders *De politieke crisis in Vlaanderen omstreeks het midden der achttiende eeuw* (Brussels, 1956); A. Vandenbulcke, *Le pouvoir et l'argent sous l'Ancien Régime. La vénalité des offices dans le conseils collatéraux des Pays-Bas espagnols (seconde moitié du XVIIe siècle)* (Kortrijk-Heule, 1992); and A. Vandenbulcke, *La chambre des compter des Pays-Bas espagnols* (Brussels, 1996).

R. de Schryver has published an exemplary biography of a prominent member of the States: *Jan van Brouchoven, graaf van Bergeyck (1644-1725). Een halve eeuw staatkunde in de Spaanse Nederlanden en in Europa* (Brussels, 1965). Concerning government leaders in the Southern Netherlands, there is L. de Ren, L. Duerloo, and J. Rogiers, *De Gouverneur-Generaal van de Oostenrijkse Nederlanden* (Brussels, 1987); F. Pichorner, *Die Statthalter Erzherzogin Maria-Elisabeth und Graf Friedrich Harrach (1725-1743)* (Vienna/Cologne, 1990); M. Galand, *Charles de Lorraine, Gouverneur général des Pays-Bas autrichiens (1744-1780)* (Brussels, 1993); G. de Boom, *Les ministres plénipotentiaires dans les Pays-Bas autrichiens, principalement Cobenzl* (Brussels, 1932); and B. Bernard, *Patrice-François de Neny (1716-1784). Portrait d'un homme d'Etat* (Brussels, 1993). With *Les institutions politiques et judiciaires de la Principauté de Liège aux Temps modernes* (Brussels, 1987), G. Hansotte offers an excellent introduction to the institutions of the prince-bishopric of Liège.

The power of the cities, whether political, socioeconomic, or cultural, is the focus of *Stad in Vlaanderen. Cultuur en Maatschappij, 1477-1787* (Brussels, 1991). A number of more focused studies are also useful in this regard, including P. Lenders, *Gent. Een stad tussen traditie en Verlichting (1750-1787). Een institutionele benadering* (Kortrijk-Heule, 1990); H. Hasquin, *Une mutation: le "Pays de Charleroi" aux XVIIe et XVIIIe siècles, aux origines de la Révolution industrielle en Belgique* (Brussels, 1971); and P. Guignet, *Le pouvoir dans le ville au XVIIIe siècle. Pratiques politiques ... de part et d'autre de la frontière franco-belge* (Paris, 1990). The pivotal period before and after the break between the North and South is sketched in "Economische heroriëntatie en reorganisatie in de Brabantse steden tijdens de scheiding der Nederlanden (1550-1650)," in *Bijdragen tot de geschiedenis*, 73 (1990, special issue).

C. Vandenbroeke's *Agriculture et alimentation* (Ghent/Leuven, 1975) gives an overview of the agrarian economy in the eighteenth century. For industry in the mid-eighteenth century, there is P. Moureaux, *Les préoccupations statistiques du gouvernement des Pays-Bas autrichiens et le dénombrement des industries, dressé en 1764* (Brussels, 1971).

The demographics of Brabant and Flanders are thoroughly examined in P.M.M. Klep, *Bevolking en arbeid in transformatie. Een onderzoek naar de ontwikkelingen in Brabant, 1700-1900* (Nijmegen, 1981); C. Bruneel, *La mortalité dans les campagnes. Le duché de Brabant aux XVIIe et XVIIIe siècles* (Leuven, 1977); and C. Vandenbroeke, "Prospektus van het historisch-demografisch onderzoek in Vlaanderen," in *Handelingen van het Genootschap voor Geschiedenis "Société d'Emulation" te Brugge*, 113 (1976): 1-85. One may also consult C. Bruneel et al., *Le dénombrement général de la population des Pays-Bas autrichiens en 1784* (Brussels, 1996) for an analysis of Joseph II's census of 1784.

Poverty in the region remains best treated by P. Bonenfant, *Le prob-lème du paupérisme en Belgique à la fin de l'Ancien Régime* (Brussels, 1934). P. Soetaert's study is also particularly informative on this issue: *De Bergen van Barmhartigheid in de Spaanse, de Oostenrijkse en de Franse Neder-landen (1618-1795)* (Brussels, 1986).

The Counter Reformation is the subject of A. Pasture's helpful book, *La restauration religieuse aux Pays-Bas catholiques sous les Archiducs Albert et Isabelle (1596-1633)* (Leuven, 1925). Much has been written about Jansenism. See, for example, J. van den Bavel and M. Schrama (eds.), *Jansenius et le jansénisme dans les Pays-Bas. Mélange Lucien Ceyssens* (Leuven, 1982). The standard works on the Jesuits are still A. Poncelet, *Histoire de la Compagnie de Jésus dans les anciens Pays-Bas*, 2 vols. (1926-1928) and P. Bonenfant, *La suppression de la Compagnie de Jésus dans les anciens Pays-Bas* (Brussels, 1926-1928).

The restrictions on cultural life are the topic of A. Puttemans, *La censure dans les Pays-Bas autrichiens* (Brussels, 1935). The prince-bish-opric of Liège in an age of Enlightenment is given broad treatment in D. Droixhe (ed.), *Livres et Lumières au pays de Liège (1730-1830)* (Liège, 1980).

Chapter 6

For a history of the Northern Netherlands between 1780 and 1830, see H. Amersfoort, *Koning en kanton* (The Hague, 1988); W.P. te Brake, *Regents and Rebels: The Revolutionary World of an Eighteenth Century Dutch City* (Oxford, 1989); J.M.F. Fritschy, *De patriotten en de financiën van de Bataafse Republiek. Hollands krediet en de smalle marges voor een nieuw beleid (1795-1801)* (The Hague, 1988); F. Grijzenhout, W.W. Mijnhardt, and N.C.F. van Sas (eds.), *Voor vaderland en vrijheid. De revolutie van de patriotten* (Amsterdam, 1987); *Herman Willem Daendels, 1762-1818* (Utrecht, 1991); D. van der Horst, *Van republiek tot koninkrijk. De vormende jaren van Anton Rein-hard Falck, 1777-1813* (Amsterdam, 1985); M.C. Jacob and W.W. Mijn-hardt (eds.), *The Dutch Republic in the Eighteenth Century: Decline, Enlightenment and Revolution* (Ithaca, 1992); M.E. Kluit, *Cornelis Felix van Maanen tot het herstel der onafhankelijkheid, 9 sept. 1769-6 dec. 1813* (Gronin-gen, 1953); "Revolutie en contrarevolutie," theme of *Tijdschrift voor Geschiedenis*, 102, nos. 3 and 4 (1989); L.J. Rogier, "Rutger Jan Schim-melpenninck," in *Terugblik en Uitzicht*, 2 (Hilversum, 1964); 69-112, N.C.F. van Sas, *Onze natuurlijkste bondgenoot. Nederland, Engeland en Europa, 1813-1831* (Groningen, 1985); S. Schama, *Patriots and Liberators: Revolution in the Netherlands, 1780-1813* (New York, 1977); J.W. Schulte Nordholt, *Voorbeeld in de verte. De invloed van de Amerikaanse revolutie in Nederland* (Baarn, 1979); G.J. Schutte, *De Nederlandse patriotten en de koloniën. Een onderzoek naar hun denkbeelden en optreden, 1770-1800* (Groningen, 1974); C.A. Tamse and E. Witte (eds.), *Staats- en natievorming in Willem I's koninkrijk (1815-1830)* (Brussels, 1992); W.R.E. Velema, *Enlightenment and Conservatism in the Dutch Republic: The Political Thought of Elie Luzac, 1721-1796* (Assen, 1993); W.M. Zappey, *De economische en politieke werkzaamheid van Johannes Goldberg* (Alphen aan den Rijn, 1967); and T.S.M. van der Zee (ed.), *1787. De Nederlandse revolutie?* (Amsterdam, 1988).

Bibliographical overviews of the South between 1780 and 1815 are to be found in *België in de 18de eeuw: kritische bibliografie/La Belgique au 18e siècle: bibliographie critique* (Brussels, 1983) and C. Bruneel (ed.), *Des révolutions à Waterloo. Bibliographie sélective d'histoire de Belgique (1789-1815) (Archief en Bibliotheekwezen in België,* Extra Issue 36, Brussels, 1989). Two recent collections offer a nicely illustrated survey of most aspects of this period: H. Hasquin (ed.), *La Belgique autrichienne 1713-1794: les Pays-Bas méridionaux sous les Habsbourg d'Autriche* (Brussels, 1987), and H. Hasquin (ed.), *La Belgique française 1792-1815* (Brussels, 1993).

The only relatively recent overview of Joseph II's government is W.W. Davis's *Joseph II: An Imperial Reformer for the Austrian Netherlands* (The Hague, 1974), and it is partially based on dated literature. Important supplements to certain aspects of Austrian rule include "Verlicht despotisme in de Nederlanden," the topic of *Documentatieblad werkgroep 18de eeuw* nos. 49 and 50 (1981); R. Crahay (ed.), *La tolérance civile* (Brussels/Mons, 1982); and L. Dhondt, "Staatsveiligheidsmodel en bureaucratisering onder Maria Theresia en Jozef II (1740-1790)," in *Tijdschrift voor Geschiedenis,* 90 (1977): 423-438. The Brabantine Revolution has enjoyed renewed attention in recent years, and J.C.A. de Clerck and P. Lierneux give a virtually complete and up-to-date bibliography of this event in *J.F. Vonck, juriste et chef démocrate de la Révolution belgique (1743-1792), suivi d'une Bibliographie de la Révolution belgique (1787-1792)* (Brussels, 1992). Fifteen authors contributed to a book on the subject, edited by J. Lorette, P. Lefèvre, and P. de Gryse, *Handelingen van het Colloquium over de Brabantse Omwenteling, 13-14 oktober 1983 – Actes sur Colloque sur la Révolution brabançonne, 13-14 octobre 1983* (Brussels, 1984). J.L. Polasky has attempted a revisionist social-historical approach in *Revolution in Brussels (1787-1793)* (Brussels, 1985). The classic text by S. Tassier, which first appeared in 1930, has recently been republished in a richly illustrated and supplemented edition: *Les démocrates belges de 1789* (Brussels, 1989).

Both the Brabantine Revolution and the French rule are covered by P. Lenders (ed.), *Het einde van het Ancien Régime in België – La fin de l'Ancien Régime en Belgique (Standen en Landen,* 93; Kortrijk -Heule, 1991). The essays are very uneven in the collection by H. van de Voorde et al., *Bastille, Boerenkrijg en Tricolore. De Franse Revolutie in de Zuidelijke Nederlanden* (Leuven, 1989). More new information can be found in J. Craeybeckx and F. Scheelings, (eds.), *De Franse Revolutie en Vlaanderen. De Oostenrijkse Nederlanden tussen Oud en Nieuw Regime* (Brussels, 1990). After a long lull, trailblazing articles on French rule in the South appeared in *Occupants, occupés (1792-1815). Colloque de Bruxelles, 29 et 30 janvier 1968* (Brussels, 1969). Critical issues are treated in R. Mortier and H. Hasquin (eds.), *Deux aspects contestés de la politique révolutionnaire en Belgique: langue et culte (Etudes sur le XVIIIe siècle,* 16; Brussels, 1989). A survey of present-day Belgian provinces under French rule is offered by H. Hasquin (ed.), *La vie culturelle dans nos provinces à l'époque française* (Brussels, 1989). The civil service and other cadres throughout the period are the topic of P. Lenders (ed.), *Le personnel politique dans la transition de l'Ancien Régime au nouveau régime en Belgique (1780-1830)* (Kortrijk-Heule, 1993).

Chapter 7

There are several good surveys of modern Belgium's political history: an encyclopedic study by P. Luykx and M. Platel. *Politieke geschiedenis van België van 1789 tot 1985*, 5th ed. (Antwerp, 1985) and a more analytical work by E. Witte and J. Craeybeckx, *La Belgique politique de 1830 à nos jours. Les tensions d'une démocratie bourgeoise* (Brussels, 1987). Covering a shorter period are H. Haag et al., *Histoire de la Belgique contemporaine, 1914-1970* (Brussels, 1974) and E. Witte, J. Burgelman et al., *Tussen restauratie en vernieuwing. Aspekten van de naoorlogse Belgische politiek (1944-1950)*, 2nd ed. (Brussels, 1990).

There are a number of studies on Belgian foreign relations: M. Dumoulin and E. Stols (eds.), *La Belgique et l'étranger aux XIXe et XXe siècles* (Louvain-la-Neuve, 1987); *Colloquium over de geschiedenis van de Belgisch-Nederlandse betrekkingen tussen 1815 en 1945* (Ghent, 1982); C.A. Tamse, *Nederland en België in Europa (1859-1871). De zelfstandigheidspolitiek van twee kleine staten* (The Hague, 1973); H. Lademacher, *Die belgische Neutralität als Problem der europäischen Politik, 1830-1914* (Bonn, 1971); and M. Dumoulin (ed.), *La Belgique et les débuts de la construction européenne. De la guerre au traité de Rome* (Louvain-la-Neuve, 1987).

Belgium's involvement in the two world wars is the subject of an extensive body of literature, including F. Wence, *Die belgische Frage in der deutschen Politik des Ersten Weltkrieges* (Hamburg, 1969); W. Wagner, *Belgien in der deutschen Politik während des Zweiten Weltkrieges* (Boppard, 1974); D. Martin and A. Colignon (eds.) *1940. Belgique. Une société en crise. Un pays en guerre* (Brussels, 1993); A. de Jonghe, *Hitler en het politieke lot van België (1940-1944)*, 2nd ed., vol. 1 (Antwerp/Utrecht, 1982); and M. Steinberg, *L'étoile et les fusil*, 3 vols. (Brussels, 1983-1986), a study on the persecution of the Jews.

Many narrowly focused studies cover Belgian colonial expansion in Central Africa. A few works with a more synthetic character include B. Emerson, *Leopold II of the Belgians: King of Colonialism* (London, 1980) and *Le centenaire de l'Etat indépendant du Congo. Recueil d'études* (Brussels, 1988).

Much research has been conducted on the history of the most important political parties. Studies include A. Verhulst and H. Hasquin (eds.), *La libéralisme en Belgique. Deux cent ans d'histoire* (Brussels, 1989); E. Gerard, *De katholieke partij in crisis. Partijpolitiek leven in België, 1918-1940* (Leuven, 1985); *1885-1985. Du parti ouvrier belge au parti socialiste* (Brussels, 1985); and W. Dewachter et al. (eds.) *Un parti dans l'histoire, 1945-1995. 50 ans d'áction du Parti Social Chrétien* (Brussels, 1995).

For the issues surrounding the ideological divisions within Belgian society – specifically the problematic of pillarization – one might consult J. Billiet (ed.), *Tussen bescherming en verovering. Sociologen en historici over zuilvorming* (Leuven, 1988); E. Lamberts (ed.), *De kruistocht tegen het liberalisme. Facetten van het ultramontanisme in België in de 19e eeuw* (Leuven, 1984); H. Hasquin (ed.), *Histoire de la laïcité, principalement en Belgique et en France* (Brussels, 1979); J. Lory, *Libéralisme et instruction primaire (1842-1879)*, 2 vols. (Leuven, 1979); and J. Tyssens, *Strijdpunt of pasmunt? Levensbeschouwelijk links en de schoolkwestie (1918-1940)* (Brussels, 1993).

Ethnic and language divisions are primarily addressed from the Flemish side. See H.J. Elias, *Geschiedenis van de Vlaamse gedachte, 1780-1940*, 4 vols. (Antwerp, 1963-1965); L. Wils, *Honderd jaar Vlaamse beweging. Geschiedenis van het Davidsfonds*, 3 vols. (Leuven, 1977-1989); A.W. Willemsen, *De Vlaamse beweging, 1830-1975*, 3 vols. (Hasselt, 1974-1979); B. De Wever, *Greep naar de macht. Vlaams-Nationalisme en Nieuwe Orde. Het VNV, 1933-1945* (Ghent/Tielt, 1994); and E. Witte (ed.), *Het probleem Brussel sinds Hertoginnedal (1963)*, 3 vols. (Brussels, 1989). Research into the history of Walloon nationalism has not yet produced important syntheses. A recent study of Belgian nationalism is H. Dumont (ed.), *Belgique et crise de l'Etat belge* (Brussels, 1989).

Economic developments are covered by, among others, *De industrie in België: twee eeuwen ontwikkeling, 1780-1980* (Brussels, 1981), G. de Brabander, *Regional Specialization, Employment and Economic Growth in Belgium between 1846 and 1970* (New York, 1981); P. Lebrun et al., *Essai sur la révolution industrielle en Belgique, 1770-1847* (Brussels, 1981); A. Mommens, *The Belgian Economy in the Twentieth Century* (London, 1994); J. Blomme, *The Economic Development of Belgian Agriculture, 1880-1980* (Leuven, 1992); and G. Vanthemsche *La sécurité sociale. Les origins du système belge* (Louvain-la-Neuve, 1994), which describes the beginnings of Belgian social legislation.

Social history is offered in works such as R.J. Lesthaege, *The Decline of Belgian Fertility, 1800-1970* (New Jersey, 1977); J. Stengers, *Emigration et immigration en Belgique aux XIXe et XXe siècles* (Brussels, 1978); C. Lis, *Social Change and the Labouring Poor: Antwerp, 1770-1860* (New Haven/London, 1986); G. Kurgan van Hentenryk and S. Jaumain (eds.), *Aux frontières des classes moyennes. La petite bourgeoisie belge avant 1914* (Brussels, 1992); P. Scholliers, *Loonindexering en sociale vrede. Koopkracht en klassenstrijd in België tijdens het interbellum* (Brussels, 1985); and D. Luyten, *Sociaal-economisch overleg in België sedert 1918* (Brussels, 1995). See also J.J. de Deken, *Social Policy in Post-War Belgium: The Development of Old Age Pensions and Housing Policies from 1945 to 1980* (San Domenico, 1994). A good introduction to the history of social legislation continues to be B.S. Chlepner, *Cent ans d'histoire sociale en Belgique*, 2nd ed. (Brussels, 1956).

A remarkable but somewhat controversial synthesis on the evolution of the country's social mentality is to be found in K. Van Isacker's *Mijn land in de kering, 1830-1980*, 2 vols. (Antwerp/Amsterdam, 1978-1983).

There is a great deal of literature on the history of the social movements. C.J. Strikwerda has provided two English-language works on this topic: *Mass Politics and the Origin of Pluralism: Catholicism, Socialism and Flemish Nationalism in Nineteenth-Century Belgium* (Lanham, MD and Leuven, 1997) and *Urban Structure, Religion and Language: Belgian Workers (1880-1914)* (Ann Arbor, 1986).

Several studies on the socialist workers' movement include J. Dhondt (ed.), *Geschiedenis van de socialistische arbeidersbeweging in België* (Antwerp, 1960-1969) and J. Puissant, *L'évolution du mouvement ouvrier socialiste dans le Borinage* (Brussels, 1982). Since 1980, a new historiography on the Christian popular movements has emerged, such as E. Gerard and P. Wynants (ed.), Histoire du mouvement ouvrier chrétien en Belgique (1891-1991), 2 vols. (Leuven, 1994); P. Pasture, *Kerk, politiek en sociale actie. De unieke positie van de christelijke arbeidersbeweging in België (1944-1973)* (Leuven, 1992) and L. Van Molle, *Chacun pour tous. Le Boerenbond Belge, 1890-1990* (Leuven, 1990). In contrast, the historiography on Belgian feminism has yet to take off. Usable works include D. De Weerdt's *En de vrouwen? Vrouw, vrouwenbeweging en feminisme in België (1830-1960)* (Ghent, 1980); L. Courtois et al. (eds.) *Femmes des années 80. Un siècle de condition féminine en Belgique, 1889-1989* (Louvain-la-Neuve, 1989), and E. Gubin (ed.) *La ville et les femmes en Belgique. Histoire et sociologie* (Brussels, 1993).

Studies devoted to religious developments include R. Aubert, *150 ans de vie des églises* (Brussels, 1980), and *Le cardinal Mercier (1851-1926), un prélat d'avant garde* (Louvain-la-Neuve, 1994); E.M. Braekman, *150 jaar protestants leven in België* (Brussels, 1981), and the more broadly oriented K. Dobbelaere et al. (eds.), *La Belgique et ses dieux: églises mouvements religieux et laïques* (Louvain-la-Neuve, 1985).

Several aspects of cultural life are analyzed in *Florilège des sciences en Belgique pendant le XIXe siècle et le début du XXe siècle*, 2 vols. (Brussels, 1968-1980); G. Charlier and J. Hanse (eds.), *Histoire illustrée des lettres françaises en Belgique* (Brussels, 1958); R.F. Lissens, *De Vlaamse letterkunde van 1780 tot heden* (Brussels/Amsterdam, 1976); W. Vanbeselaere, *De Vlaamse schilderkunst van 1850-1950, van Leys tot Permeke* (Brussels, 1976); and P. Caso, *Un siècle de peinture wallonne, de Félicien Rops à Paul Delvaux* (Brussels, 1984).

Chapter 8

In a short work, *De eenwording van Nederland. Schaalvergroting en integratie sinds 1800* (Nijmegen, 1988), H. Knippenberg and B. de Pater manage to give insight and information on how, in the course of the nineteenth and twentieth centuries, growing uniformity and intensification of communications took place in a myriad of ways. Anglophone readers will appreciate J. Mokyr's *Industrialization in the Low Countries, 1795-1850* (New Haven, 1976).

A handy survey of political history (chiefly of parliaments of cabinets) is P.J. Oud and J. Bosmans, *Staatkundige vormgeving in Nederland*, 11th ed., 2 vols. (Assen, 1990). Another largely political history is J.J. Woltjer's *Recent verleden. De geschiedenis van Nederland in de twintigste eeuw* (Amsterdam, 1992), which gives particular attention to economic policy and the influence of the state in economic and social life in the 1900s. A host of facts on the twentieth, but also to some extent on the nineteenth century, are to be found in H. Daalder, C.J.M. Schuyt, and A.P.N. Nauta (eds.), *Compendium voor politiek en samenleving in Nederland* (loose-leafed, Alphen aan den Rijn, 1986).

For the beginnings of the Dutch constitutional system and of nineteenth-century liberalism, the most important works are J.C. Boogman, *Rondom 1848. De politieke ontwikkeling van Nederland, 1840-1940* (Bussum, 1978); S. Stuurman, *Wacht op onze daden. Het liberalisme en de vernieuwing van de Nederlandse staat* (Amsterdam, 1992); and H. te Velde,

Gemeenschapszin en plichtsbesef. Liberalisme en nationalisme in Nederland, 1870-1918 (Groningen, 1992). Pillarization enjoys a rich literature, written both by historians but especially social scientists, and include the various essays of H. Daalder in *Politiek en historie. Opstellen over Nederlandse politiek en vergelijkende politieke wetenschap* (Amsterdam, 1990); A. Lijphart, *The Politics of Accommodation: Pluralism and Democracy in the Netherlands,* 2nd ed. (Berkeley, 1975); and S. Stuurman, *Verzuiling, kapitalisme en patriarchaat. Aspecten van de ontwikkeling van de moderne staat in Nederland* (Nijmegen, 1983). A good introduction to the history of the orthodox Protestant pillar is offered by J. de Bruijn (ed.), *Een land nog niet in kaart gebracht. Aspecten van het protestants-christelijk leven in Nederland in de jaren 1880-1940* (Franeker, 1987) and J. de Bruijn (ed.), *Bepaald gebied. Aspecten van het protestants-christelijk leven in Nederland in de jaren 1880-1940* (Baarn, 1989). For the Catholics, L.J. Rogier's study, *Katholieke herleving. Geschiedenis van katholiek Nederland sinds 1853* (The Hague, 1956) is still usable; see also J.M.G. Thurlings, *De wankele zuil. Nederlandse katholieken tussen assimilatie en pluralisme,* 2nd ed. (Deventer, 1978) and H. Righart, *De katholieke zuil in Europa. Een vergelijkend onderzoek naar het ontstaan van verzuiling onder katholieken in Oostenrijk, Zwitserland, België en Nederland* (Meppel, 1986). A classic study on early socialism in the Netherlands is A.J.C. Rüter, *De spoorwegstakingen van 1903. Een spiegel der arbeidersbeweging in Nederland* (1st ed., 1935; rep. Nijmegen, 1978). Although much has been published about the Dutch workers' movement, there are few satisfying works which give an overview. The most suitable are E. Hueting, F. de Jong Edz., and R. Neij, *Naar groter eenheid. De geschiedenis van het Nederlands Verbond van Vakverenigingen, 1906-1981* (Amsterdam, 1983), and M. Brinkman, M. de Keizer, and M. van Rossem (eds.), *Honderd jaar sociaal-democratie in Nederland, 1894-1994* (Amsterdam, 1994).

Only a few titles can be mentioned out of the many dealing with specific periods and issues in Dutch history. For the history of the Netherlands during the Second World War there is the definitive fourteen-volume work by L. de Jong, *Het koninkrijk der Nederlanden in de Tweede Wereldoorlog* (The Hague, 1969-1991). For the same period, see also J.C.H. Blom, *Crisis, bezetting en herstel. Tien studies over Nederland, 1930-1950* (The Hague, 1989) and G. Hirschfeld, *Nazi Rule and Dutch Collaboration: The Netherlands under German Occupation, 1940-1945* (Oxford, 1988). For the history of the Dutch welfare state there is, among others, K. Schuyt and R. van der Veen (eds.), *De verdeelde samenleving. Een inleiding in de ontwikkeling van de Nederlandse verzorgingsstaat,* 2nd ed. (Leiden, 1990). The so-called civilizing offensive is clarified by B. Kruithof, J. Noordman, and P. de Rooy (eds.), *Geschiedenis van opvoeding en onderwijs. Inleiding, bronnen, onderzoek,* 3rd ed. (Nijmegen, 1985); W.W. Mijnhardt and A.J. Wichers (eds.), *Om het algemeen volksgeluk. Twee eeuwen particulier initiatief, 1784-1984. Gedenkboek ter gelegenheid van het tweehonderdjarig bestaan van de Maatschappij tot Nut van 't Algemeen* (Edam, 1984); and A. de Regt, *Arbeidersgezinnen en beschavingsarbeid. Ontwikkelingen in Nederland, 1870-1940* (Meppel, 1984). A good introduction to the history of (early) Dutch feminism is U. Jansz., *Denken over sekse in de eerste feministische golf* (Amsterdam, 1990).

The most important introductions to the economic history of the Netherlands are R.T. Griffiths, *Industrial Retardation in the Netherlands* (The Hague, 1979); J.A. de Jonge, *De industrialisatie in Nederland tussen 1850 en 1914* (Amsterdam, 1968); and J.L. van Zanden and R.T. Griffiths, *Economische geschiedenis van Nederland in de twintigste eeuw* (Utrecht, 1989). Finally, access to colonial history is available through a number of fine, informative works that give an overview of the most important issues: J.A.A. van Doorn, *De laatste eeuw van Indië. Ontwikkeling en ondergang van een koloniaal project* (Amsterdam, 1994); C. Fasseur, *Kultuurstelsel en koloniale baten. De Nederlandse exploitatie van Java, 1840-1860* (Leiden, 1975); M. Kuitenbrouwer, *Nederland en de opkomst van het moderne imperialisme. Koloniën en buitenlandse politiek, 1870-1902* (Amsterdam, 1985); E. Locher-Scholten, *Ethiek in fragmenten. Vijf studies over koloniaal denken en doen van Nederlanders in de Indonesische archipel, 1877-1942* (Utrecht, 1981); J. Bank, *Katholieken en de Indonesische revolutie*, 2nd ed. (Dieren, 1984); and J.A.A. van Doorn and W.J. Hendrix, *Ontsporing van geweld. Het Nederlands/Indisch/Indonesisch conflict*, 2nd ed. (Dieren, 1983).

Index

Contributors

L.J.R. Milis (1940) is professor of medieval history at the University of Ghent. His particular research focus is the religion and mentalities of the early Middle Ages.

W.P. Blockmans (1945) is professor of medieval history at the University of Leiden. His research chiefly focuses on the consolidation of political power from the thirteenth to sixteenth centuries.

A.T. van Deursen (1931) is professor emeritus of modern history at the Free University of Amsterdam. *Plain Lives in a Golden Age* (1991) is an English translation of one of his many books.

C. Bruneel (1943) is professor of modern history at the Catholic University of Louvain-la-Neuve. His research interests are in the fields of economic and social history as well as historical demography.

J. Roegiers (1944) is archivist of the Catholic University of Leuven. He is also professor of early modern religious and cultural history. He has published works on the history of the University of Leuven and the political, religious and intellectual history of the Southern Netherlands, especially in the period between 1780 and 1830.

N.C.F. van Sas (1950) is professor of modern history at the University of Amsterdam. He is primarily interested in the history of the Netherlands and Europe in the "long" nineteenth century.

E. Lamberts (1941) is professor of Netherlandic history and political-religious history of the modern period. His publications are chiefly about political and social Catholicism and the historical development of universities.

J.C.H. Blom is director of the Netherlands Institute for War Documentation and professor of history at the University of Amsterdam. His research deals primarily with the history of pillarization and the period proximate to the Second World War.